Sarah Osborn's World

MEMOIRS

OF THE

L I F E

OF

Mrs. SARAH OSBORN,

WHO DIED AT

NEWPORT, RHODEISLAND,

ON THE SECOND DAY OF AUGUST, 1796.

IN THE EIGHTY THIRD YEAR OF HER AGE.

By SAMUEL HOPKINS, D. D.

PASTOR OF THE FIRST CONGREGATIONAL CHURCH IN NEWPORT.

PRINTED AT WORCESTER, MASSACHUSETTS,
By LEONARD WORCESTER.

1799.

Title page of Samuel Hopkins, *Memoirs of the Life of Mrs. Sarah Osborn* (Worcester, Mass.: Leonard Worcester, 1799). Photograph courtesy of the Newport Historical Society.

Sarah Osborn's World

The Rise of Evangelical Christianity
in Early America

CATHERINE A. BREKUS

Yale
UNIVERSITY
PRESS
NEW HAVEN & LONDON

NEW DIRECTIONS IN NARRATIVE HISTORY
John Demos and Aaron Sachs, Series Editors

The New Directions in Narrative History series includes original works of creative nonfiction across the many fields of history and related disciplines. Based on new research, the books in this series offer significant scholarly contributions while also embracing stylistic innovation as well as the classic techniques of storytelling. The works of the New Directions in Narrative History series, intended for the broadest general readership, speak to deeply human concerns about the past, present, and future of our world and its people.

Published with assistance from the foundation established in memory of Philip Hamilton McMillan of the Class of 1894, Yale College, and from the Annie Burr Lewis Fund.

Yale University Press books may be purchased in quantity for educational, business, or promotional use. For information, please e-mail sales.press@yale.edu (U.S. office) or sales@yaleup.co.uk (U.K. office).

Designed by Mary Valencia.
Set in Adobe Caslon type by Newgen North America.
Printed in the United States of America.

Library of Congress Cataloging-in-Publication Data

Brekus, Catherine A.
Sarah Osborn's world : the rise of evangelical Christianity in early
America / Catherine A. Brekus.
p. cm. — (New directions in narrative history)
Includes bibliographical references and index.
ISBN 978-0-300-18290-3 (alk. paper)
1. Osborn, Sarah, 1714–1796.   2. Christian biography—
United States.   I. Title.
BR1725.O7B74 2013
277.3′07092—dc23
[B]
2012019515

A catalogue record for this book is available from the British Library.

This paper meets the requirements of ANSI/NISO Z39.48–1992 (Permanence of Paper).

10 9 8 7 6 5 4 3 2 1

publication of this book is enabled by a grant from

Jewish Federation of Greater Hartford

For my mother, Trudy Brennan Brekus
And in memory of my father, Gordon L. Brekus (1930–2011)

Remembering speechlessly we seek the great forgotten language,
the lost lane-end into heaven, a stone, a leaf, an unfound door.
—Thomas Wolfe, *Look Homeward Angel*

Write this for a memorial in a book.

—Exodus 17:14

Contents

Preface xi

Introduction 1

PART I: A MEMOIR, 1743

ONE *Never Despair* 15

TWO *The Name of Christ* 33

THREE *An Afflicted Low Condition* 59

FOUR *Amazing Grace* 93

PART II: DIARIES AND LETTERS, 1744–1796

FIVE *The Lord Gave, and the Lord Hath Taken Away, 1744* 137

SIX *No Imaginary Thing, 1753–1755* 170

SEVEN *Pinching Poverty, 1756–1758* 191

EIGHT *Love Thy Neighbor, 1759–1763* 217

NINE *Jordan Overflowing, 1765–1774* 248

TEN *The Latter Days, 1775–1787* 289

ELEVEN *The Open Vision, 1796* 316

Epilogue: A Protestant Saint 337

List of Abbreviations 345

Notes 349

Acknowledgments 415

Index 419

Preface

This book tells the story of an eighteenth-century evangelical woman, Sarah Osborn, who recorded her experiences in thousands of pages of letters, diaries, and a memoir. These manuscripts offer a rare opportunity to hear an early American woman reflecting on the meaning of her life, and they also offer a fascinating glimpse of the world of eighteenth-century America. Although Sarah's story was uniquely her own, she was deeply shaped by her culture, and when we read her writings we can hear both her own individual voice and the voice of her community speaking through her. Like all of us, she could not transcend the historical moment in which she lived, and although no other person in the eighteenth century shared all her feelings or experiences, her life bears the indelible imprint of the ideas, practices, and material forces of her time.

Each chapter of this book combines a narrative of Sarah Osborn's life with an examination of the larger historical forces that shaped her understanding of both herself and God. Rather than trying to write a traditional biography from the cradle to the grave, I have organized this book around the fragments of her writings. By listening to her reflect on her experiences, we can come to a deeper understanding of how early Americans made sense of the religious, economic, and political transformations that were reshaping their world. Whether writing about the revivals of the Great Awakening, the consumer revolution, slavery, or the American Revolution, Sarah wrestled with the most critical issues of her age.

In order to recapture the vibrancy of Sarah Osborn's world, I have built this book around a wide variety of sources: manuscript church records, ministers' sermons, newspapers, religious periodicals, census data, philosophical writings, theological treatises, childrearing books, devotional manuals, and other men's and women's conversion narratives and diaries. My most important sources, of course, are Sarah's own religious writings, including her memoir, ten volumes of diaries, more than a hundred letters, and a short tract, *The Nature, Certainty, and Evidence of True Christianity*, which she published anonymously in 1755. I have also relied on two collections of her writings that were published after her death: Samuel Hopkins's *Memoirs of the Life of Mrs. Sarah Osborn* and Elizabeth West Hopkins's *Familiar Letters, Written by Mrs. Sarah Osborn and Miss Susanna Anthony*. Since Samuel Hopkins occasionally edited Osborn's language in order to make her conform to his vision of an ideal Christian (and his wife, Elizabeth Hopkins, may have done the same), these books must be used cautiously, but they are the only clue to what may have been in Sarah's missing manuscripts.

Unfortunately most of her diaries have been lost. Six volumes disappeared during the last years of Sarah's life, perhaps given to friends who never returned them, and others may have been destroyed after her death by a fire at Hopkins's house. (Many of his own manuscripts were consumed in the blaze.) Perhaps others were forgotten in attics or discarded as worthless.

Nevertheless, a remarkable number of her writings still survive, preserved by people who found her voice too compelling to ignore. Although it is not clear how her letters and diaries eventually ended up in several different archives on the East Coast (including libraries in Rhode Island, Connecticut, Pennsylvania, Massachusetts, and New Hampshire), they seem to have been passed around as devotional reading after her death. Several people, for example, wrote their names on the inside cover of her 1757 diary, including "Cabel J. Tenney" of Newport, Rhode Island, and "Miss Clara Allen" of Northampton, Massachusetts.

Reading Sarah's writings can be difficult because of her frequent misspellings, her lack of punctuation, and her odd capitalizations, but nothing can substitute for the experience of encountering her breathless, urgent words in their original form. In order to give readers a glimpse of her "stream of consciousness" style, I have started several chapters with excerpts from her manuscripts as they were originally written. (In other cases the quotations come from her published writings, which were edited for clarity in the eighteenth century.) In the rest of the book I have chosen to modernize the spelling and punctuation of her manuscripts in order to make them more intelligible.

Historians who write about women have to make difficult decisions about what to call their female characters. Books about famous men usually identify them by their last names: Jefferson, for example, or Lincoln.

But Sarah did not become "Osborn" until her second marriage at the age of twenty-nine, and it seems anachronistic to use the name "Osborn" when writing about her childhood or her marriage to her first husband, Samuel Wheaten, when she was known as "Mrs. Wheaten." Because women were defined in relationship to their fathers and husbands, they could have several different names in a lifetime. In most of the book I have chosen to call Sarah by her first name because it seems most true to her identity—the only name she kept from birth to death, the name she used when standing before God. All her surviving manuscripts are written in the first person, and many of her diary entries are addressed directly to God. But I have also chosen to use her last name when discussing her authorship and her participation in the religious debates of her time. My hope is that Sarah Osborn will appear in future books about the evangelical movement next to male leaders like Jonathan Edwards, George Whitefield, and John Wesley.

Reading Sarah's reflections on her life reminds us of how far away the past is—but also how close. Sarah lived at a time when modern ideas about the reality of human freedom and the goodness of everyday life were still emerging, and we may find it hard to understand her unflinching belief in human depravity, her embrace of suffering as a positive good, and her fears about loving her family and friends too much. "The past is a foreign country," the novelist L. P. Hartley once wrote. "They do things differently there." But Sarah's questions about the meaning of human life were ultimately universal ones, and her story can help us to reflect on our own understanding of the human condition. We, too, debate over how to define happiness, and we, too, wonder if there is any such thing as absolute truth. Sarah was profoundly influenced by the Enlightenment world in which she lived, a world that stood on the brink of our own, and although we may try to distance ourselves from the past by describing our culture as postmodern, we continue to wrestle with the legacy of the Enlightenment in its many forms—whether its defense of capitalism, its commitment to humanitarianism, or its optimistic faith in human nature.

After spending many years with Sarah Osborn, my feelings about her are a mixture of admiration and ambivalence: admiration for her intelligence, her kindness, and her commitment to the common good, ambivalence about her vision of a God who deprives us of genuine freedom and rejoices in violence and damnation. Her quest for absolute religious certainty—rational *proof* of God's existence—strikes me as one of the most problematic legacies of both the evangelical movement and the Enlightenment, burdening Christianity with the task of empirically demonstrating its truth. Yet I have tried to understand Sarah on her own terms, and I have been inspired by her determination to see God's goodness in every part of her life. Like the poet A. R. Ammons, she went in search of the "lowly," certain that her place was with the smallest and least significant things in the universe, but wherever she looked she found signs of grace. "Though I have looked everywhere," Ammons wrote in "Still," "I can find nothing/to give myself to:/everything is/magnificent with existence, is in/surfeit of glory: nothing is diminished,/nothing has been diminished for me." Despite wrestling with many dark nights of the soul when she felt as though God had "hidden his face," Sarah refused to give up hope.

If not for her remarkable memoir, diaries, and letters, we would know almost nothing about her. After more than 250 years, few traces of her life remain. If we pored over genealogical records, we would find that she had lived a long life that took her across the Atlantic Ocean: she was born in 1714 in London and died in 1796 in Newport, Rhode Island. If we searched for her name in the *Newport Mercury*, the city's weekly newspaper, we would discover that she had been a teacher who had considered opening a boarding school in her home. "SARAH OSBORN, Schoolmistress in Newport, proposes to keep a Boarding School," declared an advertisement in 1758. "Any person desirous of sending Children, may be accommodated, and have them instructed in Reading, Writing, Plain Work, Embroidering, Tent Stitch, Samplers, &c on reasonable Terms." And if we sat down to read Newport's many volumes of church records, we would find that she and her second husband, Henry, had been members of the First Church of Christ (later known as the First Congregational Church). Most intriguing, we would learn that in 1826, thirty years after her death, her church had organized a charity known as the Osborn Society.

But without her writings, we would have no way to make sense of these fragmentary glimpses of Sarah's life, the scattered remains of a world far removed from our own. Although we would know that she had been a teacher and a Christian, possibly an influential one, we would have no sense of her as a living, breathing person who had once walked down Newport's cobbled streets. None of these records captures the pious, intelligent, and sometimes anguished voice that we hear in the pages of her writings. None of them tells us about the everyday joys and sorrows that influenced her image of God. And none reveals her struggle to believe that a loving God had designed everything in her life—even her moments of doubt and despair—for her own good.

When Sarah Osborn died in 1796 at the age of eighty-two, frail and nearly blind, she left behind few possessions of value: a gold locket, a silver spoon inscribed with her second husband's initials, a maple desk. But more precious, in her opinion, were the thousands of diary pages she had sewn together into neat booklets, each marked with a number and date. Even after more than two centuries, her tight stitches have never come unraveled. On the cover of one of her diaries, she bequeathed her words to "the disposal of providence." Her most cherished hope was that someday her manuscripts would be read by people who shared her hunger to communicate with a personal, majestic, sovereign God. More than two centuries later, her writings can help transport us back to the world of eighteenth-century America, a world that has much to say to our own.

Introduction

*If a word in these lines ever prove useful to one soul after my decease
it will be ten thousand times more than I deserve from the hands of a
bountiful God to him alone be all the glory.*[1]

What can the story of an eighteenth-century woman's life tell us about
the rise of evangelical Christianity in America?

This is a book about Sarah Osborn, a woman born three centuries ago,
and the strange yet familiar world in which she lived. Strange, because she
rejected many of the axioms about human goodness, freedom, and self-
determination that Americans today take for granted. Familiar, because she
belonged to the first generation of evangelicals in America, and she helped
create a dynamic new religious movement that has flourished in our modern world. Her passionate language of sin, repentance, and conversion still
reverberates on the American landscape, a tribute to the enduring power of
born-again Christianity.

Few people today have ever heard of Sarah Osborn, but at a time when
virtually all women were forbidden to vote, attend college, seek ordina-
tion, or own property if they were married, she became a well-known religious leader. Her life story, as dramatic as a novel, was filled with tragedy.
Born in 1714 and raised by parents whom she later described as "severe," she
struggled with suicidal feelings in her youth; eloped at the age of seventeen
with a sailor, Samuel Wheaten, who died two years later, leaving her with
a one-year-old son to support; married a tailor, Henry Osborn, a widower
with three children, who suffered a physical or mental breakdown that left
him unable to work; and toiled long hours as a schoolteacher in order to
pay her family's bills. Despite her constant battle to achieve economic security, she remained so indigent throughout her life that her name never
appeared on Newport's tax lists. Her beloved son, her only child, died at

Two pages from Sarah Osborn's diary, March 15, 1758. Osborn cut pieces of folio paper into squares and sewed them together to make individual books. (Her stitching is visible along the side of the page.) Each diary page measured approximately 4 x 6 inches. Courtesy of the Newport Historical Society.

for thy Glory and my future
encouragement yt I may ne
ver sink under a prospect
of the frowns of Mortals
Let faith be strong and then
nothing can disquiet me but
when faith totters nothing
can establish me Lord increse
my faith this is thy glorious
gift and by this thou wilt
be glorified faith will work
by Love and purifie the heart
and influence to beter obedience
and thou shalt have the Glory
while worthless I reap the
comfort o guard me against
accursed Pride my shield my
Rock and sure defence save
me here because this will
displease and dishonour thee
o Let all the world be against
me rather then suffer me
to displease and dishonour
thee o Hold me by thy almighty

the age of eleven. Through it all, she endured chronic bouts of illness. Although it is impossible to diagnose her disease across the span of almost three centuries, her symptoms suggest that she may have suffered from either rheumatoid arthritis or multiple sclerosis.

Yet despite these tribulations, Sarah was so charismatic that many people sought her spiritual counsel. Like the followers of medieval women saints, they seemed to interpret Sarah's afflictions as a mark of her sanctity, a symbol of her closeness to a suffering Christ. Reputed to be gifted in prayer, she became more popular than any of the ordained ministers in her town. During the mid-1760s she emerged as the leader of a remarkable religious revival that brought as many as five hundred people—including large numbers of slaves—to her house each week. Although she remained poor, strangers from as far away as Canada and the West Indies sent money to help defray her expenses, eager to help the woman who had become virtually a Protestant saint.[2]

Sarah spent many hours teaching her school, reading the Bible, attending church, doing chores, and sharing the gospel, but she saw her life first and foremost as a *writing* life: she wrote early in the morning, sometimes before daybreak, putting down her quill only when it was time to feed her family and teach her students; she wrote at noontime between sessions of her school; and if she could force herself to stay awake she wrote late in the evenings by the light of her fireplace, squinting to see the pages in front of her. If she wore a pocket tied around her waist (a common piece of clothing for colonial women), she may have carried a pen and paper with her as she did her chores. Because she hoped to make a "hidden God" visible, she picked up her pen day after day, hoping to see his refracted image on the page. "O blessed be God that I have been taught to write," she rejoiced in her diary, "since that is the means that God has made the most Effectual of all other to fix my thoughts on Eternal things." When she explained that "'tis in this way of musing that the fire burns," she echoed a verse from Jeremiah: "His word is in my heart like a fire, a fire shut up in my bones. I am weary of holding it in; indeed, I cannot." Writing was almost a compulsion for her, an obsession. A fire in her bones that she could not put out. Besides composing a memoir at the age of twenty-nine, she wrote hundreds of letters and kept a diary for at least two decades, filling as many as fifty volumes and fifteen thousand pages with her heartfelt prayers to God.[3] More than two thousand pages of her manuscripts still survive.

Although Sarah did not know the formal rules of spelling, capitalization, or punctuation, she wrote with such raw power that her words seem to speak from the page. Rather than wasting time puzzling over where to put commas or periods, she wrote in a stream of consciousness style that anticipated later writers such as Virginia Woolf and James Joyce. Pouring out her thoughts in long, flowing sentences that spill into one another without a single pause or break, she recaptured the immediacy and intensity of her experiences. There are no white spaces on her pages, no moments of silence that invite readers to take a breath or collect their thoughts. Instead there is only her quiet, insistent voice telling story after story about the experiences that had shaped her understanding of God.

Sarah's faith influenced every facet of her life: her understanding of suffering, for example, and her attitude toward slavery. It affected how she thought about her gender, how she spent her money, how she educated the children in her school, and how she coped with the loss of loved ones. Although she imagined God as too sovereign and mysterious to be fully grasped by the human mind, she searched for his presence in all her experiences, hoping to come to a deeper understanding of how he was directing her life. He was the Alpha and the Omega, the beginning and the end—the reason her life bore meaning.

A history of Sarah Osborn's life and times, this book traces both her own individual story and the rise of the evangelical movement in the decades before the American Revolution. Although many people associate evangelicalism with modern religious leaders like Billy Graham and Rick Warren, its roots can be traced back to the eighteenth century.[4] In response to social, political, economic, and intellectual transformations that were transatlantic in scope, eighteenth-century Protestants throughout the Atlantic world gradually created a new kind of faith that we now call evangelicalism. The word itself was not new, and its roots stretch back to the Greek *evangelion*, meaning "gospel."[5] The sixteenth-century Protestant reformers used *evangelical* to emphasize the their reliance on the gospel message they found in scripture. Yet during the eighteenth century the word became increasingly identified with revivalists who emphasized a personal relationship with God, the joy of being born again, and the call to spread the gospel around the globe. Although Sarah described herself simply as a Protestant, she seemed to sense that her faith represented something new, and like other converts she settled on the adjective *evangelical* to describe it. After a night of prayer, for example, she wrote about her experience of "true evangelical repentance."[6]

Sarah's manuscripts offer a unique vantage point on the rise of the evangelical movement that can help us understand how and why it emerged

A letter from Sarah Osborn to Joseph Fish, dated September 5, 1759. Her letters were written on folio pages measuring 9 x 14 inches. Courtesy of the American Antiquarian Society.

in the eighteenth century. Most books about evangelicalism focus on male leaders like Jonathan Edwards or George Whitefield, but historical change takes place from the bottom up as well as the top down, and Sarah Osborn's story can help us appreciate why so many people in the eighteenth century were searching for a new kind of Christianity, a Christianity that would better meet their spiritual needs. Like thousands of other converts, Sarah was drawn to evangelicalism because it helped her make sense of changes in everyday life that did not yet have a name. Words like *capitalism, individualism, Enlightenment,* and *humanitarianism* were not coined until the late eighteenth and nineteenth centuries, but language often lags behind reality, and Sarah seems to have recognized that the austere Puritanism of her childhood was under attack by a growing faith in human goodness and individual freedom. She admired evangelical ministers because of her belief that they offered convincing answers to the most pressing questions of her day—questions about the nature of God, the meaning of suffering, and the definition of truth. Sarah wanted to know what sort of God had created the world, why evil exists, and whether there is any inherent goodness in human nature. She wondered why "the poor are always with us" (in the words of the apostle Matthew) and whether slavery could be just. She wondered whether the pursuit of happiness should be the ultimate goal of human life. And most of all, she wondered what her individual story meant in the larger scheme of the universe.

Explaining the rise of evangelicalism is not an easy task, but it is clear that the movement emerged in response to momentous changes in politics, economics, intellectual life, science, and technology that laid the foundations for our modern world. The rise of merchant capitalism sanctioned economic liberty and self-interest; a consumer revolution gave people greater freedom to make choices about their material lives than ever before; the 1689 Toleration Act in Britain guaranteed Protestants (though not Catholics) the right to worship freely without fear of state violence or persecution; technological advances led to improvements in the standard of living; scientific discoveries inspired a new faith in human progress; and ordinary people insisted that they had the right to govern themselves. In 1700 no one would have imagined that revolution was imminent, but by 1800 both the United States and France had violently rejected the divine right of kings.

Accompanying these changes were new currents of thought that historians have termed the Enlightenment—an intellectual movement that was premised on the assumption that individuals had the freedom to create a better world. As the historian Peter Gay has explained, the Enlightenment was committed to "freedom in its many forms—freedom from arbitrary power, freedom of speech, freedom of trade, freedom to realize one's talents, freedom of aesthetic response, freedom, in a word, of moral man to make his own way in the world." As we shall see, Gay's masculine language obscures the profound effects of the Enlightenment on women, but his central point remains important: Enlightenment thinkers hoped to liberate people from the shackles of the past by insisting that every hypothesis about human nature and society had to be tested by both reason and experience. With its critical spirit, its faith in progress, and its celebration of the individual, the Enlightenment marked the creation of our modern world.[7]

Since some of its most prominent thinkers were hostile to institutional religion, the Enlightenment has often been imagined as skeptical and anti-Christian.[8] Yet even though there is no doubt that the Enlightenment heralded the birth of modern secularism, it also transformed Christianity from within. (Since some historians have suggested that the Enlightenment grew out of the critical spirit of the Reformation, such cross-fertilization is not surprising.) As the historian J. G. A. Pocock reminds us, there was no single, monolithic Enlightenment in the eighteenth century but rather "a family of Enlightenments, displaying both family resemblances and family quarrels (some of them bitter and even bloody)"—and one of those quarrels centered on religion. In contrast to the French Enlightenment, which tended to be particularly radical and anti-clerical, the British Enlightenment led to the emergence of a new, liberal form of Protestantism that emphasized tolerance, reason, free will, human goodness, and God's benevolence.[9] (Since "liberal" Protestants in the eighteenth century believed that the Bible should be read literally, including the creation account in Genesis, readers should be careful not to confuse them with the political or religious liberals of modern America. *Liberal* is always a relative term.)

Historians have often portrayed evangelical Protestantism as reactionary and backward looking, a backlash against new currents of Enlightenment thought. Like its liberal counterpart, however, it has endured for more than three centuries because it represented a vector of modernity, a creative response to the transformations that were reshaping everyday life. Evangelicals condemned Enlightenment skeptics for daring to question the literal truth of the Bible and the divinity of Christ, and because they felt as though their beliefs were under attack they could sound more extreme than earlier generations of Protestants. American evangelicals, in particular—most of whom were Calvinists in the years before the American Revolution—fiercely denied that humans were free to choose their own destinies. (In England, by contrast, the Wesleyan stream of the evangelical movement preached a gospel of free will.) Emphasizing the doctrine of original sin, American evangelicals described humans as inherently inclined to evil. "I bewail the depravity of my nature, so totally corrupt," Sarah Osborn lamented in her diary in 1760.[10] Evangelicals also set themselves apart from Enlightenment thinkers by emphasizing the redemptive power of suffering and the reality of hell. Rejecting the humanism of the age, they insisted that God had created the world to glorify himself, not to make people happy.

Yet evangelicals could not ignore the intellectual challenges to their faith, and as they tried to adapt to a changing world they absorbed many Enlightenment ideas as their own. As David Bebbington has argued, "The Evangelical version of Protestantism was created by the Enlightenment."[11] Influenced by the long Christian interest in religious experience, evangelicals were especially attracted to John Locke's emphasis on firsthand experience as the basis of knowledge. "All our knowledge is founded [on] *Experience*," Locke wrote. If the Enlightenment was an Age of Reason, it was also an Age of Experience, and Enlightenment thinkers insisted that knowledge must be based on empirical proof rather than clerical authority or inherited tradition. "*How do I know this God is mine; and that I myself am not deceived?*" Sarah Osborn asked. "By the Evidences of a *work of grace* wrought in my Soul."[12] Ironically, evangelicals defended their faith against the skeptical and liberal strains of the Enlightenment by appropriating an enlightened language of experience, certainty, evidence, and sensation as their own. Unlike earlier Protestants, who had been hesitant to appear too confident about their salvation (lest they be guilty of pride), the new evangelicals of the eighteenth century claimed that they could empirically feel and know whether they had been spiritually reborn.

With Christian roots stretching back to Bernard of Clairvaux and the Protestant Reformers, this emphasis on personal religious experience was not new, and seventeenth-century Puritans had often scrutinized their lives for visible proof of God's grace. But evangelicals spoke the language of experience with a fervor that few other Christians could match.[13] They claimed that an intellectual, rational understanding of doctrine was less valuable than a personal experience of the Holy Spirit. By arguing that nothing was more important than being "born again," they gave ordinary people—including women, slaves, and Native Americans—a powerful language to justify their religious authority. Even though evangelicals (like most Enlightenment thinkers) portrayed women as naturally subordinate to men, they also argued that converts were transformed by their rebirth in Christ. Despite her fear of going beyond her "line," Sarah Osborn claimed to have been called to lead prayer meetings for slaves and to become a published author, a rare distinction for women at the time. According to surviving church records, the majority of evangelical converts in the eighteenth century were women, a pattern that has continued to our own day.

Historians have usually depicted the Enlightenment as an elite, masculine movement that marginalized women, but once we recognize that there were multiple "Enlightenments" that took place within Protestantism as well as against it, a more complicated picture emerges. Influenced by the empiricism of the Enlightenment, evangelicals crafted a theology with a potentially radical edge. By the end of the eighteenth century growing numbers of female authors would defend their right to participate in the public sphere on the grounds of their firsthand experience of God's grace.

Evangelicals absorbed other aspects of Enlightenment thought as well—including its faith in human progress, its humanitarian ideals, its emphasis on the affections, and its individualism—but always with their own distinctive stamp. They were fervent believers in progress who dreamed of a millennial age of peace and prosperity, but they denied that progress was possible without God's grace. They shared the humanitarian zeal to alleviate suffering, but they argued that there was no greater suffering than to be alienated from God—a conviction that made them more zealous about "saving" sinners than virtually any other group of Christians before them. They assumed that virtuous behavior flowed from the "affections" (the emotions), but they argued that the heart was naturally corrupt; hence true virtue depended on being born again. And perhaps most striking, they elevated the importance of the individual by defining Christianity as a personal relationship with Jesus but denied that individuals were free to determine their own destinies. Unlike Adam Smith and other Enlightenment thinkers, they condemned self-interest as another name for selfishness. True Christians should be willing to sacrifice their individual interests for the common good.

As these examples illustrate, the relationship between evangelicalism and the Enlightenment was fraught with tensions. Although early evangelicals absorbed many aspects of Enlightenment thought, they also tried to resist optimistic ideas about innate human goodness, the sufficiency of human reason, and the benefits of self-love. In many ways the evangelical faith that emerged in the eighteenth century was an "enlightened" one that was at home in an increasingly individualistic and religiously pluralistic society. Yet evangelicalism, like the Enlightenment, was never a single, coherent movement, and evangelicals often stood in an uneasy relationship to the modern world that they had helped create.

Historians like to provide precise dates for events, but major historical developments tend to emerge gradually over time, and evangelicalism was no exception. For lack of a better term I have identified evangelicalism as a *movement*, but it would be more precise to describe it as a loose coalition of leaders, ideas, and practices that took decades to come together. In the late seventeenth century, a small group of Lutherans and Reformed Protestants tried to recapture the vitality of the Protestant Reformation by emphasizing heart-centered experience over dry, systematic theologies, but their efforts did not come to fruition until the transatlantic revivals of the late 1730s and the 1740s.[14] Even then, evangelicalism remained closely connected to older forms of Protestantism, and in America there were clear continuities between seventeenth-century Puritans and their eighteenth-century evangelical descendants. Looking backward as well as forward, evangelicals were linked to the Puritans by their emphasis on God's sovereignty, their dark view of human nature, their vivid belief in heaven and hell, their reliance on the Bible, and their ambivalence about the value of everyday life. Yet in order to meet the new spiritual needs of their age, evangelicals also set themselves apart from earlier Protestants in several crucial ways: they placed more trust in the reliability of firsthand experience; they expressed greater assurance about their ability to know whether they had been "saved"; they made the converted individual, not the community or the church, the main locus of authority; they emphasized that all Christians were called to spread the gospel through missions and evangelism; they defined true religion as a matter of the heart or affections; they had a robust faith in progress; and they borrowed the techniques of the consumer revolution to spread the gospel.

In brief, evangelicalism was a heart-centered, experiential, individualistic, and evangelistic form of Protestantism that was intertwined with the rise of the modern world. Although evangelicals from different religious backgrounds sometimes disagreed on doctrinal issues (including free will and predestination), they shared a common faith in biblical authority, human sinfulness, God's sovereignty, and the possibility of redemption, and they drew firm boundaries between those who had been born again and those who had not.[15] Although other Christians were often offended by their assurance, evangelicals boldly proclaimed their salvation. Sarah Osborn, for one, was absolutely certain that she had experienced the "new birth."

Part One

A Memoir, 1743

Chapter 1

Never Despair

*Having been for some years under strong inclinations to write some
thing of what i can remember of the dealings of god with my soul from
a child hoping it may consist with the glory of god at which i trust
through grace i sinceirly aim and the good of my own soul as a means
to stir up gratitude in the most ungratefull of all hearts even mine to
a glorious and compatinate Saviour for all his benefits towards so vile
a monster in sin as i am and for the incouragement of any who may
providentialy lite on these Lines after my discease to trust in the Lord
and never dispair of his mercy since one so stuborn and rebellious as i
have thro the sovereighn riches of free grace obtain it [I have begun
this memoir] but oh Let all tremble at the thought of abusing a saviour so Least god should say Let them alone they shall never enter in to
my rest.*[1]

1743. Revivals are the talk of every tea table, sewing circle, and tavern
in New England. George Whitefield, the young evangelist famous for his
crossed eyes and honeyed tongue, preaches to thousands of people up and
down the eastern seaboard, leaving many in tears. James Davenport, another
young evangelist, protests against the "idolatry" of material things by stripping off his breeches and throwing them into a bonfire, leading to speculation that his "wild, frantic, and extravagant" behavior might be the result of
a mental breakdown. After several Massachusetts ministers complain about
"*disorderly Tumults* and *indecent Behaviors*," others insist that "there has been
a *happy* and *remarkable Revival of Religion in many Parts of this Land, thro'
an uncommon divine Influence*."*[2] Jonathan Edwards, later renowned as one
of America's greatest theologians, publishes a book defending the revivals

as a genuine work of God, perhaps even a harbinger of the millennium. Charles Chauncy, his fiercest critic, retorts that the revivals are nothing more than the product of overheated "passions."[3] The excitement grows as newspapers and periodicals report that revivals are taking place not only in New England but also in Scotland, England, Switzerland, and Germany.

And in Newport, Rhode Island, Sarah Osborn sits quietly at her desk, a pen in her hand, wondering how to tell the story of her life—how to find words for the sorrows and joys, the moments of despair and trust, that have led her to Christ. She has already written three volumes of diaries, but she wants something more than a daily record of her thoughts and feelings. Inspired by the revivals, she wishes to understand how God has been directing her life since her childhood. She is young (only twenty-nine), female, and poor, but like many other ordinary people caught up in the fervor of the awakening, she believes that her story is immensely valuable as a testimony to God's grace.

With much to say, she does not know how to begin. Which stories should she share? How can she make sense of all that has happened to her on the way to being "born again"? Dipping her pen in a pot of ink, she writes a breathless sentence that stretches all the way down the page. (Her words tumble out with such urgency that she forgets to include a subject and a verb.) Gathering up the fragments of her memories, she frames her life story around her "vile" sinfulness, God's grandeur, and the unmerited, priceless gift of "free grace" that has saved her from "despair."

Sarah fills more than 140 pages with her bittersweet memories of God's "dealings" with her. She writes about her childhood fears, her angry battles with her parents, and her desire to accept her sufferings as God's will. She writes about her marriage at the young age of seventeen, the birth of her son, and the crushing poverty that makes it difficult to buy food and firewood. She writes about her anguish over her "vile" sins and her resolutions to "lead a new life" in the midst of the awakening. And in what will become a recurring refrain, she writes about her long struggle to overcome her feelings of doubt and hopelessness, what later generations of Americans will call depression. Writing is her way not only of communicating with God but of staving off the darkness that sometimes seems about to engulf her. The lesson she has learned along her religious pilgrimage can be summarized in just a few words. "Trust in the Lord," she advises, "and never despair of his mercy."[4]

Sarah Osborn's memoir is both a meditation on her past and a declaration of a new religious identity. After years of doubt, she longs to leave her burdens behind in order to embark on a new life devoted to Christ. By casting her future with those who demand an "evangelical faith" or "evangelical repentance" (and who will someday be known simply as evangelicals), she rejects not only her former life but the tempting world of enlightened self-interest and consumer choice emerging around her.

A New Life

With the exception of a single letter, Sarah's memoir, finished in 1743, is the earliest piece of her writing that still survives. Although she had thought about writing a memoir for "some years," she had always hesitated, daunted by the challenge of narrating the story of her entire life. Unlike a diary, which could be fragmentary and episodic, a memoir was supposed to have a coherent plot, and although she knew that she wanted her story to be an archetypal tale of sin and salvation, the prodigal coming home to her father, she may have worried about how she would fit her complicated life into a single, linear framework. Instead of simply recording what had happened to her each day, she would have to construct a single, coherent "I" out of her multiple, contradictory experiences.[5]

Since Sarah was one of relatively few American or British women in the eighteenth century to write a memoir (most chose to write diaries instead), it is worth asking why she decided to subject herself to such a difficult discipline. Why, in 1743, after years of hesitation, did she finally sit down to write the story of her life?

People often decide to write about their lives during times of turmoil and disruption. By putting their stories into writing, they try to impose coherence on events that stretch the limits of their understanding: for example, the loss of a loved one, the birth of a child, or the outbreak of war. As one critic has explained, writing can be a response to "a sense of discontinuity of self—I was that, now I am this; I was there, now I am here. Keeping a life record can be an attempt to preserve continuity seemingly broken or lost."[6] In Sarah's case, she seems to have begun writing in order to make sense of two dramatic upheavals that had recently shaken her life: her spiritual awakening during the revivals and the loss of almost all her money because of bankruptcy in September 1742.

First had come the exultation of her renewed commitment to Christ. During the early 1740s, she had been an eyewitness to one of the most thrilling spectacles that had ever taken place in New England—a religious "awakening" that brought thousands of new converts into churches. Like others who have been touched by major historical events (one thinks of the American Revolution, the Civil War, or the attacks of September 11, 2001), she wanted to articulate the dizzying sensation of watching the wheels of history turn—in her case, of watching hundreds of people crying out for mercy and rejoicing at their salvation. When she realized that she, too, had been saved, she was so overwhelmed with joy that she could barely find words to describe it. It was not enough to say that she had been "born again"; she had been virtually resurrected, "restored as it were from the grave."[7]

But then, in a turn of events that was almost too bewildering to comprehend, she had plunged from the elation of feeling God's "astonishing grace" into the despair of losing the little money she had managed to save. Her husband, Henry, a tailor, had hoped to strike it rich by investing in a Newport ship, but instead he went bankrupt.[8] When she finished her memoir in 1743, she was still not sure how they would find the money to repay their creditors.

Torn by conflicting feelings of thankfulness and loss, Sarah seems to have hoped that recording her life story would help her to come to a deeper acceptance of God's plan for her. Writing would help her to remember what was really important: not her possessions, but her relationship to God. Although she wrote only obliquely about her struggles to accept God's will, she hinted at her difficulties when she confessed her desire to "stir up gratitude in the most ungrateful of all hearts, even mine." By looking back over the whole story of her life, she hoped to reassure herself that even in her darkest moments, when she had felt most alone and vulnerable, God had been invisibly guiding her and arranging everything for her own good. At the beginning of her memoir, when she explained that she hoped to inspire others to "trust in the Lord and never despair of his mercy," she may also have been speaking to herself.[9] She, too, had to remember to place her trust in God instead of succumbing to despair.

Although Sarah could have written another volume of diaries in 1743 to help her cope with her "unbelieving fears" (she would write more than forty volumes of diaries in the years ahead), she had "resolved to lead a new life," and she thought that writing a memoir was the best way to strengthen her commitment to become a new self in Christ. Beginning with her birth and moving forward, she wanted to give her past a new meaning, imagining all her former trials as nothing more than the prologue to her "astonishing" experience of "the sovereign riches of free grace." She sought both to bring her old self into line with the new person she had become and to determine the self she would be in the future. Because she had not always been an evangelical, she seems to have been afraid that she might backslide again, forgetting who she "really" was. Writing would allow her to fix her identity on a page, anchoring her to the new self she had become. If she were ever tempted to doubt the reality of her conversion or to question God's goodness and mercy, she would be able to reread her narrative. "Do not trust your slippery memories with such a multitude of remarkable passages of Providence as you have, and shall meet with in your way to heaven," advised the English Puritan John Flavel. "Certainly it were not so great a loss to lose your silver, your goods and chattels, as it is to lose your experiences which God has this way given you in the world."[10] Flawed by original sin, humans were too imperfect to remember all of their religious experiences, but if they committed them to paper they could preserve them against forgetfulness. Unlike prayer or other religious practices, writing led to the creation of material, permanent objects that could serve as commemorations of God's grace. Sarah's memoir would be a lasting testimony to the ultimate meaning of her life.

Sarah never would have used such modern language, but she seems to have approached her memoir as a project in self-fashioning, a "technology of the self."[11] Autobiography, as one critic has noted, is not only the narration of the self but the *construction* of the self. Although Sarah began her memoir by insisting that she was "impartial in this work, declaring the truth and nothing but the truth," she inevitably made choices about which details to include and which to leave out. Instead of recording her whole life as it was actually lived, her memoir reveals the "self" that she chose to share—and on a deeper level, the self that she wanted to be.[12]

Yet unlike the more liberal thinkers of her age who believed that individuals had the power to remake themselves (one thinks of Benjamin Franklin's faith in self-improvement), Sarah insisted that selfhood was bestowed, not chosen. Evangelicals absorbed parts of the Enlightenment's individualistic language as their own, but they still claimed that their identities ultimately came from Christ, not their own efforts at self-construction. Denying her own agency, Sarah believed that she was helpless to change herself, but she nonetheless hoped that writing, like listening to sermons or reading the Bible, could be a "means of grace."[13] She prayed that her memoir would be a channel of divine transformation, the means through which God would pour greater humility and obedience into her heart.

Although writing was Sarah's most cherished religious practice, it was not her only "means of grace." Besides writing a spiritual memoir (and then thousands of pages of diaries), she prayed, listened to sermons, joined church members around the table of the Lord's Supper, read the Bible and devotional literature, and visited the sick and needy. Even her modest dress and speech reflected her attempt to conform her entire identity to God's will. At a time when colonial women copied the latest dress styles from England, she wore plain clothing, and despite the popularity of salons among the better sort, she thought that the most important topic of conversation should be Christianity. Religion was not simply a way of thinking for her; it was a way of acting. By disciplining both her body and her mind, she hoped to empty herself in order to make room for God's grace. "Lord, nothing Else can, Nothing else shall satisfy my craving soul but thee," she wrote in a later diary entry. "O fill me with thyself."[14]

Becoming a new self was a painful process that involved renunciation as well as affirmation. At the same time as Sarah celebrated the birth of her new identity in Christ, she also expressed deep hostility to her former self—a "stubborn and rebellious" sinner who had disobeyed both her parents and God. Condemning herself in harsh language as a "hell deserving sinner," "*an heir of hell*," a "fool," and "a poor sinful worm" who was "unworthy of the Least mercy," she expressed amazement that God had chosen her for salvation. She was "astonished," she wrote, "at God's patience in sparing me alive and out of hell." If she had not emphasized her sinfulness, an emerging evangelical community would not have recognized her as one of their own. But the cost was high. Becoming an evangelical empowered her to construct a new self, but it also required her to destroy the person she had once been.[15]

Yet even though Sarah knew what kind of story she was *supposed* to write, she could not always make her life fit into the conventional evangelical framework of sin and redemption. Reading her memoir is like watching the collision between her real, personal experiences and the expectations of a new evangelical community, a community that was linked together not only by shared beliefs but by a shared narrative voice.

The Great Noise

The self that Sarah Osborn presented in the pages of her memoir stood in stark contrast to the enlightened, optimistic understanding of selfhood that had begun to gain ascendancy in the eighteenth-century Atlantic world. Like the evangelical ministers whom she most admired, Sarah seems to have feared that Protestants had begun to drift away from the faith of their fathers, abandoning the Puritans' stark vision of human helplessness and depravity in favor of a more positive understanding of human goodness and free will. In the late seventeenth century, ministers in both England and America complained about a "visible decay of Godliness," and by the 1730s, according to Jonathan Edwards, there was a "great noise about Arminianism."[16] (The term *Arminianism* refers to the beliefs of Jacobus Arminius, a sixteenth-century Dutch theologian who argued that humans could put themselves in position to earn God's favor by their good works. Nothing was more offensive to Calvinist sympathies than the idea that humans could do anything to save themselves from hell.) When Sarah listened to sermons or read accounts of the revivals in *The Christian History*, a popular periodical founded in 1743, the echoes of that great noise were impossible to ignore. According to ministers, the contagion of Arminianism was everywhere, and some even confessed to having once been infected with it themselves. Besides complaining that the people in his congregation "had made themselves easy for some time with the Arminian way of conversion," the Reverend Jonathan Parsons admitted that he himself "had been greatly in Love with *Arminian* Principles, and especially I abhorred the Doctrine of GOD'S ABSOLUTE SOVEREIGNTY." Joseph Park, a missionary, testified that before the revivals, "he had secretly believed there was something [good] in men to begin with, and that Gospel grace came to make [it] perfect."[17]

Since historians have been hard-pressed to find many genuine Arminians among New England's clergy, they have wondered whether revivalists overstated this religious "declension" in order to make more converts. Perhaps Arminianism was a myth or a bogey man that ministers invoked whenever they wanted to remind people not to stray from orthodoxy. After surveying New England's Congregational clergy in 1726, Cotton Mather wrote, "I cannot learn, That among all the Pastors of Two Hundred Churches, there is one Arminian."[18] Yet whether or not there were "real" Arminians in New England, people at the time clearly believed that there were, and perception can be as important as reality in shaping historical events. When ministers expressed alarm about the spreading heresy of Arminianism, they may have been exaggerating, but they were also trying to make sense of confusing religious changes that did not have a simple name.

Why were Sarah Osborn and other evangelicals in the 1740s so grimly certain that they were standing in the midst of a religious crisis? For those in New England, the first and most visible sign of religious decline was the growing popularity of Anglican worship. Of course, the evangelical

movement grew inside Anglican circles in England, and George Whitefield and John Wesley, two of the most influential evangelical leaders of
the eighteenth century, were ordained Anglican ministers. But ever since
the early 1600s, when Puritans had fled to Massachusetts Bay to escape
Anglican persecution, New England ministers had reviled Anglicans and
prohibited them from worshiping freely. (Contrary to popular myth, the
Puritans did not found New England as a haven of religious freedom, and
in order to maintain the purity of their holy commonwealth they severely
punished dissenters. Sarah's home of Rhode Island, founded by the visionary Roger Williams, was exceptional in extending tolerance to all religions.) The situation changed in 1689 when Parliament passed the Toleration Act, which extended religious freedom to all Protestants in the British
Empire. Almost immediately afterward, King's Chapel, the first Anglican
church in New England, was founded in Boston, and many of its members
ranked among the leading gentry in the colony. Even more shocking to
Puritan sensibilities was the decision of several Congregationalist ministers, including Timothy Cutler, the rector of Yale College, to conform to
the Church of England in 1722, and the decision of two more ministers to
follow their example in 1734.[19] By 1776, Massachusetts counted twenty-two
Anglican churches and Connecticut thirty-seven. (According to the historians Edwin S. Gaustad and Philip L. Barlow, "A report of 1774 reckoned
one out of every 13 citizens of Connecticut to be an Anglican.")[20] Although
some Anglican ministers in the colonies became part of the nascent evangelical movement—for example, Devereux Jarratt in Virginia—many others found evangelical piety too extreme. Rejecting the Calvinist belief in
human depravity and predestination as "not only most *absurd*, but likewise
blasphemous against *God*," they insisted that humans were saved by their
good works as well as by their faith.[21]

Since Sarah had briefly attended Newport's Trinity Church, the largest
and wealthiest church in the city, she was particularly aware of the threat
that the liberal wing of the Anglican movement posed to Calvinist theology. While she spent Sunday mornings in the First Church of Christ
listening to stern sermons about the futility of good works, she knew that
only a few blocks away the members of Trinity were listening to a more
comforting message. As the Reverend James Honeyman assured his congregation, "Our whole Duty may be brought into a very narrow Compass,"
namely, "The Love of God and our Neighbors."[22] In later years, Sarah
would condemn this kind of preaching for "rocking . . . People more and
more to sleep in the cradle of security instead of Exciting them to fly from
the wrath to come."[23]

The Friends meetinghouse in Newport, mid-nineteenth century.
Courtesy of the Newport Historical Society.

Sarah was less critical of Quakers (perhaps because one of her closest friends, Susanna Anthony, had grown up in a Quaker family), but most evangelicals judged them to be as dangerous as Anglicans. Besides denying the doctrine of original sin, Quakers claimed that the Bible was not the final revelation of God: all believers had a spark of divinity in them, an "inner light" that made it possible to receive ongoing communications from God. If this were not proof enough of their "enthusiasm," they also allowed women to lead religious meetings, a clear violation of Paul's command that women should "keep silence in the churches." Although most Quakers lived in Pennsylvania, they could be found in all of the colonies by the mid-eighteenth century, and they built a large meetinghouse in Newport.[24]

Evangelicals were also troubled by the spread of new, "enlightened" ideas about God and human nature. Since Sarah was poor and female, she did not have access to what college students were reading, but she often heard ministers criticizing the "new learning" in their sermons, and she was convinced that Christianity was under attack. Because she lived in one of the most cosmopolitan cities in America, she had a keen sense of the changing intellectual climate of the eighteenth century. Newport's shops were stocked with books imported from England, and the Philosophical Society, a group that had been founded by George Berkeley, the bishop of Cloyne and one of the eighteenth century's most famous philosophers, met regularly in Newport's taverns to discuss the latest theological and scientific works. (Berkeley had lived in Newport from 1729 until 1731.)[25] Based on booksellers' catalogues and the records of both private and circulating libraries, few educated Americans read the works of radicals like Baruch Spinoza (the virtual father of the "radical Enlightenment"), but they were attracted to moderate thinkers like John Locke, Francis Hutcheson, John Tillotson, and Anthony Ashley Cooper, the third earl of Shaftesbury.[26] None of these men ever condemned Christianity as "priestcraft" or completely discarded the authority of biblical revelation, but they undermined older Calvinist assumptions about the self and God in quieter, more subtle ways. Shaftesbury, for example, argued that all humans have an innate moral sense that inclines them to ethical behavior, an idea that threatened the doctrine of original sin, and Hutcheson insisted that humans are naturally compassionate. John Tillotson, the archbishop of Canterbury, was especially controversial—and especially popular among the "better sort" in the colonies—because of his rejection of orthodox doctrines like predestination and eternal punishment and his emphasis on good works over doctrinal disputes.[27] Tillotson's sermons, according to one historian, "were probably the most widely read works of religious literature in America between 1690 and 1750," and his positive view of reason, his focus on morality, and his tolerance left an indelible impression on colonial American religion. After George Whitefield visited Harvard in 1741, he complained that more students were reading Tillotson than Thomas Shepard, the famous Puritan divine: a charge that Harvard's students and faculty heatedly denied.[28]

Whitefield was being deliberately polemical, but he had a point. After thousands of books were donated to Harvard and Yale in the early eighteenth century, ministry students were exposed to the ideas of "enlightened" British theologians who questioned traditional Christian doctrines. Although Sarah Osborn probably did not read any of these books herself, she was almost certainly familiar with them. Her uncle, the Reverend John Guyse, devoted much of his illustrious career to defending Calvinism against rationalism, and the authors that he found most objectionable were the same ones who caused controversy in New England. Thomas Chubb's books, for example, could be found at Harvard despite his denial of original sin and his radical claim that "reason either is, or ought to be, a sufficient guide in matters of religion." "I truly wish some of our *modern*

& new Books had never *arrived* or been read there," complained Benjamin Colman, "& particularly such as *Mr. Chubb*."[29] Students could also read books by authors like William Whiston, who rejected the doctrine of the Trinity; Daniel Whitby, who referred to the doctrine of predestination as "Bull"; and Samuel Clarke, whose elevation of human reason seemed so threatening that Thomas Clap, the president of Yale, eventually removed all his books from the library. (Clarke also portrayed God as a benevolent father, not as a stern judge, and suggested that the doctrine of the Trinity was unscriptural.)[30] Although Clap's censorship may have been an over-reaction, at least one Congregationalist minister traced his flirtation with "the dangerous error of Arminius" to "reading *Arminian Books*, and some of the Writings of such as are called Freethinkers." Writing in 1738, Edward Wigglesworth, the Hollis Professor of Divinity at Harvard, commented that his students were "loath to give up" the traditional doctrine of origi-nal sin, but "they seem hardly able to bear up against the Current of our English Writers of the present, and latter part of the last Century, who are almost all against it."[31]

As Sarah Osborn knew, a small but influential group of Congrega-tionalist clergy had responded to these enlightened ideas by moving in more liberal religious directions. In the 1720s, ministers like Benjamin Wadsworth and William Brattle began preaching a more optimistic form of Calvinism that emphasized religious tolerance, the rational order of the universe, and the benevolence of God, and although they remained ortho-dox, a small number of others stretched Calvinist theology to the breaking point. Four Congregationalist ministers faced well-publicized disciplinary hearings during the 1730s because of suspicions about their beliefs, and all but one were forced out of their pulpits. Samuel Osborn's crime was claim-ing that people could be saved by doing good deeds: "Men's Obedience is a Cause of their Justification," he declared. (Despite the common surname, he was not related to Sarah.) Benjamin Kent was even bolder, denying the Calvinist doctrine of predestination. According to his accusers, "he de-nied an absolute Election, and asserted a conditional one on the foresight of good works." Other ministers managed to keep their pulpits, but not without a fight. After William Balch was accused of preaching that "Man by Nature is more inclined to Virtue than Vice," a statement that flatly contradicted Calvinist theology, he was harassed by a conservative faction within his congregation.[32]

The number of liberal-leaning pastors remained small, but the mere fact of their existence was cause for scandal. Fearful that the faith of the

Puritans was being abandoned, the Reverend John White lamented that "some of Our *Young Men*, and such as are devoted to and educated for, the *Ministry* of the *Gospel*, are under *Prejudices* against, and fall from important Articles of the *Faith* of these *Churches*, and cast a favorable Eye upon, embrace, and as far as they dare, *argue* for, *propagate*, and *preach* the *Arminian Scheme*."[33]

Underlying these new ideas were changes occurring in everyday life that contributed to a greater confidence in human agency. As the historian C. C. Goen has argued, the revivalists of the awakening seem to have been less afraid of an actual "Arminian" faction than a changing climate of opinion, "a mood of rising confidence in man's ability to gain some purchase on the divine favor by human endeavor."[34] During the 1740s traditional ideas about hierarchy and deference had begun to break down under the pressures of political, economic, and scientific change. Politically, these years witnessed the emergence of a more representative form of government that vested authority in the people as well as the monarchy. Because all the colonies elected their lower assemblies, men with the minimal property required to vote felt as though they were important political actors in their own right, not just subjects of the king.[35] Scientifically, new discoveries, especially Isaac Newton's theory of gravitation, revolutionized the way that people imagined the universe. As the historian Roy Porter has commented, nature now seemed to be "a machine made up of material particles governed by universal laws, whose motions could be given mathematical expression"—a machine that did not seem to work exactly as it had been described in the Bible.[36] (If the Bible were literally true, then why did it portray the sun revolving around the earth instead of the earth revolving around the sun?) And economically, a consumer revolution made it possible for people throughout the colonies to buy a greater variety of British goods than ever before, enabling them to make more extensive choices about their everyday lives: what to eat and drink, what to wear, what books to read, and how to decorate their houses. Shopkeepers in cities and villages and peddlers in the countryside offered so many tempting wares for sale that in 1740 a Boston physician punned that the colonies were suffering from a bad case of "Galloping Consumption."[37] (The word *consumption* had two meanings in the eighteenth century: it referred both to the purchase of goods and the disease of tuberculosis.) In the seventeenth century only the wealthiest colonists had been able to afford luxuries like "*Fine Flanders Laces*" and "the Finest Dutch Linens," but in the early 1740s, as trade with

The Potter Family of Matunuck, Rhode Island, circa 1740. The family in
this portrait demonstrates its social status by displaying some of its most
valuable goods: expensive clothing, a tea set, and a young slave.
Courtesy of the Newport Historical Society.

England rapidly expanded, the middling sort found that they, too, could
participate in a thriving marketplace.[38]

Among the most desired commodities in the eighteenth century were
slaves, and there is no doubt that white colonists gained an inflated sense
of their own personal agency because of their control over the enslaved.
Slaveholders had the power to determine virtually every aspect of slaves'
lives, including whether their children or other loved ones would be sold,
and many exercised this power ruthlessly. Psychologically, masters seem to
have regarded slaves as symbols of their status and importance, and instead
of recoiling at the power they had been given, they prided themselves on it.
According to an Anglican priest in Maryland, masters should regard themselves as "God's overseers," and slaves should "*do all Service for THEM, as
if . . . for GOD himself.*"[39]

If slavery had been limited to the South, its effects might have been
mostly regional, but in the eighteenth century, slavery could be found in
every colony. Although most slaves lived in the South (where they made up
38 percent of the population by 1750), they also toiled as household servants

or farm laborers in the North, especially in cities. In Newport in 1748, blacks made up almost 17 percent of the population.[40] Although evangelical ministers do not seem to have realized it (and in fact, many of them owned slaves themselves), ministers undermined their message of human sinfulness and helplessness by insisting that white masters had a God-given right to own and control their slaves.

Proud of their ability to influence political decisions, to improve the material quality of their lives, to make consumer choices, and to own slaves, growing numbers of Anglo-Americans found it hard to believe the things the Calvinist tradition taught them. They did not feel helpless, but capable. Not weak, but strong. Not sinful, but worthy of the material goods that filled their parlors and the slaves who toiled in their fields. Although Perry Miller may have been exaggerating when he declared that by 1730, "the greatness of man's dependency had unaccountably become a euphemism for the greatness of man," his words contain a grain of truth.[41] Even though Americans knew that many things were still tragically out of their control, including the devastatingly high rate of infant mortality, they had new confidence in their ability to shape their lives.

For Sarah Osborn, and for thousands of evangelicals like her, this was nothing less than hubris. Only God could determine an individual's destiny.

Turned Fool and Distracted

Given the growing faith in human goodness, free will, and the sufficiency of reason, it is not surprising that evangelicals were often mocked for being too extreme in their piety—too strict and self-abasing. "Some would tell me I was turned fool and distracted when I said that I had been a vile sinner," Sarah confessed in her memoir, "for everybody knew I had been a sober woman all my days." When she insisted that true Christians had to give up "amusements" like singing, dancing, gossiping, and playing cards, many of her friends wondered why she was making such a fuss about trivial self-indulgences. "Some said they should hate such religion as caused people to forsake their friends," she remembered. "Others said in a way of derision they supposed I thought they were monsters now."[42]

Hostile jokes like these stung, but far more upsetting were the critiques of Protestants who might have been expected to sympathize with the emerging evangelical movement. Not all Protestants in New England believed that the awakening was a genuine "work of God," and as the revivals

became increasingly emotional in 1742 and 1743, ministers (and their congregations) began to split into competing parties. Charles Chauncy, one of
the leading opponents of the awakening, agreed with evangelicals that the
"Spirituality of Christians" rested in their "Lowliness, and Humility," but
he angrily accused the "awakened" of lacking both. In a tract published in
1743, *Seasonable Thoughts on the State of Religion in New-England,* he complained that while converts loudly chastised themselves for their sinfulness,
they were clearly proud of their piety. Ministers like George Whitefield
were not true Christians but "pompous" zealots who went from town to
town "boasting of their own superior Goodness."[43]

Converts during the revivals were criticized for being self-righteous,
overly emotional, and "enthusiastic." As people cried out for mercy, wept
over their sins, fell into "fits," or, in the most radical cases, claimed to have
seen visions of angels or heard heavenly voices, ministers worried that the
revivals had spun out of control. Chauncy argued that *"strange Effects* upon
the *Body"* were "produced . . . by the *wild and extravagant Conduct* of some
over-heated Preachers," not by the Holy Spirit. Pointing to the example of
James Davenport, who was infamous for stamping his feet, shrieking, and
threatening his listeners with graphic descriptions of damnation, Chauncy
claimed that ministers had deliberately inflamed their listeners' passions.
Ezra Stiles, the future president of Yale, remembered later that it seemed
as if "multitudes were seriously, soberly, and solemnly out of their wits."[44]

When Sarah began writing her memoir, the bitter controversies over
the revivals (and the complaints about her own newfound piety) were never
far from her thoughts, and besides hoping to strengthen her commitment
to Christ, she also seems to have wanted to defend the rising evangelical
movement from criticism. At first she seems to have intended to keep her
memoir private until her death, hoping that it would be read by future
generations of Christians who might "providentially light" on it after she
was gone. (There was a thriving custom of manuscript exchange in early
America, and Sarah may have hoped that someday her memoir would be
passed around within evangelical circles, as indeed it was.)[45] But at some
point she decided that her memoir was too valuable to put away in a drawer
during her lifetime. In 1744, only a year after the ink on her pages had
dried, she sent it to one of her closest friends, the Reverend Joseph Fish of
Stonington, Connecticut, who responded that he had read it "with close
attention and great Delight, not observing anything in it that needed Correction." With this implicit nod of approval, she began sharing it with

friends, especially members of her female prayer group.[46] She seems to have envisioned her memoir as an extension of the transatlantic revivals, a way of preaching the gospel.

Sarah fashioned her memoir into a powerful justification of the revivals and, more broadly, evangelical theology. She portrayed the story of her life as the gospel in miniature, a story of sin and redemption that spoke to universal truths about the human condition.[47] In order to defend evangelicalism against the challenge posed by the Enlightenment, she argued that humans were weak and flawed, the reverse image of the newly emerging "modern" self. She was not autonomous or independent, but helpless; she could not earn salvation through good works, but only through grace; she could not understand God through unaided reason, but only through revelation; and she was not essentially good by nature but vile. And in response to critics of the revivals, she argued that the awakening was not the result of overheated passions, but an instance of divine grace. Sprinkling her narrative with tidbits of theological wisdom, she left no room for doubt about how she wanted her story to be read. At the end of her memoir she explained, "My intent has been all along to show how God's glorious grace has triumphed over my sins and temptations, infirmities, and everything that has risen in opposition to it."[48]

Underneath everything else, Sarah's memoir was about the transforming power of divine love. The God she imagined in the pages of her memoir was often angry and punishing, but he was also a "father" and "friend" who loved her despite her sinfulness. Because she had such a strong sense of God's power, she expressed both astonishment and gratitude for his "free grace and redeeming love."[49] His love for her—a poor, insignificant woman—seemed too remarkable to be true.

Although many evangelicals expressed amazement at their salvation, Sarah's sense of wonder seems to have been more than simply a nod to convention. She had often doubted God's love during her periods of "backsliding," and in her worst moments she feared that he had abandoned her. By writing about her tangible experiences of his love, she hoped to reassure herself that even when she felt most alone and vulnerable, he had not deserted her. "He hath said I will never Leave thee nor forsake thee," she reminded herself, quoting from Hebrews.[50] Her memoir is the story of her slow, halting steps away from feelings of worthlessness toward the breathtaking realization that God loved her.

Sarah wrote about her religious experiences for many reasons, but this was the most deeply felt: she wanted to express her love to God in return

for his goodness. Although she hoped that future Christians would read
her manuscripts, she sometimes turned away from her imagined audience
to speak directly to God. "Let me Love thee much whom I never can love
too much," she prayed. [51]

There was a mystical strain within the early evangelical movement
that imagined God as pure, overpowering, blinding love. Because evangelicals believed that the Holy Spirit dwelled within those who had been
born again, they yearned to experience moments of full communion with
God—to lose the boundaries of the self in ecstatic unity with Christ. The
Reverend Timothy Allen remembered feeling "even swallowed up in God,"
and Sarah Prince Gill longed to be "absorbed in the ocean of immensity,"
to have "no Will of my own," to be "swallowed up in him who is the bright-
ness of the father's glory." Sarah Osborn wanted to become a new self in
Christ—to be engulfed in something larger than herself. As she meditated
on the words of Psalm 32 ("Blessed is he whose transgression is forgiven,
whose sin is covered"), she felt "swallowed up with Love to the immaculate
Lamb." "The frequent language of my soul was this," she wrote, echoing
another Psalm; "Whom have I in heaven but thee? and there is none upon
earth I desire besides thee." Although these mystical moments of unity
with God were rare, they were the reason that she refused to succumb to
"despair."[52]

In contrast to Enlightenment thinkers who taught that the heart of
Christianity lay in its teachings about morality, Sarah believed that her
faith called her to something more. It was not enough to live virtuously.
A true Christian was someone who loved God more than anything in the
world, including one's self. She was willing to be called a "fool" because she,
like Paul, believed that the faithful were often despised as a "spectacle unto
the world." Writing to the Corinthians (1 Cor. 4:10), Paul had proclaimed,
"We are fools for Christ's sake."

To justify the rising evangelical movement, to create a new self, to glorify God, to express her love for him, to "trust in the Lord and never despair
of his mercy"—these were the reasons that Sarah decided to write her life
story. In the years ahead she would reread her memoir again and again,
scribble notes in the margins, underline sentences she liked, scratch out
lines she regretted writing, and even tear out some pages (unless someone
else mutilated her manuscript at a later date). But she never felt compelled
to write an entirely new version of her story. Unlike James Lackington, a
British Methodist who wrote two versions of his narrative because of his

changing understanding of his life (the first after renouncing his Methodist faith and proclaiming himself a self-made man, the second in his old
age after renewing his commitment to Christ), Sarah never wavered in her
understanding of what she wanted her life to mean.[53]

The story that Sarah chose to share would shape her identity for the
rest of her life. As we shall see in the pages ahead, it was a story about the
inevitability of human sinfulness, the redemptive nature of suffering, and
most of all, the power of God's love.

Chapter 2

The Name of Christ

Oh god the father god the son and god the holy ghost who has so wonderfully contrived and wrought out my redemption and tho thou hast thro infinite wisdom hid these things from the wise and prudent yet thou hast reveald them to babes and even to me the most ignorant and vile of all creatures whose deep rooted enmity against thee and thy Laws broke out into action as soon as i was capable of any the first i can remember of actual sins which i was guilty of was telling a lie O but that text of scripture oft rung in my ears all Lyars shall have their portion in the lake that burns with fire and brimstone i was frequently under the striveings of the spirit of god pressing me to forsake sin repent and perform duties but sometimes found them very burdensome to me such as praying and saying many other good things which i was frequently taught Blessed be god however for such instructions sometimes i loved them and was much affected with them but my corruptions prevailed dreadfully i remember partook of an angry ungratefull temper stirring in me especially when corrected by my mother but must acknowledge to the glory of god that he preserved such a tenderness of concience in me that if at any time my mother convinc'd me that she did it because it was her duty for my sin against god i could bear it patiently and wilingly yea thankfully.[1]

The most ignorant and vile of all creatures. Enmity. The lake that burns with fire and brimstone. Corruptions. These were some of the images that came to Sarah's mind when she remembered her life as a child.

There were many ways that Sarah could have begun the story of her childhood. Besides recording the basic facts that would have appeared in the church register, including her date of birth and her parents' names, she could have tried to articulate her earliest, most vivid memories of growing up. Reaching back in time, she must have been able to salvage many memories, both sweet and bitter, from the ruins of the past. Perhaps she remembered running through the grass on a warm summer evening, or quarreling with her brother, or crying over a broken toy. Or perhaps she remembered sitting next to her father, her hands clasped and her head bowed in prayer, as he gave thanks for their evening meal. Some of her memories must have taken her back to a world almost before language, a sensory world of sights, sounds, and tastes: a beam of sunlight through the trees, a soothing lullaby, a drink of cold water from the well.

Yet at a time when many Americans had begun to ask questions about the doctrine of original sin—were children fallen from the very moment of birth?—Sarah began her narrative by recounting her early memories of sin. Without even pausing to record her birthdate, she immediately lamented her "stubborn and rebellious" childhood, castigating herself with such strong language that her images of corruption, repeated again and again, become almost numbing. Besides being tainted with "original" sin, the sin she had inherited from Adam and Eve, she had committed "actual" sins at an early age. (Actual sins were those that she had deliberately committed in defiance of God's law.) She was "a monster in sin," a "liar," and "the most ignorant and vile of all creatures." Her "base ingratitude," her "deep-rooted enmity" against God, her "angry ungrateful temper," and her dreadful "corruptions" made her entirely unworthy of God's love.[2]

Sarah's account of her early life is by far the most fragmentary part of her memoir. Because she lived long before the psychological fascination with childhood, she dismissed most of her early experiences as insignificant. We know very little about the details that modern psychologists would consider crucial, especially her infancy and her early experiences of illness or loss. Nor do we know much about the fabric of her everyday life as she grew older.[3]

Most important, Sarah wrote her memoir at the age of twenty-nine, long after her childhood had ended, and she inevitably brought her adult concerns and experiences to her memories of the past. She was no longer a child, but a grown woman who had been married, widowed, and then married again, and she was the mother of a ten-year-old son and three teenaged stepsons. It was impossible for her, just as it is for us, to bring back the young girl who had once sat on a parent's lap. Rather than a transparent reflection of her past, her memoir was a conversation with it, a dialogue with her childhood self. "A self distended in time, never reaches complete reunion with itself . . . "[4]

Nevertheless, Sarah's memoir offers an evocative glimpse of both her early life and her adult attitudes toward children. Looking back, she remembered herself as a sinful, disobedient child and a rebellious "youth" (the term *adolescent* was not coined until the twentieth century) who had needed to be "corrected" for her own good. Rejecting the growing faith in human goodness, she turned her life into a lesson about the inherent sinfulness of children, the importance of childhood obedience, and the wrath of God.

The Wicked Are Estranged from the Womb

When Sarah looked back on her childhood in search of the person she would become, hoping to find the moment when the door of childhood had opened to let the future in, she remembered a day when her whole life had changed. She could not have been more than four or five, but of all the stories she could have told about her childhood, this was the one that she chose to tell first. "The first I can remember of actual sins which I was guilty of was telling a lie," she wrote. "O, but that text of scripture oft rung in my ears, 'all Liars shall have their portion in the lake that burns with fire and brimstone.'" In retrospect, she believed that committing her first "actual" sin had forced her to recognize the precariousness of the human condition—the reality of both her "deep-rooted" corruption and God's blazing wrath. Her childhood, she confessed, had proven the dark wisdom of the Psalms: "The wicked are estranged from the womb: they go astray as soon as they are born, speaking lies."[5]

Raised in a pious household, Sarah first learned about her sinfulness from her parents. Her mother, Susanna Guyse Haggar, and her father, Benjamin Haggar, were Congregationalists (also known as Independents or Dissenters) who traced their religious heritage back to the Puritans. Benjamin was a tanner (leather worker) who remained a church member for his entire life; Susanna was the daughter of a deacon in the Congregationalist Church of Hertford, England, and the sister of John Guyse, a well-known minister who led churches in both Hertford and London.

Congregationalists were a religious minority in England, making up only 1.1 percent of the population in 1700, and because of their opposition to the Anglican establishment, they were not allowed to hold political office. But their small numbers and their sense of persecution only heightened their devotion to their distinctive theology. Besides objecting to "popish" forms of worship such as stained-glass windows and special priests' vestments, they complained that the Church of England had watered down the doctrine of God's sovereignty. Influenced by John Calvin and sixteenth- and seventeenth-century English Puritans, they emphasized that humans could not earn salvation through good works, but only through God's grace.[6]

When Sarah was born in 1714, her parents knew what sort of child they wanted her to be: a good Christian who would obey God's law. They brought her to be baptized in her infancy, and when she learned her first words, they taught her to pray and "*to forsake sin.*" Since most people assumed that children were too young to experience conversion, they probably did not expect her to be "born again" until her adolescence or adulthood, but they still considered it important to ground her in the Christian tradition. If they shirked their duties, they might pay a terrible price. "You must know, *Parents*, that your *Children* are by your means *Born* under the dreadful *Wrath* of God," warned Cotton Mather. "And if they are not *New-Born* before they *Die*, it had been *good for them, that they* had *never been Born at all.*" By teaching Sarah to pray and to say "many other good things," her parents hoped to prepare her for conversion. Perhaps not surprisingly, she sometimes found her religious duties "very burdensome," but in retrospect she thanked God for giving her such pious parents. "Blessed be God for such instructions," she wrote.[7]

Sarah seems to have learned the outlines of Calvinist theology at an early age. The *Westminster Shorter Catechism*, which was published in scores of editions in the seventeenth and eighteenth centuries, listed 107 questions and answers that young children were expected to memorize. To the very first question, "What is the chief end of man," children were instructed to respond: "Man's chief end is to glorify God, and enjoy him forever." By repeating the same words every night, children were trained to accept the Christian story as the truth: a sovereign, majestic God had created the world; he had made a "Covenant of Law" with Adam and Eve requiring them to obey his commands; he had exiled them from the Garden of Eden after their willful disobedience; and as punishment, he had decreed that all their descendants would inherit the stain of original sin. From the moment of birth, humans were inherently depraved, fallen from grace. (Jonathan Edwards believed that children's first moments of life symbolized their spiritual corruption: "Children's coming into the world naked and filthy, and in their blood, and crying and impotent, is to signify their spiritual nakedness, pollution of nature and wretchedness of condition with which they are born.") But as the *Catechism* explained, a merciful God had refused to abandon humans despite their sins. Because they could not possibly atone for their crime against him—no mere mortal could make amends for an offense against an infinite being—he had intervened in history to send his only son, Jesus Christ, as a sacrifice. Through his suffering on the cross, Jesus had repaid their debt and saved them from eternal death. God made a new covenant with the world, a "Covenant of Grace." As the apostle John wrote, "For God so loved the world, that he gave his only begotten Son, that whosoever believeth in him should not perish, but have everlasting life."[8]

Looking back, Sarah remembered being overwhelmed with feelings of love and gratitude when she learned about Christ's sacrifice on the cross. "The name of Christ was sweet to me," she wrote. Although she was still too young to understand all the subtleties of Calvinist theology, she knew that Christ was a "dear redeemer" and "beloved savior" who wanted to save her from sin. She also knew that he loved little children and had welcomed them into his arms. "Suffer the little children to come unto me, and forbid them not," he had said to his disciples. "For of such is the kingdom of God."[9]

Yet even though the young Sarah found many parts of Reformed theology comforting, she was also alarmed by it. As she learned, Christ's death had not redeemed *all* of humanity but only a small group of the "elect." (As she grew older, she would learn to say that Christ's atonement had been "limited" rather than "general.") Calvinists interpreted Paul's words to the Ephesians, "He hath chosen us in him before the foundation of the world," as evidence that God had decided who would be saved at the beginning of time. Although God had predestined some people to spend eternity in bliss, he had also sentenced others to eternal torment in hell. Predestination, as John Calvin had admitted, was a "dreadful" decree, but humans could do absolutely nothing to sway God's transcendent will. They could not earn salvation by going to church, confessing their sins, or doing good works. With no power to save themselves, they were completely dependent on a transcendent and uncontrollable God.[10]

Since ministers did not believe in being "kind" to children by sugar-coating the truth, they wrote catechisms that are startlingly blunt. Contrary to what many historians have argued, they did not treat children as miniature adults who were expected to understand complicated theological ideas, and they tried to tailor their religious instruction to fit the unique needs of "infants" (those under the age of seven), "children" (ages seven to fourteen or sixteen), and "youth" (ages sixteen to twenty-five).[11] Still, they thought that it was crucial for even the youngest to be exposed to the concepts of original sin, heaven, and hell. By explaining the Bible in plain, childlike language, they tried to convey a sense of God's infinite power. When Isaac Watts (a friend of Sarah's uncle John Guyse) published his *First Catechism* in 1730, he included a frank set of questions and answers about damnation.

> Question: And what if you do not fear God, nor love him, nor seek to please him?
> Answer: Then I shall be a wicked Child, and the great God will be very angry with me.
>
> Question: Why are you afraid of God's Anger?
> Answer: Because he can kill my Body, and he can make my Soul miserable after my body is dead. . . .
>
> Question: What must become of you if you are wicked?
> Answer: If I am wicked I shall be sent down to everlasting Fire in Hell among wicked and miserable creatures.

This catechism was explicitly designed for children who were three or four years old.[12]

Even when Sarah read children's books or sang children's songs, she learned about God's hatred of sin. During the 1740s and 1750s parents began to buy amusing, entertaining books for their children like *The Little Pretty Pocket Book* or *Nurse Truelove*, but before then children's literature was almost entirely religious and didactic. *The New-England Primer*, the most commonly used schoolbook, mixed the alphabet with a strong dose of Calvinist theology. When children learned the letter "U," they were taught to recite the verse, "Upon the Wicked God shall rain an horrible Tempest." "A" reminded them that "In Adam's fall, we sinned all."[13]

Children's hymnbooks were similar. Isaac Watts's immensely popular *Divine and Moral Songs for the Use of Children*, which was printed more than seventy-five times in eighteenth-century America, mixed soothing

A — In *Adam's* Fall
We Sinned all.

B — Thy Life to Mend,
This *Book* Attend.

C — The *Cat* doth play
And after flay.

D — A *Dog* will bite
A Thief at night.

E — An *Eagles* flight
Is out of fight.

The Idle *Fool*
Is whipt at School.

The New-England Primer. Courtesy of the American Antiquarian Society.

images of God's "goodness," "power," "mercy," and "love" with more severe pictures of divine wrath. A typical example is the song "Heaven and Hell":

> There is beyond the sky
>> A heaven of joy and love;
> And holy children, when they die
>> Go to that world above.

> There is a dreadful hell,
>> And everlasting pains:
> There sinners must with devils dwell
>> In darkness, fire, and chains.

Although Sarah never recorded the exact names of the books she read as a child, she may have owned a copy of Watts's hymns. As she remembered, she was delighted when a minister kindly gave her a "Little book of spiritual songs."[14]

Two of the stories that Sarah decided to tell in her memoir, both dating from the age of seven or eight, suggest that these vivid images of divine love and divine wrath made a lasting impression on her. In the first story, she remembered her growing sense of God's "sweetness" after her mother sent her to a boarding school eight miles outside London. "I was constantly taught things that was religious and they all become sweet to me," she wrote. "I verily thought I lived a heaven upon earth. Oh how sweet was sabbaths, and for secret prayer I would not have omitted it for all the world." Often she would break down in fits of weeping as she thought about her sins.[15]

Yet as she also confessed, her overwhelming sense of God's sweetness was tinged with fear. Remembering her dread of God's wrath, she explained that she never would have dared to commit the "monstrous" sin of going to sleep without first saying a prayer: "The sin appeared so monstrous that I durst not lie down without it, for I should have been afraid the devil would have fetched me if I had."[16]

Although Sarah did not explain in her memoir why she had been sent away to school, her religious anxiety may have been heightened by troubles at home. Her parents do not seem to have been desperately poor, but they struggled throughout their lives to make ends meet. Her father had recently left the family to emigrate to New England, probably in search of greater financial opportunity, and her brother, her only sibling, went to live with her grandmother in Hartford, a few miles outside of London. Perhaps her mother decided to send the two children away so that she could go to work. (Many British boarding schools were quite cheap.)[17] If Sarah sensed that her parents were anxious about the future, she may have felt frightened and vulnerable. Despite her hope that God would save her, she dreaded that Satan might be lurking nearby.

In her second story, Sarah remembered her distress after rebuking her brother for committing a sin. "My brother did something that I thought was wicked and I reproved him sharply for it, but was much perplexed with this text of scripture: 'Thou hypocrite. First cast out the beam out of thine own eye and then thou shalt see clearly to cast the mote out of thy brother's eye.' This frighted me exceedingly. I thought I was a vile hypocrite and should never dare to reprove anybody again." Although her grandmother had told Sarah that it was her duty to speak the truth, she worried that she had not conquered her *own* depravity. Was she any better than her brother? What would happen to her if she was just as "wicked"?[18]

Sarah shared these stories because she wanted readers to understand her early "delight in the ways of holiness," but modern readers cannot help being struck by her emphasis on *fear*. Later in her memoir she would write rapturous descriptions of Christ's love, but many of her early memories of God involve a mixture of anxiety and shame. Despite a brief mention of Jesus as a "glorious and compassionate Savior" at the beginning of her memoir, she also warned her readers that if they "abused" his mercy a vengeful God might sentence them to damnation. "Let them alone," she imagined God proclaiming. "They shall never enter into my rest."[19]

Sarah may have exaggerated her religious anxiety in order to conform to religious convention. The first rule listed in *The School of Good Manners*, an etiquette book meant for children and youth, was "Fear God and Believe in Christ," and Cotton Mather urged children to memorize a verse from the Psalms: "The fear of the Lord is the beginning of wisdom."[20] Yet it also seems likely that when Sarah recalled her childhood, her memories of God's wrath were stronger than her memories of his love. She had heard many different sermons during the Sundays of her childhood, some comforting and others alarming, but because she was small and helpless she seems to have found the stories about God's anger particularly vivid. In her young imagination, God loomed as a large, forbidding figure who ruled the world with an iron hand. He had the awe-inspiring power to create and destroy, to reward and punish, to save and condemn.

Sarah's religious fears do not seem to have been unique. When John Bunyan wrote his life story more than eighty years earlier, he vividly remembered his early terror of damnation. Because his sins had "offended" the Lord, "even in my childhood He did scare and affright me with fearful dreams, and did terrify me with dreadful visions." Obsessed by thoughts of "devils and wicked spirits," he was afraid to go to sleep at night. David Brainerd, a missionary, was "terrified at the thoughts of death" at the age of seven or eight, while the Reverend Aaron Burr, the future president of Princeton, was troubled by "great terrors and horrors from a guilty Conscience and the Fears of Hell." When the Reverend John Cleaveland looked back on his childhood, he remembered that his mother "took a Considerable Deal of pains" to warn all of her children that they were "Children of wrath and exposed to Hell fire." Other children learned they were never too young to pray for God's mercy. In Jonathan Edwards's congregation in Northampton, Massachusetts, a four-year-old girl spent hours alone praying that God would save her. "I pray, beg, pardon all my sins," she was heard crying loudly. When her mother tried to soothe her, she "continued exceedingly crying, and wreathing her body to and fro, like one in anguish of spirit," until she finally managed to put her fears into words. "I am afraid I shall go to hell!" she wept. Her first images of God involved anger and vengeance. "O how fraid was I of God," remembered Hannah Heaton in her diary. "He appeared to me to be an angry terrible being."[21]

Children of Wrath, Children of Grace

For reasons that historians have only begun to explore, the rhetoric of children's sinfulness seems to have grown particularly heated in the first few decades of the eighteenth century. In some ways evangelicals simply echoed the Puritan belief that children needed to be subjected to strict discipline. Imagining the human race as part of a great chain of being that extended downward from God to the lowest form of creation, the Puritans had feared that infants were only a small step above beasts. As one minister explained, "The Highest of a lower Kind of Creatures, approaches very near to the lowest of a higher Kind." Determined to rear children who were upright both morally and physically, parents wrapped their infants in tight swaddling clothes in order to straighten their limbs and make them appear more erect, and placed them in special walking stools to prevent them from crawling. (Early Americans seem to have been disturbed by the sight of babies crawling on all fours, an activity which made them look too much like small animals.) With no seats in them, these stools forced children to learn how to stand. Parents also laced girls into stays or corsets to straighten

"Woman at clothesline." A woman (circa 1800) with a child in a standing stool.
With no seats in them, these stools were designed to make children stand upright.
Drawing by Michele Felice Cornè. Courtesy of the Newport Historical Society.

their backs, which is why children look unnaturally rigid in many colonial
paintings.[22]

As Puritan children grew older, parents fed them a steady diet of catechisms and books designed to transform them into virtuous Christians. *The
New-England Primer* included the story of a youth who spurned Christ's
offer of salvation in order to pursue a life of frivolous pleasure. Although
the young man promised to become a Christian in his old age (after he
could no longer enjoy the vanities of the world), Christ was so angered by
his disobedience that he immediately struck him dead: "Thus end the days
of woful youth, / Who won't obey nor mind the truth. They in their youth
go down to hell, Under eternal wrath to dwell. Many don't live out half
their days, For cleaving unto sinful ways."[23]

Yet Puritans had mixed these warnings with a more comforting message about their redemption. They were not humanitarians who recoiled at

the thought of children's suffering (and few seem to have been concerned about the fate of "heathen" children like Native Americans), but they did believe that virtually all their *own* children would be safe from God's punishment. Identifying themselves as the "new Israel," they proclaimed that God had entered into a special covenant with them that extended to their descendants as well. As Cotton Mather explained, "The children of Godly Parents, we are bound in a Judgment of Charity to reckon, as much belonging upon the Lord, as Themselves." Softening the doctrine of infant depravity, Mather reassured "distressed parents" that grace, like original sin, was hereditary. In theory, ministers accepted the possibility of infant damnation, but in practice they tended to be squeamish about it. Michael Wigglesworth, a Puritan poet, even claimed (without biblical evidence) that children would have "the easiest room in Hell." Most ministers avoided the topic entirely, and when real flesh-and-blood children died they were almost always imagined as rejoicing in heaven.[24]

But the religious mood began to shift in the 1710s and 1720s. Doctrine had not changed, but ministers now seemed less interested in reassuring parents and children than in shattering their complacency. The number of books and sermons about children increased significantly, and although judgments about style are hard to quantify, these sermons sound harsher than those published earlier. When Benjamin Wadsworth, a Boston minister, preached several sermons on "early piety," he described children as "*Children of Wrath by Nature*, liable to Eternal Vengeance, the Unquenchable Flames of Hell." Although doting parents might be tempted to see them as innocent, "Their Hearts naturally, are a mere nest, root, fountain of Sin, and wickedness; an *evil Treasure* from whence proceed *evil things*, viz. *Evil Thoughts, Murders, Adulteries &c.*" A few years before Sarah's family moved to Newport, a minister there urged parents not to neglect their children's religious education. "The time is coming when you will bitterly bewail it," he warned, "but it may be They will be *Dead and in Hell* first."[25]

In order to understand why ministers spoke so harshly, it is important to situate them in their own time and place. On both sides of the Atlantic, Reformed Protestants were lamenting that religion had been eclipsed by "the *Powerful Love of the World and Exorbitant Reach after Riches*." Covetousness, gambling, drinking, theft, slander, sexual licentiousness—these were only a few of the crimes that ministers identified as symptoms of religious decline, and despite their tendency to exaggerate, they were genuinely concerned that parents were failing to pass on the faith to the next generation. "Nothing is more Threatening to the Welfare of a People,

than to have their *Young Ones* generally *Ignorant, Irreligious, Di*
Wadsworth warned. "When it is so, it looks as though Iniquity wo\
abound, to the pulling down [of] heavy Judgments." Jonathan E
warned parents that unless they set a better example, their childrei
be "Cast, Gone down into Hell."[26]

Concerns about children were also heightened by changes in the family. In the seventeenth century, ministers had identified the family as a "little commonwealth," a model for the hierarchical ordering of both church
and state. To help them rear obedient, submissive children who would accept their subjection to parents, magistrates, and ultimately the king, Reformed Protestants gave enormous power to parents, especially fathers. Fathers controlled the family's property; they helped choose marriage partners
for their children; and by law they were allowed to administer "moderate
correction" to unruly children and servants. They could also request that
their children be punished by the courts. In several New England colonies
(though not in Rhode Island), children over the age of sixteen who cursed
or struck their parents could be put to death. Significantly, no child was
ever actually executed under this law, but it was a chilling reminder of paternal power in American culture.[27]

By the early eighteenth century, however, as larger socioeconomic
forces began to reshape everyday life, men began to lose their authority
over the family. Because of widespread land shortages, many fathers could
no longer provide farms for their sons, and because of the growth of a new,
market-oriented economy, they lost control of children who moved away
from home in search of greater economic opportunities. Although fathers
still tried to influence whom their children would marry, they had little
success. As historians have shown, many couples seem to have realized that
their best weapon against strong-willed fathers was pregnancy. During the
1740s and 1750s the premarital pregnancy rate in New England rose as high
as 40 percent.[28]

Whether or not evangelicals understood the underlying historical
forces that were changing the family, they were disturbed by their effects.
As Jonathan Edwards complained after arriving in Northampton in 1726,
"Family government did too much fail in the town." Instead of deferring
to their elders, the "youth of the town" were addicted to "frolicking," "fre-
quenting the tavern," and such sinful, "lewd practices" as "bundling"—the
New England custom of allowing courting couples to sleep in the same bed
with a "bundling board" between them. In a sermon Edwards preached to
young people, he condemned "taking such liberties as naturally tend to stir

up lusts," including the "shameful custom of fondling women's breasts." By sternly admonishing parents to "keep their children at home," ministers fought a losing battle to strengthen the patriarchal family.[29]

In addition to their concerns about the sanctity of the family, many ministers feared that the doctrine of original sin was under attack. One of the most controversial questions of the age was whether human nature should be understood as inherently good or stained with sin. On one side stood evangelicals like Edwards who denigrated humans as "totally corrupt, in every part, in all their faculties, and all the principles of their nature, their understandings, and wills." For Edwards, "There is nothing but sin, no good at all." On the other side stood a collection of Enlightenment thinkers, British liberals, sentimental novelists, and ordinary Protestant believers who found this kind of language extreme, perhaps even absurd. According to Francis Hutcheson, people were born with an innate moral sense, "a determination of our nature to study the good of others; or some instinct, antecedent to all reason from interest, which influences us to the love of others."[30] Although Hutcheson acknowledged the reality of evil, he believed that if not for false theories of human sinfulness people would act far more benevolently. Influenced by these ideas, sentimental novelists celebrated the quality of "sensibility," the innate human desire to sympathize with the afflicted and to alleviate suffering. Works like Samuel Richardson's extraordinarily popular novel, *Pamela; or, Virtue Rewarded* (1740) helped popularize a new gospel of human goodness.[31]

Enlightened thinkers especially objected to the doctrine of "imputation": the belief that all humans had been cursed for Adam and Eve's transgression in the Garden of Eden. It did not seem fair to imagine God punishing people for sins they had not personally committed. According to Daniel Whitby, a British theologian, the entire idea of inherited sin was "exceeding cruel, and plainly inconsistent with the Justice, Wisdom, and goodness of our gracious God." "We dare not say that millions of Infants are tortured in Hell to all eternity," an Anglican missionary protested, "for a Sin that was committed thousands of years before they were born."[32] At a time when Enlightenment thinkers defended the concept of individual rights, the doctrine of original sin seemed to make the individual irrelevant.

The debates over original sin always revolved around the same axis: the status of children. Because Enlightenment thinkers and liberal-leaning Protestants knew that infant damnation was a hard doctrine to swallow, they scored rhetorical points by forcing the orthodox to defend it. As Edwards affirmed, it was "exceeding just, that God should take the soul of a new-born infant and cast it into eternal torments."[33] To be clear, Edwards and other evangelicals never argued that *all* infants and children who died before conversion would be damned, and they assumed that many, especially those with godly parents, had been saved. (It is a tribute to the success of anti-Calvinist propaganda that even in the nineteenth century there were rumors that Calvinists had once taught that hell was paved with infants' bones.)[34] But because they preached that every individual's fate was decreed before birth, they could not avoid the logical corollary that infants as well as adults could be damned. Their critics pounced. John Taylor asked, "Must it not lessen the due Love of Parents to Children, to believe they are the vilest and most wretched Creatures in the World, the Objects of God's Wrath and Curse?" In *The Scripture-Doctrine of Original Sin Proposed to Free and Candid Examination*, a work that went through three editions in only six years, Taylor condemned the doctrine of original sin as "absurd": "And pray, consider seriously what a God he must be, who can be displeased with, and curse his innocent Creatures, even before they have a Being," he cried. "*Is this thy God, O Christian?*"[35]

Intellectuals were not the only ones who had doubts about the doctrine of original sin. Much to his frustration, Jonathan Edwards discovered that many parents in his congregation perceived their children as "innocent," and they denounced him for "frighting poor innocent children with talk of hell fire and eternal damnation."[36] In response, he accused parents of being too indulgent. But as he seems to have sensed better than almost anyone in his generation, Calvinist thought was being eroded by deeper tides of change. People who could elect their own lower assemblies, read the latest books from England, and choose what to purchase in an expanding consumer marketplace seem to have found it hard to view themselves—or their children—as either helpless or unworthy. Free to make choices that most of their parents and grandparents had never imagined, they developed a stronger sense of their own agency.

Although historians sometimes write as though evangelicals dominated eighteenth-century American life, the evangelicals did not see themselves in this way at all; rather they thought of themselves as a besieged minority trying to defend their beliefs against attack. Certain that they had been called to save the world from apostasy, they asserted their theology in deliberately provocative language. In order to defend the doctrine of original sin, Edwards claimed that children were not innocent, but "young vipers, and . . . infinitely more hateful than vipers," and Thomas Prince warned unconverted children that "God utterly abhors you and is angry with you." Sarah Osborn concluded that her childhood sins were proof that all humans "have a fountain of corruption in them that is ever flowing."[37]

Disturbed by this fierce language, historians have presented a grim picture of Puritan and evangelical attitudes toward children. They have accused them not only of "committing a crime against childhood" but of teaching children "perverted ideas of God."[38] Rather than trying to assuage children's natural anxieties about monsters, abandonment, and death, ministers seem to have deliberately heightened these fears, using the threat of hell as a crude form of social control. When Isaac Watts published his *Divine and Moral Songs for the Use of Children*, he included songs warning children not to be lazy, vain, greedy, or selfish. Even James Janeway's best-selling *A Token for Children*, which reassured devout children that they would rejoice in heaven, tried to frighten the "naughty" into obedience. "Whither do you think those Children go when they die, that will not do what they are bid, but play the Truant, and lie, and speak naughty words, and break the Sabbath?" Janeway asked. "Whither do such children go do you think?" In a response that must have sent shivers down many a spine, he answered: "Why, I will tell you, they which Lie, must to their Father the Devil into everlasting burning; they which never pray, God will pour out his wrath upon them; and when they beg and pray in Hell Fire, God will not forgive them; but there they must lie forever."[39]

Yet it is important to remember that ministers also argued that children of wrath could be transformed into children of grace. Before the revivals, few ministers believed that children were mature enough to experience conversion (the exception was children on the brink of death who suddenly understood their peril), but in the midst of the awakening they claimed that even the youngest children could be born again. As Edwards remarked, "It has heretofore been looked on as a strange thing, when any seemed to be savingly wrought upon, and remarkably changed in their childhood," but in his Northampton congregation alone, almost thirty children between the ages of ten and fourteen were converted. (There were also two converts between the ages of nine and ten and one precocious four-year-old.) He welcomed twenty of them into full membership and allowed them to join adults at the table of the Lord's Supper. Similarly, when the Reverend Samuel Blair described a revival in Pennsylvania, he marveled that two sisters, one seven and one nine, had been genuinely converted. "They speak of their Soul Experiences with a very becoming Gravity, and apparent Impression of the Things they speak of," he testified. Another minister reported that "there was a *Spirit of Prayer* upon *Young* and *Old*, especially the younger sort. And *Children* of *five, six, seven* Years, and upward, would pray to Admiration."[40] Because evangelical ministers believed that religion was a matter of the heart more than the head, they thought it was possible for children to grasp the central Christian message without a mature understanding of doctrine. Few Christian communities at the time treated children's spirituality with as much seriousness.

Although ministers often used fear to persuade children to seek salvation, they also knew how to offer reassurance. Preaching on a verse from Proverbs, "I love them that love me, and those that seek me early shall find me," the Reverend Joseph Emerson assured children that if they genuinely longed for grace, they almost certainly had been chosen for salvation. Their desire to please God—to "seek" him—was a hopeful sign that they would find him.[41] Time and again, ministers imagined blissful children being gathered up into Christ's loving arms. There was no anger as fierce as God's anger, but no love as sweet, as pure, or as boundless.

Ministers argued that it was better to tell children the hard facts about sin and damnation than to lull them into complacency. "Why should we conceal the truth from them?" asked Jonathan Edwards. Although children might find it painful to confront the reality of damnation, there were times when they "needed" to be hurt. In his words, "A child that has a dangerous wound may need the painful lance as well as grown persons. And that would be a foolish pity, in such a case, that would hold back the lance, and throw away the life."[42] "Frighting" children was for their own good.

Obey Your Parents in the Lord

Influenced by what they heard in church and read in childrearing manuals, Sarah's parents enforced a strict code of obedience. Although Sarah said very little about her mother and even less about her father, her brief portraits of them suggest that they would have admired Edwards's tenacious defense of original sin. They, too, refused to spare the lance.

It was common to praise mothers for their kindness and patience, but Sarah found that she could not conform to convention: what she remembered was not her mother's compassion but her anger. The first time she mentioned her mother (on the third page of her memoir), she described being "corrected" by her—in other words, spanked or beaten. Remembering her childhood sinfulness, she wrote: "My corruptions prevailed dreadfully. I remember [I] partook of an angry, ungrateful temper stirring in me especially when corrected by my mother." Although her words were terse, they set a pattern for the rest of her memoir. She almost always portrayed her mother as a strict disciplinarian. Perhaps because of her father's absence, she mentioned him only in passing ("my father being in New England, my mother put me to boarding school"), but as she revealed later in her memoir, *both* her parents had been "severe."[43]

Most people in early America believed that physical punishment could be an effective tool of discipline. "Correction" was not simply a penalty for bad behavior, but as the positive valence of the word suggests, a way of instilling virtue. When Martha Gerrish, an evangelical from Boston, wrote a letter to her stepdaughter about childrearing, she warned her not to "spare the rod." "Don't overlook their *pretty little Faults*, as Parents call them: but frown at the Beginnings of Sin in them," she advised. "When they prate prettily and lisp out a *Lie*, look serious, and not smile upon 'em. Don't let them be *unmannerly familiar* with you." If children were "*Stubborn*," parents should "use the *Rod* . . . let no ill habits be indulged." Taking this advice to heart, Esther Edwards Burr, the daughter of Jonathan Edwards, punished her ten-month-old by whipping her. "I have begun to govern Sally," she wrote to a friend. "She has been Whipped once on Old Adam's account." Although she found it agonizing to "chastise your *own most tender self*," she rejoiced that Sally had become much more obedient. "It did her a vast deal of good."[44]

Historians have usually explained this authoritarian style of childrearing as the logical outgrowth of the doctrine of original sin. Connecting childrearing practices to theology, they have suggested that parents who saw their children as inherently sinful would try to break the will. By itself, however, the belief in original sin has not always led to repressive childrearing practices. August Hermann Francke, for example, a German Pietist, assumed that all humans had inherited Adam's guilt, but he also claimed that very young children were not capable of deliberate misdeeds. Even Augustine, according to a recent historian, viewed children as "non-innocent" rather than depraved. Although infants were born with the inclination to commit sin, they did not become truly corrupt until they grew older.[45]

Beyond their religious motivations, parents seem to have hoped that "breaking the will" would prepare children to be good subjects of the king. Most early Americans did not want to raise children to be independent; they wanted them to accept their place in a hierarchical social order. *The School of Good Manners*, an etiquette book, listed obedience to the king as second in importance only to the fear of God. Although children were expected to resist if anyone tried to force them to do something sinful, they were also supposed to be unfailingly obedient to their parents. Reflecting on her childrearing philosophy, Martha Gerrish wrote, "We are to train up our Children in the Exercise of *Love, Respect, Obedience, & Modesty*, and not to allow them too much Familiarity in their Speech or Behavior towards us." In Osborn's words, children must "submit to and obey their own parents or other superiors in all things right."[46]

Of course, not all evangelicals believed in breaking the will, and some took a more gentle approach to childrearing. While almost everyone agreed that children needed to be "subdued," they disagreed about whether they should be trained with rewards or "severity." According to Cotton Mather, Christians should use love, not fear, to discipline their children. In *Bonifacius: An Essay upon the Good*, published anonymously in 1710, Mather swore that he would "never dispense a *blow*, except it be for an atrocious crime, or for a lesser fault obstinately persisted in." Like the philosopher John Locke, whose *Essay on Education* (1693) became a best seller in America, Mather lamented that "the slavish, raging, fighting way of education" was "a considerable article in the wrath and curse of God, upon a miserable world." Without rejecting corporal punishment outright, he insisted that parents should beat their children only as a last resort, and even then not in a "*passion* and a *fury*."[47]

The Reverend Joseph Fish, one of Sarah Osborn's closest friends as an adult, also recommended that parents treat their children with kindness. While he was not opposed to beating on principle, recommending it for "vassals, negroes and other sordid slaves when nothing else will do," he thought that it did more harm to children than good. (Although he never examined his racial assumptions, he clearly meant that it harmed *white* children.) "If *Children* are of a tender *Make*," he reasoned, "they neither *need*, nor can they *bear*, nor even be supposed to *deserve*, Severity." On the other hand, "if they are of a more hardy and stubborn *Make*, what so Likely, as *Goodness, Moderation*, and Patience, to work them into a human shape, and mold them into a Gospel Temper?" Instead of "governing" his two daughters with force, he guided them with "the gentle reins of *Love* and *Tenderness*."[48]

Since Sarah never described how often she was corrected, we do not know whether her punishments involved a quick spanking or a whipping. But it is clear that her parents, unlike Fish, believed in using severity.

What is most missing from Sarah's account of her childhood is a sense of her emotional attachment to her parents. Her attitude seems to have been profoundly ambivalent. By 1743, the year of her memoir, many people had begun to advocate bending the will rather than breaking it, but she echoed her parents' conviction that her punishments had been for her own good.[49] On one hand, she complained that her parents had been too harsh, and even as an adult she remembered her "angry, ungrateful temper" as her mother had corrected her. In a provocative slip of her pen, she implied that she *wanted* to be thankful for her strict upbringing but could not feel genuine gratitude. "I desire to be thankful I never escaped correction for the sin of Lying," she wrote in the margins of her memoir. Contrary to her desire, she may not have been able to swallow her lingering feelings of resentment. On the other hand, she also claimed that sinful, disobedient children deserved to be punished. "If at any time my mother convinced me that she did it because it was her duty for my sin against God," she explained, "I could bear it patiently and willingly, yea thankfully." Raised on the biblical wisdom that "He that spareth his rod hateth his son: but he that loveth him chasteneth him betimes," she dared not question the justice of corporal punishment.[50]

Since psychological studies have shown that young children often describe God and their parents in remarkably similar terms, Sarah's childhood experiences may have shaped her early image of God, but it would be a mistake to see her conception of him as nothing more than a projection of her mother or father. Her spiritual life was probably far more complex: children construct their image of God not only out of family relationships but also from their experiences in the world. Contrary to what one might expect, for example, many abused children today do not envision God as violent, but as caring and compassionate. Despite suffering from feelings of worthlessness, they struggle to envision a God who looks nothing like their parents.[51]

At the same time, when Sarah was very young, too young to have learned about God on her own, she seems to have imagined him as a larger, more powerful version of her mother or father. Besides being influenced by catechisms, primers, and children's songs, her images of God were also shaped by what she witnessed in her own family. She developed a more complicated understanding of God during adolescence, but as a small child she saw him as a volatile mixture of love and anger, mercy and vindictiveness. Like her father, who left his family to go to New England, God could be remote, hiding his face when she desperately called out to him in prayer. Like her mother, God could be stern, sharply reproving her for sin. And like both her parents, God could be physically violent, deliberately inflicting pain in order to make her behave.

Sarah's most vivid childhood memory involved her first exp
of God's hatred of sin. Recounting a horrifying story of his wra
claimed that when she was eight years old, he had brutally punisl
for the crime of playing on the Sabbath. As she and her mother we
ing to America to rejoin her father (her brother remained in England), she
became so sinful that God sentenced her to an excruciating ordeal: "On
board the ship I Lost my good impressions and grew vile so that I could
play upon the sabbath then. But I was convinced of that sin by an accident
that befell me, or rather what was ordered by infinite wisdom to that end.
For as I was busy boiling something for my baby [a doll], I fell into the fire
with my right hand and burned it all over, which I presently thought was
just upon me for playing [on] a sabbath day. And I was ashamed and sorry
I had done so." Despite the fact that she was only eight, still young enough
to play with dolls, she had been so vile that she had deserved to be badly
burned. Intentionally sending her into the flames, God, like her parents,
had chastised her for her sins.[52]

By claiming that her burned, blistered hand was not the result of an
accident but a sign of God's "infinite wisdom," Sarah echoed what her parents had taught her. Because Calvinists believed that "*God hath decreed and
determined whatever cometh to pass in the world*," they denied that there was
any such thing as chance or luck. Everything that happened, whether prosperity or illness, was God's providence. As one minister explained, "There
is no sickness so little, but God hath a finger in it, though it be but the
aching of the little finger." When Cotton Mather had a toothache, he immediately interpreted it as punishment for sin. "Have I not sinned with
my *Teeth?*" he asked. "How? By sinful, graceless, excessive *Eating*." His
toothache, like Sarah's burned hand, was a reminder that a transcendent
God controlled even the smallest details of human life.[53]

Sarah interpreted her agonizing burns as a sign that God had punished
her out of love. Just as she had submitted to her mother's beatings "patiently and willingly, yea thankfully" as penalty for sin, she accepted God's
afflictions with humility and gratitude, praising him in the midst of her
pain. True Christians should behave like the "Turks," a Puritan minister
explained, who, "when they are cruelly lashed, are compelled to return to
the judge that commanded it, to kiss his hand, and give him thanks, and
pay the Officer that whipped them, and so clear the Judge and Officer of
Injustice. Silently to kiss the Rod, and the Hand that whips with It, is the
noblest way of clearing the Lord of all injustice." Samuel Willard envisioned God as an angry father who stood over his children with a rod in

his hand and beat them with heavy blows. "It consists well enough with the love of God, for him to be angry with his children," he preached, quoting from Proverbs, "and when he is so, he can lay hard blows upon them, and love them still, because they are for their good and not hurt; yea, *because he loves them he chastens them. . . .* And sometimes he strikes so hard he kills them."[54] Sinners needed to be corrected, and gratitude, not anger, was the proper Christian response to affliction.

Feminine Weakness

Besides reflecting the religious expectations of her time, Sarah's emphasis on her childhood sinfulness and her need of correction accorded with contemporary stereotypes of femininity. Although she never shared her reflections on what it meant to be reared as a girl rather than as a boy, she grew to adulthood in a world that assumed women's weakness and inferiority. By the time that she was born, witchcraft trials were only a memory (the Salem crisis took place in 1692), but negative images of women as gossips, seductresses, and scolds still lingered. Despite her belief that sexual differences would someday disappear in union with Christ, Sarah also assumed that "weak" women had been ordained to be subordinate to men on earth.

On the surface, people in the eighteenth century seemed to have a relatively fluid understanding of sex. Unlike later generations of Americans, who emphasized the inherent differences between men's and women's bodies, they believed that the sexes were more alike than different. According to medical treatises, women's sexual organs were identical to men's except they were turned inside out: the vagina was an interior penis, the ovaries were testes, and the uterus was a scrotum. Anatomically, men and women were simply two representations of a single model of sexuality. By the end of the century this understanding of sex had been replaced by a less fluid model of difference, but in the 1740s most Americans still assumed that there was only one sex, the male sex, and men were the standard against which women were measured.[55]

Yet despite this belief in the similarity between the sexes, early Americans did not believe that men and women were physically or intellectually equal. Since they saw men's bodies as the norm, they believed that women were inferior, underdeveloped versions of men. Women were *lesser* men who were governed by different bodily fluids that influenced their characters. In contrast to men, whose "humors" were dry and warm, women were

dominated by cold, wet humors that supposedly made them more deceit-
ful, erratic, and passionate than men.[56] According to a misogynistic tract
that was printed eleven times in England before 1741, most women were
naturally "lewd," even those who were not prostitutes. "There are lewd
women that are no whores, and yet are ten times worse," the writer complained, "because their lewdness is more difficult to be known, and harder
to be avoided." It had all started with Eve, who had been "transformed
into a Kind of a Devil incarnate" when she ate the apple, and it had grown
worse with every generation. "History will abundantly inform us, that as
the World grew in years, so Women grew in Wickedness, each Age being
worse than the preceding."[57]

Although Puritan clergymen challenged these images of women's sinfulness as early as the seventeenth century, the stereotype proved persistent.
On one hand, women were praised for their "*Zeal*, Faith, Purity, Charity,
[and] Patience" and, as growing numbers of them swelled the pews, ministers began to argue that women were inherently more pious than men. In
1736, when Jonathan Edwards penned his famous account of the revivals in
his Northampton congregation, *A Faithful Narrative of the Surprising Work
of God*, he filled it with descriptions of godly women, including a "frivolous
girl" whose sudden conversion was "the greatest occasion of awakening to
others, of anything that ever came to pass in the town." George Whitefield
frequently corresponded with women, including the patron of the Methodists, the countess of Huntingdon, and he elevated them as models of
piety. On the other hand, both Puritans and their evangelical descendants
remained suspicious of women's "passions." As the historian Harry S. Stout
has pointed out, Whitefield often criticized young, attractive women for
their "lust," "Worldliness," and "idolatry," but "rarely did he level similar
charges against young men."[58]

Although the images of women as both naturally pious and naturally
passionate may seem contradictory, they were closely intertwined. Because
evangelicals took women's weakness for granted, they believed that women
could be easily overpowered by Satan as well as by Christ. Without the
advantages of masculine strength and rationality, women were both archetypal saints and archetypal sinners.[59]

Both evangelical men and evangelical women traced their sinfulness
back to childhood, but women's descriptions of themselves tended to be
more extreme. The differences were in degree, not kind. When George
Whitefield looked back, he remembered "such early Stirrings of Corruption in my Heart, as abundantly convince me that *I was conceived and born*

in Sin—That in me dwelleth no good Thing by Nature." Yet when White-field's narrative of his early life is placed next to women's accounts, his humility sounds comparatively mild. Whitefield described himself as a "poor soul" only once, and he never portrayed himself as "weak" or a "worm." (The word *weak* appears only twice in his book, once when he was describing his debility after an illness, and once in a quotation from the poet Joseph Addison.)[60] In contrast, Susanna Anthony began the story of her life by remembering her sins at the age of five or six. As she continued writing, she portrayed herself as utterly corrupt and polluted. Her heart was "a sink of sin, more loathsome than the most offensive carrion that swarms with hateful vermin! My understanding dark and ignorant; my will stubborn; my affections carnal, corrupt and disordered; every faculty depraved and vitiated; my whole soul deformed and polluted, filled with pride, enmity, carnality, hypocrisy, self-confidence, and all manner of sins." (The weak ending to her sentence—"all manner of sins"—is almost humorous in its deflation. After piling up so many adjectives, Anthony seems to have run out of words to express how truly terrible she was.) Hannah Heaton longed to "fly out of this blind withered naked sore stinking rotten proud selfish self love into the arms of a lovely Jesus."[61] In the battle for salvation, women's greatest enemy was the "polluted" self.

It is impossible to know whether evangelical women actually saw themselves as more sinful than men or whether they were unconsciously echoing popular stereotypes. It would be a mistake, though, to dismiss their language as nothing more than rhetoric. Sarah Osborn may have described herself as "a vile sinner," "too vile to be forgiven," and a "vile wretch" because of her sense that women were supposed to sound particularly humble, but these words inevitably affected her understanding of herself.[62] Language always shapes perceptions of reality. Indeed, Sarah seems to have recognized that the more she chastised herself for her corruption, the more corrupt she appeared to herself. Denigrating herself was a form of discipline that was designed to make her confront her dependence on God.

Evangelical men and women agreed that true Christians should be humble and self-effacing, but ironically, even when they spoke the same language their words conveyed different meanings because of popular understandings of gender. When evangelical men lamented their sinfulness and their weakness, their words sounded countercultural and almost subversive. Since the dominant discourse of the time equated masculinity with strength, rationality, and boldness, evangelical men implicitly rejected "worldly" values by emphasizing their dependence on Christ. In contrast, when women confessed that they were sinful and helpless, they reinforced feminine stereotypes rather than challenging them. There was nothing either radical or surprising about Sarah's description of herself as "the weakest, meanest, and unworthiest of all creatures."[63]

Yet it is worth remembering that evangelical women (like evangelical men) assumed that recognizing one's fallenness was the first sign of God's grace. In a book that Sarah read (probably shortly before she wrote her memoir), she learned that the "best Christians" were the most sensible of their "badness": "The good person has his Eyes opened to see himself a vile, unworthy, loathsome Wretch, and he can't but be humble and have the saddest thoughts of himself, as if the worst in the world, because he sees himself so bad: and he hasn't such a sight of others in their badness, as he has of himself in his." Paradoxically, Sarah's description of her vile heart was also an assertion of her salvation in Christ. Despite encouraging women to acknowledge their sinfulness, the evangelical movement also taught them to believe in their own self-worth.[64] There were many things that women were forbidden to do in early America, but they could still be saints, the chosen of God.

Sarah Osborn's sober reflections on her childhood lay the foundation for the rest of her memoir. From her first pages she wanted her readers to understand that sin is real, not an illusion, and even children bear its marks. All humanity has inherited a fallen world, a world of sin and sorrow, and only those who confront this hard truth can be saved. Her vision of children's corruption and wickedness could not have been more different from the new ideas of human goodness emerging around her.

The controversies over children's "innocence" grew even more heated in the years after Sarah finished her memoir. As a minister complained, the doctrine of original sin was the one "most eagerly struck at, and virulently opposed by many, in the present Age." In 1749, the Reverend Jonathan Mayhew stoked the fires of controversy by declaring that "the doctrine of total ignorance, and incapacity to judge of moral and religious truths, brought upon mankind by the apostasy of our *First Parents*, is without foundation."[65] The fights became nastier during the 1750s when a group of ministers quarreled over whether a compassionate God would sentence infants to damnation. "How can you reconcile it to the *goodness, holiness* or *justice* of God, to make them heirs of hell," Samuel Webster asked, "and send them into the world only to breathe and die, and then take them away to hell, or even send them to hell from their mother's womb before ever they have seen the light of life?" By the early nineteenth century, many refused to imagine children coming into the world stained with sin but saw them instead, in William Wordsworth's image, "trailing clouds of glory." "Heaven lies about us in our infancy," he exclaimed.[66]

But Sarah put her faith in a darker creed. In her world, a world that rejected the exaltation of childhood innocence, children were taught to lament their sinfulness, parents were urged to be strict, and God, an all-powerful father, brooded over his creation with a mixture of love and wrath, a rod always resting in his hand.

Chapter 3

An Afflicted Low Condition

I have oft thought god has so ordred it throout my days that I should be in an aflicted Low condition and enclind the hearts of others to relieve me in all my distresses on purpose to suppress that pride of my nature which doubtless would have broke out greatly to his dishonour had i had health and prosperity and so as it were Lived independent upon others i will think it best for me for the tenderness of my friends to me has always had a tendency to humble me greatly and cause me to admire the goodness of god to me.[1]

As Sarah Osborn continued to write her memoir, she put aside her childhood recollections in order to focus on the tumultuous years of her adolescence and early adulthood. From her vantage point in 1743 she could look back at a long string of trials that had tested her faith, and as she tried to make sense of the past she had to confront the difficult question of suffering. She remembered soaring moments of communion with God (moments that had lifted her out of "the foul rag and bone shop of the heart," to borrow an image from Yeats), but also dark times of doubt that had led her to the brink of despair.[2] Poverty, chronic illness, the loss of loved ones, self-hatred, suicidal thoughts—all these lay in her past.

Sarah claimed that her afflictions had not only been "ordered" by God; they were "best for her." At a time when many Enlightenment thinkers insisted that a compassionate God did not want his creation to suffer, she found it more alarming to imagine that God was *not* responsible for affliction. If there was no divine providence in the world, but only fate or luck, then human life was sheer chaos, an abyss of meaninglessness that was even more frightening than hell. Either God controlled everything, including suffering, or there was no God. Echoing the words of Psalm 119:71, "It is good for me that I have been afflicted," she portrayed her suffering in rational terms as the means to a higher good: her salvation in Christ.

Evangelicals resisted the stream of Enlightenment thought that would later be known as humanitarianism, but as Sarah Osborn's memoir reveals they were also influenced by it. Despite denying that God's actions should always be understood in rational terms as promoting human fulfillment, they absorbed some of the ideas and language they found most troubling. Christians throughout history have viewed suffering as religiously meaningful, even redemptive, but under the pressures of humanitarian thought, evangelicals ended up wedding a new vocabulary of benevolence, happiness, and "reasonableness" to an older one of divinely ordained suffering. Instead of simply defending suffering as God's will, they claimed that in the long run it would make people *happy*. As Sarah reflected on the meaning of her life, she described her afflictions as a path to holiness, a dose of strong medicine for the soul, a rational good.

The Sin of Disobedience

When Sarah sailed into the Boston port with her mother in 1723, her burned hand still tender, she must have wondered what sort of life she would have in their new home. Long before the Revolution transformed America into a rising national power, it consisted of only a few small colonies strung along the eastern seaboard. Even though Boston was one of the largest cities in the colonies, with a population of eleven thousand, its busy wharves, wide streets, and crowded shops looked small and mean in comparison to the magnificent city of London. (London's population at the time exceeded half a million.) Despite its pretensions to gentility and refinement, America was still a distant outpost of the British Empire, a borderland where thousands of immigrants hoped for a better life.[3]

Although Sarah never explained why her parents decided to move to America, they may have hoped to make a fresh start in a country that would offer them greater economic opportunity. Her father was a tanner, a skilled craftsman who made leather goods, and as he labored to support his family, he uprooted them three times in the six years after their reunion at the Boston port. After spending two and a half years in Boston, they moved a few miles south to Freetown, then across the Taunton River to Dighton, and finally to Newport, Rhode Island, where Sarah remained for the rest of her life. Her brother, who had stayed in England with his grandmother, did not come to America until twelve years later in 1735.

Sarah wrote nothing about her years in Boston, but when she remembered her adolescence in Freetown and Dighton, she made it clear that her relationship with her parents was tense. No matter how much she tried, she could not conquer the sin of "disobedience." She had been a liar, a "fool," a "wretch," and "an abuser of mercy," she confessed, and despite her burns she had not kept her promise to "lead a new life." Sometimes she was "diligent in the performance of prayer," but as her language suggested, she was only *performing*: even though she tried to speak to God, she did not feel as if her words came from the depths of her heart. Often she "agonized" that he was not listening. Fearful that she was too stubborn to be converted by "ordinary means" (for example, sermons or religious reading), she begged God to afflict her again, praying that he "would do anything with me, though ever so terrible, so that I might be drove from my evil courses and turned to God." (At first she had written that she had asked him to "give me a sight of hell with my bodily eyes," but realizing how extreme this sounded, she scratched it out.) Even falling into a blazing fire, the closest thing to hell on earth, had not been enough. She thought that she needed more sorrow and more suffering—even the unspeakable sight of hell—before she could become a true Christian.[4]

All the stories that Sarah told about her adolescence were designed to reveal God's love for her despite her "disobedience." When she remembered her stormy relationship with her parents during their unsettled years in Massachusetts, she decided that two stories were especially crucial. In the first, she remembered that at the age of thirteen she had deliberately flouted her parents' "commands" by venturing out in a canoe at night. As she drifted downstream with the tide, she lost control of the boat, and, fearful that she might drown, she knelt down on the wooden bottom and clasped her hands to pray. "All my former convictions revived, and the sin of disobedience to my parents especially appeared odious," she wrote. "I thought it was just with God to bring me into this distress for it, and with great vehemence and self-abhorrence confessed and aggravated my sins before God, pleading for an interest in the blood of Christ, and for pardon for his sake." Given her sinfulness, she thought it would be "just" for God to take away her life.[5]

Yet for the first time in her memoir, in a remarkable turning point that she never explained (and, indeed, she may not have been able to explain, even to herself), Sarah remembered a blissful, almost mystical moment when she felt consumed by Christ's "everlasting love." Alone on the water in the dark, lost in prayer, she forgot her sadness, her fears, and her anger at her parents. For a fleeting moment, the wrathful God of her childhood disappeared, eclipsed by a compassionate Jesus. Sarah finally knew what it meant to experience the gift every Christian longed for: the gift of forgiveness. "I felt a secret Joy," she exulted, "verily believing that I was forgiven and that Christ had Loved me with an everlasting love and that I should be happy with him, and Longed for the time. I was immediately resigned to the will of God, quite willing to die, and willing to Live, begging that God would dispose of me as most consisted with his Glory. And after I had thus resigned myself, soul and body, into the hands of God to do with me as seemed him good, I was as calm and serene in the temper as ever in my life." Only after this moment of communion with Christ did she try to save her life. "At Last [I] bethought myself that self-preservation was a great duty," she explained, "and therefore I ought to try to get on shore." She screamed for help for several hours until she was hoarse and exhausted, and at last neighbors paddled out to rescue her.[6]

Of all the stories that Sarah could have told about her adolescence, she seems to have chosen this one because of the sudden insight she had gleaned on the water that night. She never wanted to forget that even when God seemed angry, he was watching over her with love.

The second story she shared about these years was much like the first. After her brush with death in the canoe, she remembered that her life had become more "sweet and pleasant," but a year later, at the age of fourteen, she forgot her promise to be a more obedient child. (What happened next, she believed, was God's way of reminding her that he still held her life in his hands.) Contrary to her parents' strict "orders," she decided to cross the frozen river after a "great thaw," making her way across watery ice that seemed to sink with her every step. With the tide rising, she was surrounded by "holes as big as houses, or larger," but after a desperate search for a way back to land she finally found a narrow bridge of ice to shore. Later she realized "how just God would have been if I had been drowned for my disobedience to my parents," but even though she was "a poor sinful worm, so unworthy of the Least mercy," he had spared her. With gratitude she wrote, "I am amazed when I consider how Miraculously God preserved me."[7]

Shaped by a religious culture that saw anger as sinful, Sarah never openly admitted how much these two episodes of "disobedience" grew out of her resentment of her parents. Although many eighteenth-century Americans accepted and even encouraged expressions of anger (one thinks, for example, of southerners who defended the honor of dueling), evangelicals tried to repress it. Like John Robinson, a Puritan minister who had vividly described the "wrathful man" as a "hideous monster," with "his eyes burning, his lips fumbling, his face pale, his teeth gnashing, his mouth foaming, and other parts of his body trembling, and shaking," they reviled anger as one of the seven deadly sins. Unlike God, whose wrath was always righteous, humans were so corrupt that their anger easily turned into uncontrollable, poisonous feelings of rage. Writing in 1723, Jonathan Edwards resolved to suppress "an air of dislike, fretfulness, and anger in conversation": "When I am most conscious of provocations to ill-nature and anger," he promised himself, "I will strive most to feel and act good-naturedly."[8]

Sarah, too, tried her best to appear "good-natured." Even though many lines of her memoir pulse with anger, she struggled to repress it, burying her bitter feelings under self-blame. Instead of criticizing her parents, she insisted that *she*—a "stupid" and "ungratefull" sinner—had been at fault. Yet even though she never asked herself why she had rashly endangered her life on two occasions, she seems to have been deeply angry at her parents, and whether to get their attention, to force them to express their love, or simply to spite them, she recklessly put herself in danger.

After the family moved to Newport in 1730, Sarah's parents may have hoped that she would outgrow her rebelliousness. They had saved enough money to purchase two lots at Easton's Point, a Quaker neighborhood where many of Newport's most successful craftsmen lived, and for the first time in years the future looked bright.[9] Her father not only worked as a tanner but opened a shop in order to make extra money.

In comparison with the rural villages of Freetown and Dighton, however, Newport was a city filled with irresistible temptations. With a population of only four thousand in 1730, Newport was not yet the bustling commercial center it would become a decade later, and Thames Street, its major thoroughfare, was still a rutted, mud-caked road where hogs sometimes wandered in front of coaches. But as the members of the rising merchant class made a fortune in shipping, they built imposing new houses (one that was rumored to have running water), stocked their sideboards with silver, bought large numbers of slaves, and flaunted the latest fashions from Britain. When George Berkeley, the British philosopher, arrived in Newport in 1729, he found "a rage for finery, the men in flaming scarlet coats and waistcoats, laced and fringed with brightest glaring yellow."[10] The houses, too, were colorful, painted in dazzling hues of red, yellow, green, and blue, and they were filled with imported goods brought by Newport's ships. Taverns were so popular that a group of residents complained that "the great

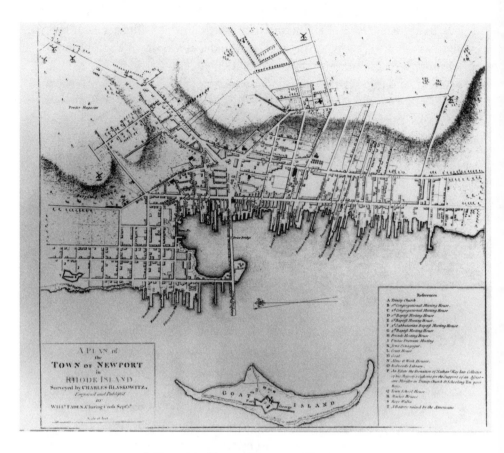

A Plan of the Town of Newport, Rhode Island.
Courtesy of the Newport Historical Society.

Increase of Taverns, Alehouses victualing houses & other houses of common entertainment" had led to "Evil practices and great abuses." When
Sarah was not tending shop for her father, she could watch a horserace on
the outskirts of town, learn the latest songs and dances from one of the
many local teachers, or parade up and down Thames Street arm in arm
with her friends. Never before had she been able to make so many choices
about how to spend her time. Rather than trying to become the obedient
child her parents wanted her to be, she decided to become someone else—
someone less sober and anxious. Forgetting her resolutions to become a
Christian, she "got into company and was full of vanity."[11]

Although all Sarah's stories hinted at her anger and unhappiness, nothing in her memoir prepared her readers for the shock of what came next. Immediately after admitting that she had "got into company," she abruptly changed the subject. "One day," she began to write, but before she could bring herself to finish her sentence, she burst out in an agony of grief, "Oh that I could mention it with weeping eyes and a bleeding heart, and after such a manner that glory may redound for the glorious God, while I with shame confess my monstrous, God-provoking, and hell-deserving sin." Struggling to compose herself, she admitted that she had been so despondent that she had considered suicide:

> *One day . . . my mother being very angry with me, and as I thought for no reason at all, my passion was raised to a dreadful degree, but durst not vent it by saying anything to her. I reflected upon many such seasons and thought myself exceedingly wronged. Satan took the advantage of me at this time, and tempted me to believe that there was no one upon earth Lived so miserable a Life as I did. Neither was hell worse. I had therefore better take away my Life and so know the worst at first, for that hell would be my portion sooner or Later, for my sins was so great they could never be pardoned. At first I started at the temptation and thought it a dreadful thing to murder myself. But Satan hurried me on, till at Last, monster that I was, I yielded so far as to think how to accomplish so hellish a design. And being in a garret, there was seemingly a voice which said, "there's a rope and there's a place," which was one of the crosspieces in the roof. "What hinders you now?"*[12]

Filled with rage and despair, Sarah imagined how easy it would be to tie the rope around her neck, climb onto a chair, and lash herself to one of the rafters. By the time her parents found her body, she would be dead, damned to a hell that could not possibly be any more terrible than her nightmarish existence on earth. Like Judas, who had hanged himself after betraying Christ, she felt worthless and ashamed, utterly forsaken by both humanity and God.

Yet at the last minute Sarah felt a sense of God's nearness, an overwhelming feeling of his presence that made her realize that she was not alone. It was as though God had collapsed the distance between them,

Sarah's account of her suicidal crisis. Photograph courtesy of Beinecke speaking to her across time and space. With her hands trembling and her eyes blurred by tears, she remembered how he had pulled her out of Satan's grasp immediately after her decision to destroy herself. "And being thus drove by the violence of temptation and my own corruptions, I thought to do it," she wrote in large, shaky handwriting. "But while in the utmost Hurry, anguish, and distress, these words come to me with great power, 'resist the devil and he will flee from you. Draw nigh to God and he will draw nigh to you.'" Recalling these words from the Epistle of James, she felt as though she heard them for the first time, and as she fell to the ground in prayer, she begged God to save her from her despair. "Oh! how then did I fall down prostrate on the floor," she remembered, "and adore the infinite goodness of a compassionate God." Breaking down into "floods of tears," she "returned thanks for so great a deliverance." Even thirteen years later, she could not remember that awful day in the garret without weeping, smearing the ink on the page.[13]

Despite the old adage that "time heals all wounds," Sarah's unsteady handwriting, her blotched ink, and even her choice of words suggest that the intervening years had not smoothed away the jagged edges of her pain. Without realizing it she slipped into the present tense as she wrote, erasing thirteen years with a single stroke of her pen. Instead of remembering the biblical words that "came" to her, she wrote, "These words *come* to me with great power." That day had been so frightening, so confusing, and so heartbreaking that she seemed to relive her despair while gripping her pen in her hand.[14]

To anyone who has ever been tormented by thoughts of suicide, Sarah's despair will seem painfully familiar. Like other people in the eighteenth century, she would have called it "melancholy," but she described it in language that matches our modern understanding of depression, or, in more clinical terms, a "major depressive state." Devastated by feelings of hopelessness, guilt, and loss, she felt as though she were being crushed beneath the weight of her sorrow. Her grief was so intense and immediate that it seemed to obliterate the future. To borrow William Styron's image of his mental breakdown, darkness had become visible, and she could no longer imagine anything beyond the unbearable pain of her present life. Consumed by her suffering, she felt as though nothing else existed. She was empty, alone, "miserable." Even hell could not be worse.[15]

Sarah Osborn lived more than a hundred years before Sigmund Freud, and she would never have used psychological language to describe her suffering: words like *repression* would have been incomprehensible to her. Yet there are striking parallels between her narrative of her suicidal crisis and modern psychological theory. Long before psychoanalysts suggested that depression should be understood as misdirected anger that has been turned inward against the self rather than outward against the world, Sarah's narrative offered a textbook example of the theory. Alice Miller has argued that children who have been forbidden to express their anger often become self-destructive and suicidal, venting their repressed rage on themselves rather than their parents.[16] Although Sarah's account of her crisis is unfortunately quite short, she claimed that her ordeal began after she struggled to stifle her resentment of her mother, who had been "very angry" with her. "My passion was raised to a dreadful degree," she remembered, "but [I] durst not vent it by saying anything to her." Reared in a religious culture that taught children to be obedient, she choked back her anger instead of daring to challenge her mother's authority. Retreating to the garret in a silent fury, she turned her explosive rage inward against herself rather than outward against her mother, desperately deciding to kill herself. Even after her crisis passed and she finally came downstairs, she seems to have disguised her true emotions. "When I had with floods of tears returned thanks for so great a deliverance, and committed myself to God's keeping," she wrote, "I came down rejoicing and perfectly calm in my temper."[17]

Although Sarah continued to struggle with bouts of despair throughout her life, she managed to overcome her suicidal feelings because of her growing faith in God's love. If, as Miller argues, a "sympathetic listener" can save someone from self-destruction, then Sarah's listener was God. She poured out her sorrows to him in prayer, and when she most needed him he sent her precious words of comfort: "Draw nigh to God and he will draw nigh to you." Even though she continued to see him as angry as well as "compassionate," she had begun to outgrow her earlier conception of him as a larger version of her parents. As she talked to her friends, listened to sermons, and, most important, read the Bible for herself, she developed a richer, more complicated image of God: he was a "king," a "conqueror," a protector, a friend, the "dearest Lord." Even though she had been ready to destroy herself, he had saved her. "Lord," she wrote, "fill me with gratitude, flaming Love too, and praise of thee, my God and King, who Like a mighty Conqueror appeared for me in the mount of difficulty and put to flight the grand enemy of my soul's salvation." Just as he had done during her two other brushes with death, he had made her see that she was worthy of being loved.[18]

Sarah almost always portrayed God in masculine terms as a father, but she occasionally used feminine imagery when writing about Scripture,

imagining God's word as a mother that nourished and comforted her. In
a letter to a friend, for example, she thanked God for sending her a reassuring biblical text at a time when she felt frightened and vulnerable.
Remembering his words "be not afraid," she felt as though she were lying
"becalmed in his bosom sucking by faith the breast of the promises given
me by a faithful God." On another occasion she remembered that she had
"sucked Large draughts of consolation" from the promise in Psalm 84:11,
"the Lord God is a sun and shield."[19]

Yet Sarah's belief in a compassionate God did not offer a simple cure
for her distress. Because evangelicals believed that true saints had an overwhelming sense of their own "vileness," she repeatedly reminded herself
that she was a "wretch" who did not deserve God's mercy. "Oh, for Jesus's
sake, suffer me not to do anything that will tend to puff up self," she prayed.
"Oh, remove all spiritual pride and keep me Low at the foot of Jesus." Her
faith both wounded and healed her, alternately aggravating and relieving
her feelings of despair.[20]

Since many evangelicals claimed to have been besieged by the temptation to commit suicide, Sarah may have decided to share her story because
it seemed to fit common expectations about the agony of religious doubt.
Even though the actual suicide rate seems to have been fairly low, many
converts claimed to have contemplated self-destruction. According to Susanna Anthony, Sarah's closest friend in Newport, Satan had tempted her
to believe that she was "an outcast, rejected of God," and she decided it
would be better to kill herself than "to live to treasure up wrath against the
day of wrath."[21] In the eyes of eighteenth-century evangelicals, considering
suicide was not necessarily a sign of a disordered mind (although in some
cases they saw it as extreme) but proof of religious fervor. As Christians
struggled to understand God's will, they were forced to ask themselves excruciating questions about whether they had been destined for heaven or
for hell. As ministers admitted, "some very godly men" had considered
killing themselves, even "the *Best of Saints* upon earth." Because Satan was
enraged by their goodness, he saved his worst "snares" for them. "When
the *Devil* has no hope of prevailing, yet he will Tempt unto Crime," the
Reverend Increase Mather explained. "He will do it, only to vex and molest
the faithful servants of GOD!"[22]

Yet even though evangelicals assumed that many sinners would be
tempted to commit suicide, they also condemned the "horrid crime of self-
murder" as the ultimate act of rebellion against God. Suicide was the most
shocking sin a person could commit—in Sarah's words, a "monstrous,

God-provoking, and hell-deserving sin." Christians were supposed to accept their sufferings as God's will, but by the act of suicide they tried to wrest their fate out of his hands.[23]

Sarah tried to make sense of her anguish in the garret by blaming both Satan and herself for her suicidal feelings. On one hand, she portrayed herself as a helpless pawn in a cosmic battle between God and Satan—a battle over who would possess her soul. Using passive language, she described Satan as the cause of her despair: "Satan took the advantage of me," she swore. "Satan hurried me on." It even seemed as though Satan spoke to her, telling her where to find a rope and reminding her of the crosspiece in the roof. Yet on the other hand, she insisted that Satan would have been helpless to hurt her if not for her inherent corruption. She had been so sinful that she had provoked God into allowing her to be tempted.[24]

Searching for a rational explanation for her suicidal crisis, Sarah concluded that God had punished her for disobeying her parents. In case any children ever read her memoir, she warned them to "submit to and obey their own parents or other superiors in all things right and not suffer passion to rise in their breasts." If she had been a more dutiful daughter, she would never have been afflicted.[25]

Yet Sarah could not completely suppress her anger against her parents. Without intending it, she gave her story two contradictory plots. On the surface, she claimed to have been such a sinful, disobedient child that God had allowed Satan to tempt her. She alone had been at fault. Yet underneath her pious confession of guilt lay a less orthodox explanation for her psychological anguish. Undermining the purely religious moral of her story, she blamed her mother, not Satan or her own depravity, for "provoking" her to suicide. At the beginning of her account, she made it clear that her crisis started when her mother had been "very angry" with her "for no reason at all," and at the end, she warned parents not to enrage their children by being too harsh. Echoing Paul's words to the Ephesians, she chided, "Oh, Let parents be entreated to be very careful that they don't provoke their children to wrath by being too severe to them since a subtle adversary will take the advantage of such seasons." Although she tried to soften the impact of these resentful words by emphasizing her own "corruptions," she could not bring herself to justify her mother's treatment of her.[26] Even fifteen years after her despair in the garret, her memory of that afternoon still angered her.

As Sarah eventually seems to have realized, she had not been able to offer a coherent explanation of her suicidal crisis. Sometime after she finished writing, she scrawled in the margins of her memoir, "Is it duty to let this criminal affair stand recorded." Perhaps she was ashamed to admit that she had thought about the terrible crime of self-murder, but since many other evangelicals openly discussed suicide, it seems more likely that she was troubled by something in the substance of her account. Others almost never mentioned a nonreligious reason for their despair, and, most important, they usually described their suicidal feelings in the context of conversion. Nathan Cole, for example, claimed that Satan made a last-ditch effort to snatch his soul after he was "born again."[27] In contrast, Sarah did not experience conversion until several years later. Without intending it, she implied that her crisis had been triggered not by her deepening relationship to God but by her uncontrollable anger at her mother.

When Samuel Hopkins published extracts from Sarah Osborn's memoir after her death, he decided to omit her account of her suicidal feelings. Besides sympathizing with her heartbreaking wish to forget the whole "criminal affair," he may have worried that other Christians might be confused or misled by the conflicting meanings embedded in her story. He must have been particularly troubled by her underlying tone of self-justification. Despite her attempt to turn the story of her suicidal crisis into a lesson about human sinfulness and God's punishments, she had also used it to voice her pent-up rage against her parents, especially her mother. At the age of fifteen or sixteen she had "durst not vent it."[28] But when she wrote her memoir at the age of twenty-nine, it spilled out on the page despite her best efforts to contain it.

Hear Ye the Rod

In the weeks and months after her suicidal crisis, Sarah slowly recovered from her despair. Taking refuge in her faith, she promised God to become a more faithful Christian. Yet as she confessed in her memoir, her "goodness" lasted only a short season. Once again she fell into sin, and once again a sovereign God chastised her with his "rod."[29]

Despite Sarah's resolutions to lead a more devout life, she could not help being drawn into the whirl of Newport social life. There was always something entertaining to see in the streets: fashionable matrons showed off their finery as they rode by in horse-drawn carriages; drunks brawled outside taverns; fiddlers strolled up and down playing for the crowds; and gamblers—many of them gentlemen—placed bets on horseraces and cockfights. While Christians went to prayer meetings with Bibles tucked under their arms, Sarah, now seventeen, amused herself by visiting friends and learning the latest card games. "After all this, oh that with deep humility of soul, with sorrow and shame I could speak of it," she wrote, "I relapsed again and was full of nothing but vanity. I used to sing songs, dance, play at cards with company as oft I could get opportunities." Defying her parents yet again, she also began "keeping company" "with a young man something against my parents' will."[30]

The young man was Samuel Wheaten. Although Sarah wrote very little about him in her memoir (we would not even know his name if not for Samuel Hopkins's account of her life), we know that he was a sailor whom she had met somewhere in the city, perhaps at a card game or dance. We also know that within a few weeks or months of their first meeting, they had fallen in love, and when he asked her to marry him she said yes.

As Sarah must have expected, her parents did not think their daughter was ready for marriage. Since most New England women did not marry until they were twenty-two or twenty-three, the Haggars probably thought she was too young.[31] They also may have worried about what sort of future she would have as a sailor's wife. Samuel spent many months of the year sailing to wherever merchants wanted to trade their goods, and he made very little money. Unless he managed to work himself up to the more lucrative position of captain, he would never be financially secure. Most important, Sarah's parents seemed to suspect that he was not completely trustworthy. "At first they Liked him," Sarah claimed, but they changed their minds because of "false reports raised of him." Perhaps they feared he would turn out to be one of the irresponsible sailors who drank away their money in the local taverns. Hoping to dampen their daughter's ardor, the Haggars swore they would never give her a marriage portion if she dared marry him. (It was customary for New England parents to give their daughters clothing, kitchen utensils, and other housekeeping goods as a marriage gift.) As Sarah remembered, "While they was angry with me they often threatened to give me nothing, which I thought was very hard."[32]

For years Sarah had stifled her anger at her parents, but when they forbade her to marry the man she loved, she became enraged. Not only did she resolve to marry Samuel, but since they refused to give her a marriage portion she decided to steal it from them. Although they did not have much cash, she found it easy to pocket things from the shelves of their shop. "I had been very diligent to work," she explained, "so was tempted by Satan and wicked companions to believe it was no sin to take anything I wanted, for it was my own by right—my parents having no other child here but me. And accordingly I did, in trifling things to the value of 30 pounds as I cast them up afterwards and was exceedingly perplexed when I found how much they amounted to."[33] Thirty pounds was a great deal of money at the time, more than she could have made by working as a seamstress or a teacher for several months.

As Sarah tried to explain to both herself and her readers how she could have sunk to the level of a thief, she put much of the blame on her "wicked companions." Although she had wanted to return the stolen items after realizing their value, her friends convinced her to remain silent:

> *Those who had persuaded me to take them and had kept them for me pleaded with me not to do it, for I must discover them and it would be base ingratitude in me so to do when they had done it all for my good. And more than that it would make a breach between my parents and me that would never be made up, for they knew they would make me a public example. And still insisted upon it: it was no sin. So at last all these things prevailed over my resolutions and I kept them [the goods] with this thought: that if ever I was able I would make restitution. But it has cost me thousands of tears since.*[34]

Under her friends' bad influence, she decided that the risks of confession were too great. Not only would her friends feel betrayed, but her parents might decide to make a "public example" of her: they might tell their neighbors or the congregation or, worse, file criminal charges against her. To even conceive of such a thing, Sarah must have already been deeply estranged from her parents, but she still seems to have wanted their love and approval. She was terrified to think that she might make a "breach" in their relationship that she would never be able to close. Most of all, she thought her friends were right to argue that her theft had not been a sin but her just due. It was not she who had been in the wrong, but her parents.

Looking back, however, Sarah realized that she had been a "vile wretch"—not only a sinner but literally a *criminal*. If not for God's grace she would have become as bad as the thieves and vagabonds who were publicly whipped on the street corners. "Oh Lord," she testified, "how just hadst thou been if thou hadst Left me entirely to myself, and if thou hadst, nothing would have been too bad for such a vile wretch as I to have committed. But blessed be God that withheld me from such sins against strangers as would have brought me to open justice and exposed myself and family to disgrace and shame." (Here she closely echoed John Bunyan, who claimed that if not for "a miracle of precious grace," he would have "laid myself open, even to the stroke of those laws, which bring some to disgrace and open shame before the face of the world.")[35] Unlike those who celebrated human goodness, she thought there was only a fine line separating the "virtuous" from the outwardly criminal.

When Samuel Hopkins read Sarah's account of her theft many years later, he found it so troubling that he decided not to include it in his published version of her memoir. Since he shared her dark view of human nature, he probably was not bothered by the fact that she had stolen from her parents; indeed, he could have used her story to emphasize God's free grace to even the worst of sinners. Had not Jesus saved the thief who was crucified next to him? Yet Hopkins seems to have feared that Sarah's words of repentance were not completely genuine. While she admitted her wrongdoing, she also tried to justify herself by pointing to her parents' unreasonableness and the evil influence of her "wicked companions." The lesson she drew from her experiences was not what he would have chosen. Addressing herself to children, she wrote, "Oh Let children tremble at the thoughts of doing any such thing, and be entreated to shun all such company as will persuade them to it." Rather than accepting full responsibility for her actions, she suggested that she had been cruelly misled by bad company.[36] As Hopkins knew (and as we shall see), she also continued to remain silent about her crime even after she supposedly had been reborn in Christ. Her parents did not realize what she had done, and she could not bring herself to confess until eleven years later.

Sarah Haggar married Samuel Wheaten on October 21, 1731, at the age of seventeen. Although she did not describe the ceremony (she recorded nothing except the date), they were probably married by a civil magistrate. Reformed Protestants, unlike Catholics, treated marriage as a civil contract rather than a sacrament, and couples were usually wed at home. Even though marriage was a covenant that symbolized Christ's love of his "elect," most Protestants did not think that clergy should preside over weddings, and until 1733 only Quaker and Anglican ministers had the legal authority to perform marriages in Rhode Island.[37] If Sarah and Samuel were like other couples, they probably put on their best clothes (but not the elaborate finery that brides and grooms wear today) and then exchanged their vows in front of a justice of the peace and a small group of well-wishers.

Although it was customary in New England for women to be married at home, it is hard to imagine that Sarah and Samuel were welcome in her parents' house. They may not have even told the Haggars of their plans. According to Rhode Island's legal code, couples could not be married until they had published their intention in a public place for fourteen days, but Sarah and Samuel may have persuaded someone to perform the ceremony in secret. In theory, the penalties for illegal marriages were stiff—magistrates could be fined or suspended from office, and couples could be whipped, fined, or imprisoned—but the laws were rarely enforced. Indeed, later in her life Sarah recorded another woman's secret marriage in her diary.[38]

After their marriage Sarah and Samuel left Newport to visit some of his friends in the country. Perhaps they did not know where else to go. Since her parents had refused to give her a marriage portion, they did not have any of the pots, spoons, furniture, or linens they needed to "go to house-keeping," and despite Sarah's theft, they may not have had enough money to pay rent.[39] Since Samuel would not go to sea again until the spring, they stayed with his friends for the first five months of their marriage.

While Sarah never expressed regret about her marriage, her first months with Samuel were filled with guilt. Instead of describing her happiness, she remembered her deep shame at her disobedience of both her parents and God. "I thought I could have Laid down my very Life to have recompensed my parents for the wrong I had done them," she wrote. "Then that sin was more clear to me than ever before. I could no longer flatter myself with hopes that it was no sin, but in bitter agonies of soul pleaded with God to forgive me for it and to give me a competency of this world so that I might make restitution." Although she decided it was not her "duty" to confess her sin to her parents unless she could repay them, she begged God to have mercy on her. Sometimes she let herself appear "merry," but inwardly she was disconsolate. "I had no real pleasure," she wrote. She loved Samuel, but she thought nothing could ease her sadness except God's grace.[40]

Samuel and Sarah returned to Newport in the spring. He needed to leave on another voyage, and she, now pregnant, may have hoped that her parents would welcome her home as a prodigal. Whether or not she suffered from the exhaustion and nausea that often accompany the first trimester of pregnancy, she may have felt vulnerable as she prepared to see them again. Would they embrace and forgive her? Would they promise to put the past behind them?

The answer, sadly, was no. According to Sarah, five months had not been long enough to heal the rift between them. "After I came home I met with much affliction in many respects," she wrote. As she had done earlier in her memoir, she briefly slipped into the present tense, remembering the past so intensely that she seemed to be experiencing it again. "My parents are more set against me than ever," she lamented, "but it was not for anything that Justified it." Since she later decided to scratch out the words "Justified it" as well as the next eight lines, which are now illegible, we do not know what she originally meant to say, but she was clearly resentful that her parents had decided to continue punishing her. Although she tried to sound less angry in the lines she allowed to remain on the page, she admitted that she had "let nature rise": "It seemed to me that the whole world was in arms against me. I thought I was the most despised creature Living upon earth. I used to pray to God in secret to relieve me but did not, as I ought, see his hand in permitting it so to be as a just punishment for my vile sins. And therefore was not humbled under it as I ought but let nature rise, and acted very imprudently in many respects. I was then with child, and often Lamented that I was Like to bring a child into such a world of sorrow."[41] After Samuel left her in Newport, she felt alone and unloved, adrift in a world that seemed to "despise" her.

In retrospect Sarah interpreted her troubles as God's punishment for her vile sins. As she explained, she should have asked herself why God had brought her more sorrow, but infuriated by her parents, she never looked inward to examine her own conscience. As ministers often warned their congregations, God's rod had a voice. "The Lord's voice crieth unto the city, and the man of wisdom shall see thy name," the prophet Micah had declared. "Hear ye the rod, and who hath appointed it." Since God never sent afflictions without reason, Christians had to search their hearts for every unknown sin. If a sinner dared to say, "It is my lot to lie under a dumb and silent rod, I do not understand its language, I cannot hear its voice, I cannot find the sin that is pointed at by it," God might be provoked into an even greater display of wrath. "It very much aggravates the affliction to God's people, when they know not the language of it," a minister admonished.[42] Suffering was rarely mysterious; it was the logical consequence of sin.

In practice this meant that an afflicted person was supposed to "accuse, judge, and condemn himself, for being the cause and procurer of his own troubles." In the words of John Flavel, a seventeenth-century British Dissenter whose works remained popular in eighteenth-century America, a suffering person should ask, "Lord, what special corruption is it that this Rod is sent to rebuke; what sinful neglect doth it come to humble me for?" Many other ministers repeated his words. "It concerns you to *consider* what you have *been*, and *done*, that has provoked the LORD thus to deal with you," one clergyman wrote in 1737. Another urged people who had met with "heavy and grievous *afflictions*" to ask, "What special article of repentance does this affliction find in me, to be repented of? What miscarriage does this *affliction* find in me, to be repented of?" Softening their language, clergymen admitted that physical or psychological suffering was not always a sign of God's anger, but they still argued that it was "safest" to beg his forgiveness. "God sometimes visits his people with affliction for the trial and exercise of their grace, and for their spiritual instruction, more than for the correction of their sin," a minister explained. "But, sin being the original and foundation of all affliction, it is safest when it is our own case, and most acceptable to God to look on sin as the procuring cause."[43]

Although Sarah did not "condemn" herself at the age of eighteen, she saw her life differently at the age of twenty-nine. As she searched for the hidden meanings in her story, she concluded that God had punished her for disobeying her parents, stealing from them, and failing to keep her vows to "lead a new life." "I blush and am ashamed when I remember my notorious ingratitude," she wrote. "Oh break this heart of flint, dearest Lord, that it may melt into tears of contrition, and never suffer me to forgive myself because thou hast forgiven me."[44] If she had been a better Christian, she would have listened more carefully to the voice of God's rod.

The Heavy News

On October 27, 1732, while Samuel was still at sea, Sarah gave birth to a son. Summing up her pregnancy, her hopes for her unborn child, and her labor in a few short words, she later wrote that she "sometimes found a disposition to dedicate my babe to God while in the womb and did so at all seasons of secret prayer. And after it was born, my husband being at sea, I could not rest till I had solemnly given it up to God in baptism. I met with many trials in my Lying in, it being an extreme cold season."[45] She was only eighteen years old.

Hidden behind these terse words lay a vast store of memories that Sarah decided not to share. Based on evidence from other women's diaries and letters, however, we can piece together a fragmentary account of what she may have experienced. If Sarah followed the pattern of other women, she spent the last weeks of her pregnancy preparing not only for the arrival of a new child (there were gowns, hats, and blankets to sew) but, more soberly, for the possibility of death. As the historian Laurel Thatcher Ulrich has found, maternal mortality was high compared to modern rates.

Whereas only one out of ten thousand women dies in childbirth today in the United States, the midwife Martha Ballard recorded "one maternal death for every 198 living births" in late-eighteenth-century Maine. (Since Ballard's records suggest that she was a particularly skilled midwife, the average rate in the colonies was probably higher. In mid-eighteenth-century London and Dublin, there were between 30 and 200 maternal deaths per thousand births.)[46] One Massachusetts woman kept a small diary in which she gratefully recorded every exhausting labor that both she and her newest infant had survived. "The Lord appeared for me and made me the living mother of another living Child," she rejoiced. "This is the third time the Lord has appeared for me in the perilous hour of Childbearing." Women referred to childbirth as *travail*. As the consequence of Eve's sin in the Garden of Eden, it was usually hard and painful, and it was often accompanied by fears of death.[47]

Since childbirth was almost entirely controlled by women (male doctors had only recently begun to contest midwives' authority), Sarah probably summoned her midwife and a group of female friends when her labor pains began. Besides bringing her the customary "groaning beer" and "groaning cakes" to sustain her during labor, they may have also brought special herbs to relieve the pain. Their job was to help her walk in order to hasten labor, to hold her and comfort her if she began shaking or vomiting, and to encourage her through the worst contractions. During the last intense stage of pushing, they may have supported her as she reclined in their laps or sat on a special birthing stool with an open seat. When her son was born, they would have cut his umbilical cord and washed him, and then the midwife would have made sure that she was not beginning to show signs of fever or other complications. Although Sarah remembered enduring many "trials" during her lying in (the time of rest following childbirth, a period that probably lasted only a few days), her problems did not involve her health but the surprisingly frigid weather. Since it was only October, she might not have bought her stock of firewood for the winter, or perhaps she was too poor to afford any. She spent her first days huddled with her son to stay warm.[48]

What Sarah remembered best about the days before and after her son's birth was her desire to bring him into covenant with God. Imitating the example of Hannah, in the first book of Samuel, who had promised to give her child to God, she dedicated her child to God while he was still in the womb. (Unable to conceive, Hannah had prayed, "O Lord of hosts, if thou wilt indeed look on the affliction of thine handmaid, and remember me, and not forget thine handmaid, but wilt give unto thy handmaid a man child, then I will give him unto the Lord all the days of his life.") Also like Hannah, Sarah chose to name her son Samuel. Perhaps she wanted to name him after his father, but since she seems to have closely identified with Hannah (and continued to allude to her in later diaries), her choice seems to have been at least partially motivated by religious considerations. Since as many as three in ten infants born in New England did not survive to their first birthday, many parents seem to have hoped that giving their children biblical names would offer them special protection. In one New England church, for example, more than 80 percent of new members enrolled between 1716 and 1758 were named after biblical heroes and heroines.[49]

Besides choosing a biblical name for her son, Sarah brought him to be baptized soon after his birth. Although Congregationalists did not believe that baptism could convey salvation, they did consider it a "seal of the covenant": a tangible sign of God's promise to redeem his chosen people. Even though God had not promised that all the children of the "elect" would be saved, he usually chose to "cast the Lines of election . . . through the loins of godly Parents."[50] Repeating what her own parents had done, Sarah wanted to bring her child under the protection of the covenant. "O how much comfort do those parents Lose who never gave their children up to God in baptism in their infancy," she wrote. "And how sad for children themselves to be deprived of the privilege of pleading with God for covenant blessings. My being dedicated to God in my infancy always put an argument into my mouth to beg of God that I might not cut myself off since I was a child of the covenant [and] from a child given to him in baptism." Although she knew that baptism did not guarantee her child's salvation, she "could not rest" until a minister had blessed Samuel and welcomed him into the church. Her sense of urgency was not unique: most parents in New England brought their infants to be baptized as soon as possible, often within two weeks of their birth, even if it meant breaking the ice on the baptismal font.[51]

Since the older Samuel was still at sea, he did not see his child until he returned to Newport the next spring. By then he had been away for many months, and unless he had met someone from home in a far-off port, he would not have known whether he was the father of a boy or a girl or, most important, whether Sarah and his child were both alive and healthy. He must have been immensely relieved to find her waiting for him with his son, who was now at least five months old. We can only imagine how many stories they must have rushed to tell each other—stories about towering waves at sea, foreign people in far-away lands, or cold winter nights nursing a child.

But Samuel could remain at home for only a few months. After spending the spring and summer of 1733 in Newport, he prepared to leave on another vessel in the fall. The merchant trade was thriving. Like many sailors, he may have traveled to other American ports such as Philadelphia or Boston, but given the length of his voyages he probably went to the British or French West Indies in order to exchange fish, lumber, and horses for molasses and sugar or, even more dangerous, all the way to West Africa to trade rum for slaves. Fragmentary evidence suggests that he may have been part of the crew of the *Bonadventure*, a sloop that left Newport in October 1733 on its way to Barbados and then Africa.[52] Neither he nor Sarah seems to have had any qualms about the justice of slavery, and he may have hoped to support his family with the profits of the slave trade. Sarah may have worried that he might become ill at sea or be captured by privateers or shipwrecked, but she tried to put her faith in God's protection. All she could do was wait, pray, and watch the harbor in search of his returning ship.

Six months later on April 1, 1734, Sarah was startled out of her sleep by an urgent knock at her door. For a brief moment she may have thought that Samuel had finally come home, but after unlatching the door and peering into the darkness she came face to face with her worst fears. "I went to bed in a house all alone, my child being at my father's, and about eleven or twelve o'clock at night was waked to hear the heavy news," she remembered.[53] It had not been possible to get word to her earlier, but her husband had died at sea the previous November. During all the months she had prayed for him, he had already been dead.

As she later groped for the right words to describe her feelings after her husband's death, she emphasized her resignation to God's will. If she had cried uncontrollably, or refused to believe that Samuel was really dead, or imagined that she saw his face in a crowd of strangers—all typical symptoms of grief—she decided not to admit it. As she knew, she was not supposed to spend too much time lamenting the loss of loved ones. In the words of John Flavel, the bereaved "must keep due bounds and moderation in [their] Sorrows, and not be too deeply concerned for these dying, short lived things." If the faithful found it difficult to accept their loss, they should beg God for greater submission. Charles Drelincourt, a seventeenth-century Calvinist, wrote a special prayer for Christians to say after losing a "beloved Person": "The Lord gave, and the Lord has taken away, grant me therefore Grace to put an end to all these Sighs, Groans and Tears, and spend my Time no longer in lamenting the loss of my beloved Object, but that I may employ myself to prepare for my removal out of this Earthly Tabernacle, into thine Eternal Rest. Amen." No matter how painful it was to lose a husband, a child, a parent, or a friend, the faithful could not succumb to despair.[54]

Whether Sarah had read Drelincourt's book by 1743 (she had definitely read it by 1760), she had heard enough sermons about death to know what she was supposed to say and feel. She admitted that "the Loss of my companion, whom I dearly loved, was great," but she also claimed to have accepted his death with a resignation that bordered on stoicism. After remembering the night she had heard the "heavy news," she continued: "But God wonderfully appeared for my support. I see his hand, and was enabled to submit with patience to his will. I daily Looked around me to see how much heavier God's hand was laid on some others than it was on me, where they was Left with a great many children and much involved in debt, and I had but one to maintain, and though poor, yet not so involved. Others I see had their friends snatched from them by sudden accidents. The consideration of these things, together with the thoughts of what I deserved, stilled me." Just as Drelincourt had recommended, she tried to imitate the example of Job—not the Job who had cursed the day of his birth but the Job who had quietly accepted the death of his seven sons. She had "deserved" worse. "With Job I could say, the Lord gave and the Lord has taken and blessed be the name of the Lord."[55]

The only clue to her sorrow is that once again, just as she had done when describing her suicidal feelings and her battles with her parents, she briefly slipped into the present tense. Remembering her sense of God's presence, she wrote, "I see his hand." Even six years after Samuel's death, her memories of that midnight knock on the door were so vivid that the boundary between past and present disappeared.[56]

Whom the Lord Loves, He Chastens

Sarah Osborn believed that she not only had to submit to Samuel's death; she needed to accept it as a sign of God's goodness. "The common Lot of good Men in this *present evil World*, is to meet with much *Evil*," Cotton Mather explained. But "*GOD has meant it unto Good.*"[57]

Christians throughout history have struggled with the question of how an all-powerful, good God could have created a world that includes evil, but the problem of suffering loomed especially large in the eighteenth century. In the midst of a scientific revolution, Enlightenment thinkers found it difficult to reconcile the existence of suffering with Isaac Newton's image of a rational, orderly universe. If God was like a clockmaker who had created the universe to run according to fixed laws, then why did suffering exist? As David Hume posed the dilemma in the 1750s, "Is he willing to prevent evil, but not able? Then he is impotent. Is he able, but not willing? Then he is malevolent. Is he both able and willing? Whence then is evil?"[58]

Sarah Osborn's understanding of suffering was shaped by a long Christian tradition that emphasized God's goodness even in the midst of evil. According to Augustine of Hippo, whose view of suffering became the dominant one in Christian communities for more than a thousand years, evil did not reflect anything in God's nature but only human sinfulness. Distinguishing Christians from the Manicheans, who portrayed God and the devil as two equal forces battling for control, Augustine insisted that God was the supreme ruler of the universe and that everything he created, from the angels to the smallest creatures in the sea, was essentially good. Although evil was real, it did not exist as a positive force or have an independent power of its own. It was best understood as a loss, a lack, a breakdown in the excellence of God's creation, or in Augustine's evocative phrase, *privatio boni*—a privation of the good. If Adam and Eve had not rebelled against God in the Garden of Eden, evil would not have entered the world, but God had refused to allow sinners to spoil his creation. By punishing them for their transgressions, he upheld the moral perfection of the universe. "The penal state is imposed to bring [the universe] into order," Augustine explained. "The penalty of sin corrects the dishonor of sin."[59]

Evangelicals echoed Augustine's interpretation of suffering as the penalty for sin, and, influenced by John Calvin, they also claimed that a sovereign God had predestined the evil and suffering that took place in the world. (Although Wesleyan evangelicals in England believed in free will, most American evangelicals were Calvinists until the nineteenth century.) Humans were incapable of making any decisions that were not controlled by God. "God not only foresaw the fall of the first man, and in him the ruin of his descendants," Calvin explained, "but also meted it out in accordance with his own decision." While people might question why God had chosen to create a world filled with anguish and loss, a world where some had been sentenced to eternal damnation even before birth, they could do nothing to change God's will. For reasons that only the almighty God could understand, he had preferred to create a universe in which humans would sin and suffer.[60]

Evangelicals did not develop a distinctly new understanding of suffering in the eighteenth century, and in many ways they simply restated themes that had been articulated more clearly by Christian thinkers who had come before them.[61] But because of the challenges posed by the Enlightenment, they took older ideas to an extreme. A new movement had begun to take shape in opposition to Calvinism, a movement later known as humanitarianism, and it offered a more optimistic assessment of human nature and divine mercy. Humanitarians were not a coherent group of thinkers who shared a single set of ideas, but they were linked by their distaste for Calvinism, their desire to alleviate suffering, and their faith in human dignity and goodness. Rejecting the doctrine of original sin, they argued that humans were inherently compassionate because they had been created in God's image. "It is . . . according to *nature* to be affected with the sufferings of other people," declared William Wollaston, a British philosopher.[62]

Humanitarians argued that God's most important characteristic was benevolence. Although God was omnipotent, he never deliberately inflicted either physical or psychological pain. According to the third earl of Shaftesbury, the appeal of Calvinist ideas could be explained in psychological terms. "We see Wrath, and Fury, and Revenge, and Terrors *in the* DEITY when we are full of Disturbances and Fears *within*," he explained, but God is actually "truly and perfectly Good." God was the very definition of compassion, the embodiment of love.[63] Indeed, *benevolence* was one of the most popular words of the eighteenth century, a shorthand for a constellation of assumptions about God's mercy and the rationality of the universe.[64]

Humanitarians also objected to the belief that suffering was the result of divine decree. Since they argued that God had given humanity the gift of free will, they explained "moral evils" like theft or murder as the misuse of human freedom. (This argument raised hard questions about why people would commit evil acts if they had been born with an inclination to virtue, but, influenced by John Locke, humanitarians answered that children were corrupted by nurture rather than nature.) As for "natural evils" like earthquakes and tornados, humanitarians saw them as an inextricable part of a larger whole that was unquestionably good. Influenced by Newton's view of the universe as a finely tuned piece of machinery, they argued that natural evils must be crucial to the functioning of the entire system. "If the whole and its parts be taken together," wrote the Anglican theologian William

e could be changed but for the worse." (King's treatise, *On the
vil*, originally published in Latin, was translated into English
d three times before 1740.) In his popular poem "An Essay on
nder Pope proclaimed, "Whatever is, is right."[65] Rather than
being flawed or fallen, the world was the best one possible.

The key word for humanitarians was *happiness*. According to John Tillotson, "the great End which Religion proposeth to itself is Happiness,"
and since God's glory was intertwined with human happiness there could
never be any competition between the two. (Skewering Calvinists, he derided their view of a jealous God as "senseless.")[66] Matthew Tindal, a British deist, argued that since God was "infinitely satisfied in himself," he did
not create humans out of a selfish desire for glory. Tindal asked, "Do we
not bring God down to ourselves, when we suppose he acts like us poor
indigent Creatures, in seeking Worship and Honor for his own sake?" If
humans broke the moral laws governing the universe, then God needed to
punish them in order to set things right, but only in proportion to the particular transgression and never in a spirit of anger. "Your common systems
of divinity," Tindal complained, "present him full of Wrath and Fury, ready
to glut himself with Revenge for the Injuries he has suffered by the breach
of his Laws," but "the ultimate End of all God's Laws, and consequently, of
all Religion, is human Happiness." If humans suffered, it was because they
had broken laws that had been designed for their own good, not because
an angry tyrant sought revenge against them. "All punishment for Punishment's sake is mere Cruelty and Malice," he objected, "which can never be
in God."[67] (When Thomas Jefferson declared in 1776 that all men had an
unalienable right to "the pursuit of happiness," he built on an idea with
deep roots in religious liberalism.)

If the celebration of God's benevolence had been limited to a few intellectuals or radicals, evangelicals could have ignored it, but images of both
God and human nature were shifting in the eighteenth century. The humanitarian movement began among the elite and well-educated, but partly
because of economic developments it gained widespread support among the
middling sorts as well. Although humanitarian ideas were not caused by the
consumer revolution (and, in fact, they predated it), the greater availability
of material goods seems to have strengthened the growing faith in divine
benevolence. As objects like candles, mirrors, lamps, and stoves ceased to
be luxuries, people in the eighteenth century increasingly prized the virtue
of being "comfortable"—a word that symbolized the new quest for material pleasures. In a world of consumer abundance filled with new amenities

that their parents or grandparents had never enjoyed, many found it hard to believe that God wanted them to suffer. In later years, Sarah would thank God for making her "comfortable as to outward things."[68]

Deliberately setting themselves against the spirit of the age, evangelicals insisted that God had created the world to glorify himself, not to promote human happiness. At first glance, this distinction may seem minor, especially because evangelicals assumed that divine glory and human happiness often went hand in hand: when saints rejoiced in heaven, they testified to both their own happiness and God's almighty power. But in fact there was a gulf between these two understandings of human life that could not be bridged. If God had created the world to display his glory, then sin, suffering, and even the existence of hell could be explained as a demonstration of his power and majesty. But if God had created the world to make humans happy, then suffering was a problem that could not be explained by simply pointing to God's sovereign will. Sensing this danger, Gilbert Tennent argued that since God was the "best of Beings," it would be illogical for him to prefer anything inferior to himself as his "last End." If humans dared imagine that their own happiness was the reason God had created the universe, they would be guilty of "Blasphemy and Idolatry"; "To make our *subjective* Happiness our last End, and not the Glory of God," he warned, "is to love our Pleasures more than God."[69] Although Sarah Osborn often wrote about her desire to be "happy," she made it clear that God, and God alone, was her "only portion and happiness." As she reminded herself, "happiness . . . is not to be found in all this world. None but God alone can fill and satisfy."[70]

In response to the humanitarian critique, evangelicals echoed the Puritan argument that God was the ultimate cause of everything that happened, even things that appeared evil. In 1706, when a promising young merchant, the son of a leading Boston family, was murdered in London, two Puritan ministers assured his grieving family that his death had been ordained by God. Warning them not to blame their sufferings on "wicked men" or the devil, the ministers insisted that God was ultimately responsible: he "*Wounds* and *Heals* as he pleaseth." As the Reverend Benjamin Wadsworth explained, the devil was only a "rod in God's hand," an "instrument" of the divine will. He was helpless to do evil without God's permission. Repeating the words of the prophet Amos, Samuel Willard asked, "Is there any Evil in the City, and the Lord hath not done it?"[71]

Although it might seem callous to tell bereaved parents that God had *wanted* their child to be murdered, these ministers meant their words to be comforting. Instead of portraying the world as a chaotic, arbitrary place where the devil ran free, they insisted that God was in control. Nothing happened without a reason—not even murder. As Willard admitted, it was hard to understand why God allowed evil to exist, but faithful Christians had no choice but to trust in him. Unlike the "wicked," who should expect damnation, true believers knew that God punished them for their own good. Usually he afflicted them in retribution for their sins, but sometimes he was motivated by other purposes: to test their faith, to make them more humble, to "wean" them from the world, to demonstrate his power, to purify them. Their afflictions were like a potent, caustic medicine that brought intense pain but also salvation. Reflecting on the fate of the young man who had been murdered, Willard promised his family that his sufferings—and their own—had been designed for their benefit: "a Godly Person shall meet with no Evil in this Life, but what shall turn to his great advantage in the issue." Because the young man had been "godly," they had "just grounds" to believe that he was safe with Christ. Quoting from Paul's letter to the Romans, Willard wrote, "I reckon that the Sufferings of this present time, are not worthy to be compared with the Glory that shall be revealed in us."[72]

Evangelicals were deeply attracted to this Puritan language of resignation, but perhaps fearing that it was too tame, they also turned humanitarian ideas upside down by making the more dramatic (and counterintuitive) claim that suffering increased human happiness. Exaggerating the rationalist tendencies that had begun to creep into late-seventeenth-century Puritanism, they made the startling assertion that the world was actually better off because of the existence of evil. (Although the Puritans had argued that God could bring good out of evil, they did not make the radical argument that an imperfect world was the best world possible.) "Upon the whole," Samuel Hopkins explained, "there is more good than if there had been no evil." If the biblical Joseph had not been sold into slavery, he would not have been able to save his people from famine, and if Jesus had not been crucified, he would not have been resurrected. In a controversial tract titled *Sin, Through Divine Interposition, an Advantage to the Universe*, Hopkins argued that sin and suffering always served a greater good: "He who rules supreme in the heavens . . . will bring good out of all this evil; and, therefore, permits it, because it is the best, the wisest way to accomplish his benevolent designs."[73] Although Hopkins was criticized for suggesting that God took pleasure in suffering and sin (an impossibility for a perfect being), he insisted that his theology was rational. Evil existed only to make the universe a better place.

When evangelicals protested that suffering, sin, and even hell were signs of God's compassion rather than his wrath, they revealed how deeply the humanitarian movement had influenced them. Instead of arguing that a sovereign God had willed the existence of hell, Hopkins felt compelled to proclaim that it was "a real good" that increased the joys of saints in heaven. When the saved looked down at the torments of the damned, they gained a greater sense of their own happiness: "The generous, benevolent mind, which desires and seeks the greatest good of the whole, the glory of God, and the greatest glory and happiness of his kingdom, must choose and be pleased with that just, eternal misery of the wicked, which is so necessary to promote this to the highest degree, and the greater and more generous and benevolent the mind is, the more pleasure will it take in such a plan." Hell was not "cruel"; it was a rational and good part of God's creation that was reserved for a small number of sinners. Like his friend Joseph Bellamy, who estimated that the ratio of the saved to the damned would ultimately be 17,000: 1, Hopkins made the utilitarian argument that Christianity was spreading so rapidly across the globe that it would soon be the most popular religion.[74] At the end of the world the happiness of the majority would far outweigh the suffering of the few.

Historians tend to portray Hopkins's stark understanding of affliction as the product of abstract theological speculation, but his ideas seem to have emerged at least partially out of popular evangelicalism. Even before he became famous (or infamous) for portraying suffering and evil as a rational part of a larger good, lay people made the same claim in their diaries and letters. For example, when Sarah Prince Gill was ill in 1744, she claimed that her suffering was "best" for her, a reason to "rejoice," and when Nathan Cole lay in bed for several months with a wounded leg, he declared that he "could not be thankful enough" for God's "Fatherly Corrections": unless he were purged of his sinfulness, he would never achieve real happiness—the kind of happiness that lay only in Christ. "Blessed be God for his *rod*," Susannah Anthony exclaimed. "How dear the sweet scourges that have quickened my too slothful place! Welcome, my father, thy chastening hand!"[75]

Sarah Osborn echoed this positive understanding of suffering as medicine or purification. "O, strike in what way else thou Pleasest," she wrote to God during an illness. "I'll adore and Kiss the Hand, the dear Hand, that smites. . . . O purge and purify me though in a furnace of affliction." Instead of shunning pain as an evil, she welcomed it as a sign of God's love: "For thy Loving kindness thou wilt not take away, nor suffer thy faithfulness to fail."

In later years when a close friend lost her child, Sarah urged her to "kiss the rod and cling to the dear Hand that Has Held it and struck the blow."[76] Although this was exactly the kind of language that humanitarians despised, it seems to have been common among early evangelicals. Preaching during a severe drought, Jonathan Edwards explained to his congregation, "We must kiss the rod and Give Glory to God under the Calamity."[77]

Sarah said relatively little about her first husband's death in her memoir (perhaps the pain was still too great), but in later years she described her loss in more positive terms. As she reflected in a diary entry, "What wise and blessed steps hath he taken, though once afflictive. When in my young and tender years, my heart was much set on the husband of my youth, he rent him from me, and likewise bereaved me of almost all that was dear to me according to the flesh, whereby he broke off my dependence on those streams for comfort, and led me to the mountain. O, 'happy rod, that brought me nearer to my God.'" (She was quoting from a hymn.) Even though Samuel's death had seemed evil at the time, in retrospect she could see that it had increased her happiness by bringing her closer to God.[78]

Sarah imagined suffering as a means of grace, a fiery furnace in which sinners were purified. "Whom the Lord Loves, He rebukes and chastens," she read in Hebrews. Although she was not a masochist—she did not *enjoy* her suffering—she longed for it in the same way that a child longs for parental attention: as a tangible sign of love.

The Widow's God

When Sarah remembered the months following Samuel's death, she praised God for sustaining her during her sorrow. With a small child to feed and clothe, she wondered how she would be able to make ends meet, but she tried to keep her faith in the "widow's God." Alluding to a verse from the Psalms, "the Lord preserveth the strangers; he relieveth the fatherless and widow," she explained, "I had then the promises of a widow's God to plead and seemed to cast myself more immediately upon his care, verily believing he would provide for me with my fatherless babe." With gratitude, she remembered that God had mercifully answered her prayers. "As before this affliction everyone seemed to be enemies to me, so now from that time all became friends." Even her parents softened. "My parents used me very tenderly, and God inclined every one that knew me to be kind to me." In what seemed like a stroke of providence, her brother finally decided to come to America, and because he was single, he and Sarah "went to housekeeping together."[79] In exchange for a roof over her head, she cooked his meals, cleaned his house, and washed his laundry.

When her brother decided to get married only three months later, Sarah feared that she would not be able to support her child on her own, and once again she prayed to God for help. "I could see no way at all how I could get a Living," she recounted. "All doors seemed to be shut. But I verily believed that God would point out a way for me." Like many indigent women in the city, she may have hoped to earn a few shillings by working in a tavern or sewing, washing, and ironing clothes, but she may have also worried that she might have to ask for poor relief. The General Assembly had created a special fund in 1730 for impoverished sailors and their families (captains were required to deduct twelve pence out of sailors' wages every month in case they fell on hard times), and she may have already asked the town for help. But on November 19, 1734, the day that she decided to move out of her brother's house, she met a "stranger" who offered her a job as a schoolteacher. "A stranger to my case who kept a school a Little way off came to me and told me she only waited for a fair wind to go to Carolina, and if it would suit me I should have her chamber, scholars, and all together."[80]

Sarah's meager salary as a teacher was not enough to pay all her bills, but she also found a job as a housekeeper. In her memoir she mentions being "placed" in a family, which may mean that she had asked the town for poor relief and that the overseers of the poor had arranged a suitable position for her rather than giving her cash. It was common for the able-bodied poor to be sent to board with families who were in need of household help. Luckily for Sarah, the family she went to live with "discovered a great deal of affection for me and in all respects used me as tenderly as if I had been a near relation." She marveled, "Thus the widow's God remarkably provided for me."[81]

But as Sarah soon discovered, God had not finished afflicting her. In May 1735 "it pleased God . . . to Lay his afflicting hand on me by a sharp humor that broke out in my hands so that for three months every finger I had was wrapped up in plasters, and [I] could help myself but very Little." While her friends took turns teaching the school, her parents probably cared for her son, who was now three.[82]

Gravely ill, Sarah decided to consult a doctor rather than a midwife about her treatment. Midwives still tended to handle women's most common complaints, but they had begun to face increasing competition from male doctors, who claimed to be better educated and more professional.

Besides charging higher fees, doctors offered more heroic treatments that were designed to force the body back into health. Influenced by Galen's ancient medical theory, they believed that the body consisted of four humors or fluids that needed to be in balance: choler (yellow bile), melancholy (black bile), blood, and phlegm. Since an excess of any of these humors caused illness, doctors used bloodletting, blistering, and cathartic drugs like ipecac (which induced vomiting) to purge the body of extra fluids. "Under the doctor's hands in the fall I was taken with violent fits," Sarah remembered, "and was quite deprived of sense by them five days. I was blistered almost all over by the doctor and my hands and arms was all raw from my fingers' ends up above my elbows and a great fever." Blistering was a painful procedure that involved applying a caustic, burning substance to the skin (often a mustard plaster). The doctor then lanced and drained the blisters to get rid of the body's excess humors.[83]

According to Samuel Hopkins, Sarah was also given large doses of mercury, a poisonous element that was commonly used in both the eighteenth and early nineteenth centuries. Doctors seem to have been attracted to mercury because of its visible, dramatic effects on the body, and as a Boston physician remarked in the 1730s, many administered "unbelievable doses" to cure everything from syphilis to pneumonia.[84] After ingesting mercury or having it rubbed into their skin, patients would salivate uncontrollably, vomit, and be seized with violent diarrhea. If they were given too high of a dose and their kidneys could not handle the burden of trying to excrete it from the body, they would die. In 1733 a British surgeon warned that patients treated with mercury often suffered "Fevers, violent Colics, Diarrheas, Dysenteries, Swellings and Erosions of the Glands, terrible Headaches, Vertigos, Tremors, Deliriums, Convulsions." Other common symptoms included loosening of the teeth, kidney disease, mental illness, and insomnia.[85] Although Sarah survived her treatment, her choice of phrasing suggests that her "violent fits" were a direct result of the care she received "under the doctor's hands." Mercury poisoning may have been the reason she fell into convulsions and was virtually comatose for five days.

We do not know the identity of the illness that led to Sarah's treatment, but it was the first bout of a disease that plagued her for the rest of her life. As she wrote in her memoir, "My fits, the humor, continued at times very violent for some years, and indeed still returns at some seasons."[86] The symptoms began in her hands but later included headaches, weakness, fatigue, and difficulty both walking and seeing. By the time she was sixty, her illness had progressed to a stage where walking was difficult and she was almost completely blind. Samuel Hopkins believed that her symptoms were caused by her exposure to mercury, "the weakening and painful effects of which attended her to the day of her death," but a single treatment with inorganic mercury, even a large quantity of it, should not have caused life-long health problems. It can take years for the body to excrete mercury, but usually not decades, and Sarah does not seem to have suffered from either hand tremors or renal failure—two of the most prominent symptoms of chronic mercury poisoning. [87]

Sarah's chronic health problems were probably not caused by her exposure to mercury at the age of twenty-one. Since she later complained about the "salt rheum" in her hands, the most likely diagnosis is rheumatoid arthritis, an autoimmune disease that damages the joints. Rheumatoid arthritis tends to afflict women more than men, and the first symptoms can include swollen inflamed joints in the hands. In the most common form of the disease, patients can spend months or even years in remission between attacks, but the symptoms grow progressively worse with each flare-up. All Sarah's symptoms fit a diagnosis of rheumatoid arthritis, especially her difficulty walking during the last twenty years of her life and her diminishing eyesight. Yet it is impossible to make a diagnosis with certainty, and all we can know is that she suffered from a chronic illness that began at the age of twenty-one and continued until her death at the age of eighty-two. Another possible diagnosis is multiple sclerosis, an autoimmune disease that damages the central nervous system and that can begin with feelings of numbness or tingling in the hands and arms.[88]

Whatever the precise nature of her illness, Sarah wanted her readers to know that she had not succumbed to despair. "All this time of illness God wonderfully provided for me. I wanted for none of the comforts of life. Neither was I cast down for his mercy held me up."[89]

By the time she recovered, Sarah had gained new insight into the beneficial nature of physical and psychological suffering. Just as God's punishments had helped her to grow in grace, her painful medical treatments had eased the worst symptoms of her disease. As with her moments of religious despair, her illness had led her to the hard truth that there could be no salvation without suffering. As one minister explained, God could be compared to a surgeon and sin to a disease. To honor his "skill," we should "quietly suffer the corrosive plasters to lie on, and . . . not offer to pluck them off, notwithstanding the smart they put us to."[90] Even though God had taken away her husband, consigned her to poverty, and afflicted her with illness, he had meant it all for her good.

One of Sarah's favorite biblical passages was from Lamentations. The third chapter begins with a cry of despair—"My strength and my hope is perished from the Lord: Remembering mine affliction and my misery, the wormwood and the gall"—but ends with trust: "The Lord is my portion, saith my soul: therefore will I hope in him." As Sarah sat at her desk writing the story of her life, she tried to mold her experiences into the confident, upward ascent of those verses. She hoped that if she could accept her suffering as a medicine that would bring her closer to God, then perhaps she would no longer be haunted by the temptation to doubt his goodness. Writing her memoir was an act of hope, a flight from despair, an affirmation of a life she had once wanted to destroy. There could be no real tragedy in a world that was completely controlled by God.

Chapter 4

Amazing Grace

Surely my heart reacht forth in burning desire after the blessed jesus oh how was i ravisht with his Love and when examining my self thrice puting the question to my soul as christ put to peter tell me oh my soul Lovest thou the Lord Jesus how did my heart melt and my eyes flow with tears in appealing to him Lord thou knowest all things thou knowest i Love thee and when inquiring into the cause of this Love I felt and from whence it flowed it still overcame me more because I could say Lord I Love thee because thou first Loved me this caused me to Loath my self and cry out Lord what a trator have I been and yet thou hast freely Loved me oh why me Lord why me why not in hell why among the Living to praise thee Lord there can be no other reason but because where my sins has abounded thy grace has much more abounded o amaising grace hast thou snatcht me as a brand out of the burning.[1]

1740 god in mercy sent his dear servant whitfield here which something stird me up but when mr tenent came soon after it pleasd god to bless his preaching so to me that it paused me but I was all the winter after exercised with dreadfull doubts and fears about my state I questiond the truth of all I had experienced and feard I had never yet past through the pangs of the new birth nor never had one spark of grace . . . i was coverd over with thick clouds for months together.[2]

In the last section of her memoir, Sarah Osborn explained that the story of her life was worth sharing only because of what it revealed about divine grace. She had written about her childhood sinfulness and her sufferings because they had prepared her for the greatest moment of her life: her rebirth in Christ.

Sarah's conversion was not like Saint Paul's on the road to Damascus or Augustine's in the garden of Milan. She did not suddenly hear God's voice calling her to repent or suddenly become a new self in Christ. Her conversion had not been that dramatic—or that easy. After an emotional religious experience in 1737 when she was twenty-three, Sarah believed that she had been born again, but by 1740, when Gilbert Tennent and George Whitefield arrived in Newport to preach the gospel, she was no longer sure. Had her earlier sense of God's love been real? Had she deluded herself?

Sarah's account of the emotional peaks and valleys of her conversion is by far the longest part of her memoir. She had written about her childhood sinfulness and her later struggles with affliction in order to show her readers (and perhaps herself) that God had always been invisibly working on her heart, but in her rush to get to the heart of her story, she had compressed the first twenty-four years of her life into forty pages. In contrast, as she began writing about her growing sense of Christ's love in the wake of her terrible illness, the pace of her narrative slowed. It would take her another hundred pages to recount the next five years. She wanted to record every thought, every feeling, and every verse of scripture that had brought her closer to God. Despite her struggles against doubt, she had finally realized that she had been truly born again. Her conversion was the reason she wrote her memoir—the reason her life mattered. She was no longer simply an ordinary woman; she was a Christian who had been given the gift of true grace.

Christians throughout history have sought conversion ("except a man be born again," Jesus testified in the Gospel of John, "he cannot see the kingdom of God"), but eighteenth-century evangelicals placed more emphasis on conversion than almost any group of Christians before them. Earlier Christians had defined conversion in multiple ways—it could mean changing one's life by going to church regularly, taking communion, studying the Bible, or living according to the Ten Commandments—but for evangelicals it meant an immediate, heartfelt change. True religion, they claimed, was "experimental." Influenced by the Enlightenment emphasis on personal experience as the foundation of knowledge, evangelicals did not view conversion as an intellectual assent to the truths of the Bible or as a slow, imperceptible turning to God; for them it was a "new sense" that was as real as the physical senses of seeing, hearing, or tasting. Because people could actually feel and know whether they had been born again, they could be virtually sure of their salvation.

For Sarah, who had always struggled with doubt, the evangelical emphasis on assurance was deeply appealing. Raised by parents who were steeped in the Puritan tradition, she seems to have absorbed Puritan understandings of conversion as gradual and often imperceptible: full assurance was possible, but rare. But a new generation of evangelicals, including young, dynamic leaders like Whitefield and Tennent, scoffed at this timidity. After arriving in Newport, they not only warned sinners that they must repent *now* but also told remarkable stories of people who had been converted so suddenly that they could identify the precise time and place of the change. Sarah envied them, and she seems to have embraced the evangelical movement as her own because she longed for their confidence. During the revivals she became convinced that if she could completely commit her life to God, she would finally be able to free herself from her worst doubts. If she could let herself believe that God loved her, then her moments of despair would be tempered by her confidence in God's love. Like thousands of other evangelicals, she could become a "new creature," a new self, in Christ.

Until the revivals, nothing about Sarah's life had seemed certain. But after she became an evangelical, she could say—with assurance—that she knew what mattered. She knew that she had been born again.

The Quest for Certainty

We know almost nothing about Sarah's life between 1735, the year of her first outbreak of rheumatoid arthritis (if that is indeed what it was), and 1737, when she became a full member of her church. Although she recorded God's care for her during the dark months of her illness, she also admitted that she had "backslidden" as her health had improved. Scrupulously honest, she confessed that she had become "intimate . . . with those whose example was very bad" and had made "bold excuses to absent myself from the public worship," but at some point she wished she had not been so frank. She scribbled over these words, as well as over seventeen other lines, which cannot be deciphered.[3] If she had been on the brink of drifting away from Christianity, she did not want future readers to know it.

Sarah was obviously troubled by her long history of "backsliding." Although she wanted her story to focus on her miraculous rebirth in Christ, she fretted over her inability to describe exactly when and how she had been born again. Looking back, she remembered feeling a strong sense of God's presence on the night she had been stranded in the canoe, but she was not positive that she had experienced conversion then. "Some *Christians* have thought the change was then wrought," she mused, but she was not sure whether she would have gone to heaven had she drowned that evening. She also thought she might have been born again on the night of her suicidal temptation, but she did not know whether she had experienced "true grace" or only a brief precursor to it. Despite her certainty that God had rescued her from hanging herself, she was not sure whether he had changed her heart. "I thought I trusted in God and used frequently in time of trials to go and pour out my complaints to him, thinking he was my only support," she wrote. "But I durst not now be positive or really conclude that I knew what it was to put my trust in God, for my conduct after this seems so inconsistent with grace that I durst not say I had one spark, but rather think I was only under a common work of the spirit, though sometimes I think I had true grace though very weak." In a frank admission of her confusion, she concluded, "God only knows how it was." She also thought she might have been converted in the weeks after her marriage, when she "had a hope again at times that Christ was mine," or during her son's baptism, when she had dedicated both herself and her child to God.[4] But each time she had fallen away from her faith. Certainty eluded her.

If Sarah had lived a hundred years earlier, she might have accepted her doubts as an inevitable part of her religious pilgrimage. Although the Protestant Reformation had been built around the conviction that converts could be sure of their salvation, ministers began toning down their rhetoric as radicals claimed to be certain that they had received new revelations from God. In 1535, for example, Anabaptists in Münster claimed that God had ordered them to practice polygamy and kill anyone who opposed them, and in 1637, Puritans in Boston had exiled Anne Hutchinson after she claimed to hear God speaking to her. (Some feared that she would turn Massachusetts Bay Colony into another bloody Münster.) In the decades after Hutchinson's trial, Puritans urged people to search for convincing evidence of their salvation, but they also warned against the possibility of self-deception. According to the *Westminster Confession*, "infallible assurance doth not so belong to the essence of faith, but that a true believer may wait long, and conflict with many difficulties before he be partaker of it." Although Puritans placed conversion at the center of the Christian life, they found that the path to assurance was often hedged with thorns.

According to the Reverend William Perkins, conversion was rarely a sudden, unexpected change; it was rather a gradual transformation of the self that could take an entire lifetime to complete. Perkins listed ten stages that converts usually experienced before knowing they had been saved, from the first, small stirrings of grace (usually under preaching) to the final stages of repentance and obedience. Although he argued that "every Christian would experience a decisive moment in his life when he first became a child of God," he also explained that conversion "is not wrought all at one instant, but in continuance of time, and that by certain measures or degrees."[5]

But there was always a mystical strain within Puritanism that prized assurance, and beginning in the late seventeenth century, in response to political, social, intellectual, and economic changes, a small but influential group of ministers reclaimed the bold language of the Reformation. When Solomon Stoddard published *A Treatise Concerning Conversion* in 1719, he argued that "Men may have the knowledge of their own conversion." Although the word *may* was crucial—he did not claim that *all* Christians would attain assurance—he believed that many would feel the spiritual change within themselves "*by Intuition or seeing of grace in their own hearts.*" Cotton Mather made the stronger assertion that when a convert was overpowered by the Holy Spirit, he would find it impossible to doubt either the reality of his own transformation or the truth of Christianity. "*Christianity* will strike such Rays of *Light* into his Mind, that he shall no more Question it, than he does, That the *Sun Shines.*" Mather imagined conversion as a heartfelt transformation that could be empirically experienced. "A Work of Grace," he wrote, "brings a Man Experimentally to *feel* the *Main Truths* which the Christian Religion is composed of."[6]

This emphasis on assurance was built on a new epistemology—a new way of thinking about human knowledge—that marked a break with the Puritan tradition. Although Puritans had always scrutinized their lives for signs of divine grace, they had also been skeptical about what they could genuinely know about themselves or God. In contrast, Stoddard and Mather admitted that self-deception was possible, but they placed far greater trust in the reliability of firsthand experience. Because of Mather's alarm about the noxious spread of "Deistical Notions," he published several tracts to prove that Christianity was true, and in each his closing flourish was an appeal to his personal, experiential knowledge of grace. "If my Saviour brings me to *Live* unto God," he argued in one tract, "then he is *Himself Alive,*" and in another he explained, "A Work of Grace upon you will be a *Witness within you* to the *Truth of Christianity.*"[7] As the historian Robert

Middlekauff has commented, the danger of Mather's approach was that it
risked making religion subjective (it is true because I feel it to be true), but
because of his anxiety about a creeping spirit of rationalism Mather did
not think that he could defend Christianity simply by affirming the truth
of the Bible. As Middlekauff explains, "Mather's conception of religious
experience was different from the founders'—it implied that when the ways
of apprehending the truth provided by science, logic, and reason did not
satisfy men, they must consult their own experience. The application of
Scripture to the believer's own condition—how he felt about it, how he
experienced it—would persuade him of its truth."[8]

During the 1730s and 1740s, this "experimental religion," as Mather
called it, flowered into a distinctive kind of evangelical faith that particularly valued experience, assurance, and evidence. During the revivals ministers not only demanded that sinners repent *now*, before it was too late, but
they urged them not to rest until they were sure of their salvation. When
Gilbert Tennent arrived in Newport in the fall of 1741, he thundered out
his condemnations of sin in such fierce language that many claimed to
have been born again on the spot (and as we shall see, he terrified Sarah
into thinking she was a hypocrite). Because the Synod of the Presbyterian
Church had recently condemned him for encouraging "Convulsion-like-
Fits" and preaching that "all true Converts are as certain of their gracious
State, as a Person is of what he knows by his outward Senses," he softened
his language, but only a bit. Although denying that every convert would
attain "a full Assurance of their good State," he still portrayed doubting
as the exception, not the norm. "All who are converted," he insisted, "ordinarily have a lesser or greater Degree of comfortable Persuasion of their
gracious State, either immediately upon their closure with Christ, or some
Time afterwards, when Faith is in Exercise, either for a short or longer
Duration." (The key word for him was *ordinarily*.) Contrary to the Synod's
accusation, he had never taught that Christians should be able to pinpoint
the exact moment of their conversion but rather that they should strive for
"Evidences" of a new heart. "Surely, those that are rightly humbled by the
Spirit of God, will not be satisfied 'til they obtain this," he concluded.[9]

The Strict Congregationalists, or "Separates" as they were more popu-
larly known, took this language of certainty to a greater extreme. Almost as
soon as evangelicalism was born it splintered into factions, with the Separates emerging as the most radical wing of the movement in America. Influenced by the heart-centered preaching of the revivals, they argued that
even uneducated men could preach if called by the Holy Spirit: God was no

respecter of persons, and he often communicated directly with the faithful through voices or visions. The Separates also insisted that true Christians could be absolutely sure of their salvation. The Separate Church in Mansfield, Connecticut, argued that "all Doubting in a Believer is sinful, being contrary to the Commands of God and hurtful to the Soul, and an hindrance to the Performance of Duty," and in nearby Canterbury, Separates claimed that "Assurance is of the Essence of Faith." Unlike Tennent, who had grudgingly admitted that a certain degree of doubt was possible, Andrew Croswell preached that "there is *no* true Believer, but hath Assurance for some Space of Time, longer or shorter." Even more controversially, some Separates asserted that true Christians could be sure not only of their own salvation but of other people's as well. Despite their claim to infallibility (or perhaps because of it), they became quite popular. "If there is such a Person as a doubting humble Christian," Ebenezer Frothingham testified, "I am sure you will find him in Hell." The Separates had founded more than a hundred new churches before 1754, including a church in Newport.[10]

In some ways, this new emphasis on assurance was the natural outgrowth of latent tendencies within the Reformed tradition, but several external developments in the transatlantic world seem to have served as a catalyst. When the Toleration Act, passed by the British Parliament in 1689, extended the freedom of worship to all Protestants regardless of denominational affiliation, churches became more concerned about a *lack* of certainty than an excess of it. In New England, for example, ministers feared that the Puritan experiment would never survive unless converts could confidently proclaim the reality of their faith in an increasingly pluralistic culture. Although few towns were as religiously diverse as Newport, where Sarah could choose whether to worship among Congregationalists, Baptists, Quakers, or Anglicans, no single denomination in the colonies enjoyed the power to coerce membership.[11]

The desire for assurance seems to have been a reaction to the proliferation not simply of religious choices but of political, economic, and social choices as well. Although psychological explanations for historical developments are necessarily speculative, it is probably not coincidental that the evangelical movement coalesced at the same time as ordinary people gained greater opportunities for individual choice than they had ever had before, the result of market expansion, the breakdown of social hierarchies, and local political independence from England. Of course, some choices, like whom to vote for in local elections, were reserved for propertied men alone, but women could also make choices about what goods to buy, what religion to practice, and, increasingly, whom to marry. While many must have been intoxicated by this new freedom, others seem to have found it overwhelming. With so many choices, how could one be sure of making the right decision?[12]

Evangelicals also placed more emphasis on assurance in response to the challenges posed by the Enlightenment. Hoping to defend orthodox Christianity against the threat of "Arminianism," they argued that true faith was a matter of firsthand experience, not abstract reason. According to Jonathan Edwards, converts gained a new spiritual "sense" that affected their perceptions of the world. As he recorded in his "Personal Narrative," he felt that new, immediate sense when reading a biblical passage that particularly moved him: "There came into my soul, and was as it were diffused through it, a sense of the glory of the divine being; a new sense, quite different from anything I ever experienced before."[13] In the popular language of the time, religious experience was "sensible": it could be empirically felt. Like Hannah Heaton, who remembered her "sensible communion with God," David Brainerd felt "sensible sweetness and joy," and Sarah Osborn experienced a "sense" of God's "excellence, glory and truth."[14]

Ironically, evangelicals borrowed this language of sensation from the same Enlightenment thinkers whom they suspected of Arminianism and deism. Edwards's understanding of a spiritual sense was influenced by the earl of Shaftesbury and Francis Hutcheson, who argued that all humans have an innate "moral sense" that helps them distinguish good from evil. Despite rejecting this positive view of human nature, Edwards agreed that knowledge comes from sense perception. When he and other evangelicals argued that Christianity was "sensible" and "experimental," they linked their movement to powerful currents of Enlightenment thought that made them sound strikingly new and modern. If the mind should be described as "White Paper, void of all Characters, without any Ideas," John Locke asked, then "How comes it to be furnished?" His answer was simple: "from Experience."[15] Echoing this language, evangelicals insisted that Christianity was based on the palpable experience of being born again.

It is likely that Sarah Osborn absorbed this experiential language from listening to her ministers, talking with like-minded Christians, and reading religious books. While there is no evidence that she ever read Locke, she did read the works of Edwards, Cotton Mather, and many other ministers who advocated an "experimental" religion. Since her church required converts to share their stories of conversion before being admitted to full membership, she also heard many lay Christians describing their religious "experiences."

Today the word *experience* has become such a common part of our language that we may find it difficult to hear its revolutionary cadences. We tend to use it as a synonym for individual subjectivity, and we describe our experiences in the same way we do our "feelings"—as interior and private. Indeed, modern-day scholars of religion have expressed skepticism about studying "the experiential dimension of religion" because personal experience is "inaccessible to strictly objective modes of inquiry."[16] But in the eighteenth century, *experience* had a more scientific connotation, and Enlightenment thinkers believed that if they scrutinized human experience they could make new discoveries about the world. Intoxicated by scientific and technological advances, they insisted that empiricism would liberate people from blind devotion to the past. All ideas had to be subjected to the test of experiment and observation.

Evangelicals did not want to be "liberated" from tradition, particularly not Christian tradition, but they, too, believed that firsthand experience could offer rational evidence about the universe. They confidently proclaimed that believers could feel and know whether they had been transformed by divine grace. In the words of David Brainerd, "I was spending some time in prayer and self-examination and the Lord by his grace so shined into my heart, that I felt his love and enjoyed full assurance of his favor for that time and my soul was unspeakably refreshed with divine and heavenly enjoyments. At this time especially as well as some others sundry passages of God's Word opened to my soul with divine clearness, power and sweetness so that I *knew* and *felt* 'twas the Word of God and that 'twas exceeding precious."[17]

Like scientists who adopted the Newtonian method in order to verify their findings, evangelicals often described their faith as experimental: it could be validated by concrete, measurable experience. Although they did not trust personal experience in the abstract—and in fact they assumed that most people viewed the world with eyes clouded by sin—they insisted that Christians gained new powers of perception during conversion. As Brainerd explained to Samuel Hopkins, "he believed it impossible for a person to be converted, and to be a real Christian, without feeling his heart, at some times at least, sensibly and greatly affected with the character of Christ." Inspired by the Holy Spirit, Christians could see and understand things as they really were. According to Sarah Prince Gill, for example, she had been "experimentally convinced" of the justice of eternal punishment.[18]

Although Gill described her sensations of grace as inward, many converts claimed to have physically felt the power of the Holy Spirit on their bodies. They cried out in fear or ecstasy, wept, trembled, and sometimes fell into "fits" or fainted. As a minister reported in *The Christian History*, the periodical that reprinted revival narratives from all over the transatlantic world, "Hundreds of souls were at one time in the meetinghouse . . . crying out in the utmost concern, what they should do to be saved!" Another minister testified that the members of his congregation had been so terrified by his sermon about Judgment Day that "the joints of their loins were loosed, and their knees smote one against the other. Great numbers cried out aloud in the anguish of their souls. Several stout men fell as though a cannon had been discharged, and a ball had made its way through their hearts. Some young women were thrown into hysteric fits." In contrast to the Puritans, who had associated anything beyond tears of repentance with "enthusiasm" (especially Quakerism), evangelicals believed that conversion was written on the body as well as in the heart. It was a tangible, physical, and sometimes violent experience that bore witness to a deeper spiritual transformation.[19]

Because of longstanding suspicions of groaning, trembling, and fainting, evangelical ministers were ambivalent about the sheer physicality of the revivals. While radicals insisted that bodily agitations were a genuine sign of the influx of grace, moderates like Jonathan Edwards tended to be more cautious. Edwards argued that "tears, tremblings, groans, loud outcries, agonies of body, or the failing of bodily strength" could not be interpreted as proof of conversion, but neither could they be dismissed as nothing more than delusion. His own wife, Sarah Pierpont Edwards, had cried out, leapt for joy, and come close to fainting during an emotional religious experience that lasted almost a week. Choosing a middle path between the skepticism of the revivals' opponents and the zeal of the Separates, Edwards reasoned that when sinners grasped the reality of hell and the boundlessness of Christ's love, they could not help feeling so overwhelmed by terror or joy that their bodies were affected.[20] On the popular level, however, few ordinary believers seem to have heeded his careful distinction between the natural and supernatural effects of the awakening. Those who had been born again often pointed to their bodily experiences—their tears, groans, and swoons—as undeniable proof of conversion. As a result, their critics accused them of treating "Wry-Faces and Grimaces, Contortions of the Body and vocal Energy, Faintings and Cryings, delusive Voices and frantic Visions" as "undeniable Evidences of Conversion, of coming to JESUS and the Power of God."[21]

What made evangelicals unique in the eighteenth century was their confidence about their ability to recognize true grace. Unlike the Puritans, who had assumed that their judgment was impaired by sin, evangelicals insisted that with the help of the Holy Spirit they could be practically certain—or in the case of the Separates, *absolutely* certain—of their salvation. Many were able to pinpoint the exact time and place that they had been born again. Nathan Cole began his memoir with the words, "I was born Feb 15th 1711 and born again Octo 1741."[22] As David Bebbington has explained, "Whereas the Puritans had held that assurance is rare, late and the fruit of struggle in the experience of believers, the Evangelicals believed it to be general, normally given at conversion and the result of simple acceptance of the gift of God."[23] Of course, the older language of anxiety and doubt did not entirely disappear. In a dark moment, Sarah Prince Gill wrote: "I find myself at an Utter Uncertainty about my spiritual state," and Nathan Cole continued to be plagued by worries about his salvation.[24] In general, though, religious expectations had shifted. Among seventeenth-century Puritans the mood tipped toward anxiety (with some converts expressing certainty), but among eighteenth-century evangelicals it tipped toward assurance (with some converts still continuing to express doubts).

Because of her struggles against despair, Sarah Osborn was deeply attracted to the evangelical language of assurance. She wanted the certainty of knowing that her life pointed to something greater and more meaningful than herself. She wanted what would always lie just outside her grasp: to be *sure*.

Sarah's lengthy description in her memoir of her discovery of God's love must be read with this evangelical context in mind. As we have seen, it is impossible to disentangle her "real" experiences from what she later decided to write about them, and the issue of retrospection is especially acute when considering her description of her conversion. Her language is so powerful and immediate that it can be tempting to imagine that she simply unspooled her life onto the page like a piece of thread, but in reality she stitched together each sentence with care. Because she wrote her memoir for God as well as for herself and other Christians, it is unlikely that she ever deliberately misrepresented her experiences, but understandably she could not help viewing her past through the lens of her new evangelical faith. As she read accounts of the revivals, heard converts' testimonies, and listened to ministers thundering out their exhortations to repent, she absorbed a new religious vocabulary of experience, assurance, and sensation that colored everything she wrote. Because she wanted to be part of a new evangelical community, she wanted to sound like other evangelicals. She wanted to belong.

Yet because her conversion had not been a dramatic turning from darkness to light but rather a slow, anguished groping toward something she could only dimly perceive, she sometimes found it difficult to fit her experiences into the popular evangelical framework. As a result, her narrative is filled with contradictions and ambiguities. On one hand, she wrote about a deeply felt religious experience that took place in 1737 as if it were her "conversion" (although she never actually used this word), and she framed it in terms that would have been familiar to evangelicals at the time: it had been a single, unmistakable moment of spiritual transformation that had changed her life. But on the other, she admitted that this experience, despite its profundity, had been followed by so many years of uncertainty that her memories of it seemed like nothing more than "dreams or delusion."[25] Her contradictory statements—her confident tone of assurance and her confusion about the timing of her conversion—reveal both her desperate desire for certainty and her difficulty in achieving it.

Experimental Religion

Regardless of whether Sarah Osborn thought that her spiritual crisis of 1737 could be positively identified as the moment of her conversion, she stocked her description of it with words, images, and scriptural references that pointed in that interpretive direction. She claimed that in the course of a week in January something remarkable had happened to her that she had felt in both her heart and her body, something that transcended language and yet demanded to be told. During a weeklong crisis that had been alternately terrifying and liberating, she had seen herself stripped down to what she really was—small, vulnerable, and utterly sinful—and she had suddenly understood the immense gulf separating her from God. She was depraved; he was perfect. She was empty; he was full. She was helpless; he was all-powerful and free. She had confronted the stark truth that she was nothing, and could do nothing, outside God. And yet just at the moment when she had felt most broken in spirit, he had healed her. "It is not possible for me to make anyone sensible what joy I was instantly filled with," she testified, "except those who experimentally know what it is."[26] As she continued writing her memoir, her challenge was to find the right words to express an experimental religion.

Sarah's spiritual crisis had begun at a vulnerable moment in the fall of 1736 when she had almost joined the Church of England. She was boarding with a family who belonged to the Trinity Church, and in November they invited her to attend worship with them. As "high church folks," they practiced a faith that she had always been taught to revile, but to her surprise she "seemed much affected both with the manner of worship and the sermons too." (By using the word *seemed*, she tried to distance herself from her earlier feelings. She had only *seemed* affected, but in retrospect she insisted that the Anglicans had not really touched her heart.) Unlike Congregationalists and Presbyterians, who had tried to purge their worship of anything that looked "Catholic," Anglicans retained much of the old symbolism, including kneeling, lighting candles, and making the sign of the cross. To Sarah, who had worshiped in a plain meetinghouse all her life, their rituals appeared strange but also deeply stirring. She was surrounded by new sights and sounds: the soft colored light that came through the stained-glass windows, the thrilling swell of the organ, the measured rhythms of the prayers that the entire congregation recited together. She was especially moved by their joyous celebration of Christmas, a holiday that her own tradition refused to observe because of its pagan origins. After watching the congregation receive communion on Christmas Day, kneeling at the altar rail and drinking wine out of tall, heavy silver cups, she decided that God had called her to be an Anglican.[27]

If Sarah had become a member of Trinity Church, she would eventually have written her life story according to a very different script. It would be a mistake to view Anglicans as less religious than Calvinists (as some historians have insinuated), and it is important to remember that both George Whitefield and John Wesley were ordained Anglican ministers. But many Anglican leaders in the colonies focused more on good behavior than on an existential confrontation with a sovereign God. Rather than imagining a vast gulf separating humans from God, they believed that conversion could occur with relatively little difficulty. Instead of limiting membership to those who had been "born again," they prided themselves on their moderation and inclusiveness, allowing all adults to join the church as long as they swore to be morally upright. Theologically they envisioned a God who seemed more benevolent than the stern Jehovah of Sarah's childhood.[28]

According to Sarah's narrative, the only reason she did not become an Anglican was that her mother, a devout Congregationalist, confronted her after hearing neighborhood gossip. When Sarah went to visit her on the Saturday after Christmas, they had exchanged only a few brief pleasantries

TRINITY CHURCH.

Trinity Church of Newport, from George Champlin Mason's *Extra Illustrated Reminiscences* (1854). Courtesy of the Newport Historical Society.

before the conversation turned combative. "I hear, daughter," her mother began, "you are turned church woman." Startled, Sarah replied that she thought she had a "duty" to worship where she was "most affected," but her mother demanded a more "rational" explanation for such a momentous decision. Why did she want to leave the church of her childhood? Did she object to Calvinism's core principles? Did she think the Anglicans "Lived more circumspect and agreeable to the rules of the gospel"? When Sarah timidly responded that she "could not profit by the preaching I had sat under," her mother asked her why she did not simply go to a different Congregationalist church. If she did not like the Second Church of Christ, then she should go to hear the Reverend Nathaniel Clap preach at the First Church of Christ. "Child," her mother scolded, "I would have you seriously consider what you are about to do, for it is my opinion you are under a strong delusion and as sure as you turn church woman *without knowing upon what grounds you turn, so sure you will turn reprobate.*" Although Sarah was an adult with a five-year-old son, her mother still had the ability to reduce her to a "child." She felt "as ignorant as a mere babe."[29]

As Sarah explained, she decided not to "turn church woman" because of her inability to give a "rational" explanation for her attraction to the Anglicans. Since she wrote her memoir at a time when evangelicals were often stereotyped as wild-eyed enthusiasts, she may have decided to include this detail as a way of defending herself against possible critics. She wanted her readers to know that for her, true faith did not involve only the affections (the feelings), but the understanding as well. (She may have wanted to distinguish herself from the radical Separates, who were fiercely anti-intellectual.) Although she did not believe that she was capable of understanding a mysterious, incomprehensible God by her intellect alone, she still thought she could find a glimmer of him by studying the Bible. If religion were reduced to rationality alone it would wither into a dry intellectualism, but those who could not give a "rational" account of their Christian beliefs were in danger of slipping into superstition. Being "affected" by the sound of an organ or the sight of a stained-glass window was no substitute for reasoned reflection on the "rules of the gospel."

After spending a sleepless night pondering her mother's words, Sarah decided the next morning that she would attend worship at the First Church. Dressed in her Sunday best, she walked along the cobbled streets near the harbor until she came to the plain, rectangular building on Carr's Lane (now Mill Street), where people had already begun to fill the pews. She had not been there for several years, but before her marriage she had sometimes gone to services there. (As she explained in her memoir, she had always preferred it to her parents' church, but they had usually insisted that they all go to meeting as a family.) This time, though, she saw the church with new eyes. She may have admired its arched windows and its soaring steeple that pointed up to God, but after seven weeks at Trinity she may have also thought that it looked surprisingly austere. After taking her seat in the gallery on one of the special benches reserved for visitors, she looked down upon rows of unpainted pews, bare walls, a sanded floor, and a high wooden pulpit. This was the way Reformed Protestants chose to worship, with no visual distractions to compete with God's word.[30]

And indeed, it was the *word* that Sarah Osborn remembered best about that day and the spiritual crisis that followed it. Nathaniel Clap was known as a stern, demanding pastor who held his congregation to a high standard of religious purity, and on that Sunday he railed against their sins. (Clap was so strict that in 1728 he had refused to baptize a child whose parents were "not of sufficiently holy conversation." In response, half the members left to form the more liberal Second Church of Christ.) Transfixed by his "terrible" words, Sarah remembered feeling as if he were speaking directly to her. He "told me the very secrets of my heart in his sermons as plain as I could have told them to him," she wrote. "His sermon was very terrible to me." Slipping between the past and present tenses, she remembered the clarity with which she had suddenly seen her life: "My sins from my cradle was ranked in order before my eyes, and my original sin as well as actual appeared doleful. I see the depravity of my nature and how I was exposed to the infinite justice of an angry God. All my former convictions was brought to my remembrance. I see how I had stifled the motions of the blessed spirit of God and resisted all the kind invitations of a compassionate savior." (By using the present tense she emphasized that she could still "see" her corruption.) Although she did not record the biblical text of Clap's sermon, he may have preached on Matthew 12:31: "All manner of sin and blasphemy shall be forgiven unto men: but the blasphemy against the Holy Ghost shall not be forgiven unto men." By the time she left the church, she was petrified that she had committed the "unpardonable sin." "I had sinned against Light and Knowledge, even against the convictions of my own conscience," she grieved. "This I knew I had done, and therefore believed I had committed that sin that could never be forgiven."[31]

For the next week Sarah was haunted by fears of damnation. Since ministers encouraged their parishioners to turn to scripture during times of trouble, she searched the Bible for words of comfort. As Cotton Mather promised, "*AFFLICTED People, who seek and who take the Delights which are to be found in the word of GOD, shall not Perish in their Affliction.*" But no matter what passage she read, she "could find nothing but terror there." The more she tried to console herself, the more frantic she became. Her eyes always seemed to land on the most alarming verses. Listing all the passages that had thrown her into despair, she strung together one terrifying text after another. Consider this, she lamented to her readers:

> *All Liars shall have their part in the Lake that burns with fire and brimstone. And this: Depart from me, ye cursed, into everlasting fire prepared for the devil and his angels. And this: consider this, ye that forget God, Least I tear you in pieces and there be none to deliver. And this: he that being often reproved hardens his neck shall suddenly be destroyed and that without remedy. And this: ye have set at naught all my counsels and would none of my reproofs. I therefore will laugh at your calamity and mock when your fear cometh. And this: it is a fearful thing to fall into the hands of the Living God. And this: who among us can dwell with everlasting burnings.*

She felt as though she could not escape from the harsh words of judgment that cursed her from every page. Like Nathan Cole, who admitted that "Hellfire was most always in my mind; and I have hundreds of times put my fingers into my pipe when I have been smoking to feel how fire felt," she was consumed by visions of hell.[32]

Fearful that she would be damned, Sarah fell into a depression that was as severe as the one that led to her earlier brush with suicide. To punish herself for her sins, she began fasting. "I thought myself so unworthy of the Least mercy that I knew not how to eat," she wrote. Nor did she sleep. "I slept no more than just to keep me alive and when I did at all it was filled with terrors." She also seems to have thought of killing herself again. Three lines of her memoir are so carefully scratched out that they are impossible to read, so we cannot know what she originally wrote, but she left a few small hints that she had contemplated suicide. As she explained, Satan had tempted her to believe she would only aggravate God by continuing to pray and read the Bible. Perhaps he had also tempted her to believe that she would be better off dead. Immediately after her crossed-out sentences, she wrote: "Oh astonishing grace that God did not strike me down into hell the very moment I thought to do so." What was it that she had "thought to do"? Whether intentionally or not, her words almost exactly echoed her earlier description of her anguish in the garret. "I thought to do it," she had written.[33]

Her narrative showed another suggestive parallel to her earlier suicidal temptation. Both times her depression seems to have been precipitated by conflicts with her mother. Her sleeplessness and anxiety had begun on the night that her mother had rebuked her for worshiping with the Anglicans. Opening old wounds, her mother had made her feel as "ignorant" as a child. Sarah seems to have felt angry and unloved, worthless in the eyes of both her mother and God.

Whatever triggered it, Sarah's crisis forced her to confront her deepest questions about the meaning of her life. At a time when "disbelief in God remained scarcely more plausible than disbelief in gravity," she did not question whether God actually existed, but she struggled to understand why she had been born. What was the meaning of her suffering and her sorrow? What was God's plan for her? Although she wanted to believe in a merciful God, she could not help worrying that her troubles were a sign of his anger or, worse, his hatred. Her deepest fear was that God despised her so much that he had predestined her to hell. When she dared hope that she might be one of the elect, Satan tormented her with doubts. "Satan assaulted me furiously," she remembered, "and told me not to flatter myself with the thoughts I should be a child of God, for I was not elected and therefore could not be saved." The thought was almost too much for her to bear. Was it possible that she had been created in order to be damned? Although she had suffered many painful ailments during her life, she claimed never to have experienced greater anguish. "Sure I am," she testified, "no affliction or pain of body whatsoever is to be compared to what I then underwent." Her burned hand, the pains of childbirth, her exposure to mercury, her raw, blistered arms—all her physical suffering paled in comparison to her torment within. "The spirit of a man will sustain his infirmity," she quoted from Proverbs, "but a wounded spirit who can bear?"[34]

After six days of agony Sarah finally found a verse of Scripture that brought her comfort. On the eve of the Sabbath, faint with hunger and exhaustion, she read a passage from Paul's first letter to the Corinthians that made her see her despair in a different light: "There hath no temptation taken you but such as is common to man: but God is faithful, who will not suffer you to be tempted above that ye are able; but will with the temptation also make a way for you to escape, that ye may be able to bear it." Even though she had heard many Christians describe moments of spiritual anguish, especially before conversion, she had been too consumed by her own pain to imagine that her doubts could be "common." Only "a minute before," she explained, "I had been thinking that there never had any been tempted Like me." Breaking down in tears of relief, she realized that a faithful God had not forsaken her. "God was pleased that moment, I see it, to give me faith, to Lay hold on it and claim it as my own," she rejoiced. "Oh how it did fill my heart and mouth with praises and my eyes with floods of tears."[35]

Sarah's description of her new sense of grace was intensely physical. Overpowered by God's love, she had felt the change not only in her heart but in every part of her body, and as she wept and trembled she found herself crying out words of praise. "My transport of joy was so great that it was more than my poor feeble frame was well able to contain," she remembered, "for my nature even fainted with excessive joy."[36]

After another sleepless night, Sarah returned to church the next morning, and this time she was overwhelmed by joy instead of fear. It was sacrament day, the monthly communion service, and after the regular meeting she stayed to watch the full members of the church gather around the table to share the bread and wine. Although Congregationalists rejected the Catholic doctrine of transubstantiation, they still believed that Christ was spiritually present in the sacrament, and as the Reverend Clap and the congregation quietly passed the plate and drank from the cup, the mood was solemn. Alone in the gallery looking down, Sarah was "filled with such a mixture of joy and grief" that once again she felt as though she might lose control of her body. (Considering that she had hardly slept or eaten in a week, she may have been close to fainting.) "I was not able to contain myself but was obliged to get down on the floor and to Lean on the bench," she remembered, "for I could neither sit nor stand." She could practically see Christ in front of her, "a crucified savior pouring out his precious blood to redeem his people *from their sins.*" Although she was careful to explain that she had seen him only "by faith" (meaning in her mind), she felt as though the boundaries between heaven and earth had virtually disappeared. "Oh, how did my heart melt and my eyes flow with tears when I thought I saw my dearest Lord in his bitter agony in the garden, and then crowned with thorns, spit upon, buffeted, beaten black and blue, and at Last nailed to an accursed tree, and all to free me from the torments I had so Lately dreaded. *It caused me bitterly to reflect upon myself and cry out, my sins, my sins, oh Lord, have been the procuring cause* of thy bitter sufferings." Suddenly she knew that Christ had died for *her* and, even more astonishing, that he longed for her love in return. "Oh, when I considered how oft he had stood knocking till his head was filled with the dew and his Locks with the drops of the night but could have no entrance into my hardened heart, I was astonished at myself that I could possibly be so cruel, and astonished at free grace and redeeming Love that I was spared to see that happy day." Borrowing the intimate language of the Song of Solomon, she exulted, "He appeared Lovely, the chiefest among ten thousands, and was ten thousand times welcome to me."[37]

Sarah Osborn's description of Jesus as an impassioned lover linked her to many other evangelicals, but a few ministers had begun to express discomfort with this kind of romantic language. On one hand, Gilbert Tennent did not hesitate to describe God as a bridegroom who "kissed" the soul "with the kisses of his Love," and George Whitefield urged his listeners to "come to the Marriage.—Do not play the Harlot any longer."[38] On the other, Isaac Watts feared that such language sounded too earthy. When he edited Elizabeth Rowe's letters for publication in 1742 (they became immensely popular under the title *Devout Exercises of the Heart in Meditation and Soliloquy, Prayer and Praise*), he expressed regret about her "passionate" language drawn from the Song of Solomon. This, he argued, was not "the happiest language in which Christians should generally discover their warm Sentiments of Religion." Because evangelicals expressed their faith in physical ways—sighing, groaning, and fainting—they were often suspected of being sexually immoral, and Watts seems to have feared that Rowe's words might be "perversely profaned by an unholy construction." (In other words, he thought they might become the target of crude jokes.) As he reassured readers in the preface to the book, "In these meditations there is no secret panting over a mortal Love in the Language of Devotion and Piety." Fifty years later, when Samuel Hopkins edited Sarah Osborn's memoir, he was so discomfited by her description of Christ as an ardent lover, drops of dew glistening in his hair, that he decided not to apologize for her imagery but simply to delete it. In the seventeenth century, Puritans had often described Christ in fervent language as a bridegroom, but in the eighteenth century, under the influence of the Enlightenment, evangelical leaders began to draw sharper boundaries between the sacred and the profane. Although Sarah could not have realized it, future generations of evangelicals would be embarrassed by the capaciousness of her religious imagination. She not only envisioned Christ as a prophet, priest, and king, but as a lover.[39]

Only a few days after her ecstasies during communion, Sarah steeled herself to visit Reverend Clap to ask to be admitted to full membership in the church. Clap was notorious for his strictness, but he also had a gentle side. When George Whitefield met him a decade later, he praised him as "the most venerable man I ever saw in my life," "a good old Puritan" who "abounds in good works; gives all away, and is wonderfully tender of little children." (Indeed, he had given Sarah a book during her childhood.) Although Sarah may have been afraid to describe her religious experiences to him, she also admired and trusted him, and she knew that if she wished to participate in the Lord's Supper she would have to convince him of her worthiness. While the First Church allowed anyone to come to services and listen to sermons, it limited communion to "visible saints" who could offer convincing evidence of their conversion. Not surprisingly, many seem to have been intimidated by this requirement, and the number of full communicants in Congregational churches tended to be small. During the 1690s many churches were so discouraged by dwindling membership that they decided to open the Lord's Supper to all adults of good moral character. But the strictest churches, including Newport's First Church, feared that open communion would dilute their religious purity. Besides demanding that prospective members make a public profession of faith to the entire congregation, they asked probing questions about their moral character. While they did not think that people could earn salvation by performing good works, they still assumed that the elect would be particularly virtuous. When Sarah wept in Clap's parlor as she tried to explain why she had come, he treated her "Like a tender father to a Little child," but he also warned that he would "inquire into" her reputation before recommending her to the rest of the church. Wiping away her tears, she assured him that she had been "*kept from open scandalous sins.*"[40]

Of all the twists and turns in Sarah's memoir, this one is especially surprising. Although it may have been technically true that she had not committed any "open" sins that had scandalized the public, she certainly knew that Clap would have been troubled by her theft from her parents. Perhaps she worried that he would counsel her to make a full confession to her mother, or maybe, despite her earlier tone of repentance, she was not yet fully convinced that her theft had been a sin. Whatever the reason for her silence, she deliberately misrepresented herself, and as she continued writing her memoir she never acknowledged to either herself or her readers what she had done. But as we have seen, Samuel Hopkins decided to strike out every passage alluding to that theft. He did not want to tarnish her reputation by letting readers know that she had not only stolen from her parents but deceived her pastor.

The evening after Sarah's visit to Clap, she stayed up all night (yet again) to read a book he had given her: Joseph Stevens's *Another and Better Country, Even an Heavenly*. She was "so delighted with it" that she read it two or three times, savoring Stevens's descriptions of a world beyond suffering. "God shall then wipe away all tears from their Eyes," Stevens promised, quoting from Isaiah, "and there shall be no more Death, neither sorrow nor crying, nor shall there be any more Pain."[41] Inspired by this book, Sarah felt an overwhelming sense of Christ's love for her. "Oh, how was I ravished with his Love," she remembered. "Surely my heart reached forth in burning desire after the blessed Jesus." After years of feeling worthless and alone, she was so stunned by her sense of God's presence that she asked, "Why me? Why me? Why [am I] not in hell?" But she fell mute as she realized that a mysterious God had always loved her despite her weakness, sinfulness, and unworthiness. "What a traitor have I been," she marveled, "and yet thou hast freely Loved me."[42] Her new vision of reality was so astonishing that she could barely believe it: God had loved her even when she had been unable to love herself.

On February 6, 1737, Sarah Wheaten was admitted to full membership in the First Church of Christ after her spiritual narrative was read aloud to the entire congregation. "I wrote my experience to the church," she explained. (Unfortunately Sarah's account does not survive in either her own personal papers or the church records, but she probably drew on it while writing her memoir.) Unlike men, who were required to make their own professions of faith, women were forbidden to speak publicly. Citing Paul's words to the Corinthians, ministers insisted that women must "keep silence in the churches" and "learn in silence with all subjection." If they were not literate enough to write their own conversion accounts, ministers would transcribe their words for them. In a symbol of her feminine submission, Sarah sat silently as the Reverend Clap recited the words she had so carefully chosen. She would never be allowed to raise her voice in her own church except to sing or respond to a prayer.[43]

At the end of the meeting, Sarah joined the other members of the church around the table for the Lord's Supper, a ritual that had always both awed and frightened her. Like many Protestants, Sarah was alarmed by Saint Paul's warning that "he that eateth and drinketh unworthily, eateth and drinketh damnation to himself," but she also believed in her "duty" to worship Christ in the sacrament. As the members of the church passed her the bread ("children's bread," she called it) and then the wine, she rejoiced at the thought of Christ's real presence in them. Christ was actually *there* with her at the table. "It was indeed sweet to me to feed by faith on the broken body of my dearest Lord," she remembered, and when she held the cup in her hands she felt as if she had been virtually transported to the foot of the cross. (During the Reformation, Catholics and Protestants had fought over whether the laity could have access to Christ's blood as well as his body, and even two centuries later Protestants like Sarah were especially devoted to the cup.) Usually she imagined God as distant and sovereign, but in this intimate moment of communion she saw him in his suffering, human form, his wounds clearly visible. Echoing the words of the apostle Thomas, who had refused to believe in Jesus's resurrection until he actually put his finger in the wounds, she wrote, "When I come to take the cup, and by faith to apply the precious properties of the blood of Christ to my soul, the scales of unbelief seemed all to drop off, and I was forced to cry out, 'my Lord and my God,' when I behold the hole in his side and the prints of the nails." (Her original sentence had concluded with the words "and hear the blessed Jesus say, 'daughter, thy sins are forgiven thee,'" but she crossed them out at some point because she did not want to imply that she had literally heard Christ's voice.) Her nearness to Jesus, her vision of his brokenness, filled her with an "ecstasy of joy."[44]

Sarah confirmed her commitment to Christ by writing a personal "covenant" with him, a Puritan practice that continued to be popular into the eighteenth century. For guidance she imitated a covenant included in the Reverend Thomas Doolittle's *Call to Delaying Sinners*, first published in 1698. Instead of copying Doolittle's covenant, Sarah reworded it to emphasize her spirit of self-denial, and in place of the resolution to "forsake all that is dear unto me in this World, rather than to turn from thee to the ways of sin," she substituted, "I will Leave, Lose, and deny all that was dear to me when it stood in competition with God, even Life itself, if he should be pleased to call for it, rather than to forsake him and his ways."[45]

Yet as she remembered later, this sentence was so distressing to write that she had to put down her pen. When she thought of everyone and everything she loved in the world, she feared that she would not be able to keep such a painful promise. "Satan in a rage flew upon me and furiously assaulted me," she remembered. "He told me that I was now a Lying to God."[46] Sarah seems to have worried that her love for her family and friends was so intense that it verged on "Idolatry," as Doolittle called it, and the thought of being forced to choose between God and her loved ones was terrifying. What if God decided to take away her son, Samuel, just as he had taken away her husband? Would she be able to keep her faith if God demanded the sacrifice of all that mattered to her?

Her unfinished covenant before her, Sarah prayed that God would give her "real and persevering grace," and in response a verse of scripture was "powerfully set home" on her mind: "My grace shall be sufficient for thee." Then she opened her Bible at random and waited for the Holy Spirit to lead her eyes to a text (a common Puritan and evangelical practice). The result was a reassuring verse from Isaiah, "Fear not; for thou shalt not be ashamed." Like earlier generations of Puritans, Sarah may have believed that parts of the Bible had been literally written with her in mind. When John Bunyan read a verse from Luke, "And yet there is room," he concluded that "when the Lord Jesus did speak these words, He then did think of me." In Sarah's case, she found Isaiah's prophecy "so adapted to every particular of my circumstances" that she transcribed every word in her memoir. In the years ahead, she would cling to this fragment of scripture as if it were a raft that would keep her from sinking. Isaiah had promised:

> *For thou shalt forget the shame of thy youth, and shalt not remember the reproach of thy widowhood any more. For thy Maker is thine husband, the Lord of Hosts is his name, and thy redeemer the Holy One of Israel, the God of the whole earth shall be called. For the Lord hath called thee as a woman forsaken and grieved in spirit, and a wife of youth, when thou wast refused, saith thy God. For a small moment have I forsaken thee; but with great mercies will I gather thee. In a little wrath I hid my face from thee for a moment but with everlasting kindness will I have mercy on thee, saith the Lord thy Redeemer.*

Sarah's feelings of shame, her widowhood, her grief, her fear of being abandoned by God—all had been foretold by Isaiah, and yet he had urged her not to be afraid. Encouraged by this verse, she finished writing her covenant with God and, to seal her promise that she would always be faithful to him, she signed it with her name. Once again, she was so overwhelmed by joy that she thought she might lose control of her body. "It seemed to me that all heavens rung with acclamations of joy that such a prodigal as I was returned to my God and father," she remembered, "and my joy was so great that my bodily strength failed and I was for some time as one whose soul was ready to break Loose and wing away into the bosom of my God."[47] In future years she would honor this date, March 1, 1737, by renewing her commitment to forsake everything for Christ.

At a time when radical evangelicals boasted that they had seen Christ in dreams, trances, or visions, Sarah offered a tamer, more scriptural description of how her heart had been changed. As she narrated her spiritual journey, she made it clear that every turning point had been precipitated by reading the Bible. When she thought she was too sinful to be saved, she had been comforted by a verse from Corinthians. When she feared that she would never be able to renounce the world for Christ, she had been strengthened by a verse from Isaiah. Even when she imagined Christ knocking at the door of her heart, she alluded to a biblical text ("Behold, I stand at the door, and knock"). Yet because so many evangelicals boasted about their "Dreams, Trances, Visions, Revelations, Impulses," she wanted to make sure that no one could tar her with the brush of "enthusiasm." When she wrote, "I saw my dearest Lord in his bitter agony in the garden," she began the sentence with "I *thought*." "I pretend to no visions or revelations," she testified.[48]

Sarah seems to have been especially nervous about being associated with the Separates. In some ways she seems to have been drawn to their sense of assurance, and her hostility toward them may have been an attempt to deny her attraction. But she did not believe that God communicated directly with people through voices and visions, and when Joseph Fish, one of her closest friends, became embroiled in conflict with an angry group of Separates in his Connecticut congregation, she immediately took his side. In response to Fish's complaint that the Separates in his church were determined to "corrupt the pure, undefiled religion of the gospel, and cast out the very bowels of vital piety," Sarah wrote sympathetically: "That the church will be overspread with errors: this indeed is a very melancholy thing, but as Luther said, it is Christ's cause. Let him see to it."[49] In the future, all her references to the Separates would be sharply negative.

Besides her desire to distance herself from the Separates, Sarah may have tried to be especially circumspect in her language because she was young and female—two traits that critics of the revivals associated with enthusiasm. According to Charles Chauncy, most of the people who fainted, or cried out during the revivals were "*Children, Women*, and *youngerly Persons. . . .* 'tis among *Children, young People* and *Women*, whose Passions are soft and tender, and more easily thrown into a Commotion, that these things chiefly prevail." Even Jonathan Edwards, one the most prominent

defenders of the revivals, implied that women were so "silly" that they easily lost control of their emotions. In *Some Thoughts on the Present Revival*,
he justified crying out during church services by including an example of
a "man of solid understanding" who had cried out, not just "a silly woman
or child." Although the revivals blurred the distinctions of gender, they did
not completely erase them, and Sarah Osborn knew that as a woman she
was particularly likely to be accused of irrationality. At the end of her memoir she scrawled a note of clarification in case anyone had misinterpreted
her language. "Once more I would mention that wherever I have spoke of
seeing such or such things I meant no other but with the eyes of my understanding or seeing by an eye of faith. Likewise, of hearing as it were a voice,
I would not be understood any real voice."[50]

Yet when Samuel Hopkins edited Sarah Osborn's memoir for publication after her death, he tinkered with her language in order to remove any
doubts about her meaning. Because her descriptions of Satan were especially vivid and immediate, he toned them down so it did not sound as
if she had actually seen or spoken to the devil in the flesh. For example,
she wrote that Satan "told me it was too late for me to find mercy," but
Hopkins clarified that this conversation had taken place only in her mind:
"And as it had been often *suggested* to me, I believe from Satan, that it was
time enough for me to repent hereafter, it was now strongly *impressed on
my mind*, that it was now too late for me to find mercy." Similarly, Hopkins
replaced her assertion "Satan assaulted me furiously with new temptations"
with the milder "I was furiously assaulted with new temptations, by Satan
I believe." Despite his belief in the reality of Satan, Hopkins did not want
her to be associated with radicals who claimed to have literally seen or
spoken to him.[51]

Like Sarah Osborn, though, Hopkins believed that true religion was
"experimental," and he did not change her descriptions of her tears, outcries, and bodily weakness. Nor did he try to tone down her expressions of
joy. In the first part of her memoir she almost never used the word *joy*, but
as she searched for the right language to describe her mystical encounter
with God, she found herself drawn to the apostle Peter's words: "ye rejoice
with joy unspeakable and full of glory." She not only remembered "great"
joy but described "ecstasies of joy" and "tears of joy" that had made her feel
as though the Holy Spirit were with her. Her rebirth in Christ had made
true joy possible—not just happiness, which could be superficial and short-
lived, but the deep contentment of knowing that she was a child of God.[52]

The Bitter Remains

Like other eighteenth-century evangelicals, Sarah Osborn sounded certain about when and where her spiritual transformation had taken place. She remembered vivid details about Clap's terrifying sermon, her inability to eat or sleep for a long, distressing week, and her unspeakable joy when she realized that Christ loved her. There seemed to be no room for doubt: she had been born again on a Saturday night in January 1737, a night that she could remember as keenly as if it had been yesterday. If she had ended her memoir by describing her new sense of God's love, it would have seemed to be a natural conclusion to her story. A sinful, rebellious child had grown into an adult who, after being chastened by affliction, had finally found her way to God.

But Sarah's pilgrimage had been more complicated than that, and as she continued writing, she admitted that she had "backslid" and doubted the reality of her former experiences. "Oh! The woeful, bitter remains of total depravity and contrariety to God," she wrote in the margins. "Lord, was there ever such a heart as mine?" Although she blamed Satan for her doubts, she blamed herself more: if not for her corruption, he would not have been allowed to torment her. "After all this I began by degrees to grow more conformed to the world," she explained. She continued to attend church, but she decided that "there was a time for all things, and singing, dancing, and now and then playing a game at cards, and telling stories with a particular friend, was all innocent diversions." (At some point she crossed out the sentence about cardplaying and gossiping, perhaps because she did not want others to know how low she had sunk.) By 1740 she had "lost almost all sense of my former experiences. I had only the bare remembrance of them and they only seemed like dreams or delusion."[53]

Sarah understood her crisis in religious rather than psychological terms, but if she had lived in a different era she might have wondered whether the words that Satan supposedly spoke to her were actually her own. Ever since childhood she had feared that she was unworthy of God's love—that it was impossible for her to be saved. Perhaps it is not surprising that even after her mystical experience of God's grace, she found it hard to believe that she could be forgiven.

By the time George Whitefield arrived in Newport in the fall of 1740, soon afterward followed by Gilbert Tennent, Sarah's faith had shrunk to only a small part of her life. Although she went to church on Sundays, on the other days of the week she played cards with her friends, went to dances, or sang the latest songs. She loved to sing, and as she recalled later, "I could sing a hundred songs of which I had wrote the first Lines in a List."[54] She was too busy gossiping with her friends, teaching school, and caring for her son to spend much time alone with her thoughts (which seems to have been the way she wanted it), but whenever she slowed down she felt empty. The joy that had once uplifted her was gone.

This may have been why she joined the throngs of people who went to hear Whitefield preach—or perhaps she just wanted to catch a glimpse of the famous man in person. Even the Rhode Island legislature adjourned in order to attend his sermon. For the past year newspapers had been filled with accounts of his preaching that seemed almost too extraordinary to be true. Not only had he supposedly preached to more than fifty thousand people in the fields of London and six thousand on the Philadelphia Common, but he had left staggering numbers of new Christians in his wake. Sometimes people cried out so loudly that they drowned out his voice. In Newport he reportedly preached to three thousand in Trinity Church, Sarah among them, and then to another thousand who followed him to the doorstep of a friend's house. (Although Whitefield probably exaggerated his audience—the entire population of Newport in 1740 was less than six thousand—all agreed that no one had ever seen such throngs in one place before.) Everyone who met him, whether friend or foe, marveled at his charisma. "I can assure you," warned one of his critics, "he is qualified to sway and keep the affections of the multitude." In Newport, like everywhere he traveled, his listeners wept.[55]

Sarah's encounter with Whitefield marked a turning point for her. "God in mercy sent his dear servant Whitefield here which something stirred me up," she remembered. As she watched people crying and following him through the streets, she seems to have realized that she had lost her sense of God's presence. Whitefield preached a faith that no longer seemed to be her own.

When Gilbert Tennent arrived shortly afterward, she spiraled into an agony of doubt about her salvation. Tennent was less polished than Whitefield, and even one of his admirers commented that "he seemed to have no regard to please the eyes of his hearers with agreeable gestures, nor their ears with delivery, nor their fancy with language." But his straight-talking sermons were terrifying. "When he sounds forth the Thunders of the Law,/He strikes the Soul with Trembling and with Awe," rhymed a Boston poet. Sarah did not record Tennent's exact words in Newport, but he often railed against hypocrisy, and after his departure she feared that she was not truly a Christian after all. "O! ye wretched, fair-faced, smooth tongued, but foul false-hearted Hypocrites!" he warned in a sermon published in 1741. "You are the Bane and Pest of Christianity. O! *Ye whited Sepulchers!* It's you, who under a Pretence of Friendship, wound Religion to the Heart, and leave it bleeding and gasping for Life. Pull off your Paint and Masks, ye Hypocrites, and appear like what ye are, incarnate Devils; it's better for the People of God to have to do with roaring, raging Devils, than Devils in Disguise; what can such as ye expect but to be cut asunder by the Sword of God's Justice, and sunk in the Damnation of Hell." For the entire winter after he left, Sarah felt as though she "had not one spark of grace." She was surrounded by converts who confidently proclaimed their salvation, but she could not be sure of God's love for her. "A dreadful uncomfortable Life it was," she remembered.[56]

Even though Sarah talked to the Reverend Clap about her doubts and renewed her covenant to God, nothing brought her comfort. Her anxiety was heightened by the unexpected death of her brother, who she feared had not been converted.[57] Although she claimed that her mourning was quickly overshadowed by her resignation to God's will, she could not help wondering about his fate, and even more alarming, her own.

Sarah visited Tennent when he returned in March 1741 to preach twenty-one sermons (a number that she carefully recorded, perhaps because she attended all of them), and at first she was comforted by his acknowledgment that Christians did not always feel God's love as intensely as they had at the moment of conversion. But when he delivered yet another of his hellfire sermons—this time against singing, dancing, playing cards, and "foolish jesting"—his words shattered her frail security. "He would not say there was no such thing as dancing Christians," she remembered, "but he had a very mean opinion of such that could bear to spend their precious time so when it is so short and the work for eternity so great."[58] Shamed by his words, she feared that if her conversion had been real she would not have slipped into her old, immoral habits so easily.

Exhausted by months of anxiety, Sarah finally decided to write down her religious experiences and ask Tennent to evaluate them. Was she a genuine Christian or not? Could he find biblical precedent for what she had experienced? She may have gotten the idea to write a letter from Tennent, who believed that he had a duty to make judgments about the souls in his care. Despite urging his fellow ministers to use "great Caution . . . in expressing our Opinion concerning others' States towards God, lest by rash judging, we strengthen the Presumptuous" or "discourage the Sincere-Hearted," he thought that he could usually determine whether someone had been reborn in Christ. The test, of course, was experience. "If their Experiences be agreeable to the Holy Scriptures," he explained, "and they be also Sound in the main Doctrines of Religion, and both be confirmed by a holy conversation, then we should judge charitably of their State." In Sarah's case, he sent her a kind letter that belied his reputation as a "son of thunder." "My dear friend," he addressed her, "I Like your experiences well. They seem to me to be scriptural and encouraging, and I think you may humbly take comfort from them and give God the glory of his pure grace." After affirming that she had "a sure interest in the great salvation," he tried to help her overcome any lingering fears by quoting several biblical passages, including a verse from Jeremiah: "Thou hast played the harlot with many lovers; yet return again to me, saith the Lord."[59]

Sarah's reliance on Tennent's guidance suggests that historians may have overstated the anti-authoritarian strain of the revivals. On the surface the revivals seem to have damaged the prestige of the clerical establishment, pitting ministers against one another. But underneath the controversies deference had not entirely disappeared. Although the laity could be contemptuous of ministers who disagreed with them, they still relied on popular religious leaders to validate their experiences. (In the nineteenth century, evangelicalism and demagoguery would often go hand in hand.) Since Sarah was well-versed in the Bible, she almost certainly knew the "precious texts" that Tennent transcribed for her, but she was reluctant to interpret them on her own. If not for his intervention, she might never have surmounted her fears. "I was as one restored as it were from the grave," she remembered.[60]

Determined to create a new Christian identity, Sarah changed almost everything about her life. She had been so unhappy before the revivals that she wanted to close the door on her past. Not only did she renounce "such vanities as singing [and] dancing," but she searched for positive ways to demonstrate her faith to others. "I earnestly pleaded with God that he would suffer me to Live no Longer an unprofitable servant," she remembered, "but would find out some way that I might be useful in the world and that I might now be as exemplary for piety as I had been for folly." She visited the sick, shared the story of her religious experiences with others, and agreed to serve as the leader of the women's society, a group that met weekly for prayer and Bible-reading. Religion became the "chief business" of her life.[61]

As Sarah reinvented herself, she made several new evangelical friends, none closer than Susanna Anthony, or "Susa," as she called her, whom she seems to have met around 1740.[62] Since Newport was a compact city, they may have been acquainted before then, but they were separated by both age and religion. Susa was twelve years younger than Sarah, so she was only about fourteen years old when they met, and she had been raised as a Quaker. In 1740, though, when Whitefield came to Newport, she joined the huge throngs gathered to hear him preach. Her sister had died recently, and in the agony of her loss, she felt as though she were "entangled in a labyrinth of darkness and confusion."[63] But after hearing Whitefield, she began a slow, tortured journey toward the evangelical movement, and in 1742 she joined both the First Church of Christ and Sarah's prayer group.

For reasons that are not entirely clear, Susa was a deeply troubled young woman whose self-loathing went far beyond anything Sarah ever expressed. We know only what Susa chose to tell us about herself, but based on her words it is hard not to wonder whether she had suffered traumas beyond her sister's death. Her self-hatred was so violent that she deliberately injured herself. "I seemed as though I should have twisted every bone out of its place," she confessed in her memoir. "And have often since wondered that I never disjointed a bone, when, through the violence of my distress, I wrung my hands, twisted every joint, and strained every nerve; biting my flesh; gnashing my teeth; throwing myself on the floor." She also starved herself. "Satan set in to persuade me I had sinfully indulged my appetite," she admitted. "And when I attempted to eat, it would be suggested, that I was then increasing my condemnation." She finally stopped punishing herself when she came to understand Christ's unconditional love, but throughout her life she suffered from bouts of melancholy. In order to devote herself to prayer she chose to remain single. Though she earned a small wage by sewing and teaching, she lived with her parents for most of her life.[64]

It is no surprise that Sarah and Susa were drawn to each other. Both knew what it meant to despise oneself, and both had experienced the healing power of God's love. "By every letter I receive from you," Sarah wrote, "I think, something more of my own heart is discovered to me." She seems to have loved and admired Susa more than almost anyone in the world. "Lord, thou knowest there is no creature upon earth more dear to me," she testified in later years in her diary. "Thou hast made her as my own soul Precious to me."[65]

Sarah also became close friends with Joseph Fish, who preached in Newport during the revival. (His cousin's husband Benjamin Church, the deacon of her church, may have introduced them.) Although Sarah had always admired and respected ministers, her feelings for Fish went much deeper. There was a spark of sympathy between them, a feeling of knowing and being known, that was religious in its intensity. As she confessed in a letter to him, "There is, as Mr. Whitefield expresses it, a sacred something that has Knot my Heart to you with stronger bonds than that of natural affection."[66] He was only eight years older than she, and although she never admitted it to herself, she seems to have been in love with him. "May faith bring home some clusters of grapes for you to feed upon, while you travel through this wilderness, this vale of tears," she wrote in a sympathetic letter. "O my very heart is melted within me with ardent desires for you: and happy shall I think myself if God will own and bless the poor weak endeavors of a feeble worthless worm to refresh you, who knows she is not worthy to wash the feet of the servants of my Lord—and blushes at the review of the freedoms I have used with one so much my superior in all respects." She always addressed him with deference but also with deep affection. In return, he called her his "dear sister" and promised that she would always be in his prayers. If not for the fact that he was already married, they might have allowed themselves to fall in love, but instead they poured their feelings into an enduring friendship that eventually included their families. "In my thoughts I am with you daily," she assured him, "and sometimes till thought itself is swallowed up and I am as it were forced to break off abruptly."[67] His spiritual guidance helped her to remember that she had become a new self, a pilgrim on the way to the promised land.

Sarah was so determined to change her life that she cut her ties to former friends. At first she hoped that some might follow her into the evangelical fold, but they resented her attempts to save them. As she remembered, "Almost anything I spoke in their hearing, though ever so innocently and without the Least thought of giving offence, was presently carried about and much game made thereof." Although she claimed to have treated her friends with "civility," it is clear that they found her arrogant. When she explained that she could not spend time with them because of more important things to do, such as visiting the sick and praying with people in distress, one of her oldest friends accused her of being a "Pharisee" who was "holier than thou" and "dreadfully puffed up with spiritual pride." Although Sarah seems to have recorded this argument in order to justify herself, she was clearly hurt. "The trial I met with in this friend and one more who I hope is a Christian," she lamented, "was more grief to me then all the scoffs and ridicules of those that plainly appear not to be acquainted with spiritual things." She spent more than four pages insisting that she never meant to appear proud, but she clearly feared that the charge might be fair.[68] On some level, she may have realized that she compensated for her feelings of worthlessness by aggrandizing herself, veering between self-loathing and self-righteousness. But when forced to choose between her hard-won faith and her former friends, she refused to look back.

The Prodigal

Only one remaining obstacle stood in the way of Sarah's dream of a new life in Christ: her guilt over the theft from her parents. Despite her reconciliation with them after Samuel's death she had never confessed to her crime, and her feelings toward them, especially her mother, seem to have been a tangle of love and resentment. Her father had died three years earlier of consumption, but during the last days of his life she had decided that she did not have a religious "duty" to admit her theft. (And indeed, it would have been an act of cruelty to burden him with the confession on his deathbed.) Instead she "begged of him to forgive me for everything I had offended concerning him in from my cradle." In a touching portrait, she remembered that he had blessed her "with the best of blessings in Christ Jesus" and called her a "dear child." It was only the second time in her memoir that she recorded her father's words to her, and unlike the earlier time, when she had noted that he had threatened to give her "nothing" if she married Samuel, she spoke of him with tenderness. Perhaps as she "stood by him and resigned his departing spirit into the hands of God," she had been able to forgive him, just as she had asked to be forgiven.[69]

During the revivals she decided that it was necessary to ask for her mother's pardon as well, and this time she was determined to make a full confession. For years she had feared that her mother would disown her if she knew the truth, but in the spring of 1742 she became convinced that she would never be able to start a new life unless she confronted her past. "Trembling," as she described herself, she sat down with pen and paper to reveal the secret that had burdened her for more than ten years. "I do with the prodigal confess I have sinned against thee," she wrote to her mother, "and am no more worthy to be called thine." In a remarkably honest letter, she admitted that she had kept her theft a secret out of pride, shame, and fear: pride, because she did not want to humble herself to her parents after their opposition to her marriage; shame, because she knew that she had committed a sin; and fear, because she worried that her parents might reject her if they knew the truth. Although it must have been hard to admit her vulnerability, Sarah told her mother that she had always been afraid of losing her love. "I was afraid it would make a breach between us that would never be made up," she confessed. If her mother wanted it, she would even sell all her possessions in order to repay the debt. "I throw myself at your mercy," she pleaded.[70]

Sarah's letter was not only an emotional plea for forgiveness; it was a declaration of her renewed commitment to Christ. As she explained to her mother, she might not have come forward if not for Eleazar Wheelock, who was "meek as a Lamb, but thunders out the awful and evangelical truths of the gospel with the courage of a Lion." Inspired by his sermon about making restitution for one's sins, she was ready to follow the biblical examples of "Zacchaeus and Peter" and "to forsake all." Despite her fear of her mother's anger, she had decided to tell the truth no matter what the cost. "I am determined to know nothing but Christ," she testified. At the end of her letter, she begged her mother to remember that they were both Christians who had been called to a life of forgiveness. Echoing the words of the Lord's Prayer, she concluded, "I do renew my petitions to you, most honored mother, for the forgiveness of my trespass against you, and beg you will be reconciled and at peace with me for the sake of him who has said, 'if you forgive men their trespasses, your heavenly father will forgive you your trespasses.'" She signed her letter, "your once rebellious but now obedient daughter till death."[71]

Writing this letter was so cathartic that Sarah "resolved with a great deal of cheerfulness to sell my household goods to make restitution having nothing else in the world." But when her mother sent her a gift the next day, unaware of the letter that would momentarily arrive on her doorstep, Sarah slipped back into her old feelings of guilt and "unworthiness." "I was almost ready to conclude I was too vile to be forgiven," she remembered.[72]

Ten days later, when her mother still had not responded to her letter, Sarah's sense of "vileness" had been replaced by rage, and instead of turning her anger inward against herself (as she had done during the suicidal crisis of her adolescence), she wrote her mother one of the angriest, most passionate letters of her life. "Is there such a breach made by my confessing my sin that it cannot be made up?" she demanded in a second letter. "Has not God said whoso covers his sins shall not prosper, but who confesses and forsakes them shall find mercy? I do with shame confess. I do judge and condemn myself and I hope freely forsake, but oh dear mother, will you shut up your bowels of compassion towards me? Can't you forgive me?

Must I suffer your displeasure now which I have so Long dreaded?" Once again she offered to sell all that she owned in order to repay the money, but this time she reminded her mother that the prodigal in the Bible had been welcomed home unconditionally. "What shall I say or do?" she demanded. "Have I wasted your substance? Did not the prodigal, too? And yet when he returned, his father's arms was open to embrace him. And when the servant could not pay his Lord without all that he had being sold, his Lord frankly forgave him the debt. But if you desire it, I am still willing to part with all to make restitution." Without explicitly accusing her mother of betraying her Christian faith, she strongly implied that if her mother were a true Christian she would show mercy to her repentant child.[73]

By the end of her letter, though, Sarah had softened. Despite her anger, she could not bear the thought of her mother's rejection. Besides offering her mother "a thousand thanks" for sending the gift, she admitted that she had been consumed by feelings of "grief" and "unworthiness." "I do again beg to be forgiven by you," she wrote, "and earnestly beg an answer that will finish this business forever for I can't be easy till it is entirely done with." After signing her letter "your very affectionate and dutiful daughter till death," she added, "I beg your prayers."[74] In three sentences, she had used the word *beg* three times.

On the next day Sarah finally received an answer to her first letter, and as she read it she was deeply ashamed of her "hard thoughts." "My dear child," her mother had written, "I long to see you. I beg you would be thoroughly easy, for assure yourself I do as freely forgive you as I pray God shall forgive me all my trespasses." Even more unexpected, she claimed that her "sweet child" had taught her something about the true meaning of grace, and she pleaded for Sarah's forgiveness in return. "[I] beg that if I have failed in my duty to you either by temporal or spiritual assistances within my poor capability, that you would forgive it Likewise." Since Sarah had spent the previous days working herself into a fury, she was so "overcome" by her mother's tenderness that she felt almost faint.[75] She wished she had never written the second letter, but it was too late.

More than a week later, when she finally received a second response, she discovered with relief that her mother had been hurt and shocked by her angry letter but once again forgave her.

I am, dear child, grieved exceedingly to think that you should entertain such a thought that I could be so cruel, so hardhearted, so barbarous, so far fallen from grace as not to be as ready to forgive you as you to ask it.

No, child. I bless God I can truly say, if my heart don't deceive me, if it had been all I possessed and what had exposed me to work for my bread as I do, I hope I neither could nor durst have denied your forgiveness and should be ready, were I able, to put a ring on your hand and shoes on your foot. Your confession is too much and more than I can well bear and beg you would not mention it anymore nor once think or Endeavor to make me any further recompense. You have done enough and more. I neither expect nor will receive.

Although she admitted that Sarah's letter had been "almost too hard," she left no doubt that she wanted to embrace her "dear child" as a prodigal.[76]

Sarah's relationship with her mother continued to be difficult at times, but she felt that she had finally made peace with a terrible part of her past. "I seemed Like one released from a dreadful burden which I would not have upon my conscience again for all this world," she remembered. Not only did she feel closer to her mother, she felt nearer to God. Because she had first learned about God as a young child, her understanding of him had always been tangled up with her feelings about her parents, and for years she had felt as though there were a "separating wall between Christ and my soul." When her mother forgave her, she gained a deeper sense of God's forgiveness as well. "Now I had peace in my own breast and peace with God," she rejoiced. "Surely I never lived nearer to God in my whole Life."[77]

By the spring of 1742, a little more than a year after Whitefield and Tennent had preached in Newport, Sarah had carved out a new identity for herself as an evangelical Christian. She was still a schoolteacher, but she no longer spent her spare time with "wicked companions." Her life was marked by a new sense of mission. Every week she led the women's society in prayer for the spread of the gospel around the world, and although she did not believe that women should be ministers, she shared her faith with her neighbors and acquaintances. After a friend criticized her for trumpeting her beliefs to the public instead of keeping them to herself, Sarah retorted that she could not possibly keep quiet when God had given her such a priceless gift. Although she had teetered on the brink of hell, God had "snatched" her as "a brand out of the burning." "Oh amazing grace that God should spare such a wretch as I," she exulted, "such an abuser of mercy." (This was a common refrain in the transatlantic evangelical movement even before John Newton wrote his famous hymn, "Amazing Grace," in 1772.) "Should I altogether hold my peace?" she asked incredulously. "It appeared to me such a monstrous piece of ingratitude that it seemed as if the very stones might cry out against me." Unlike Christians who saw religion as a private matter "betwixt God and the soul," evangelicals believed that it should be joyfully proclaimed to the world.[78]

Sarah's sense of self was still fragile, though, and she seems to have compensated for her vulnerability by proclaiming her assurance in extreme language. It was not enough to tell people that she had been born again. She wanted everyone in Newport to know that she did not have a single shred of doubt about her salvation. Not surprisingly, her words caused "offence," and she admitted that she gained a reputation as a "bold pretender" for supposedly saying that she was as "sure of heaven as if I was there" and that "God must cease to be God if he damned me." When a minister in Newport preached "very smartly" against evangelicals' arrogance, many in his congregation suspected that his sermon was about her. "Several that heard it knew who he meant," she protested in her memoir. Much to her "shock" and embarrassment, she had become a symbol of the excesses of the revivals, but she insisted that her words had been misinterpreted. Invoking the Calvinist doctrine of the perseverance of saints, she explained that after conversion it was impossible to fall from grace. Perhaps someone had heard her say, "*those* that are once interested in Christ are sure of heaven as if they were there." ("I firmly believe it still," she added.) As for claiming that God would cease to be God if he damned her, "I do not remember expressing myself in any such terms to any person on Earth," but it was possible that she had said that God "could as soon cease to be God" as to forget his covenant promises. Citing Paul's promise that those who had been "predestinated" would also be "called," "justified," and "glorified," she declared, "I *was enabled here to prove my calling.*"[79]

Was Sarah Osborn as sure about her relationship to God as she claimed to be in her memoir? Although she wanted her future readers to think so, it is possible that she proclaimed her certainty so loudly in order to convince herself. The more she testified to her assurance, the more she may have hoped to believe in it. Assurance was supposed to be God's gift to the born again, a mark of true grace.

The Way of Duty

Shortly after Sarah confessed to her mother, she made another life-changing decision. After eleven years of widowhood, she agreed to marry Henry Osborn, a tailor and member of her church. She had received two marriage proposals after Samuel's death, but she had refused each time because she did not want to marry someone who was not a Christian. In 1739 a sailor had almost convinced her to say yes, but although he had enough money to support her "comfortably," he was "not so sober as I wanted." Nor did she seem to love him. ("I could not get rid of him," she complained.) Only a week before they were supposed to be married, she changed her mind in order to avoid being "unequally yoked." (Paul had warned the Corinthians, "Be ye not unequally yoked together with unbelievers.") In 1741, during the revivals, she seems to have fallen in love for the first time since Samuel's death, but despite her pleas the man (whom she never named) refused to repent and seek Christ. "I wrestled with God in bitter agonies for him from day to day and from night to night," she remembered, but finally she said good-bye. "I could not bear the thoughts of being espoused to one that was not for Christ," she remembered. "This I found to be a great piece of self denial."[80]

In this self-sacrificing spirit, a year later Sarah agreed to marry Henry, a man who was old enough to be her father. A fifty-seven-year-old widower with three sons—Edward, eighteen, Henry, seventeen and John, fourteen—he had recently lost his wife after twenty years of marriage.[81] At first she considered refusing his proposal because "my inclination did not much Lead me to it." Besides being concerned about the almost thirty-year age difference between them—she was only twenty-eight—and the new responsibilities she would have as a stepmother, she feared that she did not have "affections enough to be found in the way of duty." Since ministers taught that God required husbands and wives to have "a very great and tender love and affection to one another," she thought that it would be sinful to marry someone she did not love. But the more she prayed about it, the clearer it seemed to her that marrying Henry was God's will. "The main thing for which I had always prayed, I trusted was in him," she explained, "namely, a principle of grace, and I found this to be a strong motive." Like other evangelicals, she believed that marriage should be a path to God, not an end in itself. The Reverend Nicholas Gilman, for example, wrote to his fiancée, "sweet Molly," urging her to remember their mutual mortality. "Though I hope to enjoy you for a season yet we are not to look upon this as our Abiding place but improve our days on earth in making ready for that happy State, where there is no marrying nor giving in marriage."[82]

Throwing herself into God's hands, Sarah begged him to send her a sign of his will. If he wanted her to marry Henry, could he help her feel more affection for him? "The more I prayed, the more I found it so," she confided, "but one day in particular, when more than ordinarily engaged in this duty of prayer, crying mightily to God for direction, I vehemently begged that God would condescend to give me some token that I might know if it was his will I should go forward. And the very instant while I was pleading, these words was with amazing power and sweetness set home upon my soul: 'Go forward. Fear not, for I am with thee.'" Convinced that the Holy Spirit had sent the words to comfort her, she picked up her Bible, opened it at random, and immediately found this exact verse in Exodus. This remarkable answer to her prayers took away her doubt about whether to marry Henry, and she found herself growing fonder of him with each passing day. "My regard for his person was greater than before," she explained, "so that I had no fears but I could Love him so as to be found in the way of my duty to him."[83]

The fact that Sarah was guided by a verse from Exodus, a book about escaping slavery, suggests the precariousness of her situation in the summer of 1742. She seems to have hoped that just as Moses had led the Israelites out of bondage, her marriage would lead her out of poverty. After her school had failed the year before, she had agreed to work as a housekeeper in exchange for room and board, but she had no steady source of income. (As always, she seems to have eked out a little extra money by sewing and baking.) She had been offered a position teaching school outside Newport, but her devotion to her church and the women's society made her disinclined to move. When Henry asked her to marry him, she found it "very remarkable that God was this way providing for me." Henry was not rich, but he made a decent living as a tailor. When they were married, on May 5, 1742, she believed that God had sent a good Christian man to give her and her son a better life. "During the whole time of the ceremony," she wrote, "I did enjoy much of God's gracious presence and was enabled to renew my engagements with the blessed Jesus and to give my whole self to him while giving my self to my husband. Oh surely Christ did sweetly manifest his Love to my soul. A happy marriage this was indeed."[84]

Only four months later, though, she and Henry went bankrupt. In the booming economy of the early 1740s, he had hoped to make a fortune by investing in a ship, but for reasons that Sarah never explained he lost his hard-earned savings instead. Since Sarah blacked out almost her entire account of their financial struggles (two pages in all), few of her words can be deciphered, but it is clear that the family was plunged into poverty. "The debts was due," she remembered, but "month in and month out we could raise no more cash." Since married women could not own any property of their own, it is likely that creditors seized her meager savings. Henry sold all the goods in his shop as a last resort (he may have been afraid of debtors' prison), but because they were forced to part with things "under price," they still owed "a hundred pounds or more."[85]

Although Sarah crossed out most of her account of their bankruptcy, probably out of shame, she left a few sentences untouched. She wanted people to know that if she and Henry were unable to repay their creditors, it had not been out of "carelessness" but from genuine poverty. Besides regretting the "wrong" they had done to others, she worried about dishonoring her "profession"—in other words, her Christian faith. "And what does the LORD require of you?" the prophet Micah had asked. "To act justly and to love mercy and to walk humbly with your God." Quoting this verse, Sarah insisted that she had always tried to treat people with "justice," but in this case she and Henry were powerless. They simply had no money to repay their debts.[86]

As always, though, Sarah affirmed that God had afflicted them for their own good. She was ashamed of their inability to repay their creditors, but not of being poor, and although she was frank about her desire for a "comfortable" life with a well-stocked cupboard, she believed that God knew what was best for her. Confident that she understood his will, she decided that he had ordained her poverty in order to "suppress that pride of my nature which doubtless would have broke out greatly to his dishonor had I had health and prosperity." Too proud to be trusted with the good things of life, she had been deprived of them in order to learn the meaning of humility. Poverty was a hard cross to bear, but in her dark moments she remembered a verse from Hebrews: "Let your conversation be without covetousness and be content with such things as you have: for he hath said, I will never Leave thee nor forsake thee."[87]

When Sarah finished writing her memoir in December 1743 she and Henry were still deeply in debt, and despite her positive tone much about their life seemed bleak. Henry's older sons, Edward and Henry, had probably already found jobs to support themselves, but John was only fourteen, and Samuel was ten. Both would need food and clothing, and there was no money to spare. Worse, Sarah left a few small hints in her memoir that her "happy marriage" was not quite what she had hoped for. Although she thanked God for answering "all my petitions throughout the course of my widowhood by giving me one who I trust is united to Christ," she added, "and is in all respects almost tender." At some point she decided to cross out that qualifying *almost* because of what she had unintentionally revealed about her feelings. She summed up her relationship to Henry thus: "My affections are so much placed on him as I desire they should be on anything here below." Although she cared for him, there was no danger of her turning him into an "idol" she would be tempted to love more than God. Sarah also praised her new stepsons for their "tender affection, both in sickness and in health," but then once again she censored herself, crossing out a description of them as "sober, well-inclined," and "in no ways addicted to the vices of the times." At some point she decided that they were not actually "sober" after all.[88]

And yet she was determined to be "content" with what she had. Poverty was hard, but not as hard as the years that she had spent searching for God. Now that she had found him, she could look forward with hope instead of backward with despair.

Sarah ended her memoir on a triumphant note. After days (or perhaps weeks) of delving into the past, she had arrived back in 1743 with a new sense of assurance about her relationship to God. Despite all she had suffered, she had found the proof—the "evidence"—of God's love for her on every page of her memoir. His grace had triumphed over her sinfulness.

But Sarah's struggle to "trust in God and never despair of his mercy" had not yet ended. Far from it. Her feelings of worthlessness were not so easily conquered, and in the years ahead there would still be dark nights of the soul when she was plagued with doubts. Yet by writing a memoir she had given her life a new religious meaning, and whenever she longed for tangible evidence of her salvation she would sit down to reread her story. Her tone of assurance always comforted her. As she wrote on the cover of the memoir twenty years later, "this Book I Have reread again and again."

By combining the Christian language of human sinfulness and divine glory with a new Enlightenment vocabulary of benevolence, happiness, rationality, and empiricism, Sarah Osborn crafted a narrative that was both uniquely her own and distinctly evangelical. Lost but now found, doubtful but now sure, dead but now reborn—this was not only Sarah's story; it was the story of all those who belonged to the first generation of evangelicals in America.

Part Two

DIARIES AND LETTERS, 1744–1796

Chapter 5

The Lord Gave, and the Lord Hath Taken Away, 1744

On Thursday afternoon, the sixth day of this month, I had the sorrowful news that my only son was sick unto death. God in his providence provided presently for me—My dear Susa Anthony to keep my house—A horse for myself and my husband to ride, and all other things comfortable. And on my way God gave me such a sense of his goodness to me in a thousand instances, that instead of sinking under my sorrow, my mind was employed in attention to, and blessing God for my mercies. . . .

On Friday morning we got to Rehoboth where I found my son much swelled with a dropsy, and pined to a mere skeleton with the jaundice, scurvy, and consumption, all combining. He rattled in his throat like a dying person, laboring for every breath. He was given over by the doctor and all his friends, who lamented him, and did the best for him in their power, as to the body. But alas! My great concern was for that precious jewel, his immortal soul. I endeavored to improve every opportunity to discourse with him, and read to him such portions of scripture as I thought suitable, with passages out of Mr. Allen's Alarm, &c. And I was enabled to pray all the day, by ejaculatory breathings, and sometimes to plead and wrestle with God on his behalf: Though alas! God was pleased to hide his dealings with him altogether. For I could discern no evidence of a work of grace wrought on his soul, for which I did pray from day to day. I did not so much as once, in all his sickness, pray for his life; but for some evidence that his soul might live.

And for want of this, I sometimes seemed to be crushed down, having a
sense of his doleful case, if not reconciled to God.[1]

Sarah Osborn wrote these painful words on September 22, 1744, eight
days after the death of her son, Samuel. He had died just a month before
his twelfth birthday.

As always, Sarah turned to writing in order to make sense of what
seemed incomprehensible. Although it was several days before she could
bear to put her thoughts on paper, she seemed to hope that the orderly act
of arranging her experiences on a page would help her see God's hand in
her life. When she sat down to write, a quill in her hand and an inkbottle
at her side, she was stunned by how much her world had changed in such a
short span of time. Just two weeks earlier, she had been spending an ordinary afternoon in her school teaching her students how to stitch a sampler
or do sums, when suddenly someone had arrived at the door to report that
her son was dying. Rushing to be with him, she found him struggling to
breathe, and by the end of the following week he was gone.

By writing down her experience, Sarah hoped to discover why God
had taken Samuel away from her and, more painfully, whether her son had
been saved. Turning her gaze inward, she also hoped to discover whether
she had endured her loss like a true Christian. She believed that Samuel's
death, like all the other events in her life, had been designed to teach her
something, but when she began writing about it she was not sure what she
was supposed to have learned. Was the story of Samuel's death supposed
to reveal something about God's mercy or, more frightening, his wrath
to sinners? Was she supposed to have gained greater insight into her own
relationship to God?

The original manuscript of this narrative does not survive, only Samuel Hopkins's published transcription, so it is not clear why Sarah wrote
it—or for whom. But she may have intended it as a memorial to her son
that would be shared with friends and family. Besides hoping to come to a
deeper understanding of her loss, she seems to have wanted to teach others
something about God's grace in the midst of affliction.

In contrast to Enlightenment thinkers who celebrated the pleasures
of everyday life, evangelicals denied that the meaning of human existence
could be found here on earth. Christians were called to love their families
and friends, but they always had to beware of turning them into "idols" that
they worshipped more than the sovereign God. It was sinful to mourn too
much for the broken things of this world.[2]

Hide Not Thy Face

If Sarah had thought that writing a memoir would satisfy her desire to make sense of her relationship to God, she soon changed her mind. By 1744 she had begun keeping a regular diary, and she also wrote hundreds of letters to friends and acquaintances. Despite her desire for certainty, there were still many days when she had "Hard struggles with unbelief," and often she echoed the cry of absence in the Psalms: "How long wilt thou forget me, O Lord? forever? How long wilt thou hide thy face from me?"[3] Still searching for evidence of God's love, she picked up her pen in order to see how he was guiding her life.

Sarah experienced Samuel's death as one of the greatest tests of her faith, a moment when God seemed to have "hidden his face" from her. Struggling with grief, she tried to bring God into her presence through the sheer power of her words, making him visible on the page. Writing about God was like lighting a candle in the dark. Suddenly, she could see him. "Hide not thy face from me in the day when I am in trouble," she read in the Psalms. "Incline thine ear unto me: in the day when I call answer me speedily."[4] She had never been more in need of the comfort of writing. Prayer was not enough; she wanted to see God in front of her, his name inscribed in ink.

Samuel was one of the most important people in Sarah's world, but he is also one of the most shadowy. Samuel Hopkins, who never met him, described him only as a "promising youth," and Sarah's other friends never mentioned him. Since Samuel left no letters or diaries of his own, we do not know how he would have chosen to describe his life, but it must have been a hard one: he had no memory of his father, who had died when he was only a year old; he had grown up watching his mother struggle to make ends meet; and unlike better-off children he knew what it meant to worry about the cost of food or firewood. In the worst times he may have gone hungry. (When he died, he was suffering from malnourishment, among other maladies.) But when Sarah bent over his bed in the evenings to pray with him, giving thanks for God's grace, he also must have known what it meant to be loved. While other mothers had many children, ten on average, Sarah had only Samuel, and she seems to have adored him. She never referred to him simply as her son, but always as her *only* son. He was her "only son," she wrote passionately in her memoir, "who had been cast upon God from the womb."[5]

By the time Samuel was eleven, he had been apprenticed out to learn a trade. Perhaps, like his stepfather, Henry, he planned to become a tailor.

Or perhaps Sarah had higher aspirations for him. Tailors tended to be lower on the economic ladder than carpenters or blacksmiths, who were paid more because of the difficulty of their crafts.[6]

Apprenticeship was a common way of teaching boys how to make a living in early America. While some relied on their fathers to teach them how to farm or practice a craft, others were indentured out to master craftsmen who promised to teach them the "art and mystery" of their trade. In a typical contract, apprentices agreed to work for seven years or until the age of twenty-one, whichever came first, and to be obedient. In return masters agreed to provide food, clothing, and in some cases education. They also agreed to provide apprentices with a new suit of clothes at the end of their term. Since boys were not usually apprenticed out until the age of twelve to fourteen, Samuel was young to learn a trade, but he probably spent most of his time doing menial chores: sweeping floors, fetching water from the well, tending the fire, or running errands for his master.[7]

Sarah may have hesitated to send her only child away from home, but her decision might have seemed like the best one for him. If she had ever hoped to send him to college (one can imagine her dreaming that he would become a respected minister like her uncle John Guyse), she had to face a more sobering reality when she and Henry went bankrupt. By indenturing Samuel to a master craftsman, she hoped to give him the skills to escape their poverty. Although it is not clear why she chose to send Samuel all the way to Rehoboth, a place that Hopkins described as a "country" town, she may have hoped to shield him from the temptations of urban life.[8] She would have shuddered at the thought of her son growing up to imitate her adolescent rebelliousness and her taste for "bad company." It is also possible that she may have had friends there. When she and her husband had been first married, they had spent several months visiting his friends in the "country."

Like other parents, Sarah may have also decided to apprentice out Samuel because of her fears of spoiling him. To explain why so many New England parents sent their children away from home, even parents who were financially well-off, Edmund S. Morgan has speculated that "Puritan parents did not trust themselves with their own children . . . they were afraid of spoiling them by too great affection."[9] Because Samuel was her only child and a living reminder of her first husband, Sarah may have worried that she would not be strict enough when he needed "correction." A firm master would help him mature into a responsible adult.

The danger was that masters might be *too* firm. As Sarah surely knew, apprentices were sometimes mistreated or abused. When Henry had been an apprentice, his master, a tailor, had tried to get out of paying for his food, lodging, or clothing, and the case had ended up in court. (His master was forced to pay more than thirty-three pounds in damages.) Years later, in 1740, Henry was called as a witness in a case involving an apprentice girl who often had been seen with whip marks on her back. Partly on the basis of his testimony, the court found the girl's mistress and master guilty of "abuse and hard usage" and released her from service.[10] If Sarah knew and trusted Samuel's master, she may have assured herself that he would be well treated, but she still may have found it frightening to place her only child in someone else's care.

Sarah's worst fears were realized on a September afternoon when she heard the "sorrowful news" that Samuel was "sick unto death." Desperate to see him while he was still alive, she rushed to tell Susanna Anthony, who quickly agreed to take care of her house and school, and then she found someone to lend her and Henry a horse for the journey. Rehoboth was twenty miles away, probably only a few hours from Newport by horseback, but as she thought of Samuel fighting for his life without her, the distance must have seemed immense.

What sustained her, as she remembered later, was her unexpected sense of God's presence. It would have been natural for her to have been overcome by anxiety or despair, but she claimed to have felt a sense of God's "goodness" instead. "On my way," she testified, "God gave me such a sense of his goodness to me in a thousand instances, that instead of sinking under my sorrow, my mind was employed in attention to, and blessing God for my mercies. Sometimes, that he [Samuel] was not snatched from me in a moment, by some awful accident—That he was not at so great a distance, but I might be allowed to go to him, with hopes of finding him yet alive."[11] Riding behind Henry for mile after mile, she thanked God for giving her the chance to see her son one last time.

It is impossible to know the degree to which Sarah's narrative reflects her true emotions during the days leading up to Samuel's death or her attempt to make sense of her grief in the days afterward. What is clear, however, is that when she finally found the strength to write about Samuel's death, she was determined to frame it as a story about God's mercy. Hoping to convince herself that Samuel had been saved, she filled her narrative with subtle allusions to biblical characters who had been healed by God. In the first sentence, "On Thursday afternoon, the sixth day of this month, I had the sorrowful news that my only son was sick unto death," she implicitly compared Samuel to Epaphroditus, an associate of the apostle Paul's who had been "sick nigh unto death: but God had mercy on him," and to Hezekiah, who had beseeched God for mercy when he had been "sick unto death." "I have heard thy prayer," God had responded; "I have seen thy tears: behold, I will heal thee."[12] Without explicitly claiming that God had shown Samuel the same compassion, she nonetheless began her story on a hopeful note. Perhaps God had answered Samuel's prayers for mercy—or her own.

When describing her horseback journey to Rehoboth, Sarah continued to weave comforting biblical allusions into her narrative. After remembering her powerful sense of God's goodness, she wrote, "And those precious promises which in the morning had supported me, still continued as a refreshing cordial; even these. 'Call upon me in the day of trouble, and I will hear thee. This poor man cried, and the Lord heard him; and saved him out of all his troubles.'" Besides alluding to the apostle Peter's assurance that God had made "exceeding great and precious promises" to save humankind from sin, she also remembered how God had pledged to save Jacob in his time of trouble. Most comforting, she recalled the calming words of Psalm 86: "For thou, Lord, art good, and ready to forgive; and plenteous in mercy unto all them that call upon thee. Give ear, O Lord, unto my prayer; and attend to the voice of my supplications. In the day of my trouble I will call upon thee: for thou wilt answer me."[13] As Sarah explained, these words "supported" her, holding her up on the long road to Rehoboth.

Yet when Sarah began to describe her reunion with Samuel, she lost her tone of composure. She would never be able to forget her first, shocking glimpse of her son on his deathbed. "I found my son much swelled with a dropsy," she wrote, "and pined to a mere skeleton with the jaundice, scurvy and consumption, all combining. He rattled in his throat, like a dying person, laboring for every breath."[14] His skin had turned yellow because his liver was not functioning properly; he had rickets because of malnourishment; his thin body was grotesquely swollen with excess fluid that his kidneys could not eliminate; and he was feverish and coughing up blood because of tuberculosis. As his lungs slowly filled with fluid, he had begun to make the ominous rattling sound that often precedes death. The doctor told Sarah what she could plainly see and hear: there was no hope.

While Samuel's doctor and his friends "lamented him, and did the best for him in their power, as to the body," Sarah tried to look beyond his physical pain in order to minister to his spiritual needs. Others could express their love by caring for Samuel's body—bathing his feverish forehead with a cool cloth, helping him take small sips of water, changing his sweat-soaked sheets—but only she could prepare him to meet his creator. "My great concern was for that precious jewel, his immortal soul," she wrote.[15] Nothing was more important than his relationship to God.

Sarah had been praying for Samuel's salvation ever since she had felt his first fluttering movements during her pregnancy. Closely identifying herself with the biblical Hannah, whose son had become a prophet, Sarah had "dedicated" her son to God after his birth, and she had also brought him to her church to be baptized. Although she knew that not all baptized infants would be saved, she believed with other Congregationalists that most would become "children of the covenant."[16]

Many bereaved parents seem to have found this covenant theology deeply reassuring. When Esther Edwards Burr, Jonathan Edwards's daughter, lost an infant, she never seems to have doubted that her child had ascended to a "glorious state."[17] Despite her grief, she could imagine her child rejoicing in heaven because of her faith in God's covenantal promises.

But Samuel was no longer an infant, and Sarah could not share this optimism. Although her memories of bringing him to the baptismal font may have brought her a small measure of comfort, she needed something more. Samuel was almost twelve years old, an age when he could be expected to affirm his identity as a child of the covenant, but he had not yet experienced conversion. There had been no passionate confessions of sinfulness, no tears of repentance, no overpowering joy.

If Samuel had lived a century earlier, few Congregationalist ministers would have suggested that he was old enough to be capable of true conversion. Writing in 1638, the Reverend Thomas Hooker claimed that a child of ten or twelve years lived the "life of a beast" and lacked the capacity "to consider of the mysteries of life and salvation."[18] Yet during the revivals of the 1730s and 1740s, many ministers claimed that God had poured out his grace on children as well as adults. They seem to have viewed children's extraordinary conversions as proof that the revivals were genuine. How else could they make sense of the sight of "Children of about ten, twelve, and fourteen Years old" crying aloud or rejoicing in Christ?[19]

Since we do not have diaries or letters written by evangelical children, it is impossible to know how they felt about the revivals. If some may have felt empowered by the message that they, like adults, were capable of genuine, life-transforming faith, others may have faced intense pressure to convert. In special children's sermons, they heard that if they did not repent, they would spend eternity in hell. "You are both by Life and Nature most abominable and guilty Sinners," thundered the Reverend Thomas Prince, "and out of Christ God utterly abhors you and is angry with you."[20] Jonathan Edwards was equally blunt. In a sermon preached to children (probably between the ages of seven and sixteen) in his congregation in 1741, he argued that "God is very angry at the sins of children," angry enough "to cast them into hell to all eternity." If they did not convert they deserved "to burn in hell forever." He ended his sermon with a chilling question: "If you should die while you are young, and death should come upon you and find you without any love to Christ, what will become of you?"[21]

We do not know whether Samuel was ever asked to answer such an alarming question, but Sarah clearly believed that children, like adults, could be damned. As she sat beside Samuel's bed, listening to the rattle of his breathing, she was tormented by anxiety about his salvation. What if God had not chosen him as one of the elect? Protestants did not believe in Purgatory, and she could not hope that he might ascend to heaven after being cleansed of sin. He was destined either to be saved or to be damned: there was no intermediate place of purification. As a Boston minister explained, "At Death the SOUL of every Man enters *immediately* into a State of unspeakable *Joys*, or unsufferable *Torments*."[22] If Samuel were not ready to meet God at the moment of his death, he would suffer for eternity. Although Sarah could not bring herself even to write the word in her diary, she was terrified that he might go to hell.

Sarah and other evangelicals did not imagine hell as a metaphor for the sinner's alienation from God; it was a horrifyingly real place where the wicked were punished. According to Gilbert Tennent, who had revived her faith during his 1741 visit to Newport, only the foolish would doubt the reality of hell. They would soon discover the enormity of their mistake. Imagining the damned, he wrote, "Hear how loudly they roar, how frightfully they screech and yell; see how they rage and foam, and gnash their teeth with desperate madness; and look how the malicious Devils torment and rack those forlorn damned Castoffs." Searching for the words to convey the terrible anguish of the damned, another minister wrote: "Fancy to yourselves a Man devoured with Worms, burning in Flames, in whose Wounds kindled brimstone is poured without Intermission, with boiling Lead, and burning Pitch, and if there be any pains more grievous, fancy it also. All these give us but an imperfect Image of the State of the Damned." Hell was "a Place and State of the blackest Darkness, the most exquisite

Torment and extremest Horror, Despair, and Raging Blasphemy. A Place of Howling, Roaring, Yelling, Shrieking."[23]

Although Puritan ministers had always preached about hell, eighteenth-century evangelicals seem to have placed even greater emphasis on its torments. During the excitement of the revivals, many ministers used fear to persuade sinners to repent. In his early sermons Jonathan Edwards had tended to emphasize God's love, but he found that he could bring far more converts into the churches by preaching about hellfire.[24] In his most famous sermon, *Sinners in the Hands of an Angry God*, he portrayed God as a forbidding judge who had no qualms about throwing the wicked into the flames. "The God that holds you over the pit of hell, much as one holds a spider, or some loathsome insect over the fire, abhors you, and is dreadfully provoked," he warned. "His wrath towards you burns like fire; he looks upon you as worthy of nothing else, but to be cast into the fire; he is of purer eyes than to bear to have you in his sight; you are ten thousand times more abominable in his eyes, than the most hateful venomous serpent is in ours." When he preached these words, "there was a great moaning and crying out throughout the whole house. What shall I do to be saved. Oh I am going to Hell. Oh what shall I do for Christ."[25] Terror was clearly an effective weapon in the evangelical arsenal.

Evangelical ministers may have particularly emphasized the reality of hell because of humanitarian challenges to the doctrine in the late seventeenth and eighteenth centuries. As Norman Fiering has commented, "it appears that hell preaching grew in frequency when the orthodox doctrine of the afterlife was seriously challenged."[26] Thomas Hobbes, for example, expressed incredulity that "the Father of Mercies . . . should punish men's transgressions without any end of time, and with all the extremity of torture, that men can imagine, and more." More cautiously, John Tillotson admitted that there was biblical support for the doctrine of eternal punishment, but in a clever twist of reasoning he denied that God always carried out his threats. "He that threatens keeps the right of punishing in his own hand," he explained, "and is not obliged to execute what he hath threatened any further than the reasons and ends of Government do require."[27] Because belief in hell was an accepted part of Christian doctrine, few New England ministers dared question it openly, but some seem to have harbored private doubts. During the 1750s, for example, Charles Chauncy began working on a treatise about universal salvation that he did not dare publish until 1784. (His work was so secret that he and his friends referred to it in code as the "pudding.")[28]

In contrast, Sarah Osborn did not seem to have any doubts about God's justice in sentencing sinners to damnation. Terrified by the thought of Samuel descending to hell, she tried to be the means of his deathbed conversion. Praying for some sign of faith, she read to him from the Bible (she did not specify which passages) as well as from Joseph Alleine's popular *An Alarm to Unconverted Sinners*.[29] First published in 1671, this book was frequently reprinted in both England and America throughout the eighteenth century. Perhaps Sarah brought it with her from Newport because of her fears that Samuel would die unconverted; or perhaps she found a copy at his lodgings. Whichever the case, she clearly hoped that Alleine's "alarming" words would change Samuel's heart.

Alleine's book was addressed to all the "miserable souls"—"the Ignorant, Carnal, and Ungodly"—who had not yet experienced conversion. Hoping to persuade sinners to repent and seek salvation, Alleine lamented that they would never go to heaven without the help of God's grace. Stringing together quotations from Revelation, Matthew, and the Psalms, he warned, "The unconverted Soul is a very Cage of unclean Birds . . . a Sepulcher full of corruption and rottenness . . . a loathsome Carcass, full of crawling Worms, and sending forth a hellish and most noisome Savor in the Nostrils of God." Anyone who secretly hoped to be saved without being spiritually reborn was deluded. "I must tell you," he protested, "Christ never died to save impenitent and unconverted sinners." Indeed, God hated sinners so much that he would rejoice at their suffering. "He laughs in himself, to see how thou wilt be taken and ensnared in the evil Day," Alleine wrote in a particularly harrowing passage. "He sees how thou wilt come down mightily in a Moment, how thou wilt wring thine Hands, and tear thine Hair, and eat thy flesh, and gnash thy Teeth for Anguish and Astonishment of Heart, when thou seest thou art fallen . . . into the Pit of Destruction." Unless they turned to God while there was still time, sinners would "dwell with everlasting Burnings!"[30]

Not all of Alleine's book was this frightening. In his closing chapters, he tried to lead his readers from despair to hope. After describing God's wrath and the horrors of hell, he vowed that even the greatest sinner could be converted and welcomed into heaven. "Verily, if thou wouldst but come in," he assured his readers, "the heavenly Host would take up their Anthems, and sing, *Glory be to God in the Highest*; the Morning-Stars would sing together, and all the Sons of God shout for joy, and celebrate this new Creation as they did the first."[31] But there was no time to waste. Sinners had to begin seeking God *now*, before death and damnation.

It is not clear what sections of Alleine's book Sarah read to her son as he lay dying. But given her anxieties about his salvation, she probably chose passages that were designed to convince him of his sinfulness and his need for God's grace. Although some people may have thought she was cruel to fill his last days with thoughts of hell, she clearly believed that she was being a good mother. The ultimate fate of his soul was far more important than any qualms about frightening him. As Alleine explained to his readers, he did not want to hurt them, but he was like a "Surgeon" who had to "cut off a putrefied Member from his well-beloved Friend; which of force he must do, but with an aching heart, a pitiful Eye, a trembling Hand."[32]

Sarah, like Alleine, may have trembled, but she knew what she had to do. The scene is almost too painful to imagine. While Samuel lay gasping for breath, she sat by his side reading the book aloud, praying for some small sign of conversion. She was desperate, frightened, overwhelmed, "crushed" by grief. "I did not so much as once, in all his sickness, pray for his life," she remembered, "but for some evidence that his soul might live. And for want of this, I sometimes seemed to be crushed down, having a sense of his doleful case, if not reconciled to God." As for Samuel, it is impossible to know whether he even understood what his mother was reading to him; her words may have skimmed the surface of his physical pain. Perhaps he slipped in and out of consciousness as he clung to life. But if he did understand, he may have spent his last days in fear. Many of Alleine's words sounded as if they could have been written especially for him: "What if the Thread of thy life should break? (Why thou knowest not but it may be the next Night, yes, the next Moment.) Where wouldst thou be then? Whither wouldst thou drop?"[33]

Because Sarah had heard many stories of people joyfully turning to Christ in their dying moments, she seems to have clung to the hope that Samuel's life would end on a triumphant note. Just a little more than a month earlier, Deborah Prince, a twenty-one-year-old Boston woman who was probably one of Sarah's acquaintances, had experienced a dramatic conversion on her deathbed. According to her father, the Reverend Thomas Prince (a well-known revivalist), she had been in despair during her final illness, which had lasted more than seven weeks, because of her sense of distance from God. "She could not come to Christ," she lamented to her father. "She could not trust in Him, she could not believe." But just when she "seemed to be dying away," leaving her family in anguish, she suddenly opened her eyes and began speaking a "new Language" of Christian love. "I Believe in him! I Rejoice in Him!" she exclaimed. When she took her last breaths, her family was too overjoyed to mourn. "Never did I see so much *Distress*, especially round a dying Bed, on a sudden turn into so much *Joy*," her father marveled later.[34] Regardless of whether Sarah had heard this particular story, she certainly had heard many others like it, and she prayed that God would show her and her son the same mercy.

Samuel lingered on the edge of death for seven agonizing days. Each day, Sarah pleaded with God for some hard, undeniable "evidence" that her son would be saved. In a new evangelical world, in which converts claimed to know the exact moment of their spiritual rebirth, she wanted nothing less than empirical proof of Samuel's salvation. Remembering the story of Jacob, who had finally received a blessing after wrestling with God all night, she resolved to "plead and wrestle" for Samuel's salvation until winning her "evidence"—perhaps a gentle smile as he listened to a biblical passage or, even better, a few last words expressing his love for Christ.[35]

But an all-powerful, mysterious God refused to divulge his will. "God was pleased to hide his dealings with him altogether," she wrote sorrowfully. "For I could discern no evidence of a work of grace wrought on his soul, for which I did plead from day to day."[36]

Sarah's confrontation with the hiddenness of God brought her to the brink of despair. While she believed that God had revealed himself in Christ, she also believed that God had not revealed *everything*: predestination, in particular, was ultimately mysterious. No mere human could fathom God's secrets. But to move beyond an understanding of God's revealed will, as the theologian Brian Gerrish has explained, "is to find oneself in a terrifying darkness, a maze without exit, a pathless waste, a bottomless whirlpool, inextricable snares, an abyss of sightless darkness."[37] Sarah stood on the edge of the unfathomable, terrified by the chasm between her small human life and the immensity of God. She had spent her life trying to know God, and yet in this moment God was hidden. If he had heard her prayers for Samuel's salvation, he "was pleased" not to answer. God was silent, inscrutable, uncontrollable, majestic, incomprehensible. Terrifying.

Sarah felt as though both she and her son had been forsaken. "I was just ready to give up, and sit down discouraged," she remembered. "My heart even almost died with fear of what would become of him."[38]

Gerrish has argued that for the Christian believer the only possible response to the hiddenness of God is to embrace Christ, who "was destined to take upon himself the agony of a man forsaken by God." This was the same advice that Susanna Anthony, in Newport, gave to Sarah in a letter. Sarah seems to have written to her friend soon after arriving in Rehoboth, describing herself as "crushed" by her "Burthen." In response, Susa urged her to put her complete faith in Christ. "Has our God and Father put this cup into your hand? Then drink it, my dear, with submission, love, and fear;—forget the cup, while you behold the hand which gives it to you." Christ had not abandoned her, she promised. "Hath he not said, you are as the apple of his eye—and will he hurt that? No! Surely, he will not!" (Susa clearly knew that Psalm 17:8—"Keep me as the apple of the eye, hide me under the shadow of thy wings"—was one of Sarah's favorite texts.) She urged Sarah not to give up hope but to continue praying. "O, arise, and by faith cast your child upon Christ," she wrote. "Tell him he is your only son, and you want a pardon for him; and will not he, who is an inexhaustible fountain,—a boundless ocean of infinite fullness, be as ready to pity the soul of your son, as he was to pity the bodies of those who came to him for healing, in the days of his flesh? Verily, the promises are to believers and their children."[39]

But even if Sarah never received "comfortable evidence" of Samuel's salvation, and even if, Susa implied, he died unconverted, God's will could not be questioned. "O do not fall out, with your Father!" Susa urged. "Kiss the hand, though it have a rod in it—it is the hand of *your* God still." While Susa knew that the hiddenness of God was frightening, she reminded Sarah that because he was ultimately in control, they had no choice but to submit to his punishments. "O my dear," Susa implored her, "you and I may, yea, must love him, because he is a *Sovereign* God!" There was nothing to do except to trust "the Father of Mercies, the God and Father of our Lord Jesus Christ!"[40]

Many Christians at the time would have recoiled at the image of God standing above Sarah with a rod in his hand, or of Sarah kissing his hand in meek submission. But Sarah claimed to have been comforted by Susa's letter, which she described as "a cordial to my drooping spirits."[41] Confronted with the awful possibility of Samuel's damnation, she tried to do as Susa told her. She turned her gaze away from God's hiddenness toward his revelation in Christ, desperately praying for mercy.

Sarah spent Samuel's last hours in an agony of fear and prayer. "In his dying moments," she remembered later, "I had an awful sense of his deplorable condition, if his naked soul should launch into a boundless eternity, without a God to go to." She felt as though the two of them were utterly helpless and defenseless—two small specks in a vast universe. "I had also a view and sense of his and my utter inability to help ourselves, and utter unworthiness that God should help us," she confessed. But strengthened

by Susa's words, she prayed that Christ would heal Samuel's soul just as
he had once healed the sick during his time on earth. Three biblical stories in particular gave her hope. When the woman of Canaan had begged
Jesus to heal her afflicted daughter, he had at first refused: "It is not meet
to take the children's bread, and to cast it to dogs." But when the woman
persisted, saying, "Truth, Lord: yet the dogs eat of the crumbs which fall
from their masters' table," Jesus had praised her for her faith and healed
her child. Comparing herself to the Canaanite woman, Sarah confessed
that she was "unworthy as a dog," but still she "pleaded for the crumbs
that fell, one of which would be sufficient for me and mine. I had a clear
discovery of the fullness and sufficiency of Christ to make satisfaction."
Sarah was also comforted by the story of the thief who had been crucified
next to Jesus. "Lord, remember me when thou comest into thy kingdom,"
the thief had pleaded. And a merciful Jesus had replied, "Verily I say unto
thee, Today shalt thou be with me in paradise." Recalling this story, Sarah
wrote, "I pleaded that he would have mercy, as on the thief on the cross,
then at the eleventh hour; apply but one drop of his precious blood, and it
was enough." Finally, Sarah once again compared herself to Jacob, one of
her favorite biblical characters. "I was enabled to fill my mouth with arguments, and in bitter agony of soul I wrestled with God for him. Surely the
pangs I then endured for his soul far exceeded those that brought him into
the world."[42] Like Jacob, she refused to stop wrestling until God gave his
blessing. Perhaps if she prayed with all her might, Samuel's defenseless,
"naked soul" might go to heaven.

Up to this point in her narrative, Sarah seemed to be preparing to
affirm that God had saved her son. From the first sentence, she had inter-
spersed her narrative with allusions to biblical figures whose prayers had
been answered or who had been healed: Epaphroditus, Hezekiah, the Canaanite woman, the thief on the cross, Jacob. In her last sentences before
recording Samuel's death, she described being "enabled" to pray for him,
suggesting that God had been helping her. By comparing her "pangs" in
prayer to labor pains, she implied that she had helped give birth to him
again, this time in Christ.

But when the moment finally came to describe Samuel's death, she
shrank back, afraid to affirm a mercy that God might not have bestowed.
Without concrete "evidence" of Samuel's conversion, she did not dare claim
that he had gone to heaven. She was afraid of sounding presumptuous,
afraid of angering God. Humbled by God's awful power, the power to save
or damn, she seemed fearful of speaking in her own voice. Her brief sen-

tences describing Samuel's death were rephrasings of biblical verses. Echoing one of the Psalms, "Cast thy burden upon the Lord, and he shall sustain thee," she wrote, "As soon as the soul had taken its flight, I was eased of my burden. I immediately cast myself, and my burden too, on God."[43] Then, repeating the words of Job, she added, "I adored him as a sovereign God, and blessed his name; for he had given, and it was he who had taken." She concluded with a heartbreaking reference to the story of Hannah and Samuel, which had always been deeply meaningful to her. In the past, Sarah had always reflected on this story from Hannah's viewpoint. Like Hannah, she had rejoiced at the birth of a son whom she had dedicated to God. This time, however, she remembered the words of Hannah's husband, Elkanah. When Hannah had been praying for a child, he had urged her to stop weeping and grieving, asking her, "Am not I better to thee than ten sons?" As Sarah remembered the sight of Samuel's lifeless body, she could no longer hope that Hannah's story would be her own. She would never see God bless her son; he would never grow into a great spiritual leader. Bereft, she clung to Jesus, her spiritual husband, for comfort. "Surely," she wrote, "he was better to me than ten sons."[44]

A Covenant God

In the great Christian story, darkness is always followed by light, suffering by redemption, death by resurrection. When ministers preached funeral sermons, they almost always concluded by imagining the dead exulting with Christ. In 1732, for example, after the death of a seventeen-year-old who had been "eminently pious," the Reverend Charles Chauncy assured her grieving parents that she was in "heavenly happiness."[45] God always saved those in covenant with him.

This was the kind of story that Sarah had longed to tell. When she had begun writing about Samuel's death, she seems to have hoped to find a way to narrate it as a parable about divine mercy. Perhaps she thought that if she relived his last days, she might find some overlooked "evidence" of his salvation. Tragically, she failed.

Yet rather than face the horrifying possibility that all her "wrestling" with God had been for naught, Sarah reframed her narrative into a story about God's mercy to *her*, not to her son. Ultimately the story she decided to tell in her diary, probably unconsciously and intuitively, was not about Samuel at all, but about her own covenant with God. Struggling with feelings of anxiety and grief, she seems to have tried to comfort herself by turning her gaze inward. Having failed to find "evidence" of Samuel's salvation, she remembered how God had upheld her during her sorrow. By writing about herself, she could still find a way to turn the story of Samuel's death into a tale of God's goodness.

If Sarah felt any of the emotions that one might expect in the wake of such a devastating loss—anger at God for taking away her only child, despair, hopelessness—she never admitted it. Instead, she claimed that as soon as Samuel died she calmly accepted God's will, renewing her trust in him despite her suffering. "I then arose from my dead child, and was quieted," she explained, "for the will of God was done, and my work was done, as it respected my child." Her model was David, who fasted and wept until his son's death but then "arose from the earth, and washed, and anointed himself, and changed his apparel, and came into the house of the Lord, and worshipped."[46] Since Samuel's fate had been sealed at his death, there was nothing more for her to do.

Yet Sarah remembered that it was at this moment, when she seemed to be most alone, that God finally ceased to hide his face. In a startling sentence that marked a pivotal point in her narrative, she claimed that after she quietly arose from Samuel's deathbed, "God was pleased to give such evidence of his love that my mouth was filled with praises." (Here she was alluding to the uplifting words of Psalm 71: "I am as a wonder unto many; but thou art my strong refuge. Let my mouth be filled with thy praise and with thy honor all the day.")[47] Even though God had not sent the kind of evidence she had so desperately prayed for only minutes earlier—evidence of Samuel's salvation—she finally felt that he was present with her. As Susanna Anthony had assured her, the God who had taken away Samuel was still *her* God. He had not forgotten or abandoned her. He loved her still.

After exhorting Samuel's friends, "who stood round lamenting him," "to take warning, and make their speedy flight to the blessed Jesus, before sickness and death overtook them," Sarah went for a solitary walk in the autumn fields. Not even Henry went with her. Leaving others to prepare Samuel's body for burial, she sought a quiet place to commune with God. "And the sweetness of that season I cannot express," she wrote. After all the distress of the preceding week, she finally found peace. Like Julian of Norwich, the medieval visionary who had heard Christ assuring her that "all shall be well, and all shall be well, and all manner of things shall be well," she suddenly saw the smallness of her suffering in comparison to God's boundless love.[48] In an almost mystical encounter, "God discovered himself to be my God, my covenant God, my Father, my Friend, my only portion and happiness, my sovereign, my all in all, my infinite fountain of all full-ness." Everything else seemed to fade into nothingness, leaving her alone with God. "And these were some of the breathings of my soul after him," she remembered: "Lord, I adore thee as my all. I rejoice in thee as my only portion. Lord, if I have thee, I have enough. Though all the streams were cut off, yet the fountain remains; I cannot be poor. Whom have I in heaven but thee? And there is none on earth I desire besides thee. Though my flesh and my heart fail; yet God is the strength of my heart and my portion forever. Blessed God, though death separate from all things here below, It cannot separate between thee and me." She had lost her child, yet she still had a "Father" and "Friend" who would never forsake her. Drawing closer to God, she renewed the covenant she had first made with him seven years earlier. "O, here I rejoiced again, chose my God again, and again renewed the dedication of myself to him, my whole soul and body, with all I have, am, or can do."[49]

In this ineffable moment of unity with God, Sarah could even accept her grief as a reflection of his goodness. Affirming her belief that God held the world in his hands, ordering everything for the best, she claimed that her anguish was for her own good. "O, his word comforted, his *rod* comforted me," she remembered. "I saw no frown in it: No, but the kind chastisement of my indulgent Father." It was a refrain that she had repeated many times in her life: she, not God, was to blame for her suffering. Without explain-ing why she thought she deserved chastisement, she comforted herself by remembering a favorite verse from Hebrews. "This portion of scripture was very sweet," she wrote, "'If ye be without chastisement, whereof all are partakers, then are ye bastards, and not sons. For whom the Lord loveth, he chasteneth.'" Samuel's death was a sign not that God had deserted her but, on the contrary, that he loved her. Echoing Psalm 19, she "cried out" to him, "I know, O Lord, thy judgments are right, and in very faithfulness thou hast afflicted me."[50]

Sarah's language in these passages was densely biblical. Struggling to express herself, she seems to have been flooded by memories of relevant biblical texts. (Since her quotations were not exact, she probably did not have a Bible open in front of her but cited verses from memory.) As al-ways, her experiences seemed less confusing and less random when she placed them within a biblical framework. When she remembered her sense of closeness to God, for example, and asked "Whom have I in heaven but thee?" she was repeating the words of Psalm 73. She had absorbed so much of the Bible that any one of her sentences could refer to several different texts at once. Indeed, when she rejoiced that God had "discovered himself to be my God, my covenant God, my Father, my Friend, my only portion and happiness, my sovereign, my all in all, my infinite fountain of all fullness," she was weaving together references from Genesis ("I will establish my covenant between me and thee"), Hebrews ("I will make a new covenant"), Romans and Galatians ("Abba, Father"), Matthew ("a friend of publicans and sinners"), the Song of Solomon ("this is my beloved, and this is my friend"), Lamentations and the Psalms ("The Lord is my portion"), and Revelation ("I will give unto him that is athirst of the fountain of the water of life freely").[51] By grafting her personal story onto the Bible, she reassured herself that her experiences were not singular. Many others before her—including David and Job—had walked the same path.

If Sarah shared her narrative with Christian friends during her life (which seems likely), they may have been particularly moved by her description of God as her "portion." Modern readers (who tend not to be as biblically literate) might miss the significance of her imagery, but Sarah's friends would have known that she was echoing several biblical texts that captured her complicated emotions. Perhaps she had in mind the comforting language of Psalm 16, "The Lord is the portion of my inheritance and of my cup. . . . Therefore my heart is glad," but she may have also been referring to the lonely words of Psalm 142: "refuge failed me; no man cared for my soul. I cried unto thee, O Lord: I said, Thou art my refuge and my portion in the land of the living." Given her grief, she also may have been repeating Jeremiah's heartrending description of being afflicted by God:

> *I AM the man that hath seen affliction by the rod of his wrath. . . . He hath hedged me about, that I cannot get out: he hath made my chain heavy. Also when I cry and shout, he shutteth out my prayer. He hath inclosed my ways with hewn stone, he hath made my paths crooked. He was unto me as a bear lying in wait, and as a lion in secret places. He hath turned aside my ways, and pulled me in pieces: he hath made me desolate. . . . He hath filled me with bitterness, he hath made me drunken with wormwood. He hath also broken my teeth with gravel stones, he hath covered me with ashes. . . . It is of the Lord's mercies that we are not consumed, because his compassions fail not. They are new every morning: great is thy faithfulness. The Lord is my portion, saith my soul; therefore I will hope in him. [Lamentations 3:1, 5–11, 15–16, 22–24]*

Although it is impossible to recapture Sarah's intentions when she described God as her portion, she may have been drawn to this evocative image because of its multiple meanings. Her words gestured toward both despair and hope. Reading her narrative, her friends would have understood that these small words encapsulated both her sense of desolation and her enduring faith.

Sarah was particularly drawn to biblical descriptions of God's covenant with his chosen people. Following the advice of ministers like Cotton Mather, who urged the afflicted to put their faith in God's covenant, she consoled herself by remembering God's promise to Abraham in the book of Genesis: "And I will establish my covenant between me and thee and thy seed after thee in their generations for an everlasting covenant, to be a God unto thee, and to thy seed after thee." Although she applied this language only to herself, avowing that "God discovered himself to be my God, my covenant God," she may have been quietly thinking of Samuel as well.[52] By asserting her own covenant with God, she implicitly raised the possibility that Samuel had shared it. Hadn't God promised that his covenant would extend to her "seed," her son?

Yet Sarah never dared ask this question openly, and a darker fear pulsed beneath her words. Perhaps unconsciously, she alluded to several biblical texts that pointed in alarming directions. When she remembered feeling "bowels of compassion" for Samuel's friends and exhorting them to "take warning, and make their speedy flight to the blessed Jesus," for example, she mixed an allusion to 1 John about keeping God's commandments with a more frightening reference to Ezekiel 33: whoever "taketh not warning" would die "in iniquity." Thirty years earlier, the Reverend Samuel Moodey, a Massachusetts minister, had used this text to warn the children in his congregation to repent. "Why will ye die, O children of New England?" he asked. "Poor Hearts; you are going to Hell indeed; but will it not be a dreadful thing to go to Hell from New England, from this Land of Light to that Dungeon of Eternal Darkness?"[53] Given Sarah's knowledge of the Bible, she may have known, on some level, that she was citing a passage that threatened "the death of the wicked," but she quickly moved away from this frightening possibility to emphasize her trust in Christ.

Several other passages in Sarah's joyful description of divine grace also hinted at God's wrath. When she remembered the beautiful words of Psalm 73, "Though my flesh and my heart fail; yet God is the strength of my heart and my portion forever," she neglected to cite the verses that followed: "For, lo, they that are far from thee shall perish: thou hast destroyed all them that go a whoring from thee." Giving her allusion to the Psalm a new, more comforting ending, she paraphrased Romans 8: "Blessed God, though death separate from all things here below, it cannot separate between thee and me." Similarly, when she described God as a "fountain," she may have been referring to the comforting words of Revelation, "I will give unto him that is athirst of the fountain of the water of life freely," but the next verses were more ominous: "He that overcometh shall inherit all things; and I will be his God, and he shall be my son. But the fearful, and unbelieving, and the abominable, and murderers, and whoremongers, and sorcerers, and idolaters, and all liars, shall have their part in the lake which burneth with fire and brimstone: which is the second death."[54] All these elisions suggest that despite her description of her rapturous feeling of God's presence in the fields, Sarah was still deeply troubled about her son.

Was Samuel in heaven or in hell? This question haunts every sentence of Sarah's narrative, even the sentences that do not explicitly mention him at all.

Suffer Me to Weep

When Sarah returned from her walk in the fields, she found her friends preparing Samuel's body for burial. They gently took off his blood-stained clothes, straightened his limbs, washed him, dressed him in his grave clothes (probably the best clothes that he owned), and lifted him into a plain wooden coffin. Then they took turns sitting next to his body to make sure there were no unexpected signs of life. Because embalming was uncommon in early America, burials usually took place within a day or two, but first it was customary to watch over the body to guarantee that the person was truly dead. After Hannah Heaton buried her eighteen-month-old daughter only a few hours after death, she was haunted by fears that she might have buried her alive. "It would dart into my soul your child was not cold," she agonized in her diary. "It might have come to again."[55] If Sarah's friends had hoped to spare her the same anxiety, they would have made sure that someone was always at Samuel's side until the final prayer had been offered and the coffin lid had been nailed shut.

Despite the solemn sight of her son lying lifeless in his coffin, Sarah claimed that in the hours before the funeral she was so "composed and comfortable" that she feared people might think her "void of natural affection."[56] While a psychologist today might interpret her stoicism as a form of denial (a common stage in grief), Sarah attributed her serenity to her abiding sense of God's presence. Even in the midst of the most wrenching loss she had ever endured, she emphasized her quiet resignation to God's sovereign will.

Since all that we have are Sarah's written words, it is impossible to know whether she was as "composed and comfortable" as she maintained. But it is clear that in her closing pages she was still trying to discern God's goodness in her suffering, and she found it in her spirit of resignation. Desperate to make sense of Samuel's death, she claimed that God had taken her son for two reasons: to make her more dependent on his divine grace and to show other Christians how to accept their afflictions without "murmuring."

Influenced by ministers, the books that she read, her friends, and the larger transatlantic evangelical community, Sarah seems to have deliberately tried to suppress her grief. Given the number of people who died prematurely in early America, whether because of childhood diseases, epidemics, or accidents ("This World is a Weeping World," one minister wrote forlornly), it is not surprising that ministers urged their congregants to bear their losses patiently. Although the Reverend Henry Gibbs denied that Christianity taught "Stoical Apathy," he also warned that grief must not become "exorbitant; bursting forth in unbecoming speeches and actions." "We are to Mourn without Murmuring, and Weep without repining," he urged, "not entertaining any hard thoughts of God, not allowing any swellings of spirit against His disposals." Other ministers stated the point more roughly. "Be *dumb*," warned the Reverend Nathaniel Appleton, "and *open not your mouths*, in the least Murmurings under this severe Correction of our heavenly Father." (He was quoting from Psalm 39:9: "I was dumb, I opened not my mouth, because thou didst it.") If they "murmured," they might suffer the same fate as the Israelites who had been punished for murmuring against God in the wilderness. (Because of their bitter complaints, God had sentenced them to wander in the wilderness for forty years before allowing them into the promised land.)[57] In hundreds of sermons published in the decades before Samuel's death, ministers urged Christians to "regulate" or "moderate" their mourning. They were told to imitate the examples of Aaron, who had "held his peace" after his two sons were devoured by the Lord's fire; Job, who covered his mouth with his hand after realizing that an all-powerful God had willed his suffering; Joseph, who had not condemned his brothers for selling him into slavery because it had been God's will; David, who had meekly testified that God could "do to me as seemeth good unto him"; and Christ himself, who, as Isaiah foretold, "was oppressed, and afflicted, yet he opened not his mouth."[58]

There were several reasons for ministers' strict prohibitions on "excessive" mourning. Because of their emphasis on God's sovereignty, they interpreted complaining about the loss of loved ones as a challenge to his will. "Christians should quietly Submit to the Holy Sovereign Will of GOD, under all the sore Afflictions they ever meet with," advised Benjamin Wadsworth. Although it was natural to grieve over the loss of loved ones, Christians would be guilty of the worst kind of hubris if they questioned God's right to decide who should live and who should die. Did they dare to imagine that they knew better than God how to govern the world?[59]

Ministers also feared that if Christians succumbed to their grief, they would forget that their suffering was supposed to be "profitable." In the midst of mourning, they should remember that God had chosen to afflict them for their own good. As Nathanael Appleton explained, God "does not *afflict willingly* nor *grieve his Children*, but only when he sees they *need* to be in heaviness, then he corrects them for their Profit, to make them *Partakers* of his *Holiness*." If they honestly believed that God had ordained their sorrows "as "*Physic*, as *Medicine* for the good of their Souls," then Christians should swallow their grief in order to praise God for his mercy.[60]

Most important, ministers warned that Christians who indulged in too much mourning might not be genuine Christians at all. *Real* Christians loved God more than anything or anyone else in the world—even more than children, friends, spouses, or parents. As the Reverend Thomas Skinner explained, we should not "set our Hearts and Affections too much upon our near Relatives, those pleasant enjoyments." Although Christians should love their families, they should not anger God by loving them "immoderately and excessively." Indeed, parents who spent too much time mourning the loss of children were almost certainly guilty of "idolatry."[61]

Although ministers generally agreed that Christians had to regulate their mourning, some were stricter than others. According to John Flavel, Christ had not meant his words "weep not" to be interpreted as "an absolute prohibition of tears and sorrow." "Christ would not have his People stupid and insensate," Flavel declared. "He only prohibits the excesses and extravagancies of our sorrows for the dead, that it should not be such a Mourning for the dead as is found among the Heathen, who sorrow without Measure, because without Hope, being ignorant of that grand relief by the Resurrection which the Gospel reveals."[62] Although Flavel insisted that Christians must submit quietly to God's will, his tone tended to be relatively gentle and comforting. By using the heathen as his antitype, he implicitly reassured his readers that their own tears were unlikely to be sinful. Even the weakest of Christians would not fall into the same "extravagancies" of despair as those who never had heard of Jesus. In contrast, Benjamin Wadsworth used more severe language by comparing excessive mourning to "Sedition or Mutiny." He envisioned a genuinely "Christian" mourner as utterly submissive, almost impossibly so. "Let us . . . lye quietly at Gods Foot," he exhorted, "under all the blows of his holy hand."[63]

Christianity, as the philosopher Charles Taylor has noted, has always been torn by conflicting attitudes toward everyday life. While Christians have affirmed the essential goodness of creation—in Genesis, God never creates anything, whether grass, stars, animals, or humans, without seeing that "it was good"—they have also believed that they must be willing to sacrifice this world's goodness for God. Ambivalent about how much they should value ordinary life, they have sometimes feared that marriage, parenthood, and work might interfere with their ability to be true Christians. Medieval Catholics, for example, claimed that priests and nuns were closer to God than the laity because of their spirit of renunciation, for they embraced poverty, celibacy, and charity in order to serve God alone. Yet in the wake of the Protestant Reformation, growing numbers of Christians insisted that it was possible to glorify God within the rhythms of ordinary life. As Taylor explains, they claimed that "the fullness of Christian existence was to be found within the activities of this life, in one's calling and in marriage and the family." Although the transformation was not immediate (as Sarah Osborn's story confirms), the Reformation gave birth to an affirmation of everyday life that has become one of the distinguishing features of the modern Western world. Enlightenment philosophers insisted that the meaning of human life could be found here on earth, not in a faraway heaven.[64]

But in the eighteenth century, when the affirmation of everyday life was still contested, many Christians seem to have feared loving their families too much. In 1753, for example, Experience Richardson, a Congregationalist from Massachusetts, worried that her continuing sorrow over her child's death was sinful. Confiding her feelings to her diary several months after her four-year-old son, Luther, had died, she fretted, "I fear I have sinned against God in distressing myself about the state of my child that is dead." She, like Sarah Osborn, seemed to be afraid that her son had not been saved. "I pray to God to give me a right spirit about this thing," she wrote plaintively. Similarly, when Hannah Heaton became severely ill, she was afraid that God was punishing her for "bitterly" mourning the deaths of her two children, an eighteen-month-old toddler and a three-week-old infant. Reflecting on her illness, she wrote in her diary, "I was in extreme misery and I believed it was for my wicked carriage under the rod." She was healed only when she promised God "never" to mourn for her children again. Although these examples may sound extreme, they were typical of many believers' experiences. Eighteenth-century evangelicals (like their Puritan ancestors) viewed losing a loved one as a spiritual test—a test that was dangerously easy to fail. When Sarah Prince Gill learned that her father was seriously ill, she knew that she should accept his impending death with "full resignation," but as she confessed to her diary, she could not do it. "Can't feel willing—My views are inexpressibly horrid," she wrote in anguish. More than a month later, as he continued to linger in "the valley of the Shadow of Death," she was still struggling with mixed feelings of sorrow, despair, and anger. "A Stubborn will raged within," she wrote. "I felt an Enmity rise against God in this his Dispensation." Only in the last half hour before his death did she accept God's will, finally proving to herself that she was a worthy Christian. "My Will [was] melted and brought to comply, and a happy Calm ensued."[65]

Sarah Osborn, too, prayed that God would give her the strength to accept her loss calmly, but as she gazed at Samuel in his coffin, his small body wrapped in a shroud, she began to lose her earlier composure. During her "last farewell at his funeral," all her repressed emotions suddenly flooded to the surface, and despite her attempts at self-control she began weeping. We can only imagine her thoughts as she looked down at his body, her cheeks wet with tears. Perhaps she remembered the small things—the way he had looked while carrying wood into the kitchen or the quiet conversations they had shared over her needlework in the evenings. Or perhaps she was haunted by the memory of his labored breathing as she had begged him to repent. "I found the bonds of natural affection very strong," she confessed, "and I wept much."[66] Although she wanted to be like David, who had accepted his child's tragic death in silence, she could not deny how deeply she had loved her son.

Although Sarah did not describe Samuel's funeral in detail, it was probably like others of the time: a simple affair that was held at a private house, with no sermon, no singing, and no testimonials. Following the example set by the Puritans, eighteenth-century Congregationalists tried to make funerals as plain as possible, stripping away all the rituals that could distract mourners from the stark reality of death. Wealthy families sometimes gave away mourning gloves, scarves, or rings as tokens of remembrance, but Sarah and Henry could not afford such expensive luxuries, and they may have marked the solemnity of the ceremony with nothing more than simple black clothing or black ribbons tied to their sleeves. After being called together by the tolling of a church bell, they and the other mourners would have listened quietly while a minister said a brief prayer, and then, after draping a pall over Samuel's coffin, they would have carried it in a slow procession to the graveyard.[67]

As she walked behind the pallbearers, weeping with every step, Sarah begged God to forgive her tears. Heartbroken at the loss of her son, she seems to have feared that God might abandon her as well, "hiding his face" from her as he had done many times before. "As I followed to the grave," she remembered, "I pleaded thus with God, 'Lord, I adore thee still as my sovereign. I do not repine at thy hand. But dear Lord, pity me, and suffer me to weep under the smart of thy rod; it is my *only son*.'" Praying that God would not be angered by her weakness, she searched her memory for a scriptural text that might ease her distress. "Then I thought on Psalm 53," she remembered. "'As a father pitieth his children, for the Lord pitieth them that fear him.' This comforted me." Still fearful that her tears might be "sinful, and the effect of an unresigned will," which she "dreaded most of all," she continued to pray for mercy until remembering that Jesus himself had wept over the loss of a loved one. "I was comforted again by reflecting, that when Martha and Mary wept for their brother Lazarus, the blessed Jesus was not angry, but wept with them." By the time that she stood at the edge of Samuel's freshly dug grave, watching the last shovels of earth cover his coffin, her thoughts had turned away from God's wrath to his humanity in Jesus. Imagining Jesus weeping over Lazarus just as she was weeping over her son, she wrote, "O, then again I adored a sympathizing savior, a glorious high priest, who was sensibly touched with the feeling of my infirmities." Strengthened by the knowledge that God still loved her despite her failings, she was finally able to dry her tears. "These and such like were the exercises of my mind, while following and laying my dust into the grave," she recorded. "And ever since I have been kept composed and cheerful."[68]

Just as she had done earlier in her narrative, Sarah filled her terse description of Samuel's funeral with biblical allusions, and this time almost all her references were hopeful. By echoing Job's cry "Have pity upon me, have pity upon me," she may have been implicitly reminding herself (and any friends who read her narrative) that God had finally answered Job's prayer, blessing him with a new family to take the place of those he had lost. (While many modern theologians tend to be troubled by Job's story, which portrays a sovereign God ruthlessly afflicting a perfectly just man, eighteenth-century evangelicals read it much more hopefully.) Just as God had taken pity on Job, he would take pity on her.

Most significant, Sarah also alluded to several biblical texts that seemed to offer hope for Samuel as well as herself. Her references to these texts were buried in sentences addressing her own relationship to Christ, not Samuel's, and she may not have been fully aware of what she was doing. When she described being comforted by Psalm 103 ("as a father pitieth his children, so the Lord pitieth them that fear him"), for example, it is not clear whether she was remembering that only four verses later the psalm promised that God would extend "his righteousness unto children's children." (Once again, she may have been quietly raising the possibility that Samuel had shared her covenant.) Given her biblical expertise, it is hard to believe that she was not aware of the hopeful references that lay submerged beneath her text, but perhaps she could not admit, even to herself, that she was still searching for evidence of Samuel's salvation—this time not in his personal experiences, but in the Bible.

Sarah's brief, mournful reference to Samuel as her *"only son"* was especially laden with meaning. Perhaps she was remembering the words of the prophet Jeremiah, "O daughter of my people, gird thee with sackcloth, and wallow thyself in ashes: make thee mourning, as for an only son, most bitter lamentation," or Amos, "I will turn your feasts into mourning . . . and I will make it as the mourning of an only son." But she may also have been thinking of the many "only sons" whom God had chosen to rescue from death, including his "only begotten son," Jesus Christ, who had been resurrected. From reading the Bible, Sarah also knew that God had spared Isaac, Abraham's "only son," as he lay upon the altar of sacrifice, and Jesus had granted the prayer of a distressed man whose only son had been possessed by an evil spirit. When the man had cried out, "Master, I beseech thee, look upon my son: for he is mine only child," Jesus had healed the child. Perhaps most meaningful for Sarah, Jesus had also taken compassion on a widow who had lost her "only son." When Jesus saw her weeping beside the funeral bier, he was so moved by her sorrow that he brought her son back to life. If Sarah was meditating on this text in the aftermath of Samuel's death (or while she was walking with a heavy heart to his grave), she may have wondered whether he, too, had been given a new life.

Yet despite the glimmers of hope lurking beneath the surface of her words, she never dared to speculate openly about what had happened to her son. All her hopes—and all her fears—about his salvation were hidden beneath her focus on her own individual relationship to God. Much of the power of her complex, multilayered narrative lies in the words that she could not bring herself to write.

In her closing sentences, Sarah tried to weave together all the disparate strands of her narrative into a coherent story, forcing her contradictory thoughts and emotions into a single framework of meaning. Abandoning her earlier attempt to tell an uplifting story about Samuel's salvation, she claimed that God had taken her son away in order to purify her, to make her more dependent on his grace, and to show other Christians how to bear the deaths of loved ones without "murmuring." "The Lord in mercy grant that I may more and more glorify him in this affliction," she wrote, echoing the words of Job. "O that my sins may be more mortified. Lord, grant I may come out of this furnace as gold purified and fitted for my master's use." (Here she echoed Isaiah's prophetic words, "I have refined thee, but not with silver; I have chosen thee in the furnace of affliction," as well as the story of the three men cast into the fiery furnace.) Once again her suffering had taught her that a covenant God would never abandon her. Quoting from Ephesians, a text that describes Christ choosing the saved even before the "foundation of the world," she praised God for sustaining her through his "glorious and special grace." If not for God's power in restraining her sinfulness, she surely would have murmured against him, rebelling against his sovereignty. In her words, "If I have behaved in any measure as becomes a child of God and any resignation has appeared in me, Lord, it is owing to the riches of thy glorious and special grace. For hadst not thou by that compelled me to act otherwise, I should have flew in thy face, murmured, fretted and repined at thee; cast away all my other comforts and mercies, and said I had none left, because thou hadst taken *one* from me." Concluding her narrative with a simple prayer of gratitude, she wrote, "Lord, these, and more than these, would have been the effects of my perverse nature. Therefore, not unto me, not unto me; but to thy glorious name be all the glory forever and ever. Amen."[69]

With these final words, Sarah placed her pen back in its stand, closed her ink bottle, and sprinkled sand on her pages to help them dry. Perhaps she also reminded herself, as she bowed her head in prayer, that she was supposed to be "composed and cheerful."

Lest My Heart Be Joined to Idols

Because we do not have Sarah's original manuscript, but only Samuel Hopkins's published version, there are many questions about her account of Samuel's death that we cannot answer. Most important, we do not know whether either Hopkins or his friend the Reverend Levi Hart, each of whom had a hand in editing her manuscripts, may have left out anything. In his brief discussion of Samuel's death, Hopkins implied that he had not published the full narrative. "She has recorded some of her exercises under this trial," he wrote, "*part of which* will be here inserted."[70] Although Hopkins does not seem to have made sweeping revisions to Sarah's manuscripts (tinkering with individual words instead), he sometimes cut entries short.

Out of sympathy for her, we might be tempted to wonder whether Sarah's original narrative was more optimistic about Samuel's salvation than what appeared in print. Yet it is unlikely that either Hopkins or Hart would have edited her account to make her sound less hopeful. Although Hopkins defended the reality of hell, he argued that children of the covenant would almost always be saved: God had "determined that real holiness and salvation shall briefly and ordinarily descend . . . from believing parents to their children. Therefore, He has ordered them all to be holy and to be numbered among the saved." Although Hopkins admitted that this covenant could be broken if parents were "negligent" about catechizing their children, he admired Sarah too much to suggest that she had been a "deficient" or "unfaithful" mother who had contributed to her child's damnation. Writing in 1792 (four years before he began editing her manuscripts for publication), and italicizing his words for emphasis, he explained, "*Real holiness and salvation are secured to the children of believers, by the covenant into which the parents enter with God as it respects their children, if the parents faithfully keep covenant, and fulfill what they profess and promise respecting their children, when they offer them in baptism.*"[71]

As for Levi Hart, who helped Hopkins edit Sarah's manuscripts, he, too, admired her, but based on his published writings he was probably troubled by her fear of mourning too much. In a sermon delivered in 1789 (before he had seen any of Sarah's writings), he denied that a verse from Ezekiel, "Forbear to cry, make no mourning for the dead," should be interpreted as a prohibition against mourning. Placing this passage in a broader context, he claimed that Ezekiel was predicting a time of such terrible divine judgments that "lamentations for deceased individuals should be lost in the general calamity." Instead of warning mourners to control their grief, Hart urged them to see their sorrows as a reflection of God's love for them. Just as they mourned over the loss of loved ones, God watched over them as a loving father.[72] Although Hart mentioned some of the same biblical texts Sarah had, including the story of Jesus weeping over Lazarus's death, he shared little of her anxiety about "murmuring." Almost fifty years younger than she (he was born in 1761), he belonged to a generation that was not as suspicious of the affirmation of everyday life, and he does not seem to have worried that loving one's family could be a form of idolatry. If he shortened or edited her narrative in any way, he probably tried to make her sound less severe.

The only other evidence that we have of Sarah's state of mind comes from her later writings. Although she seems to have hoped that writing about Samuel's death would bring her a sense of closure, it is clear that she continued to agonize over why God had decided to take away her only child. Following ministers' advice to those who had lost loved ones, she spent the weeks after Samuel's death subjecting herself to intense scrutiny, asking herself why God had afflicted her. According to John Flavel, an afflicted person should ask, "Lord, what special corruption is it that this Rod is sent to rebuke; what sinful neglect doth it come to humble me for?" The anonymous author of *A Pastoral Visit to the Afflicted*, which was published two years before Samuel's death, urged mourners to remember that God always sent affliction for a good reason: "It concerns you to *consider* what you have *been*, and *done*, that has provoked the LORD thus to deal with you."[73] When Sarah wrote her narrative, she humbly confessed that her afflictions had been for her own good, but perhaps because she was still in shock she did not ask why God was afflicting her. What had she done to "provoke" God?

Childhood deaths were all too common in early America—the result of epidemics, accidents, and ordinary illnesses that are easily cured today—and ministers often preached and wrote about how parents should respond to the loss of children. According to the author of *A Pastoral Visit to the Afflicted*, bereaved parents should ask themselves how they had angered God in relationship to their children. (The question did not seem to be *whether* they had angered God, but only how.) The possibilities were legion. Parents could be too fond and indulgent, "too *worldly*, and too *solicitous* in *providing Inheritances* for them," or not grateful enough to God for them.[74] The loss of a child (like all other tragedies in life) was never simply an accident; it was always a message from God.

Influenced by a verse from Paul's letter to the Colossians describing "inordinate affection" as "idolatry," ministers also warned parents that God would take away their children if they "over-loved them, and over-prized them," lavishing them with devotion that properly belonged to God alone. "Christians, your hearts are Christ's royal Throne," the Reverend Thomas

Brooks proclaimed, "and in this Throne Christ will be chief. . . . [H]e will
endure no competitor; if you shall attempt to Throne the Creature, be it
never so near and dear unto you, Christ will dethrone it, he will destroy
it, he will quickly lay them in a bed of dust, who shall aspire to his Royal
Throne." Although Flavel was gentler in his admonitions, he, too, believed
that a jealous God would take away children who had been made into
idols. Writing to a sister who was "bewailing the death of her dear and only
son," he implied that her child had been taken away so that nothing would
stand between her and God. "If the Jealousy of the Lord hath removed that
which drew away too much of your Heart from Him," he declared, "and
[God] hath spoken by this Rod, saying, Stand aside Child, thou art in my
way, and fillest more room in thy Parents Hearts, than belongs to thee, O
then deliver up all to him and say, Lord, take the whole heart entirely and
undividedly to thyself."[75] Although it was sinful for a parent not to love a
child, it was also sinful to love a child too much.

When Sarah looked into her heart to ask how her relationship with
Samuel might have angered God, she did not berate herself for being too
indulgent or too ambitious for his economic success. But she thought that
she was guilty of a far worse sin—a sin that she had never been able to
conquer. Two years earlier, when she had made her personal covenant
with God (using the Reverend Thomas Doolittle's published covenant as a
model), she had balked at writing the words, "I will Leave, Lose, and deny
all that was dear to me when it stood in competition with God, even Life
itself, if he should be pleased to call for it, rather than to forsake him and
his ways." "Assaulted" by Satan, she had feared that she was "Lying to God"
by promising to love him above everything else. After Samuel's death, she
seems to have believed that God had finally shown her the true contours of
her heart. Despite her covenant promises she had violated the First Com-
mandment: "Thou shalt have no other gods before me."[76]

This was Sarah's sin: she had loved her son even more than God. Because she had worshiped Samuel as an idol, God had taken him away. His
death was her fault.

In a letter to Susanna Anthony written sometime after Samuel's death
(the date is not clear, but she referred to her "late shock"), Sarah claimed
that God had repeatedly taken away her loved ones so that all her love
would belong to him alone. If not for her losses, she never would have understood that God was better to her than a husband, a father, a brother, and
even an only son. "Sometimes he will visit me with affliction," she explained
to Susa, summing up the story of her life. "He will take away the husband

of my youth, and thereby cause me to fly to the Widow's God, and rejoice in him, as the best of husbands! At another time, he will take away a tender father, and enable me to acquiesce in his dispensation, and rejoice in him, as my father's God, as my God; and a father of the fatherless! Then he will remove an only brother, and thereby cause me more fully to know, what it is to be resigned to his will, and to adore his sovereignty." All her losses had strengthened her love for God, including the death of her son. "Again, lest my heart should be joined to idols, he will have an only son! and show me at the same time, that he is better to me, than ten sons! Ah, than ten thousand sons, and all earthly enjoyments!" Although Sarah confessed that she was sometimes tempted to see God as "*evil*," she insisted that he had punished her out of love. He brought her "to the greatest extremity, that I may know assuredly, the work of my deliverance must be all his own. And when he hath subdued my stubborn will, brought me to leave all with him, to work in his own way; then he appears on the mount of difficulty, preserves his own honor, causes his name and ways to be well spoken of, instead of *evil*, as I had feared, delivers me from all my fears, and makes me to rejoice in him."[77] Despite her "idolatry," there was still reason for joy: God held the world securely in his hands, and he had ordained all the events in her life, even Samuel's death, for her own good.

Because many early American parents, like Sarah Osborn, sounded stoic when discussing their children's deaths, historians have sometimes wondered whether they loved their children as much as we do today. Yet Sarah's story suggests that the differences between our world and hers are about diverging images of God, not disparities of love. There is no doubt that Sarah loved her son, but in a religious culture that warned parents not to make their children into idols, her love was so deep that it frightened her. After his death, her silence about him was not a sign of coldness or indifference, but an indication of her overflowing love—a love so passionate that she was afraid it had been sinful.

If Sarah continued to fret over what had happened to Samuel's "naked soul," she never admitted it in her writings. But at some point she reread the section of her memoir that described her hopes for his future, and she was clearly upset by what she had written. When he had been nine years old, she had spent a day "wrestling with God for blessings for my only son," pleading that he would be saved. "O, I think I felt the pangs of the new birth for him," she rejoiced: "Having had such a sense of his miserable state by nature and what it would be if he died Christless and such a discovery of the sufficiency of Christ for him, I continued agonizing with God in prayer for a considerable time. At Last was quieted by this portion of scripture adapted and sweetly applied: all thy children shall be taught of God and great shall be the peace of thy children. Oh, this caused me to bless and praise my God that he had . . . put this poultice into my mouth to plead on behalf of my own son." The scripture that came to her mind was from Isaiah 54, perhaps her favorite chapter in the Bible. After her husband Samuel's death, there had been many times when she had felt as though Isaiah's words had been written just for her: "Fear not," he had prophesied, "for thou shalt not be ashamed . . . and shalt not remember the reproach of thy widowhood any more." This time, as she prayed for her son, she remembered Isaiah's comforting promise to the children of the covenant: "All thy children shall be taught of the LORD; and great shall be the peace of thy children." Longing for assurance that her beloved son would find "peace" in Jesus, she claimed to have received evidence of his future salvation.[78]

Sometime later when Sarah returned to these words, she scratched them out so thoroughly that they are almost impossible to decipher. (They can just be made out with the help of patience and a magnifying glass.) In the margins she explained, "I don't think I was free from impulses here." (This, too, she eventually crossed out, but not as completely.) Apparently she questioned whether she had truly felt the "pangs of the new birth" for Samuel, or whether she had been sadly deluded. Perhaps she edited her words in the eight months between finishing her memoir and Samuel's death, but it seems more likely that she made these changes afterward. She may have been afraid that her words proved that she had loved her son too much, even as an idol.

The sentence that remained after her crossings-out and emendations was far bleaker than her original words. In the new version there is no redemption, but only Sarah imagining "his miserable state by nature and what it would be if he died Christless." She still describes herself as "agonizing with God in prayer for a considerable time," but this time her prayers go unanswered.[79]

In all of Sarah Osborn's surviving manuscripts, there is only a single diary entry ever recorded on September 14, the anniversary of Samuel's death. In 1753, on a Friday morning (the same day of the week that he had died), she lamented her sinfulness. Although she did not mention Samuel by name, she may have been thinking about him when she asked her soul, "Canst thou never be diligent but when the rod or frown drives thee to thy knees?" In other diary entries written around the anniversaries of his death, she often sounded depressed. Each September as the summer slowly turned to fall and the days grew shorter, she may have remembered her vigil by Samuel's deathbed. "Everything seems to have lost its life and vigor," she grieved on September 10, 1754. "All is flat and dull. The Bible itself does not reach me!" And on September 18, 1760, she felt as if there were "an awful estrangement betwixt God and my soul. My thoughts Like the Dead fish is carried down the stream by every Petty trifle. All communion with God is broken up."[80]

Yet in all these entries, she never mentioned Samuel's death. Nor, in all of her extant writings, did she ever mention him by name again. She had spent the last week of his life weeping and praying for his salvation, but after finishing her narrative she fell silent. Like Job in the whirlwind, she fell mute before her suffering, awed and humbled by the mysterious sovereignty of God.

Chapter 6

No Imaginary Thing, 1753–1755

I Have thought much on those few Lines you began to write to me; and do not at all wonder that you expect I should improve the Opportunity to relieve you. . . . And Oh that God would now bless the poor weak Endeavours of a worthless Worm to refresh you! If so, it will rejoyce me much: But whether it please him to use a poor nothing Creature as an instrument or no, I am perswaded he will in his own Time revive you, and I rejoyce and praise him on your Behalf, by Grace; that he will turn your Captivity; and that He will bruise Satan under your feet shortly, and make him gladly quit the Field, and leave you to enjoy your God. For blessed be God, Christ Jesus is stronger than He and all his combin'd Legions; and he can't resist his Power, tho' he has audaciously struck at his Honour, and endeavour'd to impede his blesed Work in your Soul. Do's or has the bold-daring Spirit persuaded to insinuate that all Religion, is vain, imaginary, and delusive? Do's he pretend that none can know they are right?—Tell him from me, He is a Liar, and I am bold to say, I have prov'd him so, for He has told me the same Tale: But blessed be God, I do know that Religion is no imaginary Thing, but a substantial Reality. I do know that there is a GOD of boundless Perfections, Truth and Faithfulness, that will not deceive; no nor forsake the Soul that puts its Trust in him.

But now perhaps you'll say, Aye, but how do I know this God is mine; and that I myself am not deceived? I answer, by the Evidences of a Work of Grace wrought in my Soul. And now as God shall enable me, my dear Friend, I'll tell you truly what GOD has done for my Soul, and what I call Evidences of a Work of Grace.[1]

In June 1753 Sarah wrote an encouraging letter to a friend in the midst of a spiritual crisis. In the nine years since Samuel's death she had tried to channel her grief into helping others to seek salvation, determined not to let anyone else die without Christ. Counseling her friend not to despair, she promised that "a GOD of boundless Perfections" would never "forsake the Soul that puts its Trust in him."

Two years later Thomas Prince arranged for Sarah Osborn's letter to be published anonymously in Boston under the title *The Nature, Certainty and Evidence of True Christianity*. We do not know whether Osborn chose the title of her book or whether Prince chose it for her, but the words *nature, certainty*, and *evidence* connected it to both the rising evangelical movement and the Enlightenment. On one hand, her title echoed scientific works like Benjamin Robins's *Discourse Concerning the Nature and Certainty of Sir Isaac Newton's Methods of Fluxions, and of Prime and Ultimate Ratios* (1735) as well as of "enlightened" religious books like Edward Stillingfleet's *Discourse Concerning the Nature and Grounds of the Certainty of Faith*. Stillingfleet, a British Anglican, wanted to make Christianity more rational and less "enthusiastic." On the other hand, Osborn's title also resonated with evangelical works like Jonathan Edwards's *Distinguishing Marks of a Work of the Spirit of God*, which examined the "evidence" that the revivals were divinely inspired, and Jonathan Dickinson's *Witness of the Spirit*, which promised to explain the "clear and satisfying Evidences" of conversion. Her emphasis on "true" Christianity was common among evangelicals: for example, Joseph Bellamy published a treatise titled *True Religion Delineated*.[2] Although she may not have been aware of it, her title symbolized the surprising cross-fertilization of Protestantism and the Enlightenment. "*Religion* is no imaginary Thing," she testified, "but a *substantial Reality*."[3]

If Osborn's title sounded curiously "enlightened" to her readers, her subtitle, "In a Letter from a Gentlewoman in *New-England*," was even more notable. Those who dared write about weighty matters of nature, certainty, and evidence were supposed to be ministers or philosophers, not gentlewomen. Although many women in early America wrote letters, poems, and diaries, only a few ever saw their work in print. Publishing was almost entirely a masculine enterprise. Of almost seventy-four hundred works published in America between 1640 and 1755, only twenty-six were written by women, and if we eliminate books that were first published in England or France the number decreases to fourteen. If we also remove books from the list that were published posthumously, the number shrinks to eight. Since many books available for sale in the colonies were imported

Th Nature, Certainty and Evidence
of TRUE CHRISTIANITY :

IN A

LETTER

, FROM A

GENTLEWOMAN

In *Rhode-Island*,

To ANOTHER, her dear Friend, in
great *Darkness*, *Doubt* and *Concern*, of a
Religious Nature.

---

1 Cor. i. 26—31.

Deborah Haggar Coker

☞ Though this Letter was written in great
Privacy from one Friend to another; yet on
representing that by allowing it to be printed, it
would probably reach to many others in the
like afflicted Case, and by the Grace of God be
very helpful to them; the Writer was at length
prevailed on to suffer it—provided her Name
and Place of Abode remain concealed.

PROVIDENCE: Re-printed by J. CARTER.

The title page of the 1793 edition of *The Nature, Certainty and Evidence of True
Christianity*. The 1755 edition listed the author as "a gentlewoman in New England,"
but this edition, published in Providence, identified her home as Rhode Island.
Courtesy of the American Antiquarian Society.

from England, the number of books written by women in circulation was much higher than these paltry numbers suggest, but as Sarah Osborn must have realized, she was a rare phenomenon: an American female author who was alive when her work appeared in print.[4]

With few exceptions, neither evangelical ministers nor Enlightenment philosophers believed that women were equal to men, but their emphasis on individual experience led to unexpected consequences. Not only did the Enlightenment have a much stronger impact on eighteenth-century Protestantism than we have realized, but it also gave women a powerful new vocabulary to justify their religious authority.

Sharing the Gospel

We know little about Sarah's life between 1744, the year of Samuel's death, and 1753, the year that she wrote the letter that later would be published as *The Nature, Certainty and Evidence of True Christianity*. Only a few facts are clear. In 1745 she lost two of the most important people in her life: the Reverend Jonathan Helyer, a young minister whose "precious sermons" had strengthened her faith during his short tenure at her church, and, only a few months later, the Reverend Nathaniel Clap, the venerable pastor who had first welcomed her into communion. She had loved them both, and despite praying for a spirit of resignation, she felt bereft. Echoing her words after Samuel's death, she wrote in her diary, "O my God, preserve me from murmuring at thine holy hand."[5] Two of her stepsons, John and Edward, were married in 1747, and her mother, Susanna, after several years as a widow, married a wigmaker, William Caswell, and moved to South Kingstown.[6] Sarah occasionally took the ferry to visit her, but since their relationship remained rocky she may have welcomed the new distance between them. Age had not softened Susanna's sharp tongue. During one visit, she showed her daughter a letter from a male acquaintance criticizing Sarah for being "lifted up with spiritual pride." Since Sarah could be arrogant, her mother may have thought that showing her these words would do her good, but Sarah was understandably hurt. More than anything she wanted to be a good Christian, but her mother always reminded her of her failures.[7]

Besides these small glimpses of Sarah's life, we know that she spent many hours trying to convert others to her evangelical faith. After the agony of watching Samuel die, she seems to have resolved to do everything possible not to let another "naked soul" plunge into eternity without Christ.

Even before his death she had prayed with the students in her school, but afterward she prayed with them every day. As Samuel Hopkins remembered, she "seriously addressed them on the concerns of their souls, urging their attention to the Bible, to Jesus Christ, and the way of salvation by him." Often she began her day with a silent prayer that God would "subdue the stubbornness of their wills." In a diary entry written only a month after Samuel's death, she confessed, "I should rejoice if thou wouldst make poor worthless me, an instrument to do them good."[8]

The child most often in her prayers may have been Bobey (probably pronounced "Bobby"), a slave boy whom she had reared since infancy. Sarah was too poor to afford a slave, but in 1744, soon after Samuel died, several friends surprised her with Bobey's purchase. As she explained later, he was "the Gift of many Good Earthly friends. Also it was to me as something saved from shipwreck when all the rest was cast over." Her friends may have hoped to ease her grief by giving her another child to raise—a child who would someday mature into a sound financial investment. They probably never reflected on the sorrow they caused a different mother, Phillis, whose relationship with her son may have been confined to visits and glimpses on the street.[9]

Sarah believed that blacks were inferior to whites, but like most evangelicals at the time she also believed that they were spiritually equal in the sight of God. Although she raised Bobey to accept his status as property, she also encouraged him to remember that his greatest "master" was God. As they sat in front of the fireplace together in the evenings, she taught him not only how to sew, knit, and mend his own clothes but how to read the Bible and say his prayers. Later Christians would question the wisdom of teaching slaves to read, but Sarah equated religion with literacy. She refused to allow a child in her household to grow up without being able to read the Bible for himself.[10]

Sarah wrote little about her relationship with Bobey, but by the time he was ten (only a little younger than Samuel had been at his death), she had become concerned about the "bad Examples" that might lead him astray in Newport. She also seems to have feared the strength of her attachment to him. In a letter written to Joseph Fish in 1754, she explained that she and Henry wanted to apprentice him to a Christian master in the country, ideally Fish himself. "He Loves Play very well and is heedless, antic &c," Sarah admitted, "but I think he is not addicted either to Pilfer, Lie, or call Names." She and Henry were not seeking money (and in fact, they asked Fish only to supply Bobey's food and clothing in exchange for his work), but they wanted to find a place where he would be kept out of trouble. "I fear his want of business with us, will be a Hurt to Him," she explained, "for we have not wherewith to Employ Him, and I know Idleness is an inlet to everything that's bad, and I can't be willing he should be brought up in it: I want he should Learn to Labor." She also wanted him to learn his "distance" from whites. Because of Samuel's death she had embraced him as her own, but now that he was ten she realized that she could not continue treating him as part of her family. He was not her child but her slave. "I desire if he does come that no favors may be showed to him because he belongs to me," she explained to Fish. "For I choose rather he should know his distance. For his being brought up with us as our own from the cradle, and we having no other child, has doubtless made him use some freedoms with us which with strangers he would not Pretend too." In the end, though, she could not keep a maternal tone from sneaking into her letter. "I hope he will be a Good boy."[11]

Since Fish already had a slave boy to help with chores, he did not take Bobey, but Sarah and Henry arranged for him to be apprenticed out to her former brother-in-law in Berkeley (north of Providence) instead. She had known her "brother French" since her marriage to Samuel, and he was one of the few people whom she could imagine trusting with Bobey's soul. French had been "sober from his youth," she wrote to Fish, "and in a Judgment of charity I have thought some years Past truly Gracious, keeps up the worship of God in his house &c." Although he ran a tavern, a minister from Berkeley assured her that it was "orderly."[12] She wanted to make sure that Bobey would live in a respectable Christian household. She had held him as a baby, rocked his cradle, fed him, bathed him, cared for him during his illnesses, and watched him grow into boyhood, and although her love for him was tainted by racism, it was genuine. It was one of the many tragedies of slavery that she wished she loved him less.

Sarah believed that God in his providence had made her a teacher so that she would share the gospel with children, but she also felt called to evangelize women. Many members of the women's society drifted away during the 1750s, but she continued to meet with a few female friends (especially Susanna Anthony) to pray, read the Bible, and talk about God.[13] Perhaps because of her past sufferings, women in distress were ineluctably drawn to her. They wanted her to explain the secret of her faith.

We do not know the name of the woman who wrote to Sarah in the spring of 1753 asking for spiritual counsel, but she seems to have been a friend from Newport. (Sarah mentioned that they had known each other for "some years," and since she also made a brief reference to past conversations, they probably lived in close proximity.) Although Sarah's most frequent correspondent was Susanna Anthony, there is no evidence that Anthony experienced a spiritual crisis during 1753, and in fact she rejoiced in May that her love for "all the members of Christ's body" was growing deeper. Sarah's anonymous "friend" may have been someone else from either her church or the women's society. All we know for certain is that the woman was "in great *Darkness, Doubt* and *Concern* of a *Religious* Nature," and she wrote to Sarah for encouragement.[14]

Sarah responded by urging her friend to examine the "evidence" of her relationship to Christ. Borrowing the empirical language of the Enlightenment, she argued that Christians could know whether they had been saved. Her own "evidences" included her willingness to suffer affliction, her desire to do good works, and her love of holiness for its own sake. In order to distinguish herself from the Separates, she denied wanting to "establish *Assurance* as the Essence of saving Faith," but she insisted that people could be virtually certain of their salvation. "Does or has the bold-daring Spirit persuaded to insinuate that all *Religion*, is *vain, imaginary*, and *delusion?*" she asked. "Does he pretend that none can know they are right?—Tell him from me, *He is a Liar*, and I am bold to say, I have proved him so."[15]

Sarah's advice to her friend seems to have grown out of her own struggles against doubt. Despite the confident tone of her letter, she filled her 1753 diary with laments about the gulf standing between her and God. As she had done many times before, she wondered why he had "hidden his face" from her, leaving her alone in her time of need. "What a vacancy do I feel while held at a distance from my God," she confessed. "O Lord, return and Leave me not comfortless and forlorn. Lord, what can I do without thee? What shall I do? Everything is dreadful if thou art absent."[16]

Just as Sarah urged her friend to search for evidence of God's grace, she herself did the same. Because of her belief that religion was "experimental," she hoped to make "discoveries" about God by studying her experiences as well as the Bible. "Let me have some more discoveries of Eternal things, Lord," she pleaded in 1753.[17] In a poignant diary entry written when she had little money or food, she reminded herself that her past experiences offered convincing proof that a loving God would never abandon her. Addressing him directly, she wrote: "My own experience has ever Proved to me, that thou art the God that has fed me all my Life Long—the God that didst never Leave me upon the mount of difficulty, but always appeared and wrought deliverance."[18]

This was the same reassuring language that she used in her letter to her friend. If she knew how to comfort others, it was because she herself had often teetered on the edge of despair, frightened by her feelings of emptiness.

Sarah's friend liked the letter so much that she shared it with others, and somehow a copy ended up in the hands of Thomas Prince. Given the length of the letter—fifteen pages in print—Sarah seems to have viewed it as a significant piece of writing, but she was probably surprised when Prince encouraged her to publish it as a tract. Although she agreed, she requested that it appear anonymously. As a brief note on the title page explained, "Though this *Letter* was wrote in great *privacy* from *one Friend* to *another*. Yet on representing that by allowing it to be *Printed*, it would probably reach to *many others in the like afflicted Case*, and by the Grace of God be *very helpful to them*; the Writer was at length prevailed on to suffer it—provided her Name and Place of abode remain concealed."[19] Whether written by the Reverend Prince or by Samuel Kneeland, the publisher, these words portrayed Osborn as a humble, self-denying woman who had not wanted to publish her letter, but who had finally "suffered" it because of her compassion for others in spiritual distress. She was identified on the title page only as "a Gentlewoman in *New-England*," a designation that made her sound slightly more genteel than her actual status warranted. Though she was not well-to-do, Prince wanted the evangelical movement to be associated with politeness and civility.[20] Evangelical women, he implied, were refined enough to participate in the republic of letters. The woman who had written hundreds of pages of diaries and letters had finally become a published author.

A Poor, Nothing Creature

With the exception of Ann Maylem, who had published a complaint against a Newport distillery in 1742, Sarah Osborn was the only published female author in Newport during the 1750s. Many other women wrote diaries, letters, and memoirs, and some may have shared their manuscripts with friends, but Osborn's publication set her apart as a remarkable figure of religious authority. Although she described herself as "a poor nothing Creature," her friends (including Susanna Anthony and the Reverend Fish) knew that she was the anonymous "gentlewoman" whose letter had been published, and it seems likely that they broadcast the news. Many must have been surprised to discover that the schoolteacher in their midst had been singled out for the honor of publication.[21]

If Sarah had lived a hundred years earlier, her letter probably would not have been published. Only three books by American women found their way into print before 1700, including Anne Bradstreet's *Several Poems Compiled with Great Variety of Wit and Learning*, Mary Rowlandson's *Sovereignty and Goodness of God*, and Sarah Goodhue's *Copy of a Valedictory and Monitory Writing*. When Bradstreet's brother-in-law arranged for her poetry to be published in England in 1650 (without her permission), he included an elaborate preface apologizing for the book. Assuring his readers that she had not forsaken her family responsibilities in order to write, he explained, "These Poems are the fruit but of some few hours, curtailed from her sleep and other enjoyments." As the literary critic Elaine Showalter has pointed out, "no fewer than eleven men wrote testimonials and poems praising her piety and industry, prefatory materials almost as long as the thirteen poems in the book."[22]

There were many reasons for the scarcity of women authors. Besides being less literate than men, women were discouraged from "meddling" in the masculine world of theology, politics, and law. John Winthrop, the first governor of Massachusetts Bay, explained one woman's mental illness as the result of too much "reading and writing": "For if she had attended her household affairs, and such things as belong to women, and not gone out of her way and calling to meddle in such things as are proper of men, whose minds are stronger, etc., she had kept her wits." Although women were encouraged to read the Bible and write devotional diaries, they were not supposed to seek public recognition, and those who dared publish their writings instead of keeping them private were subjected to withering criticism. "Your printing of a Book, beyond the custom of your Sex, doth rankly smell," a New England minister wrote to his sister in England in 1650. Even Cotton Mather, who praised female devotional writers for their piety, insisted that the best women writers were "Patterns of *Humility*." In his words, "They have made no Noise; they have sought no Fame."[23]

The number of titles by women grew in the first four decades of the eighteenth century, with nine more books published before 1740. Eight of these focused on religious topics (the exception was Hannah Penn's letter to Governor George Keith), and as before they were usually prefaced by a man's testimonial or apology. As the publisher of Sarah Fiske's *Confession of Faith* (1704) explained, "'Tis not with a design to blazon the Fame and Reputation of any Person, that this is now presented to the Public View." Since Fiske's writings were published after her death, the editor's apology seems extreme (a dead woman could not take pride in her fame), but he seems to have been genuinely concerned about tarnishing her character. Since the greatest sign of a woman's virtue in early America was anonymity, any attempt to gain public recognition seemed morally suspect.[24]

As Fiske's example suggests, women's writings were rarely published without a minister's or husband's support and approval, and they often appeared posthumously. For example, both Sarah Goodhue's *Copy of a Valedictory and Monitory Writing* and Mary Mollineux's *Fruits of Retirement; or, Miscellaneous Poems, Moral and Divine* were published after their authors' deaths, and neither woman seems to have anticipated that her words would ever become public.[25] Rather than simply reprinting women's writings in their entirety, men often edited them to suit their own agendas. When Walter Wilmot published extracts from his deceased wife's writings, he arranged them under his own headings: for example, "Of the universal Depravity and Corruption of human Nature." His voice, not hers, dominates the text.[26]

Since ministers were concerned about passing on their faith to the next generation, they were particularly interested in publishing women's personal writings about the duty of Christian motherhood. When Nathaniel Appleton published his funeral sermon for Martha Gerrish, he included lengthy extracts from her religious letters to her children. Writing to a daughter who had not yet become a full church member, Gerrish warned, "Let me tell you,—that while you live in the Omission of any Duty, you have no Room to expect a Blessing: God will turn a deaf Ear to all your Cries; you are Exposed to His Wrath."[27] Appleton could not have said it better, which may have been part of the reason he decided to publish Gerrish's words.

There was a small increase in the number of women's writings published during the revivals in New England, with ten books by women printed between 1740 and 1750. (One of these was a housekeeping manual and another involved a legal proceeding; the rest focused on religious themes.) Since three of the ten were published posthumously and six were reprinted from England, this number does not reflect an upsurge in the number of women seeking publication, but rather a new interest among publishers in providing female models of piety during the revivals. The public was so hungry for individual religious narratives that publishers saw an opportunity to make a profit, and besides reprinting large numbers of Puritan texts they seem to have deliberately sought out women's devotional writings. Elizabeth White's narrative, first published in London in the seventeenth century, was reprinted in Boston in 1741, and Elizabeth Bury's diary, first published in London in 1720, was reprinted in Boston in 1743. Two of Elizabeth Singer Rowe's books, *The History of Joseph* and *Devout Exercises of the Heart*, both popular in evangelical circles in England, were published in 1739 and 1742. (Rowe had died in 1737.)[28]

All these books were widely read during the revivals, and although we do not know exactly why readers found them so compelling, their portraits of female piety may have been part of the reason. These works sounded reassuringly "feminine" at a time when women's religious zeal had become controversial. Angered by the female radicalism he had witnessed at a revival meeting, Charles Chauncy complained, "Many of the *young Women* would go about the House *praying* and *exhorting*" as well as "*laughing* and *singing, jumping up and down*, and *clapping* their Hands together." Although Jonathan Edwards rarely agreed with Chauncy, he, too, believed that women should keep silence in the churches, and in 1741 he presided over a church council that admonished Bathsheba Kingsley of Westfield, Massachusetts, for claiming to be "a proper person to be improved for some great thing in the church of God; and that in the exercise of some parts of the work of ministry." Describing her as a "brawling woman," Edwards complained that she had spent two years traveling from town to town exhorting sinners to repent; when ministers had tried to discourage her, she had threatened them with divine retribution. Although the church council decided not to excommunicate her, the members insisted that in the future she should "keep chiefly at home." Other ministers grumbled about disorderly women who fell into fits, interrupted sermons, and "spoke much Publicly." According to Nathan Bowen, a Massachusetts lawyer, he had seen women stride into the pulpit to harangue their "betters" in front of "large assemblies"; another man reported being disgusted by the sight of a "big-bellied Woman" who "straddled into the pulpit."[29]

Although some of these stories of female radicalism may have been exaggerated, the Separates openly defended women's right to speak publicly in meetings. Pointing to the examples of biblical heroines like the woman of Samaria, who had testified that Jesus was the Christ, and Mary Magdalene, the first witness of Christ's resurrection, the Reverend Ebenezer Frothingham argued that in his own day "God has chosen some Women, and despised Brethren, to be the first Witnesses of the Reviving of a glorious and wonderful work of God." Although they never argued that women should be ordained, the Separates allowed women to "exhort," or testify in public. In contrast to preachers, exhorters did not have the authority to interpret a biblical text, but they could share their personal stories of conversion publicly. When Joseph Fish arrived at a revival meeting in New London in 1742, he found "two or three" women exhorting the congregation, and when he began to pray aloud one of the women tried to drown out his voice with her own, "praying and Exhorting at the Same time for Several minutes."[30]

From the few books by women that were published during the 1740s and 1750s, readers would never imagine that Christian women could be contentious or arrogant—and this may have been at least part of the reason that these particular titles found their way into print. It is unlikely that Thomas Prince would have decided to publish Sarah Osborn's letter if she, like the "brawling" Bathsheba Kingsley, had "cast off that modesty, shamefacedness, and sobriety and meekness, diligence and submission, that becomes a Christian woman in her place." Osborn's descriptions of herself as "a poor nothing Creature," "utterly unworthy," and "vile" made it possible for her to be elevated as a model for other evangelical women. In a typical passage, she exclaimed, "Oh, may the Crown be set on JESUS his HEAD; while I lay my Mouth in the dust, and acknowledge I am an unprofitable servant, and utterly unworthy of all the Mercy he has showed to me." Although Osborn expressed assurance about her rebirth in Christ, she took pains to explain that her letter was not motivated by "Self-confidence, Pride, Ostentation, or vain Glory," but only her desire to glorify God. Often she wrote in the passive voice. "God *caused my Heart to go out after Him*," she explained.[31]

Since Sarah was a voracious reader who seems to have deliberately sought out books that were either by or about women, her "feminine" writing style was probably influenced by her immersion in the world of print. By reading books like Bury's *Account of the Life and Death of Mrs. Elizabeth Bury* and Hannah Housman's *Power and Pleasure of the Divine Life*, she learned how to cultivate an authorial voice that sounded properly humble and deferential. Bury, for example, described herself as "polluted," a "poor, weak, wandering Child," and "a poor, weak, unworthy, defiled Child."[32] Although Sarah never mentioned reading any of the sentimental novels that were popular during her day, they may have influenced her as well. She wrote in an emotional, fervent voice that was filled with exclamations, especially the word "O!" Since female devotional writers were also fond of sentimental language ("Oh! Let my Experience stand a Witness to them that hope in his Mercy," Elizabeth Rowe exclaimed), Sarah may have been imitating religious books, but given how many other evangelical women read sentimental novels it seems likely that she may have occasionally indulged in their pleasures as well. The daughters of two prominent ministers—Esther Edwards Burr, the daughter of Jonathan Edwards, and Sarah Prince Gill, the daughter of Thomas Prince—corresponded about reading Samuel Richardson's novels *Pamela* and *Clarissa*, and even Susanna Anthony ruefully admitted to spending a day with a novel. "I blush, Lord, I am ashamed that such amusement has engrossed almost all my thoughts this day," she wrote in her diary in 1749. (She, too, may have been reading *Clarissa*, a tearjerker published in 1748 that was wildly popular on both sides of the Atlantic.)[33] Most sentimental novels were written by men, but their focus on women's lives made them immensely popular with a female audience. It probably is not a coincidence that Sarah and Susanna Anthony decided to exchange heartfelt letters, despite living in the same neighborhood, at the same time as epistolary novels like *Pamela* and *Clarissa* were selling thousands of copies.

How did Sarah Osborn, a woman of humble means, manage to read so much? With little money to spend on luxuries, she certainly could not afford to buy the many titles she saw in Newport's shops. When she died in 1796, the inventory of her possessions listed only seven books, including two copies of the Bible: a small octavo edition and a larger, more imposing quarto one. But this small number of books did not reflect either the breadth or the depth of Sarah's reading. Despite her poverty, she satisfied her craving for books by begging friends and ministers to lend her interesting titles, dropping by neighbors' houses to read their books (as she did when she went to Deacon Nathaniel Coggeshall's house to read Daniel Defoe's *Family Instructor*, an advice manual on family relationships), and borrowing them from her church.[34] During his pastorate, Nathaniel Clap had bought religious books to share with his congregation, and after his death the church continued his custom. Although Sarah never mentioned going to Trinity Church's free library, which was open to everyone in Newport regardless of denomination, she may have also borrowed books from its impressive collection.[35]

The result of all this reading was that Osborn developed a writing style that reflected the narrative conventions of her world. When we read *The Nature, Certainty and Evidence of True Christianity*, we can hear the echoes of many different voices—Puritans examining themselves for signs of grace, sentimental novelists plumbing the depths of human emotion, evangelicals proclaiming their rebirth in Christ, female devotional writers confessing their weakness. Even when Sarah heard the news that her letter had appeared in print, she took pains not to aggrandize herself. "My poor performance was printed," she wrote in her diary on April 22, 1755. "This gave me a sense of my vileness, and earnest longings that God might be glorified thereby. It appears another solemn bond and obligation for me to lead a holy life."[36]

Sarah clearly believed that a "feminine" voice was humble and self-denying, but at a time when few women lived to see their names in print, it would be a mistake to underestimate the importance of her letter's being published. By explaining that her words could offer comfort to those who were "afflicted" with doubts, Thomas Prince implicitly suggested that a gentlewoman from New England should be regarded as a model of true grace. Anyone who read her book was encouraged to believe that her story was valuable, indeed priceless, because it offered insight into the meaning of a Christian life.

This God Is Mine

The publication of Osborn's letter reflects one of the central paradoxes of the rising evangelical movement. Evangelicals were theological conservatives who believed that women had been created subordinate to men, but they also gave women a new vocabulary of individual experience to justify their authority and leadership. "*How do I know this God is mine?*" Osborn asked. "By the *Evidences of a Work of Grace* wrought in my soul."[37] Because of her heartfelt experience of his love, she knew that God was "hers."

In addition to the long Christian history that emphasized women's secondary status in creation, evangelicals were influenced by the gendered language of the Enlightenment. A few radical Enlightenment philosophers insisted that the mind had no sex, but most were more conservative in their attitudes toward women, supporting sexual inequality rather than attacking it. According to Jean-Jacques Rousseau women belonged at home, where they should devote themselves to pleasing their husbands and raising their children. As he explained in *Emile*, "To oblige us, to do us service, to gain our love and esteem . . . these are the duties of the sex at all times, and what they ought to learn from their infancy."[38] Although evangelicals and Enlightenment philosophers agreed on few things, most were united in their belief that women were not as intelligent or as intellectually curious as men. As the Reverend Ebenezer Pemberton explained when he published some of his mother's writings, "She read the sacred Pages, and other religious Tracts, not so much to increase her *speculative Knowledge*, and gratify the Inclinations of an *inquisitive Mind*, as to learn the self-denying Mysteries of the Cross of CHRIST." Unlike men, who wrestled with hard theological questions about God's purpose in the world, women were expected to take a purely devotional interest in religion.[39]

Yet as we have seen, one of the many "enlightenments" took place within Protestantism as well as against it, and by absorbing the Enlightenment language of experience as their own, evangelicals made it possible for women to gain public recognition as informal religious leaders. Despite their emphasis on female subordination, no other religious group in pre-Revolutionary America did more to support women's authorship. (The first African Americans and Native Americans to be published were also evangelicals.) Before 1774, when there was a sudden spike in the number of "daughters of liberty" writing about politics, sixty-eight books by women were published, not including reprints; and forty-three of these (62 percent) focused on Christian themes. It is clear that the roots of women's authorship in America are religious. (Other writings by women included novels, plays, song collections, a treatise on gardening, and broadsides like Gezelena Rousby's plea for the release of her husband from debtors' prison.) Most striking, evangelicals wrote 34 percent of the books by women that were published between 1740 and 1774, seventeen of fifty titles. (For the sake of comparison, it is worth noting that Quakers, the second-largest group of female authors, published seven of these.) Evangelical women's publications included poetry, letters, and devotional writings, including Anne Dutton's *A Letter from Mrs. Anne Dutton to the Reverend G. Whitefield* and Martha Brewster's *Poems on Divers Subjects*.[40]

In a notable departure from the past, most of these evangelical female authors were alive when their words appeared in print. Sarah Osborn's *Nature, Certainty and Evidence of True Christianity* heralded a trend that continued throughout the rest of the century: fourteen of the seventeen titles were published during the authors' lifetimes. Martha Brewster, for example, was forty-seven when her poetry collection was published, and, challenging older conventions of female modesty, she refused to hide behind a cloak of anonymity. Her title page announced that the book had been written "by Martha Brewster, of Lebanon."

To justify their right to appear in print, these evangelical women appealed to their religious experience. In a book of poems honoring George Whitefield, Jane Dunlap used her preface to explain how deeply his sermons had touched her heart, and she included a poem about her joy at being born again. Though she apologized for her "homely stile," she claimed that even a woman could teach others about the meaning of a Christian life: "No eloquence does in these lines,/I'm very sure appear,/But sacred truths will always shine,/Tho' in the lowest sphere."[41] She claimed that God revealed himself not only through the Bible but through women's personal experiences of his grace.

Perhaps the most remarkable female author in the eighteenth century was Phillis Wheatley, a slave who had been kidnapped from Africa as a child. In order to gain acceptance in the republic of letters, Wheatley emphasized the depth of her Christian faith, and in 1770 she published an elegy lamenting the death of George Whitefield. Because she was young, female, and a slave when she published her first book, *Poems on Various Subjects*, in 1773, the volume included a testimonial signed by eighteen of Boston's leading gentlemen, including the governor, swearing that an "uncultivated Barbarian from Africa" had indeed written her own poems. No other female author in early America faced the same degree of skepticism or hostility. Yet as Wheatley made clear in her poems, her authority to write came from her rebirth in Christ—in other words, from God himself.[42]

Though Wheatley does not seem to have realized it, she stood in a long tradition of Christian women who justified their religious authority on the grounds of their personal experience of God's grace. Like Hildegard of Bingen, a medieval visionary, and Anne Hutchinson, the "American Jezebel" who claimed to have received divine revelations, Wheatley explained that God had chosen her to proclaim the good news. Excluded from formal avenues of power, women across the centuries had learned to emphasize the authority of their experience rather than their rationality or intelligence. Yet despite these continuities with the past, the eighteenth century marked a watershed in understandings of experience. Because Enlightenment philosophers elevated firsthand experience as the only reliable source of knowledge, even more reliable than the Bible, empirical language sounded particularly potent.

Besides being influenced by the Enlightenment language of experience, evangelicals also absorbed its individualism—one of the most enduring legacies of the eighteenth century. In earlier periods of history it had seemed almost inevitable that children would grow up to follow in their parents' footsteps: a farmer's son would usually become a farmer, a goodwife's daughter would live in the same neighborhood as her mother. But because of religious toleration, technological innovation, social and geographical mobility, and the expansion of political and economic choices, personal identity no longer seemed as fixed in the eighteenth century, and individuals gained a new sense of self-determination. As anyone who has

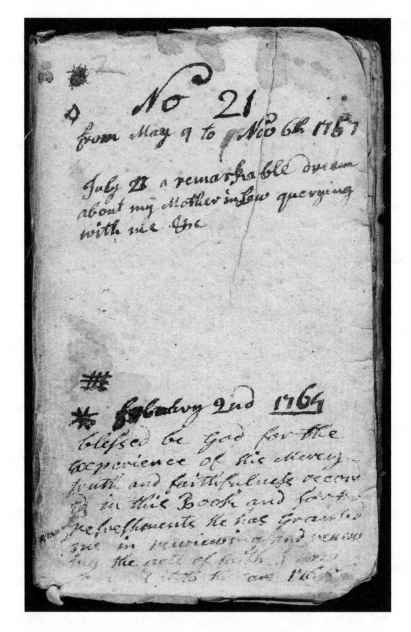

The cover of Sarah Osborn's diary no. 21. Sarah often reread her diaries in order to find evidence of God's grace in her former experiences. After reading this diary again in 1764, she wrote on the cover, "February 2nd 1764, blessed be God for the Experience of His Mercy truth and faithfulness recorded in this Book and for the refreshments He has Granted me in reviewing and renewing the acts of faith I now commit it to the same." Photograph courtesy of Beinecke Rare Book and Manuscript Library, Yale University.

seen Rembrandt's self-portraits can attest, the fascination with selfhood was not new, but in response to both changes in everyday life and new Enlightenment ideas, people seem to have gained a greater sense of their agency as individuals. "There is a profoundly radical individualism at the heart of Enlightenment thought," the historian Isaac Kramnick has argued. "Its rationalism led Enlightenment philosophy to enthrone the individual as the centre and creator of meaning, truth, and even reality."[43] Enlightenment philosophers defended the right of the sovereign individual to choose his own government, to pursue his own economic interests in the marketplace, and to worship according to the dictates of his own conscience. As this language suggests, they almost always imagined the individual as a man, but a few early feminists extended the principle of individual rights to women as well, including Mary Astell, who wrote a defense of women's education.[44]

Evangelicals were ambivalent about the individualism that was enshrined by the Enlightenment, but in response to the challenges of their time they crafted a new form of Protestantism that was based more on the converted individual than the covenanted community.[45] Since the Puritans had also encouraged people to look inward for signs of God's grace, evangelicals often sounded like them, but it was as if they were speaking the same language with a different accent. Fearful that God would break his covenant with them if they did not behave righteously, the Puritans had emphasized the morality of the entire commonwealth. When the number of converts dwindled in the early eighteenth century, they demanded communal renewal and repentance as well as individual conversion. They imagined New England in collective terms as the people of God, the "new Israel." In contrast, even though evangelicals agreed that both personal and communal transformation were important, they put their pronunciation more on the individual, arguing that one could not be a Christian without a personal experience of grace. As a minister explained, "True religion is an inward thing, a thing of the heart."[46]

The spiritual individualism embedded within the evangelical movement seems to have enhanced women's sense of personal dignity and worth. Instead of trying to suppress the gendered dimensions of their identities, they filled their conversion narratives with details about their distinctive lives as women, including marriage, childbirth, motherhood, and female friendships. In most aspects of their lives they were expected to subordinate themselves to their fathers and husbands, but in the realm of religion they turned their gaze inward to focus on their own stories. "O why me, why me," exclaimed Hannah Heaton. "Oh *Why me! Why me*, when *Thousands perish!* How is it that I should be a *Vessel of Mercy*, that have deserved to have been a *Vessel of Wrath* forever!" Like other evangelical women's writings, Sarah Osborn's *Nature, Certainty and Evidence of True Christianity* overflowed with the words *I* and *me*. "I'll tell you truly what GOD has done for my Soul," she declared at the beginning of her letter. "GOD the FATHER *manifested* himself to me." "God made with me an *everlasting Covenant.*"[47]

Yet as we have seen, there were limits to the kind of "individual" an evangelical could be, and women's writings were rarely published if they challenged gender norms. Perhaps readers were able to find more egalitarian meanings in these texts, but they nonetheless portrayed women as naturally humble and self-effacing. Osborn's title page included a scriptural citation, "1 Cor. 1: 26–31," in the center of the page, an allusion to Paul's words, "But God hath chosen the foolish things of the world to confound the wise; and God hath chosen the weak things of the world to confound the things which are mighty." Since Osborn never explicitly referred to this biblical text in her letter, it is likely that either the Reverend Prince or Samuel Kneeland (the printer) decided to include it—but they may have been inspired by her description of herself as a "poor nothing creature." At a time when few women dared publish their words, these men wanted readers to know that even the weak and the foolish—or in Osborn's case, the female—could offer insight into "the nature, certainty, and evidence of true Christianity."[48]

The publication of Osborn's letter raises crucial questions about the effects of both the early evangelical movement and the Enlightenment on women. Many historians have been sharply critical of the Enlightenment, arguing that it created "a single truth and a single rationality" that legitimated women's political, economic, and religious subordination.[49] As Enlightenment thinkers tried to establish a new "Age of Reason," they constructed their ideal of the rational self against the image of feminine religious "enthusiasm," a strategy that led to a decline in women's spiritual authority. According to Susan Juster, one of the results of the Enlightenment commitment to rationality and middle-class respectability was the "domestication" of women's religious voices. When radical female prophets like Jemima Wilkinson and Joanna Southcott published books in the late eighteenth century, they were ridiculed for their "enthusiasm," a reaction that demonstrated "the intractable hostility of Anglo-American men of letters toward women in public."[50] Few women participated in the "public sphere," the vibrant world of coffeehouses, freemasonry societies, and newspapers that laid the foundation for democratic government. Although white, property-owning men were encouraged to engage in rational political discourse, women were excluded from the public on the grounds of their supposed irrationality.[51]

On one hand, Sarah Osborn's story seems to confirm these bleak interpretations of the effect of the Enlightenment on women. Even though she published a book, she did not exert the "democratic political agency" that historians have associated with the public sphere; nor was she part of an explicitly feminist "counterpublic" that demanded a voice in public affairs. Controversial feminist writers like Mary Wollstonecraft and Judith Sargent Murray would not publish their works until the late eighteenth century.[52] It is clear that Osborn accepted (and reinforced) negative stereotypes of women's frailty and passivity, and even though she probably knew more about Reformed Protestant theology than most of the men in her church, she never defended her religious authority on the grounds of her intelligence, only her experience.

Yet on the other hand, Sarah Osborn's story suggests that the Protestant encounter with the Enlightenment made it possible for women to make their voices heard in one of the other publics that jostled for attention in eighteenth-century America—an "evangelical public of letters" that was crucial to the emergence of the movement. Evangelicals defined themselves not only around well-known leaders like George Whitefield but around common texts like Jonathan Edwards's *Faithful Narrative of the Surprising Work of God*, Thomas Prince's periodical *Christian History*, and Puritan stalwarts like Elizabeth White's *Experiences of God's Gracious Dealing with Mrs. Elizabeth White*. Although Sarah Osborn's letter never achieved the status of an evangelical classic, it was still published in five editions before her death, in Boston, Newport, Providence, Danbury, and even London, and her words helped define what it meant to be an evangelical.[53] We do not know who bought her book, but it is clear that in the early years of the evangelical movement men as well as women were eager to read about women's religious experiences. Jonathan Edwards read the works of Elizabeth Rowe and Hannah Housman, and one of the surviving copies of Osborn's letter is marked with the signature "John Perrey, his Book." We can only imagine what it meant for an eighteenth-century man to search for religious truth in a woman's book, but it seems likely that women's growing presence in the evangelical public of letters paved the way for their later activism in missionary societies, Sunday Schools, and charities. As evangelicals grew accustomed to encountering women's voices in print, they became more comfortable with women's participation in public life—provided, that is, that women never forgot Paul's words: "the man is the head of the woman."[54]

Historians have sometimes debated whether evangelicalism was liberating or oppressive for women, but this dichotomy is too simplistic. Evangelicals were not feminists before their time, but they still encouraged women to publish books, to hold religious meetings in their homes, and, in the most radical cases, to speak publicly about their beliefs. By arguing that women were silenced by the Enlightenment's emphasis on rationality, historians have underestimated the equally powerful language of experience and individualism. They have also underestimated women's ability to devise new strategies to overcome the limitations placed upon them. Despite being excluded from the republic of letters on the basis of their supposed irrationality, women found ways to enter through the door of religious experience. Sarah Osborn never claimed to be equal to men, but by testifying that she had been reborn in Christ, she portrayed herself as uniquely qualified to write about the "nature, certainty, and evidence of true Christianity." She might be female, poor, and "worthless" in the eyes of the world, but she was sure that her heartfelt religious experience, like God himself, was "no imaginary thing."

Chapter 7

Pinching Poverty, 1756–1758

I now record on purpose yt I may Give God the Glory of Providing for us in His Providence yt at this time my ways are as mr Elot expresses it Hedg'd up with thorns and grow darker and darker Daily for our Expense is unavoidably Greater then our income notwithstanding I take every Prudential step I can think of to Lessen it the Necessaries of Life being so vastly risen A considerable sum is tis Probable Lost in bad Hands beside 50 or 60 more yt can be Had in nothing of Eatables or cask yt there is no Prospect at Present of our being able to provide wood or any one Particular for winter—but the God yt Has fed me all my Life Long does know what I need and will supply all my Needs too Let Satan or unbelief say what they will He never yet made me asham'd of my Hope nor He never will He has said He will never Leave me nor forsake me.[1]

"Our Expense is unavoidably Greater than our income." "This week we knew not what to do for food." "Let us not ungratefully . . . complain of Poverty but cheerfully rely on the stores of the Providence without coveting stores of our own." "Lord, pity me."[2] Sentences like these punctuate almost everything Sarah Osborn wrote between 1756 and 1758, the opening years of the Seven Years' War.

The war pitted two of the world's great powers, France and England, against each other in a battle over who would control America's vast economic resources. Most of the fighting took place in Canada, the Ohio valley, and upstate New York, but because the stakes were so high, the hostilities spread to Europe and the West Indies as well. The war sparked an international crisis that influenced the balance of power in western Europe.

For Sarah, though, the war was less a conflict over money and territory than a cosmic battle between true religion and false. French Catholics and their "heathen" allies, the Indians, were "Bloodthirsty enemies" who were plotting to "deprive us of all our Privileges sacred and civil, to cut off the very Name of Protestantism." Like other Protestants at the time, she identified the French as the "Antichrist," and she was certain that they were part of a vast Catholic conspiracy to make the world bow down to the authority of the pope. Remembering the fate of the Protestant martyrs who had been burned at the stake during the reign of England's Mary I, Sarah swore that she would suffer anything—"Prisons, dungeons, racks and tortures, fire and faggots"—rather than forsake her faith.[3]

Little though Sarah realized it, the greatest test of her faith during the war would come not from the French Antichrist but from the grinding poverty caused by rising prices and scarce provisions. As the war dragged on, her prayers for a Protestant victory were eventually overshadowed by petitions for food, money, wood, and, most important, the courage to trust in God. Her flour barrel was often empty, her fireplace cold. Even when she worked herself to the point of exhaustion she could not pay all her debts. Although she and Henry had endured bankruptcy once before, she could not bear the thought of losing all their possessions again. She yearned to believe that God had a plan for her life, but it was hard to believe in a God who sometimes seemed to be absent. "May I trust Him?" she asked herself in her diaries. Her answer was always yes, but given how many times she repeated the question during the war, it is obvious that she found it hard not to doubt. In the darkest days of her poverty, when she and her family were forced to rely on charity, she admitted experiencing "the sharpest conflict with temptations to atheism I have endured some years." (In the eighteenth century, an atheist was not necessarily someone who doubted the existence of God, but rather one who doubted God's providential intervention in the world.)[4]

Sarah's diaries during the first years of the Seven Years' War reveal her struggles to understand the meaning of poverty in a world of consumer abundance. During the 1740s and 1750s, British manufacturers flooded the colonies with small consumer items that transformed the character of everyday life. China, clothing, ribbons, jewelry, books—all were for sale in cities like Newport, and even in rural areas people could buy merchandise from itinerant peddlers. Between 1750 and 1773 the American market for consumer items rose by an astonishing 120 percent.[5] In Newport alone, people could visit more than ninety shops along the waterfront, most marked with hanging signs, that offered goods as mundane as linen and as exotic as red wine from Lisbon.[6] Not just the rich but the middling sort could now choose among a vast array of goods that promised status, pleasure, and refinement.

Like other evangelicals, Sarah was not immune to the desire for material goods, and she welcomed the "consumer revolution" as a reflection of God's beneficence toward his creation. As long as people did not become greedy or turn their possessions into idols, they could savor the pleasures of buying a new book, choosing a new outfit, or investing in a matched set of Wedgwood plates. At the same time, however, Sarah was uneasy about the commercial world emerging around her in Newport, and although she could not clearly articulate her fears, she seems to have sensed that there was something deeper at stake than money and possessions. Searching for the right word to describe her disquiet, she often complained about "pride," but in fact the crux of the issue was *choice*. What troubled her was not the expansion of commerce but the implicit sanction of individual agency and self-interest that lay underneath it. If there was anything that Sarah knew for certain, it was that the self and God were reverse images of each other, with the sinful, helpless self standing in awe of the perfect, sovereign Creator; yet when people participated in the consumer economy, they were encouraged to imagine themselves as free agents who could fashion their identities however they pleased, gratifying their desires instead of repressing them. This kind of "choice," though alluring, was always sinful.

Sarah's insistence that her poverty was God's will must be read with this context in mind. In spite of the expansive choices offered in the consumer marketplace, she denied that she or anyone else had the power to make real choices about their economic lives. Distinguishing herself from the self-satisfied merchants in Newport who acted as though they were the masters of their own fate, she insisted that only God had the power to determine whether a person would be rich or poor.

And for reasons she only partially understood, God wanted her to be poor.

The Haves and the Have-Nots

One would not know it from reading Sarah's diaries, but the standard of living seems to have improved for most Americans in the eighteenth century because of the expansion of the market and the greater availability of material goods. As British merchants increased their exports to the colonies, the middle and lower-middle ranks could buy objects that had once seemed out of reach. Based on evidence drawn from estate inventories and archaeological digs, historians have argued that eighteenth-century Americans were eager to purchase items that would increase not only their comfort (for example, spermaceti candles) but also their social standing in the eyes of others. Hoping to imitate the British gentry, they spent their money on objects that signaled their good taste and refinement. When a team of archaeologists excavated the site of an eighteenth-century house in Newport that had once belonged to William Tate, a blacksmith, and his wife, Mary, a seamstress, they discovered remnants of creamware, fans, jewelry, and a tin-glazed punchbowl that had been imported from England. The Tates were not well off, but they seem to have aspired to gentility, and they lived in a style that earlier generations of Americans would have found luxurious.[7] Nothing could quench "Wild-Fire Fashion," a Boston writer complained in 1750: "It is *now fashionable* to live great, to indulge the Appetite, to dress rich and gay."[8]

Historians tend to be uneasy about using the word *capitalism* to describe the economic system of the eighteenth century because industrial capitalism as Karl Marx defined it did not appear in America until the 1800s. Before the economic energies unleashed by the American Revolution, many farmers continued to value cooperation over competition, and although they wanted to make enough money to ensure the security of their families, they remained suspicious of self-interest and economic rivalry.[9] Yet still it is clear that the economy of the Anglo-American world was shifting in the late seventeenth and eighteenth centuries, and increasing numbers of farmers and merchants embraced the opportunities offered by intercolonial and international trade. Fueling the acceleration of the consumer economy was mercantile capitalism—a form of capitalism characterized by strong government control of trade, the accumulation of wealth, and profit-oriented production instead of subsistence.

Although all the colonies were affected in some way by the emergence of mercantile capitalism and consumerism, cities like Newport represented the cutting edge of economic change. Merchants not only amassed vast fortunes by trading wood, molasses, furniture, and slaves throughout the Atlantic world, they showed off their financial prowess by spending staggering amounts of money—especially by earlier standards—on their houses, furniture, and clothing. (Conspicuous consumption, as Thorstein Veblen would later christen it, was not an invention of the nineteenth century.) Much of Newport's wealth came from the slave trade, a business that was violent, brutal, dangerous—and lucrative. With molasses imported from the West Indies, merchants manufactured rum that they sent to Africa to trade for slaves (paying around two hundred gallons for each male slave), and then, to complete the triangle, they sailed back to the West Indies to trade the slaves for more molasses.[10] In 1741 Godfrey Malbone used his earnings in the slave trade to build Malbone Hall, a pink sandstone mansion with a mahogany interior, six chimneys, and canals in the gardens that a traveler described as "the largest and most magnificent dwelling-house I have seen in America." It cost a hundred thousand dollars, an almost unheard-of sum at the time.[11]

Yet not everyone shared in the wealth generated by mercantile capitalism. Despite the rising standard of living, the gap between the richest and the poorest widened in the eighteenth century, especially in cities. In Newport in 1760, the wealthiest 10 percent of taxpayers paid 56 percent of taxes and the bottom 20 percent paid only 3 percent. (Since taxes were not graduated, this statistic reveals that the top 10 percent owned more than half of the taxable wealth.) Stark as these percentages are, they fail to capture the vast distance separating the "haves" from the "have-nots." Many residents of Newport were too destitute to pay taxes, but because they never asked for poor relief their numbers are impossible to count precisely. Based on town records, one historian estimates that 45 percent of Newport's white population may have lived near the poverty line.[12] When Sarah walked through the city on her way to teach school, she saw both prosperous merchants on the way to the counting house and ragged, hungry men looking for a day's work.

Frustrated by the growing number of vagrants in the cities, magistrates and ministers tried to distinguish between the "deserving" poor—the disabled, the widowed, and the elderly—and the "undeserving," who were too lazy to earn their bread. The "idle poor," according to Charles Chauncy, should not be assisted to eat. (Earlier, in 1695, Cotton Mather had argued, "*We should Let them Starve*," and in 1697, John Locke recommended that "begging drones" should be "kept at hard labor" until they reformed.)[13] Newport provided small sums of cash (known as out-relief) to the able-bodied poor or arranged for them to board with families, but the city also constructed an almshouse in 1723 to care for the aged or infirm. Sometime in the 1750s, city fathers became so concerned about the rising numbers of tramps that they built a workhouse where the "idle poor" were required to pick oakum. (This was a messy job that involved separating tar from fiber in order to make caulking for ships.) As in other New England towns, large numbers of the transient poor who were not legal residents were "warned out": forced to return to their hometowns to receive charity.[14] Land shortages, the loss of male breadwinners in the war, inflation—all exacerbated the problem of poverty, but at a time when the study of economics was still in its infancy, most people understood poverty as an individual rather than a structural problem. The solution was simple: "If we are industrious we shall never starve," Benjamin Franklin insisted.[15] The lazy had to be forced to labor, not coddled with food and a warm place to sleep.

Public discussions about poverty usually focused on how to help (or to force) men to support their families, but hidden from view was a large group of penniless women. During the 1740s female poor-relief recipients in Newport outnumbered men by two to one.[16] Early-American women made significant contributions to the family economy by spinning cloth, brewing beer, growing vegetables, and churning butter, but they were not educated to be anything other than wives and mothers, and if they lost their husbands or fathers they had limited options when it came to supporting themselves. A few became lawyers or printers, but most were forced into low-paying "women's work" as seamstresses, cooks, or teachers. For every woman in Newport like Ann Franklin, a successful printer, there were dozens of others like Hannah Lamb, a member of Sarah's prayer group who managed to stay out of the almshouse only because of her church's charity. Even though there were many female-headed households in Newport (the consequence of the appalling numbers of sailors who died at sea), in 1760 only thirty-five women earned enough money to pay taxes. (They constituted 3.6 percent of all taxpayers.)[17]

Sarah's income was too small to earn her and Henry a spot on Newport's tax list (she probably earned less than half the wages of male teachers),[18] but she felt fortunate in comparison to the many women who were forced to rely on charity. When war was formally declared in 1756 after more than a year of skirmishes on the frontier, she seems to have believed that she and her family would be able to withstand any economic hardships that might come their way. Ever since their bankruptcy fourteen years earlier, she had always managed to pay the family's debts by dint of her hard work, never too proud to bake, sew, or spin flax to supplement her teaching income. Even though she and Henry never managed to scrape up enough money to buy their own house, they were still better off than many of their friends and neighbors. When the First Church of Christ assessed pew rents in 1753, Henry Osborn was charged ten pounds a year, a figure that put him in the bottom half of the congregation but still above 21 percent of the membership. (In a typical example of early-American patriarchy, the church listed the pew in Henry's name alone even though Sarah earned the money to pay for it.) While the richest member, Thomas Coggeshall, paid thirty-six pounds for a large pew on the first floor, the poorest members, Widow Hart and her son Norman, paid only five pounds to sit in the gallery near Sarah and Henry.[19] Describing their social and economic standing to her friend Joseph Fish, Sarah explained that they did not belong to either the "politest sort" or "the vulgar," but the lower middling sort who were hardworking and "pretty sober." Grateful for enough food to eat, a warm house to live in (though rented), and a large school to teach, Sarah addressed God in her diary, "Thou in infinite Wisdom art giving me neither Poverty nor Riches and thou Hast Graciously freed me from anxious cares and Perplexing fears about futurities."[20]

Sarah would have been less sanguine if she had been able to see the hard years that lay ahead, but at the beginning of 1757, with the fighting still far from Newport, she and Henry felt secure enough to hire an assistant teacher for her school and to move to a more comfortable house. They also helped support Henry's son John and his wife, Abigail, who were "Destitute of the Necessities of Life." In a cryptic diary entry, Sarah complained that John and Abigail had been guilty of "Misconduct" in the past, but out of pity for their four children, the oldest not more than nine and the youngest a baby, she was determined to "cheerfully and thankfully relieve them."[21]

Sarah worked hard not just because she needed to support her family but because she saw teaching as her vocation. Echoing Martin Luther and John Calvin, who had rejected the monasticism of the Catholic Church, she believed that Christians must serve God in the world rather than withdraw from it. "Christians must have some Business of their own to mind," Nathaniel Clap preached. "Their Bones, or their Brains, or both must be Employed in some Good Business, whereby their Neighbors may be Advantaged, in their Souls, or Bodies, or Estates, or some of their Desirable Interests; otherwise, they will not mind the Work of the Lord." Hoping to glorify God and to serve her neighbors, Sarah prayed to be "diligent in business." In many ways she embodied what Max Weber would later term the Protestant ethic: she worked hard, spent frugally, and treated time as a commodity that should not be wasted. Between teaching, caring for her family, meeting with the women's society, and writing in her diary, she allowed herself virtually no time for leisure.[22]

Yet even Sarah's industriousness was not enough to shield her and her family from the economic distress caused by the war. By the spring of 1757 she was worried about rising prices. "Everything of the necessaries of life are so Excessively risen," she complained in her diary. Because the British military needed to buy large quantities of food for their soldiers, the price of commodities rose sharply. Overall the war benefited America's economy (the British army and navy spent more than six million pounds sterling in the colonies between 1756 and 1762), but the poor found it difficult to afford food or firewood. Prices were especially high in Newport because merchants suffered heavy financial losses during the war. Rhode Island had always been infamous for privateering, and in the 1740s many merchants had grown rich by capturing French bounty. During the Seven Years' War (known in the colonies as the French and Indian War), however, they lost more than 150 of their ships to the enemy. Because the British enforced a trade embargo with the French West Indies, they also lost one of their most important sources of revenue. (Many resorted to smuggling, but they faced stiff penalties if caught.) When the Act of Insolvent Debtors was passed in Rhode Island in 1756 to help those facing bankruptcy, it was supposed to be temporary, but by the end of the 1760s more than a hundred men had filed for protection. Handley Chipman, for example, whose wife was a member of Sarah's prayer group, lost his soap-boiling and rum-distilling business during the war, perhaps because he could no longer import molasses from the French West Indies.[23]

Sarah, too, feared that she might go bankrupt, but she hesitated to raise the tuition for her school at a time when so many people were suffering. What made her decision especially difficult was that many of the parents who sent children to her were also members of her church, her "sisters" and "brothers" in Christ. Student Polly Hammond, for example, was probably related to Elnathan Hammond, a member of the committee that assigned pew rates.[24] Parents could choose among schools in Newport, but many seem to have been attracted to Sarah's desire to make her school "a Nursery for Piety," and they not only expected her to teach Christian ethics but to embody them herself. Because Sarah took this responsibility seriously, she swore that she would rather "beg my bread from door to door or die upon a dunghill" than sully her name as a Christian. Indeed, when she had tried to raise her prices once before, she had changed her mind after hearing "cutting, bitter reflections" on whether she was a true Christian.[25]

Sarah's dilemma arose from the fact that ministers offered advice about economic life that seemed to point in contradictory directions. On one hand, they argued that the poor must do everything possible to improve their lives: although it was good to trust in God, it was sinful to be passive in the face of adversity. "*Reliance* on God is vain and *provoking* without a diligent use of *Means*," Cotton Mather insisted. "If a *drone* pretend to *trust* in Providence he does but *tempt* God." Echoing this language, Sarah wrote in her diary, "O, my God, suffer me never to live in the neglect of proper means, but use all diligence, casting my care on thee." She thought that raising her tuition was what a responsible follower of Christ should do. On the other hand, ministers also insisted that converts must subordinate their own economic interests to the common good, and Sarah feared she might be guilty of violating Christ's injunction to love her neighbor as herself. Imagining the Christian community as the body of Christ, she believed that she was linked to other believers by bonds of love that were more important than the desire for individual gain. She wrote, "Let me consider myself only as a member of the Glorious body of which my Precious Precious Christ is Head and seek the Prosperity of the whole."[26]

Sarah believed that if she were motivated by genuine economic need, she could raise her tuition with a clear conscience, but if she were driven by "covetous desires" she would have to make the best of her destitution. It was better to be a poor woman on the way to heaven than a rich one on the way to hell. Everything hinged on her motivation, but because she had such a strong sense of her sinfulness she was afraid to trust herself. Praying to God, she asked him to help her see into her own heart. "Let the Golden Rule be mine," she wrote. "Preserve me from covetousness, from extortion, from Grinding the face of the Poor."[27]

Sarah's economic scruples might suggest that she saw money or material goods as inherently corrupt, but in fact she spent most of her life praying for *more*: more money, more firewood, more flour, vegetables, and pork. Reflecting the historic influence of Calvin and Luther, Protestants insisted that poverty was not a sign of holiness but an evil that must be combated. (In contrast, the Catholic Church argued that the poor were especially blessed in the eyes of God, and many nuns and priests took vows of poverty.) Sarah assumed that money was one of the good things of the world, a sign of God's overflowing love for his creation. When Jonathan Edwards searched for an image that would capture the joy of being part of a revival, he compared it to a "market day," a day of "Great opportunity and advantage."[28] As long as people did not worship money, they could savor the contentment of a comfortably furnished house, shelves filled with books, and a well-stocked pantry. The challenge was to approach money in a spirit of stewardship, not ownership. Like everything else in the world, money ultimately belonged to God, and those who had been blessed with prosperity were supposed to use it for the common good.

Hoping to improve her fortunes, Sarah often bought tickets in the city lotteries. Lotteries were a common way to raise money for civic improvements (like paving roads) in the eighteenth century, and although some people disapproved of them as a form of gambling, Sarah believed that like everything else they were controlled by God. "I come to thee for success," she wrote to God in her diary, "for I know the whole disposal is of the Lord. Not a mite shall go to one or the other without thee." She promised that if she won, she would use the money not only for her own "comfort" but for the support of the ministry and the relief of the poor.[29]

As she soon discovered, however, winning the lottery was not part of God's plan for her life. If she wanted to raise more cash, she would have to increase her tuition. The decision was so difficult that she spent months agonizing over it. Borrowing an image from Psalm 131 ("Surely I have behaved and quieted myself, as a child that is weaned of his mother: my soul is even as a weaned child"), she prayed to be "weaned" from the world, to place her affections on God instead of the fleeting pleasures that someday she would have to leave behind. But it was not easy. Surrounded by people who spent more on fashionable carriages and imported lace than she could earn in a year, it was hard not to be envious, hard not to wish that she were one of the well-heeled matrons who had never felt the pinch of poverty. Recent historians have celebrated the "strikingly egalitarian" nature of the consumer market because "anyone with money could purchase what he or she desired," but the truth was that many people did *not* have excess money to spend, and even those who occasionally bought a penknife or a piece of ribbon knew that their purchases did not put them on equal footing with the rich. The language of consumption may have brought people together, but it also caused resentment. This was why Sarah's church wrote a new covenant in 1755 forbidding "Manifest Discontentment with our own Estate and Circumstances, together with all manifest inordinate Motions and Affections toward anything that is our Neighbors.'"[30] And it was also why Sarah spent so much time wringing her hands over raising her tuition. Envy, avarice, selfishness—these, not money, were what she feared.

In June, after three months of praying about it, she finally decided that she was "in the path of duty respecting raising my price for schooling." The word *duty* was crucial: she believed that she had a religious obligation to make sure that she could pay her bills. Although she did not want to "grind the face of the poor" by raising her tuition, she also did not want to defraud her creditors, and because of the war her situation had suddenly become desperate. The British government, angered by smuggling, had ordered all American ports closed, and from March until the end of June no ships could sail without explicit government clearance. The results were devastating. A severe drought in New England had decreased agricultural yields, and as Newport's ships sat at anchor in the harbor, forbidden to sail, Sarah feared that dwindling food supplies might lead to "famine." Shortly before deciding to raise her tuition, she admitted that "this week we knew not what to do for food." She and Henry would have gone hungry if God had not sent them "dainties from day to day: squab, pigeon, sparrowgrass [asparagus], pudding, gingerbread, tarts, Gammon &c." (It was typical for her to explain people's charity toward her as God's will.) It did not seem as though things could get any worse, but in response to her tuition increase eight of her students left for cheaper schools. "My whole school totters," she wrote fearfully.[31]

As always, Sarah relied on her diary to strengthen her faith. She often recorded her prayers in order to keep track of when (and if) they were answered. For example, at some point after asking God to help her and Henry pay their debts, she added in the margins, "blessed be God, good success." Sometimes her prayers were answered almost immediately, like the day when she wrote an anxious entry about the scarcity of firewood in Newport, and someone arrived at her door fifteen minutes later to tell her where to buy it. But even if she had to wait months before a prayer was answered, she would return to her original entry in order to make a notation. In case she was ever tempted to forget it, her diaries "proved" that God heard her prayers.[32]

As she reflected on her life, Sarah found abundant evidence of God's mercy in the midst of her troubles. Henry had not had a paying job since their bankruptcy, but because of widespread fears that French forces might attack by sea he was hired to be one of the wardens who stood watch over the harbor. "I have been able to stand alone some years without his Earning anything and then there was no way that He could earn a shilling to Help," she wrote in her diary, but now God had brought something good out of the evil of the war. Even though Henry's job was only part time, his income helped pay their rent.[33]

An even greater mercy awaited in May when Phillis, Bobey's mother, told Sarah that she had been born again in Christ. Because she was a slave, few records mention her, but based on fragmentary evidence we can piece together some facts about her life. The mother of two children, Bobey and another whose name has been lost to history, Phillis belonged to Timothy Allen, a silversmith who was a member of Ezra Stiles's church, and she was married to Gosper, a slave like herself. On June 26, 1757, she was admitted into full membership at Sarah's church, the First Church of Christ, and afterward she became the only black member of Sarah's prayer group.[34] Based on a single sentence in Sarah's diary, we can surmise that Phillis had either been owned by the Osborns at an earlier date or been hired out to them as a household servant. "This was my servant," Sarah wrote in her diary, "but is she now thine?"[35] Without more evidence, the exact nature of their relationship is murky, but they had probably known each other for at least thirteen years, ever since Phillis's infant son had become Sarah's slave. We can only imagine the pain that Phillis must have felt at being separated from her son or the anger and resentment that may have bubbled under the surface whenever she saw Sarah scold or punish him. Yet there were far worse masters in Newport, and over the years Phillis and Sarah managed to forge a close relationship—so close that they eventually had serious conversations about suffering, sin, and God. After Phillis experienced conversion, she asked Sarah to come with her as she recounted her religious experiences to the Reverend Vinal. (Phillis wanted to join Sarah's church, not her master and mistress's, perhaps because she wanted the freedom to worship without their supervision or perhaps because of her more conservative theology.) Although many slaves attended Vinal's meeting each Sunday with their masters, only two had ever been accepted into membership before. The first was Cudjo Nichols, who was baptized in 1749, perhaps on his deathbed, and the second was Primos Leandrow, a free black who had transferred his membership from Bristol in 1757. With so few black faces in the congregation, Phillis may have been apprehensive about whether Vinal would accept her as his spiritual equal, but he judged her religious experiences to be real. Only one obstacle still remained: she had to get her owner's approval before she could be baptized or partake of the Lord's Supper. It is not clear what would have happened if her master had said no, but when Sarah anxiously visited him the next day he assured her he had "no objection at all."[36] In June, when Sarah saw Phillis sitting at the Lord's Supper for the first time, she was so moved by God's grace that she could almost forget the war, suffering, and hunger that lurked outside the church doors. "O adored be thy Name for what thou Hast done for my poor Phillis," she thanked God. "She is made free indeed."[37]

A page from the Records of the First Church of Christ in Newport.
On June 26, 1757, "Phillis, a Negro woman" was baptized into the church (see line 136).
Courtesy of the Newport Historical Society.

After this remarkable sign of divine mercy, though, the rest of the summer of 1757 was grim. In churches, coffeehouses, and the streets, no one could stop talking about French Catholics and their savage Indian allies. Because almost all Protestants at the time saw the papacy as the "whore of Babylon" described in the book of Revelation, they expected the battle with France to be long, vicious, and bloody—as indeed it was. "For Christ's sake, spare a sinful People," Sarah pleaded. "O Give not thine heritage to reproach. God be merciful to us sinners." Whenever the French won a victory (and in 1757, they seemed invincible), she feared that an angry God might have forsaken his "British Israel."[38]

Both of Henry's sons, his two remaining children, joined the fighting in 1757. (His middle child, Henry, had died sometime after his marriage to Sarah, but we know nothing about the circumstances.) Because twenty-seven-year-old John needed to support his wife and four children, he signed on as a privateer in hopes of capturing a "prize," a French merchant ship laden with bounty. Privateering bordered on smuggling, but in this case the plundering was legal, and as an advertisement in the *Newport Mercury* promised, it was a quick way for poor men to "make their fortunes." Unfortunately for John, however, his voyage was a failure, and if he made any money beyond his enlistment bonus it was soon spent. (Since Sarah disapproved of privateering, she could not muster much sympathy.) Sarah had few kind words to say about John, but he seems to have been a pathetic figure: reckless, "hardened in sin," and unable to feed his family. Sarah's solution to his problems, not surprisingly, was to urge him to seek Christ, but he refused. "Turn Him to thyself for Christ's sake," she implored God.[39]

Henry's older son, Edward, thirty-three, enlisted as a soldier and sailed to Albany to fight, leaving behind his wife, Mary.[40] (Although they had been married ten years, they do not seem to have had any children.) Two months later, Sarah and Henry heard the ominous news that he had been "shot through the body in a Late Engagement with the Enemy." Nothing else was known: had he survived? Was he recovering in safety away from the fighting? Twelve agonizing days later, they learned that his wounds had been fatal. Since he had never experienced conversion, Sarah had spent every day praying for his "awakening," but just as she had done after her son Samuel's death she forced herself to accept God's will. "After I heard this news God quieted my heart," she wrote that evening, "and made it submit to His adorable sovereignty. I realized in some degree His infinite wisdom in ordering all Events and was constrained to say He does all things well. The Judge of all the Earth Has done and will do right." Henry, however, seems to have been anguished. Only one of his three children was still alive. "Sanctify thy rod to my dear consort," she begged God in her diary. "Lord, support, quicken, humble and comfort him."[41]

In the midst of their mourning, she and Henry decided to extend their compassion to a "poor girl," Almey Greenman, who came to live with them. Since Sarah wrote little about Almey (and her name does not appear in other Newport records), the relationship between them is not clear, but she could have been a girl from a poor family who was apprenticed to Sarah as a teacher; a ward of the town whose parents were too poor to care for her; or perhaps an orphan who needed a home. Although Sarah clearly hoped that Almey would provide an extra pair of hands for preparing breakfast or teaching school, she also seems to have taken a maternal interest in her. It was almost as if she and Henry wanted another chance to raise a child. "Pity the poor unsteady creature," she begged God in her diary. "Help her to bend Her mind to business and the affairs of Her Precious soul." Edward had died without being born again, but Sarah begged God to "snatch this brand out of the burning. Take away her filthy Garments and clothe Her with the Precious robe of thine own righteousness."[42] She and Henry had never known the joy of seeing their own children turn to Christ, but there were still others who needed their prayers.

Among these were John's children, and Sarah, deeply in debt, could not stop thinking about their suffering. Describing them as "Poor, Helpless, Neglected Little ones," she yearned to bring them into her own house, where she could make sure that they were fed, clothed, and reared as Christians. Although she had said more prayers for John than she could count, she feared that he would never become a good father. She begged God in her diary, "Meet with our son Even Now Whilst he is running away from God and from His Duty, Neglecting the Means of Grace and committing those things that are abominable in thy sight." Sarah never explained the nature of John's "abominable" behavior (did he fit the stereotype of the drunken, profane, hot-headed sailor?), but at the least he and Abigail seem to have been negligent parents. Later Sarah remembered that their children were "Hungry, Naked, and dragged up as Heathen in a Gospel Land, real objects of charity which Moved my compassion towards them."[43]

It is a testament to the depth of Sarah's faith—and her generosity— that she could contemplate taking in three grandchildren at a time when she and Henry could barely afford to feed themselves. His job as a watchman was only part time, and though Sarah worked herself to exhaustion they could not keep up with mounting prices. She wrote in her diary, "Our Expense is unavoidably Greater then our income, notwithstanding I take every Prudential step I can think of to Lessen it." Having little cash, she offered to pay some of her creditors with things she could make at home. "In his Providence, yesterday 2 persons took flax from me instead of money," she recorded gratefully. Despite her own struggles, though, she kept praying for her needy grandchildren, and as 1757 drew to a close she became convinced that God wanted her to take them in. At first she and Henry hoped to take the three oldest (the youngest was a baby), but either because of their own indigence or John and Abigail's resistance, they took only one instead. In March 1758, Sarah thanked God for bringing "this dear Little one under my care."[44] (Her diary entries are vague about details, and it is not clear whether the child was a boy or a girl.)

Most of Sarah's diary for 1758 has been lost, but it is clear that financially she and Henry could not afford to feed yet another mouth. While she never seems to have regretted her generosity to Almey or her grandchild,

she spent many hours worrying about money. Whenever a student withdrew from her school, she prayed for the strength to trust in God. After
a boy stopped coming in March, she reminded herself, "God fed me and
clothed me before I had Him and will again, and He knows when tis best
to remove Him." To save money she and Henry moved in April to a house
that they had to share with their landlord—their second home in two years.
They were descending the economic ladder instead of climbing it, always
in search of cheaper rent. A few bedsteads and featherbeds, chairs, skillets,
blankets, a desk—their possessions were easily bundled up and loaded onto
a wagon for a trip across town.[45]

By the winter of 1758 Sarah was so worried about money that she seriously considered opening a boarding school. She hesitated, though, because
of her fear that caring for boarders might interfere with her devotional life.
Like other evangelicals, she imagined her faith as the foundation of all her
financial decisions, not as a private concern that could be separated from
the grubby reality of money making. If opening a boarding school would
take too many hours away from reading the Bible, praying, and writing,
then she would have to find a way to make ends meet without the extra

SARAH OSBORN, Schoolmiftrefs in Newport,
propófes to keep a

Boarding School.

ANY Perfon defirous of fending Children, may
be accommodated, and have them inftructed in Reading, Writing, Plain Work, Embroidering, Tent Stitch, Samplers, &c. on rea-
fonable Terms.

An advertisement for Sarah Osborn's boarding school in the *Newport Mercury*,
December 19, 1758. Photograph courtesy of the Newport Historical Society.

income.[46] But she feared that if she did not do something soon, she would not be able to support her own family or find the extra cash to help John and Abigail, who were even poorer than she was. Because several of her students were ill, they had stopped coming to school in the fall, and she did not know how she would pay the rent. Even with all her scrimping and saving, she could not imagine stretching her small income any farther. In December 1758, after more than a year of thinking and praying about it, she placed an ad in the *Newport Mercury* announcing her plans to open a boarding school. Though willing to take both boys and girls, she especially advertised her ability to teach needlework.[47]

Even after her decision, though, she worried. She did not want to be like the rich man in the Gospel of Luke who decided to pull down his barns to build bigger ones so that he could "eat, drink, and be merry." The "fool," as Sarah branded him, had died before realizing that only God could satisfy his craving for happiness. "God alone can fill and satisfy," she reminded herself.[48]

The Needle's Eye

Given Sarah Osborn's precarious finances, her trepidation about whether to raise her tuition or open a boarding school may seem overly scrupulous. It is hard to imagine that anyone would have accused her of grinding the face of the poor when she herself was impoverished. But her anxieties about a rising spirit of "covetousness" make more sense when understood as part of a larger evangelical conversation about wealth, poverty, and, on a deeper level, self-interest and choice. If Christians were supposed to sacrifice their own interests for the good of the whole, then what did that mean for their participation in an expanding marketplace? "It is easier for a camel to go through the eye of a needle, than for a rich man to enter into the kingdom of God," Jesus had proclaimed (Matthew 19:24).

On both sides of the Atlantic, evangelicals worried that commercial success had led to a decline in religious faith. While John Guyse, Sarah's uncle, asked his congregation whether their "Plenty" had been "turned into Means and Occasions of feeding our Pride and Ambition, Intemperance, Luxury and debauchery," George Whitefield accused his listeners of worshiping Mammon rather than God. In a sermon titled *The Folly and Danger of Parting with Christ for the Pleasures and Profits of Life*, he protested that many so-called Christians cared about their "pleasures" more than God. "If they can but indulge their sensual appetite, please and pamper their bellies, satisfy the lust of the eye, the lust of the flesh, and the pride of life," they would forget who had created them.[49] Food, sex, and money—these were their gods.

Whitefield's angry words stood in a long Christian tradition of condemning avarice and luxury. Yet as he and other evangelicals seem to have sensed, there was something new about economic life in the eighteenth century that went beyond the age-old problem of greed. For centuries Christians had assumed that hierarchy was a natural part of God's creation, with some people created to be rich and some to be poor, but as more goods became available for sale in the marketplace no one seemed to know his or her "place" anymore. As early as 1719 Benjamin Colman reminded the "good people of Boston" that the most opulent goods for sale in the market were meant for those of the highest rank, not ordinary farmers and tradesmen. People with "*little Money*" should not be "*prodigal*," he admonished. "We should be willing to live low, where God has set us." Another minister complained that the "*very poor*" owned many of the same goods as those who were worth "*Hundreds of pounds*"—gold rings, jewelry, lace, silk, and ribbons. He asked angrily, "And is not this abominable Pride?" In the early years of New England, sumptuary laws had forbidden anyone except the elite to wear silk and lace, but in the new, modern world of consumption, people were free to pursue their own interests. Individual choice, not law or tradition, determined how they would spend their money.[50]

Since ideas about humanity and God and are always connected, the expansion of the marketplace changed popular understandings of both God and the self. As people could buy a greater variety of goods than ever before, adorning themselves with expensive silks and serving imported tea in their parlors, traditional Christian suspicions of self-love suddenly seemed overly strict. Especially in large cities like Newport, the burgeoning consumer economy helped pave the way for a more positive view of the self as good and worthy of gratification. The middle and upper ranks were able to buy not just what they needed but what they *wanted*, and this frank pursuit of individual desire gradually undermined older Protestant understandings of the self as sinful and unworthy.

Self-interest, freedom, choice—these would become three of the most important words in modern America, but in the eighteenth century they were laden with controversial theological meanings. Self-interest, for example, was one of the most divisive issues of the age. Influenced by the Puritans, evangelicals believed that "self-love," as they called it, was the result of the Fall. As Joseph Fish explained, "When Man forsook the Lord, he lost sight of the only Object of his Happiness, retired into *himself*, and made *himself* the Object of his Love, and the Centre of all his Desires and Actions." Writing against what he called "a new scheme of religion," Thomas Clap, the rector at Yale, condemned the belief that "the natural Tendency which Things have to promote our *own Interest*, is the sole Criterion of moral Good and Evil, Truth and Falsehood, Right and Wrong." As he explained, "For a Man to make the *sole, supreme*, or *ultimate* End of all Being and Action to be for *himself alone* or his *own* Happiness, as the *Summum Bonum*, and to regard God and all other Beings, only so far as they may *serve himself*, or be subservient to his own Happiness, or *gratify his Principle of Self-Love*, is the most absolute inversion of the *Order, Dignity* and *Perfection* of Beings: and one of the worst Principles that can be in human Nature." Even though many people did not realize how deeply their lives were tainted by self-love, true Christians knew that they must take up the cross of self-denial in order to be saved. In her closest moments of communion with God, Sarah Osborn rejoiced that she was filled with a spirit of "self-abasement" and "self-abhorrence." "Strip me entirely of self," she prayed.[51]

Other Christians, however, had a more positive view of human nature, and they argued that self-love was the foundation of their love for God. They did not love God for abstract reasons but because he offered them salvation. According to Benjamin Wadsworth, "man's . . . chief end is God's glory and his own happiness . . . and if they are not the same, yet they are so closely connected that they cannot be separated from the other." Echoing the ideas of liberal Anglicans, humanitarians, and other Enlightenment thinkers, they insisted that self-love did not have to degenerate into selfishness or pride. The Reverend Samuel Cooper of Boston, a liberal-leaning Congregationalist, scoffed at the idea that Christians should abhor themselves. "Were it possible for a rational Creature, to extinguish the Principle of Self-Love," he protested, "far from being any Virtue or Perfection, this would at once appear a gross and monstrous Defect in his Constitution. For Self-Love is at least as necessary to the Support and Happiness of the World as social." Although Cooper assumed that the self had to be disciplined, he did not think it had to be annihilated.[52]

Two other fighting words—*choice* and *freedom*—also caused divisions among eighteenth-century Protestants. In contrast to Enlightenment thinkers, who celebrated human freedom, evangelicals insisted that there were limits to their self-determination. On one hand, they urged people to "choose" salvation, and they insisted that all were free to do what they wanted. As Jonathan Edwards explained, "Let the person come by his volition or choice how he will, yet, if he is able, and there is nothing in the way to hinder his pursuing and executing his will, the man is fully and perfectly free, according to the primary and common notion of freedom." Humans were free in the sense that they could decide how to act at any particular moment—to choose, for example, whether to churn the butter or milk the cow. On the other hand, humans were *not* free in a deeper, moral sense. No matter how hard they tried, they could not make the correct moral choices without God's grace.[53]

These debates might sound like theological hair-splitting, but in fact they had a profound effect on how people imagined everyday life, including the economy. Because Anglicans, Quakers, and a few radical Congregationalists saw humans as free agents, they do not seem to have been troubled by the implicit approval of individual free choice that supported the emerging capitalist order. Their religious and economic values subtly reinforced each other: in church they learned that they could choose to be saved, and in the marketplace they learned that they could choose how to fashion their personal identities. Samuel Johnson, an American Anglican, described humans as "intelligent free Agents" who were motivated by "the Pursuit of true Happiness." Guided by "that great *Law of our Nature* (which may be called the Law of *Self-Love or Self-Esteem* . . .)," we are "laid under a Necessity of valuing ourselves and our own *Interest*, and of seeking and preserving our own *Preservation* and *Well-being* or Happiness, and whatever we find tends to it or is connected with it." To be sure, Anglicans remained committed to a Christian ethic of charity, and they often preached against the excesses of wealth. Johnson denied that individuals could be happy unless they were serving the public good: "Self and social Good must not be considered as at all interfering, but as being entirely coincident, and subservient to each other." Nevertheless, Protestants who preached a gospel of free will and self-interest seem to have unintentionally contributed to the triumph of a capitalist ethic. By 1776, when Adam Smith published *The Wealth of Nations*, many people in the Anglo-American world had already accepted his bold defense of self-interest as a positive good. "It is not from the benevolence of the butcher, the brewer, or the baker, that we expect our dinner," Smith wrote, "but from their regard to their own interest."[54]

In contrast, evangelicals were deeply troubled by self-interest. Because of their conviction that humans were innately and profoundly sinful, they scorned the argument that "self love" (little better than "atheism," in Gilbert Tennent's view) could promote the public good. In a sermon on the "Sin of Extortion," Jonathan Edwards warned merchants not to raise their

Merchants displayed their goods at the Brick Market, which was
completed in 1762. Courtesy of the Newport Historical Society.

prices simply for the sake of personal profit. They had to be guided by
a commitment to the common good: "Whenever men in their dealings
seek their own private Gains in such a manner and measure as apparently
tends to the injury of the public society, then [their] Gains are unreasonable Gains." Sarah Osborn's church, like many others, vowed to punish
members who were guilty of "Oppression, Extortion, Engrossing Commodities to enhance the Price, and manifest acts of Covetousness," but
the congregation could not control what happened outside church walls.
Repulsed by the brutishness of economic life, Edwards even toyed with the
idea that the government should regulate prices—this despite his fear that
magistrates would not be any less rapacious than individual merchants.[55]
(New England Puritans had regulated both prices and wages in the 1630s,
but they eventually abandoned their experiment because of their inability
to control economic ambitions.)

Samuel Davies, an evangelical in Virginia, argued that merchants were
the worst "Enemies" of Calvinism, and though he exaggerated, he had a
point. Prosperous men who built their fortunes through hard work and
self-discipline found it hard to accept the notion that they were powerless
to sway God's will. But it would be a mistake to argue that economic considerations determined people's religious decisions, as if religion served as

nothing more than a screen for class interests. There were many evangelicals like David Moore, a member of Sarah's church (she had tended his shop before her second marriage), who worried about mistaking their economic success for God's favor. "O pray for me that I may not Deceive myself with false hope," Moore wrote to the Reverend Eleazar Wheelock. "I am Rich and Increased in Goods and have Need of Nothing, and at the same time I may be wretched and Miserable and poor and blind and naked." Religious sensibilities were shaped not only by rank but by intangible factors of psychology and temperament. Yet it is clear that many wealthy Christians in the eighteenth century had begun to chafe under the yoke of Calvinism, and they chose to worship in churches that affirmed human goodness and agency. In Newport there were unmistakable class distinctions between those who worshipped at Trinity Church, an Anglican congregation, and those who attended the First and Second Churches of Christ. Among the people who paid the highest taxes in Newport in 1760, 45 percent were Anglicans, 20 percent were Quakers, and 15 percent were Congregationalists. (From a different angle, 53 percent of the people who paid the lowest taxes were Congregationalists, 18 percent were Quakers, and 1 percent were Anglicans).[56]

Evangelical ministers never explicitly rejected the concept of choice, and they tried to turn commercial language to their own ends by intensifying their calls to come to Christ. "Is *Jehovah* infinite in his Being and Attributes?" Gilbert Tennent asked. "Then how worthy is he of our highest Love, entirest Confidence, and freest Choice?" Yet evangelicals' understanding of choice (like their understanding of freedom) bore little resemblance to the assumption of individual agency that held sway in the marketplace. Sarah Osborn promised God to "choose thee alone for my dear and only Portion," but she thought that she could "choose" only what God had already willed for her. "God knows what is best for us," Tennent explained. "If we were left to our own Choice, we should certainly ruin ourselves." His words may have sounded counterintuitive to people who prided themselves on the tasteful, refined choices they made in the market, but that was precisely the problem: How could ministers convince their congregations that they lacked the power to control their ultimate economic or religious destinies? Concerned that a commercial sensibility had begun to erode older teachings about human sinfulness and helplessness, Jonathan Edwards warned that Christians could not "buy" salvation in the same way that they could buy things in the market: "True Wisdom is a precious Jewel: And none of our fellow Creatures can give it to us, nor can we buy it with any Price we have to give."[57]

Ironically, however, evangelicals were pioneers in using commercial techniques to spread the gospel. Like merchants who advertised their goods in local newspapers, they publicized their meetings in order to attract as many people as possible. George Whitefield arranged for the serial publication of his writings, enabling readers to buy sections of his books each week for a small price, and he offered booksellers a discount for buying in bulk. His output was prodigious: he published the first volume of his *Journal* in 1738, three more volumes in 1739, the first part of his autobiography in 1740, and the continuation of his autobiography in 1747. By the time he was in his mid-twenties, he had published an astonishing six hundred pages of life writing.[58] Like other evangelical ministers, Whitefield often sounded like a prophet denouncing luxury and corruption, but he was also an entrepreneur who knew how to "sell" religion.

Although evangelicals were profoundly ambivalent about mercantile capitalism, it would be a mistake to argue that they were opposed to a market economy. When historians have argued over how to define capitalism, some have used the terms "market exchange" and "capitalism" as if they are interchangeable, but in fact few people in early America opposed markets, which they saw as good.[59] Sarah clearly enjoyed the rare times when she could afford to purchase goods from Newport's merchants, especially books, and she sometimes used economic imagery to describe God's majesty. In a letter to Joseph Fish, for example, she prayed that God would comfort him "with the abundant incomes of his Blessed spirit." She and other evangelicals saw nothing wrong with either making money or buying things in the marketplace as long as they did not idolize wealth.[60]

Evangelicals *did* object, however, to the model of selfhood that formed the bedrock of the emerging capitalist order. Capitalism depended on a commitment to the values of acquisitive individualism, benevolent self-interest, and free choice, and it was these values, not the opportunity to buy and sell commodities, that disturbed people like Sarah Osborn. The challenge for her and other evangelicals was how to welcome the opportunities offered by the market without also accepting the capitalist values that threatened their faith.[61]

Contentment with My Own Condition

At the end of 1758, with the war still raging, Sarah and Henry had a mounting pile of debts, no house of their own, and few of the consumer luxuries that Newport's merchants proudly displayed in their homes. Yet if Sarah was ashamed of her poverty she never admitted it in her diary or letters. Because of her belief that God was guiding her life, she was convinced that she had no choice whether to be rich or poor. Although it was sometimes hard to accept, she was free only to become the person whom God wanted her to be. "Do not let me murmur against thee, and grieve thee," she beseeched him. "Thou requirest full contentment with my own condition."[62]

This was exactly the kind of attitude that Enlightenment thinkers wanted to combat. Complaining that Calvinist theology encouraged passivity and hopelessness, they argued that the poor should *not* be "content" with their situation. God was not a tyrant who predestined some to wealth and others to poverty but a benevolent father who wanted his children to reap the rewards of their labors. Writing as "Poor Richard," Benjamin Franklin insisted that "God helps them that help themselves." If poor people worked hard, saved their money, and practiced the virtues of honesty, temperance, and moderation, they could improve their lives.[63]

Like Franklin, many Anglicans, Quakers, and liberal-leaning Congregationalists were impatient with the attitude that poverty was inevitable, an unavoidable fact of life that should be accepted as God's will. Because of their faith in human agency and progress, they assumed that poverty could be overcome. In Boston a group of Congregationalists created the Society for Encouraging Industry and Employing the Poor, setting up a linen factory that was designed to help the indigent support themselves, and in Philadelphia, Quakers founded the Pennsylvania Hospital for the Sick Poor. Instead of repeating the dictum that "the poor you shall always have with you," the founders of these institutions tried to help poor people change their lives through discipline and hard manual labor.[64]

For some it worked: the "American dream" of upward mobility has its roots in eighteenth-century liberal understandings of freedom and progress. Yet there was also a dark side to the effort to uplift the poor. Reformers inflicted harsh punishments to make the poor conform to a middle-class work ethic; in some cases, as in Philadelphia's Bettering House, they even incarcerated the indigent. Some reformers also forced parents to indenture their children, breaking up families in the name of "rehabilitation." Not surprisingly, many poor people ran away from the institutions that were supposedly designed to help them.[65]

Ironically, many of the ministers who seemed most interested in aiding the poor ended up stigmatizing them as lazy, improvident, and sinful. By insisting that people had the power to change their lives, they implied that the chronically poor could be blamed for their own suffering. As early as 1719, the Reverend Benjamin Wadsworth published a sermon explaining that poverty was almost always the result of "vicious courses"— sloth, intemperance, "filthy unclean practices." (Wadsworth was one of the "catholick" Congregationalists who embraced the early Enlightenment.) In his closing pages, he assured his readers that if they lived as good Christians, they could shape their own fates. He remained too much of a Calvinist to claim that people could completely determine their destinies, but his words pointed in that direction: "We should be true to our word and promise, Just, upright and honest in all our dealings; readily and seasonably pay everyone his due; do our part honestly to support both church and state, to maintain God's worship, to relieve the poor and needy; and we should *pray to God* for his blessing on us. If we take this course, we need not fright ourselves with the fear of distressing poverty."[66] This may have been good advice for an able-bodied man in an economy that offered stable employment, but Wadsworth ignored the structural factors that kept some people poor, such as the unequal wages that made it hard for women to support their families. Even though Sarah Osborn could have been the model for his ideal Christian, she had good reason to be afraid of "distressing poverty."

Evangelicals could also sound harsh when discussing the poor, but because of their belief that God controlled everything, including economic status, they removed some of the stigma of poverty. The dispute, once again, was about choice. Although they assumed that those who were obviously immoral—the lazy, drunken, or debauched—were poor as a result of God's wrath, evangelicals also insisted that God sometimes afflicted people with poverty for his own mysterious reasons: to make them more compassionate or to teach them greater trust. Because of their circumscribed understanding of freedom and choice, evangelicals assumed that poverty could be the result of God's will instead of individual failings.[67]

To be clear, neither view of poverty was the "right" one (and it is hard to imagine what such an ideal would look like). While Enlightenment thinkers and Protestant liberals may have made the poor feel ashamed, evangelicals may have made them feel hopeless. Even though evangelical ministers insisted that hard work was a religious obligation, their theology could be twisted into a justification of passivity.

For Sarah Osborn, though, and for many others like her, the evangelical movement offered an appealing balance of resignation and exertion. Sarah had no doubt that God wanted her to be diligent, and she believed that if she worked hard, he might bless her labors with prosperity—or at least with a comfortable living. But she also assumed that an all-powerful God sometimes ordained poverty for his own reasons. As Susanna Anthony explained, the poor as well as the rich could serve God's purposes. "Blessed be God, the cause of Truth and the advancement of the redeemer's Kingdom don't absolutely depend on worldly prosperity," she wrote. "Had it done so, it had died with Him . . . who had nowhere to lay his head."[68]

Sarah believed that her benefactors learned something about Christian love whenever they gave her money, food, or firewood. Although her poverty was not good in itself, it enabled others to practice the virtues of compassion and generosity. Her suffering was a reminder of Christ's suffering on the cross—an invitation to "do unto others" as they would have done for him.

Historians have argued that as attitudes toward the poor became increasingly hostile in the mid-eighteenth century, poor people tried to resist their degradation by refusing to indenture their children, flouting codes of discipline in workhouses, and moving from place to place.[69] What they have rarely noticed, however, is that religion also helped the poor preserve their sense of dignity. Sarah knew that some people looked down on her, but when she remembered that Jesus had been born in a stable she held her head high. As long as she worked hard at her calling, she believed that there was no disgrace in being poor.

Chapter 8

Love Thy Neighbor, 1759–1763

O Let us build upon the dear the sure foundation Christ Jesus all the Good works we can O Let this be ever as oile to our wheels to make them run swift inasmuch as ye did it unto them ye did it unto me O may God reward Every kind benefactor He has rais'd to me in Every time of distress o may they never Loose their reward tho they did it to the Least of thine Let them Hear thee say dear Lord to them Precious souls Even Here in as much as ye did it ye did it unto me o reward them a thousand fold into their own bosoms and may Gratitude Ever Glow in my breasts to God and them and as I Have freely receiv'd in times of my distress so Let me freely Give as God Enables and occasion offers Lord Ever open my Hand and Heart to the sick poor and needy and make me a blessing in my day o make me extensively useful in my family in my school in the dear Dear society to all arround me Oh Let the Lord God almighty delight to own me to use me to set me apart for Himself in secret in Private and in Every way my Proper station admits.[1]

Sarah wrote these words in the midst of the Seven Years' War, a time of devastation in Newport. The war was in its fifth grueling year, and every day brought terrible news of battles lost, soldiers wounded, and loved ones killed. As food supplies dwindled and prices rose, many families were left destitute. The almshouse was filled with widows and orphans who lacked food, clothing, and a safe place to sleep.

Sarah spent many sleepless nights worrying about whether she and Henry would fall into bankruptcy again, but even though she could barely pay their rent, she was determined to help the hundreds of other impoverished and distressed people in Newport whose lives had been disrupted by the war. Praying to God in the pages of her diary, she promised to open her hand and heart to the "sick, poor, and needy"—a description that easily could have been written about Sarah herself. She, too, was chronically ill and had little money to spare, but inspired by Jesus's injunction to "love thy neighbor as thyself," she resolved to emulate characters in three biblical stories who sacrificed their own needs for the good of others: the Good Samaritan who tenderly bathed a stranger's wounds, the poor widow who gave away her last two mites to the public treasury, and the "righteous" in the Parable of the Sheep and the Goats who treated the hungry, naked, sick, and imprisoned as if they were Jesus himself. Inspired by the words of Jesus to his disciples, she transcribed them in her diary: "Inasmuch as ye have done it unto one of the least of these my brethren, ye have done it unto me." If she could not afford to give money to the poor, she could visit the sick, comfort the dying, and share the gospel with others, and if she felt too weak to leave her house she could still pray. "Make me a blessing in my day," she implored God.[2]

One of the distinctive features of the new evangelical movement was its commitment to doing good. As we have seen, evangelicals were ambivalent about the humanitarian movement because of their conviction that suffering could be redemptive, but they also absorbed its language of benevolence as their own. Although evangelicals refused to see human flourishing as the greatest good, they accepted the premise that Christians should strive to alleviate suffering and create a better world, and they had obvious affinities to a movement that echoed Jesus's ethical command to "love thy neighbor as thyself." Holding two beliefs in tension, Sarah believed that God's plan for the world included suffering, but she was also convinced that Christians were called to alleviate it. "If you have no Compassion, no Value of the bodies of Men," George Whitefield warned, "you are not, indeed, my dear Brethren, Christians, nor true Disciples of the Lord Jesus Christ."[3]

When the word *humanitarian* was coined in the nineteenth century, it was virtually an antonym to *evangelical*: a humanitarian was a religious skeptic (perhaps even an atheist) who viewed happiness as the greatest good, while an evangelical was a fervent believer in Christ's resurrection who wanted nothing more than to glorify God. Humanitarians wanted to abolish suffering; evangelicals thought suffering could be redemptive. Humanitarians believed that humans could make the world a better place; evangelicals insisted that progress was impossible without the inspiration of the Holy Spirit. Humanitarians imagined humans as essentially good; evangelicals saw them as fallen and sinful.

Yet despite these disagreements, there is no doubt that eighteenth-century evangelicals were influenced by the humanitarian currents of their age. As they created a new kind of Protestantism in dialogue with the Enlightenment, they sounded as fervent as humanitarians about creating a kinder, more compassionate world. Ultimately, though, they forged an understanding of benevolence that was uniquely their own. Convinced that there was no greater act of generosity than to save sinners from damnation, they placed more emphasis on evangelism than virtually any other group of Christians before them. Although they wanted to help the suffering body, they were even more concerned about the suffering soul. When the humanitarian command to "do good" collided with the Christian imperative to "preach the gospel," the result was an explosion of missionary zeal. Sarah felt called to give money to the poor and care for the sick, but she was even more inspired to evangelize children, slaves, and anyone who had not yet been born again. "The spirit of a man will sustain his infirmity," she quoted from Proverbs. "But a wounded spirit who can bear?"[4]

Christians have always struggled to understand what Jesus meant when he commanded his followers, "Love thy neighbor as thyself." While some Christians have interpreted his words as a radical challenge to the social order, others have concentrated more on saving sinners than on demanding structural or institutional change. Because of their dark view of human sinfulness, eighteenth-century evangelicals tended to fall on the conservative side of this religious spectrum: they insisted that the only lasting solution to the world's problems was conversion, and although they were willing to extend charity to individuals in need, they assumed that corporal punishment, torture, war, and slavery were an inevitable part of a fallen world. Sarah's compassion for the needy made her one of the most admired women in Newport, and yet in her zeal to save sinners she sometimes turned a blind eye to the entrenched evils of her time, especially slavery.

Blessed Is He That Considereth the Poor

Sarah's diary for the first few months of 1759 is missing, but based on a forlorn letter she wrote to Joseph Fish that May, it is clear that her decision to open a boarding school had saved her family from complete destitution. Writing at one o'clock in the morning, she confided, "All as to means that Holds up our Heads above water at all is a couple of boarders." Many of her students had stayed home from school during the winter because of bad weather, and then an outbreak of measles had shut it down for several weeks. One of her boarders had pleurisy, perhaps caused by pneumonia, and Sarah seems to have been afraid that she would be forced to close her doors yet again. "Poverty as an armed man has been coming on us ever since we was with you Last," she lamented, "but this Last winter it Has made swift Progress. . . . Our income Has not been Half equivalent to our unavoidable Expense that we sink Lower and Lower day by day and I can turn no way either to Lessen our charge or increase our income." She had sixty day students and ten boarders, and though she paid an assistant teacher to help her, she still felt like "a poor over-Loaded weak animal crouching under its burden." The weight pressing down on her shoulders was almost too much to bear.[5]

In the midst of all these troubles, however, she and Henry took in another of John and Abigail's children. They now had two grandchildren under their roof as well as Almey Greenman and the ten boarding students—thirteen children in all. Even with help, Sarah must have found it difficult to handle all the cooking and laundry, but whenever she thought about her grandchildren's former experiences of hunger and want, she believed that she was doing God's will. As she explained to Joseph Fish, "I can't repent it, nor cast them off so Long as tis Possible for me to Grapple with them. When I Look on them I am most strengthened. Psalm 41 and 1st oft supports me." (Her text was "Blessed is he that considereth the poor: the Lord will deliver him in time of trouble.") Even so, there were limits to what she could do. Disappointed by his failure at privateering, John had recently joined the army (probably because the colony had begun to offer large enlistment bonuses), but even though he left behind "a poor slothful wife and two more poor children as wretched as they can be," Sarah could no longer help them. Not only was she dangerously in debt, but Abigail's "sloth" in comparison to her own diligence seems to have angered her. "I don't Pretend to do for them now," she wrote in a rare expression of frustration. "I Have Given them up to shift for themselves. I can't Hold out any Longer to do for them." As she explained to Fish, she had "five to maintain wholly." (She was probably referring to herself, Henry, her two grandchildren, and Almey.)[6] John would have to find a way to support the rest of his family on his own.

The fall of 1759 and winter of 1760 brought even greater troubles. In September, Sarah heard the terrible news that Elizabeth Vinal, one of her closest friends and the minister's wife, had died in childbirth along with her newborn. The Reverend Vinal tried to "bear up with Christian Patience and Resignation to the divine will," but as Sarah confided to Fish, "He seemed

A letter from Sarah Osborn to Joseph Fish, May 3, 1759. She wrote this desperate letter about her financial problems at one o'clock in the morning. Courtesy of the American Antiquarian Society.

as though He would Have died with Her." Susanna Anthony moved into
Vinal's house to cook and clean for him and his family, and Sarah offered
to care for two of his daughters, Sarah and Becky, in her boarding school.
(Little Sarah, who was five, may have been her namesake; when she was
born in 1754, Sarah offered a prayer for both her and her mother, "dear
Elisa," in her diary.)[7] Although Sarah could not afford to take the children
for free, she charged only what they cost "out of Pocket," meaning half of
her usual tuition.[8] Caring for two grief-stricken children added to her burdens, but she was determined to keep them "as long as Providence permits
me." She and Henry now had fifteen children under their care.

Then at the end of November another tragedy struck. News came that
John, Henry's last surviving child, had died in battle at Fort George in upstate New York. After years of praying for his salvation, Sarah and Henry
had to accept that he, like his brother Edward two years earlier, had died
without being converted. Sarah's account of his death was brief, but her
terse words suggest that Henry was grief-stricken. "The bonds of nature
are strong," Sarah reflected. "It was His all, and many sorrows attend such a
Loss."[9] Years earlier, Sarah had hoped that all their children would experience the joy of being born again. Now she could not understand how she
could have been so wrong. Once again, a mysterious God had disappointed
her hopes.

Despite her earlier declaration that Abigail and her two youngest children would have to "shift for themselves," Sarah did not have the heart to
turn them away in their time of need. Having once been widowed herself, she knew the fear and anguish of losing a husband and being left to
raise a child alone. Though fearful of being plunged into "difficulties too
Great for me to Grapple with," she believed that God would help her to
scrape together enough money to keep Abigail and the grandchildren out
of the almshouse. Besides emptying her own purse of its few shillings, she
pleaded with friends and members of her church to be charitable. Anxieties in Newport were high because of an outbreak of smallpox and fears of
a food shortage, but Sarah persuaded a Mrs. Tweedy, the mother of one
of her former students, to give her forty shillings, and someone else to do-
nate wood—a necessity in a bitterly cold winter with "snow upon snow."
(Wood prices were so exorbitant that many poor people could not keep
their houses warm, and according to an irate writer in the *Newport Mercury*,
wood sellers often shortchanged their customers by delivering less than had
been paid for.)[10] Captain David Moore, a member of Sarah's church, gave

forty shillings, and "the doctor's Lady," probably Mrs. Ebenezer Gray, another church member, contributed twenty shillings as well as "meat, sauce, sugar, tea & cheese." Both Moore and Gray were among the wealthiest members of Sarah's church (their pew assessments placed them in the top 1 percent), and Moore in particular was a good friend of Sarah and Henry's who sometimes visited them at home.[11]

Sarah also went to the Town Council to ask for John's remaining salary, but to her disappointment she discovered that the family could expect only thirty-six pounds. It is not clear why Abigail did not go the council herself, but she seems to have been incapacitated in some way. Perhaps she was ill, or perhaps she was too dejected to attend to her responsibilities. Even before John's death, Sarah had described her as chronically slothful, which raises the possibility that she may have been suffering from depression or, given the large number of taverns in Newport, alcoholism. She seems to have been incapable of caring for either herself or her children. Whatever the reason, the council treated Sarah as Abigail's guardian, ordering her to pay Abigail's rent, buy her some wood, and "Let her Have the rest as I see need."[12]

Sarah clearly disliked Abigail: although she sometimes referred to her in sympathetic terms as a "poor, distressed widow," her descriptions were usually more critical—she was lazy, "obstinate," guilty of "Misconduct," and, worst of all, rearing her children to be little better than "heathens."[13] Yet even though Sarah did not see Abigail as either a good mother or a good Christian, she was committed to helping her. Besides being motivated by concern about her grandchildren, she believed it was her duty to help the poor regardless of whether they were Christian. She fed a beggar who several times knocked at her door even though he "plainly" told her that "He hates the ways of Holiness." Irritated by the frequency of his visits, she turned him away one day, but then immediately reproached herself for not being kinder to the "poor creature." Like George Whitefield, who argued that Christians must help others whether they were "friends or enemies," Sarah thought that God had called her to help "any of his poor, or the poor widow and fatherless, whether they are by his special grace or not." There was no such thing as the deserving or the undeserving poor, only people who needed help. Yearning to be as "Godlike and Christlike Here as tis Possible," she tried to imitate Jesus's generosity to the outcasts of his society. If he had treated "publicans and sinners" with compassion, then so would she.[14]

Use Me in Thy Service for Others

Given her belief that her poverty, her illness, and her sorrows had made her a better Christian, Sarah's commitment to alleviating the suffering of others might seem surprising. Why did she spend so much time helping others if she assumed that God had ordained their afflictions for their own good? And why, if she believed that she could not earn her way into heaven by doing good works, did she become renowned in Newport for her charity? Praying to God, she wrote, "As I am through boundless grace your own, use me in thy service for others."[15]

The answer turned on a hinge of Calvinist theology that valued good works as a sign—rather than a cause—of salvation. Though a subtle distinction, it was a crucial one. Sarah denied that people could earn salvation by doing good deeds, but she still assumed that the born again would show their faith by their actions. As Jonathan Edwards explained, "All true Christian grace tends to holy practice." Sarah had no doubt that "Eternal Life is the free Gift of God through Jesus Christ and not wages for our works," but from reading the Bible she was also certain that true faith "Purifies the Heart, works by Love, and is Productive of Good works."[16] Indeed, a true Christian was rarely idle. Besides helping Abigail, Sarah fed the hungry, gave money to the poor, and visited the sick and dying. While she was collecting charity for Abigail, she risked her health by visiting an ill child who seems to have had smallpox. The girl died a few days later.[17]

Historians have often noted that evangelicals had a stronger missionary and reforming impulse than earlier generations of Puritans. Puritans were committed to practicing "Christian charity," but as they built new towns and churches, organized governments, and developed trading routes, they focused more on the needs of their own communities than the plight of outsiders. Although the original seal of the Massachusetts Bay Colony included the image of a half-clothed Indian pleading "come over and help us," Puritans did not begin evangelizing Native Americans until 1646, sixteen years after the colony was founded.

Puritans began to pay greater attention to the poor outside their own churches in the late seventeenth century. In part they were motivated by necessity. After the Act of Toleration made it illegal to exile religious dissenters, they were forced to compete with other denominations, especially Anglicans and Quakers, for converts. By creating almshouses and reform societies where they mixed charitable relief with religious instruction, they not only fulfilled the moral obligation to "love thy neighbor as thyself" but also brought large numbers of people under their care and supervision. They also organized Indians into "praying towns" where they could be taught to live as Christians. In order to preserve their religious and political hegemony, the Puritans needed to find new ways to spread the gospel.

Yet their altruism was motivated by more than a desire to shore up their own authority. Puritans had always believed in being charitable, but they had a limited sense of their ability to alleviate large-scale suffering. Beginning in the late seventeenth century, however, they gradually gained a new faith in their power to improve the world, an expanded sense of possibility about effecting change. Inspired by scientific discoveries, technological advances, greater consumer choices, and their growing political influence in local governments, they seem to have become more sanguine about their ability to create a more Christian world.

Perhaps no one in New England was more influential in spreading humanitarian ideas than Cotton Mather, the illustrious pastor of Boston's North Church. After Mather was exposed to humanitarianism through his contact with German Pietists, he urged Christians to create reform societies and spread the gospel through missions. "If men would set themselves to *devise good*," he argued, "a world of *good* might be done, more than there is, in this *present evil world*." Although scoffing at the idea that humans were innately compassionate, Mather still believed that Christians were called to heal the brokenness of the world: "There needs abundance to be done, that the *miseries* of the world may have *remedies* and *abatements* provided for them; and that miserable people may be relieved and comforted." He founded societies to encourage piety, to combat "disorders" like drinking and prostitution, to help the poor, and to evangelize Indians. As he testified, "*Plain men dwelling in tents*, persons of a very *ordinary character*, may in a way of bright piety, prove persons of *extraordinary usefulness*."[18]

By the middle of the eighteenth century, humanitarian ideas had become so widely accepted that evangelicals naturally incorporated them into their own fledgling movement. With a zeal that would have delighted Mather, they gave money to the poor, founded orphanages for needy children, and started schools for Native Americans and slaves. After visiting Georgia, George Whitefield founded an orphanage that he named Bethesda after the biblical house of mercy, and in Connecticut, Eleazar Wheelock founded Moor's Charity School for Native Americans. Although some of these ventures failed (Wheelock's school ended up catering to white students), they reflected the reforming zeal of the age.[19] "Whatsoever thy Hand finds to do," John Guyse preached, quoting from Ecclesiastes, "do it with thy might." (After reading this sermon, Sarah Osborn wrote an impassioned diary entry promising to serve others.)[20] By the early nineteenth century, evangelicals in New England had founded scores of reform and benevolent organizations, including temperance and Bible societies and maternal associations.

In many ways, evangelicals would have bristled at the thought that they shared anything in common with the humanitarian movement. In contrast to philosophers like the third earl of Shaftesbury, Francis Hutcheson, and David Hume, they argued that humans were too sinful to improve the world by their own efforts. Progress was impossible without the direct guidance of the Holy Spirit. (Writing about Isaac Newton, the Reverend Nicholas Gilman attributed his revolutionary discoveries solely to the will of "Heaven.")[21] Most important, evangelicals denied that people could be truly virtuous unless motivated by a desire to glorify God. Distinguishing between "common morality" and "true virtue," Jonathan Edwards claimed that all people, even the worst of sinners, were capable of doing good deeds, but unless they were motivated by a pure, selfless love for God—"a supreme regard to God"—their works were worthless. "Nothing is of the nature of true virtue," he wrote, "in which God is not the *first* and the *last*."[22]

Evangelicals were also troubled by the attempt to promote charity on the grounds that it was pleasurable and gratifying to the giver. Influenced by Shaftesbury's theory of an innate moral sense, many philosophers, poets, and sentimental novelists claimed that the highest human virtue was "sensibility," a sympathetic identification with the sufferings of others. As one historian has explained, "The most exquisite raptures known to mankind were supposed to flow from the ability to feel for the sufferings of others, and to relieve it by acts of unselfish courage and generosity."[23] If evangelicals could have been sure that this kind of charity was indeed "unselfish," they would have welcomed it, but they recoiled at anything that looked like self-indulgence. Sarah could sound like the heroine of a sentimental novel when she prayed to "be filled with sympathy, when I see others in distress" and to "weep with those who weep," but she never waxed rhapsodic about the delights of benevolence. She thought her kindness to others should be motivated by her desire to serve God rather than the quest for individual gratification.[24]

The crucial issue for evangelicals, as always, was self-interest. As the gap between the rich and the poor grew during the early eighteenth century, many Protestant ministers tried to convince the wealthy that giving charity would not only increase their status in the eyes of the world (an appealing thought for nouveau riche merchants who felt insecure about their social standing) but it might even make them richer. As one minister promised his congregation, "the Great Benefactor" would "highly recompense" the benevolent for their charity.[25] The more they gave, the more God would shower them with blessings. In a frank defense of "private interest," the Reverend Samuel Cooper assured a group of wealthy men (all donors to the Society for Encouraging Industry and Employing the Poor) that they did not need to pretend that their largesse sprung solely from their commitment to the public good. "If Charity seeketh not her own, yet she always *finds* it," he promised, "and Self-Love may be improved as a Motive, to the Practice of this Virtue. It gains us the Confidence of Men, and enlarges our Credit in the World. It derives the Blessing of Heaven upon our secular Affairs, and entitles us to the peculiar Care of Providence." Invoking one of the most important words of the eighteenth-century Enlightenment, he insisted that being charitable would make people *happy*. "And as Happiness is the only Thing worth possessing for its own Sake; we ought to remember, that Charity is the very Temper of Happiness."[26]

Evangelicals disagreed. They insisted that giving charity was not a mark of "true holiness" unless it emanated from a spirit of genuine self-sacrifice. "A man may give all his goods to the poor, and devote his whole life to the most severe discipline," Samuel Hopkins warned, but if he were motivated by self-interest then his actions were no better than if he "indulged his sensual appetites in riot and wantonness." Hopkins's language, as usual, was extreme, but Sarah Osborn shared his antipathy to "the Hateful Principle of self-Love." She thought Christians should be charitable because of their love of God, not because they wanted to boast about their munificence or be rewarded with greater prosperity. In her own case she prayed not to "sound a trumpet before me" while helping her daughter-in-law.[27]

The greatest difference between evangelicals and humanitarians lay in their definition of charity. Though influenced by the charitable spirit of the age, Sarah did not believe that it was enough to feed the hungry, clothe the naked, visit the imprisoned, or care for the sick. All these things were important, but there was no point in making people's lives more comfortable if they would someday end up in hell. It was no good to fill a hungry man's belly if he was destined to starve for all eternity. *True* charity, in Sarah's eyes, must be aimed not only at the body but at the soul. "Our Enemies say we deny all moral Actions," George Whitefield complained, "but, blessed be God, they speak against us without Cause: Now, my dear Brethren, we highly value them; but we say, that Faith in Christ, Love of God, being born again, are of infinite more worth." Besides tending to people's physical needs in times of poverty or illness, Sarah urged them to repent and seek salvation. Part of the reason she regretted turning the beggar away from her door was that if she had fed him, she might have persuaded him to "Listen to something serious." Like Whitefield, she thought the kindest thing that she could do for others was to proclaim the gospel.[28]

As Sarah went about her daily business in Newport, drawing water from the well or stopping to buy a barrel of flour, she evangelized anyone who seemed willing to listen. (And when it came to close friends or family members like Abigail, even those who seemed determined *not* to listen.) Despite her recognition that some people found her holier than thou, she felt compelled to speak. Remaining silent would be cruel, like watching a man burn to death without trying to quench the flames.

Sarah's understanding of charity encompassed prayer as well as evangelism. As she knew, many of the "enlightened" men in Newport rejected her faith in the power of prayer to change the course of events, but she saw prayer as a form of action, a way of persuading God to intervene in history. God was a "Glorious Hearer and Answerer of prayer," she rejoiced in her diary.[29] She prayed not only for her family and her friends but also for all those who had not yet been reborn in Christ: criminals, "heathens" in other lands, children in her school, slaves, and those who had mistreated her. (This was an especially difficult discipline, but crucial to an ethic of turning the other cheek.) Even the ability to pray, though, depended on God's grace. "Lord," she testified in her diary, "thou knowest I can no more Pray in prayer myself then I can make a world."[30]

Evangelicals did not want to be associated with a movement that placed human welfare at the center of the universe, but they were strongly influenced by the humanitarian sympathies of their time. Indeed, they saw themselves as far more compassionate than reformers who focused solely on people's physical needs. When humanitarian thinkers insisted that people must do everything possible to alleviate suffering, evangelicals nodded in agreement—but what they had in mind was not only the transient suffering of illness or poverty but the eternal suffering of the damned. After John's death, Sarah collected charity for Abigail, but she also prayed for her—prayer after prayer for the salvation of the "poor widow" and her fatherless children.

Making Everyone's Burden My Own

Sarah spent the winter of 1759 – 60 knocking on doors to ask for charity for Abigail, teaching school, looking after her boarding students, caring for her two grandchildren and Vinal's two children, and worrying about her debts. She also met with her female prayer group on Wednesday evenings. (The women's society had stopped meeting for several years, probably because of lack of interest, but Sarah revived it in January 1759.) Worried that she was trying to do too much, she asked God to help her accept her limitations. "Lord, show me that thou art not Looking for Perfection in me nor Marking iniquity against me," she begged in her diary. "O Let me not Look on thee as an angry, austere Judge Looking for Perfection where thou knowest it is not to be found." Yet she could not seem to stop "poring on the distressed circumstances of others, making every one's burden my own, and thinking I am bound in duty to exert myself to do something for the relief of everyone that I know to be distressed."[31] Even though she knew, on one level, that God loved her despite her failures, she could not always live as if she believed it. Her expectations for herself were like a weight she could never shake off. In her own eyes, she could never be good enough.

Given all the pressures on her during the winter of 1760, it is no wonder that her illness flared up again. "Hard Rheumatic Pains," "strong Pains," and "stupefying" headaches left her exhausted.[32] Her usual morning schedule was to awake at five o'clock and pray for two hours, but her illness sapped her energy. "I am all sloth," she complained. "Can't awake in the Morning till near seven o'clock and then the duties of the family calls for me. The two Precious hours I used to redeem for secret converse with God are now wasted in sleep and I only catch a few confused Moments. And how does my Precious soul Grow lean from day to day." Yet except for a few days when she felt too ill to get out of bed, she kept working. Her family's survival depended on it. In the spring she managed to pay her rent and three other debts she had owed for months, but she was still "deeply in debt."[33] Praying to God for help, she wrote, "Thou knowest all my need. Thou knowest the debts we owe and How the meal in the barrel and oil in the cruse is almost Expended. Thou knowest also the wants of the widow and fatherless whom I am determined to Help if thou permit." She was "sinking under the weight of business," and "yet the Necessities of my family oblige me to covet it."[34]

Usually she would have shared her troubles with her pastor, the Reverend Vinal, but since his wife's death he had become distracted and morose. Pleading illness, he often kept the doors to his meetinghouse closed on Sundays or asked a neighboring minister to preach in his stead. Sarah explained to Joseph Fish, "His disorder is, the doctor says, a Nervous fever. He keeps about house and is better but can't bear the air." Hesitant to admit the full extent of his problems, she added only, "There is greater difficulties attends Him and us then I dare Mention." Even in her diaries, she wrote about Vinal's "indisposition" in vague terms, but most of her church suspected that his problems stemmed from alcohol abuse.[35] He had always been a heavy drinker—between 1750 and 1752, the church bought him 111 gallons of rum—but as he grieved for his dead wife, he drank so much that he could no longer hide his addiction. As the church descended into controversy and "cruel backbiting," Sarah tried to defend him from "slanderous tongues," but he acted like a shepherd who had abandoned his flock. Even though she was caring for his two daughters, he rarely visited.[36]

Exhausted, ill, and anxious about Vinal and the church, Sarah was sometimes impatient with the children in her school. She was still teaching seventy students, and despite the help of an assistant teacher, they were hard to keep under control. She begged God to subdue her "wildfire Passions," but when the children were "Giddy, Idle and unruly," she found it hard not to lose her temper. "Calm my Passions, dear Lord," she prayed, "that I do nothing rashly or speak unadvisedly with my Lips."[37]

Psychologists have often noted that as children grow into adults, they repeat behavior they learned from their parents, and Sarah was no exception. Even though she had once resented her parents' harsh style of discipline, she did not believe that the injunction to "love thy neighbor as thyself" precluded the corporal punishment of children. When her students misbehaved and she was frustrated by "the darkness of their Minds, the blindness of their understandings, the stubbornness of their wills," she used the rod to "subdue" them. As she admitted in her diary during the summer of 1760, "I was Last Evening obliged to correct a child from a sense of duty with some degree of severity in Hope of Preventing Her running to utter destruction. The Lord Sanctify the rod for Christ's sake and secure thine own Honor." When someone accused her of cruelty, she claimed to have been motivated by a sense of religious duty, not "Passion," and she also insisted that "the rod was small and tender and in no respect an unreasonable weapon." "Correct thy son while there is hope," she quoted from Proverbs, "and Let not thy soul spare for His crying."[38] Yet despite her tone of justification, she seems to have feared that she had let her anger get the best of her. She was reputed to be a kind, dedicated teacher, but when so much else was troubling her—mounting debts, Abigail's "sloth," the French Antichrist, and Vinal's alcoholism—she took out her frustration on her students. Not until several years later would she finally stop beating her students to make them behave. After reading Cotton Mather's complaint that "raving at children and beating them" was "a dreadful Judgment of God upon the World and a very abominable Practice," she was both shocked at herself and ashamed. After three decades of "correcting" children on the grounds that it was for their own good, she finally put away the rod.[39]

With all the burdens on Sarah's shoulders during the summer of 1760, it is hard to understand why she decided to take on anything more, but her pattern was to push herself to her limits whenever she felt most troubled by her imperfections. Perhaps because of her difficulty "governing" her students, she looked for another way to glorify God. In July, when she heard that two criminals in Newport would be executed for their crimes, she saw an opportunity to spread the gospel. She sent the criminals a letter urging them to repent, and soon she was spending hours in prayer for their salvation. (Once again, she seems to have modeled herself on the "righteous" in the Gospel of Matthew who visited the imprisoned.) For a month they were rarely out of her thoughts. One of them seems to have ignored her letter (perhaps exasperated by her zeal), but the other prisoner wrote back, and although it is not clear whether she was allowed to visit him in jail regularly, she was with him on the morning of his execution. "I think myself Dead in sin," he reportedly said to her, "but alive through the alone Merits of Jesus Christ."[40] At a time when so much of her life seemed bleak, Sarah was elated by her role in his conversion. Nothing was more important than bringing a sinner to Christ.

Many Enlightenment thinkers protested against the deplorable treatment of criminals, but if Sarah was troubled by Newport's overcrowded, foul-smelling prison or by a justice system that sentenced people to death for offenses like robbery, counterfeiting, and sodomy, she kept silent. In contrast to the baron de Montesquieu, who argued that a punishment should not exceed the crime, and Voltaire, who decried the use of torture, Sarah felt that the most important concern was saving criminals from damnation, not reforming prisons or making the legal codes more humane. Like most evangelicals at the time (and like Christians generally), she not only accepted violence as an integral part of the social order; she sanctified it as God's will. Because people were too sinful to resist the lure of violence, they had to be discouraged by the threat of violence in return. As proven by the existence of hell, God wanted sinners to be chastised. Public whippings on street corners, prisoners shackled in the stocks, public executions— all were a part of everyday life in Newport, and all, in Sarah's eyes, glorified God.[41]

War, too, could glorify God if it were fought against his enemies, and Sarah had no doubt that the bloodthirsty French and their heathen allies deserved to die. In his *Philosophical Dictionary*, Voltaire pointed out the absurdity of a religious man solemnly invoking the Lord "before he goes out to exterminate his neighbors," but even among Enlightenment thinkers his voice was radical. In New England, Protestants of all theological stripes described the French and Indian War as a holy crusade. Sarah asked God to "Have compassion on the souls of our Enemies if it be thy Holy will, and turn them to thyself as well as to us," but she was convinced that they were in league with Satan.[42] Because the people of New England had turned away from God, falling into covetousness, profanity, and drunkenness, God had allowed the French and their Indian allies to raze towns and commit "cruel murders," but he would save his chosen people from destruction if they reformed. "Lord, I own the Justice in all that Has befallen us," Sarah mourned in her diary. "We Have deserved this and a thousand times More at thine Hand, but Lord, have Compassion on us. Make the antichrist and the Heathen know that Zion's God has not forsaken her though He hast scourged Her."[43] Although she believed in loving her neighbor as herself, not everyone deserved the title of "neighbor," and not all her prayers for others were benign. She prayed for the conversion of the "heathen," but failing that, for their annihilation.

When Sarah heard in September that British forces had followed a surprising victory in Quebec with the capture of Montreal, she rejoiced that her prayers had been answered. After years of humiliating defeat, the army had finally driven the "Antichrist" out of Canada. (The battle had taken place in August, but it took several weeks for the news to arrive.) At the end of a day of "public rejoicing," Sarah and the women's society gathered to offer thanks for "the Mercies He Has bestowed on our Nation and Land." Although the fighting continued in Europe (the Treaty of Paris was not signed until 1763), the colonies were no longer under siege, and Sarah was confident that God would vindicate his chosen people against their Catholic enemies. "Good news from a far country," she exulted in November. "Zion's God Has again appeared for the King of Prussia and Given Him another Victory . . . what a wonder of Mercy is it."[44]

Reminding herself of God's compassion helped Sarah get through the dark days after the war. On a personal level, she and her family had little to celebrate in the fall of 1760: John and Edward were dead, Abigail was destitute, two of her grandchildren were still living in squalor, and the whole family seems to have been poorer than at any time since their bankruptcy eighteen years earlier. Sarah was in charge of managing the family's finances (the result of Henry's infirmity), and when she sat down with her account book she was alarmed. "I Have been deceived," she wrote in her diary, "for I thought we was upon full as Good Ground now as at this time twelve month. But upon Examination see we are at Least an Hundred and twenty odd pounds poorer then we was then." By November their debts had climbed to more than 170 pounds.[45]

Sarah wanted to buy ten cords of wood for the winter, but by the middle of November she had scraped up only enough money to buy four—and only two had been delivered. (A writer in the *Newport Mercury* suggested that most people needed fifteen cords to survive the winter, and the Reverend Vinal received twenty as part of his salary, so the house must have often been cold. Sarah seems to have scrimped on wood to save money.) With fifteen children to feed, she also needed to buy apples, pork, potatoes, cornmeal, and flour, but she did not know how she would afford them. (She charged extra tuition for her boarding students, but she suggested in a letter to Joseph Fish that she had set her price too low to cover the rising costs of room and board.)[46] She had borrowed small sums from friends in the past—her former employer Captain Moore had once loaned her twenty shillings—but she was already so buried in debt that she did not know how she would ever dig herself out. When two of her students withdrew from the school, she fretted that it was "breaking all to Pieces."[47] "Business is now failing every day," she wrote to God in her diary. "Grant me a Habakkuk's faith, that although all should be cut off, that I may trust and rejoice in thee." Small economic exchanges suddenly seemed so critical that she noted them in her diary. After someone repaid a long-standing debt by giving them a rancid barrel of flour, she worried that they might have to settle the dispute in court.[48]

With the weather turning colder, Sarah especially worried about her daughter-in-law, but in a rare piece of good news the Town Council agreed to pay Abigail five pounds a week to support herself and the two children still living at home. By law, Rhode Island towns were required to pay yearly pensions to the dependents of soldiers and sailors killed in war.[49] Although the sum was too paltry to lift Abigail and her children out of poverty, it still eased Sarah's burden. Every shilling from the town treasury was one less that had to begged from friends and neighbors.

If Sarah could have sold her slave Bobey, her most valuable possession, she might have been tempted to part with him in order to raise money. Sixteen years old and healthy, he was probably worth at least ninety-five dollars.[50] But he was in the last year of his apprenticeship to her former brother-in-law, and if she wanted to sell him she would have to wait until the end of 1761. Even though she and Henry had raised him "as our own from the cradle," and even though his mother, Phillis, was her "sister" in Christ, she does not seem to have had any scruples about selling him. After seeing him in November, she admitted in her diary, "I find as His time draws nearer being out with his Master, my dependence begins More and More to fix on Him, and Expectations from this withering Gourd are raised as if this would shadow me from the Heat." (She was implicitly comparing herself to the prophet Jonah, who had been sheltered by a gourd until God sent a worm to destroy it.) "When shall I cease to catch at and build upon every Prospect of Prosperity?" she asked herself. "And when shall I cease to fear and droop at every fear of disappointment?"[51] There was no guarantee that she would ever make a profit from Bobey (what if he got sick and died in the next year?), but he was her best hope for the future—the only thing of real value that she owned.

For the time being, though, she was so desperate for money that she was forced to rely on charity. Abigail Chesebrough, the twenty-six-year-old daughter of David Chesebrough, one of the wealthiest merchants in Newport, gave her a gift of eight pounds—the equivalent of the tuition Sarah received from two boarders in a week. (Since David Chesebrough was a slave trader who ranked forty-second on Newport's tax list in 1760, he and his family could afford to be generous.)[52] The Chesebroughs had left Sarah's church to join the Second Church of Christ, but they admired her piety and wanted to help.[53] Sarah also received relief from Nathaniel Coggeshall, the deacon of her church, and his wife, a member of the women's society, who had been the Osborns' friends for many years. On a cold evening in November Nathaniel appeared at the door with coal, and in December, when Sarah "begged in Jest" for firewood, his wife supplied it. (Sarah denied that she had "the Least thought of receiving wood," but the Coggeshalls realized that her joke was actually a thinly disguised plea for help.)[54] Even though they were not as affluent as the Chesebroughs, Nathaniel's distillery was quite profitable, and he and his family numbered among the wealthiest people in Sarah's church. (In comparison to the ten

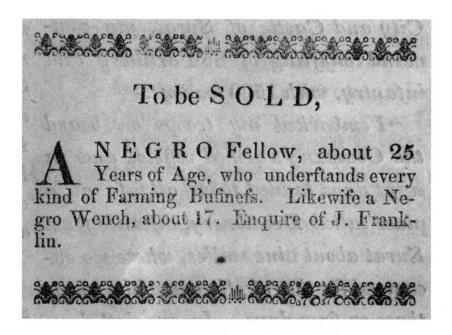

An advertisement for a slave, *Newport Mercury*, March 11, 1760.
Photograph courtesy of the Newport Historical Society.

pounds that Henry Osborn paid for his pew in 1753, Nathaniel Coggeshall and his sons were assessed twenty-two pounds.)[55] Sarah may have also relied on help from friends like Sarah Anthony, Susanna's sister, who had lent her money in the past despite her own poverty.[56] If Sarah Osborn's diaries are representative of other people's experiences, those who had the least were often the most generous in giving it away. The poor often depended on one another for food, clothing, and money.

Although Sarah always insisted that her poverty was best for her, she would have loved to be a rich woman who could open her hand and heart to the poor. When she wrote about her cousin in England, a wealthy, pious woman who was supposedly worth as much as three or four hundred thousand pounds, she could barely suppress her envy—not of her material possessions but of her ability to be charitable. Besides supporting the work of ministers (regardless of denomination) who were "eminent for Piety," her cousin and her husband often invited six people of "Lower rank" to enjoy the bounty of their table on Sunday evenings. She was the kind of woman whom Sarah longed to be—affluent, generous, and devoted to Christ. "They keep their own chariot &c &c but run into none of the foolishness of the Gentry," Sarah boasted to Joseph Fish. "A Greater Honor this to them and me than all their riches."[57]

Since the first half of Sarah's diary for 1761 has been lost, we know little about her life during the early months of the year, but it is clear that she and Henry still struggled to pay for their food and rent. (Later she remembered that in 1762 they were three hundred pounds in debt—a staggering sum that probably represented more than she could earn in a year.) "I can say safely, though not by way of Complaint, that we are really much poorer then some years ago," she admitted to Fish in February 1761. As always, though, she claimed that her poverty was good for her, a discipline that brought her closer to God. Besides making her more grateful for what she had, her poverty helped her remember her complete dependence on God's grace. "All is as well as if we Possessed thousands," she assured Fish. "'Tis sweet Living to see God Giving day by day our daily bread."[58]

Remarkably, Sarah somehow managed to pay down her debts during the year while also making significant contributions to help the poor and to support the ministry. According to church records, she gave nine pounds, nineteen shillings, to the church in 1761, almost double what she gave in 1760.[59] Her scrimping and saving must have affected the quality of her life (it is hard to imagine that she and her family ever wasted a morsel of food or a stick of wood), but she was willing to make sacrifices in order to be charitable. Psychologically, she seems to have gained a sense of assurance from her constant, almost compulsive efforts to help others. Whenever she reminded herself that faith showed itself in good works, she felt more secure about God's love for her.

Besides giving away money, Sarah also became involved in a different kind of "charity" in 1761—a moral crusade against the theater. (Any activity that led to the salvation of souls constituted charity in her eyes.) When a company of British actors arrived in Newport in the fall, she was stunned by the huge crowds who gathered to see farces like Charles Coffee's *The Devil to Pay* and sentimental comedies like Richard Steele's *The Conscious Lovers*. (Some people traveled from as far away as Boston, a two-day trip in each direction.) Ever since the sixteenth century, Puritans had railed against the theater for glamorizing evil, promoting effeminacy (the women's parts were played by men in female clothing), encouraging hypocrisy and lying, and, in general, luring people into vice, and Sarah thought that going to see a play was a form of devil worship—even when it included, as it did in Newport, occasional performances of Shakespeare.[60] Condemning the theater as a "temple of wickedness," she resolved to "oppose vice and immorality as far as in me Lies." She even promised God to break off a friendship with a woman who did not see anything wrong with "playing at cards—reading romances, seeing Plays." (Despite her desire to "Live Peaceably with all," Sarah refused to "contract or maintain intimate friendship with those that will not appear on the Lord's side.") Although she knew that she might be mocked as a scold, she was afraid that staying silent would be sinful. "Can I altogether Hold my Peace and be guiltless?" she asked. For two months, until the actors finally packed up their costumes and props to travel to their next engagement, she and other evangelicals were a constant thorn in their side, denouncing the theater as the "devil's entertainments." Their activism eventually paid off in 1767 when the colony passed an act prohibiting theatrical performances—a victory that Sarah surely savored.[61]

My Dear Servant's Soul

It is a reminder of the distance between the eighteenth century and our modern world that Sarah Osborn, who wanted to love her neighbor as herself, could spend hours writing about the theater as an abomination while turning a blind eye to a real evil in Newport. Every time she walked along the docks she saw slave ships anchored in the harbor, and everywhere she went—to neighbors' houses, to shops, to her church—she saw the faces of Africans (and their descendants) who had been violently seized from their homes and sold as chattel. The auction block stood only a few blocks away from her church. And of course she herself owned a slave, Bobey, whom she and Henry had raised from birth.

Although Sarah believed that she had a duty to treat slaves with compassion and to share the gospel with them, she did not see either the slave trade or slaveholding as sinful. Since the great patriarchs of the Bible— Abraham, Isaac, and Joseph—had all owned slaves, most Christians assumed that slavery had been ordained by God. Shaped by the racial prejudices of the time, they also assumed that Africans were an inferior race. As African slavery became economically profitable, Christians interpreted Noah's curse on his son Ham's descendants, "a servant of servants shall he be unto his brethren," as a reference to all people of African descent— this despite the fact that Ham is not described as either black or African. The Hebrew Bible never sanctions the enslavement of Africans in particular (slaves are described as war captives who can belong to any race), but by the time of Sarah Osborn's birth most Christians associated slavery with blackness.[62] Although Sarah hoped to glorify God by teaching slaves about Christianity, she did not think that her faith required her to protest against slavery in the same way that she protested against gambling, cardplaying, drinking, or theatergoing. The merchants of Newport who stumbled home drunk on Saturday nights were sinners; the merchants who attended church, lived soberly, and amassed huge fortunes in the slave trade were not.

This was why in December 1761, when Bobey's apprenticeship ended and his master, "brother French," offered to buy him, Sarah did not question the morality of selling another human being. The only sign we have that she might have felt uneasy is her odd silence about the money involved. When she had first considered selling Bobey a year earlier, she had been frank about her desire for "prosperity," but by the end of 1761 she treated the question of money as irrelevant. It is hard not to wonder whether she felt a twinge of conscience about being covetous, or whether she remembered the nights after Samuel's death when she had rocked Bobey's cradle and hoped for another chance to raise a Christian child. For many years he had been virtually a member of her family—playing on their floor, attending church with them, and knitting his stockings by their fireside.[63]

Whatever her deeper feelings, Sarah told herself (and God) that she wanted to sell Bobey because it was in his best interests, not her own. Because he was strong-willed, he would be better off living in the country than in Newport, where she and Henry might not be able to shield him from bad influences. As she confided to her diary, "I fear if we keep him He will rather be an Encumbrance than a comfort as Neither His Master or I can manage him." Even though he was "Honest and averse to drink and . . . more and more faithful," she worried that if he lived in the city they might not be able to prevent him from "Proving bad, taking to bad courses, or Going to Sea." She seemed especially concerned about the possibility that he might become a sailor—a common occupation for slaves and freed people in the urban North that was frequently associated with drunkenness and profanity.[64] Selling him, she was convinced, would be for his own good—a demonstration of her commitment to loving her neighbor.

When she broached the topic with Bobey's mother at a meeting of the women's society, however, she was shocked by Phillis's angry response:

I asked the opinion of Phillis about our selling of Bobey, which contrary to my Expectation vexed her. I really Expected as we Have not business for Him and He must be Let out from Place to Place and run to risk of

being made unsteady or quite spoiled or of going to sea, she would Have
rather Chosen to Have Him Settled under a Steady Master whom He
Loves, where He Has Lived more than Seven years, the whole family
fond of him and He of them, where He has and will Enjoy the Privi-
leges of God's House, the worship of God in the family, instructions for
His soul and all the Comforts of this Life Necessary for Him. But it was
quite Otherwise. Her reason Seems at Present to be Laid aside and a
fondness to take Place, or rather anger.[65]

Sarah and Phillis were probably as close as a white woman and an enslaved
black woman could be in the eighteenth century, but their conflict about
Bobey exposed the deep racial divide separating them. As Bobey's owner,
Sarah was certain that God wanted her to sell him, but as Bobey's mother,
Phillis was equally certain that God wanted him to return to Newport. She
and her husband, Gosper, had been separated from their son for seven years
during his apprenticeship, and although they were probably proud that he
had learned a trade, they wanted him home again. Bobey was their child,
not an object to be bought and sold.

Slaves were supposed to be deferential toward whites, but Phillis was
too "vexed" to hide her anger. How could Sarah be certain that selling
Bobey was the right decision? And how could she guarantee that Bobey
would not be sold again, this time to a cruel master?

Sarah spent ten days debating whether to sell Bobey. Although the issue of money always lurked behind her words, she seems to have convinced
herself that her motives were pure: she was thinking about Bobey's happiness, not her own. From her perspective, the only person who was acting selfishly was Phillis, whose "fondness" for her son prevented her from
seeing what was best for him. She was stunned that Phillis, of all people,
would question her judgment: Phillis, whom she had led into her church,
welcomed into her women's society, and treated as a spiritual equal despite
her racial inferiority. Hurt and offended, she wrote, "Oh, How Hard it
Has been to me to be thus Mistrusted by Phillis to whom I think I Have
never been unfaithful, by Her who I always thought Had a better opinion
of me! O Let this teach me to my dying day How ungrateful, How ungen-
erous and cruel it is for me to disbelieve my Gracious, faithful God who
never deceived me." Blinded by anger, she imagined herself, not Phillis or
Bobey, as a victim, and in an astonishing moment of hubris she implicitly

compared herself to God: just as she found it difficult to trust God despite
his goodness to her, so Phillis had "mistrusted" her without reason. Like
the Reverend Thomas Bacon, an Anglican minister who described slave
masters as "God's overseers," Sarah seems to have imagined slaves standing
in the same relationship to their masters as their masters did to God. Unless slaves were asked to do something that violated biblical law, they were
expected to submit quietly to their masters' will. In a diary entry, Sarah
reminded herself that God had "given" Bobey to her "in a covenant way."[66]
She had been divinely commissioned to oversee his life.

We have only one side of the conversation—Sarah's—but it is clear
that she and Phillis argued fiercely about Bobey. In an entry written three
days after their first clash, Sarah considered keeping him, but, as she acknowledged to God, only because her feelings of "resentment" had triumphed over "tenderness." "I Have from resentment been ready to Give
Him up to His father's and Mother's will since they can't believe that Either
His Master or I Have Honesty Enough to Speak the truth, or at all to aim
at His Good."[67] Sarah rarely sounded so bitter in her diary entries, but
whatever Phillis had said, it had stung. Sarah almost seems to have hoped
that if she kept Bobey, he would ruin his life and prove that she had spoken
the truth about the advantages of selling him. "O Let me not be Willing
to Give the child up to be Exposed to Hardships and ruin to Gratify them
[Phillis and Gosper]," she wrote angrily. "Nor yet to Encumber myself with
cares, distresses, and Perplexities at Home and abroad."[68]

Sarah's fury seems to have grown out of a sense of personal betrayal. If
she viewed herself as a particularly kind, Christian master (it is unlikely that
many other white women invited a slave to join their prayer group), she may
have resented Phillis's insinuation that she was no better than the heartless
slave owners in Newport who separated children from their parents. Or
if she relied on her relationship with Phillis to bolster her fragile sense of
self-worth, she may have been hurt—and then enraged—to discover that
even Phillis could be critical of her. Proud of her role in bringing Phillis
into her church, she seems to have expected a certain level of admiration
and deference in return. It was a shock to realize that Phillis did not have a
"better opinion" of her.[69] Although we cannot sort out all of Sarah's tangled
thoughts and emotions, she clearly felt that Phillis had been disloyal, and
her anger brought out the worst features of her character, especially her
self-righteousness. She was certain that she was *right*.

Gradually, however, Sarah calmed down enough to realize that her
"temptations to anger" might destroy one of the most important rela-

tionships in her life. After praying and worshiping with Phillis for more than three years, it pained her to think of anything coming between them. Blaming the devil, not herself, for their conflict, she wrote, "I will not Humor Satan who Has a design against us both, but will Love Her still for Jesus' sake." Although she remained adamant about selling Bobey, she vowed to do everything in her power to ease Phillis's distress. The solution, she thought, was to "Pity and make much of the poor creature and Endeavor if we do sell Him to make up to her the disappointment as far as in me Lies."[70]

We can only imagine how Phillis responded to the suggestion that Sarah could somehow "make up" for the loss of her son.

At the end of Sarah's diary entry, she recalled a biblical text that had comforted her after the loss of her own son, Samuel. She implored God, "Be better to Her than ten Sons."[71] Her allusion to this verse suggests that she may have remembered her own terrible grief after Samuel's death, and yet she refused to consider the possibility that this time the story could end differently. Even though she had the power to relieve a grieving mother's anguish, she refused to yield. It is hard to understand how she could have been so callous, but she seemed to want Phillis to prove her faith by resigning herself quietly to God's will. The problem was that Phillis insisted that the sale of her son was only *Sarah's* will.

Day after day in her diary Sarah pleaded with God to help her do what was right. As she lamented, she could "think of nothing Else." Her entries all sounded alike: "I can't control the torrent of thoughts that whirl me down the stream from the fountainhead." "I am so amused with this affair and at such a Loss to know what is duty that I can bend to nothing." (By "amused," she meant troubled or distracted.) "I am wearied out and Heartsick of thinking and weighing one thing with another."[72]

Finally, however, Sarah made a decision. In a long entry written on a Sunday before church (where she would almost certainly have to look Phillis in the eye), she tried to imagine Bobey's life if she sold him. Since her former brother-in-law was a "Steady Master" and a Christian, she had no reservations about entrusting Bobey to him. He would make sure that Bobey went to church regularly and avoided "bad courses." Yet she had to admit that dangers might lie ahead. "Should his Master die and Leave Him," she worried, "I can't conclude How it might be as to religious Privileges or other comforts He now Enjoys." If he were ever sold to a new master, he might be forbidden to practice the Christian faith. (Phillis and Gosper were probably concerned about the possibility of physical abuse as well, but Sarah focused solely on his religious vulnerability.) Bobey had not yet experienced conversion, but because he attended worship and knew how to read the Bible, Sarah hoped he would some day be born again. If she owned him, she could guarantee that he would be given every opportunity to become a Christian, but if she sold him she would have no say about his future. Could she take that chance?[73]

No, she finally realized. No, she could not. Even though she did not object to the buying and selling of slaves, nothing was more important than Bobey's soul.

As stubborn as ever, though, Sarah refused to give Phillis any credit for being right. When she wrote about her decision in her diary, she never mentioned Phillis, suggesting instead that her change of heart had grown out of her commitment to trust in God. As she agonized over Bobey's future, she asked herself, "Why can't I still trust Him in the Hands of that gracious God that at first Gave Him to me, and believe that He will take care of both Him and me?" Not only was it "ungrateful" of her to consider parting with a gift from God, but it showed her lack of faith. Bobey "shant nor he can't Go to Sea except God Pleases," she reminded herself. "He can Control Him if we can't, and his Life, his Health, his Living is in God's Hands. The whole disposing is of the Lord, and I think I had rather commit Him to Him to keep for me then to Commit Him to the Care of any Man."[74] In the religious drama she constructed, the most important roles belonged to her, Bobey, and God, with Phillis and Gosper appearing as bit players.

Yet there is no doubt that Sarah cared deeply for Phillis. Her own word was *love*—a word she rarely used in reference to anyone except Susanna Anthony (and, of course, Jesus). Sarah saw Phillis as a genuine Christian, the beloved of God. "I Bless thee, my God, from my very soul for what thou Hast done for His Mother," she wrote after deciding to keep Bobey. "She, I trust, is thine own. Thou Hast appeared for Her." On December 25, two weeks after her decision, Sarah mentioned writing a letter to a "choice friend," almost certainly Phillis, in order "to remove some disgust I think is taken at some of my conduct." She prayed that God would "compose my friend and convince I designed no slight at all but to improve all means for my Establishment in the Path of duty." She did not record the response, but when she met with the women's society on January 2, Phillis was there.[75]

As long as Sarah was the master and Phillis and Bobey were slaves, however, their relationship would always be tainted by her sense of racial superiority and their feelings of vulnerability. When Sarah asked God to transform Bobey into a "new creature," she prayed, "Though he cannot change His skin nor His Heart, thou can change His Heart in a moment."[76] Despite Sarah's belief that slaves could be spiritually equal to their masters, she also assumed that racial differences would not be erased until death. When she looked at Bobey and Phillis, she saw not only members of the body of Christ but slaves with black skin who would never be her equals on earth. As for Bobey and Phillis, we can only imagine what they saw when they looked at Sarah, but their sight was probably clouded by fear.

Slavery was one of the greatest challenges faced by early American evangelicals. Influenced by a passage from the book of Acts—God "hath made of one blood all nations of men" (17:26)—they preached the gospel to slaves, baptized them, and invited them to the communion table, but their egalitarianism usually stopped at the church door. In 1761, Sarah was no exception, but her conflict with Phillis and Bobey seems to have forced her to reflect more deeply about what it meant to love her neighbor as herself. Her anguished debate over selling Bobey was the first step in a slow, halting journey toward a new vision of race, slavery, and the meaning of the gospel.

The Fatherless

Since Sarah rarely mentioned Bobey in later diary entries, it is not clear what happened to him. Perhaps she hired him out to his former master in Berkeley, or perhaps she arranged for him to work in various businesses in the city. We do not know what trade he learned during his apprenticeship, but skilled slaves in urban areas often worked outside their masters' households. If Bobey had learned to be a tailor, for example, he might have been hired out as a tailor's assistant for months or even a year. Yet unless Sarah and Henry allowed him to keep a portion of his wages, his earnings would have belonged entirely to them.[77]

Bobey's wages may have been the reason that Sarah and Henry suddenly had fewer financial worries at the beginning of 1762. "Thou Hast Given me the utmost of my wishes," Sarah thanked God in her diary. "Thou art comfortably feeding and clothing me and all committed to my immediate charge: my dear husband in His age and the dear orphans, too. We Have a comfortable House, wood Enough, and no one under our roof is Exposed to any temporal wants—thou art enabling me Honorably to Pay rent, wages, and all other dues."[78] Sarah never explained how God had made all these things possible, but her new sense of security may have been founded on slave labor.

Sarah and Henry's fortunes improved even more in the spring when she heard the unexpected news that her uncle John Guyse had died and left her a bequest of 20 pounds sterling, the equivalent of 640 pounds in American currency.[79] Sarah had not seen Guyse since her childhood in England, but she had always been proud to be related to such a distinguished minister, and she seems to have corresponded with him regularly. Surprised by his generosity, she was determined not to be "silly" about her new prosperity. Besides using the bequest to pay off some of her debts, she immediately set aside 125 pounds to give to charity. She planned to "support the Gospel, buy books to send or Give away to children, and to relieve the needy." She also gave 22 pounds, 14 shillings, to two "poor widows," one of them almost certainly Abigail.[80] Like everything else in the world, money ultimately belonged to God, and he had given it to her in stewardship to use for the common good.

Yet Sarah was not immune to the acquisitiveness of her age, and her sudden wealth posed temptations that kept her awake at night. "Before I had tidings of my Legacy, all was well," she confessed in her diary. "I had Enough. I declared myself satisfied." But now that she had money in her pocket, she could not stop dreaming about the expensive goods that were for sale on the wharves, especially "a Handsome suit of black silk and a Prussian cloak" that she could wear as mourning for Guyse. "Satan Has taken me in Hand," she lamented. Although "Dear friends" encouraged her to buy proper mourning attire, she worried about being motivated by "Pride and a conformity to the world." The suit would cost more than 300 pounds, a hefty sum for someone who had recently relied on charity to survive, and if she bought it, only 125 pounds of her bequest would remain. On one hand, she fretted that such an expensive, "handsome" outfit was too "grand" for a lowly schoolteacher, but on the other, she also worried that her decision not to buy it would be a sign of her "unbelief," her failure to trust God to provide for her in the future. Although she knew that the "Worldly wise" would condemn her, she thought it would be better to "spend every farthing" than to hoard away her money in a spirit of doubt. (This profligacy would have surprised Max Weber, who associated the "Protestant ethic" with the steady, disciplined accumulation of capital. Although Sarah does not seem to have been representative, at least a few evangelicals tried to obey Christ's injunction to "take no thought for the morrow.")[81]

Since Sarah never wrote about the new suit and cloak again, we do not know for certain whether she decided to buy them, but probably not.

In March, finally at "peace" with regard to her uncle's bequest, she made a momentous decision about how God, the "father of the fatherless," wanted her to spend the money, and it did not involve clothing. Distressed by the sight of Henry's two youngest grandchildren, Nancy and Johnny, living in squalor with their mother, she promised God to give them a better life—a life away from Abigail.[82] If Sarah could find a place for Nancy to live as an apprentice, then Johnny could join his two other siblings at her house, and Abigail could get a job to support herself.

Not surprisingly, Abigail resisted the idea of being separated from her two younger children. Although she may have been grateful to Sarah and Henry for saving her family from the poorhouse, she also seems to have resented their interference and criticisms. Once again, we only have one side of the conversation, but if Sarah ever spoke to Abigail in the tone with which she wrote about her, their relationship must have been tense. Sarah almost never described poverty as a divine punishment for sin, but in an angry moment she wondered whether God might punish Abigail's "sloth" by refusing to show mercy to her children. "If it is thy Pleasure that they through her obstinacy as a Just Punishment for sloth and other sins shall remain miserable," she asked God, "who am I that I should oppose it?" Although she prayed for Abigail's salvation, she had little hope that she would ever be born again. "O Let Her not be Miserable through time and to Eternity through Laziness," she prayed. "But I Leave her in thy wise, Just, and faithful Hands."[83]

Sarah always described herself in her diaries as "weak" and powerless, but in fact she was a formidable opponent who knew how to get her way. After two weeks of arguing, Abigail relented under the pressure. Still dependent on Sarah and Henry's charity, she had little choice. Besides agreeing to send Johnny to live with them, she allowed "Little Nancy" to live with a Mrs. Wanscoat, probably as a household servant. (Mrs. Wanscoat did not belong to the First Church of Christ, but she was probably a member of one of the other Christian churches in Newport. Sarah would have hesitated to send Nancy to anyone who was not a devout Christian.) Perhaps Sarah worried about her ability to support all four of Abigail's children, but she may have also hoped that Mrs. Wanscoat would teach Nancy a skill that would help her in the future—for example, baking or sewing.[84]

Without knowing more about Abigail, it is hard to say whether Sarah treated her fairly. Sarah could be condescending at times, and because of her certainty that Abigail was a bad mother, she ignored her pain at being separated from her children. Given Sarah's suffering when she had lost her own son, she might have been more empathetic, but just as she claimed to know what was best for Phillis and Bobey, she also insisted that she knew what was best for Abigail and her children.

But perhaps in this case she made the best choice under difficult circumstances. If she was not exaggerating when she described her grandchildren as "hungry" and "naked," then they needed her help. Many people in Newport were poor, but Sarah claimed that "no greater Objects [of compassion] are to be found in this Place than these [children]." Abigail's "sloth" seems to have included outright neglect. As a widow with no money and no employment, she may have been too depressed to care for her family. When Sarah embraced Abigail's children as her own, she was trying to imitate God's compassion to the fatherless. They were "Dear Lambs," a gift from God.[85]

Sarah's generosity was especially remarkable in light of her faltering health. Although she felt relatively well between flare-ups of her illness, her condition deteriorated with every attack. By the spring of 1762 walking had become so difficult that her friends usually took her to church in a chaise. She could no longer visit the sick or the needy unless someone drove her, and to spare herself the exertion she seems to have moved her school into her house. In November she suffered a flare-up that was so severe she spent twelve days in bed. Thinking she might die, her friends gathered around her bedside to keep vigil. In a rare expression of pride, Sarah remembered later, "perhaps not less than fifty offered to watch."[86] She eventually recovered, but the number of people who rushed to her side was a fitting tribute to a woman who had always tried to help others in need. Many of them had probably experienced Sarah's generosity in the past.

Almost everything that we know about Sarah's declining health comes from her letters to Joseph Fish rather than her diaries. Although she prayed for help as her illness progressed, she chose her words carefully because she did not want to sound discontented or resentful. Adopting a posture of submission, she wrote in her diary, "I ask not Health nor any temporal mercy, be it what it will, if it will stand in competition with that or be anyway improved to the dishonor of God." If not for her candid descriptions in her letters to Fish we would have no idea of the true extent of her debility. In a brief aside she mentioned that she usually spent at least one day a week in bed, and as she admitted in June 1763, she had been to church only twice in the previous ten months.[87] Since the Reverend Vinal was still struggling with alcoholism the church may have been closed on many Sundays, but even when it was open, she did not have the strength to get there. Her disease often left her exhausted, and it was slowly robbing her of the ability to walk. She still taught her school, but she was forced to spend more and more time at home, her world shrinking to the four walls of her house.

At the age of forty-nine Sarah could no longer venture out into the streets to find those who needed her charity and prayers. But driven by her desire to be useful and to glorify God, she opened her doors to anyone who wanted to learn more about the gospel. Her advancing illness should have marked the end of her evangelism, but instead it was the beginning of the most remarkable chapter of her life.

Chapter 9

Jordan Overflowing, 1765–1774

*I Hope and trust out of Love to poor Perishing immortal souls and a
degree of Love and Zeal for the Glory of God I at first concented to Let
poor servants and white Lads come here on Sabbath evenings to Join
with us in family worship but Little thot of their Multiplying as at
this day even till the House will not contain them and now I know not
what to do I Have set my hand to the plow and dare not look back I
dare not dismiss and say they shall not come since they behave with all
decency and seem to esteem it a great priviledge I [can] chierfuly read
to them talk with them and sing a psalm with them but when it comes
to the duty of prayer I [refrain] Lest I bring a wound and reproach
upon religion I dare not Encourage black ones to pray thus openly Lest
they be Lift'd up with Pride and proceed from praying to Exhorting
&c Every Brother and friend declines affording me assistance in this
Point . . . shall I write my dear Pastor just to come up and pray one
Lords Day Evening Mr Styles another Mr Thurston another and Mr
Maxen another as there is a considerable Number of each Ministers
Peculiar charge as well as there own servants or shall they be sent away
without Prayer . . . Who would ever have thot that God by such a Mean
despicable worm would have Gatherd such a Number as now stately
resorts to this House every Week . . . in all three hundred and twelve
souls beside all the trancient persons that come to converse on a religious
account is this not the Lords doing is it not marvelous in our Eyes what
but his secret drawing could incline so Many to Lend a Listening Ear
to serious things why aut [else] the young and the bond as usual not*

prophaining the Lords Day Evenings by Plays and Passtimes if God has not given them a serious turn and in a degree stopt them in their Mad Carreer is there not room to Hope God is preparing his way for a Glorious revival of religion I have sometimes cheiring Hopes but as to my self none but God alone knows my conflicts and fiery trials and temptations the Lord soport guide and direct me that I may not turn out of the Path of duty to the right hand or Left. . . . O pray for me dr sir pray for me o that my God will Grant me Grace to know and do his will the weight and concern that Lies upon my spirits at this time Lest I should take any wrong steps or Encourage others to do so causes my sleep to depart from me whole Nights together and o my dear Pastor so far as in you Lies protect me and direct me what course to take would you advise me to shut up my mouth and doors and creep into obscurity will this be most for Gods Glory and the Good of souls sometimes I am tempted thus to do but Hithertoo I dare not.[1]

1765. It is a cold Sunday night in the middle of winter. Candles and firelight illuminate Sarah Osborn's house, casting a glow onto the street. More than seventy slaves and free blacks sit quietly in her kitchen as she reads the Bible to them. With few chairs in the house, most of them sit shoulder to shoulder on the floor while she perches above them on a stool, pausing occasionally to emphasize that the Bible was written for each and every one of them. Though she has difficulty walking and standing because of her advancing illness, she has never felt more alive.

Every night seems marvelous to her—a stunning testament to God's grace. Crowds of people assemble at her door almost every evening waiting to pray, read the Bible, and sing hymns with her. To handle the throng, she arranges for different groups to meet on different nights of the week: white boys, young men, "neighbor's daughters," and "Ethiopians" join her family for worship on Sundays; Baptist men gather on Mondays; blacks on Tuesdays; the women's society during their traditional time on Thursdays; and Baptist women on Fridays. Since she is reluctant to pray aloud in front of adult white men, she asks her husband, Henry, to pray with them instead.[2]

Both exhilarated and frightened by the revival at her house, Sarah writes to Joseph Fish for advice. Sometimes she worries that the sheer number of worshipers might become like "the river Jordan overflowing all the banks," and with more than three hundred people crowding into her house each week, she fears losing control, especially of the slaves. Yet because of her hope that she is witnessing the beginning of a "glorious revival of religion," she refuses "to shut up my mouth and doors and creep into obscurity."[3]

A Glorious Revival

Sarah Osborn's prayer meetings were controversial—women were not supposed to aspire to religious leadership—but her decision to invite blacks into her home was greeted with greater hostility than she had ever before encountered. Without intending it she had exposed the deep ambivalence about race that lurked underneath Newport's urbane, polite culture. Christians in Newport paid lip service to the ideal of converting blacks, but they found it disturbing to imagine that slaves—especially their *own* slaves— might become their "brothers" and "sisters" in Christ. They preferred to assume that Africans were too ignorant, stubborn, or savage to understand the gospel.

Evangelicals set themselves apart from virtually all other Christians in the eighteenth century by making a determined effort to convert the enslaved. Just as the rise of evangelicalism in dialogue with the Enlightenment gave women new opportunities for religious leadership, it inspired a small but influential group of free blacks and slaves to affirm their spiritual equality. Influenced by the Enlightenment emphasis on the authority of individual experience, evangelicals insisted that blacks could become true Christians, and they encouraged the most literate to publish their narratives of sin and redemption.

Yet white evangelicals shared something else with Enlightenment thinkers: a tragic inability to accept racial difference as anything other than a sign of inferiority. Even the most fervent preachers to the enslaved found it virtually impossible to imagine a world where blacks and whites would be political, economic, or social equals. Neither evangelicals nor Enlightenment thinkers were able to forge a new vision of race on their own. Each had something the other lacked: evangelicals a fervent belief that sin must be immediately repented, Enlightenment thinkers an equally fervent belief that freedom was a universal right. In the eighteenth century only a few radical visionaries were courageous enough to combine the Enlightenment ideal of universal equality with the Christian imperative to "love thy neighbor as thyself," and at first, Sarah Osborn was not one of them.

It is not clear exactly when and how her meetings began. None of her diaries survive for the period between April 1762 and January 1767, and although Samuel Hopkins included brief extracts from the missing diaries in his *Memoirs of the Life of Mrs. Sarah Osborn*, he was not able to read several crucial volumes dating from the early years of the revival. Sometime before Sarah died, she realized that her diaries from January 4, 1765, to October 2, 1766, had disappeared, but she "could not tell where, or by what means they were gone."[4] As a result, there are many questions about the revival that we cannot answer.

Hopkins claims that Sarah did not begin holding meetings until 1766 and 1767, when "there was an uncommon attention to religion, which turned the thoughts of many to Mrs. Osborn. They repaired to her as a known pious, benevolent Christian, to whom they could have easy access, that they might enjoy her counsel and prayers." Yet by piecing together evidence from her extensive correspondence, her 1767 diary, and Hopkins's own account of her life, we can determine that Sarah began holding religious meetings for blacks and children (probably white children) as early as June 1764. "Lord, overrule for thy own glory, both as to servants and children," she prayed. Perhaps Hopkins minimized her evangelistic role in order to shield her from criticism, but the evidence suggests that her meetings were not the consequence of the "uncommon attention to religion" but its cause. As she explained to Joseph Fish in September 1764, she was eagerly praying for a revival, and by the following April "several Ethiopians" were coming to her house every Sunday evening. In an attempt to hide her own agency, Sarah explained that they had "asked Liberty to repair to our House for the benefit of family prayer, reading, &c." But she also admitted, "I have thought it a duty to Encourage them." Although she never mentioned reading Cotton Mather's *The Negro Christianized*, which was published in 1706, she may have been influenced by his call to evangelize slaves. One of Mather's suggestions was that families should invite blacks to join them on Sunday nights for worship.[5]

If the Reverend Vinal had been available, Sarah might have sent the Africans to his house instead of her own, but he was increasingly incapacitated by his drinking. Reluctant to name the problem, Sarah wrote only that he was "Laid by frequently and we scattered as sheep without a shepherd."[6] Although Deacon Nathaniel Coggeshall strove to keep the church running, it was Sarah who took up the mantle of spiritual leadership. Despite her illness, she had a gift that others lacked.

Sarah's evangelism was fueled by her belief that the millennium might be near. Like many Americans she had interpreted France's defeat during the Seven Years' War as a blow to the Catholic Antichrist, and she searched for signs that Christ would soon return. "I know not what is before us," she wrote in 1764, "no, not for an Hour, but would fain Hope the Glory of the Latter days is beginning to dawn." Encouraged by the news of revivals in other places, she hoped that "vile Rhode Island" might be next.[7]

Sarah's meetings began only a few months after her mother's death, a painful loss that may have also felt like a release. There is no doubt that Sarah loved her "dear mother," and ever since her confession many years earlier, she had tried to be a good daughter. Yet their visits over the years had sometimes been difficult, and it may not have been a coincidence that Sarah decided to do something radical so soon after her mother's death. If Susanna had been alive to hear the news of Sarah's prayer meetings for slaves, she probably would have reprimanded her daughter for being too zealous: they had never completely agreed about what it meant to be a Christian. But now that her mother was gone, Sarah could make her own choices without fear of recrimination.[8] As she wept over her loss, she may have realized that there was no longer any reason to mute her convictions. She would follow God wherever he led.

Sarah's meetings with Africans—both enslaved and free—seem to have begun with a slave named Quaum (also known as Quamenee Church and later John Quamine), who sent her a letter describing his conversion in 1764. Quaum was the slave of Captain Benjamin Church, a merchant who had belonged to the First Church of Christ for seventeen years, but he decided to approach Osborn and Deacon Nathaniel Coggeshall instead of his own master for religious guidance, perhaps hoping that they would be less reluctant to accept him as a spiritual "brother." Most masters had little interest in welcoming their slaves to the communion table. Since Africans in Newport formed a tight-knit community, Quaum probably knew about Sarah's close relationship to Phillis, and it is even possible that he asked Phillis for help in writing his conversion narrative. He dictated his account to a literate female slave because of his poor English and his inability to write.[9]

Quaum's narrative has been lost, but Sarah sent it to Joseph Fish, and his response includes a summary of the contents. Quaum was born in Anamaboe on the Gold Coast of Africa (in modern-day Ghana) and was sold into slavery in Newport in 1754 or 1755. There he had quickly mastered the tenets of evangelical Christianity. His language, though reportedly "broken," sounded much like Sarah's. "Truly I must join you in Favorable Sentiments of what has passed within him," Fish wrote to her. "The discoveries he had of Himself,—his Sinful Life,—Total Corruption and Depravity of Nature,—utter Inability to help himself,—Unworthiness of any Favor,—Just Desert of Eternal Punishment,—Lost undone state,—Excellency and Loveliness of Christ,—Freeness of his Grace,—Perfection of his Righteousness,—Fullness and all-sufficiency &c &c are all of a Gospel Stamp; & constrain me to think that there is, in the Subject, *like Precious Faith with Saints.*" On July 28, 1765, Quaum was baptized and accepted into full communion at the First Church, the fourth black member to be accepted. Perhaps because of his devotion to the Gospel of John, which he named as a favorite book of the Bible, he renamed himself John Quamine.[10]

Although the meetings at Sarah's house began with blacks, the news of Quamine's conversion soon brought others to her door as well, including a group of white boys. Perhaps they were simply curious at first, but there was something magnetic about Sarah—a warmth and an earnestness—that drew them in. Week after week they returned, pressing into her kitchen to pray and sing with her. By the summer of 1766 she felt as though she were witnessing the miracle of the loaves and the fishes. As she explained to Fish, when she had first allowed "poor servants and white Lads" to join family worship on Sunday nights, she had "Little thought of their Multiplying as at this day even till the House will not contain them."[11]

But the crowds kept growing. Soon both blacks and whites of all ages were clamoring for the opportunity to pray at her house. Though not all were Congregationalists, Sarah welcomed them anyway. Since we do not have any accounts from the people who attended her meetings, we cannot know why they were so drawn to her, but even if asked they might have found it difficult to articulate the force of her charisma. Gifted in prayer, Sarah seems to have intuitively known how to touch people's hearts. When a group of more than thirty girls assembled at her house one night, including a girl whose father had recently died, Sarah's emotional prayer for the "fatherless" reduced them to tears.[12] Although she could be stern when speaking to those who did not share her faith, she could also be tender when consoling the ill or distressed. Her sensitivity to other people's crosses must have made her an especially appealing figure to the enslaved, who knew that she, too, had lost loved ones. Although there must have been times when her empathy failed (as it had with Phillis), she tried her best to offer comfort and hope. Her message was always the same: a loving, compassionate Jesus had offered up his own life to save them.

People seem to have been especially drawn to Sarah because of her steadfast faith in the midst of suffering. Even though she was losing her ability to walk and to see, she testified that God was her only portion—her strength and her life. Her faith seemed remarkable, a mystery that they wanted to understand.

As the Osborn house grew increasingly crowded on Sunday evenings, the meetings spilled into other homes as well. Deacon Coggeshall invited worshipers to join his family on Sunday evenings, and a "free Ethiopian" opened his doors to "young men" (probably of both races) on Sunday nights and to blacks on Thursday nights. Sarah also invited young children to visit her twice a week to recite the catechism, sing hymns, pray, and talk about God. Sometimes she read passages from *A Token for Children*, a Puritan book featuring the stories of pious children who had died young.[13]

Not everyone was welcome at Osborn's house, however, and not everyone found her a charismatic figure. Most Quakers seem to have avoided her, probably troubled by her defense of original sin, and some members of the Second Church of Christ (her mother's former church) found her overly strict. Even parents who sent their children to her for catechism classes sometimes chafed at her rigor. In a humorous aside to Fish, Sarah admitted that an Anglican couple "complained I Had Spoilt their child for she did nothing but get alone and read and pray and cry and they would not divert her all they could do."[14] Although Sarah cherished the child's visible signs of a changed heart, others in Newport rejected the notion that true religion should involve tears.

The numbers who crossed Sarah Osborn's threshold each week were astonishing. During the summer of 1766 more than 500 people crowded into her house every week, including almost 140 on Sunday nights alone. Sometimes strangers stopped by to see what was happening. Always self-effacing, she asked Fish, "Who would ever have thought that God by such a Mean despicable worm would have Gathered such a Number as now steadily resorts to this House every Week?"[15]

Sarah's interracial meetings were so large that they were impossible to ignore, and many in Newport were troubled by her violation of the codes of racial etiquette that kept blacks and whites apart. Because Sarah allowed dozens of slaves and free blacks to mix with young white men and women on Sunday evenings, some critics seem to have feared miscegenation. As she admitted to Fish, one of Newport's matrons had cut off "all intercourse with her" because "the reproachful sound of keeping a Negro House is too intolerable to be born." Fearing that her decision to allow "Neighbor's daughters" to worship with blacks on Sunday nights might "Give some occasion of offence," Sarah asked the young women to come on Monday nights instead. But she refused to stop welcoming blacks into her house. "I dare not dismiss and say they shall not come," she explained to Fish. "They behave with all decency and seem to esteem it a great privilege."[16]

Slave masters in Newport prided themselves on their benevolence, but the truth is that they were more than a little afraid of the slaves and free blacks in their midst, and they seem to have worried that Sarah Osborn's meetings would incite rebellion. The *Newport Mercury* often printed accounts of violent slaves who had revolted on shipboard or murdered their masters. In the spring of 1763, for example, the newspaper printed stories about a Newport captain who had died after his throat was cut during a slave mutiny; a twenty-one-year-old woman who had perished after a slave struck her with a flatiron and dragged her to the cellar; and a slave uprising in Berbice, a Dutch colony in Guyana, that had led to the massacre of "all the inhabitants." Masters insisted that their slaves were content, but they knew that a desire for freedom always bubbled under the surface. Between 1758 and 1775 the *Newport Mercury* printed more than sixty-five advertisements for runaway slaves, each ad accompanied by a crude drawing of a black figure in flight, a staff in hand. John Bannister, for example, a member of Sarah Osborn's church, placed an ad offering a reward for his runaway slave Caesar. Although these images were designed to serve as a quick reference point for slave catchers, the result was that the dominant visual representation of slavery involved escape.[17]

Sarah could not have chosen a worse time to encourage mass gatherings of slaves and free blacks. Although whites in Newport had always been nervous about the possibility of slave revolts, they grew especially anxious during the 1760s because of mob violence against British policies. When the British Parliament passed the Sugar Act in 1764 and the Stamp Act in 1765 in order to pay for the French and Indian War, colonists responded by burning effigies of stamp collectors, destroying houses, and tarring and feathering Loyalists. In June 1765 a mob of five hundred "Sailors, Boys, and Negroes" seized a boat from the British vessel *The Maidstone* and burned it on the Newport Common to protest against the impressment of men into the British navy. (Impressment was virtually a form of kidnapping.) Even for those who were sympathetic to the plight of impressed sailors, the "rabble" was alarming, especially because it involved "Negroes" brazenly attacking British property. Two months later a Stamp Act demonstration organized by three of Newport's leading merchants spiraled out of control

R UN-AWAY from their Mafters, (Col. Job Almy, and Cornelius Sole, both of Tiverton) on the 2d Day of November Inftant, two Negro Men, and one Indian Man, Slaves, all born in Tiverton, defcribed as follows, viz.—— *Pero*, one of the Negroes, about 25 Years of Age, is a Blackfmith by Trade, and plays on a Fiddle ; had on when he went away, a Sheeps gray Coat, with blue Cuffs, a ftriped Flannel Jacket, Leather Breeches, thick Shoes, a Hat, and a full Cap.——*Jack*, (the other Negro) about 35 Years of Age, 5 Feet 6 Inches high, has a Scar on his Forehead, and has a glaring Eye ; had on a mill'd Worfted Coat, white Holland Jacket, a ftriped Flannel ditto, Fuftian Breeches, and a Pair of thin Shoes.——*Ifaac*, (the Indian) about 28 Years old, 5 Feet 10 Inches high, was born of a Spanifh Squaw, has a Scar in his Forehead ; had on a mill'd colour'd Coat, a fhort Jacket near the fame Colour, a Pair of Tow Trowfers, and a Pair of thin Shoes.

Whoever fhall fecure one or more of faid Slaves, fo that his or their Mafter or Mafters may him or them again, fhall be well rewarded, and all neceffary Charges paid, by JOB ALMY, Tiverton, Nov. 5, 1765. CORNELIUS SOLE.

An advertisement for a runaway slave, *Newport Mercury*, November 11, 1765. Photograph courtesy of the Newport Historical Society.

when Patriots attacked the houses of two prominent Loyalists.[18] With tensions running high, any large gathering raised the specter of anarchy and violence.

A large gathering led by a *woman* conjured up images of a different kind of disorder. In a letter to Joseph Fish, Sarah asked whether she had ventured "too far beyond my Line." Although hoping that he would say no, her question was not rhetorical. Certain that "Ministers should stand in their Places and Private Christians . . . in theirs," she did not want anyone to think that she aspired to "Ministerial Office." Nor did she want worshipers at her meetings to imagine that women had the same religious authority as men. Though she was willing to pray aloud in front of women, children, and slaves, she refused to place herself in a position of leadership over adolescent boys or white men; she relied on Henry or visiting ministers to pray with them instead. She knew her "proper place." Comparing herself to the biblical woman of Samaria, she portrayed herself as nothing more than a messenger. If people believed in Christ, it was because "of his own word and not for the saying of the woman only."[19]

Sarah's meetings were controversial for another reason as well. Not only were they interracial, they were interdenominational. By 1761 she had allowed at least one Baptist woman, a former Congregationalist, to be part of the women's society, but she had always worried about compromising her religious purity. During the revivals, however, she put aside her scruples to invite both Baptists and Seventh-day Baptists to her meetings, and even a few Anglicans attended. "*Church folks*," she called them. Because Vinal was increasingly withdrawn and even hostile, she invited the Reverend Gardiner Thurston, the pastor of the Second Baptist Church, to attend instead. He was a cooper (a cask and barrel maker) who had never been to college, but he was rumored to have "the power of attracting great congregations." Like George Whitefield, Osborn believed that religious experience was more important than doctrinal disagreements, a nondenominational approach that would become a hallmark of the evangelical movement in the future. "All sorts and sects almost promiscuously come to our House," she reported. "They Have all a welcome there."[20]

But not everyone believed that it was wise to break down the barriers that had usually kept Newport's Christians apart. The Reverend Vinal disliked the Baptists because of their rejection of infant baptism, and Joseph Fish had never forgiven them for destroying his church. During the early 1740s, two-thirds of his congregation in Stonington had walked out in order to found a new Separate Baptist congregation, and even twenty years later he had not forgotten the indignity of being attacked as "the devil" and "a wolf in sheep's clothing." Besides claiming that the Baptists wanted "to Banish Learning and Order from the Churches," he accused them of mistaking frenzied emotion for grace.[21]

When Samuel Hopkins published excerpts from Sarah Osborn's diary after her death, he omitted any references to her relationship with the Baptists. Sarah imagined a future in which doctrinal differences would be less important than "essentials," but in this case Hopkins refused to let her speak for herself.[22] Too much was at stake for him: the definition of what it meant to be an evangelical. He was not willing to admit that true Christians could disagree about doctrine.

During August 1766, Sarah was as anxious as she had been during the dark days preceding her conversion. At night she lay awake wondering whether she was doing God's will. "I Have Lost six whole Nights sleep out of eleven without so much as one wink," she confessed to Fish, "a seventh slept but one hour." In a revealing analogy, she compared herself to Uriah the Hittite, who had been slaughtered on the front lines of battle because of David's betrayal.[23]

Sarah's "David" seems to have been Vinal, who had left her alone and vulnerable instead of helping with her meetings. The more that he drank, the more withdrawn and embittered he became. Sarah gently tried to raise the issue of his alcoholism by writing to him about others who struggled with the same problem, but he never responded. Although he accepted new members from her meetings, he refused to cross her threshold to preach. (When Samuel Hopkins published his account of Sarah Osborn's life, he sidestepped the issue of Vinal's involvement in her meetings by mentioning that he was not "able to attend.") Sarah sent Vinal a letter suggesting that he and other ministers (including the Reverend Thurston, the Reverend John Maxson of the Seventh-day Baptist Church, and the Reverend Ezra Stiles of the Second Church of Christ) could take turns presiding at her meetings, but he condemned her "zeal" and her willingness to expose people to the wrong kind of Christianity. (He may have been especially angry because of her earlier letter about the dangers of too much drinking.) "I received your Letter but am not able to write a proper answer," he retorted. "Your proposal of Having Proselytizing Ministers to assist in carrying on your religion I do by no means approve of. That has a worse tendency than you think. . . . Your zeal for God if you are not on your Guard will carry you astray."[24]

Sarah was shocked by Vinal's letter, but by 1766 he had become increasingly hostile and even paranoid, and he seems to have been afraid that other ministers were trying to steal his flock. After discovering that Ezra Stiles had baptized a child against his wishes, he accused Stiles of "savoring too much of a Fondness to meddle in Affairs of our Congregation, and in such a Way as has a direct Tendency to diminish our Congregation and to augment your own." He was so "jealous" of Sarah's friendship with other ministers that she hid her correspondence with them. "I Must Have a Great regard for but *one*," she complained. As his relationship with his congregation deteriorated, he wrote an angry letter demanding that they pay him in goods if they lacked cash. He threatened to leave unless they complied, and to underline his point he signed the letter "your (present) pastor."[25]

Vinal's "indisposition," as Sarah delicately called it, weighed heavily on her. Stung by his disapproval of her meetings, she struggled with doubts about her duty, even comparing herself to the prophet Jonah, who had run away from Nineveh out of fear. "Under this pressure poor Jonah fled," she lamented to Fish. She was grateful for the support of her husband, Susanna Anthony, and Deacon Coggeshall, but when two close female friends, Mrs. Chesebrough and Mrs. Grant, warned her to send the crowds away, she was tempted to shut her doors. Once again she felt as though God had hidden his face, leaving her alone with her doubts.[26]

Yet unlike Jonah, Sarah was determined not to shirk God's call, and as she prayed for guidance she felt the same sense of his mystical presence that had sustained her during other crises of faith, a feeling of oneness that collapsed the boundaries between heaven and earth. Referring to Psalm 104, she claimed that "God determined the soul to take up with nothing short of Himself and the Comforter came down and caused faith to Look above the tops of the Mountains and they flowed down at his presence."[27] Strengthened by her faith that the "Comforter" (the Holy Spirit) was hovering over her, she resolved not to let Vinal or anyone else keep her from doing God's work.

Sarah wanted to be sure that her meetings were inspired by God, and suddenly it seemed that she saw proof of his favor wherever she looked: in the young people who had stopped "profaning the Lords Day Evenings by Plays and Pastimes"; in the children who wept at the thought of dying without Christ; and most of all in the Africans who sat quietly in her kitchen listening to the gospel. When she looked at the earnest people streaming through her doors every night, some with Bibles clasped in their hands, she regained the sense of certainty that had eluded her. In October she begged in her diary, "Permit me to feed thy lambs, and devote my whole life to the service of my God."[28]

By January 1767, 525 people were coming to her house every week, including at least 70 Africans. Remarkably, more than 5 percent of Newport's black population passed through her doors every Sunday evening.[29] "We were so crowded there was scarce room to stir Hand or foot," she marveled.[30]

Since evangelical history is filled with stories of leaders who took advantage of their power to touch people's hearts, it is worth noting that Sarah's life could have turned out differently. Exhilarated by her charisma, she could have become a demagogue. No one knew this better than Sarah herself, who prayed not to be "influenced by self-confidence or vain Glory." During the revival she seems to have intensified her practice of self-discipline, privately chastising herself for being "sullen," "covetous," and "a depraved monster."[31] She did not want to forget that she was too weak and sinful to have brought about the revival on her own.

In February, Sarah finally received an answer to the long letter she had written to Joseph Fish the previous summer. Although this letter no longer survives, Sarah's response makes it clear that he urged her to reconsider her meetings. At some point during the fall he had visited her house on a Sunday evening to pray with the "poor Blacks," and he was alarmed by what he had witnessed. Besides chastising her for moving beyond her "line," he worried that the presence of large numbers of blacks would eventually lead to trouble. He also wondered how she found time for private devotion and household chores while holding meetings every evening. Sarah had looked up to Fish for more than twenty years, and if anyone could have persuaded her to close her doors, it would have been he. But even he could not shake her confidence in her call. She began her response in a conciliatory fashion by portraying herself as "a Child in the Presence of her Father," and she insisted (twice) that she did not want to be perceived as "Obstinate." "I don't reject counsel," she insisted. "Don't Let my Honored Father think I do." Yet she also made it clear that she could not heed his advice. Although she would have liked to place her meetings for blacks "into Superior Hands," no one had offered to help. (The exception was Thurston, the Baptist minister, whom she tactfully did not mention.) Denying that she had ever stepped out of her place, she explained, "I only read to them, talk to them, and sing a Psalm or Hymn with them, and then at Eight o'clock dismiss them all by Name as upon List. They call it School and I Had rather it be called almost anything that is good than Meeting." Portraying herself as a teacher and a mother rather than a pastor, she explained, "The servants appear to me no otherwise now then children though for stature Men and Women."[32]

Sarah also reassured Fish that the blacks at her meetings had never been disorderly, and in fact the enslaved among them had become more obedient. "If any disturbance or disorder Should arise Either to the breaking of public or family Peace, that would immediately Make the path of duty Plain for dismissing *at once*, but on the contrary Ministers and Magistrates send their Servants and approve. And other Masters and Mistresses frequently send me presents in token of gratitude, Express their thanks, Speaking of the good Effects that through the blessing of the Lord it Has Had upon their Servants." If good works were a sign of grace, then there was no doubt that many slaves were on the path to salvation. "Some that were unwilling to serve and saucy are become diligent and condescending," she wrote proudly.[33]

In contrast to what she had written earlier, Sarah insisted that most Christians in Newport approved of her meetings, including "Ministers and Magistrates." Perhaps the truth was more complicated, but Newport's leaders may have put aside their doubts once they realized her commitment to fostering obedience. Sarah reported that both Mrs. Chesebrough and Mrs. Grant had recently thanked her "for persisting Steadily in the path of duty against their discouragements," and although Mr. Chesebrough remained dubious, he was "quite silent." Other brothers in the church supposedly defended her meetings as divinely inspired. When she had been "affrighted at the throng" in December and had considered sending people away, Deacon Coggeshall "insisted I ought not to do it." As she explained, "Every Intimate brother and friend entreats and charges me not to dismiss So Long as things rest as they are, telling me it would be the worst day's work that Ever I did if I should, as God Himself Has thus Employed me."[34]

"God himself": this was Sarah's deepest conviction, and because of her long friendship with Fish she desperately wanted him to understand that she had been gripped by a force larger than herself. "As God Has Gathered I dare not Scatter," she avowed. When she had tried to send a group of white boys to Deacon Coggeshall's house on Sunday nights to ease the crowds, "they kept their places and would not stir," refusing to budge until she promised to meet with them on Tuesday nights. "*Still* they will come," she marveled to Fish.[35] Because the events at her house defied rational explanation—who had ever heard of boys choosing prayer over play?—she was convinced that God was working through her.

Sarah saw even her gender as proof that the revival had been inspired by God. Echoing stereotypes instead of challenging them, she suggested that a "weak" woman could never have attracted so many people by virtue of her own authority. "Christ's strength is Made perfect in my weakness," she testified. "I am nothing and can do nothing without Him." Remembering Paul's words to the Corinthians, she wrote, "He has chosen the weak things of the world."[36]

In response to Fish's concern about the pressures on her time, Sarah assured him that neither she nor her family was suffering because of her meetings. She continued to read and write early in the mornings, "without which I must *starve*," and friends and neighbors helped with housekeeping. "I Educate the children of poor Neighbors who Gladly pay me in washing, Ironing, Mending and Making," she explained. "Every dear friend is ready to set a stitch or Help me in any wise." Rebuffing Fish's suggestion that her work was "too heavy" for one person, Sarah claimed to feel stronger than she had in years. "I used to Lie by, unable to sit up, usually one day in the week for years together," she reminded him. "I have Lain by but one this winter and comparatively know nothing about weariness to what I did when I had so Great a School and ten or more children in family to attend." With her illness apparently in partial remission, she was even able to walk at times. Although she was "not able to walk abroad, yet in the House I can walk and act sometimes a Little while with almost the vigors of youth."[37] This, too, seemed to be proof of God's approval.

Sarah also argued that if she did not spend her evenings speaking about religion, she would probably be drawn into political gossip with visitors instead. It was a "*critical day*," she reminded Fish, and although she did not elaborate on her point he would certainly have understood her meaning. Tensions between Loyalists and Patriots were threatening to erupt into violence. When an angry mob harassed the Newport custom's collector, he published an advertisement ordering all protestors to "desist from such Attempts, otherwise it will be at the Peril of their Lives." Everyone seemed to be talking about politics—everyone, that is, except Sarah Osborn and the people at her meetings, who believed that the debate over "taxation without representation" should take a back seat to the quest for salvation. On Election Day in 1767 she wrote in her diary, "This day Let others choose whom they will to rule and whom they will serve but I will renewedly choose the Great Governor of the Universe to rule in and reign over me."[38]

We do not know how Fish responded to Sarah's defense of her meetings, but he seems to have visited Newport again sometime that winter, and in another letter to him in May, Sarah mentioned that his wise counsel had prevented many worshipers from joining the Baptists. Yet the relationship between the two seems to have been strained. After offering him "ten thousand thanks" for his "care and tender regard," she begged him not to end their friendship. "Permit me to beg you will not cast me off," she pleaded, even if he believed that her "Conduct" had rendered her "unworthy of farther Notice." In 1767 she broke off her relationship with the Baptists because she did not want to "Grieve nor offend" him.[39]

Yet there were limits to her deference. She continued to hold meetings at her house, and despite keeping her distance from the Reverend Thurston, she strongly defended him as a faithful minister whose "precious truths" had changed lives. When Fish published a book attacking the Separates and Baptists for creating schisms in Congregationalist churches, Sarah decided that in good conscience she could not help finance its publication by subscribing to it. Although a few members of her church had turned Baptist, she insisted that Thurston had never intended to cause controversy. He was not guilty of anything other than "affable, courteous behavior"—hardly a crime.[40]

Fish was more generous than the Reverend Vinal, and he seems to have decided that their friendship was more important than his scruples about her evangelism. Though he never actively supported her meetings, he tolerated them, and she continued to attract large crowds throughout 1767. She often used her diary to keep track of the number who attended: thirty-seven "young Handmaids" met on March 9, forty-three on March 16, forty-nine on March 23. Her Sunday meetings for blacks and young men were always the largest. Even on a stormy night in March, more than seventy blacks met in her kitchen while a group of young white men met upstairs. "Our House was Last Night filled as full as it ever was," she exclaimed in the spring.[41]

Some of her family members seem to have been caught up in the fervor. Besides Henry, Sarah's nephew William Guise Haggar (her deceased brother's son) often attended the men's group. He was a member of Ezra Stiles's church, but he had recently become a father at the age of twenty-nine, and he may have wanted to think more seriously about the meaning of his life. Although the evidence is murky, two of her step-grandchildren also may have been touched by the revival. "Bless my dear son," she prayed in her diary. "Turn and Look Him into an Evangelical flow of repentance."

(Since she had raised her grandson since childhood, she might have referred to him as her "son.")[42] In addition, her granddaughter Sally was almost certainly the "Fatherless" girl whose "turn in temper," "diligence," and kindness to others seemed like "marvelous" evidence of her spiritual transformation.[43] There is no record of whether Abigail remained in contact with her children, but Sarah never seems to have regretted her decision to separate them from their mother. Besides rescuing them from poverty, she believed that she had saved their souls.

Sarah's meetings remained controversial, however, and even Deacon Coggeshall, one of her warmest supporters, began to worry that she had pushed the boundaries of her evangelism too far. In April 1767 he warned her to stop praying aloud in front of black men. Despite their race, they were still *men*, and yet she addressed them almost as if she were a preacher. Praying for guidance, Sarah asked God whether her behavior was "offensive" or "ostentatious." Although she knew that she "ought not to pray in so public a Manner as it were in the corner of the street to be seen," she was determined to obey God's will even if it caused a scandal. "Man can't determine me," she wrote fiercely. "Man's opinion alone shant content me for or against. Tis thy approbation I want. Let me but please God and tis enough. Only Let me know by thy spirit accompanying thy word that I do so and it is enough." Later that month she confessed in her diary, "I dared not omit praying." In the margins she added, "Deacon Coggeshall had bid me omit it if I dared—and I dared not."[44]

Always on the lookout for Satan, Sarah saw his hand—or rather his "paw"—behind her troubles. Imagining him as a "Lion," she begged God to "Put his Hook in his Nose and turn him back by the way he came." Not since the days of her conversion had she felt such an intense awareness of evil. Enraged by her evangelism to the heathen, Satan was plotting "to break up my Evening exercise which has been so refreshing to me." Though Sarah rarely compared herself to biblical warriors, she swore to put on "the whole armor of God" to fight the devil. Boldly addressing him in the first person, she promised to vanquish him with the "shield of faith," "the helmet of salvation," and "the sword of the Spirit."[45]

Sarah's call to arms was inspired by Ephesians 6, a chapter that also includes Paul's restrictive "household codes" for children, wives, and slaves. "Servants, be obedient to them that are your masters according to the flesh," Paul advised, "with fear and trembling, in singleness of your heart, as unto Christ." Like Paul, Sarah did not see any contradiction between fighting "against spiritual wickedness in high places" and accepting slavery.

Though she was willing to wage war against Satan himself in order to teach slaves about Jesus, she would not fight to free them.

Ethiopia Shall Soon Stretch Out Her Hands unto God

Sarah Osborn's meetings failed to challenge the justice of slavery, but they represented a new spirit of religious outreach to enslaved and free Africans. As evangelicals absorbed, challenged, and reinterpreted Enlightenment ideas, they argued that anyone who had experienced conversion—including Africans and Native Americans—had been given new religious authority. Transformed by a "saving knowledge of Christ," they had become "new creatures."[46]

Although earlier generations of Christians in America had tried to convert slaves, their efforts had been hampered by their ambivalence about seeking religious intimacy with "the most Brutish of Creatures." Even the Quakers, who were notorious for their antislavery sentiments, seemed reluctant to worship side by side with blacks, and the Philadelphia Yearly Meeting did not allow them into membership until 1796.[47] Christians echoed the words of Acts—"God hath made of one blood, all nations of men"—but they rarely treated Africans as their spiritual equals. Few slaveholders were willing to teach their slaves how to read the Bible, a crucial requirement for membership in most Protestant churches.

In contrast, evangelicals were convinced that the most important mark of a true Christian was heartfelt religious experience, and despite their commitment to fostering biblical literacy they did not require converts to know how to read or write. There are no comprehensive statistics available on the number of blacks who were baptized or admitted to eighteenth-century churches, but it is clear that ministers increased their efforts to evangelize them during the revivals. The First Congregational Church of Salem, for example, admitted ten blacks into membership between 1739 and 1758, and by 1755 Samuel Davies, a Presbyterian minister in Virginia, had baptized more than a hundred slaves—a small number in comparison to the thousands living in his county but still remarkable in comparison to the past.[48] In the mid-eighteenth century many churches added slave names to their membership rolls for the first time.

Evangelical ministers knew that they spoke to only a small proportion of the black population, but they were exhilarated by the presence of slaves and free blacks at their meetings. Jonathan Edwards reported that many "ignorant and barbarous" slaves had been born again, a sign that the revival was "exceeding glorious," and after visiting Philadelphia in 1740, George Whitefield boasted that "Near fifty negroes came to give me thanks for what God had done to their souls." The sight of Africans flocking to hear the gospel seemed like proof that the Holy Spirit was at work and, even more remarkable, that the millennium might be near. Quoting Psalm 68:31 ("Ethiopia shall soon stretch out her hands unto God"), evangelicals rejoiced that the Bible's promise was coming true in their own day. They dreamed that Christianity would become an interracial movement uniting the globe. Imagining the millennial age, Edwards predicted that in the future "many of the Negroes and Indians will be divines, and that excellent books will be published in Africa, in Ethiopia, in Turkey."[49]

If evangelicals could have lived according to this hopeful vision of the future, they might have created a more racially egalitarian world, but when they encountered real, flesh-and-blood slaves, their visceral response was to recoil from blackness as a deformity. Like most early Americans, they associated the color black with evil and ugliness—a curse that Africans supposedly had to bear because of Ham's sin. When Sarah searched for an image to evoke the depth of her sinfulness, she described herself as black. "Though I am black," she prayed to God, "Let me be comely in thy sight." In a poem that a master wrote on his slave's gravestone, he imagined him losing his black skin in heaven: "His faithful soul has fled / To realms of heavenly light / And by the blood that Jesus shed / Is changed from Black to White."[50] To be a Christian was to be white.

Instead of challenging these stereotypes of racial inferiority, Enlightenment philosophers often reinforced them. In the abstract the principle of human equality seemed to contradict slavery, and both Montesquieu and Rousseau pointed out the absurdity of claiming that anyone had the "right" to own another human being.[51] Yet most Enlightenment philosophers scoffed at the idea of blacks ever overcoming their "savagery." When they argued that "all men" had been created equal, they usually meant that only white men were equal. As David Hume explained in 1748, "I am apt to suspect the negroes and in general all the other species of men (for there are four or five different kinds) to be naturally inferior to the whites. There never was a civilized nation of any other complexion than white, nor even any individual eminent either in action or speculation." Echoing these arguments, Immanuel Kant proclaimed whites to be superior to blacks in "mental capacities," and Linnaeus classified the "European" kind of man as "*gentle*, acute, inventive," and the African as "*crafty*, indolent, negligent."[52]

The most skeptical thinkers of the Enlightenment, including Voltaire, laid the foundation for the "scientific" racism of the nineteenth century by denying the biblical account of human origins. Instead of monogenesis— the belief that all humans had a single ancestor—they posited that humans had sprung from several races, some more advanced than others. Portraying racial differences as intractable, they reviled blacks for their dark skin and wooly hair. (Montesquieu satirized the proslavery argument by imagining slaveholders saying, "These creatures are all over black, and with such a flat nose that they can scarcely be pitied.")[53] Blacks were posited as physically and intellectually inferior by nature.

Thomas Jefferson's struggles are representative of Enlightenment thinkers' ambivalent ideas about race and slavery. In principle Jefferson opposed slavery, and in an apocalyptic passage in his *Notes on the State of Virginia*, he admitted that a righteous God might punish Americans for the sin of slaveholding: "The whole commerce between master and slave is a perpetual exercise of the most boisterous passions, the most unremitting despotism on the one part, and degrading submissions on the other. . . . And can the liberties of a nation be thought secure when we have removed their only firm basis, a conviction in the minds of the people that these liberties are of the gift of God? That they are not to be violated but with his wrath? Indeed I tremble for my country when I reflect that God is just: that his justice cannot sleep for ever." Yet Jefferson also voiced his suspicion that "the blacks, whether originally a distinct race, or made distinct by time and circumstances, are inferior to the whites in the endowments both of body and mind." Despite fathering six children with his slave Sally Hemings, he expressed deep disgust for black bodies, criticizing the "immoveable veil of black" that shadowed slaves' faces and their "very strong and disagreeable odor."[54] He was convinced that slavery was a moral evil, but he freed few of his own slaves.

Historians have pointed to these tortured debates over slavery as evidence that the "Enlightenment project" was racist at its core. Even though Enlightenment thinkers claimed to speak on behalf of all humanity, they imagined reason as the sole property of white European men, denigrating all other peoples as "racially inferior and savage." One critic has even referred to the Enlightenment as the "Enwhitenment."[55]

Yet as we have seen in the case of women, the Enlightenment involved more than the privileging of rationality, and its emphasis on individual experience had radical implications. Because evangelicals rooted religious knowledge in the experience of being born again, they gave both Native Americans and Africans a surprising degree of religious authority. A Presbyterian church ordained Samson Occom, a Mohegan, to the ministry, and the most radical "New Lights" (as those who supported the revivals were termed) seem to have allowed blacks and Native Americans to exhort publicly, an innovation that infuriated their critics. "Men, Women, Children, Servants, & Negros are now become (as they phrase it) Exhorters," scoffed Charles Brockwell, an Anglican minister.[56] By the 1760s the evangelical public of letters had expanded to include blacks and Native Americans as well as white women. Besides Phillis Wheatley, who published her first poem in the *Newport Mercury* in 1767, Samson Occom, Jupiter Hammon, James Albert Ukawsaw Gronniosaw, and John Marrant published their spiritual writings. Though their individual stories differed, they all claimed that the experience of conversion had given them the authority to appear in print. In the preface to Gronniosaw's *Narrative*, a white minister explained that "there are certain Particulars exceedingly remarkable in his Experience. God has put singular Honor upon him in the Exercise of his Faith and Patience." Samson Occom's book of hymns included "A True Christian's Experience."[57]

Yet even though white evangelicals were thrilled by the stories of African converts, they still assumed that blacks should accept slavery and racial hierarchy (like sexual hierarchy) as part of God's plan. On one hand, they condemned the slave trade as the grossest example of what was wrong with a burgeoning capitalist economy: the reduction of a person to a thing. According to Jonathan Edwards, nations did not have the right to deprive Africans of their liberty solely for material gain. On the other hand, Edwards also quoted a passage from Leviticus to justify enslaving debtors, war captives, and the children of slaves. (In later years his disciples would argue that his position was morally flawed: it could not be ethical to keep the children of those who had been violently kidnapped from Africa.) Edwards himself owned several slaves, the first purchased at a Newport auction in 1731, and when asked for his opinion on slaveholding he compared it to eating or drinking: even though it could lead to sin, Christians did not have to abstain completely from it. His comparison implicitly underlined the naturalness of slavery, which seemed as inevitable to him as taking nourishment. He never once described slavery as a sin.[58]

When Sarah Osborn began holding meetings for slaves, she, too, seems to have taken slavery for granted. Although a few scholars have suggested that she may have harbored secret abolitionist sympathies, this seems to be wishful thinking on their part.[59] Sarah never criticized slavery in her diaries or letters from the time, and although she decided not to sell Bobey, she was more concerned about slaves' salvation than their bodily freedom. Encouraging them to be content with their situation, she assured them that "they are free from cares, because it is their master's part to provide, and theirs only to do their duty." She knew that slavery often included physical abuse and exploitation, but she perpetuated the fiction that the system benefited slaves: since generous masters did the hard work of providing food, clothing, and shelter, slaves had few real "cares."[60]

Sarah set strict rules for the "black folk" who came to her house. Slaves were not welcome without the consent of their owners, and besides urging them to be "diligent and faithful to their own Masters and Mistresses," she warned them not to "Neglect their business" to attend. Because of a law against blacks and Native Americans being on the street after nine o'clock in the evening without a pass, she also instructed them to "repair as soon as possible to their own Homes at or after Nine o'clock [so] that magistrates May not be offended."[61] Fearful that some might "run into wild enthusiasm and start out of their proper places," she also tried to prevent black men from taking leadership roles. She refused to let them pray aloud "Lest they be Lifted up with Pride and proceed from praying to Exhorting &c." (The "&c" pointed in the direction of blacks preaching, a possibility that Sarah could not even bring herself to name.) As a final condition she insisted that they "come entirely Empty handed without thought of Making any recompense by way of present." Although she remained poor, even resorting to baking and selling biscuits in order to make ends meet, she did not want anyone to suspect that her evangelism to them was motivated by a desire for money.[62]

Little about Sarah's message to slaves seems to have been subversive or radical. Besides teaching them about their inherent corruption, she demanded that they repent of drinking, gambling, swearing, Sabbath breaking, and sexual "uncleanness." Even though many masters were reluctant to allow slaves to marry, Sarah insisted that anyone who had a sexual relationship outside of marriage was guilty of promiscuity. As a result, according to a letter that she wrote to Fish, "Several couples" were married who had formerly lived together "but could not bear to Live in the Sin any longer."[63] This was the kind of sin she decried at her meetings, not the sin of kidnapping Africans and forcing them into slavery.

Given Sarah's insistence that the enslaved must remember their places, it might seem surprising that they flocked to her meetings in such large numbers. Even when a "free Ethiopian" began holding weekly meetings that attracted "many of His own color," blacks continued to crowd into her house. According to a letter Sarah wrote to Fish, many slaves tried to give her gifts in return for her kindness. "I have the Hardest work to suppress their gratitude of my part," she exclaimed. Perhaps she was exaggerating, but it is probably not a coincidence that one of the slaves who attended her meetings during the 1760s, Zingo Stevens, named his infant daughter Sarah.[64] It is hard to imagine a greater sign of his admiration.

What did Sarah say or do to make such an impression on Newport's slaves and free blacks? The fact that she exposed herself to criticism by welcoming them into her house, singing and praying with them and listening to their stories, must have struck them as remarkable. Although they saw the inside of many whites' houses as they did chores, they were usually treated as if they were invisible—as if their only worth lay in their ability to sweep a floor or build a fence. At other times they were *too* visible, paraded in front of guests as a sign of their masters' wealth and status. At the Osborn house, in contrast, they were treated as more than chattel. Most white people had little interest in hearing about their suffering, but Sarah encouraged them to share their stories with her, searching for evidence of God's grace in their lives. Although she occasionally referred to blacks in derogatory terms as "Negros," she usually called them "Ethiopians," a word that recalled the biblical promise that "Ethiopia shall soon stretch out her hands unto God."[65] When slaves crowded into her house on Sunday nights, they knew that despite her defense of slavery, she expected them to play a crucial role in Christian history.

Perhaps because of her close relationship with Bobey and Phillis, Sarah also does not seem to have shared the common contempt for blacks' intelligence—a difference that the enslaved almost certainly noticed. Although she once described blacks as "children" in a letter to Fish, she never described them this way in her diaries, and her condescending language in the letter may have been a strategy to deflect Fish's criticism of her meetings. In practice she does not seem to have talked to Africans as if they were simpleminded or, as Thomas Jefferson claimed, "inferior" in reason. "I think one could scarcely be found capable of tracing and comprehending the investigations of Euclid," he argued.[66] In contrast, Sarah eventually encouraged two of the black men who attended her meetings, Bristol Yamma and John Quamine, to study at the College of New Jersey (later Princeton) in order to return to Africa as missionaries.

Even though Sarah seemed more interested in slaves' salvation than their treatment on earth, they seem to have been touched by her concern for them. Many of them had suffered traumas that she could not begin to imagine. Because Newport was one of the largest slave-trading ports in the colonies, it was home to a large population of African-born slaves who had experienced the horrors of the slave trade firsthand. Torn away from loved ones and forced to march to the African coast, they endured humiliation, beatings, and a brutal journey in chains across the Atlantic. Captains wanted to keep as much of their human cargo alive as possible, but assuming that large numbers would die, they squeezed as many as possible into cramped, unsanitary quarters below the ship's deck. (In 1762, a ship arrived at Newport after having lost a quarter of its slaves.)[67] The enslaved spent weeks shackled together, suffocated by the stench of vomit, urine, and excrement. When they finally arrived at Newport, they were displayed on the auction block and sold to the highest bidder and, in a final indignity, they were stripped of even their names. For masters who prided themselves on their resemblance to the illustrious Roman slaveholders of antiquity, there was something satisfying about having slaves with names like Caesar or Pompey.

Slaves chafed at their degradation, but because physical resistance was usually met with a whip, they tried to preserve their dignity in small ways: for example, by refusing to give up their African names. "Pompey Stevens" was also known as "Zingo" and "Jack Mason" was the same person as "Salmar Nubia." (One notable exception is John Quamine, who seems to have chosen a new name as a sign of his conversion.) As revealed by an archaeological dig that unearthed African cowry shells and beads—objects that were associated with spiritual power and protection—the enslaved may have also continued to practice traditional West African religions.[68] Yet even though slaves wanted to preserve their tribal identities (they were not "Africans" as much as they were Ashantis or Yorubas), they knew that they would have to learn white customs and beliefs in order to survive. Sarah Osborn's meetings offered them an avenue into the alien, Christian world of their masters.

Slaves may have found Sarah's support of black literacy especially appealing. Although it is not clear whether she spent any of her Sunday-night meetings teaching them to read, there is no doubt that she urged them to read the Bible for themselves. In a letter to Fish, she expressed pride that many "were now intent upon Learning to read etc. at Home and

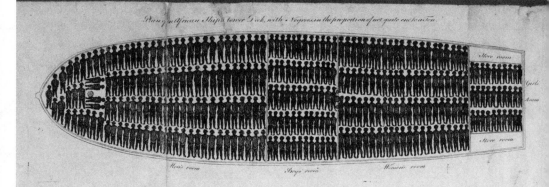

Diagram of the lower deck of a slave ship.
Courtesy of the American Antiquarian Society.

abroad."[69] Nothing symbolized white power better than the ability to read and write.

At first glance it may seem hard to understand why slaves were attracted to Sarah's theology, especially the doctrine of original sin. When John Quamine lamented his "Total Corruption and Depravity of Nature," he inadvertently reinforced negative stereotypes of slaves as inherently sinful and unruly. "I have a Great weight of Sins upon me that none but the blood of Christ can take away," a slave woman confessed to Sarah.[70] Yet even though Sarah urged slaves to denigrate themselves, she also gave them a powerful vocabulary to criticize their masters and to make sense of their suffering. The doctrine of original sin is egalitarian at its core, emphasizing that all humans—even the wealthiest and most powerful—are flawed. When Sarah described the world as a fallen, broken place in which humans selfishly pursued their own interests, slaves knew exactly what she meant. Forced labor, beatings, starvation, sexual abuse—they understood the reality of sin.

It may also be difficult to understand why slaves accepted Sarah's explanation of affliction, but many seem to have been willing to blame themselves for their suffering in exchange for the promise that it was not meaningless. Whether Sarah ever urged them to "kiss the rod" (an image that she sometimes used in her letters and diaries), she almost certainly promised that their afflictions were a sign of God's love, a "furnace" that would burn away their "dross" in preparation for salvation. At a time when all the colonies sanctioned slavery and freedom seemed like an impossible dream, many slaves seem to have been comforted by the thought that their trials might be ultimately redemptive. According to Newport Gardner (also known as Occramar Marycoo), who had been born in Africa, God had punished Africans for their idolatry in "worshipping trees, and streams, and fountains of water, and reptiles," but his chastisements were meant for their own good. When Gardner and several other black evangelicals founded the Free African Union Society, they confessed the "righteousness of GOD in bring[ing] all these evils on us and on our children & brethren."[71] Similarly, Phillis Wheatley wrote a poem in 1773 describing her enslavement as a blessing rather than a curse:

> 'Twas mercy brought me from my heathen land,
> Taught my benighted soul to understand
> That there's a God, that there's a Savior too:
> Once I redemption neither sought nor knew.

Perhaps other slaves were troubled by her determination to view slavery as a "mercy," but like Sarah Osborn, Wheatley was drawn to the image of a sovereign, all-powerful God who arranged everything for her benefit.[72] Her suffering was not pointless but a rational part of God's plan.

Besides being urged to see themselves as sinful and deserving of punishment, the slaves who attended Sarah's meetings heard a more radical message about the equality of all souls before God. When the Reverend Hezekiah Smith, a Baptist, preached at Osborn's house on the text "And yet there is room," a slave was "greatly awakened" by the realization that there would be room for him, too, at Christ's banquet. Jesus made no distinctions among persons, welcoming even "the poor, and the maimed, and the halt, and the blind" to his table.[73] Even though the rich and powerful seemed to enjoy God's favor on earth, only the born again would spend eternity in heaven. The first could be last and the last could be first—a dizzying thought for those who felt despised.

Above all, slaves may have responded to Sarah's faith that the millennium was near. She interpreted their religious yearnings as a portent of "Ethiopia's" mass conversion to Christianity and then Christ's return, a vision that promised the end of their captivity. There would be no slavery in Christ's glorious kingdom.

By the end of 1767 the revival at Sarah's house had begun to wane, and as she admitted to Fish, many children and young men now treated her meetings as a "task" or a "burden" rather than a "delight." She had managed to keep their interest for three years—a remarkable achievement for a woman with no formal religious authority—but many eventually drifted away. Male and female slaves and young white women, however, continued to come each week in large numbers. "There is seldom Less than 60 or 70 odd blacks on Lord's day evening," Sarah reported in the spring of 1768, and between thirty and fifty girls typically attended on Monday nights. Perhaps more than anyone in Newport, slaves and young white women knew that their future depended on the decisions of white men, and they seem to have been strengthened by Sarah's assurance that only God—not masters, fathers, or husbands—could determine the ultimate direction of their lives.[74]

Most of the sixty or seventy Africans who attended Sarah's meetings were never baptized or admitted into full communion. The First Church of Christ accepted eight blacks into full membership between 1765 and 1774; the Seventh-day Baptist Church baptized two blacks in 1771; and Ezra Stiles's Second Church of Christ counted seven black members in 1772.[75] (Because the records for Gardiner Thurston's Baptist Church no longer survive, we do not know whether it had any black members, but Sarah mentioned that his church reaped the benefits of the revival.) According to Ezra Stiles, there were "perhaps 26, and not above 30 professors out of Twelve hundred Negroes in Town." Although it is not clear why so few slaves were baptized, some may have been reluctant to renounce their African religious beliefs in order to become Christian, and others may have faced opposition from hostile masters who viewed baptism as a step toward freedom. Despite clerical assurances that born-again slaves did not have to be emancipated, many masters seem to have been worried about the morality of holding a fellow Christian in bondage.[76] By the nineteenth century these qualms would disappear, but only after ministers repeatedly insisted (as Sarah Osborn had done) that Christianity would make slaves more obedient.

A Woman's Influence

If Sarah was disappointed by the small numbers of slaves and free blacks who joined her church, she never admitted it in her diaries and letters. But she was obviously hurt by the Reverend Vinal's disapproval of her meetings and, worse, by his refusal to defend her from criticism. He had "refused to protect me," she lamented.[77] Praying for a spirit of forgiveness, she struggled to overcome her feelings of bitterness.

As Vinal's drinking problem became increasingly obvious to church members, Sarah debated over what to do. Drunkenness was a religious issue for her: a "temptation" rather than a disease. A "DRUNKARD," according to a writer in the *Newport Mercury*, "is indisposed to Virtue: Is a licentious Person: Makes his Belly his God: Is worse than a Brute." Although Sarah "longed to act the part of a faithful friend" by talking to Vinal about his drinking, she did not dare speak to him openly, and out of deference to his authority as her minister she did not even confess her fears to her husband. From reading her correspondence one would never know that there was a problem in her congregation. If anything she became more effusive in her praise in an attempt to hide her concerns. Writing to her friend Susanna Bannister, she claimed that "our dear Mr. Vinal" was "more than ever Enlivened."[78]

Only a year later, however, in September 1768, the First Church of Christ Committee (the governing body of the church) convened to discuss Vinal's "Excessive Use of spirituous Liquors." After weighing his excuse that he had been tempted by a "Bad habit of body" and a "weakness" in his "stomach," the committee unanimously voted to dismiss him as pastor.[79] He had led the First Church for twenty-two years, but the members were fed up with his drunkenness, his combativeness, and his frequent absences from church on Sunday.

Infuriated by his dismissal, Vinal wrote to Sarah asking for help. Even though she could not vote on church business, she was one of the most influential members of the church, and despite the tensions between them, they had once been close friends. She may have also remained close to his children, especially the two daughters who had lived at her school after their mother's tragic death. We do not have a copy of the letter that Vinal sent to her, but based on her response he seems to have mixed self-pity with recrimination. Though he thanked her for her kindness over the years, he denied ever being drunk (contradicting his earlier confession to the church), and he angrily accused the church of being (in Sarah's words) "odious, malicious, cruel, unmerciful." Portraying himself as an innocent victim, he blamed church members for treating him unfairly and plotting against him, and he urged her to take his side when a church council convened to hear his complaints.[80] (It was common for Congregational churches to invite local ministers to hold councils in order to make judgments about internal disputes. The council could not force a church to take its advice, but served in an advisory capacity.)

Sarah's long, emotional response to Vinal suggests the depth of her distress about his accusations. At the beginning of her letter she assured him that "you and yours were and are dear to me," and she admitted that the thought of doing anything to upset him caused her "sensible *pain*." "I should rather delight in comforting you," she lamented. Yet as she continued writing, she finally allowed herself to express the sadness, frustration and anger she had kept bottled up for years. Insisting that she herself had seen him in "the effects of spirituous Liquor," she remembered how many sleepless nights she had spent "sighing and weeping" on his account. "My only relief was in God alone," she wrote passionately. "To him I carried you with my own soul and cried for strength." Rejecting his language of victimization, she claimed that she had been wronged, not he: his dismissal had upset her so deeply that she had longed to die, and his lies about his drunkenness had been almost unbearable. "This cuts me to the heart," she cried. "It even tears me all to pieces, it stumbles, it grieves me almost to death, it gives my cruel foe [the devil] such an advantage against me that I don't know if Ever I shall get over it to my last breath." If he had admitted his sin she could still treat him as a friend, but lying about it was intolerable, "a thousand times worse to me than the thing itself." At the end of her letter she promised to pray for him, but she also made it clear that she had no interest in helping him restore his battered reputation. If a church council ever convened, she would "declare to every serious enquirer after truth that I do believe in my heart that the church's proceedings with you were *conscientious* and not malicious."[81]

Sarah might have responded less emotionally to Vinal's letter if she had been in better health, but by the fall of 1769 her illness had worsened again, and this time her flare-up was not followed by a period of remission. If she resented Vinal for his lies, she also resented him for consuming the little energy she still had left. She was only fifty-five, but she found walking extremely difficult, and even reading and writing were exhausting. "I am entirely cut off," she admitted to Joseph Fish, "and if I presume . . . to strain my sight a Little the pain is so Great in my Eyes, and my Head so amazed and confused that I am utterly unfitted for all duties secret and social perhaps for a week or two."[82] Since Henry also felt "poorly" (he was now eighty-four), she could not depend on him for help. She continued to meet with slaves on Sunday evenings as well as with groups of children, men, and women, but she no longer had the strength to cope with Vinal's anger and paranoia. If she ever wrote him another letter, no copy of it survives.

Without a pastor, the First Church turned the Osborn house into the spiritual center of their congregation. In many ways this had been true even before Vinal's dismissal (which is part of the reason for his hostility toward Sarah), but as the church searched for a new minister, candidates often ended up preaching at her house. The Reverend Punderson Austin delivered a sermon there on a Wednesday evening, and both he and Ephraim Judson, another candidate, vied for her favor by meeting with her "societies" of children and of blacks—Judson eleven times and Austin eighteen.[83]

At first Sarah denied having a strong opinion about who should be the new minister, but after the First Church of Christ Committee decided to add Samuel Hopkins's name to their list of candidates, she and Susanna Anthony threw their support behind him. Forty-eight years old and the pastor of a church in Great Barrington, Massachusetts, Hopkins had gained renown for his theology of "disinterested benevolence"—a view that portrayed selfless devotion to Christ as the essence of true faith. Hopkins was not reputed to be a charismatic speaker, and in fact he was later remembered for his "drawling" voice and his "*bad*" pronunciation, "*decidedly so*": he mangled the word *stone* into "stun" and *Deuteronomy* into "Deuteronowmy." He was also described as "ungainly in gait and dress."[84]

Yet Osborn and Anthony cared less about his awkward style than his theology, and they were thrilled by his unblinking defense of the doctrine of human depravity and his intense self-abasement. Here, at last, was a minister who prized selflessness as much as they did. Hopkins, in turn, made no secret of his admiration for the two of them. An earnest, morally

Rev. SAMUEL HOPKINS. D.D.

Portrait of Samuel Hopkins. Drawn and Engraved by Abner Reed,
May 1803. Frontispiece for Stephen West, ed., *Sketches of the Life of the
Late Rev. Samuel Hopkins* (Hartford: Hudson and Goodwin, 1805).
Courtesy of the American Antiquarian Society.

serious man who had often been tormented by doubts about his salvation, he wanted to learn how to be more like them: humble, self-denying, and yet supremely confident about his relationship to God. They seemed like the embodiment of his theology, living each day as if the only thing that mattered were God's will.

But not everyone in the church liked Hopkins. Although he had been one of Jonathan Edwards's students, he and several other ministers—including Joseph Bellamy, Levi Hart, and Jonathan Edwards, Jr.—were accused of preaching a "New Divinity" because of their modifications to Reformed theology. Like other evangelicals, Hopkins tried to reconcile central Calvinist insights about divine sovereignty and human sinfulness with the Enlightenment faith in reason, divine benevolence, and freedom, but his commitment to logical consistency sometimes led him to conclusions that other Protestants found absurd or even offensive. On one hand, he made crucial concessions to Enlightenment thought by arguing that God was benevolent and that Jesus had died for all, not just the elect. On the other, he exaggerated the most controversial features of Calvinist theology in order to emphasize God's sovereignty: he startled many liberal-leaning Protestants, for example, by asserting that sin was actually a rational good with positive consequences. Though not denying that sin was wrong, he argued that God chose to demonstrate his glory by bringing good out of evil. He also insisted that since people who longed for conversion were usually motivated by a selfish desire to go to heaven instead of genuine love for God, they were even more corrupt than the "heathen" who ignored the gospel. Most shocking of all, he claimed that true Christians should be willing to be damned for the glory of God. Although some members of the First Church were impressed by his radical demand for selflessness, others found him extreme, and many seem to have read the Reverend William Hart's scathing attack on his theology, *Brief Remarks on a Number of False Propositions, and Dangerous Errors, Which Are Spreading in This Country.* (The book was advertised in the *Newport Mercury*.) Hart accused Hopkins of making such impossible demands on sinners that his theology was "a ready way to throw them directly into the devil's arms."[85]

Sarah Osborn worried that Hart's "bitter" and provocative attack would alienate the congregation, especially since many were already concerned about Hopkins's strict regulations regarding infant baptism and church membership. Besides requiring church members to make a public profession of faith (a custom that Vinal had abandoned), he refused to baptize the infants of those who were not full members. As Sarah recognized, he was a controversial figure, and without the power to vote she would have to rely on all her influence to gain his election. Unlike Susanna Anthony, who filled her letters to Hopkins with typically feminine self-deprecation, Sarah tried to give him advice without appearing presumptuous, and perhaps because she was seven years older she sometimes addressed him in the manner of an affectionate older sister. Reporting that a church member had expressed admiration for one of his sermons about human sinfulness (a change from his earlier scorn for Hopkins's preaching), she wrote gently, "You will take no notice of any Hint from me Sir, but if you Please visit him as soon as you can I believe his Ear is now open to receive instruction from you."[86] Wisely, Hopkins did indeed take Sarah's "hints," and he frequently visited her at home.

When the men of the church narrowly voted against Hopkins's selection in March 1770 (the count was thirty-six to thirty-two), Sarah stubbornly refused to give up. According to Ezra Stiles, who was frank about his distaste for Hopkins's theology, she and the "Sorority" (the women's society) were "violently engaged and had great Influence." With more than sixty members, the society was a force to be reckoned with—and they knew it. On the Sunday that Hopkins preached his farewell sermon, many people in the congregation wept, with Sarah and her friends probably among them. In response, the male members met again to take a new vote, and this time they agreed to invite Hopkins to be their pastor.[87] It is not clear whether Henry was well enough to attend church that day, but many of the other men who voted—including Deacon Coggeshall, William Gyles, and Benjamin Peabody—were married to members of the women's society.[88]

Hopkins knew that Sarah Osborn's support had been crucial for his election, and in the years ahead he treated her as one of his most trusted and respected confidantes. Unlike Vinal, who had resented her leadership, he recognized her importance to the congregation by treating her house as virtually an alternate church. Because her illness made it difficult for her to walk to the meetinghouse, he sometimes preached at her house during the week, and the entire church gathered there for "prayer and Christian conference, and for the transacting of any other affairs" before the monthly celebration of the Lord's Supper. In a letter to a friend in the fall of 1770, Sarah praised Hopkins as "a dear indulgent Pastor" who had "never been one week absent from our House from His first coming here to this day."[89] He usually had tea with her on Saturday afternoons to discuss his upcoming sermon.

Of One Blood

Soon after Hopkins took charge of the First Church, Sarah Osborn stopped holding her evening prayer meetings. Although she continued to pray with the women's society on Thursday afternoons, she may have thought it would be unseemly to continue her leadership now that her church had a new, sober pastor. Because of her declining health, she may have also lacked the strength. With the help of assistants, she seems to have continued teaching her school, but Hopkins gradually took over her meetings, inviting people to his house on weeknights. Ezra Stiles, perhaps relieved that Osborn's controversial gatherings had finally come to an end, also began holding prayer meetings, including separate gatherings for men, women, and blacks. In February 1770, Stiles met with seventy young women, and by the winter of 1772 as many as ninety blacks were meeting weekly at his house—a greater number than she had ever reported.[90] Departing from Osborn's ecumenical spirit, however, neither Hopkins nor Stiles seems to have opened his doors to anyone who did not attend his own Congregational church. Sarah had always been ambivalent about Stiles because his theology was more liberal than hers, and despite praising him for his "Lovely, Engaging, benevolent temper," she criticized him for avoiding the topic of hell. His sermons were polished, agreeable, and usually comforting—and this, in Sarah's view, was exactly the problem: he cared more about pleasing the ear than telling the truth about damnation. Yet he had occasionally preached at her meetings, and she was willing to collaborate with anyone who wanted to convert Newport's Africans.[91]

In 1773, Hopkins asked Stiles to meet with John Quamine and Bristol Yamma, two of the slaves who had attended Sarah's meetings, to judge whether they could become missionaries to Africa. Although Stiles was dubious about their intellectual abilities, he was impressed by their zeal. As he recorded in his diary, Quamine "tells me that ever since he tasted the Grace of the Lord Jesus he conceived a Thought and Earnest Desire or Wish that his Relations and Countrymen in Africa might also come to the knowledge of and taste the same blessed Things."[92]

Quamine had been one of Sarah Osborn's first converts, but we know little about him and Yamma except for a few bare facts. Both men were Ashantis from Ghana who had been kidnapped by slave traders: Yamma at such a young age that he no longer remembered his family, and Quamine after being promised that he would be sent abroad for an education.

Although Yamma seems to have been single, Quamine was married and had fathered two children by 1773, a two-year old daughter and a one-year-old son.[93] His wife, Duchess Channing (later Quamine), was known as "the most celebrated cake-maker in Rhode Island," and although she belonged to Stiles's church instead of her husband's (probably because her master, William Channing, worshiped there), she was an equally devoted Christian: "intelligent, industrious, affectionate, honest, and of exemplary piety." Quamine and Duchess seem to have attended Sarah's meetings together, and Duchess fully supported his desire to become a missionary and perhaps even return to Africa.[94] Besides being determined to spread the gospel, he seems to have hoped to be reunited with long-lost family members. After Hopkins sent a letter to the Reverend Philip Quaque, an Anglican missionary in Ghana, he learned that Quamine's mother was still living, and she had shed "tears of Joy" at the news that her long-lost son was not only alive but hoped to return to his native land.[95]

Quaque discouraged Hopkins from sending Yamma and Quamine back to Ghana, insisting that their tribe was too "*Savage, Villainous, Revengeful, Malicious*" and "*Blood-thirsty*" ever to convert to Christianity, but Phillis Wheatley was more optimistic. Responding to a letter from Hopkins, she hoped that the mission might mark "the beginning of that happy period foretold by the Prophets, when all shall know the Lord from the last to the greatest."[96] She seems to have met Hopkins through Obour Tanner, a female slave in Newport who was one of her closest friends and a member of Hopkins's congregation. (Like Duchess Quamine, Tanner had probably attended Sarah's meetings.)[97]

When Quamine and Yamma bought a ticket in the Newport lottery and won three hundred dollars, Hopkins, Stiles, and Sarah Osborn believed it was providential—an extraordinary answer to their prayers. After splitting the winnings, Quamine was able to buy his freedom, but because Yamma's master refused to free him for less than two hundred dollars, he needed to raise another fifty dollars, a sum that Hopkins eventually donated himself. Hopkins and Stiles also circulated a letter asking "pious and benevolent" Christians to contribute money to send both men to the College of New Jersey to be educated. "These persons," they testified, "have good natural abilities; are apt, steady, and judicious, and speak their native language; the language of a numerous, potent nation in Guinea, to which they belong. They are not only *willing*, but *very desirous* to quit all worldly projects and risk their lives, in attempting to open a door for the propagation of Christianity, among their poor, ignorant, perishing, heathen brethren."[98]

Sarah Osborn and the women's society held a day of fasting and prayer, and by 1774 Hopkins and Stiles had raised enough money to pay for Quamine and Yamma's expenses. Drawing on the transatlantic evangelical network that had been forged during the 1740s, they received donations not only from people in New England but from London and Scotland. (The Society in Edinburgh for Promoting Christian Knowledge donated thirty pounds sterling.) In November 1774, soon after the meeting of the First Continental Congress, Quamine and Yamma set sail to embark on their education.[99]

Sarah must have been elated. Their desire to become missionaries to Africa seemed to be evidence that God himself had vindicated her meetings.

As she eagerly awaited news from Princeton, Sarah also prayed for another new convert, her cherished granddaughter Sarah, nicknamed Sally. There are no records of what happened to Sarah and Henry's three other grandchildren, but Sally seems to have been deeply affected by what she witnessed during the revival. By the summer of 1773, when she was in her early twenties, she had been born again. Although Sarah rarely went to church any longer because of her illness, she almost certainly found a way to get to the meetinghouse to see Sally's baptism and to share communion with her. There was now a second "Sarah Osborn" in the First Church. A year later, on September 1, 1774, Sally was married to Daniel Fellows, a church member who seems to have shared her desire to perpetuate her grandmother's legacy. The two of them sat in the family pew every Sunday morning.[100]

Yet even as Sarah praised God for the many happy events in her life, her past conflicts with the Reverend Vinal still weighed on her mind. During the summer and fall of 1774, Vinal continued to accuse the First Church of mistreating him, even claiming that his confession had been coerced at a time of "bodily infirmity and weakness of mind." The church had sent him a letter of admonition in 1770 and then censured him in 1771 (a serious penalty that barred him from taking communion in Congregational churches), but in response he sent harassing letters, accused Hopkins and Elnathan Hammond of slander, and even dragged Sarah's name through the mud. He claimed that she, Susanna Anthony, Deacon Coggeshall, and two other men had been guilty of drunkenness, telling lies, and other "immoralities." When a church council made up of local ministers finally convened in the summer of 1774 after years of delay, they cleared the First Church of any wrongdoing and demanded that Vinal apologize to those he had maligned, but to little effect. When the church received a halfhearted apology from him in December 1774, the members angrily voted not to accept it. "He has made no satisfaction to most of the individuals he has injured," they complained, "and has not so much as mentioned them, nor many of the abuses he has offered them." After all Sarah's kindnesses to him over the years, she must have been both stunned and wounded by his bitter accusations.[101]

But if Sarah were ever tempted to condemn Vinal for his weakness, she soon realized that she, too, had reason to be ashamed. Indeed, she feared that she had committed a far worse sin.

Until Samuel Hopkins moved to Newport he seems to have assumed that slavery had been ordained by God, and he himself had owned a female slave during his earlier pastorate in Great Barrington. Yet after meeting large numbers of slaves at the Osborn house, seeing them in chains on the public auction block near his church, and listening to their tragic stories of captivity, he became increasingly troubled by the contradictions between slavery and his Christian faith. Though he had always known that humans were corrupt, he had never understood the depth of human depravity until witnessing the suffering of Newport's slaves. It is not clear whether the realization came slowly over the course of several years or suddenly in a flash, but at some point before 1775 he became convinced that slavery was sinful, an abomination that had to be immediately repented.[102] Sarah's distress— and perhaps resistance—must have been great when he told her that the slaves who had gathered in her kitchen deserved more than an otherworldly gospel: they deserved to be free.

Historians have often puzzled over how and why Hopkins became one of the leading antislavery activists of his time and, more generally, why antislavery sentiment suddenly blossomed in the 1770s and 1780s after centuries of indifference. Although there had been isolated critiques of slavery in the past, most whites accepted it as an inevitable part of the social order. Explanations for the rise of the eighteenth-century antislavery movement have ranged widely, but many historians have been struck by the fact that it emerged in tandem with the humanitarian movement, revolutionary rhetoric, and mercantile capitalism. As we have seen, many people who prided themselves on their compassion did not oppose slavery, but by equating virtue with "sensibility" (the ability to feel others' pain), the humanitarian movement raised troubling questions about the justice of owning another human being. In London, the Society for Effecting the Abolition of the Slave Trade (composed mostly of Quakers) commissioned a seal of a kneeling slave in chains who raised his manacled hands to heaven and asked, "Am I not a man and a brother?" Although historians have sometimes denigrated eighteenth-century reformers for their sentimentality, abolitionists understood the power of sympathy. In a graphic depiction of the cruelty of slavery, Samuel Hopkins asked his listeners to imagine thousands of "poor Africans . . . Staked to the ground and burnt by inches, or hung up by their thumbs and after 8 or 9 days Expired in torments." Appealing to his listeners' emotions, he asked, "Can we, I say, See this and hold our peace?"[103]

The revolutionary demand for freedom also contributed to an emerging climate of antislavery. After the Stamp Act, the Townshend Acts, and the Boston Massacre, many colonists accused the British of "enslaving" them by depriving them of the right to political representation. The *Newport Mercury*, for example, denounced the Stamp Act for being "indisputably subversive of our inestimable Rights, and calculated to reduce us, together with Millions yet unborn, to irredeemable Slavery, and the most abject Poverty." In 1771 the newspaper unveiled a new masthead blazoned with the words "Undaunted by TYRANTS,—We'll DIE or be FREE." While Sarah Osborn seemed deaf to the absurdity of Patriots demanding their political liberty while defending slavery, other Americans recognized the hypocrisy for what it was. As an anonymous author complained in the *Newport Mercury*, it was "amazing" that colonists should rail against being "enslaved" by the British while they were guilty "of enslaving, and promoting the slavery, of thousands, and tens of thousands of their fellow creatures!!!"[104]

The rise of antislavery also coincided with the emergence of merchant capitalism, but the exact relation between the two has been the subject of debate among historians. According to David Brion Davis, many early antislavery activists were wealthy Quaker merchants who condemned "unfree" labor in order to legitimize "free" wage labor in factories. Though they couched their arguments in Christian language, they seem to have unconsciously hoped to convince wage laborers (and themselves) that factory work was superior to slavery—a conclusion that might not have been immediately obvious to the men and women who spent sixteen hours a day, seven days a week doing repetitive work in dark, crowded spaces. In contrast, Thomas Haskell has offered a more positive assessment of the relation between antislavery and capitalism, arguing that people gained a greater sense of their ability to create change through their involvement in markets. As merchants traded goods with others around the world, they may have realized both the far-reaching effects of their actions and their power to eradicate entrenched evils like slavery.[105]

Since a movement as complicated as antislavery probably did not emerge from a single cause, it is possible that both these interpretations capture some of its complicated relation to capitalism. But Hopkins's example—and the example of the Quakers—suggests that there was yet another thread in the tapestry of antislavery: a suspicion of capitalism because of its acceptance of rational self-interest as a positive good. Although there is no doubt that the rise of antislavery eventually legitimated free market capitalism, it is impossible to know whether Quakers "unconsciously" intended this, and they seem to have been deeply ambivalent about their success as merchants. At the same time as Quaker leaders condemned the evil of slavery, they also began an internal "reformation" to root out the sins of materialism, luxury, and greed. The Quaker leader John Woolman, an outspoken opponent of slavery, decried the "carnal" desire for wealth and prayed that people would "set aside all self-interest and come to be weaned from the desire of getting estates." Like Woolman, Hopkins was also suspicious of self-interest, and his theology can be understood as an almost desperate attempt to reclaim an ethic of the common good. He branded slave traders "Extortioners" who had "robbed" Africans of their rights. Many antislavery writers in the late eighteenth century condemned slavery as "barbaric traffic," a perversion of what commerce was supposed to be. Although they did not propose an alternative economic order, their impassioned opposition to slavery reflected their anxiety about the moral quandaries raised by commercial capitalism.[106]

Besides these intellectual, political, and economic explanations for the rise of antislavery, it is important to remember that white Americans were also influenced by the testimonies of slaves themselves. Hopkins's personal interactions with John Quamine, Bristol Yamma, and the other slaves whom he met at Sarah Osborn's house may have contributed more to his abolitionist stance than his fears about political tyranny or economic self-interest, and in addition to reading Phillis Wheatley's poetry (and purchasing a copy of her book for the church), he was probably familiar with the published works of other black evangelicals. (Gronniosaw's *Narrative* was advertised in the *Newport Mercury*.)[107] Not everyone who read these books was willing to acknowledge the intelligence of the enslaved, but their writings were a haunting testimony to their humanity. Although Thomas Jefferson claimed that Wheatley's poems were "below the dignity of criticism," he criticized them anyway, fearful that other readers might glimpse something that he refused to see. Hopkins thought that Wheatley was "a remarkable African."[108]

Hopkins's antislavery convictions grew out of his encounters with slaves, his suspicion of economic self-interest, his humanitarian sympathies, and his faith in human equality. As we have seen, there was nothing about evangelicalism (or Christianity more generally) that inevitably led to abolitionism, and, in fact, Christianity and slavery had coexisted since the first century. Nor was there anything about the Enlightenment that inevitably led to racial egalitarianism, and many Enlightenment thinkers treated blacks as if they were a different species. But when Hopkins combined the Christian belief that "God hath made of one blood, all nations" with the Enlightenment language of sympathy and individual rights, the result was a powerful indictment of slavery. In 1776 he preached an angry sermon that combined biblical allusions with references to the Declaration of Independence. Besides condemning slaveholders for treating Africans as chattel, defacing "the image of God in them" in order to satisfy their own greed, he excoriated them for violating the maxim that "all men are created equal and alike endowed by their Creator with certain unalienable rights, as Life, Liberty the pursuit of happiness." "Our hands are full of Blood," he thundered. Speaking as a prophet, he threatened his listeners that a vengeful God would hold them accountable for "the Blood of Millions who have perished by means of the accursed Slave trade."[109] The most radical critics of slavery in the eighteenth century were not Enlightenment thinkers but a small group of Christians (especially evangelicals and Quakers) whose absorption of selected Enlightenment ideas allowed them to think about God—and human beings—in new ways.

During the 1760s Sarah Osborn had never dared question the morality of slaveholding, but after Hopkins became convinced that slavery was sinful, she eventually concluded that he was right. Exactly how and when this happened is a mystery, and if not for a single poem that she composed sometime during the last twenty years of her life, we would not even be sure of her change of heart. Imagining heaven, she wrote:

> New wonders still! Lo, here are they,
> Unjustly brought from Africa!
> They've heard the gospel's joyful sound,
> Though lost indeed they now are found.
>
> Those we see here who once have been
> Made slaves to man by horrid sin.
> Now through rich grace in Christ are free,
> Forever set at liberty.

Hopkins reprinted this poem in his *Memoirs of Mrs. Sarah Osborn* but did not say when she composed it or when she realized that slavery was a "horrid sin." According to him, however, she began dictating poems to friends sometime in the 1770s or 1780s after her failing eyesight made it impossible for her to keep a diary any longer.[110]

Since this small poem is our only evidence, we know little about Sarah's changed attitude. Indeed, we cannot even be certain that it was Hopkins who led her to condemn slavery and not vice versa, but it seems significant that he chose not to describe her as an antislavery activist in his published memoir of her life. Since he praised her as the embodiment of his theology of disinterested benevolence, he probably would have liked to suggest that her selfless love for Christ had inevitably led her to condemn slavery. Yet he remained silent. It would not be surprising if Sarah had initially resisted his arguments. Ever since her first husband, Samuel, had died on board what was probably a slave ship, her life had been tangled up with slavery, and it may have been wrenching for her to confront the reality of her complicity with sin.

Once admitting that Hopkins was right, however, Sarah probably did not spare herself from condemnation. Given her providential imagination, she may have wondered whether a wrathful God had taken her first husband away as punishment for his decision to sail on a slave ship, and when she thought about Bobey she may have been ashamed of her belief that he had been God's gift to her—a claim that now seemed arrogant. God had "made of one blood all nations of men," and yet she had treated other human beings like property. Like Hopkins, she had always identified sin with excessive self-love, but now she saw slavery as proof that humans were capable of the worst depredations imaginable, even the selling of one another into bondage.

The census of 1774 listed six blacks in the Osborn household. They are not named, but their presence in her house may attest to Sarah's changed heart. Perhaps Bristol Yamma or John Quamine lived with her in order to save money before leaving for Princeton later in the year. Since there are no records of what happened to Bobey after 1762, we do not know whether he might have been living with her as well—or even whether he was alive—during the 1770s, but if he still belonged to Sarah she almost certainly set him free. Hopkins strongly encouraged his congregation to free their slaves, insisting that slavery was "a sin of a crimson dye" that had to be immediately repented. As for Phillis, she lived until 1779, but we do not know whether she and Sarah ever talked about their painful past.[111] We can only hope that Sarah sought her forgiveness.

Chapter 10

The Latter Days, 1775–1787

The strength and courage I mentioned, which God graciously granted me in times of danger; was not the result of any confident persuasion, that I should not be slain.—No! when the bullets were whizzing around me, I realized the next might have a commission to reach me; and if this was the way, infinite wisdom had chosen, I had no objection to make.—I chose neither life nor death, only that God might glorify himself in me; and that, whether I lived, or died, I might be the Lord's.—I know every shot was directed by unerring wisdom; and every heart of the enemy, as much at his controul, who hath said to the restless ocean, hitherto shalt thou come, and no further; and here shall thy proud waves be stayed.

Thus I rested on GOD.—Oh! Boundless grace, adorable sovereignty!—Why was I not rather called to drink, the very dregs, of the cup of his displeasure?—Why was I not made, even a terror to myself, and all around me! I, who have had so great a hand, in drawing down the judgments of God upon us!—Oh, my friend, adore, with me; and let me be reckoned, among the chief of sinners! . . .

May not all that hath befallen us, both in Church and State, serve rather to strengthen, than stagger our faith; since our divine Redeemer faithfully warned us of the coming of such things, in the latter days.— We see that not one jot or tittle of his word fails, in this part; and shall not latter-day promises, be as truly fulfilled.—May we not lift up our heads, because redemption draweth nigh![1]

Sarah Osborn dictated this letter to Joseph Fish in 1780, too ill to write it with her own hand. The Revolutionary War was still raging, but the British had left Newport after occupying the city for three years, and Sarah was finally able to communicate freely with the outside world. Remembering the worst days of the fighting, she reassured Fish that God had watched over her, and whether she lived or died she knew that she belonged to him. God was in control of everything: even the bullets that had left many dead.

For years Sarah had prayed that the millennium might be imminent, and she interpreted the war—like the revival at her house—as a sign of the latter days. Like many other Americans she believed that the war heralded the creation of a new era in human history. Newport's devastation was not meaningless but a fulfillment of biblical prophecies about the return of Christ. God's kingdom was coming.

Sarah's evangelical faith in the millennium existed in tandem with a secular discourse of American progress and American nationalism, and sometimes the two were difficult to tell apart. Evangelicals denied that humans could make progress without God's grace, but they sounded optimistic about the future, imitating the most ardent defenders of the Enlightenment by rhapsodizing about the blessings of a republican government. Secular thinkers insisted that humans could use their reason to create a more perfect world, but their descriptions of the future sounded like the heavenly kingdom, a paradise of liberty and peace. "We have it in our power to begin the world over again," Thomas Paine proclaimed. "A situation, similar to the present, hath not happened since the days of Noah until now. The birthday of a new world is at hand."[2]

Although the evangelical faith in the millennium and the secular faith in progress were not identical, the encounter between Protestantism and the Enlightenment may never have been more fateful than during the Revolutionary era. If not for the widely shared faith that a new age was possible (whether through divine providence or human agency), the American Revolution would never have taken place.

Precious Liberty

As the revival at Sarah's house waned in the late 1760s, so too did her physical strength. Her illness seems to have been in partial remission during the mid- and late 1760s, but by the early 1770s she could no longer deny the severity of her symptoms. In a letter to Mary Fish Noyes, Joseph

Fish's daughter, in 1770, she admitted that she could barely write because the "pain" was "too severe." Shocked by her declining health, she seems to have wondered whether she was near death. "Farewell, my dear sister," she wrote. It was as though she could not imagine taking another breath after being "cut off" from her ability to read and write.[3]

And yet Sarah lived for another two decades. The desire to write still burned "like a fire" in her heart, but because of her poor eyesight and physical weakness she rarely picked up her pen. Hungry to express herself, she sometimes asked friends to write letters for her or composed poems in her head. But one of the greatest joys of her life had been lost. Each day she had to reconcile herself to silence.

Because of Sarah's difficulty writing, we know little about her life during the Revolution. After her 1767 diary and her letter to Mary Fish Noyes, her only surviving writings are two letters dictated in the late 1770s, a poem from an unknown date, and the will she wrote with her own hand in 1793.[4] Yet even though Sarah's own voice almost entirely disappeared from the historical record, we can catch fleeting glimpses of her in church records, census records, and other people's letters and diaries. Besides including a brief account of her last years in his *Memoirs of the Life of Mrs. Sarah Osborn*, Samuel Hopkins also mentioned her in his correspondence with Levi Hart. Although these scraps of evidence leave many questions unanswered, they allow us to piece together an account of her experiences during the Revolution, the creation of the new republic, and the last years of her life.

Based on Sarah's letters, it is clear that she was a Patriot who interpreted the war in millennial terms. Despite disdaining local politics as a distraction from the more important business of salvation, she believed that God guided the ballot box, and in times of crisis she mixed political and religious images in her writings, freighting her words with double meanings. On the first anniversary of the Stamp Act's repeal, when ships in the harbor displayed their colors and soldiers fired a royal salute, she prayed that "Liberty, Precious Liberty were used for the Glory of God. Let not this day be remembered only by way of reveling instead of thanksgiving. Lord, bring me and others of thy children to rejoice in the Liberty wherewith Christ Has Made us free, and Let us not be again Entangled with the yoke of Bondage. Lord, free us yet More from the bondage of sin." Although Sarah emphasized that there was nothing more important than repentance, her words suggested that she wanted to be liberated from political oppression as well as the "bondage of sin."[5] She had been born in England and had always prayed for the king, but after the Stamp Act, the Coercive Acts, and the Boston Massacre, she denounced the British as the "enemy."[6]

Sarah's church rallied behind the Patriot cause. To encourage the women of his congregation not to buy British imports, Samuel Hopkins hosted a spinning bee in the parsonage with eighty spinning wheels, and he refused to admit a Mr. Malcolm, a customs' officer, to the table of the Lord's Supper on the grounds that his "Morals" were "exceptionable." Perhaps Malcolm was guilty of something more than his willingness to collect taxes for the king, but the First Church of Christ was home to few, if any, Loyalists. Like Hopkins, Ezra Stiles was an ardent Patriot, and the First and Second Churches of Christ fasted and prayed for American independence. Peter Oliver, a Loyalist sympathizer, derided Congregationalist ministers as the "black regiment" because of their militant support of the Patriot cause.[7]

Like many other Protestants at the time, Sarah seems to have believed that the British government had joined forces with the Catholic Church to deprive Protestants of their liberties. In the wake of the Stamp Act, Patriots tried to discredit the British government by accusing it of being "popish" and totalitarian, but after the 1774 Quebec Act, which granted toleration to Catholics in Canada, many argued that Parliament was engaged in a sinister plot "to destroy the British Protestant colonies; and to establish the most arbitrary and despotic government throughout America." According to an article in the *Newport Mercury*, the English ministry planned "to destroy the English constitutions and thereby lay a sure foundation, on which to build and establish POPERY." Another article reported that the pope was plotting to reestablish the Catholic Church in England "and bring George the third to kiss his Holiness's great toe, and humbly acknowledge his supremacy throughout Christendom."[8] Although these articles said more about Protestant anxieties than reality, many Americans imagined that they were engaged in an apocalyptic battle with the Antichrist. In the summer of 1773, Sarah's church bought a copy of Antonio Gavin's *Master Key to Popery*, a sensational account of corrupt priests and licentious nuns who worshiped the "beast" instead of God.[9] Any church member was allowed to borrow it. A few months later, during the commemoration of the Gunpowder Plot, a Newport mob burned effigies of the pope, the devil, Lord North, and the despised governor of Massachusetts, Thomas Hutchinson.[10]

Not all churches in Newport, however, supported the Patriots, and Anglicans in particular tended to have Loyalist sympathies. Every Sunday at Trinity Church, the largest single church in Newport, the congregation prayed for the king (the head of the church), and many members were wealthy merchants who opposed the nonimportation movement. Because of their pacifist convictions, Quakers also hesitated to endorse armed resistance to England, and Baptists were ambivalent about joining the Congregationalists—who had often persecuted them in New England—to mobilize political support for independence. In small New England towns dominated by the Congregationalist establishment, support for the Revolutionary cause was almost ubiquitous, but the religious diversity of Newport meant that it was a city of divided political loyalties.[11]

In April 1775 the first shots were fired at Lexington and Concord, killing both American minutemen and British soldiers. Some colonists still held out hope for peace, but the *Newport Mercury*'s editor, a staunch Patriot, saw no alternative to war. "Thus," he wrote, "through the sanguinary Measures of a wicked Ministry, and the Readiness of a standing Army to execute their Mandates, has commenced the American Civil War, which will hereafter fill an important page in History." He hoped that it would "speedily terminate in a full restoration of our Liberties."[12] The Second Continental Congress met in May, and George Washington was named commander-in-chief of the Continental Army in June.

It was a frightening time to bring a child into the world, but Sarah's granddaughter Sally and her husband, Daniel, welcomed their firstborn, a daughter, in July. Probably in honor of either Sarah's mother or her closest friend, Susanna Anthony, they named her Susanna. We can only imagine Sarah's happiness on the day that her great-grandchild was baptized into the covenant, or her prayers for God's protection as the fighting approached Newport.[13] With an infant at home, the war seemed especially menacing.

The British targeted Newport because of its importance as a trading port. In the summer and fall of 1775, Commander James Wallace blockaded the harbor to prevent smuggling, and he promised to "lay the town in ashes" if his ships were not supplied with provisions.[14] The British fired on the town whenever they needed food, terrifying the inhabitants. At one in the morning on a cold December night, British troops went on a rampage in neighboring Jamestown, ordering families out of their houses and "driving out the women and children, swearing they should be burnt in the houses if they did not instantly turn out." They stole beds and furniture, stripped women of their best clothes, and slaughtered oxen, cows, sheep, and hogs for food before setting the houses on fire. "This morning we were awaked with the Conflagration of Jamestown," Ezra Stiles wrote in his diary. "An awful sight!"[15]

By January 1776, Stiles estimated that "more than three quarters of the Inhabitants" had fled.[16] Besides being afraid of British troops, residents were worried about being plunged into destitution if they remained in the city. Wallace's blockade had destroyed local trade, leaving everyone from sailors to distillers without jobs. According to Samuel Hopkins, there was "an almost total stagnation of trade and business," and he was forced to rely on voluntary donations because so few in his congregation were able to contribute to his salary.[17] As the population dwindled, Sarah closed her school. She and Henry were financially stable at the beginning of the war (though still too poor to pay taxes), but they had generously donated more than 145 pounds to their church between 1770 and 1774 to create a private subscription library for the women's society. According to Samuel Hopkins, Sarah often gave more money to the church than "many wealthy persons of the same congregation." But now, with little in the way of savings, she and Henry worried about their ability to afford food and fuel.[18]

Concerned about the plight of the poor, a Quaker woman lamented that "many for want to employ are already reduced to live many days together on bran and water boiled together and a bit of bread, and some have hardly that, to eat at a time."[19] The Continental Congress had resolved to boycott anyone who raised prices to take advantage of shortages, but some of Newport's merchants could not resist the opportunity to get rich. "We hear several persons in this town are taking advantage of the times, by raising the price of the articles they deal in," complained the *Newport Mercury*, "from which base, selfish practice we advise them to desist, lest we should be obliged to hold them up to the public in a very disagreeable light." Writing several months later in August, only a month after the Declaration of Independence, Susanna Anthony worried that if everyone stayed in Newport, "numbers must perish for want of food or fuel through the winter."[20]

John Quamine and Bristol Yamma, however, had no choice but to return to Newport from Princeton. According to John Witherspoon, the president of the College of New Jersey, they were "pretty good in reading and writing and likewise have a pretty good Notion of the Principles of the Christian faith," but they had run out of money to pay their expenses.[21] Samuel Hopkins and Ezra Stiles had hoped to raise enough money to send Salmar Nubia to the college as well, but the war destroyed their plans. (Nubia was a member of Stiles's church who had almost certainly attended Sarah Osborn's meetings.) All three men were eager to return to Africa as missionaries, but in the meantime Quamine enlisted as a privateer in order to make enough money to buy his wife's freedom.[22] Before leaving he wrote

a letter to Moses Brown, a well-known Quaker abolitionist, thanking him
for his work:

> *Having some late understandings of your noble and distinguished char-*
> *acter, and boundless benevolent engagements, with regard to the un-*
> *forfeited rights, of the poor unhappy Africans in this province; and of*
> *your sundry petitions to the General Assemblies in their favors, [there]*
> *has existed [in] one of that nation, though an utter stranger, [a desire]*
> *to present thee with gratitude and thanks . . . , the only returns he is*
> *capable of, for all your ardent endeavors for the speedy salvation of his*
> *poor enslaved country men, and for what you were kindly disposed to do*
> *already of this kind, in freeing all your servants.*

This is the only one of Quamine's letters that has been found, and it suggests both his intelligence and his devotion to the emancipation of slaves.[23]

People in Newport were relieved when Captain Wallace and his fleet
left in March 1776, but in December, General Sir Henry Clinton and eight
thousand troops sailed into the harbor and occupied the city without a
fight. (This despite the boast of the *Newport Mercury* that Newport's militia
was "equal to any regulars in the King's dominion.") British troops looted
stores, raided farms for provisions, forced residents to quarter soldiers in
their homes, and tore down houses for firewood. "It is dangerous to walk
the streets after dark," a resident wrote in his diary. "Men have been beat up
by the Hessians."[24] Most people fled, but not everyone was either willing
or able to leave, including the Osborns. The population dropped precipi-
tously, from 11,000 in 1775 to 5,300 in 1776.[25] Among those who left were
Sarah and Henry's grandson, whom they seem to have sent away to begin
an apprenticeship.[26] Daniel, Sally and six-month-old Susanna stayed behind, perhaps to be close to Sarah and Henry.

Much of the beautiful city of Newport, famous for its Brick Market
and elegant houses, was reduced to dust and rubble. In a systematic cam-
paign of demoralization, the British turned the Colony House (the Rhode
Island government seat) into a barracks and desecrated the churches that
were identified with the Patriot cause, including the First Church. Turning it into a barracks and hospital, they tore down the parsonage, broke
the windows, and ripped out the pulpit and the pews. "The inside is almost wholly ruined," Samuel Hopkins lamented.[27] Sarah rarely attended
church anymore because of her difficulty walking, but after cherishing it

The Colony House, finished in 1739, was Rhode Island's statehouse.
People gathered near the front steps in 1776 to hear the Declaration
of Independence read aloud. During the Revolution the British
used it as a barracks. Courtesy of the Newport Historical Society.

as her spiritual home for more than thirty years, she was heartbroken by
its ruin. "Many distressing things passed before us," she remembered later,
especially "the destruction of the house of the Lord's." Hopkins fled to the
safety of Connecticut, where he spent the war preaching to different congregations. Sarah tried to be stoic, but she admitted that his absence was
"very trying."[28]

Sarah and Henry had endured the ravages of war before, but this time
they may have felt especially vulnerable: she was sixty-three and he was
ninety-two when the British stormed into town, and both of them were
ill and frail. Although Sally and Daniel were with them, each day brought
frightening stories of drunken soldiers and looted houses.

After the war Sarah claimed that she had suffered little during the
British occupation, and although Samuel Hopkins never explicitly claimed
that God had especially watched over her, he implied it. She "had a constant supply of the necessaries of life; and received no abuse from the British officers or soldiers, as most others did," he testified. Although soldiers
were quartered near her, "it was remarked by her and others, that they made
less disturbance and noise, than they did elsewhere; and were particularly

careful not to do anything on the Sabbath to disturb that *good woman*, as they called her. And they took care to avoid all profane words when near her."[29]

It would not have been surprising if at least a few British soldiers had been in awe of Sarah's piety, and this is what Sarah liked to remember in later years. But Hopkins had not been with her in Newport, and her true situation seems to have been more perilous. In a letter to a friend written during the war, Susanna Anthony reported that Sarah was "sick; destitute; and in affliction," and she was "in very different circumstances, from any she ever saw before.—Refuge, and helpers fail;—and she does not seem to possess that confidence, and joy, which was usual in difficulties." It was an "extremely cold" winter, but there was almost no wood for sale. Once again it seemed as if God had hidden his face. As Susa exclaimed, "Everything in Providence appears dark, respecting her!"[30]

Whether because of their concerns about their safety or their inability to pay rent, Sarah and Henry moved into John Tanner's house during the war. John and his wife, Mary, were Seventh-day Baptists, but they may have belonged to the First Church at some point, and Mary seems to have been a member of the women's society. The Tanners had been friends of the Osborns for at least twenty years, and when they decided to flee Newport, leaving behind John's successful goldsmith business, they allowed Sarah, Henry, and fifteen other people to move into their house. As one of the deacons of his church, John Tanner was responsible for the welfare of the poor, and he had a reputation for generosity.[31] Although we do not know the names of the others who sought refuge under his roof, they were probably like Henry and Sarah: poor people with nowhere else to go. Sally, Daniel, and Susanna, now one, were probably among them.[32]

In later years Tanner described his house as a "large mansion," but with seventeen people crowded into four rooms, living there must have been anything but luxurious. Sarah and Henry were grateful to have a roof over their heads, but with the lack of privacy, the shortage of basic necessities like flour and wood, and the fear of British troops, they must have often prayed for relief.[33]

Henry spent his last days at the Tanner's house. He died in 1778 at the age of ninety-three. Sarah had written little about him over the years, perhaps because he had access to her diaries, but even though she may not have loved him with the same passion she felt for her first husband, their bond had been strong. He had given her freedoms that many other men begrudged their wives, supporting her even when others had accused her of going beyond her line. She never referred to him in her diaries without using the adjective *dear*: he was never simply her "consort," but her "dear consort."[34]

Soon after Henry's death, Sally and Daniel decided they could no longer endure the strain of rearing a child in a war zone. They do not seem to have moved far, probably only across the bay to South Kingstown, but as Samuel Hopkins commented, their departure meant that Sarah, ill and "destitute," was "left *alone*."[35] Perhaps she was invited to go with them, but if so she refused. She was too devoted to her religious community to leave Newport, even if it meant enduring the violence of the British. Many of her closest friends were still in the city, including Deacon Coggeshall, and they gathered together for prayer whenever possible on Wednesday evenings.[36]

Sarah and other Patriots had much to pray for during the winter of 1777–78. The Continental Army was near starvation at Valley Forge, and because white men were so reluctant to enlist, Rhode Island's General Assembly decided to offer freedom to any male slave willing to fight. In February 1778 the Assembly passed a law promising to reimburse masters as much as 120 pounds for each slave who joined the army. Although many blacks had already enlisted to fight for the British, who had promised to emancipate anyone willing to become a redcoat, the Continental Army was nervous about arming slaves or former slaves. As many as 250 joined Rhode Island's "black battalion" before the General Assembly stopped the program in May, frightened by the possibility of a rebellion. Perhaps because of the resistance of their masters, only a few slaves from Newport seem to have enlisted.[37]

Since records are fragmentary, we do not know the exact date of either Henry's death or Sally and Daniel's decision to leave Newport, but if Sarah was alone in August during the Battle of Rhode Island, she probably counted it as a mercy. She would not have wanted them to experience the terrors she did—the screaming outside her door, the sound of gunfire, the sight of wounded soldiers dying in the streets. Like other Patriots, she may have been elated when Admiral d'Estaing arrived with the French fleet (the Treaty of Alliance between the French and the Continental Army had been ratified earlier in the year), but as the harbor filled with smoke from the constant barrage of gunfire, the mood of celebration turned to panic. Anticipating that the French would soon come ashore, the British burned down buildings to prevent them from being used as barracks, forcing many to flee. Mary Almy, a Loyalist, remembered gathering up a few bundles and running out of the city with her children. "All this time the ships were firing continually, women were shrieking, children falling down, crying," she wrote to her husband. It seemed as though the shells would never stop exploding, but then, in an event that Sarah surely saw as providential, a hurricane sent the soldiers scurrying for shelter. For two days the city was buffeted by a violent storm that toppled trees and ripped tents to shreds. Admiral d'Estaing retreated in order to repair his damaged ships, but the battle had not yet ended, and after fierce fighting between British and Continental troops on land near Quaker Hill, several miles outside the city, the British managed to keep possession of Newport. Both sides suffered heavy casualties. Mary Almy witnessed "cartloads of wretched men brought in, their wives screaming at the foot of the carts, in consort with their groans—fine youths with their arms taken off in a moment." On the Sunday after the battle, every hospital was "crowded with wounded men, no church, nothing but horror and distress."[38]

If Sarah was as frightened as everyone else, she did not admit it afterward. Instead she emphasized her submission to God's will. Certain that "every shot was directed by unerring wisdom," she resigned herself to her fate. The worst that could happen was that she would finally go to God.[39]

The British sent reinforcements to Newport after the Battle of Rhode Island, tightening their stranglehold on the city. The conditions were miserable. In December 1778 the weather turned so cold that soldiers froze to death at their posts, and because of a severe shortage of flour, millers began grinding rice for bread. British ships could not deliver more provisions because of the frozen harbor. According to Solomon Southwick, the former editor of the *Newport Mercury* (which had been shut down by the British), "The enemy at Newport are so greatly distressed that unless they have a speedy supply of provisions they must surrender, having neither shipping nor provisions to carry them off. The town goes to destruction at last." The people of Newport were on the brink of starvation, with "several who cannot get a small mouthful of bread for several days together."[40]

The British did not surrender in Newport, nor did Sarah starve. But that winter was one of the worst of her life. Perhaps it is no wonder that later she remembered her willingness to die if it had been God's will.

Sarah prayed that God would have mercy on the Americans, but despite several victories in the South, each month brought more terror. Besides defeating the Americans at Brier Creek in Georgia, the British burned down Fairfield and Norwalk in Connecticut and massacred dozens of soldiers in New Jersey with bayonets. It seemed as if God's wrath would never be sated.

As Sarah knew, God did not always answer her prayers in the way that she wanted. In the fall of 1779 she heard the devastating news that John Quamine had been killed on board a privateer during his first battle. His violent death was a terrible loss to his family, who would always remember the sacrifice he had made in the hope of earning enough money to free them. His wife, Duchess, and their three children, the youngest only two, remained slaves.[41]

Though Sarah believed that everything happened for a reason, she may have struggled to understand why God had brought Quamine from Africa, saved him from sin, and then sent him to Princeton only to shatter his missionary dream with a bullet. She would never forget him.

British troops finally evacuated Newport in October 1779 as the center of the fighting moved to the South. Before their departure they destroyed buildings, filled wells, burned Long Wharf, and took most of the church bells to sell in England, leaving only Trinity Church's behind. "The Town is in Ruins," mourned Ezra Stiles after a visit. Another resident described Newport as "a barren city, with shuttered houses, a pillaged library, books burned, and commerce practically at a standstill."[42]

When Sarah wrote to Joseph Fish in December, she was frank about what she had lost, but grateful for what still remained. "I have been stripped of my dearest enjoyments on earth, attendance on public worship, reading, writing, my dear and worthy pastor, Christian friends, Grandchildren, my dear aged Companion," she admitted, "yet have upheld under all, and in every apparent danger throughout the Captivity God mercifully granted me renewed strength and courage." John Tanner had returned after the British evacuation, and she now lived with a "kind neighbor" who read the Bible to her every night. Her friends generously continued to supply her needs. "Blessed be God," she wrote, "I have lacked for nothing." Eager to emphasize God's particular kindness to her, she claimed that even during the worst of the fighting she had been as safe as Noah in the ark, Daniel in the lions' den, and the three men in the fiery furnace. While many "righteous" people had been subjected to "the hateful din and profane swearing" of British soldiers, she had been spared "the filthy Conversation of the wicked," and even though the British had threatened to leave the entire city "in devouring flames," they had boarded their ships "as Gentle as Lambs." Comparing the people of Newport to the Israelites who had been enslaved in Babylon (and echoing Psalm 118:23), she rejoiced, "This was the Lord's doing and marvelous in our Eyes. Thus ends the captivity."[43]

As Sarah must have known, the British hardly left Newport as "Gentle as Lambs," and the fact that the she had not heard any "filthy" profanity was hardly a strong proof of God's mercy. Perhaps her life had been so bleak that this was the most positive thing she could say. As always, however, she was determined to find evidence of God's compassion in the midst of his wrath.

Evangelicals were often accused of being pessimists who saw humans as too sinful to create a better world, but despite their suspicion of human nature they had a deep faith in God's power to triumph over evil. The American Revolution was brutal and bloody, but evangelicals saw it as the fulfillment of their hopes, the dawning of a more glorious age. They were cosmic optimists who lived in constant anticipation of the millennium.[44]

The Heavenly City

Evangelicals were not alone in their hopes for the future. Many Enlightenment thinkers and liberal-leaning Protestants also dreamed of a more perfect world, but they thought humans had the power to create it on their own without divine assistance.

The Christian belief in the second coming and the Enlightenment ideal of progress were so intertwined during the Revolutionary years that it is hard to disentangle them. As the historian Carl Becker noted, Enlightenment philosophers placed their faith in "nature's God" rather than the God of revelation, but they "demolished the Heavenly City of St. Augustine only to rebuild it with more up-to-date materials." Despite their criticism of traditional Christian doctrines like original sin and eternal punishment, they crafted a secular version of the Christian narrative of salvation, substituting natural law for biblical revelation, the love of humanity for the love of God, and human perfectibility for divine redemption.[45] Their fervent utopianism was virtually a religion of its own.

Not all Enlightenment thinkers (Rousseau and Voltaire among them) believed that progress was either possible or inevitable, but the dominant mood of the eighteenth century was optimistic. In addition to technological and scientific advances like the invention of the microscope and the discovery of electricity, the spread of commerce and the rising standard of living seemed to be harbingers of a more perfect society. In France, the philosopher Anne-Robert-Jacques Turgot imagined the human race marching "towards still higher perfection," and in England, Adam Smith argued that

if people were free to pursue their own economic interests, they would create a more prosperous and peaceful world. Edward Gibbon's famous *History of the Decline and Fall of the Roman Empire* ended with the promise that
"every age of the world has increased, and still increases, the real wealth,
the happiness, the knowledge, and perhaps the virtue, of the human race."[46]
Although the past was filled with violence, poverty, and ignorance, "enlightenment" was coming.

Revolutionary leaders like John Adams and James Madison tended to
be less starry-eyed about the future than the most optimistic Enlightenment thinkers, and perhaps because of their Protestant heritage they greeted
claims of human goodness with ambivalence. (This is why they and other
Founders created checks and balances on constitutional power.) But like
Locke and Helvétius, they saw human nature as malleable, and they firmly
believed in the possibility of designing laws and institutions that would
give rise to a virtuous citizenry.[47] As Adams explained in his *Thoughts on
Government* (1776), a republican form of government "introduces knowledge among the people, and inspires them with a conscious dignity becoming Freemen. A general emulation takes place, which causes good humor,
sociability, good manners, and good morals to be general. That elevation of
sentiment inspired by such a government, makes the common people brave
and enterprising. That ambition which is inspired by it makes them sober,
industrious, and frugal." Although Adams admitted that people could be
selfish and power-hungry, he thought they could be transformed—reborn,
in a sense—by the right form of government. As Abbé Raynal proclaimed,
"the human race is what we wish to make it."[48]

Evangelicals argued that the human race was what *God* wished to
make it, but they, too, believed that humans stood on the brink of a new
era in history. Although millennialism has always been part of the Christian tradition, it has been particularly intense during times of crisis, and
eighteenth-century America was rife with speculation about the end times.
After Lexington and Concord, ministers explicitly linked the coming of
the millennium to political events, portraying the Revolution as a step toward Christ's return to earth. The Reverend Sylvanus Conant, for example,
claimed that Isaiah's prophetic question—"Shall the earth be made to bring
forth in one day, or shall a nation be born at once?"—was answered by the
American Revolution. Searching for evidence of America's destiny in the
Bible, he confidently declared to his congregation, "It is a question whether
anything has happened for these 1700 years past, that doth so literally and
extensively answer this query, as when these thirteen united States, by voice

of their deputies in Congress assembled, were led to declare the
and independent of the jurisdiction of Great-Britain, and of ?
ers on earth."[49] While some believed that Jesus would literally retun.
on Israel's throne, others claimed that he would not reign in the flesh, bu.
in the hearts of believers.[50]

These optimistic visions of the future were always mixed with under-
currents of violence. Even though both Enlightenment thinkers and evangelicals deplored the bloodshed of the past, they also assumed that violence
and suffering might be a necessary stage in the emergence of a new age.
Whereas Enlightenment thinkers imagined that the cataclysm of war could
be a way of wiping the slate clean so that a new story could be written,
evangelicals insisted that redemption always involved suffering. In a sermon preached in 1774, the Reverend Joseph Lyman reminded his congregation that God always afflicted his chosen, sending the "fire of affliction and
persecution to purge away the sins of his people." Echoing this rhetoric,
John Adams feared that it was the "Will of Heaven" for Americans to "suffer Calamities." In a letter to his wife, Abigail, he wrote: "The Furnace of
Affliction produces Refinement, in states as well as Individuals."[51]

This vision of America's destiny had deep Puritan roots. Like John
Winthrop, who described Massachusetts Bay as a "city on a hill," many
New England ministers claimed that God had made a special covenant
with America just as he had done with Israel. Portraying America as a chosen nation, a beacon to the rest of the world, they promised their congregations that they would be showered with blessings if they kept God's commandments, but punished with war, famine, epidemics, or other disasters
if they went astray. The only way to appease an angry God was through repentance. Echoing this language, Sarah Osborn not only praised the Lord
as "a Faithful covenant keeping God" but also interpreted the Revolution
as divine punishment for sin. Remembering the biblical story of Jehu, who
sought vengeance instead of peace, she confessed that God would be "Infinitely Just" if he decided to "vindicate his Injured honor" by destroying
Americans. Always eager to chastise herself for her sins, she blamed herself
as well as others for "drawing down the judgments of God upon us!" Yet she
was also hopeful that God would eventually "grant repentance and maintain His own Right in America." His afflictions were a sign of his love, and
if people repented he would restore his covenant with them. Even though
America was wallowing in "iniquity," someday it would be redeemed.[52]

It is not clear whether Sarah Osborn believed that America would
be the location of Christ's second coming, a belief that Samuel Hopkins

and other New Divinity ministers found idolatrous. But for many other Protestants, both liberal-leaning and evangelical, it was only a small step from the belief that America was a chosen nation to the conviction that it would be the site of the millennium.[53] The Reverend Ebenezer Baldwin wondered whether America might become "the Foundation of a great and mighty Empire; the largest the World ever saw," or even more marvelous, "the principal Seat of that glorious kingdom, which Christ shall erect upon Earth in the latter days."[54] Similarly, the Reverend Samuel Sherwood imagined that the millennium would begin in America and gradually spread to the rest of the globe. After the defeat of the "beast," he predicted "that peace, liberty, and righteousness might universally prevail; that salvation and strength might come to Zion; and the kingdom of our God, and the power of his Christ might be established to all the ends of the earth."[55]

It is hard to say who influenced the other more: evangelicals who absorbed Enlightenment ideas about the inevitability of progress or Enlightenment thinkers who imagined that America was destined for greatness. On one hand, Enlightenment thinkers seem to have been influenced by religious ideas about the coming of God's kingdom; as the historian Ruth Bloch has pointed out, even the Continental Congress sounded vaguely millennial when it imagined "the golden period, when liberty, with all the gentle arts of peace and humanity, shall establish her mild dominion," and "that latest period, when the streams of time shall be absorbed in the abyss of eternity." On the other hand, evangelical descriptions of the millennium sounded startlingly like Enlightenment visions of educational advancement, material abundance, and commercial expansion. According to Samuel Hopkins, people would grow in knowledge and wisdom, and "all outward worldly circumstances will then be agreeable and prosperous, and there will be for all, a sufficiency and fullness of everything needed for the body and for the comfort and convenience of every one."[56] In the dialectical encounter between Protestantism and the Enlightenment, the influence flowed in both directions.

Evangelicals did not always mean the same thing as enlightened thinkers when they looked forward to their "liberty" in "Zion," but the double meanings of these words made it possible for different audiences to unite around a common cause. In a letter to Joseph Fish, for example, Sarah wondered whether she would live to see "the dawn of that blessed day" when Christ would return to earth, and she imagined the joy of the angels in heaven "when *millions* repent; when a *nation*, is born in a day!" Although her quotation from Isaiah—"Shall the earth be made to bring forth in one day, or shall a nation be born at once?"—had political overtones, it is not clear whether she shared the popular faith that the millennium would begin in America. While others used this text to portray the Revolution as the fulfillment of divine prophecy, she may not have meant *nation* literally.[57] The difficulty in determining her meaning, however, points to the protean power of millennial language to unite people during the Revolutionary years.

Both Protestants and Enlightenment thinkers dreamed that the American Revolution might change the world: enlightened thinkers because of their faith in republican government and Protestants because of their faith in God. "When the set time to Favor Zion is come, then Christ will be avenged on Satan for all the mischief he hath done," Sarah exulted in a letter to Fish. "The old Serpent shall be bound, that he deceive the nations no more! God shall pour out his Spirit, in plentiful effusions. The knowledge of God, shall cover the earth, as the waters fill the sea.—Then Christ Jesus will reign triumphant, King of Nations, as he is now King of Saints."[58]

The Wickedness of the World

It is remarkable that Sarah Osborn could write such a jubilant letter at a time when Newport lay in ruins, but like other evangelicals she assumed that a period of tribulation would precede Christ's return. As the world sank into corruption, people would finally realize that Christ was their only hope for salvation. According to Jonathan Edwards in his *History of the Work of Redemption* (which Hopkins bought for the First Church in 1775), "'Tis reasonable to suppose that just BEFORE THE END OF THE WORLD the wickedness of the world should be at its greatest height."[59]

Sarah was not sure whether she was witnessing the end of the world or only the prelude to it, but in the terrible winter after the British evacuation she had no doubt that "wickedness" was increasing. Like Susanna Anthony, who lamented "the torrent of universal corruption" and "the dreadful degeneracy" unleashed by the war, she was shocked by "the prevalence of error and delusion" at a time when people should have been begging for God's mercy. "We remain as a people thus hardened and impenitent," she confessed to Fish.[60] If not for her confidence that God was setting the stage for his triumphant return, she would have fallen into despair.

To Sarah's eyes the world seemed to be filled with signs of God's wrath. Although she was thankful as her old friends trickled back into the city after the evacuation, she could hardly bear to listen to their stories of suffering and loss. It was "too much for my feeble frame," she admitted to Fish. When John Tanner returned to his house he came alone; his wife, Mary, had died during their exile in Hopkinton.[61] Many others chose not to return to Newport at all, including Ezra Stiles, who had become president of Yale. With as many as 500 buildings in ruins, warehouses empty, and wharves damaged, most merchants moved their shipping to Providence, taking ropewalkers, distillers, and sailors with them. From a high of 9,208 in 1774, Newport's population plunged to 5,530 in 1782, a decline of 40 percent, and many of those who remained were single women and widows with nowhere else to go. Adult white women made up 30.6 percent of the population; adult white men, 17.6 percent.[62] "The Inhabitants of the Town are greatly diminished both in numbers and Circumstances," wrote Christopher Champlin. "Commerce at a low Ebb—our Society small— our Taxes high."[63]

When Samuel Hopkins returned to Newport he found that his congregation had shrunk, its few remaining members impoverished and anxious about the possible return of British troops. Because the interior of the First Church had been gutted, Sarah Osborn's house became the spiritual center of the congregation, the place where church members baptized their infants and met for prayer. Hopkins also arranged to hold public services at the Seventh-day Baptist meetinghouse, one of the few houses of worship not destroyed by the British. No one knew why it had been spared, but some speculated that British troops had hesitated to tear down the table of the Ten Commandments mounted behind the pulpit, its letters edged in gold. (The table had been John Tanner's gift to his church.)[64] The Baptists' good fortune seemed to be proof that God had not abandoned his people, and yet Sarah and the rest of her congregation could not help wondering why he had allowed their own beautiful church to be destroyed.

Adding to the sense of devastation, the winter of 1779–80 was brutally cold, even worse than the previous year, when British soldiers had frozen at their posts. According to a historian, "For the only time in recorded history, all of the saltwater inlets, harbors and sounds of the Atlantic coastal plain, from North Carolina northeastward, froze over and remained closed to navigation for a period of a month or more." George Washington worried that his troops would die from exposure at their winter quarters in Morristown, New Jersey—or desert their posts—and ice and snow made it almost impossible to get provisions. "We were absolutely, literally starved," a soldier remembered later.[65] Many people in Newport feared they would not survive the winter.

But Sarah's friends made sure that she was well-cared for—a blessing she may have interpreted as a sign of God's enduring covenant with her. "I have known no sufferings, this hard winter, but what hath been the effect of sympathy," she wrote to Joseph Fish, "for while many others have been ready to perish, I have had a constant supply of food and fuel." Many friends helped her: not only Susanna Anthony, John Tanner, and the Coggeshalls, but a Mrs. Mary Mason, who had left the Anglican church to become a member of the First Church in 1775. Since Sarah was too ill to reopen her school, she had no source of income, but Mrs. Mason generously "supplied many of her wants."[66]

When General Rochambeau and six thousand French troops occupied Newport in July 1780 in order to make the city the base of their operations, the weary residents rallied to give them a hero's welcome, firing rockets from the Grand Parade and illuminating their houses. After years of suffering they had finally found a reason to celebrate, and the French soldiers— many from elite families—proved to be so charming that balls and parties took place almost every night.[67] For Sarah Osborn, however, the arrival of the French, many of whom were Catholic, may have seemed like further proof that "infidelity" would run rampant in the latter days. Even though the French had pledged their lives to the American cause, Samuel Hopkins accused them of bringing religious corruption and degeneracy to Newport with them. When George Washington arrived in March 1781 to meet with Rochambeau, a thrilling event that was celebrated with torch-lit processions, music, and balls, Hopkins and Osborn may have resigned themselves to the American alliance with the French, but only because of their belief that God could demonstrate his power by bringing something good out of the false "church of Rome."[68]

The French were still in Newport in May 1781 when Sarah heard the sad news that Joseph Fish had died at the age of seventy-six. Losing him after almost forty years of friendship was hard to bear, but she knew that he had died knowing the depth of her love and gratitude. There had been no unsaid words between them, no feelings of regret. Writing with the help of a friend a year earlier, she had said good-bye to him in case her illness made it impossible for her ever to write again. "I thank you, Sir, for all your past indulgence," she declared, "and for all the helps you have afforded me, in my various trials.—The Lord reward you.—May a double portion of his Spirit, rest upon you." After expressing her hope that he would always taste the Lord's sweetness, she sent him and his family her "tender love." "Farewell, my dear friend; farewell!"[69]

Sarah had kept all his letters, storing them carefully, and now that he was gone she may have especially treasured them. She had always treated her friends' letters as evidence of the communion of saints, the unity of all Christians in Jesus. Throughout the years, when she had signed her letters to Fish "your sister in Christ," she had meant those words literally. Someday, she believed, she would sing God's praises in heaven with him, and the love once expressed in their letters would last for eternity. Until then, his letters offered her a small glimpse of the cloud of witnesses waiting beyond the grave.

The war finally ended in October when Cornwallis surrendered to Washington at Yorktown. Eight thousand American soldiers had been killed during the five years of combat and as many as twenty-five thousand wounded, and the survivors knew that they might return home to find their houses or farms reduced to wreckage.[70] Soon after the victory, the people of Newport sent a petition to the General Assembly begging to be exempted from state taxes because so many of them were "destitute of the means of subsistence."[71] A French visitor described Newport as "an empty place, peopled only by groups of men who spend the whole day idling with folded arms on street corners. Most of the houses are in disrepair; the shops are miserably stocked. . . . Grass is growing in the public square in front of the State House; the streets are badly paved and muddy; rags hang from windows; and tatters cover the hideous women, the emaciated children, and the pale, thin men, whose sunken eyes and shifty looks put the observer ill at ease."[72]

Americans kept their faith in progress in the post-Revolutionary years, but they were also sobered by the difficulties of creating a new nation. The Treaty of Paris, signed in 1783, marked the formal end of the war, but tensions with England remained high. The Articles of Confederation gave so much power to individual states that the national government had little authority, and federalists and antifederalists were locked in bitter controversy over whether the United States should have a stronger, more centralized government. As commercial shipping resumed and people rushed to buy consumer goods, hard currency drained out of the country, resulting first in inflation and then in depression. Pirates from the Barbary States harassed American ships, forcing the U.S. government to pay huge tributes. Indians threatened settlers on the western frontier. And in 1787, after Daniel Shays and a mob of impoverished Revolutionary veterans tried to prevent the collection of debts, the Massachusetts state militia attacked them, imprisoning Shays and killing many others.

Protestants responded to the political wrangling, economic hardship, and social unrest of the 1780s in a variety of ways. The majority continued to insist that the millennium was coming, but they claimed that it would develop gradually over time. Timothy Dwight, the grandson of Jonathan Edwards, argued that the Revolution had been the prelude to acts of "higher importance," and others insisted that the future would bring westward expansion, commercial success, and international power. Both liberal and evangelical Protestants invested the nation with sacred meaning, portraying it (in Abraham Lincoln's later phrase) as the "last best hope on earth."[73]

But not all evangelicals believed that the nation enjoyed a special covenant with God, and not all assumed that it was destined for economic or political greatness. On the contrary, New Divinity ministers like Samuel Hopkins, Joseph Bellamy, and Levi Hart portrayed the United States as a nation like any other, and they warned that it would prosper only if its people obeyed God's moral law.[74] In the short term, according to Hopkins, the country's prospects looked bleak. As he recorded in his letters (and as he probably discussed with Sarah during their Saturday afternoon visits), Americans were guilty of "general stupidity and carelessness about the important things of religion" and "selfishness and worldliness."[75] Alarmed by books like Ethan Allen's *Reason: The Only Oracle of Man* (1784), he complained that "Deists, universalists, and deistical Christians prevail in general, and take the lead. The unclean frogs are croaking all around me, so that I can hear little else." Although Hopkins was exaggerating, deism was indeed becoming more militant after the Revolution, and he probably encountered more than a few merchants in Newport who prided themselves on their rationalistic critique of Christianity.[76]

Of all the sins Hopkins decried, the worst in his eyes was slavery. During the Revolution he had argued that the war was God's punishment for the sin of enslaving Africans (a view that few other evangelicals seem to have shared), and he warned that Americans must liberate their slaves or face even greater "calamities."[77] After the war he joined forces with Moses Brown, a Quaker, to lobby for slave emancipation in Rhode Island. Despite strong opposition, the state legislature passed a gradual emancipation act in 1784 requiring masters to free their slaves as they reached adulthood— girls at the age of eighteen, and boys at the age of twenty-one.[78] In the same year, the First Church voted to forbid slaveholders from becoming members, condemning slavery and the slave trade as "a gross violation of the Righteousness and Benevolence which are so much inculcated in the

Gospel." (Eleven years earlier, in 1773, Newport's Quakers had demanded that all members emancipate their slaves on penalty of being read out of the meeting.) Yet even Deacon Coggeshall had not freed his slaves until he had been forced to do so, and many states, including Rhode Island, seemed ambivalent about outlawing slavery in the new nation as a whole.[79] In 1787 Rhode Island passed a strict law prohibiting the slave trade—every slave ship would be fined a thousand pounds plus an extra hundred pounds for every slave on board—but the law was rarely enforced.[80] Most people in Newport cared more about making money than resisting slavery. "It is notorious that it is the African trade that prolongs the existence of this de-clining town," argued the *Newport Mercury*, "and the poor of this place well evince who benefits them most, the *African Trader* or the *Abolition Man*."[81]

Samuel Hopkins (and perhaps Sarah Osborn) condemned this kind of economic thinking as selfish, greedy, immoral—and dangerous. A righ-teous God would not be mocked. In 1787, at the same time the Consti-tutional Convention was meeting in Philadelphia, Hopkins warned his listeners that God would destroy the new nation if slavery were not im-mediately abolished. God had guided Americans to victory during the Revolution because of the Continental Congress's decision to outlaw the slave trade, but now that the Constitutional Convention seemed willing to allow slavery to continue, he was preparing to pour out his wrath. "All the blood which has been shed constantly cries to Heaven," Hopkins warned, "and all the bitter sighs, and groans, and tears of these injured, distressed, helpless poor have entered into the ears of the Lord of hosts, and are calling and waiting for the day of vengeance." God had already begun to sharpen his sword. "And is not Heaven frowning upon us *now?*" Hopkins asked. "We are as yet disappointed in our expectations of peace, prosperity, and happiness, in consequence of liberty and independence. Instead of rising to honor, dignity, and respect among the Nations, we have suddenly sunk into disgrace and contempt. Our trade labors under great disadvantages, and is coming to nothing." Debts, war with the Indians, and "violent opposition to government" (a reference to Shays's Rebellion) were all signs of God's anger, and Rhode Island, especially Newport, had "fallen into a disagree-able and very calamitous situation." Slavery was "the first wheel of com-merce in Newport, on which every other movement in business has chiefly depended," and the town had grown rich "at the expense of the blood, the liberty, and happiness of the poor Africans." (One historian has estimated that Newport merchants sold forty thousand slaves between 1760 and 1776.) Now the town was "fast going to poverty and inevitable ruin," reaping the ugly fruits of what it had sowed. God's message was frighteningly clear: if Americans allowed slavery to continue, they would "bring the guilt of this trade and the blood of the Africans on our own heads and on our children." Hopkins's grim warning alluded to Exodus 20:5: "I the Lord thy God am a jealous God, visiting the iniquity of the fathers upon the children unto the third and fourth generation of them that hate me."[82]

When the Constitutional Convention refused to outlaw slavery (and decided to count each slave as three-fifths of a person for the purpose of political representation), Hopkins felt confirmed in his belief that the world was growing more sinful as the millennium was approaching. Even though Rhode Island had outlawed the slave trade in 1774, merchants found ways to evade the law, and by 1800 the volume of trade had returned to prewar levels.[83] In a widely publicized murder case in 1791, Captain James De Wolf of Newport was accused of killing a slave woman who was ill in order to prevent her from infecting others on his ship. After separating her from his crew, tying her to a chair, and suspending her from the rigging, he decided that allowing her to remain on board at all was too great a financial risk. He bound her eyes and mouth with a handkerchief to prevent the other slaves from hearing her screams, and despite the objections of his crew he flung her, still alive, into the sea. Later he was reported to have remarked that he was "sorry he had lost so good a Chair."[84] A Newport jury indicted De Wolf, but a judge in the West Indies cleared him of any wrongdoing. He became one of the wealthiest men in Rhode Island and a member of the Rhode Island House of Representatives.[85]

Stories like these confirmed Hopkins's belief that the world was descending into a pit of corruption, and yet he was almost Panglossian in his optimism, insisting that God would bring good out of evil. Despite his conviction that slavery was "a direct and gross violation of the laws of Christ" (the ends never justified the means), he also refused to accept that a just God would allow slaves to suffer for no reason. "This dark and dreadful scene will not only have an end, but is designed by the Most High to be the means of introducing the gospel among the nations in Africa," he argued. He dreamed of a day when the nations of Africa would be prosperous, peaceful, and Christian. "Thus all this past and present evil which the Africans have suffered by the slave trade, and the slavery to which so many of them have been reduced, may be the occasion of an over-balancing good; and it may hereafter appear, as it has in the case of Joseph being sold a slave into Egypt, and the oppression and slavery of the Israelites by the Egyptians, that though the slave traders have really meant and done that which is evil, yet God has designed it all for good."[86] Few whites in the eighteenth century detested slavery as much as Samuel Hopkins, and yet few were more optimistic about the future of the enslaved.

Hopkins argued that slavery, deism, and the other evils of the world were all signs that the millennium was coming. According to his biblical calculations, it would not take place for another two hundred years— around the year 2000—but God had already begun to pour out the "sixth vial" described in the book of Revelation, and the darkness and degeneracy of the present age were heralds of Christ's spiritual return. "Ignorance, error and delusion, and open vice and wickedness abound, and are increasing," he explained, "and infidelity is rapidly spreading in the Christian world. The unclean spirits, like frogs, appear to have gone forth to all the kings' courts, and the great men in Christendom; and the greatest corruption and abominable vices are spread among them, and real Christianity is neglected, run down and opposed." (Revelation describes "unclean spirits" coming out of the Dragon's mouth like "frogs.") The world trembled on the brink of its darkest age, and yet Christians knew that they should look forward to the future with hope. "These evils," Hopkins explained, "both natural and moral, however undesirable and dreadful, in themselves, are necessary for the greatest good of the church of Christ, and to introduce the Millennium in the best manner, and there will be then, and forever, more holiness, joy and happiness, than if these evils had never taken place."[87] The millennium would be especially glorious because of the epidemics, famines, and moral depravity that had preceded it.

Hopkins believed that there were already small signs of hope that a better world was on the horizon. A group of free black men, including many who had once attended Sarah Osborn's meetings, had founded the Free African Union Society (FAUS) in 1780, an organization that revealed how deeply its members had internalized her message of piety, hard work, and thrift. One of the leaders of FAUS was Newport Gardner (Occramar Marycoo), a remarkable man who had arrived on a slave ship in 1760 at the age of fourteen. Though at first he could not speak English, "he early discovered to his owner very superior powers of mind. He *taught himself* to read, after receiving a few lessons on the elements of written language. He *taught himself* to sing, after receiving a very trivial initiation into the rudiments of music. He became so well acquainted with the science and art of music, that he composed a large number of tunes, some of which have been highly approved by musical amateurs, and was for a long time the teacher of a very numerously attended singing school in Newport."[88] Besides being a member of the First Church, he was a sexton and close friend of Samuel Hopkins. Gardner, Salmar Nubia, and more than two dozen other FAUS members saved enough money to buy their own houses, laying the groundwork for the creation of a black middle class.[89]

Because of Rhode Island's gradual emancipation act, the liberation of black soldiers, and large numbers of runaways during the Revolution, free blacks outnumbered slaves in 1790 for the first time in Newport's history, and although slave traders did a thriving business with southern planters, slavery seemed to be gradually dying out in the North.[90] Relatively few slaves had converted to Christianity, but both Hopkins and Osborn were heartened that a small community of blacks in Newport seemed interested in forming their own church. They asked Hopkins to preach to them, and despite his worries about making "enemies" among slave owners, he agreed. When he published his *System of Doctrines* in 1793, a theological tome that stretched to more than six hundred pages, the subscribers included seventeen free blacks from Newport and Providence. Among them were "Solmar" (Salmar) Nubia, Bristol Yamma, Obour Tanner, Newport Gardner and his wife, Jenny, and John Quamine's widow, "Mrs. Duchess Quamine." (By giving a black woman the honorific, "Mrs.," Hopkins made a radical statement about black equality.) Many of the black subscribers not only supported Hopkins's book but also remained committed to his vision of sending missionaries to Africa. When Sarah remembered the remarkable meetings that had begun two decades earlier in her kitchen, she may have dreamed that her legacy would be carried across the Atlantic. Although Bristol Yamma died in 1794 after an illness, Salmar Nubia and Newport Gardner hoped to return to their native land.[91]

Hopkins supported the colonization movement because of his conviction that blacks would never achieve racial equality in the United States. As he explained, "The whites are so habituated, by education and custom, to look upon and treat the blacks as an inferior class of beings, and they [the blacks] are sunk so low by their situation and the treatment they receive from us, that they never can be raised to an equality with the whites, and enjoy all the liberty and rights to which they have a just claim." Though his assessment was bleak, the members of the Free African Union Society shared it. Because many of them had been born in Africa, they felt like "strangers and outcasts in a strange land." They did not believe that the millennium would begin until their triumphant return to their "own country."[92]

In the nineteenth century, millennialists would split into two groups: postmillennialists (often theological liberals) who believed that Christ would return after a thousand years of peace, and premillennialists who believed that Christ would appear before the millennium in order to engage in an apocalyptic war against Satan. While the first group tended to emphasize gradual human progress, the second insisted that humans were too corrupt to bring about the millennium on their own. Reading the book of Revelation literally, with its violent depictions of plagues, beasts, and the Great Red Dragon, they warned that there would be unimaginable bloodshed and devastation before the world was cleansed of its sin. In the eighteenth century, however, these different positions had not yet hardened, and Hopkins did not fit neatly into either category.[93] Technically he was a postmillennialist who predicted that Jesus would not return until after a thousand years of peace, but unlike later Protestant liberals he denied that progress was possible without God's direct intervention. He was an optimist, but only because of his faith that God would not allow humans to wallow in sin forever—merely another two hundred years.

During the Revolution, Sarah Osborn seems to have thought that the millennium might be imminent, but, influenced by Hopkins, she may have eventually resigned herself to the likelihood that she would not live to see it. In 1787, the year the Constitution was ratified, she was seventy-three and in "generally low" health, and without Mrs. Mason's help she would have been unable to afford food or rent.[94] She had moved yet again, probably in search of cheaper rent, this time to live with Latham Clarke and his wife, Elizabeth.[95] Yet if Hopkins can be trusted, she continued to affirm that she lived in the best of all possible worlds. When her beloved great-grandchild Susan died, probably at the age of nine, a tragedy that may have brought back memories of her son Samuel's death many years before, she received a letter from Susanna Anthony urging her to accept her suffering as a sign of God's love. According to Susa, it was possible that God had taken Susan away to prevent her from becoming a burden on her great-grandmother's strength. "While the dear babe lived," Susa wrote, "I viewed it as growing up in the church of God, and much more than supplying our places: But when Dead, I thought, perhaps this young plant, would have drawn too much sap from the spreading, yet aged oak, and so eclipse her beauty, mar her importance, and weaken at least, her shady indulgence."[96] We do not know whether Sarah was comforted by these words, but she had always tried to believe that everything that happened to her was for the best.

As Sarah reflected on the Revolutionary years she knew that God would somehow bring good out of evil. Unlike Enlightenment thinkers she envisioned history as a spiral that sometimes circled backward rather than as a straight line moving forward, and she insisted that grace, not reason, would bring history to its glorious completion. But still, she was sure that the millennium was bearing down on the world and nothing could stop it—not the horrifying violence of the Revolution, not deism and infidelity, not even the barbaric human traffic in slaves.

Chapter 11

The Open Vision, 1796

But now, behold, the vail is rent from top to bottom. I will never any more hide my face from thee. Come, all thy desires are fulfilled; all thy imperfections are done away; and, according to thy wish, thou art made perfect in holiness. Thou shalt never find any more weariness in my service. And thou mayest now with open face behold me, constantly look on my perfections, see my glory, and the luster of it shall not confound thee. Come, here is the open vision, the full fruition thou didst long for. Come, drink in as much of God now as thy finite capacity can hold, and I will still enlarge thy capacity: Thou shalt pass from glory to glory, and be more and more transformed into the same image. Come, drink and swim, and drink again of those rivers of pleasure, which flow from the right hand of God forevermore. Here is the boundless ocean, in which thee mayest dive throughout the endless ages of eternity, and thy delights shall be forever new.

Come, search into the wonders of redeeming love and grace, which has brought so many of the apostate sons and daughters of Adam to glory: And now, in this everlasting now, give to God the glory of his sovereign grace. Come, tune thy harp, and sound upon the highest string. Shout aloud for joy; for he has given grace and glory too. Here is no danger of ostentation or spiritual pride; or of grieving any of the inhabitants of this world. No, they will all join with thee, and each for himself, and on thy behalf, give glory to God, in the highest strains. Didst thou long to be thus employed? Well, go on forever to praise and adore the glorious Three [in] One. Didst thou delight to commune with me in providences, as well as in ordinances? Well, thou mayest now learn the mysteries of them: They shall be unfolded. Unbelief shall no more molest thee.[1]

August 1796. Sarah Osborn lies in her room, her breathing labored, and listens to a friend read the Bible aloud. In her eighty-two years she has often dreamed about dying and going to heaven, but now she knows that the time is near. Weak, swollen with edema, and out of breath, she seems to be suffering from congestive heart failure, a condition often linked to rheumatoid arthritis. Soon, she tells her friends, she will be *"going home."*[2]

Sarah has imagined heaven so many times that it is as real to her as the four walls of her room. At the moment of her death she expects her soul to float away from her body, free from the "clog" that has weighed it down, before she comes face to face with Jesus, her greatest desire. She has always loved him as her "dearest Lord," her bridegroom, her shield and fortress, and her covenant God, but now she will finally "see him as he is, Enjoy him as he is, Know as I am Known." In heaven there will be no more illness, no more mourning over sin, no more weeping over the loss of loved ones, and "no more trembling fears and doubts." There will be no more oppression and no more slavery. According to Joseph Stevens, one of her favorite authors, "There the Believer is freed from all the Miseries and Sorrows of this World. There all Tears are wiped away. There the Weary are at Rest, and the Wicked cease from troubling. There is no pricking Briar nor vexing Thorn: No Discontent, no Discord, no anxious Cares, or Fears."[3] Nothing but joy.

Sarah believes that she will bask in God's love until Judgment Day, when her resurrected body will join her soul in heaven. Her bliss at that moment will be deeper than she can imagine, the zenith of her existence. Instead of the frail, crippled body that has imprisoned her on earth, she will be given a new body like Christ's. After a lifetime of lamenting her pollution and corruption, she will finally be "clean," freed from "the intolerable burden, *sin!*" She will no longer be poor, but rich in God's grace; no longer broken, but whole; no longer empty, but overflowing with love. Her body will be "Immortal, Incorruptible, Spiritual, Strong, Vigorous and Beautiful; so as to shine in the perpetual and everlasting Bloom of Youth."[4] Rejoicing with the whole communion of saints, she will spend eternity gazing at God and swimming in the boundless ocean of his love.

This Body of Sin and Death

Sarah's lyrical description of the beatific vision (inspired by Paul's Second Letter to the Corinthians) sounds like something that could have been written by a medieval Christian or a Puritan, and she imagined heaven existing outside history—an "everlasting *now*" that transcended the boundaries of time and space. But even heaven has a history, and the eighteenth century marked a watershed in the way it was imagined. Under the pressures of the Enlightenment, the growth of a consumer economy, and revolutionary politics, many eighteenth-century Americans were beginning to develop new ideas about heaven or, in some cases, reviving older ones to make sense of their changing world. Rather than envisioning heaven as a place of rest and eternal contemplation, they hoped that it would be filled with progress, activity, knowledge, and friendship—heaven as a more perfect earth.

Even as evangelicals helped popularize this new idea of heaven, they remained ambivalent about its sanctification of everyday life. Despite their desire to live in a paradise in the next world, they never wanted to forget that their greatest happiness would come from worshiping a sovereign God. With her death drawing near, Sarah's dreams of heaven always returned to the joy of seeing him face to face, a hidden God made visible.

Sarah's life had been ebbing away slowly since the end of the Revolution, her world shrinking in on her with every passing year. Deprived of almost all her former enjoyments, she could no longer read the Bible on her own, and although she managed to write down a few of her poems, she lacked the stamina to meet with the women's society. She had always imagined her body as a "clog" and a "Lump of clay" weighing down her soul, but as her illness grew worse she may have felt as though her flesh and spirit were at war. Echoing the words of Paul, she longed to escape from "this body of sin and death that so betrays me and separates between my God and me."[5]

Sarah was too ill to care for herself during her last years, but she was surrounded by people who admired and loved her. Although Newport was a religiously diverse city, she lived in a predominantly evangelical neighborhood. According to the 1790 census (which seems to have been taken from door to door), Sarah lived next door to Susanna Anthony and in close proximity to several other female members of the First Church of Christ, including Elizabeth Melville, Lydia Bissell, and Mary Smith. Also in the neighborhood were her friends Elizabeth and Latham Clarke (whose house she had once shared) and Scipio Tanner, a free black who had probably attended her religious meetings in the 1760s.[6] (He had been a slave of Sarah's friend John Tanner before being freed in Tanner's will in 1785.)[7] With all these friends only a few steps away, Sarah knew that someone would always be available to cook or clean for her. Her friends were poor (even Samuel Hopkins could barely support himself), but they were willing to share the little they had.

Yet growing old meant coping with the loss of loved ones, and Sarah outlived many of her dearest friends. When Susa died in 1791 at the age of sixty-five, Sarah felt as though she had lost a member of her family, her sister in Christ. They had shared each other's lives for more than fifty years—praying together, rejoicing together, and comforting each other in times of grief—and their bond had grown stronger with time. In times of spiritual darkness each had felt as though she could see God in the other despite being blind to his presence in her own life. When Sarah learned that Samuel Hopkins had decided to publish a memoir of Susa's life along with extracts from her diaries, she may have hoped that Susa's example of self-sacrificing love would inspire others to seek Christ. Someday, she hoped, she and Susa would "have a joyful meeting at Christ's right hand."[8]

When Mrs. Mason died in 1792, Sarah lost not only another cherished friend but one of her most generous benefactors. Though poor herself, Mrs. Mason had helped pay for Sarah's food and rent, and her loss meant that Sarah had to rely on other friends for charity. The First Church may have given her money (it often gave alms to the "poor of the church"), and the Reverend Levi Hart of Connecticut, a close friend of Samuel Hopkins, frequently sent money as well—sometimes as much as three dollars at a time. (Sarah's rent was five dollars a quarter, so this was a significant sum to her.) Perhaps Sally and Daniel tried to help, too. Sarah may have been especially touched by the unexpected generosity of strangers who sent money from places as far away as Quebec and the West Indies, inspired by the story of her remarkable life. Their donations reminded her that she was part of a transatlantic religious movement whose boundaries extended far beyond Newport.[9]

Sarah had never been more vulnerable, but according to Hopkins she also had never been happier or more confident of God's protection. When friends worried about how she would pay her rent, she is reported to have replied, "I desire to be thankful to God, I do not feel in the least anxious about it. I do not doubt of my having the whole of the money at the time in which it will be due, or near it. God has given me a constant and earnest

THE
LIFE AND CHARACTER
OF
MISS SUSANNA ANTHONY,

WHO DIED, IN *NEWPORT*, (R. I.) JUNE 23, MDCCXCI,

IN THE SIXTY FIFTH YEAR OF HER AGE.

CONSISTING CHIEFLY IN

EXTRACTS FROM HER WRITINGS,

WITH SOME **BRIEF OBSERVATIONS** ON THEM.

COMPILED
BY SAMUEL HOPKINS, D. D.
PASTOR OF THE FIRST CONGREGATIONAL CHURCH IN *NEWPORT*.

PRINTED AT *WORCESTER*, MASSACHUSETTS,
BY LEONARD WORCESTER.
MDCCXCVI.

[37]

Title page of Samuel Hopkins, comp., *The Life and Character of Miss Susanna Anthony* (Worcester, Mass.: Leonard Worcester, 1796). Hopkins published extracts from Susanna Anthony's devotional diaries after her death. It is not clear whether Sarah Osborn was still alive when the book appeared in print. Courtesy of the American Antiquarian Society.

desire to do justice, and pay when any thing is due. This is a just debt, and God has been pleased hitherto to gratify me by enabling me to pay, when it is due; and I believe he will still continue to do it. Perhaps I shall not live to the end of the quarter. I shall then leave enough to pay this debt. I desire to leave it with God."[10]

Although this stilted language does not sound like Sarah's voice, it is easy to believe that the sentiment was hers. She had always prayed for greater trust in God, and now that she could do nothing for herself she had no choice but to resign herself to his will. According to Hopkins, "She appeared in this last part of her life in a measure to enjoy the happy consequences and reward, of the sore trials, labors and conflicts, through which she passed in former years." Giving her story a happy ending, he claimed that after many years of struggling against despair and yearning for a "hidden God," she finally had been blessed with the gift of serenity. "She enjoyed an almost uninterrupted assurance of her interest in the divine favor through Jesus Christ," he testified.[11]

This is a comforting vision of Sarah Osborn in her last years, and we can only hope that in its general outlines it was true. But there seem to have been darker episodes in her life as well, times when she felt so despondent that she wanted to die. "Some years before her death," according to Hopkins, "she said to her friends, she thought the time was now come for them, and for all who knew her, to be quite willing that she should leave the world; for she was become useless in all respects, and was only a charge and burden to those by whom her bodily wants were supplied."[12] Although Hopkins portrayed these words as a sign of her joyful desire to be united with God, her language suggests that she may have feared that her friends had grown tired of caring for her or, worse, that they no longer loved her. Poor, sick, and elderly, she worried that she had become "useless" and a "burden."

Sarah's friends insisted that her life still had value, and appealing to her desire to feel useful, they assured her that her prayers had touched the lives of others. Whenever her friends and acquaintances thought of her "alive in her room" and praying for "all the people and churches of Christ," they felt as though she were holding them up, strengthening them to face their doubts and sorrows.[13] Her prayers were a beacon of hope pointing to a better world.

Yet as Sarah grew increasingly tired and weak, she dreamed less of serving Christ on earth and more of being united with him in heaven. After decades of struggling against illness, she longed to leave her sickly body behind in the grave. "Oh what a clog is this Poor crazy body," she lamented during one of the flare-ups of her disease. (In the eighteenth century, *crazy* was a synonym for *frail*.) "O blessed be God I shall Ere Long Shake off this clog."[14] Of all the books mentioned in her diaries, she especially admired Charles Drelincourt's treatise on death, with its vivid portrait of the body as a "loathsome sepulcher."[15]

Sarah's attitude toward her body was shaped not only by her own suffering but by a long history of Christian ambivalence toward the embodied self. Because of their belief that humans were created in the image of God, Christians saw the body as essentially good, and they emphasized that Jesus himself had taken human form. The resurrection would be physical as well as spiritual. Yet Christians also denigrated the body as an obstacle to the progress of the soul, and they portrayed it as the site of deadly temptations like lust, gluttony, and sloth.[16] According to the Puritans, the body was a "a manacle," "a snare," "a fetter," and a "*Shell*, which [would] soon be *broken*."[17]

Rejecting this dismal view, Enlightenment thinkers and liberal-leaning Protestants argued that the body (like the self) was essentially good. As they dismantled the doctrine of original sin, they emphasized that humans could enjoy the pleasures of the flesh as long as they refrained from overindulgence. According to John Tillotson, God had created humans with bodies as well as souls because he wanted his children to savor "Life and Happiness." By the middle of the eighteenth century, many liberal Protestants chose to highlight the New Testament's positive description of the body as the "temple of the Holy Ghost."[18]

In some ways evangelicals contributed to these more positive images of the body. Jonathan Edwards assumed that the born again would feel the change in their bodies as well as in their hearts, and by describing the conversion experience in sensual language as a new "taste" and a new "sight," he made it possible to imagine true religion as embodied. Despite arguing that the body had to be disciplined and purified through fasting, chastity, modest dress, and temperance, many evangelicals hoped that it could be an avenue to communion with God. Writing in her diary, Sarah Osborn assured God that "every room in my heart is thy own and my body is a temple for thy spirit to dwell in."[19]

Yet just as evangelicals resisted the growing faith in human goodness, they insisted that the body was "filthy" unless it had been transformed by divine grace. As Edwards explained, "The inside of the body of man is full of filthiness, [and] contains his bowels that are full of dung, which represents the corruption and filthiness that the heart of man is naturally full of." Describing the body as "a dark covering to the soul," evangelicals claimed that its "animal spirits" made it vulnerable to satanic temptation. According to Edwards, the devil "can't produce thoughts, in the soul immediately, or any other way, than by the medium of the body." Lamenting that Satan took advantage of her "bodily indisposition" to tempt her with feelings of anger or despair, Sarah Osborn denigrated the body as the "animal" part of the self, a "heavy molded . . . lump of flesh and blood" that dragged down the soul like a "dead weight." She and the women's society fasted at least once a month in order to "crucify the flesh with its affections and lusts."[20]

Ministers encouraged all their members, even children, to discipline their bodies, but their language suggested that women's bodies were particularly sinful and weak. Thomas Shepard, a Puritan, referred to the body as a "menstruous cloth," and Peter Bulkeley argued that the damned "are to [God] as the filthiness of a menstruous woman." To defend the doctrine of original sin, Jonathan Edwards argued that men were inherently "unclean" because they were born of women.[21] Although women resisted these negative images, they could not help being influenced by them. Besides comparing herself to the woman with the "bloody issue" who prayed to be made "clean," Sarah occasionally complained about suffering from "Hysteric disorders," a stereotypically "feminine" affliction. It is not clear whether she believed that her hysteria was caused by a wandering womb (the traditional interpretation) or by an affliction of the central nervous system (the interpretation that eventually gained acceptance in the eighteenth century), but in either case she claimed that her weak body was responsible for her psychological distress, or in her words, her "Melancholy Gloom." Being female meant being prone to "hysteria."[22]

When Sarah imagined her death she rejoiced at the thought of leaving behind both her body and her gender in union with Christ. At first she would exist only as a spirit, but after the resurrection she would be given a new, perfect body that would never tire or decay. Though heaven would be a place of overflowing love, there would be no courtship, marriage, or sexual desire to interfere with the worship of God.[23] Ministers never seem to have speculated on the sexual appearance of resurrected bodies, but perhaps the question was moot. Since there would be no gender differences in heaven, it mattered little whether the saints would be recognizably male or female.

Sarah had often prayed to become more like God, to be transformed into his image. "I am weary of my deformity," she confessed in her diary.

"When shall [I] be Like thee?"[24] In heaven, at last, she hoped to be granted the answer to her prayer.

A Better Earth

Since Sarah wrote so little during the last twenty years of her life, we do not know whether her ideas about heaven changed in her old age, but it is clear that in her earlier years she had absorbed new images of heaven as the perfection of everyday life. Influenced by the Enlightenment, the American Revolution, and the rise of merchant capitalism and consumerism, many Protestants no longer hoped to spend eternity in divine contemplation; rather, they envisioned engaging in the activities that had given them the most joy during their lives. During the eighteenth century they gradually created a new understanding of heaven as a better earth, a paradise where humans would continue to work, make progress, advance in knowledge, and spend time with their loved ones.[25]

When it came to the topic of heaven, the Enlightenment tended to be rather tame. Although a few radical Enlightenment thinkers denied the existence of the soul and the reality of heaven and hell, most continued to defend the idea of an afterlife.[26] Whatever doubts they harbored about Christianity, they feared that people would not behave morally unless they believed in a day of judgment. According to John Locke, ancient teachings about virtue had fallen on deaf ears until Christians had promised that good works would be rewarded with eternal life. Even Benjamin Franklin, who was frankly skeptical about Jesus's divinity, claimed that "the soul of Man is immortal, and will be treated with justice in another life respecting its conduct in this." The Constitution prohibited religious tests for political office on the federal level, but many states required political officials to believe in a "future state of rewards and punishments."[27] In a new nation that depended on a virtuous citizenry, believing in heaven and hell had never seemed more important.

Yet even though the Enlightenment did not undermine belief in the reality of heaven, it influenced the kind of heaven that people imagined. As Enlightenment thinkers insisted that humans were essentially good and that progress was possible, they blurred the boundaries between heaven and earth. Earlier Christians had imagined heaven as the opposite of earth—a place of rest instead of activity, contemplation instead of work, fulfillment in God instead of in other human beings. But eighteenth-century Protestants began to reconsider these dichotomies. If everyday life were valuable and held religious meaning, then perhaps its best features would look like heaven.

For most of Christian history, people had assumed that they would spend eternity joyfully gazing at God. Medieval artists portrayed the saints sitting in chairs around God's throne and admiring his majesty; the Protestant Reformers hoped to spend eternity enjoying the beatific vision of God. Even though Calvin and Luther argued that humans should work hard at their callings instead of withdrawing from the world into monasteries, they did not challenge the Catholic understanding of heaven as a place of eternal contemplation. In the long term, however, their emphasis on the value of work set the stage for a new understanding of the afterlife. This change came about gradually, but when Enlightenment philosophers argued that humans should always strive for improvement, many Protestants—both liberal and evangelical—decided that since work was intrinsically good, it would continue to exist in heaven. "The happiness of the redeemed in heaven will not consist in rest and indolence," Samuel Hopkins insisted, "but the contrary; in activity, and incessant, unwearying labor and service, from which they will not cease or rest." Although John Murray, the founder of Universalism, disagreed with Hopkins on almost everything, he, too, claimed that even though "the spirits of believers, at death, are said to have entered into rest," they never stopped exerting themselves. "No, they only rest from their *labors*—labors that gave pain—weariness—or grief—With respect to vitality and all its exercises, the souls born into the world of glory, may be said only then to begin to live. They do then spring to action with a vigor and alacrity hitherto unknown."[28] The more Protestants prided themselves on their industriousness, the more they resisted the idea of a contemplative heaven.

The crux of the issue seems to have been happiness. Rejecting the idea that heaven would "consist in a perpetual gazing upon God, and in idle contemplation of the glories of that place," John Tillotson assured his readers that God did not expect the saints to sit passively and adore him. "We need not doubt, but that he who is happiness itself, and hath promised to make us happy, can easily find out such employments and delights for us in the other world, as will be proper and suitable to that state." As Isaac Watts admitted, he could not imagine that saints could enjoy heaven if they had nothing to do. "I confess *Heaven* is described as a Place of *Rest*, but it can never be such a *Rest* as lays all our active Powers asleep, or renders them useless in such a vital and active World. It would diminish the Happiness of the Saints in Glory to be unemployed there."[29] As we have seen, evangelicals were ambivalent about the liberal, enlightened emphasis on happiness, but whether emphasizing the goodness of suffering or the earthly delights of heaven, they also echoed it.

Most ministers were vague about how saints would be "employed," but because of their belief that there would be degrees of glory in heaven, they imagined that the most exalted souls would work on behalf of those below them. Isaac Watts, for example, wondered whether the holiest might rule as "kings" over others. Later in the nineteenth century this medieval, hierarchical view of heaven would fade from view, an offense to the democratic sensibilities of the modern West, but it remained popular in the eighteenth century.[30] Like both Thomas Aquinas and John Calvin, Jonathan Edwards expected some of the redeemed to enjoy a fuller vision of God than others, and in case anyone worried about feelings of competition or resentment, he insisted that "the exaltation of some in glory above others, will be so far from diminishing anything of the perfect happiness and joy of the rest that are inferior, that they will be the happier for it. Such will be the union of all of them, that they will be partaker of each other's glory and happiness." Drawing on these ideas, Samuel Hopkins wondered whether some of the redeemed might serve as "public teachers" helping their inferiors attain greater degrees of glory.[31] Even in heaven, Christians would continue to spread the gospel.

Both liberals and evangelicals believed that there would be a hierarchy in heaven, but they disagreed over the reasons why. According to liberal ministers, the most virtuous would be rewarded for their good works on earth. "*Their works follow them*," explained the Reverend Samuel Webster. God would grant them greater glory "according to the degree of their virtue and goodness."[32] In contrast, evangelicals insisted that good works were worthless, and some would be more glorified than others only because of God's sovereign will.

Sarah Osborn never speculated about the place she would occupy in heaven (though she always longed for "greater degrees of grace" on earth), but she expected to be "all activity and all reverence and Love in the realms above." Because her illness sapped her energy, sometimes leaving her too exhausted to get out of bed, she dreamed of a time when she would be "forever active." Besides longing to praise, adore, and gaze at God without ever growing weary, she also imagined flying to "execute his commands," as if there might be specific tasks that he would ask her to perform.[33] According to Isaac Watts, the saints would be engaged in labor beyond "*mere Adoration and Praise*," including speaking to one another about their pilgrimages, traveling to other planets, and executing God's commissions. While John

Murray wondered whether God might send the saints on "beneficent errands" to Christians on earth, ministering to those whom they had left behind, Sarah Osborn expected to "work for eternity."[34]

The more heaven looked like earth, the more the boundaries between the two seemed to dissolve. Earlier generations of Protestants had assumed that the dead were so entranced by the heavenly vision that they had no desire to look back toward the scene of their suffering and sorrows, but many eighteenth-century ministers speculated that the saints took a keen interest in events on earth. According to Jonathan Edwards, Moses and other biblical heroes enjoyed watching "the progressive wonderful doings of God with respect to his church here in this world. . . . The church in heaven and the church on earth are more one people, one city and one family than generally is imagined." Elaborating on this point, Samuel Hopkins claimed that the saints had "a very particular knowledge of the events which take place in this world, and a much more clear and certain knowledge of the state of the church of Christ, and the conversion of sinners, than any have while in the body." As they waited for Judgment Day, the saints eagerly watched the unfolding of God's providence on earth.[35] Each day brought more glimmers of progress.

Indeed, heaven itself was imagined as a place of progress. In the past most Christians had taught that souls would attain even greater joy after being reunited with their bodies, but the resurrection would be the ultimate fulfillment of history, "the complete and total consummation of all." As a Puritan minister explained, "This is the highest pitch, that they can arrive at." To suggest otherwise was to imply that heaven was imperfect and needed improvement.[36] Yet Enlightenment thinkers like G. W. Leibniz were troubled by this static view of heaven, and it conflicted with the exhilarating faith in human progress that inspired technological advances, capitalist exchange, and revolutionary politics.[37] Over the course of the eighteenth century many ministers concluded that God would lead saints to infinitely greater joys. Although acknowledging that his view sounded unorthodox, John Tillotson insisted that heavenly perfection would continually increase, and Cotton Mather claimed that "the *Knowledge* of GOD will be *Eternally Progressive*." In a treatise on "natural religion," Gad Hitchcock argued that "the most rational and consistent notion we can form of the condition of good men in heaven is, that of continual advances in knowledge and holiness, approaching towards the Deity, and perfecting their image of him." According to Jonathan Edwards, the saints had an endlessly increasing capacity for love and delight. "As they increase in the knowledge of God and of the works of God," he wrote in his private note-book, "the more they will see of his excellency; and the more they see of his excellency . . . the more they will love him; and the more they love God, the more delight and happiness . . . will they have in him." In a remark-able departure from traditional doctrine, Edwards imagined that even *God* would make progress: he would grow in glory as humans grew in their love for him, binding them together in a reciprocal relationship that would yield greater and greater joy.[38]

Because they associated progress with knowledge, many Protestants imagined heaven as the place where their questions about God would fi-nally be answered. Without claiming that she would attain perfect knowl-edge of God, Sarah Osborn imagined heaven as the place where she would come to a deeper comprehension of how he had directed her life. "I shall see thee as thou art," she rejoiced in her diary. "Then, Lord, shall I be satis-fied, when I have the open vision, and full fruition of my God." After the death of Joseph Fish's daughter, she speculated that "our dear departed now knows the Meaning, to Her unspeakable Joy, of Many a thing she could not Here understand."[39]

In most of her writings Sarah imagined gazing at God in a timeless, unchanging state of bliss, but there are hints that she may have expected a heaven of eternal progress. In one of her descriptions of seeing God face to face, she imagined him promising that in the "boundless ocean" of his love, "thy delights shall be forever new." She would experience new joys each time she plunged into his depths, floating in an ocean of love without a shore. "All here is concord; all at peace," she wrote in a poem, "And hap-piness does still increase."[40]

As envisioned in the eighteenth century, heaven would be always new and always changing. What earlier generations seem to have most prized about heaven—its timelessness—no longer seemed as appealing. Because eighteenth-century Americans lived in a world of technological, scientific, and political innovation, many seem to have found it hard to imagine a heaven where each and every day would be the same. "There will be *new* glories to be seen in GOD to all eternity," John Murray exclaimed. "Thus the wine in our Father's kingdom is ever *new*—and *new* songs shall cel-ebrate the Giver's praise to endless ages."[41]

Of all the eighteenth-century Protestants who imagined heaven as a better earth, Charles Chauncy was the most bold. In a sermon titled *The Earth Delivered*, he argued that the "new heavens and new earth" described in Revelation would be "*this world of ours* brought back to its *paradisaick* state, or one that is better; and that the *very world we now live in*, thus changed and made new, is the place, where good men, after the resurrection, and judgment, shall live and reign with Christ forever." Although God had cursed the earth after Adam and Eve's sin in the Garden of Eden, he would restore the world to its original perfection—or make it even more glorious—after Christ's return. If Christians wanted to know what heaven would be like, they should imagine it as "the *present*" without "all the inconveniences and evils, the *curse* has subjected it to." Although Chauncy's ideas never seem to have become popular, they reflected a growing desire to collapse the boundaries between heaven and earth.[42]

The Communion of Saints

Evangelicals helped create the image of heaven as an earthly paradise, but they insisted that their happiness would come first and foremost from gazing at God. Torn between their desire to see their loved ones again and their fear of idolatry, they were especially ambivalent about imagining heaven as a place where families and friends would be reunited.

Christians had always assumed that they would spend eternity with a generalized "communion of saints"—the apostles, the martyrs, and all the ordinary believers who had devoted their lives to God—but in the eighteenth century they increasingly looked forward to being reunited with their lost loved ones. This was not a new idea (it had been popular in early Roman Christianity and during the Renaissance), but the Protestant Reformers had insisted that the joy of seeing departed family members and friends was only a pale shadow of the joy of seeing the almighty God. Without completely rejecting the image of heaven as a new home (Calvin expected to see Luther there), they worried about its exclusiveness and this-worldliness, and they argued that a person could be supremely happy in heaven even if completely alone with God. As Calvin explained, "If God contains the fullness of all good things in himself like an inexhaustible fountain, nothing beyond him is to be sought by those who strive after the highest good and all the elements of happiness." Echoing medieval ideas, Calvin imagined that the greatest joy of heaven would be the beatific vision of God, the eternal delight of gazing at Christ. As he explained, "Nothing is more desirable for the consummation of our happiness, than that we should behold the serene countenance of God."[43]

Puritans shared this Christocentric view of heaven, and although they assumed that they would see their loved ones among the communion of

saints, they particularly emphasized their desire to see Christ "face to face."
(The apostle Paul had written, "For now we see through a glass, darkly; but
then face to face: now I know in part; but then shall I know even as also
I am known.") In his popular *The Saints Everlasting Rest*, Richard Baxter
warned that "we must be careful not to look for that in the saints which is
alone in Christ," and in his *Meditations on Death*, Increase Mather barely
mentioned reunions with loved ones at all. "In Heaven the Infinitely Glorious GOD is to be Enjoyed," he proclaimed. "He is the Portion of his
Children and a greater Portion cannot be."[44]

During the eighteenth century, however, many Protestants revived the
Renaissance emphasis on the joy of heavenly reunions, imagining touching
scenes of loved ones coming together never to be parted again. Not surprisingly, liberals led the way. Influenced by Enlightenment ideas, they claimed
that God had created heaven—like earth—to make humans happy, and he
wanted them to spend eternity surrounded by family and friends. In a sermon comforting those who had lost "pious friends and relatives," Charles
Chauncy promised that their separation would be brief: "They are gone
to the very Place, we call our *Home*; to the very Place, whither we are has-
tening ourselves." When a grieving Simeon Howard preached his wife's
funeral sermon, he imagined that they would someday be joined in love
again, a reunion that would last for all eternity. Samuel Webster was so
passionate about portraying heaven as a better home that he cluttered his
sentences with exclamation points, a style that made his sermon sound like
a sentimental novel: "O how often are we called to mourning in this dying
world! But happy saints who have got to heaven! They shall no more be
afflicted with such sorrowful bereavements! For Oh, there all are immortal!
Nor shall any of their dear friends ever be parted from them more! But as
fast as they come there, abide with them, and are parted from them no
more forever!"[45]

This vision of heaven was based on the implicit assumption that something akin to individual identity would persist even in the afterlife. Even
though most Protestants denied that sexual difference would endure in
heaven, they still imagined that the resurrected saints would be recognizably themselves. This idea was not new, but at a time when Americans
defended the right of sovereign individuals to choose their own government and pursue their own economic interests, it became more important.
Influenced by the nascent individualism of the Enlightenment, both liberals and evangelicals emphasized that selfhood would not be lost in heaven;
rather, it would be made perfect. Since liberals saw the self as essentially

good, they thought it would endure for eternity. And since evangelicals believed that the foundation of Christianity was a personal experience of divine grace, they assumed that the born-again self would last forever. As Jonathan Edwards explained, the saints would never forget "what passed in their life upon earth."[46]

Evangelicals usually criticized liberals for caring too much about human happiness, but they, too, were drawn to the hope of seeing lost loved ones in heaven. Elizabeth Rowe, one of Sarah Osborn's favorite authors, published a best-selling book, *Friendship in Death*, which portrayed families and friends meeting again in heaven, including a man who was greeted by his beloved wife in a dazzling sapphire and gold "Chariot."[47] Osborn's poem on heaven included the verse, "Though bonds of nature now do cease,/Our happiness it does increase,/To see our godly parents here,/And relatives to Christ most dear." Often she imagined heaven as her "home," as if heaven would be something like the house where she and other Christians had once met to worship God.[48]

Evangelicals looked forward to loving one another in heaven with a freedom that they had never enjoyed on earth. The sinfulness that had divided them—the backbiting, selfishness, and greed—would be washed away by Christ's atoning blood, and the schisms that had rent Christ's body would finally be healed. Devoted to serving God, they would no longer fear loving one another as idols in competition with him. Sarah Osborn imagined God as promising that her friends would never "ensnare" her, "even as *they* were wont to do. They shall never turn off thy eyes from me."[49]

In her poem on heaven, Osborn envisioned it as a loving community that would spend eternity adoring God with her. Besides being reunited with her "dear companions," "godly parents," and "relatives," she hoped to see many others whose salvation seemed less sure, including Africans, Jews, and "the charming infant race." Many of them would be brought to heaven through God's "rich and sovereign grace."[50]

Yet evangelicals also insisted that Christians must confront the terrible possibility that they might not see all their loved ones in heaven—a burden Sarah had carried ever since her son's death. Liberal-leaning Protestants assumed that most people would be saved if they tried to live virtuously, and two of the most prominent liberals, Charles Chauncy and John Murray, argued that *everyone* would eventually be saved. (Chauncy insisted that sinners would be punished before being admitted into heaven, but he and Murray both preached universal salvation.)[51] In contrast, evangelicals insisted that one of the pleasures of heaven would be gazing into hell, a

spectacle that would reveal God's almighty power. Although Enlightenment thinkers rejected this teaching as cruel and even sadistic, it had deep
roots stretching back to the first centuries of Christian history. In a sermon
delivered to children, Edwards warned that even their own parents would
rejoice at the sight of their damnation: "When they shall behold you with a
frightened, amazed countenance, trembling and astonished, and shall hear
you groan and gnash your teeth; these things will not move them at all to
pity you, but you will see them with a holy joyfulness in their countenances,
and with songs in their mouths."[52]

Since Sarah rarely wrote about hell, it is not clear whether she shared
the belief that the saints would take pleasure in the sufferings of the damned.
By the 1770s and 1780s this idea had begun to fade from view, an affront
to humanitarian sympathies. Yet evangelicals continued to insist that the
point of heaven was to glorify God, and Sarah argued that heaven was only
heaven because God was there. One of her favorite psalms was "Whom
have I in heaven but thee? and there is none upon earth that I desire beside
thee." Just as she had once turned her eyes away from her dead son and toward Christ, she refused to meditate for too long on the prospect of seeing
loved ones in heaven, focusing instead on God alone. Perhaps to remind
herself of the true source of happiness, she asked in her diary, "What is the
Hope of Enjoying departed friends or angels compared with the Enjoy-
ment of the Ever blessed God?" Isaac Watts gently reminded his readers
that their love for one another must always be rooted in their greater love
for God: "God, who is the first Cause, must be the last End of all, and no
Creatures, as divided from him, can make us either holy or happy."[53]

More than anything else, Sarah Osborn longed to see God "face to
face," to gaze at his "matchless beauty" forever. Like other evangelicals,
she echoed medieval language by imagining that the greatest joy of heaven
would be the "open vision," the "full fruition" of God. Gilbert Tennent
promised that every redeemed soul would "*see God as he is, face to face*," and
the Reverend Aaron Burr imagined that "the beatific Vision of *Jehovah*,
shall transport their Souls, and fill them with ineffable Ecstasy."[54] In a diary entry addressed directly to God, Sarah wrote, "O Lord, hasten the time
when I shall enjoy thee, behold thy glory, see thee as thou art, when all
veils and walls of separation shall be forever broken down, and I shall gaze,
adore and praise, as glorified saints and angels do." Once he was no longer
hidden, she would never turn away from his "Lovely Glorious face."[55]

If Sarah ever dared hope that she would be reunited with her two beloved Samuels, father and son, she may have tried to discipline her emo-

tions. She knew that not everyone would be saved, and to die was to leave behind the flawed relationships of a fallen world for something far better: Christ's perfect, eternal love. Although she hoped to see the "charming infant race" in heaven, Samuel had not been an infant when he died, and we do not know whether she ever overcame her fear that his "naked soul" had been launched "into a boundless eternity, without a God to go to." Losing him seems to have been the greatest sorrow of her life.[56]

Despite her passionate love for her family and her friends, Sarah had always told herself that nothing mattered except God. Other people were only "creatures," and "Creatures are Empty broken cisterns." As she assured God, "Tis thou, thou fountain of all felicity, that art able to fill my soul."[57]

A Life of Wonders

Sarah had spent most of her life meditating on the joys of dying in Christ, but as the time of her death drew nearer she could not keep herself from feeling a twinge of fear. Though assuring her friends that she had "no reason to be apprehensive for the future state," she was afraid of dishonoring God by complaining or questioning his goodness. In some of her final words to her friends, she is reported to have said, "The trials of my situation are great; to be in want of breath, is very distressing; pray for me, that I may have patience and resignation: I desire them above all things. O pray for me that, in these last hours of my life, I may not cause you all to blush that I have professed Christianity."[58] She wanted her death, like her life, to demonstrate her trust in God.

In the past Sarah had tried to blunt the hard edge of her fear by forcing herself to meditate on the physical reality of death, the wasting away of her body in its last hours and minutes. In a graphic passage in her diary she asked, "What though my eye strings crack, my blood chill, hands, feet and all grow cold, and all nature is convulsed and distressed, while the soul is breaking loose: Is this to be compared to the body of sin and death, under which I groan; but shall then be delivered from, and bid a final adieu to forever!"[59] Although it was terrifying to imagine her body decaying, she thought it was better to confront her death openly than to pretend, like Newport's foolish sinners, that "the king of terrors" would never knock on her door.

Sarah's meditations on death always ended with the comforting thought that Jesus would be waiting for her on the other side of the grave, his arms open to embrace her. Leaving behind all of her "trials," sorrows and sins, she would finally be with her savior. "The day of one's death [is better] than the day of one's birth," she reminded herself, quoting from Ecclesiastes. Often she reflected on the comforting words of Psalm 23: "Yea, though I walk through the valley of the shadow of death, I will fear no evil: for thou art with me; thy rod and thy staff they comfort me."[60]

Sarah Osborn died on August 2, 1796, alone in her room. Her friends had been keeping watch over her, but after leaving for a few minutes to let her sleep, they returned to find that her breathing had stopped. It was the kind of death she had always wanted: "calm and serene, without the least perceivable struggle or groan." As was the tradition in early America, the church bell rang to commemorate her passing: six strokes as a sign that she had been a woman, and then another eighty-two for each year of her age.[61]

Two days later "an uncommon concourse of people" gathered at her funeral to say good-bye. As her coffin lay in the meetinghouse, Samuel Hopkins preached on a text from Ephesians: "I therefore, the prisoner of the Lord, beseech you, that ye walk worthy of the vocation wherewith ye are called." He could not have chosen a better epitaph for someone who had always tried to live a life worthy of Christ. To comfort the crowd of "truly Afflicted Acquaintance and Friends," he reminded them that she had finally attained her heart's desire: "We cannot doubt that she has gone to REST: that she has gone to that State where her Heart has long been: that she has gone to the Possession of those Objects on which her Affections have long been placed—that she has gone to JESUS CHRIST, and the General Assembly and Church of the First Born which are written in Heaven."[62]

In a will that Sarah made two years before her death, she directed that her possessions be sold and the money put out to interest. (She also mentioned setting aside a few items, presumably for her friends and family, but the "papers" to which she referred no longer exist.) Always charitable, she wanted the interest to be divided in half to support the poor of the First Church and the pastor, but there was hardly enough money to pay her last debts and her funeral expenses. She had a few small things of value, but most of her possessions were described as "old": an old maple desk, old kitchen chairs, two old Windsor Chairs ("1 of them very much broken"), an old feather Bed, three old pillowcases, an old fire screen, an old brush, two old combs, old knives and forks, an old candle stand, an old shovel, an old tea table, old blankets, an old coffee mill, an old gown, "a parcel of Old

Trumpery." She had less than a dollar in cash, and the total value of her estate was $44.61. Though better off than many of Newport's poor, she had less money at her death than some of the slaves and free blacks who had once attended her religious meetings. When her neighbor Scipio Tanner died in 1819, his estate was valued at $59.15.[63]

Sarah bequeathed her most cherished possessions, her diaries and other manuscripts, to Samuel Hopkins with instructions to use them as he wished.[64] Since Hopkins had already edited Susanna Anthony's devotional diaries for publication, she probably hoped that he would publish hers as well. Despite her fear of appearing proud, she had always hoped that future generations of Christians would be inspired by her words, and nothing in her last years may have given her more satisfaction than imagining her story in print. By the end of her life she could barely see her own writings anymore, but her friends may have read passages aloud to her, and perhaps for the sake of her future readers she decided to add a few words to the last page of her 1743 memoir. In large handwriting that resembles that in her will (the result of her poor eyesight), she summed up the story of her life: "My Life has been a Life of Wonders, but the greatest wonder is that I am out of Hell."[65]

Like many of the great men of her time, Sarah Osborn hoped that her life would be celebrated by posterity—but with a crucial difference. Radical Enlightenment thinkers placed a high value on historical memory because of their conviction that it was the only path to immortality. According to Denis Diderot, for example, there was no such thing as the soul, and people could live forever only if they were remembered by future generations. In contrast, Sarah believed that no one would ever be forgotten, no matter how obscure he or she had been on earth. A merciful God would remember every detail of their lives for eternity. "Not a single tear or Groan will be Lost," she testified in her diary. "They are all in the book of the Lord."[66] Sarah hoped her words would inspire people to seek Christ and to trust him in times of doubt, but if her name were wiped off the face of the earth, her story would still endure. Books made of paper and ink could be destroyed, but the "book of the Lord" would last forever.

Sarah could not be sure what waited for her on the other side of death, but whether heaven turned out to be a place of contemplation, progress, or joyful reunions, she expected to delight in the open vision of God. Quoting from Job, she wrote, "I know that my Redeemer liveth, and though after my skin worms destroy this body, yet in my flesh shall I see God." Overjoyed by the thought of the revelation to come, she exulted, "O transporting thought! O glorious resurrection! Then I shall gaze to eternity. Then I shall drink my fill. Then I shall be like him, for I shall see him as he is."[67]

Heaven would finish the work that had begun with her conversion, the creation of a new self.

Epilogue: A Protestant Saint

Precious in the sight of the Lord is the death of his saints.

Psalm 116:15

Protestants have never believed in saints in the same way Catholics do. During the Protestant Reformation, Martin Luther and John Calvin condemned the Catholic belief in saints as idolatry, insisting that only God was worthy of veneration. Even the holiest people in history could not intercede with God or perform miracles after death. All God's chosen people were "saints," members of God's heavenly kingdom.

But when the Reverend Levi Hart, one of Sarah Osborn's most generous supporters, heard the news of her death in August 1796, he wrote a letter to Samuel Hopkins asking whether it were possible for the dead to pray for the living. Since the letter no longer survives, we do not know whether he mentioned Osborn by name, but based on Hopkins's response he seems to have wondered whether she still prayed for her friends now that she was in heaven: whether she could stand as an intercessor between heaven and earth. Although he must have known that he was venturing into dangerous territory, Sarah had been such an extraordinary woman that he could not help feeling that she might have an exalted relationship to God.[1]

Not surprisingly, Hopkins was offended by Hart's "papist" speculation. He explained that since the dead were completely happy in the presence of God, they had nothing left to pray for. But perhaps he understood the impulse behind Hart's question. He, too, had been awed by Sarah's faith, and in the years after her death he did more than anyone else to elevate her as an icon of evangelical piety. He considered her a saint in the Protestant sense of the term, as a true Christian who had devoted her life to God. Only a month after her death, he published "Sketch of the Character of Mrs. Sarah

FAMILIAR LETTERS,

WRITTEN BY

Mrs. SARAH OSBORN,

AND

Miss SUSANNA ANTHONY,

LATE OF NEWPORT,

RHODE-ISLAND.

PUBLISHED ACCORDING TO ACT OF CONGRESS.

NEWPORT, (R. I.) PRINTED AT THE OFFICE OF
THE NEWPORT MERCURY.
1807.

The title page of *Familiar Letters, Written by Mrs. Sarah Osborn, and Miss Susanna Anthony, Late of Newport, Rhode-Island* (Newport: Newport Mercury, 1807). Courtesy of the American Antiquarian Society.

Osborn" in the *Theological Magazine*, and with Hart's help he chose parts of her memoir and diaries to publish as *Memoirs of the Life of Mrs. Sarah Osborn* in 1799. (The publisher printed a thousand copies; a second edition was published in 1814.) After Hopkins's death, his wife, Elizabeth, continued his work by publishing *Familiar Letters, Written by Mrs. Sarah Osborn, and Miss Susanna Anthony, Late of Newport, Rhode-Island.* Though we do not know how widely Osborn's writings were read, they were reprinted in several evangelical journals in the early nineteenth century.[2]

Sarah Osborn was particularly remembered by the women of the First Church of Christ, who changed the name of the Female Praying Society to the Osborn Society in 1826, and by the Africans who had once attended the religious meetings at her house. She had always dreamed that some of them would return to Africa to spread the gospel, and in 1826 Newport Gardner and thirty-five other blacks (twenty from Newport) finally set sail for Liberia. On the day before his departure, Gardner wrote a letter to the deacon of the First Church remembering how Osborn, Susanna Anthony, and the Reverend Hopkins had once helped him. Even though all three had been dead for more than twenty years, he had always treasured their memories. Tragically, it was one of the last letters he would ever write: he died soon after arriving in Liberia.[3]

When another wave of revivals swept through the nation during the 1820s and 1830s, evangelicals looked back in their history for inspiration, and some seem to have read and admired Osborn's writings. The Reverend Gardiner Spring published an article on "Christian Sanctification" in 1834 in which he referred to Sarah Osborn and Susanna Anthony as though they were religious heroes. "When we advert to the names of David and Paul," he wrote, "of [John] Owens and [John] Howe, of [Richard] Baxter and [Henry] Martyn, of Susanna Anthony and Sarah Osborn, whose light will shine through a long line of succeeding generations; we may no longer feel that the sons and daughters of Adam may not become splendid examples of moral excellence."[4]

Nineteenth-century evangelicals shared much in common with Sarah Osborn, and words such as *experience, certainty, proof,* and *evidence* were a common part of the evangelical vocabulary. Methodists held experience meetings; Baptists preached experimental religion; and clergy from many denominations confidently proclaimed that true Christians could be virtually sure of their salvation. Given the widespread popularity of this language among men as well as women, it would be an exaggeration to suggest that it was gendered, but it strongly appealed to those who were excluded from formal positions of power, whether white women, lower-class men, or male and female slaves.

Yet Sarah had been a Calvinist, and by the 1830s her style of evangelicalism had been eclipsed by a new faith in good works and free will. The British evangelical movement had always included an Arminian wing associated with Charles and John Wesley, and these "Methodists," as they called themselves, became enormously popular in nineteenth-century America. Although there were only three hundred Methodists in the colonies in 1771, their numbers had exploded to two hundred thousand by 1816. By 1850 they were the single largest Protestant denomination in the United States.[5]

The Methodists' message of free will was ideally suited to the new world of nineteenth-century America, and in hindsight the decline of Calvinism seems almost inevitable. As the changes that had begun in the eighteenth century accelerated after the Revolution, many Americans found it increasingly difficult to accept that they were either innately sinful or helpless to determine their own destinies. Not only had they defeated the British, the most powerful empire in the world, on the bloodstained battlefields of Saratoga and Yorktown, but they had created a republican system of government based on the premise that ordinary people were virtuous enough to govern themselves—an idea that undermined older teachings about human depravity. After the Revolution they also laid the groundwork for a capitalist economy that generated immense new wealth. Even more than the consumer revolution and merchant capitalism, the rise of industrial capitalism was built on an implicit model of the individual as free and self-determining.

In response to these challenges, Calvinists continued to search for creative ways to reconcile their beliefs with Enlightenment thought. Building on the innovations of Samuel Hopkins and other New Divinity ministers, they softened the doctrine of original sin by claiming that all people were born with an innate moral sense. Though this was a startling reversal of their earlier thinking, they needed to find a new foundation for social order in a democratic culture that celebrated religious freedom and capitalist accumulation. If it were true that everyone had the capacity to behave virtuously, then no one need worry about the future of the republic.[6] Leaving behind their suspicion of both democracy and capitalism, evangelicals became vocal supporters of a new economic and political order based on freedom, self-interest, and choice. During the twentieth century they would even try to rewrite history by claiming Jonathan Edwards as a supporter of free market capitalism.[7]

In another departure from the past, Calvinists gradually shifted their emphasis away from God's glory to human happiness. Without renouncing the idea that suffering was redemptive, they softened their language in order to focus on God's compassion for the afflicted rather than his anger at their sinfulness. Similarly, even though doctrines like predestination and eternal damnation did not disappear, ministers clamed that a loving, benevolent God wanted everyone to be saved. If sinners went to hell, it was because of their own refusal to seek God's forgiveness.

By the end of the nineteenth century Sarah Osborn seemed like an anachronism, a relic of an evangelical past that few wanted to remember. The same qualities that had made her such an admirable figure during her lifetime—her denial of free will, her acceptance of suffering as a positive good, her emphasis on human depravity, her intense self-abasement— struck later evangelicals as extreme. When a member of the First Church wrote a history of the congregation in 1891, he praised Osborn for her activism in the church, especially her meetings for Africans, but he denigrated her piety as "morbid."[8]

A few women's historians tried to recover Sarah Osborn's memory during the 1970s and 1980s, but they, too, seemed ambivalent about her religion. A literary critic complained that her moments of doubt had been linked to "hysterics and excessive agitation," disparaging her collected writings as "sentimental," "moralistic," and "replete with tear-stained emotion." The historian Mary Beth Norton was more sympathetic, and she helped lift Osborn's name out of obscurity by transcribing and publishing several of her letters to Joseph Fish. But she seems to have been influenced by Betty Friedan's *The Feminine Mystique*, the revolutionary book that chronicled the unhappiness of 1960s suburban housewives, and she portrayed Osborn as a restless, discontented woman who was driven less by faith than by a desire for personal authority and "freedom." Reflecting on Osborn's description of her meetings with Africans as "sweet refreshing evenings, my resting reaping times," Norton commented, "Behind these words one can discern a lifetime of drudgery, dutiful wifely submission, and feminine inconsequentiality suddenly transformed by God's miraculous will into a life of leadership, purpose, and social importance." According to Norton, Sarah Osborn understood her meetings "in terms more personal than spiritual."[9] Whether this interpretation holds a grain of truth (Sarah herself would have found it condescending), it reveals the distance between Sarah Osborn's world and ours. In the wake of the Enlightenment we may find it easier to dismiss her faith as "morbid," "sentimental," or a repressed desire for freedom than to appreciate her desire to glorify God.

Sarah Osborn's story reveals how deeply the Christian tradition was shaped by the forces of modernity. Even when religious leaders tried to reject the Enlightenment, they implicitly defined themselves in relationship to it, allowing Enlightenment thinkers to set the terms of the debate. The evangelical movement is often portrayed as backward looking, but there was no religion in the Western world—including Catholicism and Judaism—that remained unaffected by the Enlightenment language of freedom, progress, and human goodness.

If Sarah could have foreseen the transformation of evangelicalism in the nineteenth century, she almost certainly would have condemned it as a decline, a rejection of the principles that had stood at the center of her life. Yet as we think about the relationship between the evangelical movement and the Enlightenment, our own reaction might be less clear-cut. Different readers will find their own meanings in Sarah's story, but during the many years that I have spent reading her manuscripts, I have often reflected on the way her faith burdened as well as uplifted her. Though I have come to a deeper appreciation of what was lost when Christianity encountered the Enlightenment, I have also recognized what was gained.

The Enlightenment used to be imagined as one of the greatest triumphs of human history, an intellectual revolution that swept away the cobwebs of the past in favor of democracy, humanitarianism, religious toleration, and capitalism. But in recent years critics have been far more cynical about its legacy. Liberals have argued that the Enlightenment commitment to "universal" rights was based on a white, European, and male model of humanity that stigmatized women, racial minorities, and the "uncivilized" as irrational. Despite its rhetoric of freedom, the Enlightenment laid the groundwork for Western totalitarianism, sexism, imperialism, and racism. Conservatives, meanwhile, have argued that it led to secularization and the silencing of religion in the public sphere. By imagining the universe in mechanistic terms, Enlightenment thinkers made it seem naive to believe in a sovereign, personal God who sustained the world. The Enlightenment is now frequently referred to as the "Enlightenment project," a derogatory phrase that suggests that Enlightenment thinkers marched in lockstep to achieve a single (oppressive) goal.[10]

Yet as we have seen, the Enlightenment was not a single movement, and its effects on Christianity were far more diverse than its critics have acknowledged. Many Enlightenment thinkers stigmatized poverty as a moral failing, but they also defended the humanitarian ideals that laid the groundwork for the rise of the antislavery movement. They promoted a crude faith in progress that was used to justify war and violence, but they also refused to imagine suffering as God's retribution for sin. They underestimated the possibility that self-interest could degenerate into avarice and selfishness, but they also insisted that humans have a natural capacity to do good works. And they denigrated women and racial minorities as inferior and inherently irrational, but they also gave them a powerful language of experience to justify their authority. This language was devalued in the nineteenth century as it became increasingly identified with subjectivity, emotion, femininity, and racial inferiority, but it has never lost its power. In the twentieth century both feminist and black theologians would argue that their experiences could offer insight into the nature of God.

This does not mean that everything about the Enlightenment was positive. Far from it. Yet as Sarah Osborn knew, we live in an imperfect world, and even our best works bear the marks of our human frailties. When evangelicals in the eighteenth and nineteenth centuries tried to craft a new kind of Protestantism that would make sense in an increasingly democratic, capitalist, individualistic, and consumer-oriented culture, they may have forsaken parts of the Christian heritage that they should have tried harder to preserve. Yet they also encouraged people to believe in their freedom to create a more just, compassionate world, and they affirmed the goodness of everyday life. As evangelicals absorbed Enlightenment ideas, they stopped seeing their love for family and friends as a dangerous form of idolatry. Instead of feeling compelled to describe loved ones as "empty, broken cisterns," they argued that their love for others was a reflection of the boundless love of God.[11]

As much as the evangelical movement has changed since the eighteenth century, crucial features have remained the same. Evangelicals have always struggled to define their relationship to the modern world, but they have never lost their missionary zeal, their sense of assurance, their reliance on the Bible, their determination to draw strict lines between Christians and unbelievers, and their emphasis on a personal relationship with Jesus. Nor have they ever doubted that sinners must be "born again." For more than two centuries they have shared the same conviction that stood at the heart of Sarah's life: a broken world needs to be redeemed by Christ.

When we think about the many people in the past who have been praised as "saints," they have usually been radical in their pursuit of God, taking up their cross with a fervor bordering on the extreme. Sarah Osborn was no exception. Her friends thought of her as a saint because of her humility, her generosity to those in need, her ethic of self-sacrifice, and her patience under suffering. If few tried to emulate her, it was because they were almost frightened by her willingness to sacrifice everything for the glory of God. She had spent her life trying to love God with the intensity that Jesus had commanded—with all her heart, all her soul, and all her mind.[12] God was her refuge and her hiding place, her rock and her fortress, her portion, her comforter, her savior.

If Sarah Osborn's voice still has the power to inspire people today, it is because of her vision of the world as flawed, transient, and yet infused with grace. "Never despair," she wrote in her memoir. She had experienced many sorrows along her pilgrimage, but even in the midst of illness, poverty, and war, she had never lost her faith in the goodness of creation. Everywhere she looked, she saw evidence of God's love, proof that a fallen world always trembled on the brink of resurrection.

Abbreviations

ARCHIVAL LOCATIONS

AAS American Antiquarian Society, Worcester, Massachusetts.
 BL Beinecke Rare Book and Manuscript Library, Yale University, New Haven, Connecticut.
BPL Boston Public Library, Boston, Massachusetts.
CHS Connecticut Historical Society, Hartford, Connecticut.
HSP Historical Society of Pennsylvania, Philadelphia, Pennsylvania.
MHS Massachusetts Historical Society, Boston, Massachusetts.
NHS Newport Historical Society, Newport, Rhode Island.
RIHS Rhode Island Historical Society, Providence, Rhode Island.
SML Sterling Memorial Library, Yale University, New Haven, Connecticut.

SARAH OSBORN'S MANUSCRIPTS

Sarah Osborn's writings have been preserved in the following collections: SO, Diaries, 1753–1772, NHS; SO, Diaries and Memoir, 1757–1769, BL; SO, Letters, 1743–1770, 1779, AAS; SO, Diaries, 1754, 1760–1761, CHS; SO, 5 Letters, 1769–1770, Simon Gratz Manuscript Collection, HSP; and SO to Eleazar Wheelock (May 5, 1742), in the Eleazar Wheelock Papers, Dartmouth College, Hanover, N.H. The diaries are cited by date in the endnotes. For locations, see the list below.

Memoir (1743): BL.
Diaries
July 8, 1753–March 1, 1754   Cover marked "No. 14," NHS.
March 5–October 16, 1754   Cover marked "No. 15," CHS.
January 1–May 7, 1757   Cover marked "No. 20," NHS.
May 9–November 6, 1757   Cover marked "No. 21," BL.
February 19–April 2, 1758   No cover, NHS.
November [no date] 1759–April 30, 1760   No cover, NHS.

June 22, 1760–January 18, 1761   Cover marked "No. 27," CHS.
September 28, 1761–February 18, 1762   Cover marked "No. 29," BL.
February 21–April 29, 1762   Cover marked "No. 30," BL.
January 11–June 2, 1767   No cover, NHS.

First Church of Christ Records

The First Church of Christ in Newport was later known as the First Congregational Church, and its records are catalogued under the later name.

FCCR-BM   First Congregational Church, Records of Baptisms and Marriages, 1744–1821, Vault A, no. 832, NHS.
FCCR-CB   First Congregational Church Records, Committee Book, 1743–99, Vault A, no. 836B, NHS.
FCCR-418, Folder 4   Records of the First Congregational Church of Newport, MSS 418, Folder 4: Contribution Book, 1763–75, RIHS.
FCCR-418, Folder 5   Records of the First Congregational Church of Newport, MSS 418, Folder 5: Contribution Book, 1775–76, 1780, 1805–7, RIHS.
FCCR-418, Folder 6   Records of the First Congregational Church of Newport, MSS 418, Folder 6, RIHS.
FCCR-418, Folder 9   Records of the First Congregational Church of Newport, MSS 418, Folder 9, RIHS.
FCCR-DRC   First Congregational Church Records, Documents Relating to the Church, 1729–99, Vault A, Box 40, Folder 1, NHS.

People

JE   Jonathan Edwards
JF   Joseph Fish
SA   Susanna Anthony
SH   Samuel Hopkins
SO   Sarah Osborn

Publications

Bushman, *GA*   Richard L. Bushman, ed., *The Great Awakening: Documents on the Revival of Religion, 1740–1745* (New York: Atheneum, 1970).
CH   Thomas Prince, ed., *The Christian History: Containing Accounts of the Revival and Propagation of Religion in Great-Britain & America.* Periodical (Boston: S. Kneeland and T. Green, 1743–45).
FL   *Familiar Letters, Written by Mrs. Sarah Osborn, and Miss Susanna Anthony, Late of Newport, Rhode-Island* (Newport: Newport Mercury, 1807).

LD   Franklin Bowditch Dexter, ed., *The Literary Diary of Ezra Stiles*, 3 vols. (New York: Scribner's, 1901).

NM   *Newport Mercury* (Newport, R.I.)

Kramnick, *PER*   Isaac Kramnick, ed., *The Portable Enlightenment Reader* (New York: Penguin, 1995).

SH, *Memoirs*   Samuel Hopkins, *Memoirs of the Life of Mrs. Sarah Osborn* (Worcester, Mass.: Leonard Worcester, 1799).

SH, *Life and Character*   Samuel Hopkins, comp., *The Life and Character of Miss Susanna Anthony* (Worcester, Mass.: Leonard Worcester, 1796).

SO, *Nature*   Sarah Osborn, *The Nature, Certainty and Evidence of True Christianity* (Boston: Samuel Kneeland, 1755).

WJE   *Works of Jonathan Edwards*, 26 vols. (New Haven: Yale University Press, 1957–2008), Perry Miller, John E. Smith, and Harry S. Stout, general editors.

WJE Online   *Works of Jonathan Edwards Online* (Jonathan Edwards Center, Yale University, 2008–), http://edwards.yale.edu/archive

WSH   Edwards Amasa Park, ed., *The Works of Samuel Hopkins*, 3 vols. (Boston: Doctrinal Tract and Book Society, 1865).

Notes

All quotations from the Bible are from the King James Version, which was in common use in eighteenth-century New England.

INTRODUCTION

1. SO, Memoir, [135]. Osborn's memoir is paginated only to page 53, but I have specified later page numbers so that readers can find quotations by counting forward.

2. For other studies of Osborn, see Mary Beth Norton, "'My Resting Reaping Times': Sarah Osborn's Defense of Her 'Unfeminine' Activities," *Signs* 2, no. 2 (1976): 515–29; Charles E. Hambrick-Stowe, "The Spiritual Pilgrimage of Sarah Osborn (1714–1796)," *Church History* 61, no. 4 (December 1992): 408–21; Sheryl Anne Kujawa, "'A Precious Season at the Throne of Grace': Sarah Haggar Wheaten Osborn, 1714–1796" (Ph.D. diss., Boston College, 1993); Sheryl Anne Kujawa, "Religion, Education and Gender in Eighteenth-Century Rhode Island: Sarah Haggar Wheaten Osborn, 1714–1796 (Ph.D. diss., Teachers College, Columbia University, 1993); Barbara Lacey, "The Bonds of Friendship: Sarah Osborn of Newport and the Reverend Joseph Fish of North Stonington, 1743–1779," *Rhode Island History* 45 (November 1986): 126–36.

3. SO, Diary (March 5–October 16, 1754), undated entry at end of diary. Hopkins gave conflicting accounts of the number of diaries that Osborn wrote, specifying forty-two in a letter to Levi Hart and more than fifty in his memoir of her life. See SH to Levi Hart, January 11, 1797, Simon Gratz Manuscript Collection: American Colonial Clergy, Case 8/Box 23, HSP, and SH, *Memoirs*, 358. Several of Hopkins's letters to Osborn are preserved in the Samuel Hopkins Papers, Andover Library, Andover Newton Theological School, Newton, Mass. See also the letter from SO to Eleazar Wheelock (May 5, 1742) in the Eleazar Wheelock Papers, Dartmouth College, Hanover, N.H. A microfilm copy is available at Wheaton College, Wheaton, Ill., Reel 1, item 742305.

4. See Harry S. Stout, *The Divine Dramatist: George Whitefield and the Rise of Modern Evangelicalism* (Grand Rapids, Mich.: Eerdmans, 1991); D. Bruce Hindmarsh, *The Evangelical Conversion Narrative: Spiritual Autobiography in Early Modern England* (New York: Oxford University Press, 2005); D. W. Bebbington, *Evangelicalism in Modern Britain: A History from the 1730s to the 1980s* (Boston: Unwin Hyman, 1989); Mark A. Noll, *The Rise of Evangelicalism : The Age of Edwards, Whitefield, and the Wesleys* (Downers Grove, Ill.: InterVarsity Press, 2003); Thomas S. Kidd, *The Great Awakening: The Roots of Evangelical Christianity in Colonial America* (New Haven: Yale University Press, 2007); George M. Marsden, *Jonathan Edwards: A Life* (New Haven: Yale University Press, 2003). See also W. R. Ward, *Early Evangelicalism: A Global Intellectual History, 1670–1789* (New York: Cambridge University Press, 2006).

5. Hindmarsh, *Evangelical Conversion Narrative*, 13.

6. SO, Diary, July 20, 1757.

7. Peter Gay, *The Enlightenment: An Interpretation*, vol. 1 (New York: Knopf, 1966), 3. See also Roy Porter, *The Creation of the Modern World: The Untold Story of the British Enlightenment* (New York: Norton, 2000).

8. See, e.g., Gay, *Enlightenment*, 338; Paul Hazard, *The European Mind: The Critical Years, 1680–1715* (New Haven: Yale University Press, 1953); Lester G. Crocker, *The Age of Enlightenment* (New York: Walker, 1969), 1; Robert A. Ferguson, *The American Enlightenment, 1750–1820* (Cambridge: Harvard University Press, 1997), 22; Jonathan Irvine Israel, *Radical Enlightenment: Philosophy and the Making of Modernity, 1650–1750* (New York: Oxford University Press, 2001).

9. J. G. A. Pocock, *Barbarism and Religion*, vol. 1 (New York: Cambridge University Press, 1999), 9. See also Roland N. Stromberg, *Religious Liberalism in Eighteenth-Century England* (London: Oxford University Press, 1954). Roy Porter argues that the "Enlightenment in Britain took place within, rather than against, Protestantism" (*Creation of the Modern World*, 99). An excellent resource on the Enlightenment is Alan Charles Kors, ed., *Encyclopedia of the Enlightenment*, 4 vols. (New York: Oxford University Press, 2003). On the multiplicity of Enlightenments, see Roy Porter and Mikuláš Teich, eds., *The Enlightenment in National Context* (New York: Cambridge University Press, 1981).

10. SO, Diary, March 26, 1760, 223. On evangelicalism as a vector of the modern world, see Hindmarsh, *Evangelical Conversion Narrative*, vi.

11. Bebbington, *Evangelicalism in Modern Britain*, 74. On the relationship between evangelicalism and the Enlightenment, see Hindmarsh, *Evangelical Conversion Narrative* and Noll, *Rise of Evangelicalism*. See also David Hempton, *Methodism: Empire of the Spirit* (New Haven: Yale University Press, 2005), 52; Frederick A. Dreyer, *The Genesis of Methodism* (Bethlehem, Pa.: Lehigh University Press, 1999); and Brian Stanley, "Christian Missions and the Enlightenment: A Reevaluation," in *Christian Missions and the Enlightenment*, ed. Brian Stanley (Grand Rapids, Mich.: Eerdmans, 2001), 1–21.

12. John Locke, *An Essay Concerning Human Understanding*, 4 vols. (1690; rpt. London: Awnsham and John Churchill, 1706), vol. 1, p. 51; see also Roy Porter, *The Enlightenment*, 2nd ed. (New York: Palgrave, 2001), 2. SO, *Nature*, 3. On seventeenth- and eighteenth-century attitudes toward experience, see Martin Jay, *Songs of Experience: Modern American and European Variations on a Universal Theme* (Berkeley: University of California Press, 2005), 9–78.

13. See Bernard McGinn, "The Language of Inner Experience in Christian Mysticism," *Spiritus: A Journal of Christian Spirituality* 1, no. 1 (2001): 156–71; Susan Elizabeth Schreiner, *Are You Alone Wise? The Search for Certainty in the Early Modern Era* (New York: Oxford University Press, 2011), 209–60. On the Puritans, see Geoffrey F. Nuttall, *The Holy Spirit in Puritan Faith and Experience* (New York: Oxford University Press, 1946).

14. On the roots of evangelicalism in the seventeenth century, see Ward, *Early Evangelicalism*.

15. The most commonly cited definition of evangelicalism is David Bebbington's "quadrilateral": crucicentrism, Biblicism, conversionism, and activism (*Evangelicalism in Modern Britain*, 1–17).

Chapter One. Never Despair

1. SO, Memoir, 1–2.

2. Bushman, *GA*, 52, 128–29.

3. JE, *Some Thoughts Concerning the Present Revival*, in *WJE*, 4: 289–530. Charles Chauncy, *A Letter from a Gentleman in Boston, to Mr. George Wishart* (Edinburgh, 1742), in Bushman, *GA*, 116–21.

4. SO, Memoir, 1.

5. See Diane Bjorklund, *Interpreting the Self: Two Hundred Years of American Autobiography* (Chicago: University of Chicago Press, 1998), 7. See also Margo Culley, *A Day at a Time : The Diary Literature of American Women from 1764 to the Present* (New York: Feminist Press, 1985), 12.

6. Culley, *A Day at a Time*, 8.

7. SO, Memoir, [86].

8. Ibid., 20, [130–31].

9. Ibid., 1.

10. Ibid., [132], 26, 1. John Flavel, *The Mystery of Providence* (1678; rpt. London: Banner of Truth Trust, 1963), 220.

11. See Luther H. Martin, Huck Gutman, and Patrick H. Hutton, eds., *Technologies of the Self: A Seminar with Michel Foucault* (Amherst: University of Massachusetts Press, 1988), 16–49, and Stephen Greenblatt, *Renaissance Self-Fashioning : From More to Shakespeare* (Chicago: University of Chicago Press, 1980). See also Tom Webster, "Writing to Redundancy: Approaches to Spiritual Journals and Early Modern Spirituality," *Historical Journal* 39, no. 1 (1996): 40; James Olney, "Autobiography and the Cultural Moment: A Thematic, His-

torical, and Bibliographical Introduction," in *Autobiography: Essays Theoretical and Critical*, ed. James Olney (Princeton: Princeton University Press, 1980), 22.

12. Georges Gusdorf, "Conditions and Limits of Autobiography," in Olney, *Autobiography*, 44; SO, Memoir, 2.

13. On Franklin, see Daniel Walker Howe, *Making the American Self: Jonathan Edwards to Abraham Lincoln* (Cambridge: Harvard University Press, 1997), 28. On evangelical understandings of the self, see D. Bruce Hindmarsh, *The Evangelical Conversion Narrative: Spiritual Autobiography in Early Modern England* (New York: Oxford University Press, 2005). SO, Memoir, 38.

14. SO, Diary, January 12, 1757.

15. SO, Memoir, 1, [58], [62], 9, 15–16. Stephen Greenblatt has argued that self-fashioning "always involves some experience of threat, some effacement or undermining, some loss of self" (*Renaissance Self-Fashioning*, 9). See also Margo Todd, "Puritan Self-Fashioning: The Diary of Samuel Ward," *Journal of British Studies* 31, no. 3 (1992): 263.

16. JE, *A Faithful Narrative of the Surprising Work of God*, in *WJE*, 4: 148. On fears of religious decline, see Perry Miller, *The New England Mind: The Seventeenth Century* (Cambridge: Harvard University Press, 1939); Miller, *The New England Mind: From Colony to Province* (Cambridge: Harvard University Press, 1953).

17. Quoted in *WJE* 4: 6.

18. Edmund S. Morgan, *The Gentle Puritan: A Life of Ezra Stiles, 1727–1795* (New Haven: Yale University Press, 1962), 19. See also Gerald J. Goodwin, "The Myth of 'Arminian-Calvinism' in Eighteenth-Century New England," *New England Quarterly* 41, no. 2 (1968): 213–37. Cotton Mather is quoted in Conrad Wright, *The Beginnings of Unitarianism in America* (Boston: Starr King, 1955), 9.

19. Wright, *Beginnings of Unitarianism*, 18.

20. Edwin S. Gaustad and Philip L. Barlow, *New Historical Atlas of Religion in America* (New York: Oxford University Press, 2001), 17.

21. Devereux Jarratt, *A Brief Narrative of the Revival of Religion in Virginia* (London: R. Hawes, 1778); John Checkley, *Choice Dialogues Between a Godly Minister and an Honest Country Man* (Boston: Thomas Fleet, 1720), 13.

22. James Honeyman, *Faults on All Sides* (Newport: E. Nearegras and J. Franklin, 1728), 6.

23. SO, Diary, November 25, 1759.

24. Rebecca Larson, *Daughters of Light: Quaker Women Preaching and Prophesying in the Colonies and Abroad, 1700–1775* (New York: Knopf, 1999).

25. Elaine Forman Crane, *A Dependent People: Newport, Rhode Island, in the Revolutionary Era* (New York: Fordham University Press, 1985), 3. On early Enlightenment ideas in America, see Norman Fiering, "The First American Enlightenment: Tillotson, Leverett, and Philosophical Anglicanism," *New England Quarterly* 54, no. 3 (1981): 338; John Corrigan, *The Prism of Piety:*

Catholick Congregational Clergy at the Beginning of the Enlightenment (New York: Oxford University Press, 1991).

26. See Jonathan Irvine Israel, *Radical Enlightenment: Philosophy and the Making of Modernity, 1650–1750* (New York: Oxford University Press, 2001); David Lundberg and Henry May, "The Enlightened Reader in America," *American Quarterly* 28, no. 2 (1976): 262–93.

27. See Anthony Ashley Cooper, Earl of Shaftesbury, *Characteristicks of Men, Manners, Opinions, Times,* 3 vols. (London: John Darby, 1711); Francis Hutcheson, *An Essay on the Nature and Conduct of the Passions and Affections* (London: J. Darby and T. Browne, 1728). On Tillotson, see Frank Lambert, *Inventing the "Great Awakening"* (Princeton: Princeton University Press, 1999), 41–42.

28. Fiering, "First American Enlightenment," 309, 336; Bushman, *GA,* 35–38.

29. Thomas Chubb, *A Discourse Concerning Reason, with Regard to Religion and Divine Revelation* (London: T. Cox, 1733), 7; Benjamin Colman to William Hooper, February 15, 1739/40, quoted in Wright, *Beginnings of Unitarianism,* 22.

30. On Whiston, see John Redwood, *Reason, Ridicule, and Religion: The Age of Enlightenment in England, 1660–1750* (London: Thames and Hudson, 1976), 165–67. See Daniel Whitby, *A Discourse Concerning . . . the True Import of the Words Election and Reprobation,* 2nd ed. (London: Aaron Ward and Richard Hett, 1735), 75; Samuel Clarke, *A Demonstration of the Being and Attributes of God* (London: Will. Botham, 1705); Clarke, *The Scripture Doctrine of the Trinity* (London: James Knapton, 1712); David D. Hall, "Learned Culture in the Eighteenth Century," in *The Colonial Book in the Atlantic World,* ed. Hugh Amory and David D. Hall (New York: Cambridge University Press 2000), 430.

31. [Samuel Moodey], *A Faithful Narrative of God's Gracious Dealings with a Person Lately Recovered from the Dangerous Error of Arminius* (Boston, 1737), cited in Wright, *Beginnings of Unitarianism,* 22; Edward Wigglesworth, *An Enquiry into the Truth of the Imputation of the Guilt of Adam's First Sin to His Posterity* (Boston: J. Draper, 1738), i. See also Roland N. Stromberg, *Religious Liberalism in Eighteenth-Century England* (London: Oxford University Press, 1954).

32. Samuel Osborn, *The Case and Complaint of Mr. Samuel Osborn* (Boston, 1743), cited in Wright, *Beginnings of Unitarianism in America,* 25. On Kent, see Levi A. Field, *An Historical Sketch of the First Congregational Church in Marlborough, Mass* (Worcester, 1859), cited ibid., 23. On Balch, see *Letters from the First Church in Glocester to the Second in Bradford, with their Answers* (Boston, 1744), cited ibid., 61.

33. John White, *New England's Lamentatons (sic)* (Boston, 1734), quoted in Wright, *Beginnings of Unitarianism,* 21.

34. *WJE* 4: 10.

35. See Jon Butler, *Becoming America: The Revolution Before 1776* (Cambridge: Harvard University Press, 2000), 99.

36. Roy Porter, *The Creation of the Modern World: The Untold Story of the British Enlightenment* (New York: Norton, 2000), 52.

37. [William Douglass], *A Discourse Concerning the Currencies of the British Plantations in America* (Boston, 1740), cited in T. H. Breen, *The Marketplace of Revolution: How Consumer Politics Shaped American Independence* (New York: Oxford University Press, 2004), 75. On greater freedom of choice, see also T. H. Breen and Timothy Hall, "Structuring Provincial Imagination: The Rhetoric and Experience of Social Change in Eighteenth-Century New England," *American Historical Review* 103, no. 5 (1998): 1411–39.

38. Breen, *Marketplace of Revolution*, 38–39. See also John Brewer and Roy Porter, eds. *Consumption and the World of Goods* (New York: Routledge, 1993); Neil McKendrick, John Brewer, and J. H. Plumb, *The Birth of a Consumer Society: The Commercialization of Eighteenth-Century England* (Bloomington: Indiana University Press, 1982); Carole Shammas, *The Pre-Industrial Consumer in England and America* (New York: Oxford University Press, 1990); Butler, *Becoming America*, 50–88.

39. Thomas Bacon, "A Sermon to Maryland Slaves, 1749," in *Religion in American History: A Reader*, ed. Jon Butler and Harry S. Stout (New York: Oxford University Press, 1998), 83.

40. For statistics on southern slavery, see Peter Kolchin, *American Slavery, 1619–1877* (New York: Hill and Wang, 1993), 240; Crane, *Dependent People*, 76.

41. Miller, *New England Mind: From Colony to Province*, 485.

42. SO, Memoir, [59], [123].

43. Charles Chauncy, *Seasonable Thoughts on the State of Religion in New-England* (Boston: Rogers and Fowle, 1743), 218–19, 48, 51. On the schisms that erupted during the awakening, see C. C. Goen, *Revivalism and Separatism in New England, 1740–1800: Strict Congregationalist and Separate Baptists in the Great Awakening* (New Haven: Yale University Press, 1962).

44. Chauncy, *Seasonable Thoughts*, 99; Ezra Stiles, *A Discourse on the Christian Union* (Boston: Edes and Gill, 1761), 50.

45. SO, Memoir, 1, [134]. David Shields, "The Manuscript in the British American World of Print," *Proceedings of the American Antiquarian Society* 102, no. 2 (1993): 403–16.

46. JF to SO, June 13, 1751, Benjamin Silliman Family Papers, Group 450, Series 1, Box 1, Manuscripts and Archives, SML.

47. Hindmarsh, *Evangelical Conversion Narrative*, 345.

48. SO, Memoir, [136].

49. Ibid., 51.

50. Ibid., [133].

51. SO, Diary, October 4, 1757.

52. SO, Memoir, [64]; Psalm 23:25.

53. On Lackington, see Hindmarsh, *Evangelical Conversion Narrative*, 340–42, 348, and D. Bruce Hindmarsh, "Reshaping Individualism: The Private Christian, Eighteenth-Century Religion and the Enlightenment," in *The Rise of the Laity in Evangelical Protestantism*, ed. Deryck W. Lovegrove (New York: Routledge, 2002), 77–78, 81.

CHAPTER TWO. THE NAME OF CHRIST

1. SO, Memoir, 2–4.

2. Ibid., 3, 1, 5, 2.

3. On childhood in early America, see Gerald F. Moran and Maris Vinovskis, *Religion, Family, and the Life Course: Explorations in the Social History of Early America* (Ann Arbor: University of Michigan Press, 1992); John Demos, *A Little Commonwealth: Family Life in Plymouth Colony* (New York: Oxford University Press, 1970); Edmund S. Morgan, *The Puritan Family: Religion and Domestic Relations in Seventeenth-Century New England*, rev. ed. (New York: Harper and Row, 1966); Philip J. Greven, *The Protestant Temperament: Patterns of Child-Rearing, Religious Experience, and the Self in Early America* (Chicago: University of Chicago Press, 1988).

4. Louis K. Dupré, *The Enlightenment and the Intellectual Foundations of Modern Culture* (New Haven: Yale University Press, 2004), 66.

5. I have borrowed the image of the "door of childhood" from Graham Greene, *The Power and the Glory* (1940; rpt. New York: Penguin, 1990), 12; SO, Memoir, 3, quoting Psalm 58:3.

6. SH, *Memoirs*, 5; Colin Haydon, "Religious Minorities in England," in *A Companion to Eighteenth-Century Britain*, ed. H. T. Dickinson (Malden, Mass.: Blackwell, 2002), 241–42.

7. Cotton Mather, *A Family Well-Ordered* (Boston: B. Green and J. Allen, 1699), 10–11. SO, Memoir, 3.

8. The Westminster Assembly, *The Shorter Catechism* (Boston: B. Harris and J. Allen, 1693), 3; *WJE* 11: 54; John 3:16.

9. SO, Memoir, 5; Mark 10:14.

10. Ephesians 1:4; John Calvin, *Institutes of the Christian Religion*, ed. John T. McNeill, trans. Ford Lewis Battles, Library of Christian Classics vol. 21 (Louisville: Westminster John Knox Press, 1960), 3.23.7. On early American Calvinist theology see Mark A. Noll, *America's God : From Jonathan Edwards to Abraham Lincoln* (New York: Oxford University Press, 2002), 31–50; Harry S. Stout, *The New England Soul: Preaching and Religious Culture in Colonial New England* (New York: Oxford University Press, 1986); E. Brooks Holifield, *Theology in America: Christian Thought from the Age of the Puritans to the Civil War* (New Haven: Yale University Press, 2003), 25–78.

11. Influenced by Philippe Ariès's groundbreaking book, *Centuries of Childhood* (New York: Vintage, 1962), which argued that childhood was not "dis-

covered" until the seventeenth century, many have argued that early American children were perceived as miniature adults. For an example, see Karin Lee Fishbeck Calvert, *Children in the House: The Material Culture of Early Childhood, 1600–1900* (Boston: Northeastern University Press, 1992). For challenges to this view, see Ross W. Beales, "In Search of the Historical Child: Miniature Adulthood and Youth in Colonial New England," *American Quarterly* 27, no. 4 (October 1975): 379–98; Moran and Vinovskis, *Religion, Family, and the Life Course*, 118. On eighteenth-century understandings of children's development, see Kenneth Keniston, "Psychological Development and Historical Change," in *Growing Up in America: Historical Experiences*, ed. Harvey J. Graff (Detroit: Wayne State University Press, 1987), 64, and Joseph F. Kett, "The Stages of Life," in *The American Family in Social-Historical Perspective*, 2d ed., ed. Michael Gordon (New York: St. Martin's, 1978), 166.

12. Isaac Watts, *The First Catechism of the Principles of Religion; or, The Catechism for a Young Child, to Be Begun at Three or Four Years Old* (London, 1730; rpt. Norwich, Conn.: J. Trumbull, 1788), 4–5, 6–7. See also John Cotton, *Spiritual Milk for Boston Babes* (Cambridge: Hezekiah Usher, 1656), 6.

13. *The New-England Primer Enlarged* (Boston: S. Kneeland and T. Green, 1727).

14. Isaac Watts, *Divine and Moral Songs for the Use of Children*, 27; see also C. John Somerville, *The Rise and Fall of Childhood* (Beverly Hills: Sage, 1982), 142. SO, Memoir, 8.

15. SO, Memoir, 4.

16. Ibid.

17. J. H. Plumb, "The New World of Children in Eighteenth-Century England," *Past and Present* 67 (May 1975): 76.

18. SO, Memoir, 5–6.

19. Ibid., 1–2.

20. *The School of Good Manners* (1715; rpt. New London, Conn.: T. Green, 1754), 1; Cotton Mather, *Bonifacius: An Essay upon the Good*, ed. David Levin (Cambridge: Harvard University Press, 1966), 45.

21. John Bunyan, *Grace Abounding to the Chief of Sinners* (Grand Rapids, Mich.: Baker, 1986), 18; JE, *The Life of David Brainerd*, in *WJE* 7: 101; Burr quoted in *The Great Awakening at Yale College*, ed. Stephen Nissenbaum (Belmont, Calif.: Wadsworth, 1972), 15; John Cleaveland, Memoir, vol. 2, in the Cleaveland Family Papers, 1742–1891, Phillips Library, Peabody Essex Museum, Salem, Mass.; JE, *A Faithful Narrative*, in *WJE* 4: 200, 201–5; Barbara E. Lacey, ed. *The World of Hannah Heaton: The Diary of an Eighteenth-Century New England Farm Woman* (DeKalb: Northern Illinois University Press 2003), 3.

22. Joseph Fish, *Angels Ministring to the People of God* (Newport: J. Franklin, 1755), 4–5; Calvert, *Children in the House*, 19–38.

23. "A Dialogue Between Christ, Youth, and the Devil," in *New-England Primer Enlarged*, n.p.

24. Cotton Mather, *Help for Distressed Parents* (Boston: John Allen, 1695), 13; Michael Wigglesworth, *The Day of Doom* (1662; rpt. Whitefish, Mont.: Kessinger, 2003), 55. See also Peter Gregg Slater, *Children in the New England Mind: In Death and in Life* (Hamden, Conn.: Archon, 1977), 40.

25. Benjamin Wadsworth, "The Nature of Early Piety," in *A Course of Sermons on Early Piety. By the Eight Ministers Who Carry on the Thursday Lecture in Boston* (Boston: S. Kneeland, 1721), 10; Benjamin Bass, *Parents and Children Advised and Exhorted to Their Duty* (Newport: [James Franklin], 1730), 3.

26. Samuel Wigglesworth, *An Essay for Reviving Religion* (Boston, 1733), in *The Great Awakening: Documents Illustrating the Crisis and Its Consequences*, ed. Alan Heimert and Perry Miller (Indianapolis: Bobbs-Merrill, 1967), 6; Wadsworth, "Nature of Early Piety," 29; JE, "Sermon on Ephesians 6:4," February 1748, Jonathan Edwards Collection (1696–1972), BL.

27. On "paternal power," see Mary Beth Norton, *Founding Mothers and Fathers: Gendered Power and the Forming of American Society* (New York: Knopf 1996), 96–137.

28. See Daniel Scott Smith, "Parental Power and Marriage Patterns: An Analysis of Historical Trends in Hingham, Massachusetts," in *The American Family*, ed. Michael Gordon (New York: St. Martin's, 1973), 255–68; Steven Mintz and Susan Kellogg, *Domestic Revolutions: A Social History of American Family Life* (New York: Free Press), 17–21.

29. JE, *Faithful Narrative*, 146; JE, "Sermon on Job 14:2," quoted in Helen Petter Westra, "Cornerstones, Cannons, and Covenants: The Puritan Clergy as Cultural Guardians," *Pro Rege* (September 1990): 28.

30. JE, *The Justice of God in the Damnation of Sinners*, in *WJE* 19: 344–45; Hutcheson quoted in Norman Fiering, "Irresistible Compassion: As Aspect of Eighteenth-Century Sympathy and Humanitarianism," *Journal of the History of Ideas* 37, no. 2 (1976): 207. On Hutcheson see Michael B. Gill, *The British Moralists on Human Nature and the Birth of Secular Ethics* (New York: Cambridge University Press, 2006), 135–200.

31. Fiering, "Irresistible Compassion," 205; Janet M. Todd, *Sensibility : An Introduction* (New York: Methuen, 1986).

32. Daniel Whitby, *A Discourse* (London, 1710), quoted in H. Shelton Smith, *Changing Conceptions of Original Sin: A Study in American Theology Since 1750* (New York: Scribner's, 1955), 12–13; John Beach, *An Appeal to the Unprejudiced* (Boston: [n.p.], 1737), 6.

33. *WJE* 13: 169.

34. See, e.g., Lyman Beecher, *Sermons Delivered on Various Occasions* (Boston, 1828), 17, quoted in Slater, *Children in the New England Mind*, 83; Beecher, "Future Punishment of Infants Not a Doctrine of Calvinism," *Spirit of the Pilgrims* (January–March 1828): 89–90.

35. John Taylor, *The Scripture-Doctrine of Original Sin Proposed to Free and Candid Examination* (London: M. Waugh, 1767), 4th ed., part 3, p. 274, part 2,

p. 153; Taylor uses the word *absurd* in part 2, pp. 112, 141, and 148. On attitudes toward original sin, see Smith, *Changing Conceptions of Original Sin*; Clyde A. Holbrook, "Original Sin and the Enlightenment," in *The Heritage of Christian Thought: Essays in Honor of Robert Lowry Calhoun*, ed. Robert E. Cushman and Egil Grislis (New York: Harper and Row, 1965); Merle Curti, *Human Nature in American Thought: A History* (Madison: University of Wisconsin Press, 1980); Conrad Wright, *The Beginnings of Unitarianism in America* (Boston: Starr King Press, 1955), 59–90.

36. JE, *Some Thoughts Concerning the Present Revival*, in *WJE* 4: 394.

37. Ibid.; Thomas Prince, "The Great and Solemn Obligations to Early Piety," cited in Sandford Fleming, *Children and Puritanism: The Place of Children in the Life and Thought of the New England Churches, 1620–1847* (New Haven: Yale University Press, 1933), 97; SO, Memoir, [119].

38. Arthur W. Calhoun, *A Social History of the American Family: From Colonial Times to the Present* (Cleveland: Arthur H. Clark, 1917), 1: 111; Fleming, *Children and Puritanism*, 153.

39. Watts, *Divine and Moral Songs*; James Janeway, *A Token for Children* (Boston: T. Hancock, 1728), viii.

40. JE, *Faithful Narrative*, 158; Kenneth P. Minkema, "Old Age and Religion in the Writings and Life of Jonathan Edwards," *Church History* 70, no. 4. (December 2001): 688; "The Rev. Mr. Blair's Account of the Revival of Religion at New-Londonderry in Pennsylvania," *CH* (October 13, 1744): 85; John White, "The said account we have thought proper to insert as follows," *CH* (April 7, 1744): 58.

41. Joseph Emerson, *Early Piety Encouraged* (Boston: J. Draper, 1738).

42. JE, *Some Thoughts Concerning the Present Revival*, 394.

43. SO, Memoir, 3–4, 18.

44. Gerrish reprinted in Nathaniel Appleton, *The Christian Glorying in Tribulation from a Sense of Its Happy Fruits. A Discourse Occasion'd by the Death of that Pious and Afflicted Gentlewoman Mrs. Martha Gerrish. . . . To Which Are Annexed Some of Mrs. Gerrish's Letters* (Boston: J. Draper, 1736), 63; *The Journal of Esther Edwards Burr, 1754–1757*, ed. Carol F. Karlsen and Laurie Crumpacker (New Haven: Yale University Press, 1984), 95, 107.

45. See Marcia J. Bunge, "Education and the Child in Eighteenth-Century German Pietism: Perspectives from the Work of A. H. Francke," and Martha Ellen Stortz, "'Where or When Was Your Servant Innocent?' Augustine on Childhood," in *The Child in Christian Thought*, ed. Marcia J. Bunge (Grand Rapids, Mich.: Eerdmans, 2001), 247–278, 78–102. On "breaking the will," see Greven, *Protestant Temperament*, 32–42.

46. *School of Good Manners*, 1; Gerrish reprinted in Appleton, *Christian Glorying in Tribulation*, 52; SO, Memoir, 18.

47. Mather, *Bonifacius*. 48. See John Locke, *Some Thoughts Concerning Education*, in *The Educational Writings of John Locke*, ed. James L. Axtell (New York: Cambridge University Press, 1968), 150.

48. Fish quoted in Joy Day Buel and Richard Buel, Jr., *The Way of Duty: A Woman and Her Family in Revolutionary America* (New York: Norton, 1984), 9, 209.

49. Philip Greven argues that there were three styles of childrearing present in early America: the evangelical, the moderate, and the genteel. Yet almost all of his examples of the "moderate" style date from the 1740s or later, suggesting that the 1740s marked a watershed. See Greven, *Protestant Temperament*.

50. SO, Memoir, 3–4; Proverbs 13:24.

51. The literature on children's images of God is vast. For an introduction, see Bradley R. Hertel and Michael J. Donahue, "Parental Influences on God Images Among Children: Testing Durkheim's Metaphoric Parallelism," *Journal for the Scientific Study of Religion* 34, no. 2 (June 1995): 186–199; Jane R. Dickie et al., "Parent-Child Relationships and Children's Images of God," *Journal for the Scientific Study of Religion* 36, no. 1 (March 1997): 25–43. On abused children, see W. Brad Johnson and Mark C. Eastburg, "God, Parent, and Self Concepts in Abused and Nonabused Children," *Journal of Psychology and Christianity* 11, no. 3 (1992): 235–43.

52. SO, Memoir, 6–7.

53. Increase Mather, *The Times of Men are in the Hands of God* (Boston: John Foster, 1675), 7; Thomas Brooks, *The Silent Soul* (Boston: Boone, 1728), 12 (originally published as *The Mute Christian Under the Smarting Rod*); Cotton Mather, *Diary of Cotton Mather* (New York: Ungar, 1957), 1: 24.

54. Brooks, *Silent Soul*, 17; Samuel Willard, *The Mourner's Cordial Against Excessive Sorrow* (Boston: Benjamin Harris, 1691), 16–17.

55. Thomas Laqueur, *Making Sex : Body and Gender from the Greeks to Freud* (Cambridge: Harvard University Press, 1990), 4; Ava Chamberlain, "The Immaculate Ovum: Jonathan Edwards and the Construction of the Female Body," *William and Mary Quarterly* 57, no. 2 (2000): 289–322.

56. Laqueur, *Making Sex*, 108; John D'Emilio and Estelle B. Freedman, *Intimate Matters: A History of Sexuality in America* (New York: Harper and Row, 1988), 15–38.

57. *Look E're You Leap; or, A History of the Lives and Intrigues of Lewd Women*, 11th ed. (London: J. Clarke, C. Hitch, J. Hodges, T. King, and T. Harris, 1741), 23, 16–17.

58. Benjamin Colman, *The Duty and Honour of Aged Women* (Boston: B. Green, 1711), 5; Edwards, *Faithful Narrative*, 149. Harry S. Stout, *The Divine Dramatist: George Whitefield and the Rise of Modern Evangelicalism* (Grand Rapids, Mich.: Eerdmans, 1991), 163. On images of women in sermons, see Laurel Thatcher Ulrich, "Vertuous Women Found: New England Ministerial Literature, 1668–1735," *American Quarterly* 28, no. 1 (1976): 20–40.

59. See Elizabeth Reis, "The Devil, the Body, and the Feminine Soul in Puritan New England," *Journal of American History* 82 (1995): 15–36.

60. George Whitefield, *A Brief and General Account of the First Part of the Life of the Reverend Mr. George Whitefield* (Boston: S. Kneeland and T. Green, 1740), 2, 10.

61. SH, *Life and Character*, 14, 69; Lacey, *World of Hannah Heaton*, 56. My reading of these texts differs from those that emphasize men's and women's different voices. Mary G. Mason argues that Augustine's *Confessions*, "where the self is presented as the stage for a battle of opposing forces and where a climactic victory for one voice—spirit defeating flesh—completes the drama of the self, simply does not accord with the deepest realities of women's experience and so is inappropriate as a model for women's life writing" ("The Other Voice: Autobiographies of Women Writers," in *Autobiography: Essays Theoretical and Critical*, ed. James Olney [Princeton: Princeton University Press, 1980], 210). But in fact, most evangelical women's writings follow this pattern exactly.

62. SO, Memoir, [99], 37.

63. Ibid., 135.

64. Samuel Russell, *Man's Liableness to Be Deceiv'd About Religion, Shewn and Caution'd Against* (New London: T. Green, 1742). The copy at AAS is inscribed with Osborn's signature.

65. Samuel Niles, *The True Scripture-Doctrine of Original Sin Stated and Defended* (Boston, 1757), 40; Jonathan Mayhew, *Seven Sermons* (Boston, 1749), 38.

66. Samuel Webster, *A Winter Evening's Conversation upon the Doctrine of Original Sin* (New Haven: James Parker, 1757), 5; William Wordsworth, "Ode: Intimations of Immortality," in *The Norton Anthology of Poetry*, rev. ed., ed. Alexander W. Allison et al. (New York: Norton, 1975), 602.

Chapter Three. An Afflicted Low Condition

1. SO, Memoir, [133].

2. William Butler Yeats, "The Circus Animals' Desertion," in *The Norton Anthology of Poetry*, rev. ed. (New York: Norton, 1975), 935.

3. On Boston's population, see Gary Nash, *The Urban Crucible: The Northern Seaports and the Origins of the American Revolution*, abridged ed. (Cambridge: Harvard University Press, 1986), 71. For London see J. F. Merritt, "Perceptions and Portrayals of London, 1598–1720," in *Imagining Early Modern London: Perceptions and Portrayals of the City from Stow to Strype, 1598–1720*, ed. J. F. Merritt (London: Cambridge University Press, 2001), 1.

4. SO, Memoir, 8–10.

5. Ibid., 10–11.

6. Ibid., 11–12.

7. Ibid., 13–15.

8. John Robinson, *The Works of John Robinson, a Pastor of the Pilgrim Fathers*, ed. Robert Ashton (Boston: Doctrinal Book and Tract Society, 1851),

quoted in Carol Zisowitz Stearns and Peter N. Stearns, *Anger: The Struggle for Emotional Control in America's History* (Chicago: University of Chicago Press, 1986), 19; JE, "Personal Resolutions," in *Jonathan Edwards: Representative Selections*, ed. Clarence H. Faust and Thomas H. Johnson (New York: Hill and Wang, 1962), 43. See also Philip J. Greven, *The Protestant Temperament: Patterns of Child-Rearing, Religious Experience, and the Self in Early America* (Chicago: University of Chicago Press, 1988), 109–23, 250–55, 318–20; John Demos, *A Little Commonwealth: Family Life in Plymouth Colony* (New York: Oxford University Press, 1970), 137–38.

9. For a transcript of the mortgage deed, see Jane Fletcher Fiske, *Gleanings from Newport County Files, 1659–1783* (Boxford, Mass.: n.p., 1998), no. 571. (There are no page numbers in this book, but excerpts from the county files are numbered.)

10. On indoor water, see Sheila Skemp, "A Social and Cultural History of Newport, Rhode Island, 1720–1765" (Ph.D. diss., University of Iowa, 1974), 19. For Berkeley see Alexander Campbell Fraser, *Life and Letters of George Berkeley* (Oxford: Clarendon, 1871), 157.

11. Petitions of the Rhode Island General Assembly, 1725–1860, Archives, State House, Providence, R.I., quoted in Skemp, "Social and Cultural History of Newport," 20; SO, Memoir, 16. See also Lynne Withey, *Urban Growth in Colonial Rhode Island: Newport and Providence in the Eighteenth Century* (Albany: State University of New York Press, 1984); Elaine Forman Crane, *A Dependent People: Newport, Rhode Island in the Revolutionary Era* (New York: Fordham University Press, 1985); Elaine Forman Crane, *Ebb Tide in New England: Women, Seaports, and Social Change, 1630–1800* (Boston: Northeastern University Press, 1998).

12. SO, Memoir, 16–17.

13. Ibid., 17–18, citing James 4:7–8.

14. Ibid., 17.

15. American Psychiatric Association, *Diagnostic and Statistical Manual of Mental Disorders*, 4th ed. (DSM-IV) (Washington, D.C.: American Psychiatric Association, 1994), 320–27; William Styron, *Darkness Visible: A Memoir of Madness* (New York: Random House, 1990).

16. Alice Miller, *For Your Own Good: Hidden Cruelty in Child-Rearing and the Roots of Violence*, trans. Hildegarde and Hunter Hannum (New York: Farrar, Straus and Giroux, 1983), 106.

17. SO, Memoir, 16–18.

18. Miller, *For Your Own Good*, 129; SO, Memoir, 20.

19. SO to JF, December 10, 1755, AAS; SO to JF, December 26, 1760, AAS.

20. SO, Memoir, 2, 9.

21. Greven, *Protestant Temperament*, 83. SH, *Life and Character*, 26.

22. Increase Mather, *A Call to the Tempted: A Sermon on the Horrid Crime of Self-Murder* (1724; Boston: B. Green, 1734), 8.

23. I. Mather, *Call to the Tempted*; SO, Memoir, 16–17.

24. SO, Memoir, 16–19.

25. Ibid., 18.

26. Ibid., 16, 18.

27. Ibid., 17; Michael J. Crawford, "The Spiritual Travels of Nathan Cole," *William and Mary Quarterly* 33, no. 1 (1976): 101–3.

28. Hopkins erases the entire episode with the sentence "After some sore trials and temptations, I was more comfortable . . . " (SH, *Memoirs*, 14). Compare his account with SO, Memoir, 16–18.

29. SO, Memoir, 21–23, citing Micah 6:9.

30. SO, Memoir, 23.

31. On women's average age at marriage, see Robert V. Wells, "Quaker Marriage Patterns in a Colonial Perspective," in *A Heritage of Her Own: Toward a New Social History of American Women*, ed. Nancy F. Cott and Elizabeth H. Pleck (New York: Simon and Schuster, 1979), 82. See also Daniel Scott Smith, "Parental Power and Marriage Patterns," *Journal of Marriage and the Family* 35 (1973): 326.

32. SO, Memoir, 24. On the "marriage portion," see Jane C. Nylander, *Our Own Snug Fireside: Images of the New England Home, 1760–1860* (New York: Knopf, 1993), 59–62.

33. SO, Memoir, 24.

34. Ibid., 25.

35. Ibid., 26–27; John Bunyan, *Grace Abounding to the Chief of Sinners* (1666; Grand Rapids, Mich.: Baker, 1986), 19.

36. SO, Memoir, 25–26, citing Proverbs 28:24 and Proverbs 19:26. See SH, *Memoirs*, 15.

37. In her memoir (SO, Memoir, 27), Osborn said that she was married in "her eighteenth year," or at the age of seventeen. She did not turn eighteen until the following February. For marriage laws, see Samuel Greene Arnold, *History of the State of Rhode Island and Providence Plantations*, vol. 2: *1700–1790* (New York: Appleton, 1860), 3.

38. SO, Diary, November 16, 1760.

39. SO, Memoir, 27. On "going to housekeeping," see Nylander, *Our Own Snug Fireside*, 54–62.

40. SO, Memoir, 26–28.

41. Ibid., 29–30.

42. Thomas Brooks, *The Silent Soul* (Boston: Boone, 1728), 21–22. See also John Willison, *The Afflicted Man's Companion* (Philadelphia: W. Young, 1788), 22, and Benjamin Grosvenor, *The Mourner* (Philadelphia: Aitken, 1781), 55. The Bible citation is Micah 6:9.

43. John Flavel, *A Token for Mourners; or, The Advice of Christ to a Distressed Mother, Bewailing the Death of Her Dear and Only Son* (London: Thomas Pankhurst, 1694), 20–21; *A Pastoral Visit to the Afflicted* (Boston, 1737), 4; Cot-

ton Mather, *Bonifacius: An Essay Upon the Good*, ed. David Levin (Cambridge: Harvard University Press, 1966), 38; Willison, *Afflicted Man's Companion*, 20.

44. SO, Memoir, 29.

45. Ibid., 30–31.

46. Laurel Thatcher Ulrich, *A Midwife's Tale: The Life of Martha Ballard, Based on Her Diary, 1785–1812* (New York: Vintage, 1991), 170, 72.

47. Mary Cleaveland, Diary, October 14, 1751, Essex Institute, Salem, Mass. On childbirth, see Laurel Thatcher Ulrich, *Good Wives: Image and Reality in the Lives of Women in Northern New England, 1650–1750* (New York: Knopf 1982), 126–45; Ulrich, *Midwife's Tale*, 183–203.

48. SO, Memoir, 31. On childbirth in colonial times see Ulrich, *Good Wives*, 127; Ulrich, *Midwife's Tale*, 183–87, 189.

49. SO, Memoir, 30. On infant mortality, see Gerald F. Moran and Maris Vinovskis, *Religion, Family, and the Life Course: Explorations in the Social History of Early America* (Ann Arbor: University of Michigan Press, 1992), 215. On biblical naming, see Harry S. Stout and Catherine A. Brekus, "A New England Congregation: Center Church, New Haven, 1638–1989," in *American Congregations*, ed. James Lewis and James Wind (Chicago: University of Chicago Press, 1994), 38.

50. Increase Mather, *Pray for the Rising Generation* (Cambridge, Mass.: Samuel Green, 1678), 12. On baptism, see Anne S. Brown and David D. Hall, "Family Strategies and Religious Practice: Baptism and the Lord's Supper in Early New England," in *Lived Religion in America: Toward a History of Practice*, ed. David D. Hall (Princeton: Princeton University Press, 1997), 41–68, and E. Brooks Holifield, *The Covenant Sealed: The Development of Puritan Sacramental Theology in Old and New England, 1570–1720* (New Haven: Yale University Press, 1974).

51. SO, Memoir, 31, 33–34.

52. Based on available records, the *Bonadventure* is the best match for the dates of Samuel's voyage. The ship left Newport on October 11, 1733, and did not return until 1734. Unfortunately there is no listing of the month when it returned to port. See *The Trans-Atlantic Slave Trade: A Database on CD-ROM*, ed. David Eltis, Stephen D. Behrendt, David Richardson, and Herbert S. Klein (New York: Cambridge University Press, 1999).

53. SO, Memoir, 32.

54. Flavel, *Token for Mourners*, 15, 8–9; Charles Drelincourt, *The Christian's Defence Against the Fears of Death, with Directions How to Die Well* (Boston: Thomas Fleet, 1744), 52–53, original in italics.

55. SO, Memoir, 32–33, quoting Job 1:21. Osborn mentions reading "Drelincourt on Death" in SO, Diary, October 19, 1760.

56. SO, Memoir, 32.

57. Cotton Mather, *The Nightingale: An Essay on the Songs Among Thorns* (Boston: B. Green, 1724), 10.

58. David Hume, *Dialogues Concerning Natural Religion*, in *The Problem of Evil: A Reader*, ed. Mark J. Larrimore (Malden, Mass.: Blackwell, 2001), 220. On the history of Christian interpretations of suffering and evil, see John Hick, *Evil and the God of Love* (London: Macmillan, 1966); Susan Elizabeth Schreiner, *Where Shall Wisdom Be Found? Calvin's Exegesis of Job from Medieval and Modern Perspectives* (Chicago: University of Chicago Press, 1994); Kenneth Surin, *Theology and the Problem of Evil* (Oxford: Blackwell, 1986).

59. Augustine, *Free Will*, 3.9.26, cited in Hick, *Evil and the God of Love*, 94.

60. John Calvin, *Institutes of the Christian Religion*, ed. John T. McNeill, trans. Ford Lewis Battles, Library of Christian Classics, vol. 21 (Louisville: Westminster John Knox Press, 1960), 3.23.7.

61. One example is Gregory of Nyssa, a fourth-century bishop who emphasized the "*liberating* nature of affliction" (Schreiner, *Where Shall Wisdom Be Found?* 29).

62. William Wollaston, *The Religion of Nature Delineated* (London, 1722), cited in Norman Fiering, *Jonathan Edwards's Moral Thought and Its British Context* (Chapel Hill: University of North Carolina Press, 1981), 249. See also Norman Fiering, "Irresistible Compassion: An Aspect of Eighteenth-Century Sympathy and Humanitarianism," *Journal of the History of Ideas* 37, no. 2 (1976): 205.

63. Anthony Ashley Cooper, third earl of Shaftesbury, "A Letter Concerning Enthusiasm," in his *Characteristicks of Men, Manners, Opinions, Times*, 3 vols. (London: John Darby, 1711), 1: 33.

64. See William Whiston, *The Eternity of Hell-Torments Considered* (1740; 2d ed., London: John Whiston and Ben. White, 1752), 20. On benevolence, see Norman Sykes, "The Theology of Divine Benevolence," *Historical Magazine of the Protestant Episcopal Church* 16 (1947): 278–91. On humanitarianism, see Fiering, *Jonathan Edwards's Moral Thought*, 200–260; Fiering, "Irresistible Compassion," 195–218; Daniel Wickberg, "Humanitarianism," in *Encyclopedia of American Cultural and Intellectual History*, ed. Mary Kupiec Cayton and Peter W. Williams (New York: Scribner's, 2001), vol. 2, pp. 689–97; Karen Haltunnen, "Humanitarianism and the Pornography of Pain in Anglo-American Culture," *American Historical Review* 100, no. 2 (April 1995): 303–34; Ava Chamberlain, "The Theology of Cruelty: A New Look at the Rise of Arminianism in Eighteenth-Century New England," *Harvard Theological Review* 85, no. 3 (1992): 335–56.

65. William King, *An Essay on the Origin of Evil* (London: W. Thurlbourn, 1731), 143 (the statistic on reprintings comes from WorldCat.org); Alexander Pope, "An Essay on Man," in *The Enlightenment and English Literature: Prose and Poetry of the Eighteenth Century, with Selected Modern Critical Essays*, ed. John L. Mahoney (Lexington, Mass.: Heath, 1980), 64. This optimism was satirized by Voltaire in *Candide* (1759).

66. John Tillotson, *Sixteen Sermons Preached on Several Subjects and Occasions* (London: Ri. Chiswell, 1700), 191, 194.

67. Matthew Tindal, *Christianity as Old as the Creation* (London: n.p., 1730), 33–34, 36, 90. See also Stephen Lalor, *Matthew Tindal, Freethinker: An Eighteenth-Century Assault on Religion* (New York: Continuum, 2006), 156–57. On eighteenth-century views of happiness, see David S. Shields, "Happiness in Society: The Development of an Eighteenth-Century American Poetic Ideal," *American Literature* 55, no. 4 (December 1983): 541–59.

68. John E. Crowley, *The Invention of Comfort: Sensibilities and Design in Early Modern Britain and Early America* (Baltimore: Johns Hopkins University Press, 2001); SO, Diary, April 24, 1754.

69. Gilbert Tennent, *Twenty-Three Sermons upon the Chief End of Man* (Philadelphia: William Bradford, 1743), 15, 18.

70. SH, *Memoirs*, [68]. SO, April 2, 1757.

71. Benjamin Wadsworth, *Considerations, to Prevent Murmuring and Promote Patience in Christians, Under Afflictive Providences* (Boston: B. Green, 1706), 6–7; Samuel Willard, *The Just Man's Prerogative* (Boston, B. Green, 1706), 10.

72. Willard, *Just Man's Prerogative*, 14–18, 5, 21–22.

73. Samuel Hopkins, *Sin Through Divine Interposition, an Advantage to the Universe*, in *WSH* 2: 504, 511. E. Brooks Holifield argues that Puritans responded to the early Enlightenment by moving in a rationalistic direction: "In trying to defend tradition against what they saw as rationalistic reduction, they of necessity accentuated the function of reason in theology" (*Theology in America: Christian Thought from the Age of the Puritans to the Civil War* [New Haven: Yale University Press, 2003], 69).

74. SH, *An Inquiry Concerning the Future State of Those Who Die in Their Sins* in *WSH* 2: 465, 472–73; Joseph Bellamy, *Sermons upon the Following Subjects, viz. The Divinity of Jesus Christ, The Millenium* [sic], *The Wisdom of God, in the Permission of Sin* (Boston: Edes and Gill, 1758), 65–66.

75. Sue Lane McCulley and Dorothy Zayatz Baker, eds., *The Silent and Soft Communion: The Spiritual Narratives of Sarah Pierpont Edwards and Sarah Prince Gill* (Knoxville: University of Tennessee Press 2005), 27; Crawford, "Spiritual Travels of Nathan Cole," 112; SH, *Life and Character*, 57.

76. SO, Diary, March 28, 1754, May 20, 1757; SO to "Mrs. Noice" [Abigail Noyes], January 16, 1767, AAS. See also SO, Diary, July 12, 1757, April 25, 1760.

77. JE, *Prayer and Supplication to God in a Time of Sore Drought 1730*, *WJE Online* 44.

78. SH, *Memoirs*, 196. She was quoting from John Mason, *Spiritual Songs; or, Songs of Praise with Penitential Cries to Almighty God upon Several Occasions*, 11th ed. (London: J. and B. Sprint, 1718), 100.

79. SO, Memoir, 33–34, citing Psalm 146:9.

80. Ibid., 34–35. On the 1730 law, see *Acts and Laws of His Majesty's Colony of Rhode Island and Providence Plantations* (Newport, 1744), 94–95; Skemp, "Social and Cultural History of Newport," 117.

81. SO, Memoir, 35. On women's work in New England seaports, see Crane, *Ebb Tide in New England*, 98–138. On Newport's methods of poor relief, see Withey, *Urban Growth in Colonial Rhode Island*, 56–63.

82. SO, Memoir, 35.

83. Ibid. On humoral theory see Ulrich, *Midwife's Tale*, 55–56. On medicine in colonial New England, see *Medicine in Colonial Massachusetts, 1620–1820*, ed. Philip Cash, Eric H. Christianson, and J. Worth Estes (Boston: Colonial Society of Massachusetts, 1980); *Medicine and Healing*, ed. Peter Benes (Boston: Boston University Press, 1990); Volney Steele, *Bleed, Blister, and Purge: A History of Medicine on the American Frontier* (Missoula, Mont.: Mountain Press, 2005), 323.

84. William Douglass, quoted in Eric Christianson, "Medicine in New England," in *Medicine in the New World: New Spain, New France, and New England*, ed. Ronald L. Numbers (Knoxville: University of Tennessee Press, 1987), 141. See Leonard J. Goldwater, *Mercury: A History of Quicksilver* (Baltimore: York Press, 1972), 239–48.

85. Henry Bradley, *A Treatise on Mercury, Shewing the Danger of Taking it Crude for All Manner of Disorders*, 2d ed. (London: J. Roberts, 1733), 27. See also Charles E. Rosenberg, "The Therapeutic Revolution: Medicine, Meaning, and Social Change in Nineteenth-Century America," in *Sickness and Health in America*, ed. Judith Walzer Leavitt and Ronald L. Numbers (Madison: University of Wisconsin Press, 1985), 43; John W. Francis, *An Inaugural Dissertation on Mercury Embracing its Medical History, Curative Action and Abuse in Certain Diseases* (New York: C. S. Van Winkle, 1811), 32; N. J. Lanford and R. E. Ferner, "Toxicity of Mercury," *Journal of Human Hypertension* 13 (1999): 651–56.

86. SO, Memoir, 36.

87. SH, *Memoirs*, 58–59. Historians have identified Isaac Newton's tremulous handwriting as possible evidence of mercury intoxication, but Osborn's handwriting was straight and steady; see L. W. Johnson and M. L. Wolbarsht, "Mercury Poisoning: A Probable Cause of Isaac Newton's Physical and Mental Ills," *Notes and Records of the Royal Society of London* 34, no. 1 (July 1979): 1–9; Leonard J. Goldwater, "Newton and Mercury Poisoning," *Science* (November 13, 1981): 742. As revealed by the 1950s Minamata disaster in Japan, organic mercury is especially toxic. Sarah Osborn took an inorganic form, probably either mercuric chloride or mercurous chloride, also known as calomel.

88. Osborn mentions taking medicine "for the salt rheum in my hands which I have been exercised with this twelve years" (SO to JF, May 4, 1747, AAS). On rheumatoid arthritis, see the Web site of the Arthritis Foundation: http://www.arthritis.org/disease-center.php?disease_id=31. On multiple scle-

rosis, see the Web site of the National Multiple Sclerosis Society: http://www
.nationalmssociety.org.

89. SO, Memoir, 36.

90. Samuel Shaw, *The Voice of One Crying in the Wilderness* (1665; rpt. Boston: Rogers and Fowle, 1746), 65.

CHAPTER FOUR. AMAZING GRACE

1. SO, Memoir, [57–58].

2. Ibid., [76].

3. Ibid., 38.

4. Ibid., 13, 21–22, 28, 31.

5. Westminster Assembly, *The Confession of Faith, Together with the Larger Catechism* (Boston: S. Kneeland, 1723), 31; William Perkins, *Works* (Cambridge: J. Legat, 1616), 1: 637. See also Jerald C. Brauer, "Conversion: From Puritanism to Revivalism," *Journal of Religion* 58, no. 3 (July 1978): 234.

6. Solomon Stoddard, *A Treatise Concerning Conversion* (Boston: Franklin, 1719), 78, 85; Cotton Mather, *Christianity Demonstrated* (Boston: Timothy Green, 1710), 23, 26. See also James Spencer Lamborn, "Blessed Assurance? Depraved Saints, Philosophers, and the Problem of Knowledge for Self and State in New England, 1630–1820" (Ph.D. diss., Miami University, 2002), 212.

7. Cotton Mather, *Reason Satisfied and Faith Established* (Boston: J. Allen, 1712), iii, 39; Mather, *Christianity Demonstrated*, 47.

8. Robert Middlekauff, *The Mathers: Three Generations of Puritan Intellectuals, 1596–1728* (New York: Oxford University Press, 1971), 306–7.

9. On Mather's "experimental religion," see Middlekauf, *Mathers*, 305–19. Gilbert Tennent, *Remarks upon a Protestation* (1741), reprinted in *The Great Awakening: Documents Illustrating the Crisis and its Consequences*, ed. Alan Heimert and Perry Miller (Indianapolis: Bobbs-Merrill, 1967), 171, 173.

10. *The Result of a Council of the Consociated Churches of the County of Windham* (Boston, 1747), 7, 17; Andrew Croswell, *A Letter from the Revd Mr. Croswell, to the Revd Mr. Turell, in Answer to His Direction to His People* (Boston: Rogers and Fowle, 1742), 10, emphasis mine; Ebenezer Frothingham, *The Articles of Faith and Practice, with the Covenant, That Is Confessed by the Separate Church of Christ in General in This Land* (Newport: J. Franklin, 1750), 114. On the Separates, see C. C. Goen, *Revivalism and Separatism in New England, 1740–1800: Strict Congregationalists and Separate Baptists in the Great Awakening* (New Haven : Yale University Press, 1962).

11. On the Toleration Act, see Harry S. Stout, *The New England Soul: Preaching and Religious Culture in Colonial New England* (New York: Oxford University Press, 1986), 111.

12. See T. H. Breen and Timothy Hall, "Structuring Provincial Imagination: The Rhetoric and Experience of Social Change in Eighteenth-Century

New England," *American Historical Review* 103, no. 5 (December 1998): 1411–39; T. H. Breen, *The Marketplace of Revolution: How Consumer Politics Shaped American Independence* (New York: Oxford University Press, 2004).

13. JE, *A Treatise Concerning Religious Affections*, in *WJE* 2: 93–461; JE, "Personal Narrative," in *WJE* 16: 792. Bruce Kuklick describes Edwards as "an experimental Calvinist": he believed that the "supernatural was conveyed in experience" (*Churchmen and Philosophers: From Jonathan Edwards to John Dewey* [New Haven: Yale University Press, 1985], 32).

14. Barbara E. Lacey, ed., *The World of Hannah Heaton: The Diary of an Eighteenth-Century New England Farm Woman* (DeKalb: Northern Illinois University Press 2003), 16; JE, *Life of David Brainerd*, in *WJE* 7: 161; SO, Diary, July 8, 1753.

15. John Locke, *An Essay Concerning Human Understanding* (1690; rpt. London: Awnsham and J. Churchill, 1706), 1: 51. See Avihu Zakai, *Jonathan Edwards' Philosophy of History: The Re-Enchantment of the World in the Age of Enlightenment* (Princeton: Princeton University Press, 2003). Leon Chai, *Jonathan Edwards and the Limits of Enlightenment Philosophy* (New York: Oxford University Press, 1998).

16. See, e.g., Robert H. Sharf, "Experience," in *Critical Terms for Religious Studies*, ed. Mark C. Taylor (Chicago: University of Chicago Press, 1998), 95; Wayne Proudfoot, *Religious Experience* (Berkeley: University of California Press, 1985); Ann Taves, *Fits, Trances, and Visions: Experiencing Religion and Explaining Experience from Wesley to James* (Princeton: Princeton University Press, 1999).

17. JE, *Life of David Brainerd*, 143.

18. Edwards A. Park, ed., "Memoir of Samuel Hopkins," in *WSH* 1: 16; Sue Lane McCulley and Dorothy Zayatz Baker, eds., *The Silent and Soft Communion: The Spiritual Narratives of Sarah Pierpont Edwards and Sarah Prince Gill* (Knoxville: University of Tennessee Press 2005), 25.

19. Joseph Tracy, *The Great Awakening: A History of the Revival of Religion in the Time of Edwards and Whitefield* (Boston: Tappan and Dennet, 1842), 161, 138. See Taves, *Fits, Trances, and Visions*, 48–50.

20. JE, *Distinguishing Marks*, in *WJE* 4: 230. For Sarah Edwards's account of her religious experience, see McCulley and Baker, *Silent and Soft Communion*, 1–16.

21. *A True and Genuine Account of a Wonderful WANDERING SPIRIT* (1741), in Heimert and Miller, *Great Awakening*, 149.

22. Michael Crawford, "The Spiritual Travels of Nathan Cole," *William and Mary Quarterly* 33, no. 1 (January 1976): 92. On the new understanding of conversion, see Kenneth P. Minkema, "A Great Awakening Conversion: The Relation of Samuel Belcher," *William and Mary Quarterly* 44 (January 1987): 121–26.

23. D. W. Bebbington, *Evangelicalism in Modern Britain: A History from the 1730s to the 1980s* (London: Unwin Hyman, 1989), 43.

24. McCulley and Baker, eds., *Silent and Soft Communion*, 88; Crawford, "Spiritual Travels of Nathan Cole," 101.

25. SO, Memoir, [71].

26. Ibid., 49.

27. Ibid., 39.

28. See J. Sears McGee, "Conversion and the Imitation of Christ in Anglican and Puritan Writing," *Journal of British Studies* 15, no. 2 (Spring 1976): 24–25.

29. SO, Memoir, 40.

30. On Newport's First Church of Christ, see Horace S. Brown, "Congregationalism in Newport, Rhode Island," 6, typescript, Vault A, no. 1646, NHS.

31. On Clap, see *Sibley's Harvard Graduates*, ed. Clifford K. Shipton (Cambridge: Harvard University Press, 1933), 4: 36; SO, Memoir, 41–42.

32. Cotton Mather, *The Nightingale: An Essay on the Songs Among Thorns* (Boston: B. Green, 1724), 3; SO, Memoir, 42–43; Crawford, "Spiritual Travels of Nathan Cole," 94.

33. SO, Memoir, 44, 17.

34. James Turner, *Without God, Without Creed: The Origins of Unbelief in America* (Baltimore: Johns Hopkins University Press, 1985), 44; SO, Memoir, 46–47, citing Proverbs 18:14.

35. SO, Memoir, 49–50.

36. Ibid., 50.

37. Ibid., 51–52.

38. Tennent quoted ibid., [79]; George Whitefield, *The Marriage of Cana* (1742) in Bushman, *GA*, 33.

39. Elizabeth Rowe, *Devout Exercises of the Heart in Meditation and Soliloquy, Prayer and Praise*, 4th ed. (Boston: Rogers and Fowle, 1742), x–xi. Compare SO, Memoir, 51, to SH, *Memoirs*, 28.

40. *George Whitefield's Journals* (London: Banner of Truth Trust, 1960), 452–53; SO, Memoir, 8, 54–55.

41. Joseph Stevens, *Another and Better Country, Even an Heavenly* (Boston: S. Kneeland, 1723), 55.

42. SO, Memoir, [57].

43. Ibid., [62].

44. Ibid., [62–63]; 1 Corinthians 11:29; John 20:28. Osborn's account echoed ministers' advice to imagine Christ as really present at the table. See Jabez Earle, *Sacramental Exercises, for the Christian's Employment Before, At, and After the Lord's Supper* (Boston: Fleet, 1725).

45. Compare SO, Memoir, [64], to Thomas Doolittle, *A Call to Delaying Sinners* (Boston: Benjamin Eliot, 1700), 140.

46. SO, Memoir, [64].

47. John Bunyan, *Grace Abounding to the Chief of Sinners* (Grand Rapids, Mich.: Baker, 1986), 40, citing Luke 14:22; SO, Memoir, [65–67], quoting Isaiah 54:4–10.

48. SO, Memoir, 51, [141], quoting Revelation 3:20; Andrew Croswell, *A Letter from the Revd Mr. Croswell, to the Revd Mr. Turell* (Boston: Rogers and Fowle, 1742), 11.

49. JF to SO, December 20, 1743, Benjamin Silliman Family Papers, Group 450, Series 1, Box 1, Manuscripts and Archives, SML; SO to JF, November 9, 1743, AAS.

50. Charles Chauncy, *Seasonable Thoughts on the State of Religion in New-England* (Boston: Rogers and Fowle, 1743), 104–5; JE, *Some Thoughts Concerning the Present Revival*, in *WJE* 4: 312; SO, Memoir, 141 (this page is ripped).

51. Compare SO Memoir, 42, 47 to SH, *Memoirs*, 21–22, 25.

52. SO, Memoir, [65], [58], [62], [69], quoting 1 Peter 1:8. I have borrowed this language from Grant Wacker, *Heaven Below : Early Pentecostals and American Culture* (Cambridge: Harvard University Press, 2001), 67.

53. SO, Memoir, [70–71].

54. Ibid., [80].

55. Tracy, *Great Awakening*, 86, 59; Thomas S. Kidd, *The Great Awakening: The Roots of Evangelical Christianity in Colonial America* (New Haven: Yale University Press, 2007), 45–47; *George Whitefield's Journals*, 452–55. On Newport's population, see Elaine Forman Crane, *A Dependent People: Newport, Rhode Island in the Revolutionary Era* (New York: Fordham University Press, 1985), 76.

56. Thomas Prince, *An Account of the Revival of Religion in Boston* (rpt. Boston, 1823), cited in Edwin S. Gaustad, *The Great Awakening in New England* (Chicago: Quadrangle, 1957), 33; *On the Reverend Mr. Gilbert Tennent's Powerful and Successful Preaching* (Boston, 1741), in Heimert and Miller, *Great Awakening*, 193; Gilbert Tennent, *The Espousals; or, A Passionate Perswasive to a Marriage with the Lamb of God* (Boston: Thomas Fleet, 1741), 39–40; SO, Memoir, [76], [78].

57. SO, Memoir, [87].

58. Ibid., [78–80].

59. Gilbert Tennent, *The Examiner, Examined; or, Gilbert Tennent, Harmonious* (Philadelphia: William Bradford, 1743), 98; SO, Memoir, [84]. Tennent was quoting Jeremiah 3:1.

60. SO, Memoir, [86].

61. Ibid., [81], [87], [89].

62. Susa did not become a member of Sarah's church until 1742, but Elizabeth Hopkins claims that they were corresponding as early as 1740. See *FL*, 2.

63. SH, *Life and Character*, 18

64. Ibid., 22, 25.

65. *FL*, 31; SO, Diary, October 13, 1754.

66. SO, Diary, May 29, 1753. See also Barbara Lacey, "The Bonds of Friendship: Sarah Osborn of Newport and the Reverend Joseph Fish of North Stonington, 1743–1779," *Rhode Island History* 45 (November 1986): 126–36.

67. SO to JF, May 29, 1753, January 27, 1755, AAS.

68. SO, Memoir, [122–25], [128].

69. Ibid., [72]. In a passage that she later crossed out, Sarah claimed that she "was so comfortable with the belief I had that his change was out of a world of sin" that she could not mourn, but felt "secret joy that he was released" (ibid., 72). She may have crossed out this passage because she did not want to sound like radicals who claimed to know whether others had been saved.

70. Ibid., [92], [95–96].

71. Ibid., [92–98].

72. Ibid., [98–100].

73. Ibid., [101].

74. Ibid., [103].

75. Ibid., [106], [105].

76. Ibid., [106–8].

77. Ibid., [94], [109].

78. Ibid., [93], [125–26], 9.

79. Ibid., [119–21], citing Romans 8:30. Since she had recently decided against joining Trinity Church, her critic may have been its rector, the Reverend James Honeyman, who opposed the revivals.

80. SO, Memoir, [74–75], [90–91], citing 2 Corinthians 6:14. These passages are crossed out in her memoir and only some sentences can be deciphered.

81. Information about Henry Osborn and his family comes from Alden Gamaliel Beamon, comp., *Rhode Island Vital Records, New Series*, vol. 11: *Births, 1590–1930, from Newport Common Burial Ground Inscriptions* (East Princeton, Mass.: Rhode Island Families Association, 1985), and James N. Arnold, *Vital Record of Rhode Island, 1636–1850. First Series: Births, Marriages and Deaths*, vol. 4 (Providence: Narragansett Historical Publishing, 1893). Henry was born in 1685 and married his first wife, Margaret Miller, in 1721. She died on September 22, 1741, at the age of forty-one. One of their children, Samuel, died at the age of a year and ten months.

82. SO, Memoir, [110]; Benjamin Wadsworth, *The Well-Ordered Family* (Boston: Benjamin Green, 1712), 24–25; William Kidder, "The Diary of Nicholas Gilman" (M.A. thesis, University of New Hampshire, 1972), 375.

83. SO, Memoir, [110–11].

84. Ibid., [111], [114].

85. Ibid., [129–31].

86. Ibid., [132–33], citing Micah 6:8.

87. Ibid., [133], quoting Hebrews 13:5.

88. Ibid., [114–15].

CHAPTER FIVE. THE LORD GAVE, AND
THE LORD HATH TAKEN AWAY

1. SH, *Memoirs*, 65–67.

2. On the affirmation of everyday life, see Charles Taylor, *Sources of the Self: The Making of the Modern Identity* (Cambridge: Harvard University Press, 1989), 211–33.

3. SO, Diary, November 17, 1760; Psalm 13:1.

4. Psalm 102:2.

5. SO, Memoir, [112].

6. See W. J. Rorabaugh, *The Craft Apprentice: From Franklin to the Machine Age in America* (New York: Oxford University Press, 1986), 6.

7. Ibid., 11. See also Carl Bridenbaugh, *The Colonial Craftsman* (New York: Dover, 1990).

8. SH, *Memoirs*, 65.

9. Edmund S. Morgan, *The Puritan Family: Religion and Domestic Relations in Seventeenth-Century New England*, rev. ed. (New York: Harper and Row, 1966), 77. See also John Demos, *A Little Commonwealth: Family Life in Plymouth Colony* (New York: Oxford University Press, 1970), 71–75.

10. Jane Fletcher Fiske, *Gleanings from Newport County Files, 1659–1783* (Boxford, Mass.: n.p., 1998), nos. 125, 710.

11. SH, *Memoirs*, 66.

12. Ibid., 65. On Epaphroditus, see Philippians 2:27. On Hezekiah, see 2 Kings 20, 2 Chronicles 32:24, and Isaiah 38:1.

13. SH, *Memoirs*, 65–66; 2 Peter 1; Jeremiah 30:7–8; Psalm 86:5–7.

14. SH, *Memoirs*, 66.

15. Ibid., 66.

16. SO, Memoir, 30. See Cotton Mather, *Help for Distressed Parents* (Boston: John Allen, 1695), 13.

17. Esther Edwards Burr to JE, November 2, 1757, cited in David E. Stannard, *The Puritan Way of Death: A Study in Religion, Culture, and Social Change* (New York: Oxford University Press, 1977), 150.

18. Thomas Hooker, *The Unbeleevers Preparing for Christ* (London, 1638), quoted in Ross W. Beales, "In Search of the Historical Child: Miniature Adulthood and Youth in Colonial New England," *American Quarterly* 27, no. 4 (October 1975): 386.

19. *CH* (June 30, 1744): 137.

20. Thomas Prince, "The Great and Solemn Obligations to Early Piety," cited in Sandford Fleming, *Children and Puritanism: The Place of Children in the Life and Thought of the New England Churches, 1620–1847* (New Haven: Yale University Press, 1933), 97.

21. JE, "Sermon on 2 Kings 2:23–24" (1741), Jonathan Edwards Collection (1696–1972), BL.

22. John Webb, *Twenty-Four Sermons* (Boston: J. Draper, 1726), 25.

23. Gilbert Tennent, *A Solemn Warning to the Secure World, from the God of Terrible Majesty* (Boston: S. Kneeland and T. Green, 1735), 171; Charles Drelincourt, *The Christian's Defence Against the Fears of Death, with Directions How to Die Well* (Boston: Thomas Fleet, 1744), 15; Samuel Moodey, *The Gospel Way of Escaping the Doleful State of the Damned* (Boston: S. Kneeland and T. Green, 1739), 10.

24. See *WJE* 14: 27–28.

25. JE, *Sinners in the Hands of an Angry God*, in *WJE* 22: 411–12; Stephen Williams, Diary, July 8, 1741 (typescript), cited in George M. Marsden, *Jonathan Edwards: A Life* (New Haven: Yale University Press, 2003), 220.

26. Norman Fiering, *Jonathan Edwards's Moral Thought and Its British Context* (Chapel Hill: University of North Carolina Press, 1981), 204. See also Perry Miller, *Jonathan Edwards* ([New York]: Sloane Associates, 1949), 155.

27. Thomas Hobbes, *Leviathan* (London, 1651), and John Tillotson, *Of the Eternity of Hell Torments* (London, 1708), cited in Philip C. Almond, *Heaven and Hell in Enlightenment England* (New York: Cambridge University Press, 1994), 150, 156.

28. See Edward M. Griffin, *Old Brick: Charles Chauncy of Boston, 1705–1787* (Minneapolis: University of Minnesota Press, 1980), 127; Charles Chauncy, *The Mystery Hid from Ages and Generations, Made Manifest by the Gospel Revelation; or, The Salvation of All Men* (London: Charles Dilly, 1784).

29. SH, *Memoirs*, 66.

30. Joseph Alleine, *An Alarm to Unconverted Sinners* (Philadelphia: B. Franklin, 1741), ii, 54, 94.

31. Ibid., 139–40.

32. Ibid., 13.

33. SH, *Memoirs*, 67; Alleine, *Alarm to Unconverted Sinners*, 109.

34. Thomas Prince, *The Sovereign God Acknowledged and Blessed, Both in Giving and Taking Away. A Sermon Occasioned by the Decease of Mrs. Deborah Prince* (Boston: Rogers and Fowle, 1744), 29–32. Sarah knew Thomas Prince; see SH, *Memoirs*, 157.

35. SH, *Memoirs*, 66.

36. Ibid., 66–67.

37. B. A. Gerrish, "'To the Unknown God': Luther and Calvin on the Hiddenness of God," in Gerrish, *The Old Protestantism and the New: Essays on the Reformation Heritage* (Chicago: University of Chicago Press, 1982), 144.

38. SH, *Memoirs*, 67.

39. Gerrish, "'To the Unknown God,'" 148; *FL*, 84. The same imagery of "the apple of his eye" appears in Deuteronomy 32:10.

40. *FL*, 85.

41. SH, *Memoirs*, 67.

42. Ibid.

43. SH, *Memoirs*, 68, citing Psalm 55:22.

44. Ibid., citing 1 Samuel 8.

45. Charles Chauncy, *Early Piety Recommended and Exemplify'd* (Boston: S. Kneeland and T. Green, 1732), 19.

46. SH, *Memoirs*, 68, citing 2 Samuel 12:20.

47. Ibid., citing Psalm 71:7–8.

48. Ibid.; Julian of Norwich, *Revelations of Divine Love* (London: Methuen, 1901), 57.

49. SH, *Memoirs*, 69.

50. Ibid., citing Hebrews 12:8 and Psalm 119:75.

51. Ibid., 68.

52. Cotton Mather, *Nehemiah* (Boston: Bartholomew Green, 1710), 4. The biblical text is Genesis 17:7; see also Hebrews 8. SH, *Memoirs*, 68.

53. SH, *Memoirs*, 68; Samuel Moodey, *Judas the Traitor Hung Up in Chains* (Boston, 1714), iii.

54. SH, *Memoirs*, 68–69; Psalm 73:26–27; Revelation 6–8.

55. Barbara E. Lacey, ed. *The World of Hannah Heaton: The Diary of an Eighteenth-Century New England Farm Woman* (DeKalb: Northern Illinois University Press 2003), 24.

56. SH, *Memoirs*, 69.

57. Henry Gibbs, *Bethany; or, The House of Mourning* (Boston: T. Green, 1714), 4, 9, 12–13, 11; Nathanael Appleton, *A Great Man Fallen in Israel* (Boston: B. Green, 1724), 34. See also Benjamin Wadsworth, *Considerations, to Prevent Murmuring and Promote Patience in Christians, Under Afflictive Providences* (Boston: B. Green, 1706), 14, citing Numbers 14; Flavel, *A Token for Mourners; or, The Advice of Christ to a Distressed Mother, Bewailing the Death of Her Dear and Only Son* (London: Thomas Pankhurst, 1694), 13.

58. See Gibbs, *Bethany*, 11; Flavel, *Token for Mourners*, 13; John Willison, *The Afflicted Man's Companion* (Philadelphia: W. Young, 1788), 205, citing Leviticus 10:3 and Job 40:4; Thomas Brooks, *The Silent Soul* (1659; rpt. Boston: Boone, 1728), 12, citing Genesis 45:8; Benjamin Wadsworth, *Hearty Submission and Resignation to the Will of God* (Boston: B. Green, 1716), 3, citing 2 Samuel 15:26; Brooks, *Silent Soul*, 47, citing Isaiah 53:7.

59. Wadsworth, *Considerations, to Prevent Murmuring*, 3, 13.

60. Ibid., 14; Appleton, *Great Man Fallen in Israel*, 34–35.

61. Thomas Skinner, *The Mourner Admonished* (Boston: Rogers and Fowle, 1746), 28–29; Gibbs, *Bethany*, 12.

62. Flavel, *Token for Mourners*, 8–9. Luke records three occasions when Jesus said "weep not": 7:13, 8:52, 23:28. Flavel's text was Luke 7:13.

63. Wadsworth, *Considerations, to Prevent Murmuring*, 24–25.

64. Taylor, *Sources of the Self*, 218.

65. Diary of Experience (Wight) Richardson [transcript], February 1753, MHS; Lacey, *World of Hannah Heaton*, 25; Sue Lane McCulley and Dorothy

Zayatz Baker, eds., *The Silent and Soft Communion: The Spiritual Narratives of Sarah Pierpont Edwards and Sarah Prince Gill* (Knoxville: University of Tennessee Press, 2005), 75.

66. SH, *Memoirs*, 69.

67. On eighteenth-century funerals, see Gillian B. Anderson, "The Funeral of Samuel Cooper," *New England Quarterly* 50, no. 4 (December 1977): 644–59.

68. SH, *Memoirs*, 70, quoting Hebrews 4:15.

69. Ibid., 70.

70. Ibid., 65, emphasis mine.

71. SH, "The Nature and Design of Infant Baptism," in *WSH* 2: 122, 129, 124.

72. Levi Hart, *A Sermon on the Sacred Obligations of Christian Ministers to Improve Their Personal Sorrows for the Benefit of Their People* (New London: T. Green, 1789), 6. His text was Ezekiel 24:15–18.

73. Flavel, *Token for Mourners*, 21; *A Pastoral Visit to the Afflicted* (Boston: n.p., 1737), 4.

74. *Pastoral Visit to the Afflicted*, 7.

75. Thomas Brooks, *The Silent Soul* (Boston: Boone, 1728), 126, and the Epistle Dedicatory (this book was first published in the seventeenth century); Flavel, "The Epistle Dedicatory," *Token for Mourners*, n.p.

76. SO, Memoir, [64], citing Exodus 20:3.

77. *FL*, 49–51.

78. SO, Memoir, [113].

79. Ibid.

80. SO, Diary, September 14, 1753, September 10, 1754, September 18, 1760.

Chapter Six. No Imaginary Thing

1. SO, *Nature*, 2–4.

2. Benjamin Robins, *A Discourse Concerning the Nature and Certainty of Sir Isaac Newton's Methods of Fluxions, and of Prime and Ultimate Ratios* (London : printed for W. Innys and R. Manby, 1735); Edward Stillingfleet, *A Discourse Concerning the Nature and Grounds of the Certainty of Faith* (London: Henry Mortlock, 1688); JE, *The Distinguishing Marks of a Work of the Spirit of God* (Boston: S. Kneeland and T. Green, 1741); Jonathan Dickinson, *The Witness of the Spirit* (Boston: S. Kneeland and T. Green, 1740). 4; Joseph Bellamy, *True Religion Delineated; or, Experimental Religion* (Boston: S. Kneeland, 1750);

3. SO, *Nature*, 3.

4. According to the digital collection *Early American Imprints, Series I: Evans, 1639–1800*, 7,373 titles were published in America during these years. This number includes titles that were printed more than once. The eight titles are: Mary Rowlandson, *Sovereignty and Goodness of God* (Cambridge: Samuel

Green, 1682); Bathsheba Bowers, *An Alarm Sounded to Prepare the Inhabitants of the World to Meet the Lord in the Way of his Judgments* (New York: William Bradford, 1709); Mercy Wheeler, *An Address to Young People* (Boston: n.p., 1733); Elizabeth Mixer, *An Account of Some Spiritual Experiences and Rapturous and Pious Expressions* (New London: T. Green, 1736); Ann Maylem, *A Short Narrative of the Unjust Proceedings of Mr. George Gardner of Newport Distiller, Against Ann Maylem Widow* (Newport: Ann Franklin, 1742); Sarah Parsons Moorhead, *To the Reverend Mr. James Davenport* (Boston: Charles Harrison, 1742); Sophia Hume, *An Exhortation to the Inhabitants of the Province of South Carolina* (Philadelphia: William Bradford, 1747); and SO, *Nature*. Counting the number of books written by women and published in America is complicated. The Evans collection includes a category titled "women as authors," but this category contains many books that were about women but not written by them. I have chosen to count only first editions because some books, especially Mary Rowlandson's narrative, were published in many editions. I have not included works that contained extracts from women's writings: for example, Cotton Mather, *Memorials of Early Piety. Occurring in the Holy Life and Joyful Death of Mrs. Jerusha Oliver. With Some Account of her Christian Experiences, Extracted from Her Reserved Papers: And Published, for the Service of Christianity* (Boston: T. Green, 1711).

5. SH, *Memoirs*, 92–93.

6. Susannah Haggar's marriage is mentioned in a court case. See Jane Fletcher Fiske, *Gleanings from Newport County Files, 1659–1783* (Boxford, Mass.: n.p., 1998), no. 810. On the marriages of John and Edward Osborn, see James N. Arnold, *Vital Record of Rhode Island, 1636–1850. First Series: Births, Marriages and Deaths*, vol. 8 (Providence: Narragansett Historical Publishing, 1896), 423.

7. SH, *Memoirs*, 96.

8. Ibid., 64, 89.

9. SO, Diary, December 15, 1761. On Bobey's birthdate, see SO to JF, May 16, 1754, AAS. Osborn described Bobey as ten years old in 1754, which means that he was born in 1743 or 1744.

10. SO to JF, May 16, 1754, AAS.

11. Ibid.

12. SO to JF, June 4, 1754, AAS.

13. Samuel Hopkins claimed that the women's society met regularly for more than fifty years after its founding in 1741 (SH, *Memoirs*, 71). But in a letter to Joseph Fish, Osborn explained that it had been dropped for several years (SO to JF, May 10, 1761, AAS).

14. SH, *Life and Character*, 113; SO, *Nature*, title page.

15. SO, *Nature*, 3.

16. SO, Diary, November 17, 1760, August 21, August 18, 1753.

17. Ibid., December 16, 1753. See also SH, *Memoirs*, 130.

18. SO, Diary, July 29, 1753.

19. SO, *Nature*, title page. The 1755 edition had slightly different wording on the title page from that of later editions. For example, the 1793 edition changed "was wrote" to "was written."

20. On Thomas Prince's involvement in the publication of Osborn's letter, see SH, *Memoirs*, 157.

21. Maylem, *Short Narrative*; SO, *Nature*, 3.

22. Anne Bradstreet, *Several Poems Compiled with Great Variety of Wit and Learning* (Boston: John Foster, 1678); Rowlandson, *Sovereignty and Goodness of God*; Sarah Goodhue, *The Copy of a Valedictory and Monitory Writing* (Cambridge, Mass.: n.p., 1681); Preface to Anne Bradstreet, *The Tenth Muse Lately Sprung Up in America* (London: Stephen Bowtell, 1650); Elaine Showalter, *A Jury of Her Peers: American Women Writers from Anne Bradstreet to Annie Proulx* (New York: Knopf, 2009), 3.

23. James Kendall Hosmer, ed., *Winthrop's Journal, "History of New England," 1630–1649* (New York: Scribner's, 1908), 2: 225; *The Copy of a Letter Written by Mr. Thomas Parker* (London: J. Field, 1650), 13; Cotton Mather, *Awakening Thoughts on the Sleep of Death* (Boston: Timothy Green, 1712), iv.

24. Hannah Callowhill Penn, *London, 26th of the 3d month, 1724* (Philadelphia: Samuel Keimer, 1724); Sarah Fiske, *A Confession of Faith; or, A Summary of Divinity Drawn Up by a Young Gentlewoman, in the 25th Year of Her Age* (Boston: B. Green, 1704), i.

25. Goodhue, *Copy of a Valedictory and Monitory Writing*; Mary Mollineux, *Fruits of Retirement; or, Miscellaneous Poems, Moral and Divine* (Philadelphia: Samuel Keimer, 1729).

26. Ebenezer Prime, *A Sermon Preached in Oyster Bay Feb. 27, 1743–4: At the Funeral of Mrs. Freelove Wilmot, Consort of the Rev. Mr. Walter Wilmot* (New York: J. Parker, 1744), 62.

27. Nathaniel Appleton, *The Christian Glorying in Tribulation from a Sense of Its Happy Fruits. A Discourse Occasion'd by the Death of that Pious and Afflicted Gentlewoman Mrs. Martha Gerrish. . . . To Which Are Annexed Some of Mrs. Gerrish's Letters* (Boston: J. Draper, 1736), 66.

28. Elizabeth White, *The Experiences of God's Gracious Dealing with Mrs. Elizabeth White* (Boston: S. Kneeland and T. Green, 1741); Elizabeth Bury, *An Account of the Life and Death of Mrs. Elizabeth Bury* (Boston: D. Henchman, 1743); Elizabeth Singer Rowe, *The History of Joseph. A Poem* (Philadelphia: B. Franklin, 1739); Elizabeth Singer Rowe, *Devout Exercises of the Heart in Meditation and Soliloquy, Prayer and Praise* (Boston: J. Blanchard, 1742).

29. Charles Chauncy, *Seasonable Thoughts on the State of Religion in New-England* (Boston: Rogers and Fowle, for Samuel Eliot in Cornhill, 1743), 240; "Advice to Mr. and Mrs. Kingsley," JE Papers, Andover Newton Theological

School, Newton Centre, Mass.; Nathan Bowen, "Extracts from Interleaved Almanacs of Nathan Bowen, 1742–1799," *Essex Institute of Historical Collections* 41 (1955): 169; *South Carolina Gazette*, June 21, 1742, quoted in Timothy D. Hall, *Contested Boundaries: Itinerancy and the Reshaping of the Colonial American Religious World* (Durham, N.C.: Duke University Press, 1994), 58. On women during the revivals, see Catherine A. Brekus, *Strangers and Pilgrims : Female Preaching in America, 1740–1845* (Chapel Hill: University of North Carolina Press, 1998), 23–67.

30. Ebenezer Frothingham, *The Articles of Faith and Practice, with the Covenant, That Is Confessed by the Separate Churches of Christ in General in This Land* (Newport: J. Franklin, 1750), 360–61; Joshua Hempstead, *The Diary of Joshua Hempstead* (New London: n.p., 1901), 402–3.

31. SO, *Nature*, 3, 4, 13, 5.

32. Bury, *Account of the Life and Death*, 123, 96; Hannah Housman, *The Power and Pleasure of the Divine Life* (Boston: S. Kneeland, 1755). Both books were originally printed in England: Bury's in 1720 in Bristol and Housman's in 1744 in London. Osborn mentioned Bury's book in SO to JF, February 4, 1747/8, AAS, and also in Diary, July 17, 1757. She mentioned Housman in Diary, March 10, 1758.

33. Rowe, *Devout Exercises*, 132; Carol F. Karlsen and Laurie Crumpacker, eds., *The Journal of Esther Edwards Burr, 1754–1757* (New Haven: Yale University Press, 1984), 98–99; SA, Diary, July 18, 1749, MS 66939, CHS.

34. SO, Diary, October 23, 1761. Since Defoe's manual was not published in America until 1792, she must have read a copy imported from England. See Daniel Defoe, *The Family Instructor*, 13th ed. (London: Tho. Longman, Ch. Hitch and L. Hawes, 1751).

35. See Sydney V. James, *Colonial Rhode Island: A History* (New York: Scribner's, 1975), 199; George C. Mason, *Annals of the Redwood Library and Athenaeum, Newport, R.I.* (Newport: Redwood Library, 1891), 3.

36. SH, *Memoirs*, 159.

37. SO, *Nature*, 3.

38. Jean-Jacques Rousseau, *Emilius; or, A Treatise of Education* (Edinburgh: A. Donaldson, 1768), quoted in Linda Kerber, "The Republican Mother: Women and the Enlightenment—An American Perspective," *American Quarterly* 28, no. 2 (Summer 1976): 194.

39. Ebenezer Pemberton, *Meditations on Divine Subjects: By Mrs. Mary Lloyd* (New York: J. Parker, 1750), 22.

40. Gezelena Rousby, *To the Freeholders and Freemen of the City of New-York* (New York: n.p., 1769); Anne Dutton, *A Letter from Mrs. Anne Dutton to the Reverend G. Whitefield* (Philadelphia: William Bradford, 1743); Martha Brewster, *Poems on Divers Subjects* (New London: Edes and Gill, 1757).

41. Jane Dunlap, *Poems upon Several Sermons Preached by the Rev'd, and Renowned, George Whitefield, While in Boston* (Boston: Ezekiel Russell, 1771), 19.

42. Phillis Wheatley, *An Elegiac Poem . . . On the Death of George Whitefield* (Boston: Ezekiel Russell, 1770); Phillis Wheatley, *Poems on Various Subjects, Religious and Moral* (London: A. Bell, 1773).

43. Kramnick, *PER*, xv.

44. See William Kolbrener and Michal Michelson, eds., *Mary Astell: Reason, Gender, Faith* (Burlington, Vt.: Ashgate, 2007).

45. See D. Bruce Hindmarsh, "Reshaping Individualism: The Private Christian, Eighteenth-Century Religion and the Enlightenment," in *The Rise of the Laity in Evangelical Protestantism*, ed. Deryck W. Lovegrove (New York: Routledge, 2002), 74; Harry S. Stout, *The Divine Dramatist: George Whitefield and the Rise of Modern Evangelicalism* (Grand Rapids, Mich.: Eerdmans, 1991), 205; Jerald C. Brauer, "Conversion: From Puritanism to Revivalism," *Journal of Religion* 58, no. 3 (July 1978): 241. In *The Self and the Sacred: Conversion and Autobiography in Early American Protestantism* (Knoxville: University of Tennessee Press, 1998), Rodger M. Payne argues that eighteenth-century evangelicals "were able to embrace and sacralize the concept of the autonomous self" (8). Although I agree with Payne that evangelicals emphasized the individual, the word *autonomous* overstates the case.

46. Josiah Smith, *A Sermon, on the Character, Preaching &c. of the Rev. Mr. Whitefield* (1740), in *The Great Awakening: Documents Illustrating the Crisis and Its Consequences*, ed. Alan Heimert and Perry Miller (Indianapolis: Bobbs-Merrill, 1967), 65.

47. D. Bruce Hindmarsh, *The Evangelical Conversion Narrative: Spiritual Autobiography in Early Modern England* (New York: Oxford University Press, 2005), 146–48; Barbara E. Lacey, ed., *The World of Hannah Heaton: The Diary of an Eighteenth-Century New England Farm Woman* (DeKalb: Northern Illinois University Press 2003), 16; SO, *Nature*, 3, 5–6.

48. SO, *Nature*, title page.

49. Caroline Belsey, "Afterword: A Future for Materialist-Feminist Criticism," in *The Matter of Difference: Materialist-Feminist Criticism of Shakespeare*, ed. Valerie Wayne (Ithaca: Cornell University Press, 1991), 262. On the sexually egalitarian possibilities of the Enlightenment, see Margaret C. Jacob, "Freemasonry, Women, and the Paradox of the Enlightenment," in *Women and the Enlightenment*, ed. Margaret Hunt, Margaret Jacob, Phyllis Mack, and Ruth Perry (New York: Haworth, 1984); Jonathan Irvine Israel, *Radical Enlightenment: Philosophy and the Making of Modernity, 1650–1750* (New York: Oxford University Press, 2001), 82–96.

50. Susan Juster, *Doomsayers: Anglo-American Prophecy in the Age of Revolution* (Philadelphia: University of Pennsylvania Press, 2003), 218. See also Jane Shaw, "Religious Experience and the Formation of the Early Enlightenment Self," in *Rewriting the Self: Histories from the Renaissance to the Present*, ed. Roy Porter (New York: Routledge, 1997), 70–71; Phyllis Mack, "Women and the Enlightenment: An Introduction," in *Women and the Enlightenment*, 9–10.

51. See Jürgen Habermas, *The Structural Transformation of the Public Sphere: An Inquiry into a Category of Bourgeois Society* (Cambridge: MIT Press, 1989); Joan B. Landes, *Women and the Public Sphere in the Age of the French Revolution* (Ithaca: Cornell University Press, 1988), 135.

52. On "democratic political agency" as a feature of the public sphere, see Ruth H. Bloch, "Inside and Outside the Public Sphere," *William and Mary Quarterly* 62, no. 1 (January 2005): 99. On counterpublics, see Joanna Brooks, "The Early American Public Sphere and the Emergence of a Black Print Counterpublic," *William and Mary Quarterly* 62, no. 1 (January 2005), 67–92.

53. The editions were Boston: S. Kneeland, 1755; London: Thomas Bayley, 1763; Newport: S. Hall, 1764; Danbury, Conn.: N. Douglas, 1793; and Providence: J. Carter, 1793.

54. *WJE* 26: 98–103; see the copy of SO, *Nature*, at AAS; 1 Corinthians 11:3.

CHAPTER SEVEN. PINCHING POVERTY

1. SO, Diary, October 3, 1757. The reference to "Mr. Elot" is to Joseph Eliot, *A Copy of a Letter Found in the Study of the Reverend Mr. Joseph Belcher, Late of Dedham, Since His Decease* (Boston: B. Green, 1725), 3.

2. SO, Diary, October 3, June 7, October 17, October 13, 1757.

3. SO, Diary, August 19, 1757, November 22, 1759, February 11, 1757.

4. SO, Diary, May 10, 1757; SO to JF, November 2, 1761, AAS.

5. See T. H. Breen, "'Baubles of Britain': The American and Consumer Revolutions of the Eighteenth Century," *Past and Present* 119 (May 1988): 78. See also Breen, "Narrative of Commercial Life: Consumption, Ideology, and Community on the Eve of the American Revolution," *William and Mary Quarterly* 50, no. 3 (July 1993): 471–501; Breen, *The Marketplace of Revolution: How Consumer Politics Shaped American Independence* (New York: Oxford University Press, 2004); John Brewer and Roy Porter, eds., *Consumption and the World of Goods* (New York: Routledge, 1993); Neil McKendrick, John Brewer, and J. H. Plumb, *The Birth of a Consumer Society: The Commercialization of Eighteenth-Century England* (Bloomington: Indiana University Press, 1982).

6. See Sheila Skemp, "A Social and Cultural History of Newport, Rhode Island, 1720–1765" (Ph.D. diss., University of Iowa, 1974), 361; *NM*, June 19, 1758, May 23, 1763; George Champlin Mason, *Reminiscences of Newport* (Newport: Charles E. Hammett, Jr., 1884), 178.

7. On the standard of living, see Lorena S. Walsh, "Urban Amenities and Rural Sufficiency: Living Standards and Consumer Behavior in the Colonial Chesapeake, 1643–1777," *Journal of Economic History* 43 (March 1983): 109–117; Gloria L. Main, "The Standard of Living in Southern New England, 1640–1773," *William and Mary Quarterly* 45, no. 1 (January 1988): 124–34; Gloria L. Main and Jackson T. Main, "The Red Queen in New England?" *William and*

Mary Quarterly 56, no. 1 (January 1999): 121–50. For a different perspective, see Billy G. Smith, "Toward a History of the Standard of Living in British North America: Comment," *William and Mary Quarterly* 45, no. 1 (January 1988): 163–66. On the Tates, see Stephen A. Mrozowski, *The Archaeology of Class in Urban America* (New York: Cambridge University Press, 2006), 49, 57–58. On the eighteenth-century economy, see Jon Butler, *Becoming America: The Revolution Before 1776* (Cambridge: Harvard University Press, 2000), 50–88.

8. "M. F.," *Boston Weekly News-Letter*, July 19 and 26, 1750, quoted in Breen, *Marketplace of Revolution*, 153.

9. See Daniel Vickers, "Competency and Competition: Economic Culture in Early America," *William and Mary Quarterly* 47 (January 1990): 1–33; James A. Henretta, *The Origins of American Capitalism: Collected Essays* (Boston: Northeastern University Press, 1991). On capitalism and Puritanism, see Mark Valeri, *Heavenly Merchandize: How Religion Shaped Commerce in Puritan America* (Princeton: Princeton University Press, 2010); Stephen Innes, *Creating the Commonwealth: The Economic Culture of Puritan New England* (New York: Norton, 1995); Mark A. Peterson, *The Price of Redemption: The Spiritual Economy of Puritan New England* (Stanford: Stanford University Press, 1997). See also Cathy D. Matson, *The Economy of Early America: Historical Perspectives and New Directions* (University Park: Pennsylvania State University Press, 2006), 57. According to the *Oxford English Dictionary*, the word *capitalism* was first used in 1854. It was not commonly used until Karl Marx published the first volume of *Das Kapital* in 1867.

10. See Roderick Terry, "Some Old Papers Relating to the Newport Slave Trade," *Bulletin of the Newport Historical Society* 62 (July 1927): 19.

11. Albert Bushnell Hart, ed., *Hamilton's Itinerarium* (Saint Louis: W. K. Bixby, 1907), 125. See also Skemp, "Social and Cultural History of Newport," 222. Alexander Boyd Hawes, *Off Soundings: Aspects of the Maritime History of Rhode Island* (Chevy Chase, Md.: Posterity Press, 1999), 153.

12. Lynne Withey, *Urban Growth in Colonial Rhode Island: Newport and Providence in the Eighteenth Century* (Albany: State University of New York Press, 1984), 51, 56; Richard Henry Rudolph, "The Merchants of Newport, Rhode Island, 1763–1786" (Ph.D. diss., University of Connecticut, 1975), 31.

13. Charles Chauncy, *The Idle Poor Secluded from the Bread of Charity by the Christian Law* (Boston: Thomas Fleet, 1752), 7, 17; Cotton Mather, *Durable Riches* (Boston: John Allen, 1695), 20; John Locke, *On the Reform of the Poor Laws* (1697), reprinted in *The Enlightenment: A Comprehensive Anthology*, ed. Peter Gay (New York: Simon and Schuster, 1973), 101–2. Here I disagree with Lisa Levenstein, who has argued that the distinction between the deserving and undeserving poor was a product of the nineteenth century. See Levenstein, "Deserving/Undeserving Poor," in *Poverty in the United States: An Encyclopedia of History, Politics, and Policy*, ed. Gwendolyn Mink and Alice O'Connor (Santa Barbara, Calif.: ABC Clio, 2004), 1: 226–30.

14. On Newport's almshouse, see Skemp, "Social and Cultural History of Newport," 349; Withey, *Urban Growth in Colonial Rhode Island*, 61–62. On the warning-out system, see Ruth Wallis Herndon, *Unwelcome Americans: Living on the Margin in Early New England* (Philadelphia: University of Pennsylvania Press, 2001), 2.

15. Benjamin Franklin, *Poor Richard's Almanack*, reprinted in Kramnick, *PER*, 489.

16. Withey, *Urban Growth in Colonial Rhode Island*, 55.

17. See Elaine Forman Crane, *A Dependent People: Newport, Rhode Island, in the Revolutionary Era* (New York: Fordham University Press, 1985), 72. On poor women in colonial America, see Daniel Scott Smith, "Female Householding in Late Eighteenth-Century America and the Problem of Poverty," *Journal of Social History* 28, no. 1 (1994): 83–107; Karin Wulf, "Gender and the Political Economy of Poor Relief in Colonial Philadelphia," in *Down and Out in Early America*, ed. Billy G. Smith (University Park: Pennsylvania State University Press, 2004), 163–88. On Hannah Lamb see SO, Diary, January 2, 1762, and First Congregational Church of Newport Records, 1744, Vault A, no. 836D, NHS.

18. On women's wages, see Gloria L. Main, "Gender, Work, and Wages in Colonial New England," *William and Mary Quarterly* 51, no. 1 (1994): 44.

19. There were seventy-three pews assigned in 1753. Fifty-three percent of the church members were assessed higher rates than the Osborns. See the October 1753 pew assessments in FCCR-DRC.

20. SO to JF, 1751; SO, Diary, January 9, 1757.

21. See SO, Diary, undated entry for April 1757; also Diary, April 3, 1757. John Osborn married Abigail Grey on June 19, 1748 (James N. Arnold, *Vital Record of Rhode Island, 1636–1850. First Series: Births, Marriages and Deaths*, vol. 8 [Providence: Narragansett Historical Publishing, 1896], 471).

22. Nathaniel Clap, *The Duty of all Christians Urged* (New London: T. Green, 1720), 25; SO, Diary, December 10, 1759; Max Weber, *The Protestant Ethic and the Spirit of Capitalism*, trans. Talcott Parsons (New York: Scribner's, 1958).

23. SO, Diary, April 13, 1757; Fred Anderson, *Crucible of War: The Seven Years' War and the Fate of Empire in British North America, 1754–1766* (New York: Knopf, 2000), 563; Rudolph, "Merchants of Newport, Rhode Island," 56; Peter J. Coleman, "The Insolvent Debtor in Rhode Island, 1745–1828," *William and Mary Quarterly* 22, no. 3 (1965): 420–23. Osborn mentions "Mrs. Cheapman" in SO, Diary, January 2, 1762. The Chipmans were members of her church. See the Pew Assessments for 1753, First Congregational Church of Newport Records, 1743–1831, Vault A, no. 833, NHS; and FCCR-CB.

24. See the references to Elnathan Hammond in FCCR-CB, including April 1745 and December 29, 1747. Polly Hammond is mentioned in SO, Diary, July 26, 1760.

25. SO, Diary, April 19, 1760. See the two undated letters from SO to JF about the controversy over raising her tuition, Folder 1, AAS. Internal evidence suggests that these letters were written in 1755.

26. Cotton Mather, quoted in John E. Crowley, *This Sheba, Self: The Conceptualization of Economic Life in Eighteenth-Century America* (Baltimore: Johns Hopkins University Press, 1974), 4; SH, *Memoirs*, 217; SO, Diary, June 11, 1757.

27. SO, Diary, April 14, 1757.

28. On Luther and Calvin, see Carter Lindberg, "Luther on Poverty," *Lutheran Quarterly* 15, no. 1 (Spring 2001): 85–101; Bonnie L. Pattison, *Poverty in the Theology of John Calvin* (Eugene, Ore.: Wipf and Stock, 2006). JE, *Having No Part in the Saving Influences of God's Spirit* (Sermon on Acts 8: 21), 1735, *WJE Online*.

29. SO, Diary, February 18, 1757. On Newport's lotteries, see Skemp, "Social and Cultural History of Newport," 214–15.

30. See Breen, *Marketplace of Revolution*, 24–25. The covenant appears in FCCR-BM, 59.

31. SO, Diary, June 14, 1757; Anderson, *Crucible of War*, 182–83, 563; SO, Diary, June 7, June 9, 1757.

32. SO, Diary, August 2, 1757; SH, *Memoirs*, 174. For an example of a notation made a year after the original prayer, see SO, Diary, March 6, 1758.

33. SO, Diary, June 24, 1757.

34. We know that Phillis had two children only because of a brief entry in Sarah Osborn's diary. Praying for Phillis, she wrote: "O appear for Her offspring, both of them" (SO, Diary, December 15, 1761). The other child may have belonged to Timothy Allen, Phillis's master. On Allen, see *LD* 1: 84, 140, 327, 428, 504. Gosper is mentioned in SO, Diary, October 19, 1761. It is clear that Gosper was Bobey's father; see SO, Diary, December 4, 1761. I am assuming that Phillis and Gosper were married because otherwise the church would not have accepted her as a full member. On Phillis's acceptance into the church, see FCCR-BM. Phillis is listed as a member of Sarah's women's society in SO, Diary, December 4, 1761, and January 2, 1762.

35. SO, Diary, May 2, 1757.

36. Ibid. On Leandrow, see FCCR-BM. The church records (FCCR-BM) for July 3, 1749, contain this entry: "Baptized Cudjo, a Negro Man servant of Mr. Nichols, upon His Bed, at his Masters House, he having first owned the Covenant for Baptism in presence of some of the Church." On the meetings with the Reverend Vinal and the Allens, see SO, Diary, May 2, 1757.

37. SO, Diary, September 19, 1757.

38. Ibid., August 9, 1757. On Protestant understandings of the French and Indian War, see Nathan O. Hatch, *The Sacred Cause of Liberty: Republican Thought and the Millennium in Revolutionary New England* (New Haven: Yale University Press, 1977); Harry S. Stout, *The New England Soul: Preaching*

and Religious Culture in Colonial New England (New York: Oxford University Press, 1986), 233–58.

39. SO, Diary, July 13, 1757; *NM*, January 2, 1759; SO, Diary, September 26, 1757.

40. Edward married Mary Young in 1747 (Arnold, *Vital Record*, First Series, vol. 8, p. 423).

41. SO, Diary, August 7, August 19, 1757. Edward served with Captain John Whiting under Colonel Samuel Angell; see Howard M. Chapin, *Rhode Island in the Colonial Wars: A List of Rhode Island Soldiers and Sailors in King George's War, 1740–1748* (Baltimore: Genealogical Publishing, 1994), 107.

42. SO, Diary, September 15, September 17, 1757.

43. Ibid., February 21, 1758, September 26, 1757; SO to JF, May 3, 1759, AAS.

44. SO, Diary, October 3, October 13, 1757, March 21, 1758.

45. Ibid., April 27, 1757, March 4, 1758. The list of possessions is drawn from SO, Will and Inventory, Probate Book no. 3, pp. 11–12, Newport City Hill, Newport, R.I.

46. On opening a boarding school, see SO, Diary, March 15, March 19, March 21, March 23, April 2, 1757.

47. *NM*, December 19, 1758.

48. Luke 12:19; SO, Diary, April 2, 1757.

49. John Guyse, *A Collection of Seventeen Practical Sermons on Various and Important Subjects* (London: Edward Dilley, 1761), 21; George Whitefield, *Sermons on Various Subjects* (Philadelphia: Benjamin Franklin, 1740), 2: 10; George Whitefield, *The Folly and Danger of Parting with Christ for the Pleasures and Profits of Life* (London: C. Whitefield, 1740), 30.

50. Benjamin Colman, *Some Reasons and Arguments Offered to the Good People of Boston and Adjacent Places, for the Setting Up Markets in Boston* (Boston: J. Franklin, 1719), 11–12; Benjamin Wadsworth, *Vicious Courses, Procuring Poverty* (Boston: John Allen, 1719), 23. See also Ann Smart Martin, "Frontier Boys and Country Cousins: The Context for Choice in Eighteenth-Century Consumerism," in *Historical Archaeology and the Study of American Culture*, ed. Lu Ann De Cunzo and Bernard L. Herman (Knoxville: University of Tennessee Press, 1996), 71–102.

51. Joseph Fish, *Christ Jesus the Physician, and His Blood the Balm* (New London: Timothy Green, 1760), 10; Thomas Clap, *A Brief History and Vindication of the Doctrines Received and Established in the Churches of New England* (New Haven: James Parker, 1755), 20; Thomas Clap, *An Essay on the Nature and Foundation of Moral Virtue and Obligation* (New Haven: B. Mecom, 1765), 16–17; SO, Diary, May 2, January 16, 1757. On self-interest, see Mark R. Valeri, *Law and Providence in Joseph Bellamy's New England: The Origins of the New Divinity in Revolutionary America* (New York: Oxford University Press, 1994), 96–100; Crowley, *This Sheba, Self*, 15–19; Albert O. Hirschman, *The Passions*

and the Interests: Political Arguments for Capitalism Before Its Triumph (Princeton: Princeton University Press, 1977); Richard L. Bushman, *From Puritan to Yankee: Character and the Social Order in Connecticut, 1690–1765* (Cambridge: Harvard University Press, 1967), 276–80. James D. German argues that because Jonathan Edwards and his followers believed that God could bring good out of the evil of self-interest, they implicitly legitimized it. Yet as he himself points out, they also argued that those who were motivated purely by self-interest would be damned, which hardly seems like legitimization. Despite their belief that evil served God's larger purposes, these evangelicals did not see evil as actually good. See James D. German, "The Social Utility of Wicked Self-Love: Calvinism, Capitalism, and Public Policy in Revolutionary New England," *Journal of American History* 82, no. 3 (1995): 965–98.

52. Benjamin Wadsworth, Sermon preached September 13, 1696, in "Nineteen Sermons," Harvard University Archives, quoted in John Corrigan, *The Prism of Piety: Catholick Congregational Clergy at the Beginning of the Enlightenment* (New York: Oxford University Press, 1991), 105; Samuel Cooper, *A Sermon Preached in Boston, New-England, Before the Society for Encouraging Industry, and Employing the Poor* (Boston: J. Draper, 1753), 2.

53. JE, *Freedom of the Will*, in *WJE*, 1: 163–64.

54. Samuel Johnson, *Ethices Elementa* (Boston: Rogers and Fowle, 1746), 9, 12; Adam Smith, *The Wealth of Nations* (1776), in Kramnick, *PER*, 507. See also Corrigan, *Prism of Piety*, 116.

55. Gilbert Tennent, *The Espousals; or, A Passionate Perswasive to a Marriage with the Lamb of God* (New York: J. Peter Zenger, 1735), 46; JE, *The Sin of Extortion* (Sermon on Ezekiel 22:12), 1747, *WJE Online*; rules of discipline, FCCR-BM; Mark Valeri, "The Economic Thought of Jonathan Edwards," *Church History* 60, no. 1 (1991): 52–53.

56. Letter from Samuel Davies to Joseph Bellamy, July 4, 1751, Joseph Bellamy Papers, Case Memorial Library, Hartford Seminary, Hartford, Connecticut, quoted in Valeri, *Law and Providence*, 87; letter from David Moore to Eleazar Wheelock, May 6, 1742, Eleazar Wheelock Papers, Dartmouth Library, available on microfilm at Wheaton College, Reel 1, no. 742306.2. On taxes, see the statistics in Withey, *Urban Growth in Colonial Rhode Island*, 128. See also Daniel Walker Howe, "The Decline of Calvinism: An Approach to Its Study," *Comparative Studies in Society and History* 14, no. 3 (June 1972): 316–17.

57. Gilbert Tennent, *Twenty-Three Sermons upon the Chief End of Man* (Philadelphia: William Bradford, 1744), 174–75, 210; SO, Diary, April 24, 1757; Samuel Hopkins, *The Life and Character of the Late Reverend Mr. Jonathan Edwards* (Boston: S. Kneeland, 1765), 103.

58. D. Bruce Hindmarsh, *The Evangelical Conversion Narrative: Spiritual Autobiography in Early Modern England* (New York: Oxford University Press, 2005), 108. See also Frank Lambert, *Pedlar in Divinity: George Whitefield and*

the Transatlantic Revivals, 1737–1770 (Princeton: Princeton University Press, 1994), 80–81.

59. Michael Merrill, "Putting 'Capitalism' in Its Place: A Review of Recent Literature," *William and Mary Quarterly* 52, no. 2 (1995): 317. On the arguments over defining capitalism, see the introduction to Matson, *Economy of Early America*, 33–34. On the attraction of the market, see Daniel Walker Howe, "Charles Sellers, the Market Revolution, and the Shaping of Identity in Whig-Jacksonian America," in *God and Mammon: Protestants, Money, and the Market, 1790–1860*, ed. Mark A. Noll (New York: Oxford University Press, 2002), 59. See also Joyce Oldham Appleby, "The Vexed Story of Capitalism Told by American Historians," *Journal of the Early Republic* 21, no. 1 (2001): 1–18.

60. SO to JF, September 17, 1750, AAS.

61. Here I disagree with Charles Sellers, who has argued that "every popular cultural or political movement in the early republic arose originally against the market." He exaggerates when he portrays Sarah Osborn as opposed to the market, though she was certainly worried about self-interest. See Charles Grier Sellers, *The Market Revolution: Jacksonian America, 1815–1846* (New York: Oxford University Press, 1991), 205–8. Katherine Carte Engel coins the term "moral capitalism" to describe the Moravians' acceptance of profit making in the eighteenth century, but she does not consider the tensions between Moravian theology and capitalist values; see Katherine Carte Engel, "The Strangers' Store: Moral Capitalism in Moravian Bethlehem, 1753–1775," *Early American Studies* 1, no. 1 (2003): 90–126. Richard Bushman argues that in Connecticut, evangelicalism appealed to merchants who felt guilty about their economic success. See Bushman, *From Puritan to Yankee*.

62. SH, *Memoirs*, 231.

63. Benjamin Franklin, *Poor Richard's Almanack*, in Kramnick, *PER*, 489.

64. Cooper, *Sermon Preached in Boston*; Simon P. Newman, *Embodied History: The Lives of the Poor in Early Philadelphia* (Philadelphia: University of Pennsylvania Press, 2003); Gary B. Nash, "Poverty and Poor Relief in Pre-Revolutionary Philadelphia," *William and Mary Quarterly* 33, no. 1 (January 1976): 3–30.

65. See Gary B. Nash, "Poverty and Politics in Early American History," in *Down and Out in Early America*, 1–37.

66. Wadsworth, *Vicious Courses*, 24, 31.

67. Here I disagree with J. Richard Olivas, "'God Helps Those Who Help Themselves': Religious Explanations of Poverty in Colonial Massachusetts, 1630–1776," in *Down and Out in Early America*, 262–88. Olivas argues that "ministers by the 1750s had completely abandoned the idea that God caused poverty, believing instead that people were poor because they were unwilling to work" (265). Olivas equates a few liberal ministers, especially Benjamin Colman and Charles Chauncy, with the entire Congregationalist clergy.

68. SA to SH, June 14, 1770, in Susanna Anthony, 34 Letters, 1749–1776, Simon Gratz Manuscript Collection, HSP.

69. See Newman, *Embodied History*, 143–48; Nash, "Poverty and Politics," 19–20.

CHAPTER EIGHT. LOVE THY NEIGHBOR

1. SO, Diary, October 21, 1761.

2. Ibid.; Ibid., March 11, 1757; Luke 10:25–37, 21:2, Mark 12:42, Matthew 25:40; SO, Diary, October 21, 1761. For examples of Osborn's visiting the sick, see SO, Diary, November 13, 1761, and SH, *Memoirs*, 266.

3. George Whitefield, *The Great Duty of Charity Recommended* (London: C. Whitefield, 1740), 22.

4. SO, Memoir, 46, quoting Proverbs 18:14. On the humanitarian impulses within early evangelicalism, see D. W. Bebbington, *Evangelicalism in Modern Britain: A History from the 1730s to the 1980s* (Boston: Unwin Hyman, 1989), 69–72.

5. SO to JF, May 3, 1759, AAS. On the number of students, see SO, Diary, May 20, 1759.

6. SO to JF, May 3, 1759, AAS. It is not clear when the second child came to live with Sarah and Henry, but probably sometime between January and May 1759. In Sarah's diary for 1758, she did not mention taking in another child, but by the time she wrote to Joseph Fish in May 1759, two of John's children were living with her. In 1759, Rhode Island was forced to offer men bounties to enlist in the army. Some were offered as much as twenty pounds plus a ten-pound bonus if Canada was defeated. See Fred Anderson, *Crucible of War: The Seven Years' War and the Fate of Empire in British North America, 1754–1766* (New York: Knopf, 2000), 320.

7. On Vinal's death, see SO to JF, September 5, 1759, AAS. Sarah Vinal was born on June 29, 1754. See the information available electronically on the Family History Library Web site maintained by the Church of Jesus Christ of Latter-day Saints: www.familysearch.org (accessed November 17, 2011). For Sarah Osborn's diary entries, see SO, June 30, June 25, 1754.

8. SO to JF, February 14, 1760, AAS.

9. SO, Diary, November 28, 1759; SO to JF, February 14, 1760, AAS.

10. SO, Diary, December 31, December 1, December 21, 1759; *NM*, December 19, 1758, April 22, 1760.

11. SO, Diary, January 3, 1760. Ebenezer Gray was the only doctor listed in the 1753 pew assessments. He was assessed thirty pounds that year. Moore was a distinguished member of the church who served on many committees. He was assessed twenty pounds in 1753. See the pew assessments in FCCR-DRC, October 1753.

12. SO, Diary, January 8, 1760.

13. Ibid., December 1, 1759, March 18, 1762, April 3, 1757; SO to JF, May 3, 1759, AAS.

14. SO, Diary, January 2, 1760; Whitefield, *Great Duty of Charity Recommended*, 3; SO, Diary, November 12, 1761. The Bible quotation is from Matthew 9:10–11.

15. SO, Diary, November 14, 1761.

16. JE, *Charity and Its Fruits*, in *WJE* 8: 294; SO, Diary, undated entry, probably July 11, 1757, November 17, 1753.

17. SO, Diary, December 10, December 18, 1759. For other examples of her visiting the sick, see Diary, November 13, 1761, and SH, *Memoirs*, 266.

18. Cotton Mather, *Bonifacius: An Essay upon the Good*, ed. David Levin (Cambridge: Harvard University Press, 1966), 17, 32. See also Kenneth Silverman, *The Life and Times of Cotton Mather* (New York: Harper and Row, 1984), 227–60; Robert Middlekauff, *The Mathers: Three Generations of Puritan Intellectuals, 1596–1728* (New York: Oxford University Press, 1971), 270–76.

19. On Bethesda, see Harry S. Stout, *The Divine Dramatist: George Whitefield and the Rise of Modern Evangelicalism* (Grand Rapids, Mich.: Eerdmans, 1991). Eleazar Wheelock, *A Plain and Faithful Narrative of the Original Design, Rise, Progress and Present State of the Indian Charity-school at Lebanon, in Connecticut* (Boston: Richard and Samuel Draper, 1763).

20. John Guyse, *A Collection of Seventeen Practical Sermons on Various and Important Subjects* (London: Edward Dilley, 1761), 183, quoting from Ecclesiastes 9:10. See SO, Diary, November 14, 1761.

21. Nicholas Gilman to Col. Robert Hale of Beverly, Mass., February 13, 1737/38, reprinted as Appendix 4 of William Kidder, "The Diary of Nicholas Gilman" (M.A. thesis, University of New Hampshire, 1972), 381–82.

22. JE, *The Nature of True Virtue*, in *WJE* 8: 560.

23. Carolyn D. Williams, "'The Luxury of Doing Good': Benevolence, Sensibility, and the Royal Humane Society," in *Pleasure in the Eighteenth Century*, ed. Roy Porter and Marie Mulvey Roberts (New York: New York University Press, 1996), 77. On the relationship between sensibility and humanitarian reform, see Paul Langford, *A Polite and Commercial People: England, 1727–1783* (New York: Oxford University Press, 1989), 461–518.

24. SO, Diary, December 23, 1764.

25. Joseph Allin, *What Shall I Render!* (Boston, 1722), cited in Christine Leigh Heyrman, "The Fashion Among More Superior People: Charity and Social Change in Provincial New England, 1700–1740," *American Quarterly* 34, no. 2 (1982): 113.

26. Samuel Cooper, *A Sermon Preached in Boston, New-England, Before the Society for Encouraging Industry, and Employing the Poor* (Boston: J. Draper, 1753), 21–22. In his early career, even Jonathan Edwards used this line of reasoning, but by 1749 he had concluded that "God oftentimes gives those men that He hates great outward prosperity"; see JE, *God Oftentimes Gives Those He*

Hates Great Outward Prosperity (Sermon on Luke 12:16–21), 1749, *WJE Online*. See also Mark Valeri, "The Economic Thought of Jonathan Edwards," *Church History* 60, no. 1 (1991): 52.

27. Samuel Hopkins, *An Inquiry into the Nature of True Holiness* (Newport: Solomon Southwick, 1773), 69; SO to JF, December 26, 1760, AAS; SO, Diary, January 3, 1760.

28. Whitefield, *Great Duty of Charity*, 24, 16; SO, Diary, January 2, 1760.

29. SO, Diary May 2, 1757; see also November 1, 1753.

30. Ibid., February 16, 1760.

31. Osborn mentions the women's society in SO to JF, December 26, 1760, AAS. SO, Diary, undated entry at the end of July 1760.

32. SO, Diary, December 17, December 29, 1759, January 2, 1760.

33. Ibid., July 27, March 6, March 7, April 27, 1760. See also SH, *Memoirs*, 250–51.

34. SO, Diary, March 29, April 25, 1760.

35. SO to JF, February 14, 1760, AAS; SO, Diary, February 3, 1760.

36. The statistic about Vinal's alcohol consumption comes from Charles E. Hammett, Jr., "A Sketch of the History of the Congregational Churches of Newport, R.I." (1891), 130, typescript available at NHS, Vault A, no. 1257. SO, Diary, February 11, April 14, 1760; see also Diary, February 28, 1760.

37. SO, Diary, April 19, June 23, 1760.

38. Ibid., April 5, August 10, 1760 (quoting Proverbs 19:18).

39. For a student's memories of Osborn, see Mary (Fish) Noyes Silliman Dickinson, "Reminiscences" (1801), copy of original made by Benjamin Silliman in 1856, Silliman Family Papers, Manuscript Group 450, Series 3, Box 35, Folders 62, 63, 64, Manuscripts and Archives, SML. On Mather, see SO, Diary, February 3, 1767.

40. SO, Diary, August 22, 1760. For more on the criminals, see Diary, August 10, August 14, August 21, 1760. In an undated entry following her entry for July 27, 1760, Osborn identifies the criminals as "Parks" and "Hawkins." Since there are no extant issues for *NM* during the summer of 1760, the nature of their crime is not clear.

41. For Enlightenment critiques of prisons and the treatment of criminals, see Montesquieu, *Spirit of the Laws* (1748); Cesare Beccaria, *Essay on Crimes and Justice* (1764); Voltaire, *Philosophical Dictionary* (1764); and Voltaire, *Commentary on the Book of Crimes and Punishments* (1766), excerpts from each of which are reprinted in Kramnick, *PER*, 515–35.

42. Voltaire, *Philosophical Dictionary* (1764), reprinted in *The Enlightenment: A Comprehensive Anthology*, ed. Peter Gay (New York: Touchstone, 1973), 247; SO, Diary, June 25, 1760.

43. SO, Diary, August 19, August 13, 1757.

44. Ibid., September 26, 1760; on the capture of Quebec, see ibid., June 25, 1760. Ibid., November 7, 1760.

45. Ibid., July 25, November 25, 1760.

46. Ibid., November 11, 1760; *NM*, April 22, 1760. On Vinal's wood allowance, see the First Congregational Church of Newport Records, 1743–1831, Vault A, no. 833, NHS, for the following dates: April 7, 1760, July 20, 1761, August 23, 1762, May 27, 1765. SO to JF, May 3, 1759.

47. SO, Diary, September 30, 1757, October 18, November 17, November 18, 1760.

48. SH, *Memoirs*, 252; SO, Diary, October 23, September 30, 1760.

49. Newport Town Council Records, vol. 13: 1760–1763, entries for November 3 and December 1, 1760, NHS; *Acts and Laws of His Majesty's Colony of Rhode-Island* (Boston: Jon Allen, 1719), 92–93.

50. In 1757, Ezra Stiles paid ninety dollars for a fourteen-year-old slave boy and ninety-five dollars for another boy. Bobey was probably worth more because he was older and knew a craft. See Ezra Stiles, Miscellaneous Papers, Reel 14, 185: 28, 29, in the Papers of Ezra Stiles (New Haven: Yale University Library, 1976), microfilm.

51. SO to JF, May 16, 1754, AAS; SO, Diary, November 13, 1760.

52. SO, Diary, October 23, 1760; Elaine Forman Crane, *A Dependent People: Newport, Rhode Island, in the Revolutionary Era* (New York: Fordham University Press, 1985), 32, 26. When Chesebrough died in 1782, Ezra Stiles estimated that he was worth ten thousand pounds sterling (*LD* 3: 11).

53. It is not clear when the Chesebrough family left the First Church of Christ, but it was before 1753. They were assigned a church pew at the First Church in 1744, but not in 1753. Abigail became a full member of the Second Church of Christ in 1756 (*LD* 1: 53). Abigail especially could afford to be generous because she had secretly married Alexander Grant, Esq., the son of a British nobleman, in October (SO, Diary, November 16, 1760).

54. SO, Diary, November 19, December 12, 1760.

55. Elaine Forman Crane lists Coggeshall as a merchant who imported molasses to make rum (*A Dependent People*, 29). See the 1753 pew assessments in FCCR-DRC. Nathaniel was the great-grandson of John Coggeshall (1601–47), the first president of the Colony of Providence Plantations. On Nathaniel Coggeshall's leadership in the church, see the FCCR-CB. Sarah Osborn mentions Mrs. Coggeshall as a member of her women's society in SO, Diary January 2, 1762.

56. See SO, Diary, September 30, 1757.

57. SO to JF, August 28, 1762, AAS.

58. SO to JF, undated letter of December 1764, AAS; SO to JF, February 5, 1761, AAS.

59. SO, Diary, December 31, 1761. For a list of her donations, see First Congregational Church of Newport Records, Contribution Book, 1754–1763, MSS 418, RIHS.

60. George Champlin Mason, *Reminiscences of Newport* (Newport: Charles E. Hammett, Jr., 1884), 121; Stout, *Divine Dramatist*, 22–24.

61. SO, Diary, October 16, October 24, October 21, 1761. See Sheila Skemp, "A Social and Cultural History of Newport, Rhode Island, 1720–1765" (Ph.D. diss., University of Iowa, 1974), 232. The act was repealed in 1793. See Mason, *Reminiscences of Newport*, 123.

62. See Stephen R. Haynes, *Noah's Curse: The Biblical Justification of American Slavery* (New York: Oxford University Press, 2002).

63. SO to JF, May 16, 1754, AAS.

64. SO, Diary, November 13, 1760, December 1, December 13, 1761.

65. Ibid., December 4, 1761.

66. Ibid.; Thomas Bacon, "A Sermon to Maryland Slaves" (1749), in *Religion in American History: A Reader*, ed. Jon Butler and Harry S. Stout (New York: Oxford University Press, 1998), 73–87; SO, Diary, December 13, 1761.

67. SO, Diary, December 7, 1761.

68. Ibid.

69. Ibid.

70. Ibid., December 9, 1761.

71. Ibid., quoting 1 Samuel 8.

72. Ibid., December 8, December 10, December 12, December 13, 1761.

73. Ibid., December 13, December 15, 1761.

74. Ibid., December 13, 1761.

75. Ibid., December 9, December 15, December 25, 1761, January 2, 1762.

76. Ibid., December 15, 1761.

77. Osborn's last mention of Bobey occurred ibid., January 13, 1762, when she prayed for "Poor Bobey" along with her friends and "Kind Benefactors."

78. Ibid., January 26, 1762.

79. Ibid., March 6, 1762; SO to JF, August 28, 1762, AAS. The estimate in American currency is Sarah Osborn's. I have not been able to locate any correspondence between Osborn and Guyse.

80. SO, Diary, February 24, February 21, March 6, 1762.

81. Ibid., March 6, 1762; Max Weber, *The Protestant Ethic and the Spirit of Capitalism*, trans. Talcott Parsons (New York: Scribner's, 1958).The Bible quotation is from Matthew 6:34.

82. SO, Diary, March 18, 1762, quoting Psalm 68:5.

83. Ibid.

84. Ibid. Johnny seems to have moved to Sarah and Henry's house in early April. See ibid., April 5, 1762, in which she asks God to bless the "young one" who has come into her family.

85. SO to JF, May 3, 1759, AAS; SO, Diary, March 18, 1762.

86. SO to JF, May 16, 1762, AAS; SH, *Memoirs*, 297.

87. SO, Diary, November 27, 1761; SO to JF, June 2, 1763, AAS. See also Mary Beth Norton, "'My Resting Reaping Times': Sarah Osborn's Defense of Her 'Unfeminine' Activities," *Signs* 2, no. 2 (1976): 527–28.

CHAPTER NINE. JORDAN OVERFLOWING

1. SO to JF, undated letter, AAS, probably written in 1765.
2. SO to JF, June 12, 1766, AAS; SO to JF, June 29, 1766, AAS.
3. SO to JF, undated letter, AAS, probably written in 1765.
4. SH, *Memoirs*, 326.
5. Ibid., 76, 320; SO to JF, September 3, 1764, AAS; SO to JF, April 21, 1765, AAS; Cotton Mather, *The Negro Christianized* (Boston: B. Green, 1706).
6. SO to JF, February 14, 1760, AAS.
7. SO to Mary Fish Noyes, July 13, 1764, AAS. See also SO to JF, November 2, 1761, AAS. On millennialism in New England, see Ruth H. Bloch, *Visionary Republic: Millennial Themes in American Thought, 1756–1800* (New York: Cambridge University Press, 1985); Nathan O. Hatch, *The Sacred Cause of Liberty: Republican Thought and the Millennium in Revolutionary New England* (New Haven: Yale University Press, 1977); Fred Anderson, *Crucible of War: The Seven Years' War and the Fate of Empire in British North America, 1754–1766* (New York: Knopf, 2000), 373–76.
8. Susanna Haggar died on March 21, 1764; see SO to JF, December 1764, AAS.
9. *LD* 1: 367. Quaum had attended Sarah Osborn's meetings in the 1760s; see SH, *Memoirs*, 78n.
10. *LD* 1: 366; JF to SO, September 4, 1765, AAS. See the list of members in FCCR-BM, 26.
11. SO to JF, undated letter, AAS. Osborn mentions blacks meeting in the kitchen in SO, Diary, April 8, 1767.
12. SO, Diary, March 4, 1767.
13. SO to JF, June 12, 1766, AAS; SO to JF, June 29, 1766, AAS; James Janeway, *A Token for Children* (1671; rpt. Boston: Nicholas Boone, 1700).
14. Mary Beth Norton, "'My Resting Reaping Times': Sarah Osborn's Defense of Her 'Unfeminine' Activities," *Signs* 2, no. 2 (1976): 525. Sarah mentioned that the children of Friends (Quakers) did not attend her meetings. SO to JF, June 12, 1766, AAS.
15. SO, Diary, January 27, 1767; SO to JF, undated letter, AAS. Osborn mentioned the presence of strangers in Diary, April 11, 1767.
16. SO to JF, August 9, 1766, AAS.
17. *NM*, June 6, April 25, 1763, September 10, 1764. See also Barbara E. Lacey, "Visual Images of Blacks in Early American Imprints," *William and Mary Quarterly* 53, no. 1 (1996): 137–80. I counted sixty-five advertisements in the extant issues of *NM*.

18. *NM*, June 10, 1765. See also Richard Henry Rudolph, "The Merchants of Newport, Rhode Island, 1763–1786" (Ph.D. diss., University of Connecticut, 1975), 151–57.

19. SO to JF, June 12, 1766, AAS; SO, Diary, January 20, 1767, June 12, 1766.

20. Norton, "'My Resting Reaping Times,'" 524; George G. Channing, *Early Recollections of Newport, R. I., from the Year 1793 to 1811* (Newport: A. J. Ward, C. E. Hammett, 1868), 103; SO to SH, July 29, 1769, in Sarah Osborn, 5 Letters, 1769–70, Simon Gratz Manuscript Collection [hereafter Gratz Collection], HSP.

21. Joseph Fish, *The Church of Christ a Firm and Durable House* (New London: Timothy Green, 1767), 157n; JF to SO, September 13, 1761, Benjamin Silliman Family Papers, Group 450, Series 1, Box 1, Manuscripts and Archives, SML.

22. Hopkins failed to mention that Osborn had once held separate meetings for Baptist men and women two days each week. See SH, *Memoirs*, 81–82; SO to JF, June 12, 1766, AAS.

23. SO to JF, August 9, 1766, AAS.

24. SH, *Memoirs*, 78; SO to JF, undated letter [August 1766], AAS; SO to William Vinal, tentatively dated 1771–74, in FCCR-418, Folder 9. In a later letter to Vinal, Osborn mentioned a letter she had written in the spring of 1766.

25. Letter from William Vinal to Ezra Stiles, January 31, 1766, Washburn Collection, 14: 15–16, MHS; SO to JF, undated letter [August 1766], AAS; letter from William Vinal to the First Society, November 3, 1766, in FCCR-DRC.

26. SO to JF, September 13, 1766, AAS. (This letter was a continuation of an undated letter from August 1766.) Norton, "'My Resting Reaping Times,'" 523.

27. SO to JF, September 13, 1766, AAS, quoting Psalm 104:8.

28. Ibid.; SH, *Memoirs*, 327.

29. SO, Diary, January 27, 1767; SO to JF, January 27, 1767, AAS. The black population of Newport in 1755 was 1,234. For population figures, see Elaine Forman Crane, *A Dependent People: Newport, Rhode Island, in the Revolutionary Era* (New York: Fordham University Press, 1985), 76. Sydney James is skeptical of these figures, which he considers too low: "There was no incentive for the citizens anywhere in the colony to make known the numbers of their slaves, who either were or might become taxable property" (Sydney V. James, *Colonial Rhode Island: A History* [New York: Scribner's, 1975], 255n).

30. SO, Diary, April 7, 1767.

31. Ibid., January 27, 1767. See also ibid., January 29, February 2, 1767.

32. Norton, "'My Resting Reaping Times,'" 526, 529, 523.

33. Ibid., 523–24.

34. Ibid., 526, 523.

35. Ibid., 526.

36. Ibid., 527, quoting from 1 Corinthians 1:27.

37. Ibid., 527–28.

38. See *NM*, November 24–December 1, 1766; SO, Diary, May 6, 1767.

39. SO to JF, May 26, 1767, AAS; SO to JF, September 15, 1767, AAS.

40. SO to JF, April 17, 1768, AAS.

41. SO, Diary, March 10, March 17, March 24, March 9, March 23, 1767.

42. In 1771, William Haggar was listed as a "halfway member" of Stiles's church who could not yet take communion (*LD* 1: 83). Based on one of her diary entries, Sarah Osborn's step-grandson may have been studying for the ministry: "Turn and Look Him into an Evangelical flow of repentance that shall never be repented of and arouse Him to His Work, and O, Let it yet Prosper in His Hands and Souls be Gathered by Him into the fold of Christ. O yet cause that vine to flourish for thy Mercies sake" (February 27, 1767). I could not find any records of an Osborn who was ordained to ministry in the late eighteenth century.

43. SO, Diary, May 27, 1767.

44. Ibid., April 14, April 24, 1767.

45. Ibid., March 17, 1767; SH, *Memoirs*, 331.

46. George Whitefield, *Journals* (1740), in Bushman, *GA*, 31. On evangelical attitudes toward slavery, see Thomas S. Kidd, *The Great Awakening: The Roots of Evangelical Christianity in Colonial America* (New Haven: Yale University Press, 2007), 213–33.

47. Cotton Mather, *The Negro Christianized* (Boston: B. Green, 1706), 1; Sydney V. James, *A People Among Peoples: Quaker Benevolence in Eighteenth-Century America* (Cambridge: Harvard University Press, 1963), 234.

48. See Lorenzo J. Greene, *The Negro in Colonial New England, 1620–1776* (New York: Columbia University Press, 1942), 268; Mark A. Noll, *The Rise of Evangelicalism: The Age of Edwards, Whitefield, and the Wesleys* (Downers Grove, Ill.: InterVarsity Press, 2003), 164; Lester B. Scherer, *Slavery and the Churches in Early America, 1619–1819* (Grand Rapids, Mich.: Eerdmans, 1975), 86.

49. JE, *Some Thoughts Concerning the Revival*, in *WJE* 4: 346; Whitefield, *Journals* (1740), in Bushman, *GA*, 26; JE, *A History of the Work of Redemption*, in *WJE* 9: 480.

50. SO, Diary, March 17, 1757, March 13, 1758 (quoting from Song of Solomon 1:5); James G. Basker, *Amazing Grace: An Anthology of Poems About Slavery, 1660–1810* (New Haven: Yale University Press, 2002), 292.

51. Jean-Jacques Rousseau, *The Social Contract*, in *The Enlightenment: A Comprehensive Anthology*, ed. Peter Gay (New York: Simon and Schuster, 1973), 328; baron de Montesquieu, *The Spirit of the Laws* (1748), in *The Age of Enlightenment*, ed. Lester G. Crocker (New York: Harper and Row, 1969), 197–99.

52. David Hume, *Of National Character* (1748), quoted in Richard H. Popkin, "The Philosophical Basis of Eighteenth-Century Racism," in *Racism in the Eighteenth Century*, ed. Harold E. Pagliaro, Studies in Eighteenth-Century

Culture (Cleveland: Case Western Reserve University Press, 1973), 245–46; Immanuel Kant, *Observations on the Feeling of the Beautiful and Sublime* (1764), in Kramnick, *PER*, 638; Carolus Linnaeus, *A General System of Nature* (1806), quoted in Popkin, "Philosophical Basis of Eighteenth-Century Racism," 248.

53. Montesquieu, *Spirit of the Laws*, 199. On the "different" races, see Colin Kidd, *The Forging of Races: Race and Scripture in the Protestant Atlantic World, 1600–2000* (New York: Cambridge University Press, 2006), 85–86.

54. Thomas Jefferson, *Notes on the State of Virginia* (London: John Stockdale, 1787), 270, 239, 230–31. On Jefferson, see David Brion Davis, *The Problem of Slavery in the Age of Revolution, 1770–1823* (Ithaca, N.Y.: Cornell University Press, 1975), 171–84.

55. On "Enwhitenment," see Emmanuel Chukwudi Eze, ed., *Race and the Enlightenment: A Reader* (Cambridge, Mass.: Blackwell, 1997), 4. See also Sabine Broeck, "When Light Becomes White: Reading Enlightenment Through Jamaica Kincaid's Writing," *Callaloo* 25, no. 3 (Summer 2002): 824.

56. Joanna Brooks, *American Lazarus: Religion and the Rise of African-American and Native American Literatures* (New York: Oxford University Press, 2003), 21–49, 51–86; letter from Charles Brockwell to the Secretary of the Society for the Propagation of the Gospel, Salem, Mass., February 18, 1742, quoted in David S. Lovejoy, *Religious Enthusiasm and the Great Awakening* (Englewood Cliffs, N.J.: Prentice-Hall, 1969), 65.

57. Phillis Wheatley, "On Messrs. Hussy and Coffin," *NM*, December 21, 1767; James Albert Ukawsaw Gronniosaw, *Narrative of the Most Remarkable Particulars in the Life of James Albert Ukawsaw Gronniosaw, an African Prince, Written by Himself* (Newport: S. Southwick, 1774), iv; Samson Occom, *Divine Hymns, or Spiritual Songs* (Portland: Thomas Clark, 1803), 10; John Marrant, *A Sermon Preached on the 24th Day of June 1789* (Boston: Thomas and John Fleet, 1789); Joanna Brooks and John Saillant, eds., *"Face Zion Forward": First Writers of the Black Atlantic, 1785–1798* (Boston: Northeastern University Press 2002). See also Philip Gould, "Early Black Atlantic Writing and the Cultures of Enlightenment," in *Beyond Douglass: New Perspectives on Early African-American Literature*, ed. Michael J. Drexler and Ed White (Lewisburg, Pa.: Bucknell University Press, 2008), 107–21.

58. See Kenneth P. Minkema and Harry S. Stout, "The Edwardsean Tradition and the Antislavery Debate, 1740–1865," *Journal of American History 92*, no. 1 (June 2005): 49–50; Kenneth P. Minkema, "Jonathan Edwards on Slavery and the Slave Trade," *William and Mary Quarterly* 54, no. 4 (1997): 831–32. Edwards was influenced by Leviticus 25:44–45.

59. David Grimsted has suggested that Sarah Osborn may have harbored abolitionist sympathies during the 1760s—a claim that has been repeated by many other scholars. For one example see Benjamin L. Carp, *Rebels Rising: Cities and the American Revolution* (New York: Oxford University Press, 2007), 136. Grimsted claims that Osborn may have "forwarded the first an-

tislavery article to appear in the paper [the *Newport Mercury*], a sermon of England's bishop of Gloucester, bitterly critical that 'rational creatures, possessing all our qualities but that of color' should be treated precisely as 'herds of cattle.' The letter to the printer enclosing the sermon, much in Osborn's style, lamented the writer's inability to do much about the shame that blacks were not offered Christ's easy yoke without 'the cruel yoke of bondage,' but hoped that the paper would show 'the firmness of mind to oppose the Vox Populi' so 'that posterity may see that there are some in these days who publicly declared their abhorrence of so flagitious a commerce.'" Grimsted finds it significant that the phrase "yoke of bondage" appeared in Osborn's diary a month earlier (entry for March 18, 1767). Grimsted's argument is marred by several problems. First, he claims that Gloucester's antislavery article appeared in the April 20, 1767, issue of *NM* at the same time as Osborn's meetings for slaves, but the article did not appear until February 24, 1781. (If an extract from Gloucester's writings also appeared in an earlier issue, I could not locate it.) In addition, the 1781 article was not accompanied by a letter, and I could find no article in *NM* matching Grimsted's quotations. It is unlikely that Osborn could have written a letter to the newspaper in 1781 because by then she was nearly blind and rarely able to write. And finally, even if Gloucester's antislavery writings appeared in *NM* sometime during the 1760s along with a letter, Grimsted's quotations from it do not sound like Osborn's style. She did not use Latin phrasing ("Vox Populi"), and I have not found the word *flagitious* in any of her extant writings. The "yoke of bondage" was a common phrase in early America. An electronic search of *Early American Imprints, Series 1: Evans, 1639–1800* (a database that includes almost all of the works published in America before 1800) yielded 236 hits (accessed July 7, 2010). See David Grimsted, "Anglo-American Racism and Phillis Wheatley's 'Sable Veil,' 'Lengthned Chain,' and 'Knitted Heart,'" in *Women in the Age of the American Revolution*, ed. Ronald Hoffman and Peter J. Albert (Charlottesville: University Press of Virginia, 1989), 379–80.

60. SO, Diary, July 19, 1764.

61. SO to JF, June 12, 1766, AAS; SH, *Memoirs*, 77. The law was first passed in 1704 and reenacted in 1750 and 1770. See Samuel Greene Arnold, *History of the State of Rhode Island and Providence Plantations* (New York: Appleton, 1860), 2: 15, and John Russell Bartlett, *Records of the Colony of Rhode Island and Providence Plantations in New England* (Providence: A. C. Greene and Brothers, 1858), 3: 492.

62. SO, Diary, January 11, 1767; SO to JF, undated letter, AAS; SO, Diary, May 10, 1767; SH, *Memoirs*, 77.

63. Norton, "'My Resting Reaping Times,'" 524.

64. The "free Ethiopian" may have been Primos Leandrow, who had been admitted to Osborn's church on March 20, 1757 (see FCCR-BM, 60); SO to JF, June 12, 1766, AAS; Akeia A. F. Benard, "The Free African American Cul-

tural Landscape: Newport, R.I., 1774–1826" (Ph.D. diss., University of Connecticut, 2008), 218.

65. For "negro," see SO, Diary, November 30, 1761; for "Ethiopians," see SO to JF, April 21, 1765, AAS; SO to JF, June 12, 1766, AAS.

66. Norton, "'My Resting Reaping Times,'" 523; Jefferson, *Notes on the State of Virginia*, 266.

67. *NM*, December 13, 1762. The newspaper reported that Captain John Gardner had lost 38 of his 153 slaves on the journey from Africa. On Newport's slave trade, see Sarah Deutsch, "The Elusive Guineamen: Newport Slavers, 1735–1774," *New England Quarterly* 55, no. 2 (1982): 229–53; Jay Coughtry, *The Notorious Triangle: Rhode Island and the African Slave Trade, 1700–1807* (Philadelphia: Temple University Press, 1981).

68. Benard, "Free African American Cultural Landscape," 103; Linda France Stine, Melanie A. Cabak, and Mark D. Groove, "Blue Beads as African-American Cultural Symbols," *Historical Archaeology* 30, no. 3 (1996): 49–75.

69. Norton, "'My Resting Reaping Times,'" 524.

70. Ibid.; SO to JF, September 4, 1765, AAS.

71. On "kissing the rod," see SO to "Mrs. Noice" [Abigail Noyes], January 16, 1767, AAS. For Gardner's words about idolatry, see *The Works of Samuel Hopkins*, ed. Edwards Amasa Park (Boston: Doctrinal Tract and Book Society, 1852), 154n. William Henry Robinson, ed., *The Proceedings of the Free African Union Society and the African Benevolent Society, Newport, Rhode Island, 1780–1824* (Providence: Urban League of Rhode Island, 1976), 25.

72. Phillis Wheatley, "On Being Brought from Africa to America," in her *Poems on Various Subjects, Religious and Moral* (London: A. Bell, 1773), 18.

73. Hezekiah Smith, quoted in Carp, *Rebels Rising*, 138. Smith's text was Luke 14:22.

74. SO to JF, December 7, 1767, AAS; SO to JF, April 28, 1768, AAS; Norton, "'My Resting Reaping Times,'" 520.

75. FCCR-BM records the names of eight black members admitted between 1765 and 1774: Quamenee Church (1765), Bristol Coggeshall (1768), Obour Tanner (1768), Phillis Hammond (1771), Phillis Morrison (1771), Jenny Folgier (1771), Cato Coggeshall (1771), and Wishee Buckmaster (1774). Using James N. Arnold, *Vital Record of Rhode Island 1636–1850. First Series: Births, Marriages and Deaths*, vol. 8 (Providence: Narragansett Historical Publishing, 1896), Benard also lists several other slaves as members, but their names appear in the list of baptisms, not full membership. They were probably the children of black members. She lists Abraham Coggeshall (1771), Isaac Coggeshall (1771), Sarah Coggeshall (1771), Pompey Stevens (1771), and Phyllis Coggeshall (1774). See Appendix to Benard, "Free African American Cultural Landscape." According to Ezra Stiles, there were 6 or 7 black members in the First Church of Christ in 1772 There were 364 members total in 1771. (*LD* 1: 214, 144). Scipio

Tanner and Arthur ("Tikey") Flagg were baptized and admitted into full membership in the Seventh-day Baptist Church in 1771. See "The Seventh-day Baptist Church at Newport, Rhode Island," *Seventh-day Baptist Memorial* 2 (January and April 1853): 77.

76. See SO to JF, April 21, 1765, AAS, in which Osborn mentioned "some considerable ingathering" at Mr. Thurston's church. On baptism, see Jon Butler, *Awash in a Sea of Faith: Christianizing the American People* (Cambridge: Harvard University Press, 1990), 132–33.

77. SO, Diary, January 31, 1767.

78. *NM*, September 5, 1763; SO, Diary, January 31, 1767; SO to Susanna Bannister, April 7, 1767, AAS.

79. FCCR-BM, September 12, September 21, 1768.

80. Letter to William Vinal, tentatively dated 1771–74, in FCCR-418, Folder 9. The RIHS does not list the author of this letter, but it is in Sarah Osborn's handwriting. It was probably written in the fall of 1768 or the winter or spring of 1769. She mentioned that it had been in "August" that she had first heard that the Church Council would hold a meeting about Vinal's intemperance.

81. Ibid.

82. SO to JF, July 9, 1769, AAS; SO to JF, April 28, 1768, AAS; SH, *Memoirs*, 342.

83. "Sermon notes, August 1768–August 1770," in FCCR-418, Folder 9; SO to JF, June 18, 1769, AAS. See also SO to JF, July 9, 1769, AAS.

84. Letter from Thomas M. Vinson to E. A. Park, August 11, 1851, Vinson Family Papers, 1789–1929, MHS; Channing, *Early Recollections*, 90.

85. William Hart, *Brief Remarks on a Number of False Propositions, and Dangerous Errors, Which Are Spreading in This Country* (New-London: Timothy Green, 1769), 30, advertised in *NM*, October 30, 1769. On Hopkins, see William Breitenbach, "Unregenerate Doings: Selflessness and Selfishness in New Divinity Theology," *American Quarterly* 34, no. 5 (1982): 479–502; Joseph A. Conforti, *Samuel Hopkins and the New Divinity Movement: Calvinism, the Congregational Ministry, and Reform in New England Between the Great Awakenings* (Grand Rapids, Mich.: Eerdmans, 1981); Peter Dan Jauhiainen, "An Enlightenment Calvinist: Samuel Hopkins and the Pursuit of Benevolence" (Ph.D. diss., University of Iowa, 1997); William Breitenbach, "The Consistent Calvinism of the New Divinity Movement," *William and Mary Quarterly* 41, no. 2 (1984): 241–64.

86. SO to SH, January 22, 1770, in Sarah Osborn, 5 Letters, 1769–70, Gratz Collection. Hopkins had an extensive correspondence with both Osborn and Anthony. See Susanna Anthony, 34 Letters, 1749–1776, Gratz Collection, and Sarah Osborn, 5 Letters, 1769–70, Gratz Collection.

87. *LD* 1: 41, 44. The estimate of the women's society comes from SH, *Memoirs*, 71. On Hopkins's farewell sermon, see Stephen West, ed., *Sketches of*

the Life of the Late Rev. Samuel Hopkins (Hartford: Hudson and Goodwin 1805), 72–74. Conforti, *Samuel Hopkins and the New Divinity Movement*, 103–6.

88. FCCR-CB, March 23, 1770, Vault A, no. 836b. For members of the women's society, see SO, Diary, November 21, 1760, January 28, 1762.

89. FCCR-BM, August 3, 1770; SO to Mary Fish Noyes, September 1, 1770, AAS.

90. *LD* 1: 33, 36, 213. Ezra Stiles's meetings began in 1770.

91. SO, Diary, November 25, 1759. Osborn mentions Stiles's participation in her meetings in SO to SH, July 29, 1769, in Sarah Osborn, 5 Letters, 1769–70, Gratz Collection.

92. Hopkins notes that Yamma and Quamine had attended Osborn's meetings in the 1760s (SH, *Memoirs*, 78n); *LD* 1: 367.

93. On Yamma, see SH to Philip Quaque, December 10, 1773, Gratz Collection: American Colonial Clergy, Case 9/Box 16. On Quamine, see Benard, "Free African American Cultural Landscape," 212. Benard lists three children born before 1773, but since two were named "Bettey," it seems likely that the first one died. The couple had another child in 1777. Stiles baptized Quamine and Duchess Channing's infant Charles in January 1772 (*LD* 1: 207). See also Ezra Stiles, "Members of the Second Congregational Church in Newport, 1728–1770," Gratz Collection.

94. On Duchess as a cake maker, see Channing, *Early Recollections*, 170–71n. William Ellery Channing wrote the description of her as "intelligent, industrious," etc., for her gravestone; see Charles Timothy Brooks, *William Ellery Channing: A Centennial Memory* (Boston: Roberts Bros., 1880), 56.

95. Samuel Hopkins, Extract from a letter written by the Rev. Philip Quaque to Hopkins about John Quamine, August 30, 1773, Joseph Bellamy Papers, CHS. Philip Quaque was the first African to be ordained as an Anglican priest.

96. Hopkins, Extract from a letter written by the Rev. Philip Quaque; Phillis Wheatley to SH, February 9, 1774, Gratz Collection: American Poets, Case 7/Box 10. See also Phillis Wheatley to SH, May 6, 1774, Ms.Ch.A. 6.20, BPL.

97. Obour Tanner was baptized and admitted to the First Church of Christ in 1768. FCCR-BM, July 10, 1768. For more on Wheatley's relationship with her, see their correspondence in *Phillis Wheatley: Complete Writings*, ed. Vincent Caretta (New York: Penguin, 2001).

98. Letter from Ezra Stiles and Samuel Hopkins, "To all who are desirous to promote the kingdom of Christ on earth, in the salvation of sinners," August 31, 1773, Joseph Bellamy Papers, CHS; Conforti, *Samuel Hopkins and the New Divinity Movement*, 145; Ezra Stiles and Samuel Hopkins, *To the Public* (Newport: n.p., 1776).

99. *LD* 1: 489, 486; Stiles and Hopkins, *To the Public*, 4; Conforti, *Samuel Hopkins and the New Divinity Movement*, 144–46.

100. Arnold, *Vital Record*, First Series, vol. 8, p. 404; "Admissions, 1744–1796," FCCR-BM; First Congregational Church of Newport Records, MSS 418, Folder 4: Contribution Book, 1763–75.

101. For the history of this episode, see FCCR-BM for the following dates: June 29, 1770; September 6, 1771; June 23, 1773; August 17, 1773; April 29, 1774; July 1, 1774; and December 5, 1774. Letter from William Vinal, to the First Church of Christ, November 30, 1774, First Congregational Church of Newport Records, Vault A, Box 169, Folder 6, NHS. See also the letter from Susanna Anthony to Samuel Hopkins, no date, Ms.Ch.A.4.16, BPL.

102. See Jauhiainen, "Enlightenment Calvinist," 290. Hopkins wrote a letter to Levi Hart in January 1775 arguing for immediate abolition: SH to Levi Hart, January 25, 1775, CHS. This is the earliest evidence we have of his antislavery position according to Jonathan D. Sassi, "'This Whole Country Have Their Hands Full of Blood This Day': Transcription and Introduction of an Antislavery Sermon Manuscript Attributed to the Reverend Samuel Hopkins," *Proceedings of the American Antiquarian Society* 112, no. 1 (2004): 60. It is not clear when Hopkins began to preach against slavery. Stanley K. Schultz argues that it may have been in January 1770 ("The Making of a Reformer: The Reverend Samuel Hopkins as an Eighteenth-Century Abolitionist," *Proceedings of the American Philosophical Society* 115, no. 5 [1971]: 356n). His evidence is that Hopkins wrote in his diary, "Have been worried about my preaching yesterday. I believe it was the truth, but perhaps I had better not preached it then." It seems likely that Hopkins was concerned about alienating the First Church either because of his controversies with William Hart or his strict stance on infant baptism and church membership. During the same month that Hopkins made this entry in his diary, Susanna Anthony sent him a letter alluding to his argument with William Hart (SA to SH, January 22, 1770, in Susanna Anthony, 34 Letters, 1749–1776, HSP). Hopkins was not appointed pastor of the church until April 11, 1770, and it is doubtful that he would have been elected if he had preached an antislavery sermon during his probation.

103. Julia A. Stern, *The Plight of Feeling: Sympathy and Dissent in the Early American Novel* (Chicago: University of Chicago Press, 1997), 218; Sassi, "'This Whole Country Have Their Hands Full of Blood,'" 87.

104. *NM*, October 21, 1765, June 17, 1771, January 4–January 11, 1768.

105. Thomas L. Haskell, "Capitalism and the Origins of the Humanitarian Sensibility, Part 1"; Thomas L. Haskell, "Capitalism and the Origins of the Humanitarian Sensibility, Part 2"; David Brion Davis, "Reflections on Abolitionism and Ideological Hegemony," all in Thomas Bender, ed. *The Antislavery Debate: Capitalism and Abolitionism as a Problem in Historical Interpretation* (Berkeley: University of California Press, 1992), 107–79.

106. John Woolman, *The Journal and Major Essays of John Woolman*, ed. Phillips P. Moulton (Richmond, Ind.: Friends United Press, 1971), 92; Philip Gould, *Barbaric Traffic: Commerce and Antislavery in the Eighteenth-Century*

Atlantic World (Cambridge: Harvard University Press, 2003); Sassi, "'This Whole Country Have Their Hands Full of Blood,'" 68–69.

107. The First Congregational Church of Newport Records include a list of books purchased for the First Congregational Society during Hopkins's tenure (1770–75), including a copy of Phillis Wheatley's poems (FCCR-DRC, April 15, 1774). The ad appeared in *NM*, August 22, 1774.

108. Jefferson, *Notes on the State of Virginia*, 234; Samuel Hopkins to Philip Quaque, December 10, 1773, Gratz Collection: American Colonial Clergy, Case 9/Box 16.

109. Sassi, "'This Whole Country Have Their Hands Full of Blood,'" 71, 81, 66. On the dating of this sermon, see page 34.

110. SH, *Memoirs*, 278, 373.

111. *Census of the Inhabitants of the Colony of Rhode Island and Providence Plantation Taken by the Order of the General Assembly* (Providence: Anthony Knowles, 1858), 24; SH, "A Dialogue Concerning the Slavery of the Africans," in *WSH* 2: 571; Death and Burial Records, NHS.

Chapter Ten. The Latter Days

1. *FL*, 155–56, 158. This letter is not dated, but since it refers to a letter that Sarah Osborn wrote to Joseph Fish on December 2, 1779, and since Osborn refers to "this hard winter," it was written sometime during the winter of 1780. That winter became legendary for its cold temperatures.

2. Thomas Paine, *Common Sense* (Newburyport, Mass.: Samuel Phillips, 1776), 54.

3. SO to Mary Fish Noyes, September 1, 1770, AAS.

4. SO to JF, December 28, 1779, AAS; *FL*, 154–60. (I am assuming that the letter reprinted in *FL* was dictated, but the original does not survive.) SH, *Memoirs*, 374–80. Sarah Osborn, Will, Probate Book No. 3, 11–12, Newport City Hall, Newport, Rhode Island.

5. SO, Diary, March 18, 1767. On the celebration, see *NM*, March 16–23, 1767. On the double meanings of liberty, see Ruth H. Bloch, *Visionary Republic: Millennial Themes in American Thought, 1756–1800* (New York: Cambridge University Press, 1985), 63; Harry S. Stout, *The New England Soul: Preaching and Religious Culture in Colonial New England* (New York: Oxford University Press, 1986), 298–99.

6. SO to JF, December 28, 1779, AAS.

7. *NM*, June 13, 1774; *LD* 1: 106, 39; Stout, *New England Soul*, 266.

8. *NM*, September 26, August 29, November 14, 1774. See Bloch, *Visionary Republic*, 57–58.

9. The list of books purchased for the First Church of Christ during Hopkins's tenure, 1770–75, includes "Master Key of Popery." See FCCR-DRC, June 23, 1773.

10. *NM*, November 7, 1774.

11. See Benjamin L. Carp, *Rebels Rising: Cities and the American Revolution* (New York: Oxford University Press, 2007), 121.

12. *NM*, April 24, 1774.

13. James N. Arnold, *Vital Record of Rhode Island 1636–1850. First Series: Births, Marriages and Deaths*, vol. 8 (Providence: Narragansett Historical Publishing, 1896), 404.

14. Florence Parker Simister, *The Fire's Center: Rhode Island in the Revolutionary Era, 1763–1790* (Providence: Rhode Island Bicentennial Foundation, 1979), 66; Elaine Forman Crane, *A Dependent People: Newport, Rhode Island, in the Revolutionary Era* (New York: Fordham University Press, 1985), 122.

15. *NM*, December 11, 1775; *LD* 1: 642.

16. *LD* 1: 649.

17. FCCR-DRC, November 15, 1774. See also SH to the Congregational Churches of New England, no date, ibid.

18. Their donation may have been left over from Guyse's bequest, or perhaps Sarah inherited the money after her mother's death. The church records list multiple contributions from Sarah Osborn for a "privet subscription" as well as a contribution from Sarah Anthony for "a sunscription [*sic*] for the Woman's." Private subscription libraries were common in the eighteenth century. There are no records of what books were purchased. See FCCR-418, Folder 4. SH, *Memoirs*, 370.

19. Mary Callendar to Moses Brown, January 24, 1776, quoted in Lynne Withey, *Urban Growth in Colonial Rhode Island: Newport and Providence in the Eighteenth Century* (Albany: State University of New York Press, 1984), 83.

20. *NM*, November 28, 1774; SA to SH, August 29, 1776, in Susanna Anthony, 34 Letters, 1749–1776, Simon Gratz Manuscript Collection [hereafter Gratz Collection], HSP.

21. Letter from John Witherspoon to SH, February 27, 1775, quoted in Joseph A. Conforti, *Samuel Hopkins and the New Divinity Movement: Calvinism, the Congregational Ministry, and Reform in New England Between the Great Awakenings* (Grand Rapids, Mich.: Eerdmans, 1981), 146.

22. On Nubia, see Ezra Stiles and Samuel Hopkins, *To the Public* (Newport: n.p., 1776). SH to Levi Hart, June 10, 1791, in Samuel Hopkins, 4 Letters, 1770, 1791, 1796, and no date, Gratz Collection. See also Ralph E. Luker, "'Under Our Own Vine and Fig Tree': From African Unionism to Black Denominationalism in Newport, Rhode Island, 1760–1876," *Slavery and Abolition* 12, no. 2 (1991): 23–48. Conforti, *Samuel Hopkins and the New Divinity Movement*, 146–48.

23. John Quamine to Moses Brown, June 5, 1776, cited in Mack Thompson, *Moses Brown: Reluctant Reformer* (Chapel Hill: University of North Carolina Press, 1962), 105.

24. *NM*, February 20, 1775; diary of Fleet S. Greene, quoted in Simister, *Fire's Center*, 113; Withey, *Urban Growth in Colonial Rhode Island*, 82.

25. C. P. B. Jefferys, *Newport: A Short History* (Newport: Newport Historical Society, 1992), 30.

26. Levi Hart recorded in his diary in 1776 that Sarah Osborn wanted to find "a proper place for a grandson of hers." In 1777 he noted that she had found him a place and needed no more assistance. See Levi Hart, Diary, November 11, 1776, January 13, 1777, in Gratz Collection: New Lights Sermon Collection, Box 6.

27. Letter from SH to the Congregational Churches of New England, no date, FCCR-DRC. See William Gerald McLoughlin, *Rhode Island: A History* (New York: Norton, 1986), 95. On the destruction of the First Church of Christ, see Edward Peterson, *History of Rhode Island* (New York: John S. Taylor, 1853), 324.

28. SO to JF, December 2, 1779, AAS.

29. SH, *Memoirs*, 354–55.

30. *FL*, 130, 131, 134.

31. SO, Diary, June 29, 1757. On Tanner, see his obituary in *NM*, January 22, 1785; "John Tanner," *Seventh-day Baptist Memorial* 3 (July 1854): 104–11; Dan A. Sanford, "Entering into Covenant: The History of Seventh Day Baptists in Newport," *Newport History* 66, no. 1 (Winter 1994), 45; and the Records of the Seventh-day Baptist Church, 1708–38, 1816, NHS.

32. Hopkins claimed that Daniel and Sally Fellows stayed in Newport with the Osborns, and Stiles included them on his list of people who stayed in Newport after the British siege. See *LD* 2: 133. The Fellowses are not listed as heads of a household in "The Occupants of the Houses in Newport, R.I., During the Revolution," *Newport Historical Magazine* 2 (July 1881): 41–45. They probably lived with the Osborns. According to Charles Hammett, Mary Anthony lived with Sarah Osborn during the Revolution. See Charles E. Hammett, Jr., "A Sketch of the History of the Congregational Churches of Newport, R.I." (Typescript, 1891), 242, Vault A, no. 1257, NHS.

33. "The Occupants of the Houses in Newport, R.I., During the Revolution," 44; "John Tanner," *Seventh-day Baptist Memorial*, 110.

34. For examples, see SO, Diary, March 6, August 16, September 26, 1757, January 15, 1762, February 20, 1767. Sheryl Kujawa quotes one of Osborn's undated letters to Fish that she claims offers a description of Henry's death ("Religion, Education and Gender in Eighteenth-Century Rhode Island: Sarah Haggar Wheaten Osborn, 1714–1796 [Ph.D. diss., Teachers College, Columbia University, 1993], 337). In fact, Sarah was quoting from a letter by Elizabeth Prentice about the death of Prentice's husband.

35. Sarah Fellows appears in the 1820 census in South Kingstown, Washington County, Rhode Island. See Heritage Quest Online, http://persi

.heritagequestonline.com (accessed September 15, 2010). SH, *Memoirs*, 355; SH to Mrs. Pemberton, January 7, 1778, MHS.

36. SO to JF, December 28, 1779, AAS; SH, *Memoirs*, 83. Susanna Anthony left Newport in 1775 after her mother's death plunged her and her sisters into poverty. Hopkins seems to have arranged for her to serve as a housekeeper in Connecticut, but she had returned to Newport by the summer of 1776. See SA to SH, May 3, July 21, September 4, 1775, January 26, 1776, August 29, 1776, all in Susanna Anthony, 34 Letters, 1749–1776, Gratz Collection.

37. See Lorenzo J. Greene, "Some Observations on the Black Regiment of Rhode Island in the American Revolution," *Journal of Negro History* 37, no. 2 (April 1952): 142–72.

38. "Mrs. Mary Almy's Letters About the Siege of Newport, 29 July–24 August 1778," typescript, 7–8, NHS; Simister, *Fire's Center*, 129–66.

39. *FL*, 156.

40. Solomon Southwick to William Vernon, quoted in Simister, *Fire's Center*, 153.

41. *LD* 2: 378; Luker, "'Under Our Own Vine and Fig Tree,'" 26. For the age of Quamine's children, see Akeia A. F. Benard, "The Free African American Cultural Landscape: Newport, R.I., 1774–1826" (Ph.D. diss., University of Connecticut, 2008), Appendix. Duchess Quamine eventually bought her own freedom. See *Encyclopedia of African American Business*, ed. Jessie Carney Smith and Millicent Lownes Jackson (Westport, Conn.: Greenwood, 2006), 1: 142; George G. Channing, *Early Recollections of Newport, R.I., from the Year 1793 to 1811* (Newport: A. J. Ward, C. E. Hammett, 1868), 170–71n.

42. *LD* 2: 427; William Ellery, quoted in Simister, *Fire's Center*, 155.

43. SO to JF, December 28, 1779, AAS. On Tanner's return, see Sanford, "Entering into Covenant," 45.

44. Perry Miller describes the Puritans as "cosmic optimists" in spite of their faith in original sin in Miller, *The New England Mind: The Seventeenth Century* (New York: Macmillan, 1939), 18.

45. Carl L. Becker, *The Heavenly City of the Eighteenth-Century Philosophers*, 2nd ed. (New Haven: Yale University Press, 2003), 31, 130. On the Christian roots of the idea of progress, see Ernest Lee Tuveson, *Millennium and Utopia: A Study in the Background of the Idea of Progress* (Berkeley: University of California Press, 1949); David Spadafora, *The Idea of Progress in Eighteenth-Century Britain* (New Haven: Yale University Press, 1990).

46. Jean-Jacques Rousseau, "Discourse on Arts and Sciences" (1751), in Kramnick, *PER*, 363–69; Voltaire, *Essay on the Manners and Spirits of Nations* (1754), ibid., 369–75; Anne-Robert-Jacques Turgot, "On the Successive Advances of the Human Mind" (1750), ibid., 362; Adam Smith, *The Wealth of Nations* (1776), ibid., 505–15; Edward Gibbon, *The History of the Decline and Fall of the Roman Empire*, in *The Age of Enlightenment*, ed. Lester G. Crocker (New York: Walker, 1969), 300. See also Clare Jackson, "Progress and Opti-

mism," in *The Enlightenment World*, ed. Martin Fitzpatrick (New York: Rout-ledge, 2004), 177–93; Roger Nisbet, *History of the Idea of Progress* (New York: Basic, 1980).

47. See excerpts from Claude-Adrien Helvétius, *A Treatise on Man: His Intellectual Faculties and His Education* (1772), in Kramnick, *PER*, 287–96; John Locke, *Some Thoughts Concerning Education* (1693), ibid., 222–28. On ideas about the pliability of the human mind, see Spadafora, *Idea of Progress in Eighteenth-Century Britain*, 135–78.

48. John Adams, *Thoughts on Government: Applicable to the Present State of the American Colonies* (Boston: John Gill, 1776), 15; Abbé Raynal, *History of the Two Indies* (1772), quoted in J. B. Bury, *The Idea of Progress* (New York: Macmillan, 1932), 169.

49. Sylvanus Conant, *An Anniversary Sermon Preached at Plymouth, Dec. 23, 1776* (Boston, 1777), quoted in Stout, *New England Soul*, 308.

50. See, e.g., Joseph Bellamy, "The Millennium," in *The Works of Joseph Bellamy* (Boston: Doctrinal Book and Tract Society, 1853), 454.

51. Joseph Lyman, *A Sermon Preached at Hatfield December 15th, 1774* (Boston: Edes and Gill, 1775), 9; Adams quoted in Sacvan Bercovitch, *The American Jeremiad* (Madison: University of Wisconsin Press, 1978), 119.

52. SO, Diary, August 31, 1753; *FL*, 156; SO to JF, December 28, 1779, AAS. On covenant theology, see Stout, *New England Soul*; Miller, *New England Mind: Seventeenth Century*.

53. See Mark Valeri, "The New Divinity and the American Revolution," *William and Mary Quarterly* 46, no. 4 (1989): 741–69.

54. Ebenezer Baldwin, *The Duty of Rejoicing Under Calamities and Afflic-tions* (New York, 1776), quoted in Stout, *New England Soul*, 308. On the timing of this political form of millennialism, see Bloch, *Visionary Republic*, 82; Stout, *New England Soul*, 306 and 383n.

55. Samuel Sherwood, *The Church's Flight into the Wilderness* (New York: S. Loudon, 1776), 39.

56. The Continental Congress quoted in Bloch, *Visionary Republic*, 75; SH, *Treatise on the Millennium* (Boston: Isaiah Thomas, 1793), 69. Bloch argues that most Americans were less influenced by Enlightenment ideal of progress than by millennialism (see p. 77), but the two sets of ideas often overlapped during the Revolution, making it difficult to draw neat lines between them.

57. *FL*, 159; Stout, *New England Soul*, 307–8.

58. *FL*, 159.

59. JE, "History of Redemption," Notebook A, Works of Edwards tran-scription, BL, cited in George M. Marsden, *Jonathan Edwards: A Life* (New Haven: Yale University Press, 2003), 485. The list of books purchased for the First Church of Christ during Hopkins's tenure, 1770–75, includes Edwards's *History of the Work of Redemption*. See FCCR-DRC, March 18, 1775.

60. *FL*, 109, 157; SO to JF, December 28, 1779, AAS.

61. On Mary Tanner's death see "John Tanner," *Seventh-day Baptist Memorial*, 106.

62. See Crane, *Dependent People*, 144, 159; Withey, *Urban Growth in Colonial Rhode Island*, 115.

63. Champlin quoted in Withey, *Urban Growth in Colonial New England*, 88.

64. SH to Stephen West, June 23, 1780, in Samuel Hopkins, Letters, Gratz Collection, Case 6/Box 10. For records of baptisms at Sarah Osborn's house, see FCCR-BM, November 18, 1779, 28, and August 4, 1780, 28. See also Arnold, *Vital Record*, First Series, vol. 8, p. 400. On Tanner, see Sanford, "Entering into Covenant," 28n, 33.

65. Ray Raphael, "America's Worst Winter Ever," HistoryNet.Com http://www.historynet.com/americas-worst-winter-ever.htm/1 (accessed September 2, 2010).

66. *FL*, 156–57; SH, *Memoirs*, 355. See also SH to Levi Hart, April 23, 1787, Gratz Collection: American Colonial Clergy, Case 8/Box 23.

67. See Arthur Tuckerman, *When Rochambeau Stepped Ashore* (Newport: The Preservation Society of Newport County, 1955); George Champlin Mason, *Reminiscences of Newport* (Newport: Charles E. Hammett, Jr., 1884), 77.

68. See Edwards Amasa Park, *Memoir of the Life and Character of Samuel Hopkins* (Boston: Doctrinal Tract and Book Society, 1854), 91.

69. *FL*, 160.

70. See John Shy, *A People Numerous and Armed: Reflections on the Military Struggle for American Independence*, rev. ed. (Ann Arbor: University of Michigan Press, 1990), 249–50.

71. "Memorial of the Town of Newport to the General Assembly," October 1781, quoted in Richard Henry Rudolph, "The Merchants of Newport, Rhode Island, 1763–1786" (Ph.D. diss., University of Connecticut, 1975), 318.

72. Jean Pierre Brissot de Warville, *New Travels in the United States of America, 1788*, ed. Durand Echeverria (Cambridge: Harvard University Press, 1964), 128.

73. Timothy Dwight, *A Sermon Preached at Northampton* (Hartford, 1781), quoted in Bloch, *Visionary Republic*, 101; Abraham Lincoln, Annual Message to Congress, Dec. 1, 1862, available online, http://showcase.netins.net/web/creative/lincoln/speeches/congress.htm (accessed September 20, 2010).

74. See Valeri, "New Divinity and the American Revolution," 769.

75. SH to Stephen West, June 23, 1780, in Samuel Hopkins, Letters, Gratz Collection, Case 6/Box 10; SH to Levi Hart, April 23, 1787, Gratz Collection: American Colonial Clergy, Case 8/Box 23.

76. SH to Levi Hart, November 27, 1787, Gratz Collection: American Colonial Clergy, Case 8/Box 23. See Kerry S. Walters, *Rational Infidels: The American Deists* (Durango, Colo.: Longwood Academic, 1992).

77. SH, *A Dialogue Concerning the Slavery of the Africans* (1776), in *WSH* 2: 551. Levi Hart also opposed slavery. See John Saillant, "'Some Thoughts on the Subject of Feeing the Negro Slaves in the Colony of Connecticut, Humbly Offered to the Consideration of All Friends to Liberty and Justice,' by Levi Hart," *New England Quarterly* 75, no. 1 (March 2002), 107–28.

78. See Sydney V. James, *Colonial Rhode Island: A History* (New York: Scribner's, 1975), 366; *NM*, June 27, 1774.

79. FCCR-BM, March 5, 1784. Three months before passing this resolution against slavery, the church voted "That whereas deacon Coggeshall did, more than two years ago, promise before the church, that he would secure the freedom of his black girl, Sarah, that she should be free upon his decease, it is the opinion of this church that he ought without delay, to deliver to us a paper properly authenticated, securing to said girl her freedom, as abovesaid" (ibid., January 30, 1784). On Quakers, see Luker, "'Under Our Own Vine and Fig Tree,'" 25.

80. Rudolph, "Merchants of Newport, Rhode Island," 340.

81. *NM*, September 2, 1790.

82. SH, *The Slave Trade and Slavery* (1787), in *WSH* 2: 615, 619, 620, 621. See also SH, *A Dialogue Concerning the Slavery of the Africans* (1776), in *WSH* 2: 587. For the estimate of the slave trade in Newport, see Crane, *Dependent People*, 23.

83. By 1800 "slaving voyages equaled the volume of the 1770s" (Withey, *Urban Growth in Colonial Rhode Island*, 97).

84. James DeWolf Papers, Vault A, Box 43A, Folder 24, NHS.

85. On James DeWolf, see the film *Traces of the Trade: A Story from the Deep North*, http://www.tracesofthetrade.org/ (accessed November 24, 2010).

86. SH, *Dialogue Concerning the Slavery of the Africans*, 557; SH, *A Discourse upon the Slave Trade and the Slavery of the Africans* (1793) in *WSH* 2: 607.

87. SH, *Treatise on the Millennium*, 145, 152–53; Revelation 16:13–16.

88. John Ferguson, *Memoir of the Life and Character of Rev. Samuel Hopkins* (Boston: Leonard W. Kimball, 1830), 90. For more on Gardner, see Edwards Amasa Park, ed. *The Works of Samuel Hopkins* (Boston: Doctrinal Tract and Book Society, 1852), 1: 154–56.

89. See Benard, "Free African American Cultural Landscape," 76–77, 92. On the Free African Union Society, see William Henry Robinson, ed., *The Proceedings of the Free African Union Society and the African Benevolent Society, Newport, Rhode Island, 1780–1824* (Providence: Urban League of Rhode Island, 1976); Free African Union Society, Minutes, Vault A, no. 1674c, NHS.

90. See Crane, *Dependent People*, 161.

91. SH to Stephen West, June 23, 1780, Samuel Hopkins, Letters, Gratz Collection, Case 6/Box 10; SH, *System of Doctrines* (Boston: Isaiah Thomas and Ebenezer T. Andrews, 1793), 1: xi. On Yamma's illness and death, see SH

to Levi Hart, July 29, 1793, and June 9, 1794, Gratz Collection: American Colonial Clergy, Case 8/Box 23. After Gardner won the lottery in 1791, he was able to buy his freedom. See SH to Levi Hart, April 27, 1791, Gratz Collection: American Colonial Clergy, Case 8/Box 23; SH to Levi Hart, June 10, 1791, in Samuel Hopkins, 4 Letters, 1770, 1791, 1796, no date, Gratz Collection.

92. SH, *Discourse upon the Slave Trade*, 610–611; Conforti, *Samuel Hopkins and the New Divinity Movement*, 148–54; Robinson, *Proceedings of the Free African Union Society*, 19.

93. On the fluidity between premillennialism and postmillennialism, see Bloch, *Visionary Republic*, 131.

94. SH to Levi Hart, July 12, 1787, and SH to Levi Hart, April 23, 1787, both in Gratz Collection: American Colonial Clergy, Case 8/Box 23.

95. See "The Rhode Island Census of 1782," in *The New England Historical and Genealogical Register*, vol. 127, no 1 (January 1973): 13. Latham Clarke may have been the same person as the "Spooner" Clark who seems to have shared Sarah Osborn's church pew (Pew 61) in the 1770s when she was no longer able to attend church. He is listed in FCCR-418, Folder 4, entry for March 15, 1772, and Folder 5, entry for November 26, 1775.

96. *FL*, 12–13. Susan was baptized in 1775, and Susanna Anthony probably wrote this letter in 1784. She referred to the effort to repair the meetinghouse, and the church held a lottery to fund the repairs in 1784. Arnold, *Vital Record*, First Series, vol. 8, p. 404; *NM*, December 18, 1784.

CHAPTER ELEVEN. THE OPEN VISION

1. SH, *Memoirs*, 124–25.

2. Ibid, 361.

3. SO, Diary, July 11, 1753; SO to JF, September 5, 1759, AAS; Joseph Stevens, *Another and Better Country, Even an Heavenly* (Boston: S. Kneeland, 1723), 20.

4. *FL*, 167; Samuel Buell, *The Happiness of the Blessed in Heaven* (New York: J. Parker, and Company, 1760), 6.

5. SO, Diary, July 12, July 9th, September 2, 1753, October 1, 1760. The Bible reference is Romans 7:24.

6. *Heads of Families at the First Census of the United States Taken in the Year 1790* (Washington: Government Printing Office, 1908). Since the names listed for Newport are not in alphabetical order, the list seems to be organized according to neighborhood. Elizabeth Melville, Lydia Bissell, and Mary Smith are included in the "List of Admissions, 1744–1796," in FCCR-BM.

7. Sarah Osborn was listed as living with the Clarkes in the Rhode Island census of 1782. See "The Rhode Island Census of 1782," in *New England Historical and Genealogical Register* 127, no. 1 (January 1973): 13. On Scipio Tanner, see "John Tanner," *Seventh-day Baptist Memorial* 3 (July 1854): 111.

8. *FL*, 25.

9. For an example of the First Church of Christ giving charity to a poor member, see FCCR-BM June 3, 1785. On Sarah Osborn's rent, see SH, *Memoirs*, 354, 357, and the letters from SH to Levi Hart in the Simon Gratz Manuscript Collection [hereafter Gratz Collection]: American Colonial Clergy, Case 8/Box 23, HSP, for the following dates: February 26, 1789, February 23, 1792, August 22, 1792, June 9, 1794, July 10, 1794, March 31, 1795, and March 30, 1796. See also SH to Levi Hart, January 26, 1793, in Samuel Hopkins, Letters, Gratz Collection, Case 6/Box 10; SH to Levi Hart, March 8, 1792, Ms.525, BPL; SH to Levi Hart, July 27, 1793, in FCCR-418, Folder 6.

10. SH, *Memoirs*, 357.

11. Ibid., 353.

12. Ibid., 360.

13. Ibid., 360.

14. SO, Diary, July 8, 1753, April 18, 1760, July 12, 1753.

15. Charles Drelincourt, *The Christian's Defence Against the Fears of Death, with Directions How to Die Well* (Boston: Thomas Fleet, 1744), 28. Osborn mentions this book in her diary on October 19, 1760.

16. See David Tripp, "The Image of the Body in the Formative Phases of the Protestant Reformation," in *Religion and the Body*, ed. Sarah Coakley (New York: Cambridge University Press, 1997), 131–52.

17. Cotton Mather, *The Soul upon the Wing* (Boston: B. Green 1722), 11.

18. John Tillotson, *Several Discourses of Death and Judgment* (London: R. Chiswell, 1701), 9: 41–42. See also John Corrigan, *The Prism of Piety: Catholick Congregational Clergy at the Beginning of the Enlightenment* (New York: Oxford University Press, 1991), 61. The Bible reference is from 1 Corinthians 6:19. On eighteenth-century attitudes toward the body, see Roy Porter, *Flesh in the Age of Reason* (New York: Allen Lane, 2003).

19. SO, Diary, July 8, 1753.

20. JE, *Typological Writings*, in *WJE* 11: 92; Isaac Watts, *Death and Heaven*, 4th ed. (London: James Brackstone, 1742), 166; JE, *Ethical Writings*, in *WJE* 8: 378–79; JE, *Religious Affections*, in *WJE* 2: 288–89; SO, Diary, March 27, April 11, 1754; SH, *Memoirs*, 149. On the "animal" nature of the body, see Shaw, *The Voice of One Crying in the Wilderness* (1665; rpt. Boston: Rogers and Fowle, 1746), 104–5.

21. Shepard quoted in Corrigan, *Prism of Piety*, 38; Bulkeley quoted in Marilyn J. Westerkamp, "Puritan Women, Spiritual Power, and the Question of Sexuality," in *The Religious History of American Women: Reimagining the Past*, ed. Catherine A. Brekus (Chapel Hill: University of North Carolina Press, 2007), 61; JE, *Original Sin*, in *WJE* 3: 270, quoting Job 14:1–4.

22. SO, Diary, July 27, 1753, July 25, 1760. See also Diary, March 28, 1754, February 18, 1757. On hysteria, see Mark S. Micale, *Approaching Hysteria: Disease and Its Interpretations* (Princeton: Princeton University Press, 1995);

G. S. Rousseau, "'A Strange Pathology': Hysteria in the Early Modern World, 1500–1800," in *Hysteria Beyond Freud*, ed. Sander L. Gilman et al. (Berkeley: University of California Press, 1993), 91–224.

23. See Samuel Willard, *A Compleat Body of Divinity* (Boston: B. Green and S. Kneeland, 1726), 2: 529; Cotton Mather, *Meditations on the Glory of the Heavenly World* (Boston: Benjamin Eliot, 1711), 107.

24. SO, Diary, March 8, 1767.

25. On heaven as a better earth, see Jeffrey Burton Russell, *Paradise Mislaid: How We Lost Heaven—and How We Can Regain It* (New York: Oxford University Press, 2006), 60–61.

26. See John McManners, *Death and the Enlightenment: Changing Attitudes to Death Among Christians and Unbelievers in Eighteenth-Century France* (New York: Oxford University Press, 1981), 186. On radical Enlightenment challenges to the idea of an afterlife, see Jonathan Irvine Israel, *Radical Enlightenment: Philosophy and the Making of Modernity, 1650–1750* (New York: Oxford University Press, 2001), 79.

27. John Locke, *Reasonableness of Christianity*, 2nd ed. (London: John Churchill, 1696), 290–91; letter from Benjamin Franklin to Ezra Stiles (1790), in Kramnick, *PER*, 166; James H. Hutson, *Forgotten Features of the Founding: The Recovery of Religious Themes in the Early American Republic* (Lanham, Md.: Lexington, 2003), 17.

28. On medieval and Reformation visions of heaven, see Colleen McDannell and Bernhard Lang, *Heaven: A History* (New Haven: Yale University Press, 1988), 69–180. SH, *System of Doctrines*, in *WSH* 2: 59–60. John Murray, *Grace and Glory; or, Heaven Given only to Saints* (Newburyport, Mass.: John McCall, 1788), 24–25.

29. *The Works of the Most Reverend Dr. John Tillotson* (Edinburgh: W. Ruddiman and Company, 1772), 1: 149–50; Watts, *Death and Heaven*, 116.

30. Watts, *Death and Heaven*, 127.

31. JE, *Miscellanies*, in *WJE* 13: 482; SH, *System of Doctrines*, in *WSH*, 2: 60.

32. Samuel Webster, *The Blessedness of Those Who Die in the Lord, Considered* (Boston: Edes and Son, 1792), 16.

33. SH, *Memoirs*, 185; SO, Diary, undated entry (late July or early August), 1760; SO, Diary, July 12, 1753.

34. Watts, *Death and Heaven*, 122, 124, 126; Murray, *Grace and Glory*, 31; *FL*, 36.

35. JE, *Miscellanies*, in *WJE* 13: 478; SH, *System of Doctrines*, in *WSH* 2: 44.

36. Willard, *Compleat Body of Divinity*, 538–39; McDannell and Lang, *Heaven*, 91.

37. On Leibniz, see McManners, *Death and the Enlightenment*, 132; McDannell and Lang, *Heaven*, 277.

38. John Tillotson, "Concerning our Imitation of the Divine Perfections," in *The Works of John Tillotson* (Edinburgh: G. Hamilton, 1748), 6:

274; Cotton Mather, *Coelestinus* (Boston: S. Kneeland, 1723), 145; Gad Hitchcock, *Natural Religion Aided by Revelation and Perfected in Christianity* (Boston: T. and J. Fleet, 1779), 19; *WJE* 13: 275–76. See also Amy Platinga Pauw, "'Heaven Is a World of Love': Edwards on Heaven and the Trinity," *Calvin Theological Journal* 30 (1995): 399; Sang Hyun Lee, *The Philosophical Theology of Jonathan Edwards* (Princeton: Princeton University Press, 1988), 170–210.

39. SO, Diary, April 15, 1760; SH, *Memoirs*, 119; SO to "Mrs. Noice" [Mary Noyes], January 16, 1767, AAS.

40. SH, *Memoirs*, 124–25, 380.

41. Murray, *Grace and Glory*, 32.

42. Charles Chauncy, *The Earth Delivered* (Boston: Edes and Gill, 1756), 15–16. See also Edward M. Griffin, *Old Brick: Charles Chauncy of Boston, 1705–1787* (Minneapolis: University of Minnesota Press, 1980), 125.

43. John Calvin, *Institutes of the Christian Religion*, ed. John T. McNeill, trans. Ford Lewis Battles, Library of Christian Classics vol. 21 (Louisville: Westminster John Knox Press, 1960), 3.25.10; Calvin, *Commentaries on the Last Four Books of Moses, Arranged in the Form of a Harmony*, trans. Charles William Bingham, vol. 2 (Edinburgh: Calvin Translation Society, 1853), entry on Numbers 6:24, p. 246.

44. 1 Corinthians 13:12; Richard Baxter, *The Saints Everlasting Rest* (New York: American Tract Society, n.d.), 72; Increase Mather, *Meditations on Death* (Boston: Timothy Green, 1707). 167.

45. Charles Chauncy, *Joy: The Duty of Survivors, on the Death of Pious Friends and Relatives* (Boston: S. Kneeland and T. Green, 1741), 14–15; Simeon Howard, *A Discourse Occasioned by the Death of Mrs. Elizabeth Howard* (Boston: T. and J. Fleet, 1777), 26. Webster, *Blessedness of Those Who Die in the Lord*, 14. Roy Porter argues that "the traditional primacy of the beatific vision was replaced by an accent on human love, expressed through family, friends and neighbours" (*Flesh in the Age of Reason*, 106).

46. JE, *Miscellanies*, *WJE* 13: 275.

47. Elizabeth Rowe, *Friendship in Death: In Twenty Letters from the Dead to the Living* (London: T. Worrall, 1728), 11.

48. SH, *Memoirs*, 377. For other examples of Osborn's hoping to see loved ones in heaven, see ibid., 210; SO, Diary, August 31, 1760. On heaven as a "home," see Diary, June 8, 1754, October 14, 1753, January 30, 1760.

49. SH, *Memoirs*, 126.

50. Ibid., 375–80.

51. See Griffin, *Old Brick*, 171–72; Charles Chauncy, *The Mystery Hid from Ages and Generations* (London: Charles Dilly, 1784).

52. JE, "The End of the Wicked Contemplated by the Righteous," quoted in David Levin, *Jonathan Edwards: A Profile* (New York: Hill and Wang, 1969), 223.

53. Psalm 73:25; SO, Diary, December 2, 1759; Isaac Watts, *Nearness to God the Felicity of Creatures*, in Watts, *Sermons on Various Subjects* (London: John Clark, 1721), 357.

54. Gilbert Tennent, *The Good Man's Character and Reward Represented, and His Loss Deplor'd* (Philadelphia: William Bradford, 1756), 27, 28–29; Aaron Burr, *A Servant of God Dismissed from Labour to Rest* (New York: Hugh Gaine, 1757), 11.

55. SH, *Memoirs*, 157; SO to JF, September 5, 1759, AAS.

56. SH, *Memoirs*, 377.

57. SO, Diary, June 21, 1754.

58. SH, *Memoirs*, 362.

59. Ibid., 137.

60. SO, Diary, April 2, 1754 (quoting Ecclesiastes 7:1); SH, *Memoirs*, 136–37. For two examples of references to Psalm 23, see SO, Diary, July 16, 1753, March 13, 1760.

61. SH, *Memoirs*, 363. On church bells, see Edwin Tunis, *Colonial Craftsmen and the Beginnings of American Industry* (Baltimore: Johns Hopkins University Press, 1999), 142.

62. Ephesians 4:1; SH, *Memoirs*, 363; *NM*, August 9, 1796.

63. SO, Will, Probate Book No. 3, 11–12, Newport City Hall, Newport, R.I.; Benard, "Free African American Cultural Landscape," 95.

64. Stephen West, ed., *Sketches of the Life of the Late Rev. Samuel Hopkins* (Hartford: Hudson and Goodwin, 1805), 104.

65. SO, Memoir, [143].

66. McManners, *Death and the Enlightenment*, 167, 172; Carl L. Becker, *The Heavenly City of the Eighteenth-Century Philosophers*, 2nd ed. (New Haven: Yale University Press, 2003), 123; SO, Diary, April 8, 1762.

67. SO, Diary, October 9, 1755, quoting Job 19:25.

EPILOGUE. A PROTESTANT SAINT

1. SH to Levi Hart, August 18, 1796, Simon Gratz Manuscript Collection [hereafter Gratz Collection]: American Colonial Clergy, Case 8/Box 23, HSP.

2. Ibid. On Hopkins's reliance on Hart to help him choose which entries to publish see SH to Levi Hart, December 17, 1796, January 11, 1797, September 12, 1798, Gratz Collection: American Colonial Clergy, Case 8/Box 23. The second edition of SH, *Memoirs*, was published by N. Elliot in 1814. Crito [Samuel Hopkins], "Sketch of the Character of Mrs. Sarah Osborn," *Theological Magazine* 2, no. 1 (September–October 1796): 1–4. See SO, *Nature*, in *Massachusetts Missionary Magazine* (Boston), 2, no. 4 (1804): 163–66. SH, excerpt from *Memoirs*, in *The Weekly Recorder, A Newspaper Conveying Important Intelligence* (Chillicothe, Ohio), February 19, 1819, 220. Elizabeth West Hopkins was not named on the title page of *FL*, but she was clearly the editor.

See Elizabeth Hopkins to Levi Hart, Jan. 12, 1787, Gratz Collection: American Colonial Clergy, Case 8/Box 23.

3. First Congregational Church, Records of the Osborn House, Vault A, no. 1999, NHS; Letter from Occramar Marycoo (Newport Gardner) to Samuel Vinson, January 2, 1826, Vault A, Box 106, Folder 13, NHS; *NM*, December 17, 1825, January 14 1826; *Rhode Island Republican*, June 15, 1826.

4. Gardiner Spring, "Christian Sanctification," in *The Literary and Theological Review* (New York: Appleton, 1834), 1: 115.

5. See Nathan O. Hatch, "The Puzzle of American Methodism," *Church History* 63, no. 2 (June 1994): 178.

6. See Mark A. Noll, *America's God: From Jonathan Edwards to Abraham Lincoln* (New York: Oxford University Press, 2002), 103.

7. See the essays in Mark A. Noll, ed., *God and Mammon: Protestants, Money, and the Market, 1790–1860* (New York: Oxford University Press, 2002); Mark Valeri, "The Economic Thought of Jonathan Edwards," *Church History* 60, no. 1 (1991): 39n5.

8. Charles E. Hammett, Jr., "A Sketch of the History of the Congregational Churches of Newport, R.I." (Typescript, 1891), 107, Vault A, no. 1257, NHS.

9. Jacqueline Hornstein, "Sarah Osborn," in *American Women Writers: A Critical Reference Guide from Colonial Times to the Present*, ed. Lina Mainiero (New York: Ungar, 1979–82), 3: 311; Mary Beth Norton, "'My Resting Reaping Times': Sarah Osborn's Defense of Her 'Unfeminine' Activities," *Signs* 2, no. 2 (1976): 521–22.

10. See James Schmidt, "What Enlightenment Project?" *Political Theory* 28, no. 6 (December 2000): 734–57.

11. SO, Diary, June 21, 1754.

12. See Matthew 22:37.

Acknowledgments

This book began many years ago when I came across a reference to Sarah Osborn's manuscripts in the catalogue of the Beinecke Rare Book and Manuscript Library at Yale. I was having difficulty finding sources for my dissertation, a study of female preaching in early America, and I decided to look at any book or manuscript collection that might be even remotely related. What I found was far beyond my expectations: a memoir so compelling that I sat in Beinecke's light-filled reading room until closing time, enthralled by my introduction to Sarah Osborn. For a month I put aside my research on female preaching while I immersed myself in Sarah's world. Even though I soon realized that she would make only a small appearance in my dissertation, I knew that I would return to her someday. I have always imagined the study of history as part of the humanities, an opportunity to reflect on the varieties of human experience across time and space, and Sarah's manuscripts are filled with her thoughts about the human condition. Her voice is unforgettable. I will always be thankful that she decided to share the story of her life.

I began working on this book in earnest more than ten years ago, and I have incurred many debts since then. When I discovered that Sarah Osborn's manuscripts at the Beinecke Library were only a fraction of her surviving corpus, I was both excited and daunted: excited by the prospect of reading more about her, but daunted by the challenge of piecing together the fragments of her writings. Her manuscripts are scattered in different archives in Rhode Island, Connecticut, Massachusetts, and Pennsylvania, and often I had to read them out of order: for example, half of her diary for 1757 is at the Beinecke and the other half is at the Newport Historical Society. Without the help of the staff of many different archives, I would never have been able to write this book. I am grateful to Thomas Knoles and Jaclyn Penny at the American Antiquarian Society, Joan Youngken and

Jennifer Robinson at the Newport Historical Society, and the staffs of the Rhode Island Historical Society, the Connecticut Historical Society, the Massachusetts Historical Society, the Manuscripts and Archives department of Sterling Memorial Library at Yale University, the Beinecke Rare Book and Manuscript Library at Yale University, the Historical Society of Pennsylvania, the Boston Public Library, and the Archives and Special Collections department of the Buswell Memorial Library at Wheaton College.

My work was generously supported by a John Simon Guggenheim Memorial Foundation Fellowship and a Henry Luce III Faculty Fellowship in Theology from the Association of Theological Schools. Sharing my research with the other Luce Fellows—a remarkable group of historians, ethicists, biblical scholars, and theologians—was an invaluable experience that helped me clarify my ideas. It was a pleasure to be part of such a vibrant intellectual community. I am also grateful to the University of Chicago Divinity School for providing research assistance. Paula Gallito, Monica Cawvey, Amy Artman and Philippa Koch contributed to this book in many ways: compiling bibliographies, tracking down obscure references, and reading eighteenth-century sources.

I have benefited from the opportunity to share my research with students and faculty at many colleges and universities, including Wheaton College, Miami University of Ohio, the University of Tennessee, and Duke University. My conversations with Mark Noll, Peter Williams, Jonathan Yeager, Grant Wacker, Richard Jaffe, and Tom Tweed helped me to think more deeply about the rise of evangelicalism, the legacy of the Enlightenment, and the category of experience. Peter Jauhiainen shared his research on Samuel Hopkins with me, and the members of the History of Christian Practice project, led by Laurie Maffly-Kipp, Leigh Schmidt, and Mark Valeri, encouraged me to think about the practice of devotional writing. All of the historians involved in that project—Anthea Butler, Heather Curtis, Kathryn Lofton, Michael McNally, Rick Ostrander, Sally Promey, Roberto Lint Sagarena, Tisa Wenger, and David Yoo—offered astute comments on my work. I have been privileged to be part of a supportive community of scholars who share my interest in women's religious history, including Elizabeth Alvarez, Amy Artman, Anthea Butler, Kathleen Cummings, Heather Curtis, Pamela Jones, Amy Koehlinger, Susanna Morrill, Kristy Nabhan-Warren, and Sarah McFarland Taylor.

I am especially grateful to the many colleagues who read the book in manuscript. Ann Braude, Jonathan Ebel, Harry S. Stout, Jonathan Yeager, and Malika Zeghal commented on individual chapters, and Kathleen

Cummings, Mark Noll, Bruce Hindmarsh, Philippa Koch, and W. Clark Gilpin read the entire book. I could not have asked for more insightful or generous readers.

I would like to thank John Demos and Alan Sachs for including this book in their series New Directions in Narrative History, and my editor at Yale University Press, Christopher Rogers, for his encouragement. Everyone at the Press has been a pleasure to work with, including Christina Tucker, who provided valuable help with images, and Susan Laity, whose graceful copyediting made this a far better book. I am also deeply grateful to Andrew Wylie, my literary agent, and Scott Moyers for their indispensable support and advice.

I am fortunate to work with a marvelous group of colleagues at the Divinity School. Susan Schreiner shared her research on certainty and experience in the early modern era; Curtis Evans encouraged me to keep writing; and even in retirement Martin Marty gave me the gift of his immense curiosity. Clark Gilpin, my first dean at the University of Chicago Divinity School, has been a cherished colleague for more than twenty years. Clark and I have taught classes together, co-edited a book, and traded ideas during workshops and hallway conversations, and his creativity has never ceased to inspire me. Richard Rosengarten, my second dean, and Margaret Mitchell, my third, have made the Divinity School a wonderful place to work. I have deeply appreciated their friendship.

Many other friends have encouraged me along the way. Tom Tweed was my high school teacher for only a brief time many years ago, but he has never stopped teaching me about either the study of religion or the meaning of intellectual generosity. Jon Butler believed in this book from the beginning, certain that the story of an obscure eighteenth-century woman would garner a wide readership. More than two decades ago Harry Stout introduced me to the historical study of religion in an extraordinary course titled "Puritanism and the American Religious Imagination"—a course whose themes continue to fascinate me. I have always treasured his advice, friendship, and kindness. Ellen and Phillip Boiselle have been so important to me that I think of them as part of my extended family. Ever since we met at Yale, Ellen has been the truest of friends, always there to share my joys and sorrows. I am also grateful to Carol and Kevin Sontheimer for their enduring support.

My deepest thanks go to several people who have never let me forget the abundance of love and grace in the world: my husband, Erik Sontheimer; our two daughters, Claire and Rachel; and my parents, to whom this book is dedicated.

Index

The abbreviation SO refers to Sarah Osborn.

Adams, Abigail, 303

Adams, John, 302–3

Addison, Joseph, 56

African Americans, free, 265, 294–95, 300, 313; and Enlightenment, 266–67, 342–43; and evangelical movement, 174, 184, 250, 254–55, 265–66, 268, 273–75, 281, 286, 294, 312–13, 340; and literacy, 271–72, 294; missionaries, 270, 281–83, 294, 300, 313, 339; published authors, 184, 268, 286; and racism, 174, 266–68, 270, 272. *See also* antislavery movement; Free African Union Society; slaves

Alleine, Joseph, 137, 146–47

Allen, Clara, xii

Allen, Ethan, 309

Allen, Timothy, 31, 202

Almy, Mary, 298–99

Ammons, A. R., xiv

Anabaptists, 96

Anglicans, 21–23, 74, 99, 224, 292–93; and SO, 105, 107, 110, 254, 257; theology of, 36, 105, 209–10, 212, 214

Anthony, Sarah, 235

Anthony, Susanna (Susa), 56, 69, 87, 123, 216, 222, 235, 277, 280, 283, 294, 297, 305, 314, 319–20, 335; correspondence with SO, xii, 148–50, 152, 166, 176, 182, 314, 338–39; friendship with SO, 23, 123, 137, 141, 175, 177, 242, 259, 293, 307, 318–19

antislavery movement, 286, 295, 309–10, 313; and capitalism, 285–86; and Enlightenment, 286–87, 343; and S. Hopkins, 284–87, 309–11; and Quakers, 265, 284–86, 309–10

Appleton, Nathaniel, 157–58, 179

Aquinas, Thomas, 326

Arminianism, 21, 25–26, 100, 340

Arminius, Jacobus, 21, 25

Articles of Confederation, 308

assurance. *See* conversion; evangelical movement; Osborn, Sarah: conversion of

Astell, Mary, 187

Augustine of Hippo, 50, 82, 94

Austin, Punderson, 277

Bacon, Thomas, 240

Balch, William, 25

Baldwin, Ebenezer, 304

Ballard, Martha, 78

Bannister, John, 255

Bannister, Susanna, 275

baptism: disputes over, 108, 257, 259, 279; of slaves, 202–3, 243, 253, 265, 274–75. *See also* children

Baptists, 99, 293, 339; Separate, 257–58; Seventh-day, 257, 297, 306; and SO's prayer meetings, 257–58, 260, 263, 274

Barlow, Philip L., 22

Baxter, Richard, 330, 339

Bebbington, David, 9, 103

Becker, Carl, 301

Bellamy, Joseph, 87, 171, 279, 309

benevolence: and Enlightenment, 8, 46, 59–60, 133, 214, 219, 227, 279; and evangelical movement, 60, 84, 86–87, 105, 133, 210, 213, 218–19, 226–27, 277, 279, 288, 341; of God, 8, 25, 59–60, 83–84, 86–87, 105, 133, 201, 214, 279, 341; and humanitarianism, 83–84, 87, 218–19, 226. *See also* Osborn, Sarah: and evangelical Christianity

Berkeley, George, 24, 63

Bernard of Clairvaux, 9

Bissell, Lydia, 318

Blair, Samuel, 48

Bloch, Ruth, 304

Bobey (slave), 201–2; and SO, 174–75, 234, 237–43, 246, 269–70, 288

Boston Massacre, 285, 292

Bowen, Nathan, 180

Bradstreet, Anne, 178

Brainerd, David, 42, 100–101

Brattle, William, 25

Brewster, Martha, 184

Brockwell, Charles, 268

Brooks, Thomas, 165–66

Brown, Moses, 294, 309

Bulkeley, Peter, 323

Bunyan, John, 41–42, 74, 116

Burr, Aaron, 42, 332

Burr, Esther Edwards, 50, 143, 182

Burr, Sally, 50

Bury, Elizabeth, 179–81

Caesar (slave), 255

Calvin, John, 36–37, 82, 197, 199, 214, 325–26, 329, 337

Calvinism, 9, 36, 38, 47, 82, 224, 279; challenges to, 21–22, 24–25, 28, 47, 83–84, 211–12, 214–15, 340–41; and SO, 37, 53, 105, 107, 129

capitalism, 194–95, 210, 340; and anti-slavery movement, 268, 284–86; and Enlightenment, xiii, 342; and evangelical movement, 7, 213, 268, 286, 324, 327, 340–41, 343

Caswell, William, 173

Catholics, 7, 74, 105, 111, 115, 159, 197, 199, 292, 307, 325, 337; and Seven Years' War, 192, 203, 232, 252

Champlin, Christopher, 306

Channing, Duchess. *See* Quamine, Duchess

Channing, William, 282

charity. *See* benevolence

Chauncy, Charles, 16, 29, 117, 145, 151, 180, 195, 328–31

Chesebrough, Abigail, 234

Chesebrough, David, 234, 261

Chesebrough, Mrs., 259, 261

children, 57–58; apprenticeship of, 139–41, 174–75, 204, 245, 295; baptism of, 79, 143, 164, 257, 279; conversions of, 48–49, 143–44, 149; and covenant theology, 143, 155, 164; death of, 143–44, 158–60, 165–67; and evangelical movement, 35–38, 41–50, 57–58, 144, 225, 323, 331–33; literature for, 36, 38–41, 48, 254; punishment of, 49–53, 230–31. *See also* Osborn, Sarah: prayer meetings of

Chipman, Handley, 198

Chubb, Thomas, 24–25

Church, Benjamin, 123, 252

Church, Quamenee. *See* Quamine, John

Church of England. *See* Anglicans

Clap, Nathaniel, 107–8, 111, 113–14, 119, 173, 182, 197

Clap, Thomas, 25, 209

Clarke, Elizabeth, 314, 318
Clarke, Latham, 314, 318
Clarke, Samuel, 25
Cleaveland, John, 42
Clinton, Henry, 295
Coercive Acts (1774), 292
Coffee, Charles, 236
Coggeshall, Nathaniel, 182, 235, 251–52, 254, 280, 283, 310; friendship with SO, 234, 259, 261, 264, 298, 307
Coggeshall, Thomas, 197
Cole, Nathan, 71, 87, 103, 109
Colman, Benjamin, 25, 208
communion, 94; exclusion from, 283, 292; and slaves, 202, 243, 252–53, 274; and SO, 105, 111, 113–15, 173
Conant, Sylvanus, 302–3
Congregationalists, 21–22, 35–36, 79, 99, 105, 107, 111, 113, 143, 160, 212, 253, 257, 263, 275–76, 283, 292–93; and African Americans, 265, 274; liberal, 25, 210, 214–15; Strict (*see* Separates). *See also* First Church of Christ
Constitution, U.S., 324
consumer revolution, xi, 26, 192–95, 200, 208, 308; and evangelical movement, 7, 11, 17, 99–100, 193, 207–8, 212–13, 318, 324, 343; and God, 84–85, 193, 208, 211; and human nature, 28, 47, 193, 207–8, 210–13, 225, 340
conversion: and African Americans, 202, 250, 265, 268, 271, 281, 313; and assurance, 96–100, 103–4, 121, 129, 148, 150; and authority, 11, 180–81, 265, 268; and children, 36, 47–48, 143–44; and church membership, 113–14; as crisis, 69, 71, 105, 110–11; at death, 146–47; and evangelical movement, 1, 10–11, 94–95, 100–101, 104, 143–45, 187, 219, 231–32, 265, 279, 282, 322; and individualism, 187; and language of experience, 94, 97–98, 100–101, 171, 265, 268, 322; narratives of, 19,

100, 103–4, 114, 252, 268; and Native Americans, 265; physical effects of, 29, 42, 102, 111, 116, 322; and Puritans, 95–97, 187; and revivals, 21, 29, 48, 55, 98, 102–3, 129, 143–45; and SO's prayer meetings, 252–53, 274, 281; and women, 55, 180–81, 187. *See also* Osborn, Sarah: conversion of
Cooper, Samuel, 209, 227
Cornwallis, Charles, 308
covenant theology, 36–37, 155, 168, 187–88, 303, 309; and children, 44, 78–79, 143, 151, 162, 164, 168
Croswell, Andrew, 99
Cutler, Timothy, 22

Davenport, James, 15, 29
Davies, Samuel, 211, 265
Davis, David Brion, 285
death: and the body, 318, 322–23, 333; and burial, 156, 160–61; and children, 48, 77–78, 144, 165–67; evangelical views of, 80–81, 85, 88, 138–39, 141–42, 144, 146–47, 150–53, 155–57, 159–60, 162–69, 204, 222–223, 314, 317, 333–34. *See also* heaven; mourning
Declaration of Independence, 287, 294
Defoe, Daniel, 182
deism, 84, 97, 100, 309, 312, 315
De Wolf, James, 311
Dickinson, Jonathan, 171
Diderot, Denis, 335
Doolittle, Thomas, 115, 166
Drelincourt, Charles, 80–81, 322
Dunlap, Jane, 184–85
Dutton, Anne, 184
Dwight, Timothy, 309

Edwards, Jonathan, xiii, 7, 21, 50, 63, 88, 100, 143, 171, 182, 189, 209–12, 224, 226, 265–66, 268, 279, 305, 309, 322–23, 326–28, 331, 341; and children, 37, 42, 45–50, 144, 332; and revivals, 15,

Edwards, Jonathan (*continued*)
55, 102, 117–18, 145, 199; and women,
117–18, 180, 189, 323
Edwards, Jonathan, Jr., 279
Edwards, Sarah Pierpont, 102
Emerson, Joseph, 49
empiricism. *See* experience
Enlightenment, xiii, 7–8, 10–11, 24, 159,
183–84, 335, 342–43; and antislavery
movement, 286–87; and benevolence,
8, 46, 59–60, 133, 214, 219, 227, 279;
and the body, 322; and capitalism,
xiii, 342; and evangelical movement,
8–11, 17, 19–20, 30, 60, 85, 94, 100,
112, 133, 138, 171, 183–85, 187, 190, 265,
267, 273, 279, 287, 290, 301, 304–5,
324, 330, 339, 342–43; and evil, 46, 82,
83–84, 100, 225; and gender, 183; and
happiness, 227, 326, 330; and heaven,
324, 327; and hell, 145, 324, 332; and
modernity, 8, 11, 30, 100, 159, 342; and
poverty, 214–15, 343; and progress, 8,
10, 226, 301–2, 304–5, 324–25, 327,
342–43; and racism, 250, 266–67, 287,
342–43; and self-interest, 10, 343; and
suffering, 46, 59–60, 82, 226, 303, 326,
343; and violence, 231–32, 303, 343;
and women, 8, 10, 173, 183, 187–90,
267, 342–43. *See also* experience;
humanitarianism; human nature;
individualism
Estaing, Admiral d' (Jean-Baptiste-
Charles-Henri-Hector), 298–99
evangelical movement, xiii, 5, 7, 9–11,
21–23, 30, 102, 128, 157, 283, 301–2,
309, 319, 339–40, 342–43; and assurance, 11–12, 95, 99–100, 102–3, 117,
129, 133, 176, 343; and the Bible, 8, 11,
38, 98, 116, 122, 157, 162, 237, 265–66,
287, 302, 343; and the body, 322–23;
and born-again Christianity, 1, 5,
9–10, 12, 31, 36, 48, 71, 94–95, 98,
100, 102–3, 105, 265, 267–68, 274–75,

331, 343; and Calvinism, 9, 82, 224,
279; and capitalism, 7, 213, 268, 286,
324, 327, 340–41, 343; and consumer
revolution, 7, 11, 17, 47, 99–100, 193,
207–8, 212–13, 343; and Enlightenment, 8–11, 17, 19–20, 30, 60, 85,
94, 100, 112, 133, 138, 171, 183–85, 187,
190, 265, 267, 273, 279, 287, 290, 301,
304–5, 324, 330, 339, 342–43; and
family, 45–46, 138, 159, 164–65, 343;
and gender, 5, 187–88, 262, 340; and
humanitarianism, 7, 10, 60, 83, 85–88,
145, 218–219, 225–28, 286–87, 343;
and millennialism, 10, 16, 252, 266,
274, 290, 301–2, 304, 309, 313–14; and
missions, 11, 190, 219, 224–25, 228,
270, 281–83, 294, 313, 343; and modern
world, 1, 5, 7, 11, 30, 100–101, 208,
342–43; and mourning, 85, 138, 148,
157–60, 164–65; and Native Americans, 10, 184, 265, 268; and progress,
7, 10–11, 218, 226, 290, 301, 304, 314,
327–28, 342; and Puritanism, 7, 9,
11, 86, 102, 112, 116, 187, 189, 208; and
republicanism, 290, 302–3, 340; and
self-interest, 10, 193, 207, 210, 226–27,
340; and slavery, 28, 219, 237, 268, 287,
309; and violence, 231–32, 302–3. *See
also* African Americans, free; benevolence; children; conversion; death;
experience; happiness; heaven; hell;
human nature; individualism; revivals;
slaves; suffering; women
evil: Christian interpretations of, 9, 46,
81–82, 85–87, 167, 199, 201, 225, 264,
267, 273, 279, 301, 311–12, 314; Enlightenment interpretations of, 46, 82,
83–84, 100, 225; and slavery, 219, 237,
266–67, 273, 285–86, 310–12
experience: and conversion, 94, 96–97,
100–102, 202; and Enlightenment,
xiii, 8–10, 94, 97–98, 100–101, 133,
173, 176, 184–85, 190, 250, 265, 267,

343; and evangelical movement, xiii, 9–10, 94, 97–98, 100–104, 122, 133, 173, 176, 183–85, 187, 189–90, 250, 257, 265, 267–68, 331, 339, 343; and individualism, 11, 185, 187, 190
—and authority, 10–11, 173, 183–85, 187, 189–90, 265, 267–68, 343; and African Americans, 202, 250, 265, 267–68, 343; and Native Americans, 265, 267–68; and SO, 100, 103–4, 113–14, 119, 121–22, 133, 138, 148, 176, 189–90, 257, 339; and women, 10–11, 173, 183–85, 187, 189–90, 265, 267, 343

family: evangelical views of, 45–46, 130, 138, 159, 164–65, 329–32, 343; historical changes in, 45–46, 165, 185
Fellows, Daniel, 283, 293, 295–98, 319
Fellows, Sally. *See* Osborn, Sally
Fellows, Susanna (SO's step-great-granddaughter), 293, 295, 297–98, 314
Fiering, Norman, 145
First Church of Christ, xiv, 22, 107, 113, 123, 129, 182, 223, 263, 279, 296, 339; and American Revolution, 292, 295, 306; and S. Hopkins, 277, 279, 281, 305, 339; and slaves and free African Americans, 202–3, 237, 239–40, 252–53, 274–75, 309, 313, 339; and W. Vinal, 230, 275, 277, 283; women's society, 123, 131, 202, 239, 297, 339
Fish, Joseph, 51, 117, 181, 208–9, 257, 263, 291, 307; correspondence with SO, 174–75, 197, 219–21, 230, 233, 236, 246, 248–49, 251–55, 257–63, 269–71, 274, 277, 290, 300, 304–6; friendship with SO, 123–24, 177, 213, 308
Fiske, Sarah, 178–79
Flavel, John, 19, 76, 80, 158, 165–66
Francke, August Hermann, 50
Franklin, Ann, 196
Franklin, Benjamin, 19, 196, 214, 324

Free African Union Society, 273, 312–13
French, "Brother" (SO's brother-in-law), 175, 238
French and Indian War. *See* Seven Years' War
Freud, Sigmund, 67
Friedan, Betty, 341
Frothingham, Ebenezer, 99, 180

Gardner, Jenny, 313
Gardner, Newport (Occramar Marycoo), 273, 312–13, 339
Gaustad, Edwin S., 22
Gavin, Antonio, 292
Gay, Peter, 8
gender: and Enlightenment, 183; and evangelical movement, 5, 187–88, 262, 340; and female body, 323; and language of humility, 56–57; and revivals, 117–18, 262; and sexuality, 54–55
George III (king of England), 292
Gerrish, Brian, 148
Gerrish, Martha, 50–51, 179
Gibbon, Edward, 302
Gibbs, Henry, 157
Gill, Sarah Prince, 31, 87, 101, 103, 160, 182
Gilman, Nicholas, 130, 226
Goen, C. C., 26
Goodhue, Sarah, 178–79
Gosper (slave), 202, 239–42
Graham, Billy, 5
Grant, Mrs., 259, 261
Gray, Mrs. Ebenezer, 223
Great Awakening. *See* revivals
Greenman, Almey, 204–5, 220
grief. *See* mourning
Gronniosaw, James Albert Ukawsaw, 268, 286
Guyse, John (SO's uncle), 24, 35, 38, 140, 207, 226, 244–45
Gyles, William, 280

Haggar, Benjamin (SO's father), 35–36, 40–41, 60, 79–80, 95, 108, 125, 167; SO's relationship with, 49–53, 61–64, 68, 70–77, 88–89, 113–14, 125

Haggar, Susanna Guyse (SO's mother), 35–36, 40–41, 60, 79, 95, 108, 252, 293; SO's relationship with, 49–53, 61–63, 65, 68, 70–77, 88–89, 105, 107, 110, 113–14, 125–28, 173

Haggar, William Guise, 263

Hammon, Jupiter, 268

Hammond, Elnathan, 198, 283

Hammond, Polly, 198

happiness, xiii, 9; and Enlightenment, 227, 326, 330; and evangelical movement, 60, 85–88, 133, 151, 153–54, 207, 209, 218, 227, 287, 310, 322, 325–26, 328–29, 331–32, 341; and humanitarianism, 60, 84, 218; and liberal Protestantism, 209–10, 227, 322, 325–26, 331

Hart, Levi, 164, 279, 291, 309, 319, 337

Hart, Norman, 197

Hart, "Widow," 197

Hart, William, 279

Hartley, L. P., xiii

Haskell, Thomas, 285

Heaton, Hannah, 42, 55, 100, 156, 159–60, 187–88

heaven: and the body, 317, 321, 322–23, 327; and Catholics, 325; and children, 38, 40, 44, 48, 58, 143–44, 146, 151, 156, 331–33; and evangelical movement, 11, 69, 85–87, 274, 279, 318, 325–26, 329–32, 337; and family, 321, 329–33; and progress, 318, 324–30, 335. *See also* Osborn, Sarah: views on

hell: and children, 38, 40, 42–48, 57, 144, 146–47, 156, 164; and Enlightenment, 145, 324, 332; and evangelical movement, 9, 11, 37, 85, 87, 144–46, 227, 232, 331–32, 341; and revivals, 102, 121, 145. *See also* Osborn, Sarah: views on

Helvétius, Claude-Adrien, 302

Helyer, Jonathan, 173

Hemings, Sally, 267

Hildegard of Bingen, 185

Hitchcock, Gad, 327

Hobbes, Thomas, 145

Honeyman, James, 22

Hooker, Thomas, 143

Hopkins, Elizabeth West, xii, 339

Hopkins, Samuel, 86–87, 101, 118, 227, 292, 294–96, 307, 319–20, 325–27, 341; and antislavery movement, 284–88, 309–13, 339; and First Church, 277–80, 283, 295, 305–6; millennialism of, 303–4, 311–12, 314; relationship with SO, 90–91, 174, 251, 258, 277, 279–81, 294, 296–98, 314, 319, 321, 334, 337; and slaves, 281–84, 286, 294

—and SO's manuscripts, xii, 138–40, 163–64, 251, 335, 339–40; alterations to, xii, 71, 74, 112–14, 118, 164, 258; *Memoirs of the Life of Mrs. Sarah Osborn*, xii, 71–72, 74, 118, 251, 258, 287–88, 291, 339

Housman, Hannah, 181, 189

Howard, Simeon, 330

Howe, John, 339

humanitarianism, 83–86, 145, 332; and antislavery, 284, 286, 343; and benevolence, 218–19, 225–28; and Enlightenment, xiii, 7, 10, 60, 83, 86–88, 145, 209, 226, 342–43; and evangelical movement, 7, 10, 60, 83, 85–88, 145, 218–19, 225–28, 343; and suffering, 43–44, 60, 83, 218, 228

human nature: Enlightenment views of, xiii, 7, 20, 23–25, 30, 46–47, 57, 83–84, 138, 209, 218, 279, 301–2, 322, 324, 342–43; evangelical views of, xiii, 7, 9, 11, 19–25, 28, 30, 36–38, 46–47, 50, 57, 76–77, 82–83, 85, 138, 193, 208–10, 212–13, 218, 225–26, 272, 277, 279, 284, 301–2, 309, 314–15, 323–24, 330–31, 340–41, 343; and human agency, 26, 28, 47, 187, 193, 209–10, 212–15, 288, 290, 340, 342; and prog-

ress, 226, 290, 302, 314–15, 324, 342.
 See also consumer revolution
Hume, David, 82, 226, 266
Huntingdon, Countess of (Selina Has-
 tings), 55
Hutcheson, Francis, 24, 46, 100, 226
Hutchinson, Anne, 96, 185
Hutchinson, Thomas, 292

Indians. *See* Native Americans
individualism, 7–8, 99; and consumer
 revolution, 193, 199, 208, 210, 212–13,
 340, 343; and Enlightenment, 10, 19,
 48, 173, 185, 187, 190, 250, 267, 287, 330;
 and evangelical movement, 10–11, 19,
 162, 173, 183, 185, 187–88, 190, 213, 250,
 267–68, 330, 343; and experience, 101,
 173, 183, 185, 190, 250, 267–68

Janeway, James, 48, 254
Jarratt, Devereux, 22
Jefferson, Thomas, 84, 267, 270, 286
Johnson, Samuel, 210
Joyce, James, 5
Judson, Ephraim, 277
Julian of Norwich, 152
Juster, Susan, 188

Kant, Immanuel, 266
Keith, George, 178
Kent, Benjamin, 25
King, William, 83–84
Kingsley, Bathsheba, 180–81
Kneeland, Samuel, 177, 188
Kramnick, Isaac, 187

Lackington, James, 31–32
Lamb, Hannah, 196
Leandro, Primos, 202
Leibniz, G. W., 327
Lincoln, Abraham, 309
Linnaeus, Carl, 266
Locke, John, 9, 24, 51, 83, 100, 195, 302,
 324

Lord's Supper. *See* communion
Luther, Martin, 117, 197, 199, 325, 329,
 337
Lutherans, 11
Lyman, Joseph, 303

Madison, James, 302
Malbone, Godfrey, 195
Manicheans, 82
Marrant, John, 268
Martyn, Henry, 339
Marx, Karl, 194
Mary I (queen of England), 192
Marycoo, Occramar. *See* Gardner,
 Newport
Mason, Jack. *See* Nubia, Salmar
Mason, Mary, 307, 314, 319
Mather, Cotton, 21, 53, 81, 97–98, 100,
 108–9, 155, 178, 195, 199, 225, 251, 327;
 and children, 36, 41, 44, 51, 231
Mather, Increase, 69, 330
Maxson, John, 248, 258
Mayhew, Jonathan, 57
Maylem, Ann, 177
medicine, 89–91, 142
Melville, Elizabeth, 318
Methodists, 339–40
Middlekauff, Robert, 97–98
midwives, 78, 89
millennialism, 10, 16, 252, 266, 274,
 290, 301–2, 304, 309, 313–14; and
 American Revolution, 290–91, 301–2,
 304–5, 309, 314; and S. Hopkins,
 311–14; and slavery, 311–13. *See also*
 Osborn, Sarah: views on
Miller, Alice, 68
Miller, Perry, 28
missions, 11, 190, 219, 224–25, 228, 343; to
 Africa, 270, 281–83, 294, 313
modernity, xiii, 8, 19, 30, 159, 208; and
 Enlightenment, 8, 11, 30, 100, 159, 342;
 and evangelical movement, 1, 5, 7, 11,
 30, 100–101, 208, 342–43
Mollineux, Mary, 179

Montesquieu, baron de (Charles-Louis
    de Secondat), 231, 266–67
Moodey, Samuel, 155
Moore, David, 211, 222–23, 233
Morgan, Edmund S., 140
mourning: and evangelical movement, 85,
    138, 148, 157–60, 164–65, 316–17, 330.
    See also death; Osborn, Sarah
Murray, John, 325–28, 331
Murray, Judith Sargent, 189

Native Americans, 192, 203, 232, 308, 310;
    and evangelical movement, 10, 184,
    265, 268; and Puritans, 224–25
New Divinity, 279, 304, 309, 340
New-England Primer, 38–39, 43
New Lights, 268
Newton, Isaac, 26, 82–83, 101, 171, 226
Newton, John, 128
Nichols, Cudjo, 202
North, Frederick, Lord, 292
Norton, Mary Beth, 341
Noyes, Mary Fish, 290–91
Nubia, Salmar (Jack Mason), 271, 294,
    313

Occom, Samson, 268
Oliver, Peter, 292
Original Sin. *See* human nature
Osborn, Abigail (SO's stepdaughter-in-
    law), 197, 203, 205, 207, 220, 222–24,
    227–29, 231, 233, 244–46, 264
Osborn, Edward (SO's stepson), 130,
    132–33, 173, 203; death of, 204, 222, 233
Osborn, Henry (SO's second husband),
    xiv, 1, 18, 129–33, 139–41, 152, 160,
    174–75, 196–97, 201, 203–6, 213,
    222–23, 233–34, 236–38, 277, 280,
    294–97; death of, 297–98; SO's prayer
    meetings, 245, 249, 257, 263; sons'
    deaths, 203–4, 222–23, 228, 233
Osborn, Henry (SO's stepson), 130,
    132–33; death of, 203

Osborn, John (SO's stepson), 130, 132–33,
    173, 197, 203–5, 207, 220; death of,
    222–23, 228, 233
Osborn, Johnny (SO's step-grandson),
    245–46
Osborn, Mary (SO's stepdaughter-in-
    law), 204
Osborn, Nancy (SO's step-grand-
    daughter), 245–46
Osborn, Sally (Sarah) (SO's step-
    granddaughter), 264, 283, 293, 295–98,
    319
Osborn, Samuel (minister), 25
Osborn, Sarah: adolescence of, 59–65,
    71–74; and American Revolution, xi,
    18, 289–301, 303, 305–8, 314–15; and
    Anglicanism, 105, 107, 110; and Cal-
    vinism, 37, 53, 105, 107, 129; childhood
    of, 1, 16, 33–37, 40–41, 44, 48–53,
    57, 93–94; and communion, 105, 111,
    113–15, 173; and covenant theology,
    115–16, 121, 129, 151–55, 162–64, 166,
    240, 293, 307, 317; death of, xv, 182,
    317–18, 321, 323, 333–35, 337; and First
    Church, xiv, 95, 100, 107, 113–14, 123,
    129, 131, 143, 173, 198, 202, 222–23, 234,
    245, 277, 279–81, 283, 307, 318–19, 334,
    339, 341; illness of, 4, 59, 89–92, 94,
    110, 218, 229–30, 246–47, 249, 251,
    254, 262, 277, 280–81, 288, 290–91,
    295, 307, 314, 317–18, 321–23, 326,
    344; and mourning, 80, 116, 121, 139,
    141, 147, 151, 153, 154, 156–57, 161–62,
    164–65, 169, 171, 174, 204, 222, 241,
    244; poetry of, 287–88, 291, 318, 328,
    331; religious anxieties of, 41, 95,
    119–22, 139, 176–77, 192; and Seven
    Years' War, 191–92, 203–4, 222,
    232–33; suicidal crisis of, 59, 65–71,
    96, 109–10, 126; theft from parents,
    72–77, 113–14, 125–28; and women's
    history, 341–42; and women's society,
    30, 128, 131, 175–76, 196–98, 202, 229,

232, 234, 238–42, 257, 280–81, 283, 294, 297, 323, 339

—conversion of, 17–20, 61, 71, 93–96, 100, 103–5, 107–22, 129, 146–50, 204, 231–32, 242; and assurance, 103–4, 117, 129, 133, 148, 150–51, 168, 173, 176, 182, 228, 260

—correspondence of, xi, xiv, 4, 17, 123–28, 139, 189, 231, 242, 280; with Susanna Anthony, xii, 148–50, 152, 166, 176, 182, 314, 338–39; with Fish, 174–75, 197, 219–21, 230, 233, 236, 246, 248–49, 251–55, 257–63, 269–71, 274, 277, 290, 300, 304–6

—diaries of, xi–xv, 2–4, 16, 18, 139, 168–69, 174, 176–77, 197, 201–2, 219, 226, 228, 230, 235–36, 240–41, 246, 251, 260, 269–70, 288, 291, 297, 322–23, 328, 332–33, 335, 339

—economic hardship of, 1, 4, 16–18, 40, 59, 88–89, 92, 131–32, 139–40, 176, 191–93, 195–201, 205–7, 213–20, 224, 229, 231, 233–34, 236, 238, 294, 314, 318–19, 321, 334–35, 344; and inheritance from uncle, 244–45

—and evangelical Christianity, xiii, 1, 5, 7, 10, 16–17, 20–21, 25, 28–31, 95, 100, 103–4, 107, 117–19, 128, 171, 190, 339–42; and benevolence, 217–20, 222–24, 226–29, 235–36, 244–47, 264, 334; and evangelism, 219, 227–28, 231–32, 236, 238, 247, 258, 260, 263–64, 269; and Tennent, 93–94, 119–22; and the theater, 236–38; and Whitefield, 93–94, 119–20, 123–24, 128

—family of: brother, 40–41, 53, 60, 88–89, 120, 167; brother-in-law (French), 175, 238; cousin, 235–36; grandmother, 41, 60; parents (Haggar), 35–36, 40–41, 49–53, 60–65, 68, 70–77, 79–80, 88–89, 95, 105, 107–8, 110, 113–14, 125–28, 167, 173, 252, 293; stepdaughters-in-law, 197, 203–5, 207,

220, 222–24, 227–29, 231, 233, 244–46, 264; step-grandchildren, 197, 203, 205, 220, 223, 229, 233, 245–46, 263–64, 283, 293, 295–98, 300, 319; step-great-granddaughter (Fellows), 293, 295, 297–98, 314; stepsons, 130, 132–33, 173, 197, 203–5, 207, 220, 222–23, 228, 233; uncle (Guyse), 24, 35, 38, 140, 207, 226, 244–45

—friends of, 64, 71–74, 123–25, 128, 174–77, 237, 300, 305–8, 318–19, 321, 333, 337, 344; Susanna Anthony, 23, 123, 137, 141, 175, 177, 242, 259, 293, 307, 318–19; N. Coggeshall, 234, 259, 261, 264, 298, 307; Fish, 123–24, 177, 213, 308; S. Hopkins, 90–91, 174, 277, 279–81, 294, 296–298, 314, 319, 321, 334, 337; Phillis, 242, 252, 270, 288; Stiles, 258–59, 280–81; E. Vinal, 220, 222; W. Vinal, 220, 222, 229, 257–59, 263, 275–77, 280, 283–84

—marriages of: H. Osborn, xiv, 1, 129–33, 139–41, 152, 160, 174–75, 196–97, 201, 203–6, 213, 222–23, 228, 233–34, 236–38, 245, 249, 257, 263, 277, 280, 294–98, 300; Wheaten, xiii, 1, 16, 72, 74–77, 79–81, 88, 92, 96, 116, 125, 130, 139–40, 166–68, 288, 332

—memoir of, xi–xii, 16–20, 29–35, 40–41, 57, 61, 67, 70–72, 74–76, 92–95, 103, 112–15, 117, 129, 132–33, 139, 167, 335, 339, 344

—prayer meetings of, 4, 248–55, 257–61, 281, 290; African Americans at, 4, 10, 249–55, 259–61, 263–65, 268–75, 277, 281–84, 294, 312, 313, 319, 335, 339, 341; anxiety over, 258–59, 264, 275; Baptists, 257–58, 260, 263, 274; children at, 249, 251, 253–54, 259, 274, 277; criticism of, 250, 254–55, 257, 259, 264, 275; interdenominational, 254, 257–58, 281; interracial, 250, 254–55; men, 249, 253; millennialism of, 252, 274; young

Osborn, Sarah: prayer meetings of
(*continued*)
men, 248–49, 253, 259, 261–63, 274,
277, 312; young women, 248–49,
253–55, 259, 263, 274, 277, 281
—publication of work of, xii, 177, 182–84,
188, 335; *The Nature, Certainty and
Evidence of True Christianity*, xii,
170–73, 177, 181–82, 184, 188–90
—school of, xiv, 4, 89, 120, 131, 141,
174–75, 196–201, 204, 206–7, 230,
247, 262, 294, 307; boarding school,
206–7, 219–20, 222, 229–31, 233, 281
—and scripture, 4, 20, 33, 35, 41, 68–69,
78–79, 81, 88, 92, 94, 107–10, 116–17,
122, 127, 131–32, 137, 139, 141–43, 146,
148–56, 160–63, 168–69, 174–76, 182,
207, 218, 220, 223–24, 230–31, 233–34,
237, 241–42, 249, 257–59, 262, 264,
270–71, 300, 303, 304–5, 317–18, 332,
334–36
—and slavery, 5, 7, 80, 219, 237–43,
264–65, 268–70, 275, 284–85, 287–88,
305, 310, 315; and Bobey, 174–75, 234,
237–43, 269–70, 288; and Phillis,
201–3, 234, 238–43, 252–53, 270, 288
—son of (Wheaten), 16, 77–79, 80,
88–89, 96, 107, 116, 120, 131, 139–41;
illness and death of, 137–39, 141–44,
146–57, 159–69, 171, 173–75, 204, 238,
241, 331–33
—views on: the body, 317, 321–24, 326,
333–34, 336; children, 35, 37, 51–52,
57–58, 70, 140, 144, 331; consumerism,
193, 211–13, 244; God, xiii–xiv, 4–5,
7, 16, 30, 32, 37, 40–41, 52–53, 58–62,
68–69, 73–74, 77, 81, 85, 91–93, 104,
110–11, 114–15, 128, 132, 138–39, 142,
148–57, 161–63, 165–67, 169–71, 176,
192–93, 200, 204, 214–16, 229, 232,
236, 259–60, 289–90, 300–301, 303,
314, 317, 319, 321, 328, 331–33, 335–36,
344; heaven, 96, 129, 144, 150, 156, 224,
287, 308, 317–18, 323–24, 326, 331–33,

335; hell, 61, 65, 109–10, 114, 128,
144–47, 155–56, 281, 332, 335; human
nature, xiii, 7, 9, 16, 19–20, 22, 28, 30,
32–35, 37, 41, 48, 53, 57, 69–70, 74,
76, 108, 119, 168, 193, 209, 212, 260,
272–73, 277, 288–89, 315, 317, 333, 336,
341, 343–44; millennium, 252, 274,
290–91, 305, 314–15; poverty, 7, 132,
214–16, 223–24, 235, 245, 317; race,
174, 242–43, 266, 269, 331; suffering,
xiii, 4–5, 7, 16, 53, 59–61, 67, 70, 76,
82, 87–88, 91–92, 94, 110–11, 133,
138–39, 141, 149, 151–54, 157, 160–61,
163, 165–67, 169, 176, 216, 218, 224,
254, 270–71, 273, 300, 314, 341, 344;
violence, 231–32
—writing style of, xii, 5; crossouts, 95,
115, 119, 131–33, 168, 188; experiential language, 9, 12, 100, 103–4, 107,
113–14, 119, 121–22, 133, 138, 148, 176,
189–90, 257, 339; mystical language,
31, 61, 152–53, 259, 316, 318, 332; present tense, 67, 75, 81, 108; sentimental,
181–83
Osborn Society, xiv, 339
Owens, John, 339

Paine, Thomas, 290
Park, Joseph, 21
Parsons, Jonathan, 21
Peabody, Benjamin, 280
Pemberton, Ebenezer, 183
Penn, Hannah, 178
Perkins, William, 97
Perrey, John, 189
Phillis (slave), 174, 201–3; and SO, 234,
238–43, 252–53, 270, 288
Pietists, German, 50, 225
Pocock, J. G. A., 8
Pope, Alexander, 84
Porter, Roy, 26
poverty, 195–96, 198; and Christianity,
198–201, 207–8, 214–17, 223, 225; and
Enlightenment, 214–15, 343

predestination, doctrine of, 25, 37, 47, 53, 82–83, 85–86, 129, 148, 214, 341

Presbyterians, 98, 105, 268

Prince, Deborah, 147–48

Prince, Thomas, 47, 144, 147–48, 182, 189; and publication of SO's *Nature, Certainty and Evidence of True Christianity*, 171, 177, 181, 183, 188

privateering, 80, 198; and John Osborn, 203–4, 220; and J. Quamine, 294, 300

progress: and Enlightenment, 8, 10, 226, 301–2, 304–5, 324–25, 327, 342–43; and evangelical movement, 7, 10–11, 218, 226, 290, 301, 304, 314, 327–28, 342; and heaven, 318, 324, 327–28, 335; and humanitarians, 218; and liberal Protestants, 214, 314; and millennialism, 290, 304, 314; and nationalism, 290, 304, 308

Protestantism, liberal, 8, 25, 46, 84, 209, 214–15, 279, 301, 304, 309, 313–14, 322, 324–31

Puritanism, 22, 35–36, 55, 115–16, 145, 160, 179, 182, 187, 189, 211, 224–25, 303, 318, 322–23, 327, 329–30; and assurance, 95–97, 99, 103; and children, 42–44, 48, 140, 254; evangelical movement, 7, 9, 11, 86, 102, 112, 116, 187, 189, 208; and human nature, 21, 26, 63, 208, 225, 236; and suffering, 85–86, 225

Quakers, 23, 74, 99, 102, 184, 210, 212, 214, 224, 254, 293–94; and slavery, 265, 284–87, 294, 309–10

Quamine, Duchess (Duchess Channing), 282, 300, 313

Quamine, John (Quaum; Quamenee Church), 286, 294–95, 300; conversion of, 252–53, 271–72; education of, 270, 282–83, 288, 294; and mission to Africa, 270, 281–83, 313; and SO's prayer meetings, 252–53

Quaque, Philip, 282

Quaum (slave). *See* Quamine, John

Quebec Act (1774), 292

Raynal, Abbé, 302

Reformation, Protestant, 8, 9, 11, 115, 325, 329, 337; and affirmation of everyday life, 159, 197, 325; and certainty of salvation, 96–97

Reformed Protestants, 11, 37, 44–45, 74, 99, 108, 189, 279

Rembrandt, 187

revivals, xi, 5, 11, 15–17, 21, 26, 28–30, 48, 95, 98, 102, 120–23, 125, 128, 130, 143–45, 171, 252, 339; and criticism of, 28–29, 98, 102, 117–18, 129; free African Americans, 268; and Native Americans, 268; and slaves, 266, 268; and women, 179, 250, 268. *See also* Osborn, Sarah: prayer meetings of

Revolution, American, 7, 60, 194, 318, 324, 327, 340; and African Americans, 294, 298, 300, 312–13; and antislavery movement, 284–85, 309–311; and millennialism, 290–92, 301–5, 309, 314–15; and Newport, 290, 292–300, 305–8

Richardson, Experience, 159

Richardson, Luther, 159

Richardson, Samuel, 46, 182

Robins, Benjamin, 171

Robinson, John, 63

Rochambeau, General (Jean-Baptiste Donatien de Vimeur), 307

Rousby, Gezelena, 184

Rousseau, Jean-Jacques, 183, 266, 301

Rowe, Elizabeth Singer, 112, 180–81, 189, 331

Rowlandson, Mary, 178

scientific revolution, 7, 24, 26, 82, 101, 171, 225, 301, 327–28

self-interest: and capitalism, 7, 194, 210, 286; and Enlightenment, 10, 343; and evangelical movement, 10, 193, 207,

self-interest (*continued*)
210, 226–27, 340; and human nature, 193, 208, 210, 343; and liberal Protestants, 210
Separate Baptists. *See* Baptists
Separates (Strict Congregationalists), 98–99, 102–3, 117, 176, 263; and women, 180
Seventh-day Baptists. *See* Baptists
Seven Years' War, 191–92, 196–98, 201, 203, 217, 222, 231–232, 252, 255
sex. *See* gender
Shaftesbury, third earl of (Anthony Ashley Cooper), 83, 100, 226
Shakespeare, William, 236
Shays, Daniel, 308, 310
Shepard, Thomas, 24, 323
Sherwood, Samuel, 304
Showalter, Elaine, 178
Skinner, Thomas, 158
slavery, 80, 309; and emancipation, 309–10, 313; and Enlightenment, 266–67, 287, 343; and evangelical movement, 28, 219, 237, 268, 287, 309; as a moral evil, 267, 287, 309–12; in Newport, 27–28, 194–95, 235, 237–38, 252, 255, 268, 271, 281–82, 284, 286, 310–11. *See also* antislavery movement
slaves, 4, 51, 63, 174–75, 185, 234, 298, 312–13; baptism of, 202–3, 243, 253, 265, 274–75; as commodities, 27, 239, 241–42, 268, 288; and evangelical movement, 10, 28, 174, 185, 201–2, 225, 237–39, 241–43, 250, 252, 254, 265–66, 268, 270, 272–75, 281–84, 286–88, 309–10, 313, 340; and literacy, 266, 271–72, 312; and missions to Africa, 281–83, 294, 313, 339; and Quakers, 265, 285–87, 295, 309–10; publications of, 268, 286; and racism, 237, 250, 266, 268–69; runaway, 255–56; and trauma of slave trade, 271–72, 310–11
Smith, Adam, 10, 210, 301

Smith, Hezekiah, 274
Smith, Mary, 318
Society of Friends. *See* Quakers
Southcott, Joanna, 188
Southwick, Solomon, 299
Spinoza, Baruch, 24
Spring, Gardiner, 339
Stamp Act (1765), 255, 285, 291–92
Steele, Richard, 236
Stevens, Joseph, 114, 317
Stevens, Pompey. *See* Stevens, Zingo
Stevens, Sarah, 270
Stevens, Zingo (Pompey), 270–71
Stiles, Ezra, 29, 202, 248, 263, 292–94, 300, 306; and African Americans, 274, 281–83, 294; and SO, 258–59, 280–81
Stillingfleet, Edward, 171
Stoddard, Solomon, 97
Stout, Harry S., 55
Styron, William, 67
suffering: and Enlightenment, 46, 59–60, 82, 226, 303, 326, 343; and evangelical movement, 9–10, 60, 70, 76–77, 82–83, 85–87, 146, 157–58, 218–19, 225–26, 228, 303, 326, 341; and humanitarianism, 10, 44, 60, 83–87, 218–19, 225, 228; as redemptive, 32, 59–60, 86–88, 151, 158, 218, 273, 303, 311, 341; of slaves, 270–71, 273, 284, 311. *See also* Osborn, Sarah: views on
Sugar Act (1764), 255
sumptuary laws, 208

Tanner, John, 297, 300, 306–7, 319
Tanner, Mary, 297, 306
Tanner, Obour, 282, 313
Tanner, Scipio, 319, 335
Tate, Mary, 194
Tate, William, 194
Taylor, Charles, 159
Taylor, John, 47

Tennent, Gilbert, 85, 93–95, 98–99, 112, 119–22, 128, 144, 210, 212, 332

Tenney, Cabel J., xii

theater, SO's crusade against, 236–38

Thurston, Gardiner, 248, 257–58, 260, 263, 274

Tillotson, John, 24, 84, 145, 322, 325, 327

Tindal, Matthew, 84

Toleration Act (1689), 7, 22, 99, 224

Townshend Acts (1767), 285

Treaty of Paris (1783), 308

Turgot, Anne-Robert-Jacques, 301

Tweedy, Mrs., 222

Ulrich, Laurel Thatcher, 77

Universalism, 309, 325

universal salvation, 145, 331

Veblen, Thorstein, 194

Vinal, Becky, 222, 229–30, 276

Vinal, Elizabeth, 220, 222, 230, 276

Vinal, Sarah, 222, 229–30, 276

Vinal, William: alcoholism of, 230–31, 246, 251, 258–59, 275–76; and First Church, 202, 233, 275–77, 279, 283–284; and SO, 220, 222, 229, 257–59, 263, 275–77, 280, 283–84

Voltaire, 231–32, 267, 301

Wadsworth, Benjamin, 25, 44–45, 85, 158–59, 209, 215

Wallace, James, 293–95

Wanscoat, Mrs., 245

Warren, Rick, 5

Washington, George, 293, 306–8

Watts, Isaac, 38, 40, 48, 112, 325–26, 332

Weber, Max, 197, 244

Webster, Samuel, 57, 326, 330

Wesley, Charles, 340

Wesley, John, xiii, 22, 105, 340

Wesleyans, 9, 82

Westminster Confession, 96

Westminster Shorter Catechism, 36–37

Wheaten, Samuel (SO's first husband), xiii, 1, 16, 72, 74–77, 79, 140; death of, 80–81, 88, 92, 116, 125, 130, 139, 166–68, 288, 332

Wheaten, Samuel (SO's son), 16, 77–79, 80, 88–89, 96, 107, 116, 120, 131, 139–41; illness and death of, 137–39, 141–44, 146–53, 155–57, 159–69, 171, 173–75, 204, 238, 241, 331–33

Wheatley, Phillis, 185, 268, 273, 282, 286

Wheelock, Eleazar, 126, 212, 225

Whiston, William, 25

Whitby, Daniel, 25, 46

White, Elizabeth, 179, 189

White, John, 26

Whitefield, George, xiii, 7, 15, 22, 24, 29, 55–56, 93–95, 105, 112–13, 119–20, 123–24, 128, 184–85, 189, 207–8, 213, 223, 225, 227–28, 257, 266

Wigglesworth, Edward, 25

Wigglesworth, Michael, 44

Wilkinson, Jemima, 188

Willard, Samuel, 53–54, 85–86

Williams, Roger, 22

Wilmot, Walter, 179

Winthrop, John, 178, 303

Witherspoon, John, 294

Wollaston, William, 83

Wollstonecraft, Mary, 189

Women: and childbirth, 77–78, 89; and Enlightenment, 8, 10, 173, 183, 187–90, 267, 342–43; as pious, 55, 57, 179–80; and poverty, 196, 215, 217, 223; and property, 131–32; and Quakers, 23, 184; and Separates, 180; as weak, 54–57, 189, 262, 323

—and evangelical movement, 10, 57, 173, 177, 180–81, 183–85, 187–90, 250, 268, 323, 340; and enthusiasm, 117–18, 188–89; and experiential language, 183–85, 189–90, 250, 340, 343; and religious authority, 183–85, 188–89,

Women: and evangelical movement
  (*continued*)
  250, 257, 260–62, 264, 280 (*see also*
  Osborn, Sarah: prayer meetings of);
  and speaking in churches, 114, 180–81,
  268
—writing and publications of, 56, 171,
  173, 177–85, 188–90, 280

Woolf, Virginia, 5
Woolman, John, 286
Wordsworth, William, 58

Yamma, Bristol, 270, 281–83, 286, 288,
  294, 313
Yeats, W. B., 59